ECONOMIC HISTORY OF THE AMERICAN PEOPLE

ECONOMIC HISTORY

OF THE

AMERICAN PEOPLE

BY

ERNEST L. BOGART

and

DONALD L. KEMMERER

UNIVERSITY OF ILLINOIS

LONGMANS, GREEN AND CO.

NEW YORK · LONDON · TORONTO

LONGMANS, GREEN AND CO., INC.
55 FIFTH AVENUE, NEW YORK 3

LONGMANS, GREEN AND CO. Ltd.
6 & 7 CLIFFORD STREET, LONDON W 1

LONGMANS, GREEN AND CO.
20 CRANFIELD ROAD, TORONTO 16

BOGART & KEMMERER

ECONOMIC HISTORY OF THE AMERICAN PEOPLE

First edition, September 1942
Seven printings
Second edition, rewritten September 1947
June 1948, November 1949
August 1951, November 1953
May 1955

Printed in the United States of America
VAN REES PRESS • NEW YORK

PREFACE

This book, the longest lived of the now numerous American economic histories, first appeared in 1907. Since then it has been repeatedly revised, its title has been changed (1930), and in 1942 a new author, Dr. Kemmerer, was added. In this edition Dr. Bogart has been primarily responsible for the chapters on colonization, agriculture, transportation, commerce, mercantilism, and social progress, and Dr. Kemmerer has dealt with those on the westward movement, slavery, labor, finance, manufacturing, and trusts. Yet the authors have been in such frequent consultation that the present revision should be regarded as a truly co-operative undertaking. The whole subject has been re-examined and every effort made to incorporate the results of recent scholarship. Numerous changes have been made, only a few of which can be mentioned here. The material on the Revolution and the Civil War has been drastically cut, less space is devoted to the tariff, the evolution of the factory system has been more carefully traced, the authors' views on some aspects of slavery and of the westward movement have, frankly, altered, the material on capital has been introduced earlier in the book and has been worked into the text more thoroughly, a new chapter on Social Progress before 1860 has been added, the former chapter on the United States as a World Power has been cut and combined with that on Commerce, a special chapter on Trusts has been added, and the chapters dealing with the period since 1914 have been largely rewritten and brought down to date. Additional maps, charts, and illustrations have been included in the belief that such visual aids are essential. The bibliography has been thoroughly revised and condensed and has been placed at the end of the book. Finally, the treatment of the subject has been brought down to the end of 1946.

CONTENTS

Part I—COLONIAL DEVELOPMENT, 1492–1789

CHAPTER   PAGE

I. THE ECONOMICS OF COLONIZATION . . . 1

II. COLONIAL AGRICULTURE 27

III. COLONIAL INDUSTRIES 53

IV. POPULATION AND LABOR 77

V. COLONIAL COMMERCE AND EXCHANGE . 98

Omit VI. Colonial Finance . . . . 125 *Omit*

VII. ENGLISH COLONIAL THEORY AND POLICY

TO 1763 146

VIII. FROM REVOLUTION TO CONSTITUTION . 164

Part II—THE WESTWARD MOVEMENT, 1789–1860

IX. NEUTRALITY AND FOREIGN COMMERCE . 190

X. THE WESTWARD MOVEMENT . . . 214

XI. THE AGRICULTURAL REVOLUTION . . 242

XII. THE TRANSPORTATION REVOLUTION . . 268   *MID TERM*

XIII. EXPANSION OF DOMESTIC COMMERCE AND

EXCHANGE 295

XIV. MONEY, BANKING AND FINANCE . . 316

XV. THE INDUSTRIAL REVOLUTION . . 339

XVI. POPULATION AND LABOR . . . 362

XVII. THE ECONOMICS OF SLAVERY . . 386

XVIII. SOCIAL PROGRESS TO 1860 . . . 411 — *OMIT!*

Part III—Industrialization, 1860–1914

CHAPTER   PAGE

XIX. Agricultural Expansion . . . 438

XX. The Rise of Large-scale
Manufacturing 466

XXI. The Trust Movement 488

XXII. Population, Immigration and Labor . 507

XXIII. Competition in Transportation and
Communication 532

XXIV. Specialization in Domestic and
Foreign Commerce 559

XXV. Money and Banking 581

Part IV—World Power, 1914–1946

XXVI. Mechanized Agriculture . . . 601

XXVII. Manufactures 629

XXVIII. Population and Labor 656

XXIX. New Agencies of Transportation and
Communication 680

XXX. Widened Horizons of Domestic and
Foreign Commerce 705

XXXI. Financing Three Emergencies . . 732

XXXII. Social Progress, 1860-1946 . . . 762

Bibliographical Notes . . . 785

Index of Maps, Charts, and Tables . 837

General Index 841

Part I—Colonial Development
1492-1789

CHAPTER I

THE ECONOMICS OF COLONIZATION

Trade of Europe with the Orient. Near the close of the fifteenth century there occurred a change in the trade activities and relations of the leading countries of Europe so profound that it has been called the Commercial Revolution. Just as the Renaissance brought about a new learning and the Reformation a new spirit in religion, so the Commercial Revolution was the manifestation of the stirring of the same intellectual forces in the economic domain. Among the changes included in this list, which help explain its name, were improvements in the art of navigation, alteration of the routes of trade, shift of trade centers from the Mediterranean to the Atlantic seaboard, introduction of new commodities into the European market, and a raising of the standard of living. Each of these may be briefly described.

The most important phase of the trade expansion of Europe during this period was that with the Orient. Europeans developed a taste for oriental wares, and certain things were in especial demand. Foremost among these were edible spices, precious stones, drugs, perfumes, and dyes, all of which had an importance scarcely believable today. There were also produced in the same eastern lands manufactured goods of peculiar delicacy or excellence which were in great demand in Europe, such as metalware and fabrics.

For all these valuable goods from the Orient, Europe had only a few commodities which contained sufficient value in a small bulk to be shipped eastward. Woolen cloth, coral, and certain metals, such as arsenic, antimony, quicksilver, tin, copper, and lead, were highly valued in Asia; but these alone could not pay for the Eastern goods consumed in Europe, and the balance had to be paid in gold and silver.

Hence the precious metals were drained off and metallic money grew so scarce in Europe that each coin had a very much greater purchasing power than the same quantity of gold or silver has today.

In these facts is to be found the explanation of the eager search for gold and silver which was one of the strong motives for the exploration of the New World.

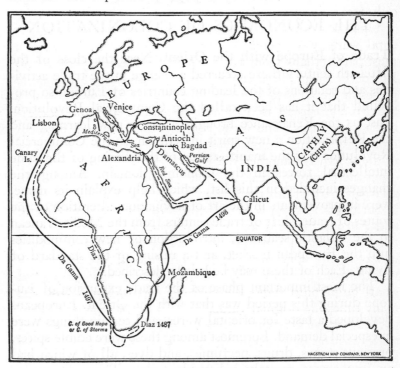

MEDIEVAL TRADE ROUTES

Trade routes. Not merely was the distance between Europe and Asia long, but the difficulties of intercourse were increased by barriers of mountain and desert. The routes of trade were determined by the physical features of the intervening areas, and led through the few gaps which existed. In the fifteenth century the two continents were linked by three general routes over which the oriental trade passed—the southern, the central, and the northern. All of these had their termini in the Mediterranean. (See map above.)

On all these routes, transshipments were frequent, losses from brigands and pirates were high, and the Turks, through whose territory all routes led, imposed tariffs, demanded registration fees, and collected tolls at the ports and along the roads. It was not the hostility of the Turks that determined Western merchants to seek new trade routes with the East, but their cupidity. This, however, was not the only factor.

Upon arrival at the eastern Mediterranean ports, the oriental wares were taken over by European traders, for the most part Italians from the city states of Venice, Genoa, and Florence. From these centers trade routes led through the passes in the Alps to all parts of Europe, or by ship through the Mediterranean to England, Flanders, and the Scandinavian countries. The Venetians especially had a practical monopoly of this profitable commerce. Thus a strong motive in the search for another route to the East was the desire of other merchants to break the Venetian monopoly and to have a larger share in this trade.

Such was the character of the trade between the Orient and Europe. Months and even years might elapse between the time when, say, pepper was packed in Ceylon and when it was finally consumed in London. So difficult and costly was the transportation that only articles of high value and small bulk could stand the charges, and the final cost was many times the original value.

And yet so insistent was the demand, that this oriental trade was the most extensive and the most lucrative known to Europe during the Middle Ages (843–1500). It was clear that the demand for oriental luxuries, which was moreover growing in Europe, could no longer be met by the old avenues of trade. A new route must be found by which these goods could more safely and cheaply be furnished to Europe.

If to the pressure of a demand for spices, the draining off of the precious metals, the interference with old routes by the Turks, and the monopoly of the Italian cities, there be added the motives related to religion, crusading, conquest, and adventure, sufficient explanation is afforded of the eager search for another route to the Indies which stimulated so many voyages of discovery during the fifteenth and sixteenth centuries.

A century of exploration. The pioneer work in the great explorations was done by the Portuguese, and consisted for the most part of a series of discoveries on the west coast of Africa. Finally, however, in 1497 Vasco da Gama sailed

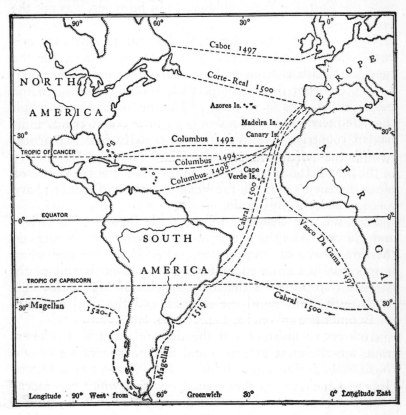

ROUTES OF DISCOVERIES

around the Cape of Good Hope and then across the Indian Ocean to India. The Portuguese explorations thus resulted in the discovery of a new all-water route to the Orient.

Even before Da Gama had sailed eastward to India, Ferdinand and Isabella of Spain had commissioned a Genoese navigator, Christopher Columbus, to sail westward toward the same goal. Although geographers generally believed that the earth was a sphere, to Columbus is due the credit of translating theory into action and of having the courage to sail boldly into the "sea of darkness" in order to reach the Indies. For the common sailor this held many terrors, such as the presence of great sea serpents, boiling water if one pushed too far south, the danger of sailing off into space, and other improbabilities. But, in spite of such superstitions, Columbus in 1492 sailed upon his memorable voyage with three small vessels, and after seventy long days came upon an island which he supposed to be one of those off the coast of Asia, but which has been identified as one of the Bahama group.

One of the significant results of these discoveries was to move the routes of commerce for Europe from the inland seas and the edge of the Atlantic to the open oceans. Until this period maritime commerce had been carried on chiefly within the Mediterranean, the Black, and the Baltic seas; sailors stuck close to the coast lines and seldom ventured far from sight of land. Now, with the new discoveries and improved methods of navigation, they sailed forth boldly upon the oceans and learned that these provided the most convenient pathways to other lands. With this change the Mediterranean city states of Venice and Genoa lost their importance and the countries which looked out upon the Atlantic—Portugal, Spain, Holland, France, and England— were given new opportunities.

Economic motives for exploration and colonization. The discovery of America was followed by a century of exploration, which led to a better geographical knowledge of the New World and of its relation to Europe and to the Orient. In explaining the remarkable outburst of maritime activity which characterized the leading nations of Europe during the sixteenth century, it will be helpful to examine the motives which actuated them. These were different among different nations and varied with each of these from time to time, but in the main they can be reduced to three—economic, political, and religious—although they were generally inextricably mingled.

Route to India. The main impulse in the work of exploration and colonization was economic, and of all the economic motives the search for a cheaper route to India was the first and for a long time the most potent. It was this which sent Columbus to the west across the Atlantic, and this motive held in the Spanish mind until Balboa proved that America was a new continent and Magellan discovered the only passage to the East. The way to the Orient had now been pointed out, but so strong was the idea of the territoriality of the ocean, according to which the routes first discovered by Da Gama and Magellan belonged to Portugal and Spain respectively, that the other nations thought it necessary to find routes of their own. Another century, consequently, saw a fruitless search for a northeast passage around the north of Europe and for a northwest passage through the American barrier.

The first explorations were made by the Spanish. The French were close on the heels of the Spanish in this work, but the most persistent in their efforts to find a northwest passage were the English. For this there were several reasons. In the first place, such a short cut would bring England nearer to the East with its treasures, and in the second place, it would avoid trespassing on the Portuguese and Spanish ocean routes. The discovery of a northwest passage by the English would have the advantage not only of securing to England a route entirely her own, but it would have the additional advantage, by passing through a cold climate, of opening up a market for England's great staple, woolen cloth.

Precious metals. The acquisition of the precious metals came to occupy first place as a motive to exploration after the discovery of the treasures in Mexico and Peru and the opening up of the silver mines in those countries. The conquest of Mexico (1519–21) by Cortés, one of the most extraordinary episodes in modern history, cannot be told here.[1]

The main purpose in conquering this territory was to obtain the vast store of gold and silver articles which the natives had been accumulating for centuries and which were now promptly shipped to Spain. Rumors soon reached the Spaniards of even greater wealth among the Incas of Peru, and

---

[1] The story is most interestingly told by W. H. Prescott, *History of the Conquest of Mexico.*

to gain this, Pizarro, with a company of 183 men, was sent to conquer that country (1531–34). This was done with much cruelty and the treasures of the Incas were plundered and sent back to Spain. Not merely were the accumulated stores of the precious metals appropriated, but the mines were developed and a steady stream of treasure flowed from the New World to Spain.

A powerful reason for the eagerness with which the precious metals were sought and for the overwhelming importance attached to their acquisition was their relative scarcity in Europe and the need for a larger supply for monetary use. The accumulations which existed under the Roman Empire had been in part exported to the Orient, in part lost by burial in forgotten hoards, in part used in the arts, or dissipated in other ways. At the same time the developing commerce had created additional demands, so that the value or purchasing power of each metallic monetary unit had increased enormously. The gold and silver mines in Europe were quite inadequate to meet this demand. To these purely economic factors may be added a political one. A state which had possession of stores of gold or silver held sinews of power not within the control of poorer states. Wealth was power, and of all forms of wealth easily disposable stocks of the precious metals conferred the most power. The incentive to gain gold and silver and to control the sources of supply was therefore very strong.

Fisheries. Even before it was seen that gold was lacking in the northern country, other motives became more important in leading to the exploration of the New World, and among these the fisheries ranked high. Danish, English, French, and perhaps other fishermen had caught cod off the banks of Newfoundland before America was discovered. When Cabot, returning from his first voyage in 1497, reported the opportunities for cod fishing off Newfoundland, he aroused great interest and was accompanied to those waters on his next voyage by three or four small ships from Bristol. These Devonshire fishermen were followed within six years by Spanish and Portuguese, Normans and Bretons, and thereafter for a century and a half these daring and rugged men fished in the icy waters off the banks. They set up their drying stages on the shores where the enormous hauls of cod were dried, much as they are today. These found a ready market in Europe, which was still wholly Catholic at the beginning of the sixteenth century and where consequently fish was in great demand as food on the numerous days—two or three a week—when the eating of meat was forbidden.

Fur trade. A new turn was given to French enterprise by the discovery of the St. Lawrence River by Jacques Cartier in 1534 and by the contacts which were established with the natives, and a new motive was given for exploration and trading. Although French explorers discovered neither gold nor the northwest passage, they found in the fur trade a traffic which yielded enormous returns. Jesuit priests followed the fur traders and soldiers accompanied them, and these three groups were the characteristic inhabitants of forest settlements. The inhospitable climate did not tempt to agriculture; they were too far from the sea to make fishing profitable; there was no market for the lumber; and manufacturing did not exist. Consequently, the scanty population of New France consisted principally of rovers.

The fur trade, which was carried on throughout this imperial stretch of territory by the French, was important and lucrative in itself, but it also had far-reaching consequences, for it engendered hostilities both with the Indians and with the Dutch and English. The Indians were the most successful trappers, and each spring they would bring to the trading post the furs which they had caught during the preceding winter. In exchange for the valuable beaver, otter, fox, and other pelts, they received cloth, blankets, hatchets, pots and pans, and sometimes firearms, ammunition, and rum, though the exchange of these last three was usually forbidden by the trading companies.[2] To the Indians, who were virtually living in the stone age, the metal wares of the white man

2 "The following may be quoted as prices (not, however, official) paid by the Hudson's Bay Company's factors about 1775, at its inland posts: a gun, 20 beaver skins; a strand blanket, 10 beaver skins; a one-pound axe, 3 beaver skins; half a pint of gunpowder or 10 balls, 1 beaver skin. The principal profits accrued from the sale of knives, beads, flint, steel awls, and other small articles. Tobacco fetched one beaver skin per foot of 'Spencer's Twist,' and rum 'not very strong,' two beaver skins per bottle." B. Willson, *The Great Company* (London, 1900), II, 65, note.

must have seemed a great bargain in exchange for a few furs. Each party benefited from this exchange.

Raw materials. As the colonies developed, new economic motives led the European countries to regard them with more and more favor. Among these motives may be mentioned the desire for sources of supply of raw materials and for markets for home manufactures. The early reports of explorers in the New World gave glowing accounts of the natural productiveness of the country, and it was thought that many raw materials and other products which the people of Europe needed might be obtained there. According to seventeenth-century ideas, England was much too dependent upon other nations for essential articles. She imported her naval stores from Norway and Poland; copper from Sweden; iron from Spain; wines, salt, and canvas from France; spices from the Indies. All these and other articles, it was thought, might be obtained from American colonies if the colonies were developed. At the same time the interchange of goods between England and the New World would stimulate the growth of an English merchant marine and train up a sturdy set of English seamen.

Markets. With the settlement of the new colonies these came to be valued also as markets for the developing industries of the mother countries. As early as 1606 the "colony at Virginia" was advocated as a place "fit for the vent of our wares." At first it was thought that the Indians might be customers for English textiles, but after this was seen to be futile it was hoped that English settlers might become prosperous enough to buy largely from the mother country.

Outlet for population. A final economic motive for exploration and colonization, which was emphasized in contemporary writings, was that the new settlements would furnish an outlet for the surplus population of England. Throughout the sixteenth and seventeenth centuries many complaints were heard about the excessive population. "There were never," exclaimed a contemporary writer, "more people, never less employment, never more idleness, never so much excess." Was there any basis for such complaints? Relatively, there was a surplus, for the demand for labor had declined and the supply, that is, the number of people in the country, had increased. The cessation of the European wars left many adventurers and younger sons of the nobility without an occupation, and these thought to recoup their fortunes in the New World. At the same time the substitution of sheep pastures for cultivated farms threw multitudes of able-bodied men out of work and led to an alarming increase in the number of "rogues, beggars, and sturdy vagabonds," many of whom became highwaymen. These changes were followed by a severe depression in the 1630's and crop failures in 1629 and 1633. In these circumstances the American colonies afforded a welcome refuge for what seemed a surplus population. Indeed the movement for colonization, as distinguished from governmental plans for appropriation and exploitation, came largely from these displaced groups.

Religious motives. Already, in the recital of the economic motives to exploration and colonization, the influence of religious motives has necessarily been noted. The religious motive was strong, especially in the minds of the Catholic sovereigns and missionaries. "We come in search of Christians and spices," said Da Gama. Among the Spanish the spread of the Gospel and the conversion of the natives to Christianity was a constant ideal which upheld the priests in the establishment of missions and similar work. In the towns monasteries were built, in the villages friars preached and carried on parish work, and among the wild Indians missions were established where agriculture and industrial arts were taught at the same time that religion was inculcated.

Far to the north equally devoted French priests and curés carried the Gospel to the Indians of that section and sought to improve living conditions. Missions were established throughout the territory covered by the fur traders, and where villages existed the curés carried on their spiritual ministrations along with a certain amount of industrial and agricultural guidance. No history of New Spain or New France would be complete which did not testify to the self-sacrifice and heroism of the priests and missionaries in that country. Most of the work was carried on by the Jesuits, but the Franciscan and other orders were also represented.

The Protestant English found a religious satisfaction in plundering treasure ships of Catholic Spain, and they also proclaimed the salvation of the Indians as one of the purposes of exploration. Captain John Smith declared that the first object of the Virginia Plantation was "to preach and baptize into the Christian Religion, and by the propagation of the Gospell, to recover out of the arms of the Devill, a number of poor and miserable soules wrapt up unto death in almost invincible ignorance."

The desire on the part of liberal-minded men to find a place where they could worship God according to the dictates of their own consciences also operated as a motive to colonization. Only the British let persecuted religious sects establish settlements in the New World. These people proved to be excellent colonizing material. More than one of the English colonies was settled by persons who migrated to the colonies to escape religious persecution at home. Separatists and Puritans settled in Massachusetts that they might worship after their own fashion. Roger Williams withdrew to Rhode Island to secure liberty of conscience. Maryland was founded as a refuge for English Catholics, while French Protestants (Huguenots) fled to the Carolinas. The Quakers and other sects found homes in Pennsylvania and other colonies.

Political motives were present in nearly all the schemes for colonizing North America. The settlement of the Carolinas and later of Georgia was regarded as a check to the northward advance of the Spanish, while similar outposts were established in the North to resist the encroachments of the French. Rivalry with Spain was a note that ran through all the work of exploration and settlement, not only on the part of England, but also of France and Holland, and a similar struggle later took place among these three nations. Political disaffection at home, as during the decade of the "great migration" from England (1630's), just before the English civil war, also sent many settlers across the Atlantic in search of political liberty and of freedom from oppressive political conditions.

Colonization. Four nations—Spain, France, Holland, and England—had carried on the work of exploration of that part of the New World now included within the United States and had sought to dominate it. The claims of nations in 1750 are shown on the accompanying map. As the sixteenth century had been one of exploration, so the seventeenth was one of colonization, and in this work each of the nations named took a part. A century of exploration had been necessary to inform the peoples of Europe as to the character and extent of the New World, and to develop an appreciation of the best methods by which they could develop and utilize its resources to advantage.

The possession of colonies exerted a profound influence upon the European countries, completely transforming their economic interests and activities. This becomes very clear if the character of European commerce before the great discoveries be contrasted with that which developed after this event. Before the sixteenth century there were only two important branches of world commerce—the intra-European and that between Europe and the Orient. The latter has already been described and need not be set forth again. More important was the intra-European, including England, but this was largely local, moving by land or small coasting vessels, and was carried on by many small merchants.

The new discoveries immensely quickened both these branches of commerce and also called into life two new ones. The first of these was that between Europe and the New World. The new lands across the Atlantic furnished the Old World with some of the products formerly obtained at great expense from the East, such as sugar, cocoa, and dyes; or they yielded articles which were scarce or unknown, such as the precious metals, furs, tobacco, and other things. The last branch of commerce, which developed later, was that between the New World and the west coast of Africa, by which slaves, ivory, gold dust, and ostrich feathers were obtained in exchange for rum, cloth, trinkets, and other wares. Both of these branches of trade were very lucrative and furnished the colonizing nations with valuable goods in wide demand.

Colonization and distant trading called for requirements different from those necessary for the more restricted commerce of the period prior to the discoveries. "It needed,"

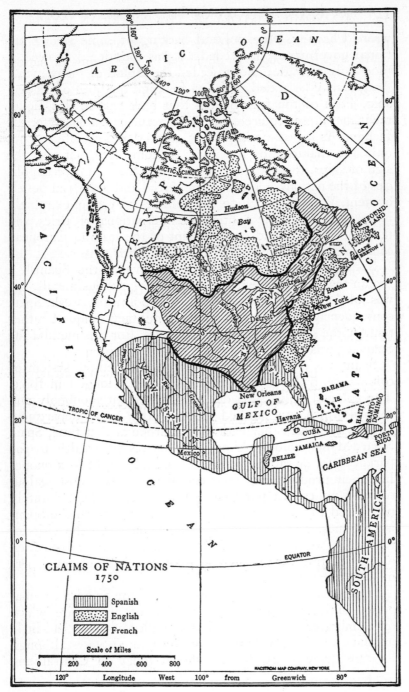

CLAIMS OF NATIONS
1750

	Spanish
	English
	French

Scale of Miles

0   200   400   600   800

HAGSTROM MAP COMPANY, NEW YORK

120°   Longitude   West   100°   from   Greenwich   80°

wrote Cheyney, "the political backing of some strong national government; it needed, or was considered to need, a monopoly of trade; and it needed the capital of many men." And, it may be added, it called for high qualities of leadership. Each of the four nations that took part in this movement met these requirements in different but in characteristic fashion. As it became important, distant trading affected not only the character of the wares of commerce, but also the size of ships, the emphasis upon trade, the commercial policies of the nations, and their commercial and industrial development. We may conclude that colonies played an extremely important rôle in the politics, the international rivalries, and the economic life and development of the leading European countries in the seventeenth and eighteenth centuries.

Spanish colonial policy. Chance gave to the Spanish a region that was wonderfully rich in the precious metals, but was inhabited by a race physically and politically weak. Spain consequently won her dominion by military conquest rather than by the slow subjugation of the soil. For this method the Spaniard was well fitted by character and training.

Spain was the first nation to develop a definite system of colonial control and regulation and kept it longest in force. The colonial policy was one of government monopoly and control which was applied to practically every department of activity. Like other nations of Europe at that time, Spain regarded her colonies simply as sources of wealth to the parent state, or rather to the crown, and sought to monopolize their products and their commerce by the most jealous colonial policy. In pursuance of this policy she absolutely prohibited the intercourse of foreign nations with the Spanish colonies. Not only the settlement, but even the visits of foreigners were forbidden. Even Spaniards were forbidden to visit or trade with their own colonies without royal permission.

It is not necessary to trace the story of the Spanish colonial policy until the complete dissolution of an empire which once embraced half the world. The policy of Spain had little influence on the development of the United States although its consequences are vividly shown today in Central and

South America, and it affected Texas and California in lesser degree. Yet it illustrates vividly one extreme type of colonial policy, with which may be contrasted the commercial relations of the other colonies with their mother countries.

Dutch colonization. Settlements of the Dutch, French, and English differed in one essential respect from those of the Spanish, and that was the lack of a numerous and developed native population with whom the first colonists might carry on commerce and whose labor they could utilize. Failing this, they were compelled to bring in other settlers to develop the land and its resources. Each nation solved this problem differently. In order to find a shorter route to the Orient, the Dutch had in 1607 sent Henry Hudson to America, where he discovered the river which bears his name. A trading post called New Amsterdam was established on Manhattan Island, now New York City, which was bought a few years later from the natives for $24. Meanwhile the Dutch interests had been taken over by the Dutch West India Company, founded in 1621, which at first thought to develop the fur trade in a similar fashion to the spice trade of the East. The Company retained a monopoly of the trade in furs, which were in great demand in Europe, and required that all imports and exports be carried only on company ships.

It soon became evident, however, that encouragement must be given to colonists, and a land policy was gradually developed. The first settlers were simply servants of the Company and cultivated its land. But in 1629, in order to stimulate settlement, it was enacted that any shareholder who would bring, at his own expense, 50 persons over fifteen years of age and settle them on the land should receive a grant of four miles on the seacoast or two miles on a navigable river, with no limit toward the interior. Such grantees would receive the title of *patroon* and be given certain feudal rights. Free colonists who could pay their own way to America were to be given all the land they could cultivate and exemption from taxation for ten years. The illiberal conditions offered to tenants, who could not hope to become owners of the land they tilled for the patroons, and the continuing monopoly of the fur trade, prevented the growth of the colony. The terms of settlement made only slight appeal to farmers, who were given no voice in the government.

The reasons for the failure of Dutch colonization are now apparent. The selfish trade policy, which sacrificed every other consideration to the aim of immediate profit, was in general incompatible with true colonization or settlement by permanent home-builders. But even if the colonial policy had been more capable, it is doubtful whether the Dutch could have developed a permanent colony in North America at the mouth of the Hudson River. By the middle of the seventeenth century the commercial and maritime pre-eminence of the Dutch had yielded to the English and they were unable to resist their more powerful neighbor. In 1664 England took over New Netherlands and the strategic Hudson River Valley.

French colonization. The work of exploiting and colonizing the territory in the New World was entrusted by the French to commercial companies from 1598, when the first company was formed, until 1663. Of these the most important was the one founded by Richelieu in 1628 along the lines laid down by Champlain and known as the Company of the One Hundred Associates of New France.[3] In spite of its great powers it was unsuccessful in promoting colonization, and in 1663 the company surrendered its charter.

The government of New France for the next hundred years was administered by the crown and was even more des-·potic and centralized than had been that of the Company. The free development of the colonists was prevented by minute and often unintelligible restrictions; thus, in 1709, the number of horses that could be kept by the *habitants* around Montreal was limited in order to encourage the breeding of horned cattle, and in 1745 a royal ordinance forbade the building of houses throughout the colony except on plots of land of specified size. Agriculture did not thrive in the cold, inhospitable regions of the north, whose forests and streams were better suited to the fur trade. Moreover, the European demand for furs made this the most profitable

---

[3] A good summary of its powers is given by E. P. Cheyney, *European Background of American History* (New York, 1904), 157-60.

occupation. The energies of the colonists were accordingly devoted to trading with the Indians for furs; this led to far-reaching exploration of the interior of the continent, not to establish settlements but to tap new sources of Indian trade. Instead of building homes they established forts and trading posts at strategic points where river routes and land routes crossed; instead of sending out colonists with their families, they sent soldiers and traders. Since the continuance of the fur trade depended upon keeping the country a wilderness, the spread of agricultural settlements was not encouraged. Although the French people bore heavy burdens on account of the colonies, these did not show commensurate increase in wealth or military strength. They were unable therefore to resist the expansion of the English, when the interests of the two nations clashed.

The mastery of the English. Last of the important European colonizing countries, England entered the field. Her rise to power was an event full of potentialities. Of the four nations that struggled for supremacy in the territory now included in the United States, England was the only one that succeeded in maintaining a permanent foothold. The Dutch were eliminated in the seventeenth century, the French in the eighteenth, and the Spanish in the nineteenth. The extent of the English colonies in North America after 1763 is shown on the map on page 18. What were the reasons which enabled the latest comer to succeed where the others made such an indifferent showing? Partly responsible, at least, was the incapacity of her rivals.

But the causes were not merely negative; there were also positive factors in English institutions and character which fitted her peculiarly for the work of colonization as it was carried on in the seventeenth century. Colonization called for leadership and organization, and it also required capital in considerable amounts and labor of a superior type. In all these respects England was probably superior to any contemporary nation in Europe. By the seventeenth century England had attained an advanced stage of economic development marked by capitalistic organization. There existed a commercial class with economic strength and initiative, and free capital and labor were available for new enterprises.

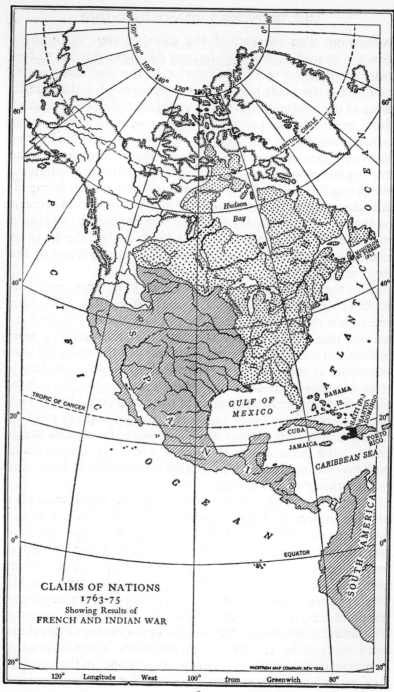

CLAIMS OF NATIONS
1763-75
Showing Results of
FRENCH AND INDIAN WAR

When the work of colonization was begun by Englishmen, it was undertaken by these men as a civilian enterprise for the sake of profit.

Capital was available in considerable amounts for the first time in the history of the country. The profits from trade and loot have already been mentioned, but sheep-raising and other home enterprises were also proving lucrative, and capital was accumulating. Indications of this fact are found in the legalization of usury, and the development of banking by the goldsmiths. Capitalists were seeking new forms of investment and turned eagerly and naturally to commercial ventures with distant lands.

But after all the most important factor in the work of colonization was the human element, and in this respect England enjoyed the greatest advantage. "It is a fact of deep significance in the history of migration," says Beard,[4] "that serfdom practically disappeared in England more than two hundred years before its last legal traces were removed from the Continent." At the same time agrarian changes, such as enclosures for sheep-raising, were displacing these free men from their accustomed work and turning them loose as beggars or sending them into the towns. "Of all European countries, England alone had an abundance of men and women accustomed to hard labor in the fields and yet cut loose from bondage to the soil. It was a dubious freedom which they enjoyed—so dubious that it prepared them for migration to the New World in spite of all the hazards."

Into the political and religious background of the period of colonization it is not necessary to go, except to note that in no country was there greater political freedom, and, during most of the time, greater religious toleration than in England. The governing class was, moreover, interested in mercantile affairs and eager to promote them. In short, the seed of English colonization was nurtured in congenial soil. The English colonies in North America are shown on the map on page 13.

Trading companies. Settlement of the English colonies and trading with them was not carried on by the government, as in Spain, nor by a single monopolistic company, as in New

[4] *Rise of American Civilization* (2 vols., New York, 1927), I, 23.

Netherlands, but by groups of individuals associated together in trading companies, which differed in no essential respect from modern business corporations. As a method by which many colonies were actually founded in North America, these companies were important in American history. The business of founding a settlement in the New World was both difficult and expensive and beyond the means of ordinary individuals, as the first attempts of Gilbert and Raleigh demonstrated. To travel so far from home and to transport the necessary supplies and equipment called for a considerable initial outlay. Since the country was undeveloped, the colonists must take with them clothing, household utensils and furniture, farm implements and tools of all sorts, domestic animals, and even, in the early days, sufficient food to tide them over the initial period until they could raise their own crops. The capital required for these purposes was furnished by the chartered company, but so remote or illusory were the profits that none of the companies repaid the original investment to the stockholders, and most of them failed. It was finally realized that as an investment the founding of a colony was unlikely to yield any financial return to the promoters at home.

Jamestown. The first permanent English settlement in America was authorized by the charter of 1606, which created two companies, one made up of "Knights, Gentlemen, Merchants, and other Adventurers" coming mostly from London, and the other composed of a similar group having its center in Plymouth. These two groups comprised seasoned navigators, merchants interested in foreign trade, and some persons of wealth and influence. They were known respectively as the London and Plymouth Companies.

The former founded Jamestown, the first permanent English settlement in America.

The instructions which the company sent with the colonists directed them to cultivate the soil, to search for a passage to India, to look for gold mines, and to develop trade with the Indians. It is evident from these instructions that the object was profits to the stockholders rather than true settlement and colonization by permanent home-building residents. For the first two years of its existence the venture was a complete failure whether regarded as a colony or as a business enterprise, but in 1609 the Company was reorganized and was given a definite grant of land of 400 miles of coast with the land behind "throughout from sea to sea, west and northwest." The colony was now treated by the stockholders in London as a true plantation and steps were taken to manage it as an investment proposition. The methods followed are well illustrated by the Company's land policy. For each £12.10s. paid in the stockholder was entitled to 100 acres of land, while an equal amount was given to every adventurer who went to Virginia in person, and the same for each laborer transported to the colony by a stockholder. For those settlers who were transported to the colony at Company expense a different arrangement was made. These were to be furnished with supplies of clothing, furniture, tools, and arms, and in return were to work for seven years—extended under subsequent charters to twelve years—on the Company's land; all proceeds were to be put into a common store from which the needs of the workers were to be met and the remainder distributed to the stockholders. The lack of incentive under this plan and the difficulty of its supervision made it a miserable failure.

By 1619 this system was discontinued and the land came into the ownership of individual settlers. The verdict passed by Captain John Smith upon the inefficiency of the method of a common store has not been reversed by subsequent experience: "When our people were fed out of the common store, and laboured jointly together, glad was he (who) could slip from his labour or slumber over his task he cared not how; nay, the most honest among them would hardly take so much true pains in a week, as now for themselves they will do in a day; neither cared they for the increase, presuming that howsoever the harvest prospered, the general store must maintain them, so that we reaped not so much corn from the labour of thirty, as now three or four do provide for themselves."

Plymouth and Massachusetts Bay. The next permanent English settlement in North America was made by the Pilgrims at Plymouth. This was a joint stock company to which seventy London merchants contributed their capital of £7000 and the colonists their labour. Each emigrant over sixteen who "adventured" himself was credited with one share, valued at £10; two children between ten and sixteen were counted as the equivalent of one adult. For contributions of money or goods the colonists were credited with additional shares. The bulk of the capital was, however, contributed by the London merchants as an investment. So far as the motives of the subscribers to the capital of this joint stock company were concerned, there seems to have been little difference between these London merchants and those who had fourteen years earlier financed the Jamestown settlement. They secured their risky venture by an agreement on the part of the whole body of colonists to work for the company for seven years and to put their produce into a common store from which they were to receive their food and clothing. At the end of the seven-year period "ye capital and profits, viz., the houses, lands, goods and chatles, be equally divided betwixte ye adventurers, and planters; wch done, every man shall be free from other of them of any debt or detrimente concerning this adventure." [5]

It will be seen that this was a more generous arrangement than that which the Virginia company had made with its laborers, who were mere indentured servants and received nothing at the end of the seven years except their freedom. The Plymouth colonists on the other hand were stockholders along with the capitalists and divided with them equally the profits of the venture. Quite as important, from a political standpoint, the colonists were to elect their own officials and direct their own efforts.

A larger colony established under the company system was that of Massachusetts Bay. This was settled by a group of Nonconformists, called Puritans, who bought up the stock of the Massachusetts company which in 1629 had obtained a liberal charter from Charles I. Taking their charter with them, they emigrated to their new home, thus escaping the distant control of English directors and managing their own affairs much as a modern corporation would do. The organ-

---

[5] Art. 5 of "Articles of Agreement of Plymouth Plantation" in W. Bradford's *History of the Plimouth Plantation*, 57. See also Bogart and Thompson, *Readings in the Economic History of the United States* (New York, 1916), 3.

izers belonged primarily to the small merchant class, though among the members were many peasants, craftsmen, and other workers. While the desire to obtain greater religious freedom was a motive for many, the opportunity for economic improvement was also a strong factor in attracting colonists. The colony prospered; many settlers came over in the Great Migration beginning in 1630, and by 1643 it had a population of over 16,000.

Colonization as business investment. It must not be supposed that the settlements at Jamestown and Plymouth were the first attempts at colonization. They are of historic importance because they were the first *permanent* settlements. Sir Humphrey Gilbert and Sir Walter Raleigh had made brave though fruitless efforts to develop the southern area; in the north more than forty recorded voyages had preceded the Pilgrims to various parts of New England, and the name Plymouth had already been given to the harbor which the Mayflower entered.[6]

These settlements were of measureless value to the country, but to the investors of capital they represented serious loss. It is estimated that about £100,000 was spent on the Virginia experiment, not a penny of which was ever recovered by the stockholders. The investors in the Plymouth Company, in despair after seven years of waiting, agreed to cancel their claims for £1800, or one-quarter of their original capital. The reasons for the failure of the company system are fairly obvious. One was the insufficiency of the capital invested—large as that was—for the expensive task of colonization. Another was the impatience of the stockholders, who wished quick returns. Distant management by company officials, ignorant of the conditions and the needs of the settlers, often provoked discord. And finally, the land system imposed upon the colonists was quite unsuited to a continent with limitless opportunities for development. The company system was useful in providing the organizations and the means for the initial experiments, but it soon gave way to other methods.

The proprietary colonies. While Virginia was developing as a royal province and the charter colonies of New England

[6] H. F. Howe, *Prologue to New England* (New York, 1943), 3.

were being planted, a different experiment in colonization was tried in the intervening territory. This was by grants of land to private individuals. The proprietor was generally a man of large means who undertook the planting of a colony for profit, as one might establish a distant estate or plantation. These estates were usually aristocratic or feudal in type, although this was modified and democratized by the environment and the economic and social forces of a new country. The proprietor occasionally lived part of the time in England and part of the time in the territory that had been granted him.

Like the chartered companies, the proprietor furnished the capital for the work of colonization, and expected to obtain his profits from the sale of the land to settlers, from quit-rents, and other sources such as fees, a share in any precious metals that might be discovered, and import duties. In order to obtain settlers, they issued prospectuses, gave away land to the first settlers, and attracted immigration by methods made familiar to us today by real-estate companies. In spite of the liberal terms of settlement the colonists quarreled with the proprietors, and all but three finally relinquished their claims so that their colonies became royal provinces. It is not necessary to describe the settlement of the other original thirteen colonies on the narrow strip of English soil in North America, for their history is familiar and offers no new features of economic interest. The work of colonization was slow and arduous, and its significance became apparent only after the task was completed.

The West Indies. In a half circle at the eastern end of the Caribbean Sea lies the group of islands known as the Lesser Antilles. Of these the English occupied St. Christopher and Barbados, at the two extremes, in 1625; a few years later they settled Nevis, Antigua, and other small islands in this group. The Bahama Islands were colonized in 1646, and in 1655 Jamaica was conquered from the Spanish. Down to 1640, probably twice as many emigrants from England settled in the West Indies—from Bermuda off the coast of Virginia to Trinidad off the coast of Venezuela—as on the continent. Considerable English capital was invested in sugar and tobacco growing in these islands, and by many

English merchants they were esteemed more highly than the northern colonies. Their commercial relations with the continental colonies, moreover, were extremely close, and a profitable trade existed between them. It would be a mistake to think of the thirteen continental English colonies as constituting either an economic or a political unit during the seventeenth and the first half of the eighteenth centuries, or as separated from the island colonies. A strong bond united both the fishing stations of Newfoundland and the sugar islands of the West Indies to the continental colonies, and the economic development of the latter cannot be traced apart from their relations with the former.

The growth of solidarity. For a hundred years the human seeds of colonization had been flung, more or less at random, upon the American continent. In some places they had found congenial soil and had flourished; in others the seed had found an inhospitable environment and had shriveled. On the whole, however, the Atlantic coast region had proved a fertile colonial seedbed. As one approaches the eastern coast of North America, it is possible at almost any point to find an entrance into safe harbors, deep tidal rivers, or protected sounds and bays, in striking contrast to the closed wall of the Pacific coast. The many navigable rivers afforded easy access for a considerable distance into the interior until the fall line (the first falls or rapids) was reached, and only in New England was this so near the coast as to confine settlement to the shore line. The strip of tidewater land varied in width from 50 miles in New England to 250 miles in the Carolinas.

The contracted area and the stony nature of the land, which cost an infinite amount of labor to clear, held the New England colonists to their first settlements. Such an environment compelled small permanent farms, but these gave such small profits that the settlers looked to auxiliary occupations like fishing or trading to make a living. Farther south the larger available areas of fertile land invited the cultivation of profitable staple crops by exhausting extensive methods. This resulted in wide dispersion of the population and also continuous change of location. The river systems and peninsulas tended to separate the various colonists and to deepen individual differences, but the ocean constituted a common highway which bound them together.

The effect of the Appalachian mountain chain, which constituted a difficult barrier and which was moreover rendered all but impassable by a thick forest growth, was to hem the population in and hold it to the stretch of territory between the mountains and the seacoast. For the first one hundred and fifty years of colonial history the English settlers were thus held together, and were also protected at most points by natural barriers against the Indians and the French. For the development of solidarity and of a spirit of unity the geographical conditions of settlement were of great importance. The unanimity with which the colonists acted at the outbreak of the Revolution can be explained in large part by the physical environment in which they had developed.

CHAPTER II

COLONIAL AGRICULTURE

The natural resources. The accounts of the explorers and the early colonists of North America are filled with descriptions of rich natural resources, which seemed to them inexhaustible. These observers were deeply impressed with the dense forests, teeming with game and bird life, the rivers filled with fish "so that a man might pass upon their backs dry-shod from one bank to the other," and other products of a fertile country whose riches the native Indians had barely scratched. If the colonists were to turn the natural wealth of a new country to advantage, if they were to purchase the manufactured wares of the Old World with the raw products of the New, they must utilize their superiority in this one respect and devote themselves to the exploitation of the natural resources.

The articles most immediately available were fish and furs and forest products, and to these the first colonists turned even before they began a settled agriculture. With the clearing of the land and the beginning of a more settled life, agricultural products began to be raised from the soil. But in this process the same exploitative methods were used as characterized the mining of the precious metals, the ruthless destruction of the forest, or the slaughter of the fur-bearing animals. In every case a quick return was desired at the smallest possible expenditure of labor and capital, and this required the prodigal and wasteful use of the agent that was being developed. This is the key to an understanding of the agricultural history of the colonial period, and indeed of all our economic life as a nation. Land was the most plentiful resource in the colonies and it was accordingly used extravagantly; treated almost as a free good, it was spent freely.

Such a transition was not an easy one for it meant the sacrifice of old habits by an especially conservative group. More-

27

over, many of the settlers were not farmers but gentlemen unaccustomed to manual labor, artisans and townsmen who were faced with the necessity of learning a new art in the midst of an unfamiliar wilderness. The first settlers could not support themselves in this land of unlimited resources and were saved from starvation only by the importation of food in supply ships and in some cases by the aid of Indians. Only gradually did they learn the necessary compromise between the agriculture of the Old World and that of the New. However, after an initial painful period of adjustment in all the colonies, they were able to raise sufficient food and agricultural products for their own needs and in time to produce an excess for export. In working out this experiment of colonization the settlers developed new methods and types of agriculture, which were a resultant of the prevailing European practices that they brought with them and of the Indian methods that they learned at first hand.

English agriculture. The colonists were generally equipped with a knowledge of crops, of implements, and of methods to which they had been accustomed in their homes, and this knowledge they first sought to apply to the new conditions. The principal cultivated plants of Europe, and more particularly of England, at the beginning of the seventeenth century were few: of grains there were barley, oats, rye, and wheat; of vegetables, beans, cabbages, onions, peas, and vetches; of fruits, apples, plums, pears, and several kinds of berries. The list of tools was still shorter: those drawn by domestic animals were the plow, the harrow, and the cart; of hand implements there were the hoe, the rake, the spade, and the sickle, essentially the same as had been used by the Egyptians four thousand years earlier; the ax, the flail, and the hand fan completed the list.

The methods and practices of agriculture were equally primitive: the two-field or three-field system was in general use; according to the latter one field would be planted with wheat, rye, or some other crop sowed in the fall and harvested the next summer, the second with barley, oats, peas, or similar crops planted in the spring and harvested in the fall, while the third field would lie fallow. By rotating the fields each was given a chance to recuperate. Fertilizing was done by turning the cattle into the stubble after the crops had been harvested. No improvement of cattle or other livestock was possible, as they were all herded together on common pasture. The lack of winter food made it customary to slaughter most of the increase in the fall and salt down the meat for winter use.

Simultaneously with the settlement of America there began improvements in the agriculture of England through the introduction of the turnip and other root crops and of the clovers and artificial grasses. These made possible a more scientific rotation of crops and the abandonment of the wasteful two-field and three-field systems; and they also provided a winter food for livestock which made it possible to carry them through the winter. English settlers during the colonial period naturally brought with them a knowledge of the contemporary English agricultural practices. Important contributions were also made by settlers from the continent of Europe. The Swedes introduced the log cabin, the Dutch were excellent dairy farmers and introduced forage grasses even before the English, the Scotch-Irish popularized oatmeal and white potatoes, but the Germans were the best farmers and practised scientific agriculture, with rotation of crops and the use of animal manure.

Native plants. The list of plants native to the country now comprised in the United States and cultivated by the Indians is a comparatively long one and includes many food crops in general use today and some that are not. Most important was maize, but the following were also generally grown: beans [1] of most edible varieties such as kidney beans, scarlet runner, and lima beans, onions, sweet potatoes, squashes (practically all varieties), pumpkins, watermelons, sunflowers (whose seeds were used for bread and also for oil), and Jerusalem artichokes. The white potato, though a native of Peru, was never known to the North American Indians. This and other native American plants, such as peanuts from Brazil and tomatoes and garden peppers from Central America, seem to have been introduced into Europe by the

---

[1] Early travelers sometimes mistook these for peas, but the latter were probably unknown to the Indians, being first introduced by Europeans. In all this list, beans and onions were the only ones known to England or Europe.

Spaniards, and from Europe into North America. Indeed, many native American domestic plants were widely distributed, not only by the Spanish, but also by the Portuguese, French, and others. Tobacco, though not a food plant, was highly esteemed by the natives and was later of great economic importance to the colonists. It was used by the Indians not merely for smoking but also for medicinal purposes, and entered largely into their religious and other ceremonial rites. Gourds of many kinds were grown and were used as containers for water, seeds, and other things, as dippers and drinking vessels, mixing bowls, and as ornaments.

The following table gives a partial list of plants of American origin: [2]

PLANTS OF AMERICAN ORIGIN

	Very ancient cultivation in America	Cultivated before discovery of America, but of no great antiquity	Cultivated only since discovery of America
Cultivated for underground parts	Sweet potato	Cassava Jerusalem artichoke Potato Onion	
Cultivated for stem and leaves	Tobacco	American aloe Grasses	Quinine Orchard grass
Cultivated for fruit		Pumpkin Squash Gourds Watermelon Red pepper Tomato Pineapple	Strawberry Blackberry Cranberry Raspberry Currant (black) Grape Plum Persimmon
Cultivated for seeds	Maize	Beans (many kinds) Barbados cotton Peanut Sunflower	

The lack of a variety of cereals was made up by the possession of the most valuable of them all, maize or Indian corn.[3] The Indians had developed nearly all the principal

[2] Based on A. Candolle, *Origin of Cultivated Plants*, 444, and G. K. Holmes, "Aboriginal Agriculture: the American Indians," in L. H. Bailey's *Cyclopedia of American Agriculture* (4 vols., New York, 1909), IV, 25-27.

[3] The English word for bread grain was and is corn; hence the new variety of grain which the Englishmen found the Indians using was called "Indian corn."

varieties of corn that we have today. Its chief value lay not so much in its large yield, as in its pre-eminent adaptability to a primitive agriculture. It was not necessary to clear or to plow the soil, but the seed could be dropped into a rudely made scratch or hole in the ground, amid the stumps, and it then took care of itself. Its large size limited the number of plants which could come to maturity in a given space, and consequently little tillage was necessary; in the case of the smaller cereals, on the other hand, it was necessary to till the entire surface of the field. Corn kept the ground clear of weeds because of its tall foliage. When ripe, it did not have to be harvested immediately, as do other cereals, but could hang for weeks upon the stalk until it was convenient to gather it. The harvesting, finally, could be done by hand without cutting the stalk, and when harvested it did not have to be threshed or winnowed.

Indian agricultural methods. At the time of the discovery of America the cultivation of corn extended from the Great Lakes in the north to the Plata River in Argentina in the south, and formed the staple crop of all those tribes in North America which practiced agriculture. Although the methods varied somewhat in different sections of the country a general description of these may be given. Because of the lack of domesticable animals in America, the Indians never passed through the pastoral stage. In the Great Plains area and to the north they lived chiefly by hunting; but east of the Mississippi most of the tribes had settled down to a more or less sedentary agricultural life with permanent villages and ordered, peaceful relations with other tribes, interrupted only occasionally by war. In the south, where the climate was genial, the Indians depended less upon game and natural products and more upon the results of the artificial propagation of vegetable products, until permanent agriculture was relied upon almost entirely for the means of subsistence. In the southern part of what is now the United States probably three-fourths of the Indian diet was vegetal. It was a fortunate circumstance that the early colonial settlements were made in regions of relatively high native culture, involving particularly the cultivation and use of maize, sweet potatoes, and tobacco.

In order to obtain a correct notion of primitive agriculture, the idea of a modern farm, with its cleared and well-planted fields, must be abandoned and a very different picture presented. With their primitive tools of wood or bone or stone, and without the aid of domesticated animals, the Indians could only make a partial clearing in the forest. This they did by killing the standing trees, either by girdling them with grooved stone axes or by building fires around their bases. The underbrush was then cleared or burned off, and the maize or corn and other seeds planted amid the blackened trunks. Such a field presented a picture of desolation rather than of orderly agriculture. Gradually, however, the trees fell, when they were burned into suitable lengths, rolled into a heap, and reduced to ashes; in this way the land was cleared with a minimum of labor. After the land was cleared, the men broke up and made even the surface of the ground, using a kind of mattock or hoe made by tying a chipped stone, a large clam shell, or the horn of a deer to a stick. Following the men came the women, who, with the aid of planting sticks, made holes in the newly prepared earth in rows about four feet apart each way. In each of these holes from four to six kernels of corn and two or three beans were planted one inch apart, and were then covered with earth. Frequently beans and squashes were planted between the rows of corn. A little later the growing plants were hilled.

No fertilizers seem to have been used except in New York and New England, where the Indians followed the practice of dropping a fish into the hill where they planted their corn. In spite of the rude tillage, a large yield was obtained because of the fertility of the soil. Hariot estimated that the average yield per acre in Virginia was, by London measure, 200 bushels of corn, peas, beans, and pumpkins, while Smith reported for New England about 45 bushels to the acre of corn alone.

The debt of the colonists to the Indians was a real and great one. Not only did they, in many instances, obtain needed food from the natives—sometimes, it must regretfully be recorded, by force or theft—but they also learned from them well-tried methods of growing the crops. Along other lines, too, they profited from Indian practices. After they had appropriated and put to use the best methods the Indians could teach them, they came to rely less upon this advice and more upon their own ingenuity and importations of new knowledge from the Old World. But without Indian aid the lot of the first settlers would have been even more difficult than it actually was.

Colonial agriculture. Those who are conversant with present methods of corn production will recognize in Indian corn culture as just described much that is familiar even after the lapse of three hundred years. When the early settlers became acquainted with the virtues of corn, they not only adopted it as a food but they appropriated bodily the Indian methods of preparing the ground, planting the seed, hilling and cultivating the growing crop, harvesting and husking the ripe grain, shelling the dried corn, and finally of preparing it in many ways as food for consumption, even adopting the Indian names, as hominy, succotash, and others. In the case of maple sugar and of tobacco there was a similar appropriation of Indian methods and practices. It is clear that in regard to these important crops our ancestors were greatly influenced by the aboriginal model they saw, and this may be accepted as evidence both of the progress achieved by the Indians and the good sense of the early settlers in recognizing the excellence of these methods. The Indian farmers, ignorant though they were of scientific principles of propagation, succeeded in establishing many useful variations in their food plants. They carried such plants as maize, beans, and squashes very far from the original wild types and gave them a wider range in climatic adaptation than any comparable plants of the Old World. Carrier estimates that "our agriculture today is at least one-third native American." [4]

Problems of selection and adaptation. In solving this problem the colonists were, however, met by many others. It was not enough to adopt the Indian practices and crops; they must also ascertain what plants and animals from the Old World would thrive in the new environment. They came to a country whose climate and soil were unfamiliar to them. The various qualities of the native plants with which they were confronted had to be determined by experience.

[4] Lyman Carrier, *The Beginnings of American Agriculture* (New York, 1923), 41.

Seeds and plants from every part of Europe and even from Asia and the West Indies, which were brought here by sailors, had first to be tried in each colony before it was known in what soil or climate they would best flourish.

For a century and a half this process of experimentation, adaptation, acclimatization, and selection continued in all the American colonies, and so successfully that in the next hundred years only one new plant, namely sorghum, was added to the list of foods grown in the United States, and that about the middle of the nineteenth century. Hemp, indigo, rice, cotton, madder, millet, spelt, lentils, lucerne, sainfoin, and other products, were tried and failed in New England. In the southern colonies wine and silk culture, and such products as ginger, lemons, olives, figs, almonds, and spices were tried, but were found unsuited to that climate. On the other hand, many European crops proved to be especially adapted to the new environment and became fully acclimatized, such as wheat, barley, oats, peas, vetches, etc.

There was, however, practically no improvement in the plants, vegetables, and fruits by culture and selection, after they were once introduced, except in the case of tobacco, rice, and indigo, of which the quality and preparation for market were distinctly bettered. Agricultural technique showed practically no improvement until after 1750. About that time Jared Eliot published his *Essays on Field Husbandry,* urging the growing of turnips as a forage crop and lamenting the insufficient use of manure as a fertilizer. Unfortunately his advice was not heeded. Agriculture was still so much of an art, with no scientific principles to guide the farmers, that its introduction into a new country was a matter of experimentation, of trial and error. The introduction of new crops into America during the colonial period was an agricultural experiment not only on the largest scale that the world had ever seen but one which was carried on with the greatest persistence for two hundred years.

Colonial agriculture extensive. Had the land been limited in extent the colonists might have found it necessary to resort to the practice of fallowing, or the later methods of rotating grain crops with clover and turnips, as was done in England, or of fertilizing; but the vast extent of available land made them prefer the more careless but immediately profitable methods of the Indians.

Rotation of crops was unknown and manures were but little used. The Swedish botanist Kalm, writing of New Jersey in 1748, said: "This easy method of getting a rich crop has spoiled the English and other European inhabitants, and induced them to adopt the same method of agriculture which the Indians make use of; that is, to sow uncultivated grounds, as long as they will produce a crop without manuring, but to turn them into pastures as soon as they can bear no more, and to take in hand new spots of grounds, covered since time immemorial with woods. This is likewise the reason why agriculture is so imperfect here... In a word, the cornfields, the meadows, the forests, the cattle, etc., are treated with great carelessness by the inhabitants."

Contemporary critics invariably directed their criticism against what they considered the wasteful and unintelligent methods of agriculture practiced in all the colonies. The author of *American Husbandry*, writing in 1775, censured severely the general practice of planting the same crop year after year and advised rotation of crops to prevent the exhaustion of the land: "they have not a just idea of the importance of throwing their lands into a proper arrangement, so that one may be a preparation for another." He complained of the lack of fences to keep out the cattle, of poor preparation of the land—"worse ploughing is nowhere to be seen"—of the insufficient and slovenly tillage—"many of their corn-fields are so full of weeds that in some it is difficult to know what is the crop"—and of the poorness of their implements.

Was this criticism justified? In Europe during the seventeenth and eighteenth centuries, under the pressure of a growing population, farmers had learned new methods of *intensive* agriculture and had introduced enclosure, manures, deep root crops, and a more scientific rotation, and other improvements. During this same period the American farmers had learned from the Indians the economy of *extensive* agriculture, which they found both easier and cheaper.

It must be remembered that the soil was extremely rich and did not require very careful tillage to yield large returns. And when the productiveness of the soil was reduced it was cheaper to take up fresh land, of which there were practically unlimited quantities, than to restore the exhausted qualities—or at least so it seemed to the colonist. When one piece lost its fertility, more land was made ready. By such a tedious process, piece by piece and under pressure, much of the land in the coastal region was prepared for agriculture. That is, with the one-crop system, they practiced rotation of fields instead of rotation of crops. In the colonies land was the cheapest factor of production and it was used prodigally; labor, on the other hand, was the scarcest and most expensive factor and everything possible was done to economize it. Here there was more land than the people could use, while farm laborers were scarce and often could not be hired at any wage. From the standpoint of the colonial farmer this was good agriculture, but it shocked the visitor from abroad who was accustomed to an agriculture based upon dear land and cheap labor; and in the long run it was poor agriculture, but the colonial pioneer did not look far ahead. "The American planters and farmers," shrewdly commented the author of *American Husbandry*, "are the greatest slovens in Christendom; their eyes are fixed upon the present gain, and they are blind to futurity."

The agricultural progress of the colonial period showed great variations from time to time and from one region to another and can probably be best portrayed by describing the conditions in the three main regions, for the differences of climate and consequently of crops were so great that the systems of agriculture were quite diverse.

Agriculture in New England. The character of agriculture and the nature of the crops produced in New England were determined by the climate and the soil of that region. The lowland belt between the ocean and the mountains is only from fifty to eighty miles wide, and the shore line is broken by many indentations, affording safe harbors and tempting the inhabitants to maritime enterprises. The glaciated soil was covered with a heavy deposit of boulders, which had to be cleared off with endless labor before cultivation of the land could begin. Once cleared, the land could be cultivated a long time without exhausting its fertility;

the necessary phosphate was supplied by using fish for fertilizer in the Indian fashion. Manure was not to be had in sufficient quantities for fertilizing, as the cattle were not housed, except for a couple of months in the winter, nor kept confined in fields; the settlers did not use the little they had.

The short summer and severe winter permitted the growth of only such crops as would flourish under these conditions —the bread grains, vegetables like cabbages, turnips, squash, onions, beans, parsnips, carrots, pumpkins, cucumbers, some of which were introduced from Europe, and fruits like apples, pears, plums, quinces, cherries, bush fruits, and nuts. Orchards were soon planted on every farm, and cider became a favorite beverage. Potatoes were not common in New England until the middle of the eighteenth century, and tomatoes were unknown. The white potato, though introduced later than most of the plants already named, has come to rank next to the cereal crops in importance. Carried from South America to Europe by the Spaniards it was accepted only slowly as a food, being called "devil's apple" because it grew underground. It first gained popularity with the Irish and became such a staple food with them that it was called by their name. When it was carried back to the English colonies (about 1720) it was not considered edible, as it was thought to be poisonous, but the Irish settlers in New Hampshire soon dispelled that belief, and by the end of the colonial period the white potato was a general article of diet.

All of these crops required intensive cultivation and, consequently, gardens were rarely planted in New England except for the most easily grown vegetables. These facts— the contracted area, the high labor cost of the land, and the nature of the crops—all made for small farms. And what nature prescribed, the character of the colonists favored, for most of those who settled in New England came from the class of small farmers and artisans, though representatives of the upper classes and the professions were not lacking.

A striking lack among the native flora was nutritive forage plants. As the Indians had no domestic animals, they had never developed hay and pasture plants and until these were introduced from Europe, the cattle fared badly. The native grasses grew rank and high—"as high as a man's head"—but they lacked sufficient nutriment for winter feeding. It was not until the middle of the seventeenth century that the various clovers were introduced into England, but they were soon after brought to the English colonies in America where they were eagerly welcomed. Indeed the recognition of the value of timothy as a forage crop by American farmers and its widespread use has led some writers to the conclusion that this was a native grass.[5] These cultivated grasses were of value not only as forage for cattle, but also as a welcome alternation between grain crops on land which otherwise would have lain fallow; there was thus introduced a rudimentary system of crop rotation.

Domestic animals. There were in North America, prior to its discovery by Columbus, no domestic animals, nor any capable of domestication except "a dog which howled but did not bark." It was therefore necessary for the colonists to import all the cattle, horses, sheep, swine, poultry, and other livestock. The immigrants to New England were accustomed to the care of sheep and cattle and to the consumption of their meat, and brought remarkably large numbers of horses, sheep, and cattle with them. Cattle-raising was, however, never so important an industry in New England as it became in the southern colonies, but dairying had reached a considerable development by the time of the Revolution; cheese was made and also butter, well-salted because of lack of refrigeration. Hogs were early introduced and adapted themselves to their new environment more readily than any other domestic animal; they multiplied so rapidly that it became possible to ship quantities of barreled pork to the West Indies. Sheep also were imported into New England, but had a hard struggle against wild animals, Indians, and the severe climate. The clipped wool averaged perhaps 2½ pounds per sheep and the fleece was a third the length of that from the best sheep in England; the colonists were able, however, to supply their own needs for wool.

Horses were imported at an early date and multiplied

---

[5] I.e., Carver in Bailey's *Cyclopedia of American Agriculture*, IV, 47. I have followed Carrier, *The Beginnings of American Agriculture*, 241, and Bidwell and Falconer, *Agriculture in the Northern United States* (Washington, 1925), 104.

rapidly on the free range, so that by the middle of the seventeenth century there was a surplus of horses which formed the basis of a very profitable and increasing export trade to the West Indies. On the sugar plantations of these islands there was a strong demand for horses and cattle for draft purposes, to haul the cane from the fields, to transport sugar and supplies, and to turn the heavy cylinders in the cane-crushing mills. Horses were also of great value to the colonists for purposes of rapid transportation. Until the building of roads and bridges made it possible to use wagons, most land travel was on horseback, and for this purpose a special breed known as Narragansett pacers was in especial demand because of their easy gait. With the cessation of the need for saddle horses this breed disappeared. Heavy draft horses were unknown. Horse-breeding was conducted in Connecticut and Rhode Island on a considerable scale during all the colonial period, for which the original stock seems to have come from England, Flanders, and possibly Ireland.

The cattle, horses, sheep, and swine brought over from England were smaller than our present representatives. After importation, the severe climate and the hardships they suffered on the commons or open range in winter, the promiscuous crossing, and the general lack of care caused a deterioration in the livestock.[6] The author of *American Husbandry* reserved his severest criticism for this feature of American farming: "Most of the farmers in this country are, in whatever concerns cattle, the most ignorant set of men in the world. Nor do I know of any country in which animals are worse treated. Horses are in general, even valuable ones, worked hard and starved; they plough, cart, and ride them to death, at the same time that they give very little heed to their food; after the hardest day's work, all the nourishment they are like to have is to be turned into a wood, where the shoots and weeds form the chief of the pasture; unles it be after the hay is in, when they get a share of the after-grass... This bad treatment extends to draft oxen; to their cows, sheep, and swine." [7]

---

[6] "Every day their cattle are harassed by labour, and each generation decreases in goodness and size, by being kept short of food." Peter Kalm, *Travels into North America* (2nd ed., London, 1772), 401.

[7] *American Husbandry* (2 vols., London, 1775), I, 80.

Farm implements. One of the greatest obstacles to agricultural progress was the scarcity and rudeness of the farming implements that the colonists had. According to Flint,[8] the Pilgrims had no plows for twelve years after they landed, and as late as 1637 there were but 37 in the colony of Massachusetts Bay. Towns often paid a bounty to anyone who would keep a plow in repair, in order to do the plowing for the community.

FARMING TOOLS, 1790

This meager list represents practically all the agricultural implements used by American farmers at the end of the eighteenth century. Notice the clumsy plow, with wrought-iron share, wooden mold-board, and heavy beam and handles; the wooden rake and fork; the primitive scythe, sickle, and flail. Great manual strength was necessary to use these tools, and the work was most exhausting.

The early colonial wooden plow, with moldboard of wood, partially covered with strips of iron, was not heavy but it was blunt and friction was excessive; it was usually necessary to have a man at the beam to bear down in order to prevent the plow from being thrown out of the ground. Even in cleared fields a farmer could plow in a day only about one acre, in which the furrows stood up on edge and had to be leveled for cultivation by a heavy harrow. Because of the great strength needed to draw such a plow, oxen were preferred to horses throughout the colonial period. In addition to this implement the colonial farmer had a spade, a hoe, a scythe,

[8] *Eighty Years Progress*, 27.

a reaping hook, a flail, a clumsy fork, and generally a harrow. All of these were rudely made of wood; almost the only metal available was bog iron, which was sometimes brittle. The hoe was actually of more significance than the plow for a considerable period for several reasons: until the colonists were adequately supplied with draft animals, only hand tools could be used; so long as stones and stumps cluttered the fields, it was difficult to use plows or other animal-drawn implements; many of their crops called for intertillage and for this the hoe was well adapted. This, with the spade and rake, was the most useful tool until the land was cleared.

Planting was done by hand, grain being sown broadcast and corn being dropped into shallow holes. In the middle of the eighteenth century Jared Eliot invented a grain drill that would drill manure with the wheat, but it does not seem to have been generally adopted. For mowing, the New England farmer used a sickle or a scythe and for threshing a hand flail. With a sickle a man could reap about three-fourths of an acre of wheat in a day, and with a flail he could thresh five or six bushels.[9] In the southern colonies grain was usually trodden out from the husks by horses or cattle that were driven around the threshing floor. The scarcity and poor character of tools was an important influence in promoting exploitative agriculture; the land was wastefully used when the capital instruments were so inefficient. Until the very end of the colonial period there were no machines that worked automatically or with the power of draft animals alone. Farm labor was carried on for the most part by human muscles and was hard and backbreaking.

Agriculture in the middle colonies. The more favorable climate and the more fertile and less stony soil of the middle colonies made agriculture the dominant interest there as it could not be in New England, while the denser population around New York, Philadelphia, and Baltimore furnished better markets. Agriculture was less primitive, the land was more thoroughly cleared and better plowed and cultivated, and the buildings and tools were superior. It was less uniform, however, since each element of the heterogeneous population, representative of every nation of northern Eu-

[9] Leo Rogin, The Introduction of Farm Machinery (Berkeley, 1931), 125, 138.

rope except Russia, introduced its own plants and livestock and used its own peculiar implements and methods. The Germans of Pennsylvania, arriving on the scene later than the first pioneers in Massachusetts and Virginia, introduced more thorough and skilful methods and probably exhibited the best agriculture in the colonies. They cleared the ground of every stump, cultivated the crops thoroughly, following careful European methods rather than the exploitative practices of their neighbors, and housed their cattle in the winter.

The crops were much the same as in New England, though relatively less attention was given to corn and more to wheat and oats; rye, barley, and buckwheat were also grown. After the pioneering stage had passed, wheat became the principal crop. So large was the production and export of these staples that the middle group was called the "bread colonies." By the middle of the eighteenth century 80,000 barrels of flour a year were being shipped from New York, though Pennsylvania was the chief granary of the continent; the exports of flour from this province were given in 1775 as 350,000 barrels. Potatoes and apples flourished in New York, while New Jersey and Delaware were soon famous for their peaches. The author of *American Husbandry*, coming from a country where this fruit was a hothouse product, was impressed by their abundance as well as their flavor: "Peaches are of a fine flavor and in such amazing plenty that whole stocks of hogs on a farm eat as many as they will, and yet the quantity that rot under the trees is astonishing. . . . Watermelons also are in such plenty that there is not a farmer or even a cottager without a plot of ground planted with them."

The cattle of the middle colonies showed almost as diverse origin as their owners. From Holland the Dutch settlers of New Amsterdam had brought the belted cattle of their native country, Swedish cattle had been introduced into Delaware, and the hybrid stock of New England, which were themselves a mixture of English, Danish, and possibly Spanish strains, filtered into New York. Large herds were soon to be found on the rich meadow lands of New Jersey, Pennsylvania, and New York. Hogs multiplied everywhere, running wild in the woods and living on mast and roots. Sheep were raised by the Germans in Pennsylvania, who used their wool for their domestic industry. Horse-breeding was certainly not so important as it was in New England, though the splendid Conestoga draft horses were developed here.

The implements seem not to have differed from those already described for New England.

The agriculture of both New England and the middle colonies was self-sufficing, that is, it provided the farmer with practically everything he needed. Except for salt and iron, the northern farmer could subsist on the product of his farm; from it he obtained meat, dairy products, breadstuffs, vegetables, and fruit, and even sugar (maple) and cider or whisky. His clothing was made from the flax and wool that he produced, and that his wife spun and wove; his shoes and boots would probably be made by an itinerant shoemaker out of leather skinned and tanned on the farm. Many a northern farmer "lived on his own" in this fashion during the colonial period.

Agriculture in the South. Wheat was the first crop planted by the Jamestown settlers within two weeks after their arrival in 1607. It was not successful and the colonists soon turned their attention to corn as a food product. After they had been instructed in the native methods of growing this crop, they were so successful that by 1631 there was a surplus for export, for which they sought an outlet in the West Indies and elsewhere. The raising of food products was threatened, however, by the introduction of tobacco by John Rolfe in 1612. This had long been grown in the Spanish West Indies and about 1565 its use had been introduced by John Hawkins into England, where a great demand for it had developed; by 1612 the English people were expending £200,000 a year for tobacco, most of which came from the West Indies.

The first tobacco grown was inferior to the Spanish, but a new method of curing it greatly improved its flavor and soon the demand for Virginia tobacco forced the price up and the resulting high profits stimulated its production and export. The exports were 20,000 pounds in 1619, and 500,000 in 1627; by 1700 they were 28,000,000, and by 1775 they were 85,000,000. The settlers turned with one accord to the raising of tobacco, and the forests could not be cleared off fast enough; in 1617 even the roads and marketplace of Jamestown were planted with tobacco.

In spite of the "Counter Blaste to Tobacco" by James I, who disapproved of its use, production continued to increase rapidly. It was estimated that the same amount of labor devoted to the growing of tobacco would yield a money return six times as great as when applied to wheat production. Tobacco had a great advantage over almost every other export from the colonies except furs—it had a high value in a small bulk and so its export did not involve high transportation costs; it also produced a high yield per acre, and its keeping qualities were good.

Tobacco consequently became the staple crop of Virginia and Maryland during the colonial period and also was grown in the Carolinas. The concentration on tobacco soon brought overproduction; its price fell below its cost. From 3s. a pound in 1617 the price fell to a half-penny in 1666. Efforts were made to stabilize prices by price-fixing legislation, by limiting the planting, by destruction of the surplus, and in other ways, but without much success, and prices fluctuated greatly. Thus the American farmer met with the problem of a market surplus in the production of this export crop at the very beginning of his history and tried to solve it by methods used again in the 1930's. As in the case of corn the Indian methods of cultivation were adopted with little change: a piece of land was cleared by felling the trees and burning them, and amid the blackened stumps the tobacco was planted until the rich but thin virgin soil was exhausted, when it was devoted to other crops. The life of a field for tobacco-growing was from three to eight years according to the fertility of the soil. Such a wasteful method made southern agriculture essentially migratory and necessitated the control and use of considerable areas of land. It must not be supposed, however, that tobacco was the only crop. Wheat, corn, and other crops were planted in the fields abandoned by tobacco, which required virgin soil, and the acreage devoted to these, with orchards and pasture, easily exceeded that planted in tobacco. Corn and corn-fed animals furnished the main food supplies.

Tobacco-growing also required large numbers of laborers. The demand for labor was met during the seventeenth century primarily by the use of indentured servants, but after about 1680 slaves became more important. The price of tobacco had fallen so low that a cheaper kind of labor had to be found to make ends meet, and the planters thought they found the answer in slave labor. The nature of the crop determined therefore the character both of the land system and of the labor system. It also determined the location of the plantations, and held them to the river banks; since tobacco was an export crop, it was convenient for the ships to sail up the broad rivers to the planter's wharf to be loaded. The first plantations were settled along the James, the York, and other rivers and along the shores of the bays and inlets; late comers were compelled to take the land father away from the water and to get their tobacco on board ship as best they could.

Rice was probably introduced into South Carolina as early as 1669, but was not successfully raised until almost thirty years later, when an improved Madagascar variety was introduced. Grown at first on the uplands, it was soon transferred to the low swampy coast lands where it flourished through the long hot summers. By 1775 the planters were exporting from "Charlestown" 125,000 barrels annually. Indigo, the other great export crop of South Carolina, which looks somewhat like the asparagus plant, dates from 1741, when Eliza Lucas, daughter of an English planter, after several discouraging experiments, succeeded in producing a dye equal to the West Indian product. Its production was stimulated by the grant by Parliament in 1748 of a bounty of 6d. a pound, and for the next thirty years the export of indigo was a source of increasing wealth. For the ten years prior to the Revolution the average exports were 700,000 pounds annually, at prices ranging from 2s. to 5s. a pound. The production of rice and indigo dovetailed so as to provide a twelve-month routine for slave labor, and consequently afforded an economic basis for slavery as did tobacco in Virginia. Cotton was raised for home use in all the southern colonies, and by the time of the Revolution was grown quite extensively. Its commercial production was, however, limited by the high cost of separating the lint from the seeds.

Corn and wheat were also always grown, and the former was the chief reliance as a food product. Sweet potatoes were universally raised and were a favorite article of diet. Apples and pears were successfully grown by grafting English varieties on the native crabtree. Peaches also flourished and were found on every plantation.

Livestock in the South. The livestock industry was especially distinctive of the Carolinas, though it flourished also in the other southern colonies. Cattle were brought to Jamestown, soon after its settlement, from England and Ireland, and later Spanish cattle from the West Indies were added. By 1639 there were 30,000 head in the colony. The cattle were allowed to run wild in the forests, finding their own forage for the most part. Sometimes hunting parties were organized which pursued the wild cattle as though they were deer. Practically all the unenclosed land formed one vast common upon which anyone could pasture his stock, and the farmer whose crops might be injured by the cattle was compelled to fence his farm in order to keep the cattle out; the cattle owner was under no compulsion to fence his livestock in. Later, as livestock multiplied, regulation became necessary.

Similar conditions prevailed in the Carolinas; by 1775 the author of *American Husbandry* described the large herds, often numbering 2000 cattle, which a single individual might own in North Carolina—"such herds of cattle and swine," he added, "are to be found in no other colony." This was the beginning of cattle-ranching in the present United States, and all the accompaniments that later became so familiar in the Far West were introduced here, such as round-ups, branding, open range, disputes with the planters, and so forth. Cattle were concentrated at "cowpens," which were enclosures in the rough frontier settlements like the cow-towns of the later western ranges. From these districts cattle were driven to Charleston, Norfolk, Baltimore, and Philadelphia.

Hogs were also allowed to run at large in the forests where they found excellent food and, reverting to a half-wild state, were later known as "razorbacks." They multiplied very rapidly and there soon began an export trade in pork; even thus early Virginia hams and bacon came to have a high reputation. Sheep did not flourish during the early colonial period in the South on account of the wolves, but by the end of the seventeenth century flocks began to be common. Goats, on the other hand, which could protect themselves, increased almost as rapidly as swine, but lost ground when sheep-raising became possible. Neither of these, however, was so important as cattle.

Horses were not very highly regarded at first, since the lack of roads made their use impracticable for transportation except as pack horses, while oxen were preferred as draft animals on the farm. With the growth in wealth of the colonists they came to be prized as saddle horses. Purry,[10] writing in 1731 of South Carolina, stated that "horses, the best kind in the world, are so plentiful, that you seldom see anybody travel on foot."

Implements. There was the same lack of implements in the southern colonies as in those to the north; capital in all its forms was everywhere scarce. Even as late as 1648, when there were 15,000 white people and 300 slaves in Virginia, there were only 150 plows. The methods used in growing tobacco required that most of the work be done by hand, for which a hoe was the favorite tool. In general the farm implements were the same as those used in New England and the middle colonies.

Land acquisition and tenure. The claims of the European nations [11] to the lands of the New World were based upon priority of discovery and exploration, of conquest, and of settlement. Of these the last-named was the most important and the decisive factor in giving title. Thus the papal bull dividing the newly discovered lands between Spain and Portugal did not deter other nations from taking possession of territory they wanted. Nor was greater regard paid to the rights of the original possessors of the land—the Indians— though some of the proprietors, like William Penn, or the

---

[10] J. P. Purry, et al, A Description of the Province of South Carolina, Drawn up at Charles Town, 1731. Sir Peter Force, Tracts and other Papers (Washington, 1837), II, no. xi, 9. See Bogart and Thompson, Readings, 41.

[11] See map on page 13.

colonies, like New York and New Jersey, made treaties with the Indians, by which they ceded their possessions to the white man; and after the establishment of the Union, the federal government was always careful to make treaties with the Indian tribes in which cessions of the land were made. But the early settlers were usually satisfied with titles to ownership based upon royal grants and did not inquire too closely into the right of the European monarchs to claim and to dispose of the land.

The land system of New England was characterized by grants to companies or to groups rather than to individuals, by community or town settlement, and by freehold tenure in small parcels of land which individuals received in turn from the proprietors. The procedure in general was somewhat as follows: A group of individuals, known as a propriety, would petition the legislative body or the governor for a grant, usually a tract of land six miles square, to be chartered as a town (township). The proprietors would then divide the land among themselves, reserving, however, enough for commons, burying ground, church and school lots, and for the builders of the first gristmill and sawmill. They had the responsibility, also, of constructing the necessary roads and providing for religious and educational facilities. As an economic system of land tenure these communal holdings had obvious defects, but the social and political results were beneficial, for they developed habits of group action and of compact social life. The eighteenth century saw a breakdown of this socio-politico-economic organization. Proprietors obtained grants for purely speculative purposes with no thought of settling the land. Land jobbers in New England peddled their proprietors' "rights" in neighboring colonies, and conflicts between speculators and actual settlers were not infrequent. But gradually the land was settled and brought under cultivation.

In the middle colonies of New York, New Jersey, Pennsylvania, and Maryland the proprietary system, which aimed to attract settlers, existed. Under this system the land was granted or sold to individuals rather than to groups, which sharply distinguished it from the "propriety" of New England. Most of the land under this system was originally disposed of on some basis of feudal tenure, such as the payment of a permanent quitrent, but as time went on there was a tendency to make outright grants of land in fee simple and to make the allotments of manageable size like those in the northern colonies. In both cases the existence of large numbers of small farms worked by their owners produced a democratic type of society. This system led to an individualistic type of colony quite different from the compact community settlement of New England, and not infrequently resulted in an undesirable dispersion of the population. Large holdings were to be found in Pennsylvania and especially in New York.

It has often been stated that large plantations were the typical estates to be found in the South. Such a broad generalization needs qualification. Large plantations never prevailed generally throughout the southern colonies, and in the seventeenth century were not typical even in Virginia or the Carolinas, where small farms, worked by their owners, were the rule. By the eighteenth century, however, the plantation type of agriculture required large holdings and the great plantations were developed in the tobacco and rice districts. The great abundance of land in proportion to population made such a development much easier there than in the more restricted area of New England with its rapidly growing population.

The difference between New England and the South was mainly the result of economic causes: the fertile soil and the presence of a few staples for which there was a good market abroad, and which lent themselves to extensive cultivation, made the large plantation profitable in the southern colonies. They consequently developed a commercial type of agriculture, which demanded a large supply of cheap labor. The average size of a seventeenth-century farm in nine counties in Virginia was 365 [12] acres; by the eighteenth century the average was much greater and there were some enormous estates, though the amount under cultivation was only a fraction of the land held. In New England the average farm was probably not far from 150 acres, except in the stock-raising district of Rhode Island where it was necessarily

[12] T. J. Wertenbaker, *The Planters of Old Virginia* (Princeton, 1922), 53.

larger. It must not be supposed that the whole of these holdings was under cultivation; much of the greater part was held
for speculation or for future use. Thus in 1686 William
Fitzhugh of Virginia had one plantation of 1000 acres, but
only 300 acres were cleared. Even on a New England farm
of 150 acres, probably not more than 10 or 15 acres could be
cultivated with the inefficient implements and limited labor
available.

The issuance of a patent or title deed for the land granted
was usually conditional on actual occupation and the payment
of a small annual quitrent. This was an annual charge payable to the grantor. It was a relic of the medieval custom,
according to which the serf originally paid part of his produce,
later a fixed sum of money, to the lord of the manor each
year for military protection. Quitrents varied from time to
time, generally becoming higher as the value of the land
increased. A frequent charge was 2s. per hundred acres. In
a country in which land was so plentiful and the proprietor
furnished no protection, the quitrent was out of place and
unpopular; its collection consequently was found extremely
difficult. Just before the Revolution quitrents in Virginia,
where they were most efficiently administered, yielded only
£10,000 to £15,000 a year. As a form of revenue quitrents
were universally unsatisfactory. These feudal charges never
existed in New England, where alone in America a settler
could obtain absolute title to an unencumbered estate.

Inheritance in the South and in parts of other colonies
followed the law of primogeniture, according to which
the eldest son inherited all the landed property; in New
England and Pennsylvania, while the right of the eldest son
was still recognized, he received only a double portion, the
rest of the property being divided equally among the other
children. The principle of entail, by which the inheritance of
a piece of property was limited to members of the family
only, was also applied. The repeal of these feudal devices,
both of which were undesirable, began with the Revolution,
and by the end of the eighteenth century they had everywhere
been abolished.

Conclusion. The agricultural problems presented to the
colonists were several. The one first solved was how to pro-

duce the necessary food supplies, and in answering this the aid of the Indians was invaluable. Practically the only contribution of Indian culture to our American civilization was in agriculture, but in this field it was noteworthy. The Indians had succeeded in bringing wild plants under control and practiced plant-breeding and seed selection. Because of the absence of domesticable animals and of adequate tools their farm operations resembled horticulture rather than agriculture, but they were well adapted to the crops raised. They also knew how to preserve food—meat, vegetables, and fruit by drying, either over a fire or in the sun, and berries, nuts, and similar edibles by mixing with honey or syrup. In the semi-arid country of the Far West they practiced irrigation, and on the plains had developed great skill in hunting and in dressing skins. All this knowledge was quickly appropriated by the white settlers.

The next problems to be solved were those of determining the best crops for each section and the most profitable methods of production, and of obtaining the necessary capital in the form of farm implements. The first of these could be answered only by experimentation, and here assistance was given not only by company directors in England and by individual farmers in America, but by every ship captain who brought back seed from the foreign ports at which he touched. Although the process was wholly one of trial and error, it was very successful in determining the crops best suited to each locality. The farm practices were a resultant of Indian and European methods, and of the economic combination of the factors of production as they existed in the colonies. It is difficult to generalize broadly for such different regions and for so long a period, but colonial agriculture as a whole may fairly be called exploitative. In sacrificing the land and conserving labor, the colonists were simply following the line of least resistance and largest returns.

It is impossible to make a general statement that will cover the different conditions existing in the various colonies respecting the organization of agriculture. It may be said, however, that in New England and in most of the colonies to the southern boundary of Pennsylvania self-sufficing farming was the rule; that is to say, the farmer practised general farming, raising practically everything that was needed for his own support. The investment of capital was small, being limited to a few agricultural implements and a small supply of livestock, and the needed labor was supplied by his family and himself. Organization of such a farm presented problems like those that faced Robinson Crusoe: the colonial farmer applied the resources at his command to the satisfaction of his own immediate needs and those of his family. South of Pennsylvania, where commercial crops were grown, the organization was different; here the problem of labor was pressing and prices had to be watched. On the whole, however, the colonial farmer worked out his problems primarily with a view to his own needs. But, in doing this, he paid little heed to the welfare of subsequent generations; he practised an exhaustive agriculture and failed to restore the worn-out lands either by crop rotation or by the application of manure.

The methods of distributing and granting title to the land were also determined by the conditions of the new environment. On the whole, as might be expected in a country of boundless extent, the acquisition of land was easy and inexpensive. If unable to obtain land in one of the settled colonies, the colonist moved out to the frontier and squatted on the land. Sometimes he was given his holding without payment or was given a prior right to purchase at the regular price. Efforts to perpetuate the feudal practices of Europe proved unsuccessful and ultimately gave way to freedom in ownership and exchange of land. Only in respect to the treatment of Indian occupants can colonial procedure be seriously called into question.

CHAPTER III

COLONIAL INDUSTRIES

Early experiments. One of the motives that led to the founding of the English colonies in North America was the desire to establish there industries which would furnish the mother country with articles she was then importing from other countries. The emigrants who were first sent out were miners and artisans and tradesmen rather than farmers. One of the first broadsides of the Virginia company, calling for settlers, solicited "blacksmiths, coopers, carpenters, shipwrights, turners, all who work any kind of metal, men who make bricks, architects, bakers, weavers, shoemakers, sawyers, and those who spin wool."

Workmen were brought from Europe to set up the manufacture of pitch and tar, potash, and glass. And in response to the urgings of the company directors in London some of the first exports from the colonies were a cargo from Virginia in 1608 of pitch, tar, iron, ore, potash, and clapboards. Captain John Smith, who understood better the conditions of colonizing, sent back word that "it were better to give five hundred pound a tun for those grosse Commodities in Denmarke, than send for them hither, till more necessary things be provided." But even Smith himself seemed to have conceived manufacturing to be the logical occupation of the colonists, for in his *True and Sincere Declaration*,[1] published in 1610, he asked that there be sent to Virginia, in addition to the workers enumerated above, "iron men for the furnace and hammer, gunfounders, tile-makers, salt-makers, rope-makers, sope-ashe men, minerall men, silke-dressers," and other artisans. These intentions were persevered in, for in 1620 Sir Edwin Sandys stated at a meeting of the Company that 150 persons had been sent over to set up ironworks, and

---

[1] The fuller title of this work was "A True and Sincere declaration of the purpose and ends of the Plantation begun in Virginia," etc.

that the settlers had been urged to make naval stores and lumber products, soap ashes, cordage, and other things needed in England. But, by this time, the profitableness of tobacco had made all such exhortations futile and thereafter manufactures languished in Virginia.

It is not necessary to rehearse the early experiences in the other colonies, for in all of them the outcome was the same. The industries to which the colonists devoted themselves were those which yielded the largest immediate returns. They concentrated on the extractive industries—lumbering, fishing, trapping, mining, and agriculture. Lacking skilled labor and any but simple tools, the colonists added little value to the raw materials they produced. The industries were also conducted on a small scale, partly because of the lack of labor and capital in the new world, and partly because markets were small and scattered and transportation was expensive. Under such conditions only a relatively small output and only a limited degree of specialization was possible.

Forest industries. The natural resource that existed in all the colonies, from Maine to Georgia, in almost inexhaustible abundance, readily accessible and easy to transport, and for which a steady and large market existed in Europe, was the forests. Practically the whole coast was clothed with timber, except in the occasional Indian clearings, and this was especially dense near the watercourses along which the early settlements were made. On the other hand, there was a great and growing demand for forest products in Europe. By the middle of the sixteenth century complaints began to be heard of the destruction of the forests and by the beginning of the seventeenth century firewood had become almost a luxury in many parts of western Europe, and the price of building materials had risen to prohibitive heights. This was true not only of materials for houses, but also for ships, a fact pregnant with danger in view of the growing interests of England overseas. The cutting down of the forests, moreover, threatened the iron industry, in which the smelting was done by charcoal, the tanning industry which needed oak bark, and other manufactures which depended upon forest supplies.

When the English settlements were planted in North America, it was only natural that both statesmen at home

and settlers in the colonies should see in the forests a resource which could be utilized to the advantage of both
parties. The colonists had much to learn about the trees and
the products for which they were best suited. Some knowledge they brought with them from Europe, and some they
undoubtedly gained from the Indians, but experience taught
them their most valuable lessons, as in the case of agriculture. Upon the forest resources were based four principal
industries—lumbering and lumber products, shipbuilding
and ship timber, the production of naval stores, and the
making of potash.

Lumber products. The dearness of iron and the backwardness of the metallurgical arts, together with the plentifulness
and cheapness of wood, resulted in making many articles of
wood which today are made of metal. Most of the agricultural implements were made of wood, as were the majority
of household articles, such as furniture of all sorts, wooden
trenchers or plates, bowls, buckets, churns, butter-paddles,
cheese-hoops, looms, spinning wheels, washboards, mortars
for grinding grain, pegs, and many other things. The houses,
barns, and fences were of course made of wood, and wood
was also used exclusively as fuel. In addition to the domestic
needs there was a steady demand for many of these articles
for export to the West Indies, and especially for cooperage
stock for the sugar and wine islands.

The process of making sugar, as it was then carried on
in the West Indies, was very crude. The juice from the
sugar cane was boiled until it was ready to crystallize; the
crystals constituted a coarse brown impure sugar called "mus-
covado," and the remaining liquid was molasses. The barrels
or containers for both these products must not only be tight
enough to hold the contents, but must keep out the moisture;
a single porous stave might ruin the contents of a sugar
barrel. Only the best lumber was used for these barrel staves,
and the sugar barrels were never used a second time for
that purpose. Casks or pipes were also used as containers for
the wine produced in the Madeira and Canary Islands. There
was consequently a constant market for all the barrel staves,
heads, and hoops and pipe staves for wine casks that the
colonists could produce. The profits from this source must

have been great for even by hand a man could make 15,000 barrel staves or clapboards in a year, which, according to Gent, were worth £4 per thousand in the colonies and £20 per thousand in the Canaries. All these were shipped in great quantity, and even knockdown houses, ready to be set up on their arrival, were exported to the West Indies. Barrels were also needed for the fish, meat, flour, naval stores, and whale oil which were shipped out of the colonies. Red and white oak were the principal hard woods used for cooperage stock.[2] Cedar, spruce, and fir were among the soft woods used for lumber and boards.

In order to utilize the forest resources, it was necessary to have sawmills, and these were built early. The first mill in the colonies is supposed to have been built near York, Maine, in 1623, which was forty years before sawmills were introduced into England. One hundred years later the little Piscataqua River in New Hampshire alone was turning the wheels of seventy sawmills, from which flowed a stream of 6,000,000 feet a year of planks and other products.

Shipbuilding. A second important industry built up on the basis of the forest resources was shipbuilding. Here again there existed the combination of a scarcity of shipbuilding materials in Europe, especially in England, and a cheap and abundant supply in the colonies. There was thus a strong demand from England for ships, masts, spars, and naval stores of all kinds, and at the same time there was a need in the colonies themselves for ships to carry on their expanding commerce. The colonists were well qualified to meet this demand, for they had large supplies of excellent ship timber at the very water's edge. Masts of white pine or fir, logs of oak fifty feet long, clear of knots, and straight-grained for ship timber and planks, pitch pine for tar and turpentine, and hemp for cordage furnished almost all the materials needed in the construction of a wooden sailing vessel.

The wasteful seventeenth-century assumption that the supply of these ship timbers was inexhaustible gave way in

2 Southern staves of red oak were preferred for sugar hogsheads and white oak for rum casks; New England supplied principally boards and scantlings to the West Indies.

the eighteenth century, as they grew scarcer, to a policy of conservation. Trees suitable for masts of twenty-four inches in diameter at the base or larger were marked with a broad arrow and reserved for the use of the royal navy, under a penalty of $500 if used for other purposes. Special mast vessels were built to transport these splendid timbers, and sometimes great rafts of masts and spars were bound roughly together in the form of a ship's hull and sailed to England where they arrived after weeks or even months. A great mast three feet in diameter at the butt, delivered at Portsmouth, England, brought in about $500 to the colonial owner. Even more important than the straight timber for masts and planks, however, was the need for logs of exceptional and peculiar size and shape for certain parts of the ship's anatomy. Knees, futtocks, stem, cathead, and other special pieces had to be taken from trees of crooked shape, with the right curvature or with two diverging branches or other peculiarities. These could not be spliced but must be a natural growth in one piece. The necessity of using these "compass" timbers limited the size of the ships and the number of ships that could be built.

Compared with modern steamships of 80,000 tons, the fishing vessels of 10 tons and even the larger ships engaged in the West Indian and transatlantic trade seem tiny indeed. Toward the end of the eighteenth century the average tonnage of colonial vessels in the West Indian trade was only 68, and of ships entering England from America 176. The cost of building was very low. Governor Bellomont of New York reported in 1700 that it cost 40 per cent less to build ships in the colonies than in England. The first half of the eighteenth century was the most prosperous period of colonial shipbuilding; after that costs rose sharply although still lagging behind English costs. By 1774 about 210,000 tons, or nearly one-third of the tonnage afloat under the British flag, had been built in American shipyards. These were situated not merely in every seaport town of New England, but even in villages along navigable streams up to the fall line. New York, Pennsylvania, and Maryland also built vessels, but New England probably launched annually twice as great a tonnage as all these other colonies combined. The number of American ships in 1775 was estimated at 2000, manned by 33,000 seamen.

Naval stores. Closely allied to shipbuilding was the production of naval stores, as pitch, tar, turpentine, and resin were called. These were "key" commodities in the days of wooden sailing vessels, for they were used in almost every part of the ship. The planks of the vessel were coated with resin and pitch to preserve them against marine borers and dry rot, and the spaces between the planks were calked with oakum and melted pitch; the rope rigging was also treated with tar to prevent its decay. Until iron steamships replaced the wooden sailing vessels, these naval stores were essential to the shipping of the world. The northern countries of Europe bordering on the Baltic had a practical monopoly of their production and England had obtained her supplies from them, but when the Swedish company which controlled their supply attempted to raise their prices, Parliament turned for relief to the North American colonies. By act of 1705 generous bounties were given of £4 per ton on all tar and pitch imported, £3 per ton on resin and turpentine, £6 per ton for hemp, and £1 per ton for masts, yards, and bowsprits, representing roughly the difference in cost of transportation between America and the Baltic region. Between that date and 1776, when they ceased, over £1,500,000 were paid to the American colonies in bounties.

The supply of naval stores was drawn from two sources, of which one was incidental to the clearing of the land and the other was the result of commercial production. In regions remote from the sea it was customary in clearing the land of pine and other resinous woods to boil out the tar they contained in rudely constructed kilns. Such an industry was simply a utilization of a waste product and ceased when the land was cleared. It was, however, of some importance while it lasted, for in a single year around 1700 over 6000 barrels of naval stores were shipped from Boston. The other source of supply was the regular commercial industry carried on in the production of naval stores, chiefly in North Carolina; for this purpose the yellow pine was used. The exports of tar amounted to only 872 barrels in 1704, but increased to 82,084 in 1718 under the stimulus of the bounty. This was more than England needed and the price dropped dis-astrously. As a result, the bounties were cut in half. In 1770 the quantity of tar exported from all the colonies was 76,000 barrels; of pitch, 22,000; and of turpentine, 16,000 barrels, worth in all nearly $1,000,000.

Potash. The fourth industry based upon the forest resources was the making of potash, but this, too, was largely incidental to the work of clearing the land for agriculture. Potash was made from the ashes of oak, ash, birch, and other hardwoods, and was therefore produced chiefly in the northern colonies. Wood ashes were collected from the trees which were cut down and burned when the land was cleared; these were then boiled with water in huge open kettles until the water evaporated and nothing was left except a thick brownish salt, called pot-ash. To make pearl ash this residue was placed in a hot oven until the carbon was burned out, leaving a lighter and more valuable substance. Potash and pearl ash were in great demand in England for bleaching, soapmaking, glassmaking, and other manufactures, and also as fertilizers, and were early placed on the list of enumerated commodities which must be sent to England only. The profits from the sale of these products were generally sufficient to pay the cost of clearing a given piece of land, especially in districts so remote from transportation that the lumber itself could not be marketed.

The fisheries. A second important group of industries was built up on the abundant ocean and river resources. Fish were found in all the rivers and along the entire Atlantic coast, but between Long Island and Newfoundland was discovered one of the richest fishing grounds in the world. Here the submerged coastal plain or continental shelf provided a large area of shallow water, rich in marine plant food, to which resorted cod, mackerel, herring, halibut, and many other varieties of fish; while the deeply indented shore line and the many islands furnished numerous harbors in which the fishermen could find refuge from the storms, or land to dry and cure their catch before taking it to market. These waters, cooled by the ocean current from the Arctic seas, were also frequented by whales, and toward the end of the seventeenth century the whaling industry was added to that of fishing.

There was a large and increasing demand in the West Indies and Europe for fish as food, especially in the Catholic countries, while in the colonies fish were so general an article of diet that servants in Massachusetts are said to have stipulated that they should not be given salmon more than twice a week. In order to meet this demand, European fishermen had pushed westward, reaching Iceland by 1300 and the Newfoundland banks by 1500. Many years before the first English settlement in North America, English fishermen had frequented the New England coast and established summer fishing stations, where they landed and dried their fish. To the settlers at Plymouth Captain John Smith gave some blunt but sensible advice, "the main staple from hence to be extracted . . . is fish," and it was from the fisheries in truth that New England gained its greatest wealth. The industry was developed early, and throughout the whole of the colonial period remained a lucrative one.

The fish were sorted into three grades, the best merchantable ones being exported to the Catholic countries of southern Europe; the middlings being shipped to the Canaries, the Madeiras, and Jamaica, or consumed at home; and the poorest, which consisted of the small, thin, and broken fish, being sold to the sugar planters in the West Indies as food for the Negro slaves. In 1770 two-thirds of the dried fish was exported to southern Europe. In 1713 a Gloucester shipbuilder constructed a new type of ship, the schooner, which was better adapted to deep-sea fishing than the older vessels, and after this the cod, mackerel, and whale fisheries took on new importance. Gloucester and Marblehead were the leading fishing ports of the eighteenth century.

The *whaling industry* was at first carried on close to the shore with small boats, but after 1700 New England seamen followed the whales into the deeper waters of the ocean. As the whales deserted the Atlantic coast they were followed to the Arctic and even to the Antarctic oceans by the whalers. Spermaceti, sperm oil, whalebone, and other products of the whale were in great demand, and upon the spermaceti oil

was based a colonial candlemaking industry of some importance. At the outbreak of the Revolution over 300 vessels
and 4000 seamen were engaged in the whaling industry, the
center of which was located in Nantucket and New Bedford.
The fishing industry was confined exclusively to New England; during the colonial period not a vessel engaged in
either the cod or whale fisheries was owned south of Connecticut. For that section it possessed great economic significance. The development of the cod and mackerel fisheries
provided New England with a needed staple for foreign
trade; they made the inhabitants a commercial and seagoing
people, giving them a wider outlook, and breaking down the
isolation of a purely agricultural community; whale-fishing
brought in larger vessels and the practice of making longer
voyages. Well might Edmund Burke exclaim, "No sea but
what is vexed by their fisheries; no climate that is not witness
to their toils." The fisheries were indeed a "nursery of seamen" and seamen of a particularly hardy breed; the training
these New England men received placed them among the
best and most daring sailors.

Industries based on agricultural resources. The rude pioneer life and the hard manual toil must have made it extremely difficult for the colonists to keep themselves
adequately supplied with suitable clothing, and the need was
accentuated in New England by the long and severe winters.
It was not possible to depend upon imported textiles, for
these were expensive and the colonists were poor. Spinning
wheels, usually of the hand-wheel type, and hand looms
were early introduced into all the colonies, and spinning and
weaving of coarse "homespun" woolen and linen cloth were
carried on in every household.

The raw materials for making textiles were neither abundant nor cheap, and a great deal of labor was required in the
processes of making cloth, in both of which respects cloth-
making differed from the ordinary colonial industries. But in
this case the urgent necessities of the colonists compelled
them to undertake this work on their own account. England
forbade the export of raw wool from that country and placed
an export duty on woolen broadcloth, and after 1660 prohibited the importation by the colonists of the cheaper Dutch

woolens. But this attempt to monopolize the manufacture for English artisans forced the colonists to rely on their own efforts rather than to buy English textiles.

Cloth-making was a household industry for the most part; in every farmhouse kitchen could be heard the hum of the spinning wheel on which the carded wool or prepared flax was drawn out into long even yarn or thread, a single one at a time. Weaving was a more elaborate process, requiring larger equipment and more skill and strength, and was frequently done by the men; it was consequently less exclusively a household industry. The next step in cloth-making was likewise a man's job. When cloth first came off the loom it was loose and uneven and had to be pounded and shrunk to prepare it for use. This was known as fulling. Special heavy equipment operated by water power was required for the job. Fulling mills were usually carried on as separate trades, but after the cloth had been fulled the further processes of dyeing and the rude operations necessary to finish the cloth for country use were carried on within the home again. The smelly dye tub was as common an article of furniture as the churn. Coloring matter came from the fields and forests— yellow from sassafras, red from madder root, brown from the bark of red oak or hickory, and blue from indigo, the last usually being obtained from a peddler. Rough druggets, jeans, and homespun made of wool and cotton, linsey-woolseys made of linen and wool, and fustians made of cotton and flax were the principal products.

Linen was more common than wool, for it was used not only for clothing but also for various household purposes for which cotton is used today, as bed linen, table linen, towels, and similar articles. European flax was introduced in 1629, but the colonists were never able to raise enough to supply all the linen they required. Hemp succeeded better, but the manufactures of this material were less important and less extensive, though the need for cordage led to the giving of bounties for the production of hemp in several of the colonies.

Cotton was but little used during the colonial period, and that was generally imported from the West Indies. By the time of the Revolution, however, some long-staple cotton was being raised in the southern colonies for domestic use. Because the cotton thread was not strong enough to serve both as warp and woof it was usually combined with flax.

The textile manufactures of the colonies grew to such a point that they led to investigations by the Board of Trade and Plantations at various times. Judging from the reports, it may be concluded that, taking them altogether, the colonists probably made about three-fourths of the textile goods for domestic consumption, but these were almost exclusively of the coarser grades for country use. The finer qualities of linens, woolens, and other goods continued to be imported from England and Ireland throughout this period, and were generally seen in the cities.

Leathermaking was carried on both as a household industry and in separate establishments of some size. After the livestock industry was developed, there was a plentiful supply of hides of cattle and sheep, and the skins of deer, raccoon, fox, wolf, and beaver were also utilized for garments. Almost as essential as the raw material itself were the tanbark, tallow, and other materials used in tanning the hides and preparing the leather for market, but these, too, were to be had in abundance. The demand for leather products was large and continuous, for in a primitive and self-sufficing community leather is used for many things which in a more advanced stage are made of other materials. Thus not only were harness, saddlery, traces, belts for wheels, boots and shoes, gloves, and similar articles made of leather, but also vests, doublets, and breeches for men, and jerkins, petticoats, and aprons for women. Hinges for doors, straps in lieu of springs for coaches, and even bed supports were made of leather. The first tannery in New England was erected at Lynn in 1629, and here there came shortly a shoemaker who laid the foundation of the shoe industry for which the city is still famous. A hundred years later Massachusetts shoes were being sent to the southern colonies and to the West Indies.

Papermaking is more deserving of the appellation of manufactures than several of the other industries mentioned, for it required a considerable capital equipment and skilled labor. During the colonial period, paper was made from linen rags, which were cut, ground to pulp, made into sheets, and dried in much the same way that handmade paper is manufactured today. The industry was introduced into Philadelphia in 1690 by a Dutch immigrant, one William Rittenhouse, and that city became the center of papermaking. It supplied more raw material than any other colonial city, not only by reason of its size but also because its inhabitants wore more linen, while the citizens of Boston preferred wool on account of the colder climate. This was, moreover, a more highly specialized craft than brewing or tanning, and the Dutch and the Germans understood it better than the English. With paper manufacture went the printing business; Benjamin Franklin, the printer, gained part of his fortune from investments in eighteen paper mills.

Brewing was a household industry in most of the colonies, but it was also carried on as a specialized trade. Barley, wheat, Indian corn, and rice were all malted for fermentation, and most of the beer and ale was consumed immediately, as it would not keep. The manufacture of cider was also large in the northern colonies. But most important of all was the making of *rum* which was distilled from West Indian molasses. On the sugar plantations of those islands molasses was a by-product of the making of sugar, but as there was little demand for this product in its natural state the problem arose as to what disposition to make of it. The English planters distilled their molasses into rum, but the French and Dutch planters could not do this, for the rum would compete with the French brandy and Holland gin of the home countries. The molasses in those islands was, therefore, treated as a waste and was run into the creeks or the ocean, but here it became a serious nuisance under the hot tropical sun. When permission was given to sell the molasses, the Yankee traders were able to buy it for a trifle—two or three shillings a hogshead—and upon this cheap raw material they soon built up a flourishing and lucrative distilling business. The distillation of molasses into rum probably came nearest to our modern system of manufacturing of all the colonial industries. As the demand grew, the price of molasses rose. The consumption of molasses as such was small, although some was used in New England and in the fisheries as a cheap substitute for sugar, but for the rum there was an enormous demand. The imports of molasses and of rum into the continental colonies far exceeded those of any other West Indian products. In 1769 almost 4,000,000 gallons of molasses and 3,000,000 gallons of rum were imported [3]; since one gallon of molasses would make one gallon of rum, there was thus available a total of about 7,000,000 gallons of rum, or between two and three gallons per capita. A considerable amount was consumed in the colonies, but a large part was exported to Africa where it was bartered for slaves, ivory, gold dust, and other products, or was sent to Canada and Newfoundland and used on the fishing vessels. It was also used in trade with the Indians, although this was officially forbidden. The rum-distilling industry was localized in New England, especially in Massachusetts, Connecticut, and Rhode Island; the wealth of Newport was derived largely from the rum and slave trade.

Corn and *gristmills* for grinding grain into flour were found in all the colonies. Country gristmills, run by water power, were among the earliest establishments in a new community, where they ground on toll, usually about one-sixth of the grain, for the neighboring farmers. These were small, but during the eighteenth century large merchant mills, converting over a hundred bushels of grain a day into flour, manufactured flour for the export trade. Bake ovens were sometimes associated with them, in which ships' biscuit was baked. The importance of these industries in the middle colonies is evidenced by the fact that in 1764-66 practically half of the exports from New York and Pennsylvania consisted of flour and biscuits.

Mineral industries. Iron was found in practically all the colonies, in the form of either bog iron or iron ore. Bog iron was a brownish scum dug or raked from the bottom of swamps and ponds, chiefly in Massachusetts. Utensils made of it were esteemed for their toughness and lightness. Deposits of iron ore existed from Connecticut to Georgia. The high cost of importing iron manufactures, such as agricultural implements, anchors and chains for ships, firearms, nails and horseshoes, kitchen utensils, and other necessities,

[3] Lord Sheffield, *Observations,* 109, 112.

together with an abundant supply of fuel for smelting at home, early stimulated the colonists to develop these resources and to supply themselves with these essential commodities.

The *iron* industry may be divided into two branches, of which the first consists of the smelting of the crude ore and its conversion into pig or bar iron, and the second of the manufacture of various finished articles from the refined iron.

Colonial annals refer repeatedly to ironworks, though it is difficult to get an adequate picture at any time. A furnace was built in 1622 near Jamestown, which was said to have cost over $20,000, but it was destroyed by the Indians and not rebuilt. A more successful smelting furnace was erected near Lynn in Massachusetts in 1643, and five years later a forge for refining the iron was set up, and soon after a foundry for casting. During the seventeenth century Massachusetts was the center of the iron industry, but Rhode Island and Connecticut took precedence as better deposits of iron ore were discovered there. In the eighteenth century the smelting of iron ore was developed on a fairly large scale in New York, New Jersey, and Pennsylvania. The statements of the governors of various colonies to the Board of Trade in 1731 reported some six furnaces and nineteen forges, but this was undoubtedly an understatement, due partly to ignorance and partly to a desire not to create antagonism.[4] They produced, said the report, "not a fourth part of the iron that is requisite for the use of the inhabitants." Twenty years later the colonies reported five furnaces, ten forges, and four rolling and slitting mills. At these mills wrought-iron bars were rolled into flat sheets or strips and then slit into rods for nail making.

The manufacture of the finished articles was carried on in workshops, for there were no factories. In these shops the colonists produced handmade iron manufactures for their immediate needs, such as pots and kettles, chains, tires for wagon wheels and sleigh runners, anvils, guns, shovels, hoes, scythes, and numerous other articles.

[4] *Report of the Lords Commissioners for Trade and Plantations to the House of Commons*, 1732. In Bogart and Thompson, *Readings*, 60.

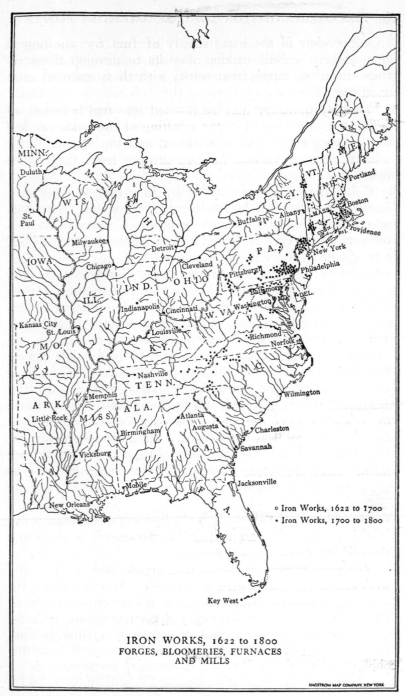

IRON WORKS, 1622 to 1800
FORGES, BLOOMERIES, FURNACES
AND MILLS

o Iron Works, 1622 to 1700
• Iron Works, 1700 to 1800

HAGSTROM MAP COMPANY, NEW YORK

One product of the iron industry was made in the home. This was nails. Nail making was done during the winter when there was little farm work; a small furnace was set up in the chimney corner where the iron rods were heated, so that they could be cut into appropriate lengths and then hammered into shape by hand. Nails were in constant demand among the pioneers for construction and repair work.

Other mineral industries for which there was an abundant supply of raw materials and whose products were in demand were the making of *brick* and *glass*. The first of these was heavy and bulky but of small value, while the other was subject to heavy loss through breakage. Consequently, the colonists were forced to produce these articles for themselves if they wished them in any quantity.

Bricks were needed for fireplaces and chimneys and were also used for houses as the colonists were able to afford them. Clay suitable for this purpose was found almost everywhere, and soft and glazed brick, and roof and enameled tiles were made; the processes were those of the workshop.

Glass was always a scarce and highly desired article at this time, but the industry required highly specialized skilled labor. The first glass furnace was erected at Jamestown in 1609; the largest one was built by Baron Stiegel near Lancaster, Pennsylvania, and earned $13,000 a year at the outset. After local needs had been satisfied, however, it languished and died for lack of an adequate market. Many attempts to manufacture glass were made during the colonial period but they were rarely successful unless conducted on a small scale.

Limited specialization. It is a well-known economic principle that "specialization is limited by the extent of the market," which means that no one can afford to specialize in one craft if there is little demand for its products. For example, the isolated colonial pioneer was a "jack-of-all-trades" who made his own shoes as well as many other necessities; later the countryside was served by an itinerant cobbler who had to travel from one village to another to find enough business to keep occupied at his trade; still later the cobbler settled down in some community large enough to keep him busy the year around; and eventually, in modern times, the shoe factory appeared, in which many specialists work, each making only one small part of many shoes which it is now possible to sell over a wide area. In small colonial communities most men were farmers and jacks-of-all-trades to a high degree. Gradually a few developed part-time specialties, which generally required some unusual skill or knowledge or equipment in the making of a product for which there was considerable demand. Tryon says that in eighteenth-century Pennsylvania, "soon after a new settlement was made a sawmill, a gristmill, a distillery and a brewery would appear; so the period of the grater, the mortar, handmill, sawpit...was usually short. A blacksmith, carpenter, shoemaker, hat-maker and other handicraftsmen would also be plying their trades in a short time." [5] Tanneries, too, appeared early because tanning requires skill, and leather was widely used. Sometimes a gristmill and a sawmill or a fulling mill would be combined, thus assuring the owner of plenty of business the year around.

Specialization was, of course, most pronounced in the more populous seaports like Boston, New York, or Philadelphia. Although these cities were never large—the biggest had a population of 13,000 in 1730 and barely reached 30,000 just before the Revolution—the number of handicrafts there was surprisingly large, if contemporary accounts are to be trusted. A Pennsylvania writer [6] mentioned 51 handicrafts besides the building trades as followed in Philadelphia around 1700. The list included, in addition to the industries already described, such workers as tailors, hatters, button makers, wigmakers, stocking-weavers, snuff makers, gunpowder makers, and silversmiths.

In spite of the long list of trades and industries carried on in workshops and mills, it is necessary to emphasize the extent to which northern farms and even southern plantations provided for their own needs. The colonial household was self-sufficing to a degree which it is difficult for us, living in an age of specialization, to picture. Most of the clothing and household linen was made at home, furniture and many farm tools were the product of household manufacture, food

---

[5] R. Tryon, *Household Manufactures in the United States* (Chicago, 1917), 190.
[6] G. Thomas, *History of Pennsylvania* (Philadelphia, 1900), 32-34.

and drink were grown on the farm and prepared there for home consumption.

Sources of power. Unquestionably most of the power for colonial industries was provided by human backs, arms, and legs. Where industry is primitive and conducted on a small scale, as in smithies, small shops, mines, ropewalks, mills and saw pits, much of the power is necessarily supplied in this way. Of course, ingenious laborsaving devices were invented ranging from the harnessing of a tiny brook to a "pounding mill" to grind grain in a mortar to the use of the ocean tides. Steedmills, or treadmills operated by a walking horse were fairly common. A few wind-driven sawmills and gristmills were set up near the larger seaports and towns, but, as these communities grew, buildings were erected which cut off the wind, and the mills had to be moved or abandoned.

More popular was the water mill. The simplest variety to construct was the so-called "float" mill, which could be built beside almost any river, large or small. It was driven by the water striking the vanes at the bottom of the wheel. Not much power was generated by these mills, and so an improved variety, the overshot wheel, was preferred. This was turned by water flowing rapidly down a millrace and striking the wheel from above. Such a wheel was not always feasible, for unless a natural falls could be found, it was necessary to dam up the river to get the required height and speed of water, and the cost of doing this was considerable. For economic as well as engineering reasons, water mills of this kind were generally found on small rivers. One of the first overshot mills of which there is record was built near Dorchester around 1630. Sometimes local communities were so anxious to have a good mill that they would make generous concessions to whoever would build and operate one: in 1645 the people of Roxbury offered a miller £20 in merchantable pay, 16 acres of land and tax exemption for seven years. By the eighteenth century water mills were in fairly widespread use and there were several large ones grinding grain for export. The colonists always had to contend with the weather and seasonal problems connected with the use of windmills and water mills.

The use of steam came later. Efficient steam power was not developed in England or in this country until the time of the Revolution, although there were isolated cases of its use to pump water out of mines. In operations where fuel was required wood and charcoal were almost exclusively used. The scarcity of firewood for home, shop, and forge became a serious problem in Boston as early as 1700. About the only users of coal were blacksmiths and a few wealthy townspeople and they imported their supplies from England. The first American coal mine of significance was a small bituminous one opened near Richmond, Virginia, about 1750. In short, power devices were capital, and capital, like labor, was scarce.

Shortage of capital. The extractive industries were the most important because of the relative scarcities of what economists call the three agents of production, namely land, labor, and capital. Most plentiful of these agents was land, which includes also the natural resources of the forest and the sea. Labor was scarce, but capital was probably scarcest of all. Two kinds of capital were required, working capital and capital goods. Working capital was needed to pay for raw materials, to hire workers, to carry current inventories, and to pay costs of shipping. Working capital was relatively more important then than it is today. The other kind of capital needed was tools and equipment. Economists call these means of production, capital goods, or just "capital" in contrast to "consumers' goods" like food and clothing. Although more consumers' goods can be produced in the long run by making equipment first—more fish can be caught if you take time out to make a net first—such a roundabout method of production may result in less consumers' goods—fish, for example—for the time being. Capital is thus the result of abstaining from expending money or effort for something that will satisfy an immediate want and instead devoting that money or effort to making capital goods. This is called saving, and capital is the result of saving. Since most colonists led a self-sufficient existence and needed most of their waking hours just to get the necessities of life like food, clothing, heat, and shelter, they had little chance to save, little time to add to their meager supply of equipment. While the nec-

essary tools in most colonial mills or shops were relatively
few in number—specialization was limited by the extent of
the market—at least some capital was sorely needed and it
often paid good profits. A sawmill that cost between $500 and
$1000 would turn out 1000 feet of lumber a day and net the
owner between five and ten dollars. Some of these profits
were frequently employed in enlarging the mill—up to about
four saws—or in building additional mills in other favorable
localities.[7] It is easy to see how the opportunities of the New
World absorbed capital as a desert soaks up water. Because
savings were scarce and capital in great demand, interest rates
were high. Eight per cent was a common rate for a well-
secured loan in New Jersey about 1720.

In their anxiety for more capital the colonists often made
the error of confusing money and capital. This is easy to do
because savings and borrowings are usually reckoned in terms
of money. Money savings are sometimes referred to as
"liquid" capital because they represent a claim on a surplus
of consumers' goods which can be traded for help in manufacturing or for equipment itself. It was easy to believe that
the capital scarcity was really a money scarcity and could be
relieved by printing more money. Where the pressing need
was for working capital, that was especially true. Indeed, if
the English and Europeans had been willing to trade their
goods and tools for colonial paper bills and never try to buy
other goods and services with that money, the colonial scarcity of capital could have been alleviated. But that was the
equivalent of expecting a gift of capital, which was obviously
unreasonable. Since the colonial stock of goods was small
relative to the money supply, the value of that money sank,
and prices rose. The growth of capital is made possible not
by the accumulation of money ground from a printing press
but by the willingness of people to live simply in order to
accumulate first surplus consumers' goods and then capital
goods.

It is not plenty of money, nor is it mere hard work that
makes possible a high standard of living. We produce more
goods today than our colonial ancestors did or than any other
people in the world do, not because our laborers work harder

[7] C. Nettels, *Roots of American Civilization* (New York, 1938), 245.

or are more skilful, but because they have more and better tools and are assisted by power-driven machines. Capital is thus a prime essential for a high standard of living. The accumulation of our present capital resources has been a long and gradual process. The colonists acquired capital in various ways: by trading a surplus of sea, farm, or forest resources and saving some of the proceeds; by borrowing the savings of others; by making their own tools; and by devoting some of the profits of their businesses to the expansion of those businesses. From the outset merchants accumulated the largest amounts of capital. In 1643 a Boston trader could survive the loss of $7000 in one bad venture; a generation later some thirty Massachusetts merchants were reputedly worth $50,000 to $100,000 each and Peter Faneuil was able to carry individual accounts of $50,000. However, the colonial merchants were not interested in the promotion of manufacturing except of the crudest kind. The capital for the most conspicuous examples of large-scale manufacturing came from abroad. The early ironworks in Virginia were financed entirely from England; those at Lynn in Massachusetts were supported in part by English capital. Baron Stiegel's iron and glass enterprises in Pennsylvania were largely financed by German capital, and Peter Hasenclever's imposing iron and textile mills were also backed by foreign capital.[8] Most of these pretentious foreign enterprises were unsuccessful. Capital for expanding the smaller but usually more successful ironworks, glassworks, paper mills, and shipbuilding concerns was obtained by regularly plowing back some of the profits. Throughout our economic history this has probably been the most important and dependable source of capital.

The business unit during this period was generally the single entrepreneur or partnership. Joint stock companies were rare, and corporations for business purposes were virtually unknown.

Government regulation of industry. The development of colonial industries was also influenced by the English and colonial governments, which encouraged some industries and discouraged others. England encouraged those colonial in-

[8] V. Clark, *History of Manufactures in the United States* (3 vols., New York, 1929), I, 144-47.

dustries which would be of advantage to her own industries and in pursuance of this end she encouraged the production of ships and shipbuilding materials, of naval stores and of iron, and directed that certain products could be sent only to England while others were denied admittance. Prior to 1660, when the most important of the Navigation Acts was passed, the colonists had obtained many of their manufactures from Holland, paying for them with the raw products of the New World. The prohibition of this trade had the effect of stimulating shipbuilding and the production of ship materials in New England, and also the household manufacture of various articles which they had previously bought in the free market of Holland. They could not now buy these in England because the grain, the fish, and other products of New England were not admitted into England in exchange. Of the northern colonies the Board of Trade reported [9] in 1731, "They have no staple commodities of their own growth to exchange for our manufactures, which puts them under great necessity, as well as under greater temptation, of providing them for themselves." In the southern colonies, on the other hand, the presence of staple products which could be readily exchanged for English manufactures rendered less necessary the varied household industry by which New England supplied most of its own needs. From the standpoint of manufactures there was a sharp contrast between the colonies north of the Potomac River and those south of it.

As certain industries developed in the colonies, the opposition of English manufacturers was aroused and legislation was passed to limit or prevent their growth. There were three outstanding instances of this kind. In the first case an act of 1699 forbade the exportation of wool or woolen manufactures of any sort from the colony in which they were produced to any outside market; it did not prohibit the manufacture of woolen goods, but only their export and sale in competition with English products. It thus made the colonial woolen industry essentially a household industry for home and local needs. The second instance was the Act of

---

[9] Report printed in D. Macpherson, *Annals of Commerce, Manufactures, Fisheries, and Navigation* (London, 1805), III, 190.

1732, which attempted in similar fashion to localize the hat-making industry by providing that no hat made in the colonies could be exported to any other colony, and that only those who had served an apprenticeship could engage in hat manufacture. Finally, in 1750, there was an absolute prohibition of iron manufactures. In other ways, too, the mother country endeavored to prevent the development in the colonies of manufactures, by forbidding the emigration from England of skilled artisans or the exportation of machinery and tools, or raw material. Such legislation appears harsh, but on the other hand, as has already been pointed out, bounties were offered for the production of certain articles which were needed in England, as naval stores, masts, and similar things.

Colonial legislatures also busied themselves with regulation of industry. If an article were needed, the inhabitants were sometimes ordered to produce it; thus the planting of flax and hemp was required by Virginia and Connecticut, and the spinning of a certain amount of yarn by each family was prescribed by a Massachusetts law of 1655. Generally, however, production was stimulated by offering bounties: these were offered for the growing of hemp at one time or another by seven colonies; and for the growing of flax by three. The production of duck and sailcloth was especially promoted in New England. In some of the colonies the English bounties, as on shipbuilding and naval stores, were paralleled. Sometimes land grants or subsidies were given to reward persons who would set up needed industries, as saltworks, ironworks, fulling mills, tanning plants, grist- and sawmills, and other establishments; most of these were in New England.

Conclusion. During the colonial period manufactures were still largely in the handicraft stage, and goods were produced primarily for local and home use. Manufacturing proper—that is, the production of goods outside the home for sale in the market or for export—never developed very far. Even Bishop, the diligent historian of American manufactures, admits that the history of the efforts made during the first one hundred years to introduce the manufacturing arts into the American colonies, is "little more than a record of unsuccessful enterprise." Such industries as were carried on were removed only a few steps from the extractive industries which furnished the raw materials. Many of the colonial industries were carried on in the home and were household industries rather than manufactures. In the busy life of the colonists these industrial activities must have crowded agriculture closely, for there were few who devoted themselves exclusively to these pursuits. The development of pure manufactures was seriously handicapped by conditions in the colonies.

Since the colonies were poor, there was always a lack of capital. Skilled labor was also wanting, for the best artisans probably did not migrate to America, and it must be remembered that in the pre-machine age the skill of the worker, acquired only by long apprenticeship, was a fundamental condition of industry. Of importance also were the absence of considerable markets, owing to the sparseness of population, the insufficiency of money and of means of transportation, and the lack of technical knowledge. In such circumstances there could be no division of labor or high degree of specialization, and costs remained high.

The direction of colonial industries was determined primarily by economic considerations. British regulation and colonial legislation deflected the colonists only slightly from the lines dictated by environment and opportunity. The pioneer settler, faced by immediate necessities, understood his own needs better than did legislative bodies. Household rather than social economy dictated the kinds of production carried on. When the conditions of pioneer life are considered, one cannot but be impressed by the progress made, for the colonists were engaged in the triple task of earning a livelihood, accumulating capital goods, and raising their standard of living. That they succeeded along all three lines is evidence of unremitting industry and great native ability, as well as of a favorable environment.

CHAPTER IV
POPULATION AND LABOR

The growth of population. The growth of population in new colonies, especially when these are far distant from the mother country, is bound to be slow. In the early American settlements the mortality was so great that the population had to be continually replenished by additions from England or the European mainland. Most of the first settlers were Englishmen. There was a considerable influx of English people into New England during the troubled period of 1630-40 when Cavalier and Roundhead were struggling for supremacy in England, and in 1640 there were approximately 25,000 whites in British North America, of whom 60 per cent were in New England and most of the rest in Virginia. The next twenty years saw more settlers leaving England, most of whom went to Virginia, so that by 1660 the population had increased to 80,000, of whom half were in Virginia and Maryland. From this time on the middle colonies began to gain somewhat in importance, and in 1688 they had about one-fifth of the population.

But while the population was gaining in size, it was also growing in diversity, for other racial elements than the English were coming in. The Dutch had settlements extending from Fort Nassau (now Gloucester, New Jersey), some four miles below Philadelphia, to Fort Orange (now Albany, New York). They conquered the Swedes who had already established themselves on the lower Delaware, but in turn submitted to the English in 1664. The wars waged by Louis XIV of France in central Europe, which devastated the country and decimated the population, forced thousands of settlers from the Palatinate, Alsace, Swabia, Saxony, and other principalities to seek refuge in this country. William Penn made special efforts to attract them, and so great was the immigration of Germans into Pennsylvania that in 1766

Benjamin Franklin estimated that one-third of the inhabitants of that colony were German. They were known as Pennsylvania Dutch, the "Dutch" being a mispronunciation of Deutsch, which is the German word for German. French Huguenots (French Protestants), denied an asylum even in the French Canadian colonies after the revocation of the Edict of Nantes (1685), added another valuable element to the already mixed population of the colonies. They were an especially talented class of people whose influence was out of all proportion to their numbers. South Carolina was a favorite haven for them. In the early eighteenth century the Scotch-Irish began coming over in large numbers: by 1775 it is estimated that there were 100,000 of them in Pennsylvania alone. They were people of Scottish origin whose forefathers had migrated to northern Ireland. Economic conditions, chief of which was higher rents, forced many to seek new homes in America. A large part headed for the frontier where land was free and rents almost unknown: there the cost of land lay rather in economic hardship and Indian fighting. Other parts of Europe which contributed to the American melting pot in this period were Switzerland, Scotland, Ireland, and Wales, but none sent large numbers.

The majority of the population was of English stock and where several nationalities were found, which was chiefly in the middle colonies, there was a steady and on the whole successful pressure to assimilate them into a unified whole. This was not difficult, since the majority of immigrants, that is, those not from the British Isles, were from northern and western Europe and of Protestant beliefs. Bancroft speaks of the colonies in 1775 as inhabited by persons only "one-fifth of whom had for mother tongue some other language than English." The population was most homogeneous in New England where at the time of the Revolution about 98 per cent of the people were English or of unmixed English descent.

How much of the colonial population came from overseas and how much was owing to natural increase it is impossible to say, but in view of the dangers and difficulties of ocean travel, it is probable that after the first settlements the increase was mainly natural. The objections of some of the

European governments to the emigration of their citizens, the poverty of the people, the expense and dangers of the long voyage, the uncertainties and hardships of life in pioneer settlements, and the tales of suffering by disappointed settlers —all operated to deter any but the bravest spirits from attempting to better their lot in the New World.

Franklin, when he estimated in 1755 that there were "near a million souls" in the colonies, thought that scarcely 80,000 had been brought over by sea. On the other hand, every encouragement was given to the natural increase of the population. Subsistence was cheap, there was plenty of land for all comers, and a large family was an asset rather than a burden because even children could aid in the work to be done. Peter Kalm,[1] the Swedish traveler, collected some remarkable cases of large families, of which one may be cited: In 1739 Mrs. Marcia Hazard died at South Kingston, aged 100. "She could count altogether 500 children, grandchildren, great-grandchildren, and great-great-grandchildren; when she died 205 persons of them were alive."

As a result of the absence of any economic check to propagation, the population doubled about every twenty-five years, and this in spite of a tragic infant mortality which probably ran as high as 40 per cent. This rate of growth obtained during most of the colonial period, as the accompanying table shows, and for another century after that. Thus, if the student of American economic history will remember that the country had a population of 2,500,000 at the outbreak of the American Revolution, he can estimate the population of the nation a century backwards or forwards and have some conception of its size at any time.

AMERICAN POPULATION GROWTH, 1641-1775 *

Year	Estimate
1641	50,000
1659	80,000
1688	200,000
1702	270,000
1727	502,000
1750	1,260,000
1775	2,418,000

* Greene and Harrington, *American Population Before Federal Census of 1790* (New York, 1933), 3-5.
[1] *Travels into North America.* Cited in Bogart and Thompson, *Readings*, 110.

Spread of population. The distribution of the population differed from time to time. The first settlements at Jamestown and Plymouth were widely separated, but by the close of the seventeenth century the gap had been filled by the settlement of Pennsylvania and New Jersey, while the southern limit had been extended to South Carolina. At the same time settlers had pushed up the rivers into the interior in New England, New York, and Virginia.

During the eighteenth century the first westward movement carried the frontier of settlement to the crest of the Appalachians, while Georgia was added to the settled area on the south. By 1754 the region east of the mountains was partly settled and the three sections—north, middle, and south—were about equally populated. The white population of New England was 425,000; of the middle colonies, 353,000; and of the southern, 387,000. The Negro population of the three sections was 14,400, 27,500, and 222,000 respectively. The population was still almost entirely rural and there were as yet no large cities. A decade later, Boston, the largest city in the colonies, had only 16,000, Philadelphia, 13,000, and New York, 11,000. Farther south the population was more widely dispersed owing to the larger available area between sea and mountains, the extensive methods of tobacco culture, and the use made of headrights in obtaining large land holdings.

Fortunately for the English colonists they had settled in a part of the country which afforded the geographic isolation necessary for the development of national life. The mountains and the ocean formed at first the natural boundaries of their settlements, and also served as frontier defenses against the French and the Spanish.

How labor shortage was overcome. In a new country the tasks to be performed are so many that labor by contrast always seems scarce. This was certainly true of the colonies, where the demand for labor was exceptionally great. To clear the land of trees, stumps, and stones, to cultivate the fields with the clumsy agricultural implements, to guard the growing crops against weeds and cattle, to produce food, to make clothing and household necessities, to cut roads through the forests, to build houses and barns, and perhaps to repel the attacks of hostile Indians—all these called for unremitting toil of the severest kind. The insufficiency of the labor supply when confronted with so many and such urgent tasks caused wages to rise. Contemporary writers are virtually unanimous in saying that wages in the colonies were higher than in England or on the continent. For example, in 1651 iron-workers at Lynn were being paid two to three times as much as similar workers in England; in 1695 it was reported that wages in New England were six times as high as those in Sweden, and about the time of the Revolution American spinners and weavers were receiving, at a conservative esti-mate, at least half as much again as English ones.[2] Such higher wages were owing not only to the greater scarcity of labor, but also to its greater productivity in a new country. Higher wages cannot be paid unless more goods are produced.

The shortage of labor, then, was one of the chief difficul-ties the colonists had to solve. They met it in various ways: the farmer or independent proprietor, his wife, and his fam-ily worked long hours, and there was a willing spirit of co-operation among neighbors when some large task had to be done. In the southern and middle colonies the custom of indentured servitude was developed and later, in the South, Negro slavery provided an ever-present supply of labor. Each of these solutions deserves closer examination.

The independent proprietor as a worker. The main source of labor in New England and the middle colonies was the skill and muscle of the colonist himself. The typical inde-pendent farmer had only himself and his family to depend upon for most of the tasks that had to be done. In such cir-cumstances a large family was an asset, for it furnished needed laborers. This labor supply was generally of a high order, because it was composed of the descendants of selected and energetic individuals who had ventured to the New World to establish homes for themselves. But it may be doubted whether they were more efficient than their contem-poraries in Europe, since they lagged behind them in tech-nical knowledge and improved tools, and since, of necessity, they had to be jacks-of-all-trades, hence masters of none.

In one respect the independent proprietor showed great

2 V. Clark, *op. cit.*, I, 155.

ability—in organizing the factors of land, capital, and labor in his capacity as enterpriser. Though the labor at his disposal might be that of only himself and his family, he exercised skill and resourcefulness in combining it with the other factors of production so as to make it as efficient as possible. The colonists' preference for extractive industries and their inclination to "butcher the soil," in short, their tendency to skim off the cream of the country's seemingly inexhaustible natural resources, have been discussed elsewhere. These were a way of overcoming the shortage of labor by getting the maximum product from a limited amount of labor.

Owing to the scarcity of laborers who could be hired to work for pay, it was a general practice in New England and the middle colonies and to a less extent in the South for the colonists to exchange labor with one another. Were a house to be erected, a barn to be raised, or a ship built and launched, the settler called upon his neighbors to assist him in the larger operations that were beyond his strength or skill, or that called for the associated effort of several workers. The typical event which called for this co-operative system of labor was a house- or barn-raising; this was made a social occasion, the women attending to provide a bountiful repast, while the men strove with one another in a spirit of emulation. It did not take long at such a time to erect the frame, rafters, and ridgepole of a building, and the event made a happy break in busy lives. Later, the more usual method for a man who wished to build a house was to agree with a carpenter or mason for so many days' work, the owner working with the more specialized craftsman and under his direction.

While labor was still very scarce and even the voluntary co-operation of neighbors could not always be depended on, legislation provided for the impressment of labor for such necessary services as harvesting crops. In New England artificers and mechanics might be compelled by the constable to leave their crafts and assist in the harvest fields of their neighbors. The obtaining of the food supply thus ranked in importance with military protection. In the South there was a larger proportion of servants—under which term was included not only hired laborers, but also indentured servants and slaves—and consequently the exchange of labor among independent proprietors or plantation owners was never so important.

Free laborers and free artisans. The number of free laborers for hire was never large but was greatest in New England where slavery had the least foothold, where industries were most diversified, and where population was densest. Occasionally some of the new arrivals in the colonies were without means or lacked the energy to engage in industry or farming on their own account and therefore hired themselves out as free laborers. Persons who became free laborers were accustomed to turning their hands to almost anything that offered. Weeden gives an account of one John Marshall, who was a good typical specimen of such laborers. He "received about 4 shillings a day at Braintree from 1697 to 1711. He farmed a little, made laths in the winter, was painter and carpenter, was messenger, and burned bricks, bought and sold live stock. He was a non-commissioned officer in the Braintree Company, and a constable of the precinct. In one day he could make 300 laths." However, the abundance of free land and the large returns to the cultivator tempted most men to become independent farmers on a small scale rather than remain hired laborers.

As population increased and towns grew up, there was enough work in some trades to support a specialist—in contrast to the jack-of-all-trades or free laborer—and there appeared a class of free artisans who worked for hire. This class included carpenters, masons, tilers, millwrights, wheelwrights, ship carpenters, thatchers, and many others. Apprentices came in time to be associated with the master artisans, as a method of recruiting and training the younger generation of craftsmen. Apprenticeship existed in the colonies much as in England and was regulated by statute. On account of the scarcity of labor, the term was frequently reduced below the usual seven years, half-trained artisans began to labor as journeymen, and sometimes workmanship suffered.

In spite of the scarcity of labor, the wages of hired workers were regulated by legislation. In accordance with English custom, provision was made for fixing wages and prices by law, or by giving the town authorities power to fix wages.

This was hardly calculated to increase the number of free workers who were few enough anyway.

Indentured servants. Another result of the scarcity of labor in the colonies was the development of schemes for obtaining a more or less permanent labor force, either by paying the cost of transporting servants to the colonies, or by buying the persons of the workers. The former gave rise to the system of indentured servants, and the latter to that of slavery. The indentured servants fell into two groups, voluntary and involuntary; the former were those who came to this country of their own free will, whereas the latter were sent regardless of their wishes.

The voluntary servitude of indentured servants was based upon a free contract with a company or an individual for a definite term of service in return for the payment of the servant's transportation to America and his maintenance during the period of service. The indentured servants were free persons who migrated for the purpose of improving their conditions. Not being able to pay their passage, they sold themselves into temporary bondage to the person advancing the money.

At first they came chiefly from England, but later large numbers were brought over from Ireland, Scotland, Wales, and Germany. So great was the colonial demand for these servants that a regular business, centered in London and Bristol, soon developed in England for supplying them. It was carried on by merchants engaged in the colonial trade, by shipmasters, or by emigration brokers, who assumed the expense of transportation in the sure prospect of reimbursing themselves with a profit when the bond servants were landed in America. So great indeed were the profits that soon an illicit trade sprang up and thousands of children and even adults were "spirited" away by so-called "crimps." Ten thousand persons were said to have been kidnaped from England in 1680.

The length of the term of service fixed by the indenture [3] was a matter of contract and differed from time to time and

[3] This name was given to this form of contract because it was usually written in duplicate on a large sheet which was separated into halves by a jagged cut, called an indent.

from one colony to another. The services of the transported servants were sold by the shipmasters to the employer. In some cases there seems to have existed a variation: for example, the so-called redemptioners were allowed a certain number of days in which to dispose of themselves to the best advantage; if they failed in this, their services were sold in the usual fashion. The cost to the purchaser averaged about £10 to £12. In general, the servants transported before 1650 were bound for long terms of from seven to ten years or more; after the settlement of New York, New Jersey, Pennsylvania, and the Carolinas, the demand increased and the term of service was reduced to four years. As the business of transporting bond servants grew, the contract or indenture received legal recognition, and its terms were stated with more definiteness. The personality of the servant was recognized by the statutes, a feature which was not true of the slave, so that before the law and the courts his position was little different from that of the freeman.

Involuntary servitude. The other group of indentured servants consisted of persons who were condemned to servitude in the colonies for some offense. This class was composed principally of paupers, vagrants, "loose and disorderly persons," and criminals, who were sent to the colonies by royal order or court sentence, or later by judges under the English penal statutes. The transportation of these persons to America seems to have been dictated at first largely by motives of humanity. There were at this time three hundred crimes in the English calendar for which capital punishment was inflicted, and justices often mercifully substituted transportation for death; at the same time the need of men in the colonies afforded an excuse for evasion of the death penalty.

During the eighteenth century, by virtue of acts of Parliament, a convict was permitted to have his sentence commuted, in case of the death penalty, to fourteen years' service, while a seven years' service might be substituted for whipping and branding. While most of the convicts thus sent over were convicted of some crime, many of them were guilty of nothing more serious than debt, and some were political prisoners who had engaged in some rebellious movement.

Acts were passed by the colonies designed to prevent the importation of convicts, and in 1671 came an order in England to put an end to the traffic. It seems not to have been observed, however, and in 1717 Parliament, against the protests of the Virginia merchants, enacted a statute providing for the transportation of convicts to America. Between this date and 1775 some 40,000 such persons were sent to America. The provinces of Virginia and Maryland received most of these convicts, although they were not unknown elsewhere. Many of the planters preferred the convicts to bond servants, as their terms were longer and their rights fewer.

One authority estimates that probably one-half of all the new arrivals of the colonial period landed as indentured servants. Fifteen hundred a year is the estimate of Governor Berkeley of Virginia in 1664. This class of labor outnumbered Negro slaves for the first century but not after that, because the white man's term of bondage was shorter and the slave population grew rapidly after 1680. Indentured servitude was, in general, the most reliable source of labor in the seventeenth century, but in the eighteenth century it gave way to slavery in the southern colonies. It was always popular in Pennsylvania.

Treatment of servants. The treatment of servants was as varied as the character of the masters. At first, a sort of good fellowship existed between masters and men, but as the numbers became greater their relations were regulated more definitely by statute. The general condition of the bond servants was certainly a hard one, as is shown by the character of the laws to protect them. No servant could be sold out of the province in which he had agreed to serve, without his consent; he must be furnished with sufficient and wholesome food, clothing, and lodging; it appeared that the food allowed was often a coarse diet of Indian meal and water sweetened with molasses, while lodging and clothing were poor and insufficient. Finally, the law provided that if a servant fell ill during his service, he must be cared for; the sick servant was often neglected, lest the doctor's charges exceed the value of his remaining service. The servant was also protected against unjust cruelty and bodily maiming; it must be remembered, however, that this was an age of flogging, and corporal punishment was meted out to soldiers and sailors, criminals, and children, as well as servants.

On the other hand, the interests of the master who had invested his capital in servants were even more carefully protected. The great danger to which he was exposed was the loss of runaway servants, who fled to escape service or were tempted away with higher wages by rival employers. Both the runaway and those who harbored him were punished by severe penalties. Ordinarily a servant who ran away was compelled to serve double time for the period missed.

Economic appraisal of the system. The importation of bond servants into the colonies under the system of indenture was advantageous from many points of view. Labor was scarce in the New World and wages high but labor was cheap in the Old World and some nations complained of a surplus population. Indentured servitude made it possible for poor emigrants to finance their transportation by the only way open to them, that of exchanging their labor for their passage. The immigrant could thus pay for his passage by working at high New World wage-rates instead of at low Old World wage-rates. It afforded many persons a method of escape from miserable conditions at home and gave them a chance to share in the opportunities of the New World.

While at first many of these laborers belonged to the lowest industrial group, some of them were skilled artisans, and a few belonged to the educated class. To the capable and industrious the future was assured. At the end of their terms of service the indentured servants generally became free laborers or independent proprietors and were merged in the white population of the colonies, many becoming highly respected citizens.

In Pennsylvania and New Jersey indentured servants whose terms had expired were granted fifty and seventy-five acres of land to cultivate in their own right. In the southern colonies "freedom dues" consisted of clothing, tools, and a store of food, costing the master from £5 to £10 at the end of the servant's term. Another advantage of the system was that it generally had the effect of an industrial or agricultural apprenticeship and provided for the training and assimilation of a large mass of newcomers under unaccustomed conditions.

Some indeed there were who "have enough money to pay for their passage, especially Germans, yet will not pay, but choose to be sold in order to have time to gain a knowledge of the language and the manner of living in the country."[4]

From the standpoint of the employers also the system had great advantages. In the first place, it permitted the organization of labor under intelligent direction for definite purposes. The long terms of service with contract labor introduced an element of certainty, which was very important for those undertaking rather hazardous enterprises in a new country, the returns from which were distant. This was especially true of larger undertakings like tobacco-growing. For these reasons indentured servants were generally preferred to free laborers.

Certain disadvantages inhered in the system: often badly crowded and unsanitary ships caused the premature death of many even before they caught sight of the promised land; the kidnaping and sale of children was indefensible; and the abuse of power by harsh or greedy masters was difficult to prevent.

On the whole, however, the balance was decidedly in favor of the system. Ballagh, writing with special reference to Virginia, sums up the matter fairly as follows: "Designed not merely as a labor supply, but as an immigration agency, it had generally the effect of industrial apprenticeship, greatly strengthened the position of capitalist employers, and developed a class of industrially efficient freemen. It supplied almost the entire force of skilled labor in the colonies for more than half a century and continued to be a source of high-grade labor long into the eighteenth century. It provided for the growth of a strong yeoman class and prevented the absorption of land into great estates; and it furnished a great number of independent settlers and citizens, particularly for the back country; it had a marked effect on the political as well as the economic development of the country."[5]

Slaves in the New World. One other answer was given to the problem of labor scarcity in the colonies, and that was

[4] *American Husbandry* (London, 1775), I, 170.
[5] *White Servitude in the Colony of Virginia* (Baltimore, 1895), 90.

the institution of human slavery. The native Indians were enslaved by the white settlers, not only in Spanish America but also in Virginia and New England. They proved poor workers, however, and their place was soon taken by Negro slaves. This solution of the labor problem was much more important and far-reaching in its effects than the institution of indentured servants, which was transitional and temporary; but slavery did not occur on a large scale until white servitude had nearly run its course.

Slavery and the slave trade have existed ever since a settled life made the compulsory labor of captives more desirable than their extermination. It has existed among all ancient peoples wherever the land was abundant as compared with the supply of labor; but in medieval Europe it was modified to serfdom and was gradually dying out as the population became denser and the necessity for compulsory labor passed away. With the discovery of the New World, however, the old problem was again presented. Negro slavery still existed in Africa and since about 1482 a regular traffic in slaves had been carried on by the Portuguese between Africa and Europe. There was little place for slaves in Europe, however, except in the domestic service of the wealthy, but with the discovery of the New World there was opened a new field for their labor and a new opportunity for their disposal. The immediate purpose of colonization was the exploitation of a continent. But for this purpose labor must be had. The early colonists, especially the Spanish, were too impatient to wait for the slow process of filling up the land by settlement; they wished immediate returns. Slavery offered one solution to this problem.

At first the slave trade was carried on by the Portuguese and Spanish but later the Dutch and English (1562) engaged in the traffic. Thus for a century prior to the settlement of the Jamestown colony slavery had existed in the West Indies and a regular traffic in slaves had developed between Africa and the islands of North America. It was very naturally introduced into the English colonies on the continent from the West Indies; later, a direct trade with Africa sprang up.

Slavery in the English colonies. The first Negro slaves in the English colonies are generally said to have been landed at Jamestown in 1619 by a Dutch [6] privateer; after that, the number increased but slowly, and in 1671 there were only 2000 slaves in Virginia out of a population of 40,000. Slaves were at first difficult to obtain, for the Dutch held a near monopoly of the slave trade, which it took two wars for the English to break and still longer to develop to a point where they could meet the demands of all the English colonies. Beginning about 1680, slaves began to flow into Virginia, and by 1700 they had become more important to the economic life of that colony than the indentured servant. Thirty years later a quarter of Virginia's population consisted of Negroes and the plantation system was well established.

Meanwhile rice production was found practical in South Carolina about 1694 and provided a further demand for slaves. The addition of indigo as a supplementary staple, about 1741, gave another resource adapted to slave labor and intensified the system. "The typical estate came to be a plantation with about thirty working hands, cultivating rice in the swampy lands and indigo in the drier fields, in a steady routine which lasted nearly the whole year through. The nature of the climate and the work to be done precluded, as in Jamaica, the use of any but Negro labor in the gangs. The prevalence of malaria in the hot months caused most of the planters to abandon their estates for much of the year to the care of overseers and foremen. In contrast to this, the usual type of estate in the Virginia plantation districts had only five or ten working hands, of whom part were likely to be white redemptioners; and the master and his family were usually on the estate the year round.... In Georgia, the rulers of the colony tried hard to keep out slave labor; but about 1750 had to yield to the inevitable. Thereafter the sea-island district of Georgia tended to assume the same complexion as that which the South Carolina low-lands had acquired." [7]

The treatment of the slaves was more patriarchal in char-

---

[6] For the controversy as to the responsibility for first introducing slaves into the English continental colonies, see J. C. Ballagh, *Slavery in Virginia*, 8 n.; A. Brown, *Genesis of the United States* (Boston, 1890), II, 886; P. A. Bruce, *Economic History of Virginia* (2 vols., New York, 1935), II, 67 ff.

[7] U. B. Phillips, "Plantation and Frontier," in *A Documentary History of American Industrial Society* (Cleveland, 1910), I, 81.

acter in the tobacco colonies; but in the rice fields of South Carolina, under a system of absenteeism, the worst excesses were found. The constant fear of uprisings, owing to the numerical superiority of the slaves, and their propensity to run away, led here to the harshest legislation against them. Herded together in gangs, with few women and no home life, they showed slavery at its worst.

The slave trade. The slave trade developed with the growing demand for slaves until it came to be one of the important branches of commerce. The monopoly enjoyed by the Dutch was more or less taken over by the Royal African Company between 1672 and 1697. Finally, as a result of protests by English traders and American shipowners, the trade was thrown open and many merchants of the northern colonies engaged in the traffic. The slave trade was important to the northern colonies because it was tied up with the West Indian trade and with the manufacture of rum. A three-cornered trade developed in the eighteenth century in accordance with which molasses was brought from the West Indies to New England, where it was manufactured into rum; this, together with some other articles for barter like iron utensils and textiles, was taken to Africa and exchanged for slaves and perhaps gold dust and ivory; the slaves were transported to the West Indies or the southern colonies where they were sold. The trip between Africa and the West Indies was called the "middle passage" since it was the second leg of the triangle, and it was often attended by frightful suffering and mortality among the slaves. Newport was the largest slave market, though the slave trade was also carried on from Boston, Salem, New York, and other places. Many colonial fortunes were based upon this trade, and even so respectable a citizen of Boston as Peter Faneuil owned a slave ship.

Ship captains bought slaves in Africa from local traders or tribal chieftains. Sometimes the natives had been brought to the coast from as far as 1,000 miles inland. A Negro might become a slave because of birth, debt, or most likely, capture in a native war. A sturdy male could be bought on the Gold Coast in 1749 for $50 and sold for $150 in the British West Indies. The price varied according to the age, health, sex, and reputation of the tribe of the native. Senegalese were considered especially intelligent and suitable for domestic service; Mandingoes were gentle but inclined to thieve; Whydahs and Pawpaws were generally husky, industrious, cheerful, and submissive; Eboes were unpopular because they were sickly and prone to suicide; and Gaboons were said to die on the slightest provocation. It has been estimated that an average of 8 to 10 per cent of every shipload died on the voyage: [8] the wonder is that the mortality was not greater, for ships were generally small and the slaves were forced to lie chained and close together on shallow ill-ventilated decks. Virginians learned in time that slaves were most likely to survive the colder temperatures of the American mainland if they were acclimatized in the West Indies first.

It is difficult to ascertain, even approximately, the number of Negroes whom the slave traders carried off from Africa and brought to America. Johnson estimates that during the fifty years preceding the Revolution the annual importations into the continental American colonies "must have averaged 10,000, and possibly much more than that number." [9] According to Du Bois 7,000,000 were brought from Africa to all the Americas in the eighteenth century.[10] As a result of these importations and of the natural increase of the resident slave population, the number of slaves in the colonies grew steadily—from about 59,000 in 1714 to 293,000 in 1754 (Bancroft) and to 386,000 in 1760 (Channing); the first federal census of 1790 showed a total of 697,877 in the country.

Attitude toward slavery. Slavery existed in all the colonies, but to a very different degree in different sections. In New England it had obtained the smallest foothold and was disappearing, not so much by reason of a moral sentiment against it as because, owing to the varied industrial and commercial development of that section, it was economically unprofitable. The Quakers of Pennsylvania were opposed to slavery, but in New York and New Jersey, from 8 to 10 per cent of the population was composed of slaves, who were

[8] U. B. Phillips, *American Negro Slavery* (New York, 1940), 38-44.
[9] E. R. Johnson and others, *History of Domestic and Foreign Commerce of the United States* (2 vols., Washington, 1915), I, 102.
[10] Quoted in R. Kuczynski, *Population Movements* (Oxford, 1936), 12.

treated with great leniency. South of Mason and Dixon's line the situation was quite different. Of the 386,000 slaves in the colonies in 1760, over three-fourths lived in the South; the proportion in the different colonies varied from 15 per cent of the population in North Carolina to 50 per cent in Virginia, and 70 per cent in South Carolina.

Many colonists were at first opposed to the introduction of slavery and various acts were passed, in Massachusetts and Pennsylvania, in Virginia and Maryland, in South Carolina and Georgia, forbidding or restricting it. Among the English, however, by whom the slave trade had already long been carried on with the West Indies, there were no such scruples. About 1663 a British Committee on Foreign Plantations declared that "black slaves are the most useful appurtenances of a plantation." In 1733 the Lords Commissioners for Trade and Plantations stated that "the colonies could not possibly subsist" without an adequate supply of slaves. Laws passed in the colonies to restrict the slave trade were generally disallowed by the Crown, and royal governors were warned that the colonists would not be permitted to "discourage a traffic so beneficial to the nation." Gradually, as it was seen to be profitable, the objections of the colonists died away, and there was little scruple about owning slaves or engaging in the slave trade, except among the Quakers of Pennsylvania.

Economic appraisal of slavery. If slavery is regarded solely as an economic institution and as a method of supplying quickly the necessary labor in the colonies, some justification can be found for the point of view held in the seventeenth and eighteenth centuries. The advantages lay all with the slaveowners, for the wishes and well-being of the slave were not taken into consideration, and we are not here concerned with the unrighteous profits made by the slave traders. Slaves were preferred to hired laborers and even to indentured servants since their terms of service were for life, there was no interruption to the work by reason of the departure of the worker, and the children became the property of the masters. The cost of maintenance of the slave was less than that of the white servant, and there were no "freedom dues" to be paid at the end of his term of service. And finally, the management of the slaves was easier, for the Negroes were usually more docile and tractable than the white servants.

Southern agriculture demanded little beyond physical strength, endurance, and the ability to use simple tools. In the hot pestilential rice fields the Negroes were practically the only laborers who could endure the climate, and in this case a remarkable combination of circumstances brought to the work men adapted to it. For untold centuries the Negroes on the Guinea coast had lived in steaming hot jungles, and here they had developed immunity to malaria and other diseases to which the white man was susceptible. Brought from the Congo River to the swamps of South Carolina they suffered little loss of health, but were able to live under conditions insupportable by white laborers. Had it not been for this circumstance, rice culture would probably have ceased, or its methods would have been changed.

The effect of the introduction of servile labor was to aid in the rapid clearing of the land and in the production of new wealth. Without the system of slavery and the sister institution of white servitude, it may be said that the development of the South would have been much slower and very different in kind.

An interesting problem presents itself at this point, as to who obtained the labor surplus of the slave above all the costs. Gray concludes that the surplus profits accruing from slave labor were divided about equally between the slave traders and the planters, the competition of white servants tending to prevent monopoly prices on the part of the traders and the necessities of the planters leading them to bid for new Negroes about as much as they could afford to pay.[11]

The relation of the worker to industry. Thus far the kinds of laborers have been described, but the character and organization of industry must also be emphasized again. Most of the labor was agricultural, since this was the principal occupation, but as towns grew and increased in size, industry began to be separated from agriculture and industrial workers to become more important. Industry was for the

---

[11] L. C. Gray, *History of Agriculture in the Southern United States to 1860* (2 vols, New York, 1941), I, 371.

most part in the custom-order stage during the early part of the colonial period; the home of the worker was the work-shop and here goods were produced on order from the customer. The mechanic was both laborer and merchant. Gradually, as the population increased, as towns were estab-lished, and the market grew in size, the master workman gathered journeymen about him. He also, in addition to custom or "bespoke" work, began to produce cheaper goods for sale without waiting for orders. This retail-order stage had been reached by the time of the Revolution.

Besides these stationary workers there were also itinerant workers, especially in those industries that required only hand tools and skill, like the itinerant shoemaker or tailor. The itinerant worker went from house to house, where he worked up the raw material belonging to his customers in return for board, lodging, and a small wage. In those indus-tries, however, where any considerable fixed capital was re-quired, as in blacksmithing, weaving, baking, etc., the worker set up his own shop and the customer came to him. With the growth of population, of industry, and of better means of transportation, the itinerant mechanic tended to become a stationary worker.

So long as goods were produced only on order, as "be-spoke" work, the master workman found it to his interest to turn out only good wares in order to hold his customers. But when custom work began to be displaced by "shop work," or the making of goods for sale in the general mar-ket without waiting for orders, then the danger arose that cheap and poorly made wares would be placed on the mar-ket. To guard against this, inspectors, supervisors, and other similar officers were appointed in various crafts to insure the quality of the goods produced. So, too, when master work-men began to hire journeymen, disputes over wages arose. But these were considered less important than the regula-tions of prices and quality, which were designed to protect the consumer. Perhaps the most general colonial regulation, which covered price, wage, quality, and weight, was the "assize of bread." Thus Massachusetts, in 1696, provided that the weight of the penny loaf should vary according to a fixed scale as the price of wheat moved up or down, and although the bakers frequently complained that the assize did not permit them to earn a living wage, regulation rather than competition was held to be necessary to protect the interests of the general public. This was in harmony with the mercantilistic ideas of that period.

Conclusions. Despite a population that doubled each generation, one of the chief problems of the colonists was the shortage of labor. This they overcame in part by concentrating on the extractive industries, by seeking the co-operation of their neighbors, and by utilizing indentured servants or slaves whenever they could afford to do so.

The colonists were for the most part an energetic, thrifty, high-minded, hospitable people. There were considerable divergencies in the different sections of the country, corresponding to differences in race, occupation, and environment. Most of the population had been drawn from the middle and lower classes, and the extremes of the Old World, whether of wealth or poverty, social rank or servile condition, were not reproduced in America. Society, removed from artificial trammels and placed in a new environment, tended to produce less inequality.

In New England, the population was remarkably homogeneous; persevering industry, in the face of an inhospitable environment, had secured for them general well-being, unmarked by either wealth or poverty. There was essential equality of condition, though the ministry and other professions constituted a virtual aristocracy of learning and birth. The population of the middle colonies was of all the sections the most heterogeneous, being composed of several nationalities. It was here, and especially in Pennsylvania, that the institution of indentured servitude was most popular. Except for fishing, the occupations and general well-being were similar to those of New England, but the disposition of the people was not so stern and they were more given to social amusements.

The southern colonies, peopled almost exclusively by English settlers, were democratic in the beginning, but the introduction of slavery caused the stratification of the population into clearly marked social classes, at the head of which stood the large plantation owners and at the foot the Negro slaves.

The character of southern agriculture and the existence of slavery dispersed the population and prevented the growth of towns, so that there was little intercourse. In general the life in the colonies was simple and often rude, with few extremes of poverty or wealth, little in the way of luxuries, but an assured subsistence as the reward of industry.

CHAPTER V

COLONIAL COMMERCE AND EXCHANGE

Geographic conditions of commerce. Commerce exists because of differences between peoples, regions, and resources. Communities similar in all these respects do not trade with each other; but when they differ, then exchange of dissimilar commodities develops. Such exchange stimulates the specialization of various areas in the production of those commodities in which they have the greatest relative advantages. But before these advantages can be realized and the commodities brought to market, various connective agencies must be provided, such as transportation, credit facilities, and a whole complex of agencies for assembling, moving, storing, and selling goods. In the present chapter only the exchange of commodities will be discussed.

During the seventeenth century, trade sprang up at once between the colonies and the mother countries, since these represented different climatic areas, vastly different natural products, and differing stages of economic development. Domestic trade within the colonies, on the other hand, did not develop on any considerable scale until the separation of occupations and the division of labor had proceeded far enough to create a dependence of different groups upon one another, and until the development of staples in the different sections provided the materials of commerce. Agriculture was the major industry and the colonists busied themselves with cutting down the forests and extending the cultivable area. Most of the settlements were small self-contained economic units, which produced for themselves nearly all of the articles which they consumed. Between such neighboring communities, whose products were similar, there was little occasion for trade.

The eighteenth century was characterized by growing territorial specialization, by the improvement of transportation, and by the extension of the market. Foreign and domestic trade consequently grew in volume and variety. Partly because of these changes, and partly because of the geographic barriers and the physical difficulties of intercourse in an undeveloped country, foreign trade was of greater immediate importance than domestic commerce and was of greater economic significance throughout the whole of the colonial period.

Waterways. Domestic trade among the different colonies and with the back country was carried on either by water or by land. During nearly all the colonial period the majority of the colonists lived within reach of navigable water; separated from each other by dense forests and tribes of hostile Indians, they found this the safest and easiest highway. Although there are sixteen rivers in New England, the fall line of the rivers, the point where navigation is first interrupted, is comparatively near the coast, and transportation could not be carried far upstream, except on the Connecticut River, which is navigable as far as Hartford, forty miles from the coast. But the lack of navigable rivers was compensated by the broken coast line, which afforded many fine harbors, and by the presence of Long Island Sound whose long stretch of sheltered water permitted the residents of that section to carry on traffic with considerable immunity from the storms of the open ocean.

In the middle colonies New York had the finest tidal river in the Hudson, which was navigable for ocean vessels as far north as Albany, one hundred and fifty miles from its mouth. Farther south such long arms of the sea as Delaware and Chesapeake bays, together with such rivers as the Delaware, Susquehanna, Potomac, and Savannah, brought even the inland plantations within easy reach of seafaring vessels.

There were thus five principal localities of settlement from which radiated most of the colonial commerce. These were eastern Massachusetts; the Connecticut River Valley and Long Island Sound; New York Bay and the Hudson River; Delaware Bay and the Delaware River; and Chesapeake Bay with the Susquehanna and Potomac rivers. Three of these—New York, Delaware, and Chesapeake bays—

were the most important gateways to the interior of the country. The two largest entrances of all into the interior, the Mississippi River and the St. Lawrence with the Great Lakes, played no direct part in the economic development of the English colonies during the colonial period, although they later became very important. Wherever a river emptied into the sea commercial seaports were established, such as Boston, New York, Baltimore, Charleston, and Savannah; and where the navigation up the river was interrupted by the fall line, inland commercial towns sprang up, such as Hartford, Albany, Trenton, Richmond, Raleigh, Columbia, and Augusta (see map).

THE FALL LINE OF RIVERS

Towns sprang up at the fall line of most of the rivers, owing to the presence there of water power and to the interruption to navigation at that point.

In the southern colonies, the deep, slow-flowing streams were navigable for a considerable distance from the sea, and beyond the fall line, where navigation was interrupted, there were fertile hinterlands. When trader and settler pushed toward the mountains in the colonial period they followed the river courses. With the light bark canoe, the art of building which they early learned from the Indians, it was possible to penetrate far inland on the interior streams. To pass the mountains, however, it was necessary to carry the canoe with its contents from the rivers flowing into the Atlantic to those emptying into the Mississippi. The portage, as this carry between the waters was called, thus became a point of the greatest interest and value to the early colonist and fur trader. Forts were soon established on the important portages, which were always the lowest and easiest ways over the watersheds. More recently roads and railways have followed the same lines, and the original Indian portages are now marked in many places by populous cities.

Colonial roads. As the population pushed inland, other means of communication than those by water became necessary, and Indian trails were used. These followed the lines marked out since time immemorial by bison, deer, and other animals along the watersheds. Down to the time of the Revolution the roads were very poor, being constructed without system by the different localities; although in Massachusetts the General Court in 1639 had ordered each town to construct a highway to connect with that of the adjoining town. To build roads was a task of enormous difficulty in a country where forests had to be cut and marshes crossed, and where able-bodied men were so few. Roads were laid out to avoid every natural obstacle and were consequently very tortuous. They were also very steep, for it was found easier to build roads along the ridges of the high lands where the forest was not so dense than to cut through the tangled morass of the low swampy valleys; these were the so-called "ridge roads." Good roads were a luxury whose construction was deferred until other still more essential tasks had been performed.

It must be remembered, too, that the engineering science of road-building was not known even in England at that time; not until 1790 did McAdam and Telford build their first hard roads in that country. The colonial road was the ordinary earth road, deep with dust in summer and during the thaws of winter and spring a veritable mud slough of despond. Wagons were a rarity, but sledges were used for rough hauling; longer journeys were made on horseback. In the North it was possible to travel with comfort or to go long distances by land only in the winter, when the snow made sleighing possible.

The cost of transportation by land was enormous and was much heavier than by water. It was usually prohibitive beyond 100 or 150 miles, except for articles of the first necessity, as salt or iron, or of small bulk, as tea; the charge for hauling a cord of wood twenty miles was $3, for hauling a barrel of flour 150 miles it was $5. In such circumstances both freight and passenger traffic were infrequent and men

Philadelphia STAGE-WAGGON, and New-York STAGE BOAT performs their Stages twice a Week.

JOHN BUTLER, with his waggon, sets out on Mondays from his House, at the Sign of the Death of the Fox, in Strawberry ally, and drives the same day to Trenton Ferry, when Francis Holman meets him, and proceeds on Tuesday to Brunswick, and the passengers and goods being shifted into the waggon of Isaac Fitzrandolph, he takes them to the New Blazing-Star to Jacob Fitzrandolph's the same day, where Rubin Fitzrandolph, with a boat well filled, will receive them, and take them to New-York that night. John Butler returning to Philadelphia on Tuesday with the passengers and goods delivered to him by Francis Holman, will again set out for Trenton Ferry on Thursday, and Francis Holman, &c. will carry his passengers and goods, with the same expedition as above to New-York.   Toctf.

From Dunbar's *History of Travel in America*

To Advertise a "Stage-Waggon"

This advertisement was in a New York newspaper in 1750. The improvement of the roads permitted the substitution of a comfortable stagecoach for this primitive wagon. The fast stagecoach between New York and Philadelphia—"the flying machine"—introduced in 1778, reduced the time to one and one-half days.

lived and died without traveling twenty miles from the place of their residence. Communities in neighboring counties were quite isolated from each other.

Travel was not only uncomfortable and expensive, it was positively dangerous as well. Few bridges existed in the colonies, and the shallower rivers had to be forded, while the broader and deeper ones were crossed by means of ferries. It was stated in Pennsylvania at the end of the colonial period that it was not uncommon for men to make their wills before starting to a state convention. Travel by stagecoach did not become important until the end of the eighteenth century, when roads were improved; the first stage between New York and Philadelphia was not established until 1750, and the trip took three days to cover a distance of ninety miles.

The Indian fur trade. Communication with the unsettled country was always important because of the fur trade during the whole colonial period. The fur trade was not carried on among the colonists themselves, but with the Indians. As wild animals abounded in the primeval forests of North America, trade in their valuable skins and furs was early developed and throughout the colonial period remained an important frontier industry. From the Indians the traders obtained valuable pelts in exchange for blankets, shirts, hatchets, iron pots, beads and trinkets, and other manufactured articles. The colonists were forbidden by the British government to furnish the Indians with firearms, powder, or rum,[1] but the Indian traders refused to be bound by legislation. Trapping and fur trading were early carried on in the New England colonies; but as the fur-bearing animals near the coast were killed off the New Englanders attempted to gain a share in the rich hunting grounds on the upper Hudson and Delaware, which were monopolized by the Dutch and Swedes. This struggle for the lucrative fur trade was a fruitful cause of dispute even at this early time between 1640 and 1660. With the decline of the fur trade in New England at the close of the seventeenth century, fishing took its place as the most important industry, and leadership in fur trading passed to New York. This colony then became the most important fur trading center because of its advantageous situation at the mouth of the Hudson River.

Competition between the French and the English was keen and became embittered as the latter pushed up the Hudson and along the Mohawk to the Great Lakes. Unlike

---

[1] *Cf.* "Abstract of the Lawes of New England," 1641, in which it is provided: "In trucking or trading with the Indians no man shall give them for any commodity of theirs, Silver or Gold, or any weapons of war, either guns or gunpowder, nor sword, nor any other munition, which might come to be used against ourselves." In Peter Force, *Tracts and other Papers* (Washington, 1844), IV, no. lx, 10.

the English, the French assimilated with the native Indians in Canada as did the Spanish in Mexico; they lived the Indian life, married Indian women, and acquired the confidence and liking of the native tribes, with the exception of the Iroquois whose hatred they had early won and who consequently favored the English. In spite of the fact that the goods which they bartered for furs were inferior to those supplied by the English, the French were able to gain an increasing proportion of the fur trade. William Clarke, writing in 1755,[2] declared that "the first and most immediate consequence of the present measures of the French, if they are allowed to pursue them—will be the engrossing the whole Furr and Pelt trade." He estimated that the furs and pelts imported into England amounted to about £90,000 per annum, while those imported by France were no less than £135,000 per annum. The struggle over this lucrative fur trade, as the English pushed across the Alleghenies to the Ohio country and there came in conflict with the French, was one of the chief immediate causes of the French and Indian War (1754-63).

A considerable Indian trade was also developed on the southern frontiers from Pennsylvania southward. Even in the time of William Penn the fur trade had been carried on by the early settlers in Pennsylvania, helped by the friendly relations established by the Quakers with the Indians. Later, as the German and Scotch-Irish settlers pushed out new frontiers, they too came to have an interest in the western fur trade. The capital for this trade was supplied by Philadelphia merchants, and the profits were large. In Virginia the trade took on such dimensions that pack-horse caravans were required to carry goods to the Indian tribes on the southwest frontier, especially the Cherokees in western Carolina, and to bring back the skins and furs. This trade was less a fur trade than one in skins and leather, for the bulk of the peltries consisted of deerskins. It was speedily taken over by a small group of rich private merchants, who furnished the considerable capital that was necessary as the trade extended to more distant points. In this trade William Byrd and other leading Virginians amassed fortunes which

---

[2] *Observations on the late and present conduct of the French* (Boston, 1755), 14.

they later invested in land and slaves. But the real center of the southern trade was Charleston, from which it was carried 1000 miles into the continent. In 1731 there were collected in that city from all quarters as many as 225,000 deerskins alone. The first fortunes in Carolina were made in the Indian trade, which was exceedingly advantageous to the English adventurer. For a few trinkets, beads, looking glasses, bright-colored cloaks and blankets, hatchets, guns, powder and shot, and rum, he could obtain on the Savannah or the Catawba rivers peltries which he could sell in Charleston at many times the cost of the goods exchanged.

Closely associated with this business was the Indian slave trade.[3] The enslavement of Indians had existed in other colonies, but only in South Carolina was the traffic conducted on a commercial scale. In 1708 there were 1400 Indian slaves in that colony out of a total population of 9580. They were not highly esteemed as workers, however, and a good Negro was held to be worth two Indians. Consequently they were shipped out of the colony whenever possible and Negro slaves imported instead.

But the English were not the only nation which coveted the lucrative fur trade. In the area between the Appalachian mountains, the Ohio and Mississippi rivers, and the Gulf of Mexico the Indians came in contact with Frenchmen from Louisiana, Spaniards from Florida, and Englishmen from Virginia and the Carolinas. This triangular competition among Spaniards, Frenchmen, and Englishmen for the Indian trade—they tried to obtain the alliance of the southern Indian tribes for the purpose of controlling this trade—was an important but generally neglected phase of the struggle for power in North America among these three European nations. The English fur traders welcomed the settlement of Georgia in 1732, for this colony would serve as a military garrison against the Spaniards and as a base for the southwestern fur trade. Augusta soon became a general resort for Indian traders. It was estimated that soon after its establishment there were purchased from the Indians in the single year 1735 2000 pack-horse loads of skins and

3 V. W. Crane, *The Southern Frontier*, 1670-1732. (Durham, Duke Univ. Press, 1928), 109, 112.

other articles.[4] In 1768, the year of largest export, shipments were 306,000 pounds of deerskins and 40,000 pounds of leather.[5]

The fur trade possessed great economic significance in the early history of this country, because it furnished a ready, cheap, and yet valuable article of use and of export for the colonies. Owing to the disparity placed upon the value of furs by the Indians and the white traders in terms of the commodities bartered by the latter, the trade was enormously profitable to the white man during the whole of the colonial period. It had an even more profound effect upon the Indians, for it completely disrupted their somewhat sedentary agricultural organization; furnished with firearms and later with horses, the Indian became a hunter and a nomad.

But more than this, it furnished the initial incentive to westward exploration and settlement. The trader brought back from his wanderings glowing accounts of the rich lands which he had seen and thus stimulated a movement to the most desirable western lands. As population became more dense and game more scarce, the fur traders followed the retreating supply of fur-bearing animals across the Alleghenies and farther west. The trading posts were taken over by the more permanent settlers and the frontier was pushed by the hunter and trapper ever farther from the coast. The history of North American expansion, it has been said, might almost be written in terms of the fur trade. Certainly there is to be found in the struggle for the control of this trade one of the causes for the expulsion of the French from this country by the English. In order to secure the diminishing supply for her own use, England in 1764 placed hides and skins on

---

[4] C. C. Jones, Jr., *History of Georgia* (Charleston, 1883), I, 143, 217.
The following prices were agreed upon between Oglethorpe and the Creeks, and probably represent maximum prices paid for skins:

1 white blanket	1 buckskin	1 knife	1 doeskin
1 blue blanket	5 buckskins	1 hoe	2 buckskins
1 white shirt	2 buckskins	1 axe	1 buckskin
1 gun	10 buckskins	1 small hatchet	1 buckskin
1 pistol	5 buckskins	18 flints	1 buckskin
2 measures of powder	1 buckskin	brass buttons, per lb.	1 buckskin
60 bullets	2 buckskins		

Doeskins were estimated at half the value of buckskin.

[5] B. Romans, *A Concise Natural History of East and West Florida* (London, 1775), 104.

the list of enumerated articles. In 1770 the exports of furs and peltries from all the North American English colonies, including Canada, were valued at about $670,000.

Intercolonial trade. Although the Indian trade penetrated far into the interior, most of the continental intercolonial trade was carried on by water along the coast. This became increasingly important during the colonial period and was probably greater in volume though less in value than either the trade to Great Britain or that to the West Indies.

Owing to the Navigation Acts, discussion of colonial commerce has usually been confined to overseas trade and the domestic trade has been neglected. Both the geography and the products conspired to cause the development of intercolonial trade, especially in the northern and middle colonies. The fur trade, just described, was carried on by a large number of traders, operating with small capital, and was very diffused; it was necessary therefore to collect the furs from scattered posts both inland and on the coast. Many other articles, like the dried and salt fish of New England, the cereals and meat of the middle colonies, or the tobacco, hides, and naval stores of the South had similarly to be brought together in quantity in the shipping towns, and for this purpose a great number of small sailing vessels was called into existence, which navigated every bay and river. The New Englanders were especially active in boat-building and their first vessel, the *Blessing of the Bay*, was launched at Medford in 1631.

A second form of the intercolonial trade was the distribution of the imported foreign goods, which was carried on by the same vessels that assembled outgoing cargoes. The import trade was concentrated in Philadelphia, New York, Boston, and Charleston, and from these cities manufactured wares and other commodities of English and European origin were carried to smaller seacoast towns and from there into the interior.

The third branch of this traffic, and the largest in volume, consisted in the interchange of commodities among the colonies themselves, especially between the northern and southern groups. Not infrequently New England fishing vessels would load up in the winter, when the fishing season was over, with household manufactures, hardware, fish, liquor, and other products and peddle these along the southern coast and at the plantation wharves for tobacco, rice, naval stores, and other southern staples. The intercolonial trade was chiefly in the hands of men from New England, and, later, from New York and Pennsylvania. British vessels took very small part in this trade, so that it remained almost a colonial monopoly with little outside competition. This explains in part the vigorous growth of the seaport towns. To these centers the products of the smaller towns and of the other colonies were conveyed and from them foreign merchandise and local products were obtained. Colonies like Maine, New Hampshire, Connecticut, New Jersey, and Delaware had little direct overseas trade, but took part in the intercolonial coastwise trade.

The extent and character of the intercolonial trade may be indicated by the following scattered examples: New York sent bread and flour to New England, the Carolinas, and Georgia; beer to Boston; refined sugar to the southern colonies; iron to Massachusetts; brick to the neighboring colonies; woolen goods and hats to the South. Pennsylvania also supplied the other colonies with a variety of goods, exporting flour, bread, and starch north and south; beer to Canada and the southern colonies; ships and pleasure carriages to neighboring colonies; iron and ironware to Massachusetts, to the West Indies, and other colonies; stoves to Boston; stoneware, leather, paper, cordage, and other articles to various colonies.

Domestic marketing organization. This was very simple, for during the colonial period little specialization existed in retail trade or methods. Merchandizing or the distribution of goods was effected by three agencies. Of these the most important was the general store. Much of the retail trade was carried on by barter, and for this purpose an essential institution was the general country store, which collected the surplus products of the colonists, such as grain, provisions, cheese, butter, potash, feathers, tow cloth, and similar goods and gave them in exchange European goods—imported dress goods, crockery, glassware, powder and shot, and bar iron— or West Indian wares such as molasses, rum, sugar, salt, and indigo. Practically all transactions at the country stores were by barter, thus dispensing with the use of metallic money, which was always scarce, and avoiding the use of the fluctuating paper or bank money. The storekeeper, who might be an innkeeper in the North or a planter in the South, usually resold the produce he received to a merchant in the nearest town, from whom he received his foreign wares. With the growth of population in the eighteenth century somewhat more specialized stores began to develop in the towns, but the general store was found in country districts throughout this period.

Markets and fairs constituted a second agency of distribution. In accordance with usages to which the colonists had been accustomed in their European homes, legislation was early passed establishing these, regulating the conditions of exchange, and even authorizing the fixing of prices. Markets were generally to be found in the cities and towns of Pennsylvania and other northern colonies, to which the farmers brought their country produce twice a week. A good description of trade in Philadelphia in 1748 has been left us by Peter Kalm, a Swedish botanist, who was sent to this country by his government to report on conditions. According to him fairs were held twice a year, on May 16 and November 16, and every Wednesday and Saturday were market days. The markets were held in two places, but the principal one was near the courthouse. Here the people of Pennsylvania and New Jersey brought their country produce and obtained the manufactures of the town. The markets began at four or five o'clock in the morning and were usually over by noon.

Fairs were to be found in practically all of the colonies; at these fairs foreign merchandise was sold as well as the wares of the different colonies. They met the business needs of an age that could not support permanent organizations for the exchange of goods. Such gatherings fell somewhat into disrepute in the eighteenth century on account of the drinking and disorder that attended them, but they were revived before the Revolution.

A final agency of commercial intercourse was the peddler, who was to be found principally in the country districts of the North. In a period of poor transportation he performed an indispensable service as distributor of small notions, drugs, and other easily carried wares, which he dispensed along with news in remote districts. He made his appearance in the eighteenth century and attained considerable importance in the early nineteenth, but sharp business practices—such as the proverbial wooden nutmegs of the Connecticut peddler— diminished his usefulness and, reinforced by the opposition of a growing class of storekeepers, led to restrictive legislation.

Foreign commerce. Although the transatlantic trade probably did not exceed the coastwise trade in volume, it unquestionably surpassed it in importance, for upon this depended the supplying of the colonies with capital goods and with the more developed manufactures of the Old World. The Atlantic Ocean was the great thoroughfare of commerce and served as a connecting link between Europe and America rather than as a barrier to intercourse. From the standpoint of trade the colonies were the frontier of Europe, and from them the countries of the Old World planned to obtain needed raw materials and exotic foodstuffs. The colonies, on the other hand, possessed rich natural resources which were of value to them primarily as articles of exchange for manufactures and other commodities not produced locally, and which were at the same time in great demand in Europe. There was thus laid the basis for a profitable trade between the two continents. This was in accordance with a principle that where trade is carried on between different producing areas each will specialize in those lines in which it enjoys the greatest advantage. This foreign trade was vital to the welfare and progress of the colonies, for it enabled them to obtain capital goods and supplies of consumers' goods in less time and at less expense than if they had been compelled to manufacture these for themselves. As Kirkland well puts it[6]: "Their needs determined the character of colonial imports; the variety and richness of their production set the nature of colonial exports. In the mirror of foreign trade not legislation but economic conditions were reflected."

[6] E. C. Kirkland, *A History of American Economic Life* (New York, 1939), 109. By permission of the publishers, F. S. Crofts and Company.

During the seventeenth century the transatlantic trade was comparatively small. The colonists necessarily devoted their main energies to making a living, establishing homes for themselves, and supplying their own most urgent wants. There was, moreover, a considerable suspension in the intercourse between the colonies and England during the period from 1640 to 1660, owing to the Civil Wars in England. New England exported furs and lumber and ships to the mother country, but her fish and grain had to seek other outlets which were found in the West Indies, Holland, and southern Europe. In exchange there were brought back manufactured commodities, cordage, wool, and iron from England and Holland, molasses, sugar, and silver from the West Indies, and wine from the Canaries. The middle colonies exported furs, grain, meat, and lumber to practically the same markets, and received about the same imports. The foreign commerce of the southern colonies far exceeded that of either of the other two sections. From Virginia and Maryland was shipped chiefly tobacco, although peltries and grain were also exported from this section. The main markets for these were England and Holland, from which were received in exchange clothing and manufactured commodities of every description, wines, iron, seed, and other necessaries. The Carolinas sent skins and furs to England, and corn, cattle, meat, and lumber to the West Indies. Georgia was not yet founded. By the end of the century, in 1700, the exports from all the colonies to England amounted to £400,000, and the imports from England to £345,000. Statistics for the total foreign trade are not available.

During the eighteenth century the range and value of overseas commerce was greatly extended; not only did it grow in amount, but it changed somewhat in character. From New England the exports of furs declined, but the fishing industry provided new products in their place, while the manufacture of rum formed the basis for an extremely lucrative trade. The middle colonies increased greatly their exports of grains, meat, and other provisions, most of the grain now going to Spain and Portugal, and the other foodstuffs to the West Indies. The southern colonies added new staples, rice, indigo, and naval stores, to the ever-popular tobacco.

By 1763 over half of the exports from New England were products of the fisheries; about three-fourths of those from the middle colonies were wheat, flour, and biscuit; and over three-fourths of those from Virginia and Maryland consisted of tobacco. In exchange the American colonists received English manufactures and European goods from England, salt from Spain, wine from the Azores and the Madeiras, and sugar, molasses, rum, and cotton from the West Indies. The imports of sugar grew rapidly owing to the spread of the drinking of chocolate and later of tea and coffee. The import trade, upon which depended the economic and cultural development of the colonists, was the all-essential factor; the export trade was but the means of paying for imported goods.

The balance of trade. On the basis of the trade carried on with the rest of the world the English colonies fell into three sharply distinguished groups: (1) the continental colonies north of and including Pennsylvania; (2) those south of Pennsylvania, and (3) the West Indies. The trade of those three regions with England was given as follows for 1770:

TRADE OF COLONIES WITH ENGLAND, 1770		
Colonies	Exports to England	Imports from England *
Northern group	£178,000	£1,410,000
Southern group	932,000	839,000
West Indies	2,350,000	897,000
Total	£3,460,000	£3,146,000

* If to these imports there be added £200,000 as the value of slaves imported (according to Lord Sheffield's calculations in his *Observations*, 2d ed., p. 246), and the difference of £114,000 for invisible items such as ocean freights, middlemen's commissions, and other services, an exact balance will be obtained. Since the invisible items must have been considerably larger than the sum named, it may be concluded that a steady investment of English capital was being made in the colonies.

(1) It will at once be noted that the northern group of colonies bought from England about eight times as much as they sold to the mother country. How was this possible? Benjamin Franklin explained it by the indirect trade which this section carried on with the Mediterranean countries of Europe, the West Indies, and Africa. To the West Indies they sent about one-half of their total exports,[7] consisting of

[7] This proportion was given for 1769 by T. Pitkin, *Statistical View*, 20.

1. With Southern Europe

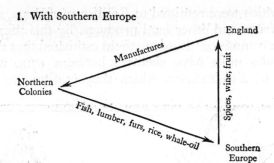

2. With West Indies

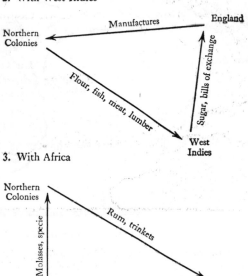

3. With Africa

"THREE-CORNERED TRADE"

fish, lumber, meat, and other products; about one-quarter
went to Spain, Portugal, and Italy; and part of the balance
to the other countries. England received directly but a small
fraction of the total exports. But most of the products received in exchange by northern traders found their way to
England to pay for the manufactured goods which the colonists wished to possess. Thus from the West Indies and from
southern Europe they obtained currency and bills of ex-

change which were remitted to English merchants, as well as tropical fruits and other local products. By this "foreign and circuitous commerce" Lord Sheffield estimated that the northern colonies must have obtained between 1700 and 1776 upwards of £30,000,000, which they remitted to England

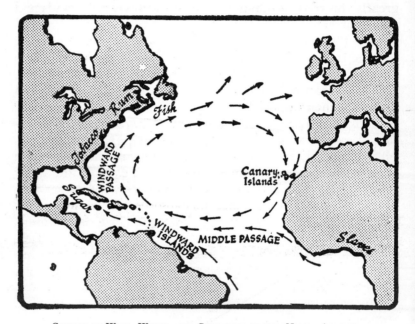

CIRCUIT OF WIND, WATER, AND COMMERCE IN THE NORTH ATLANTIC

H. R. Muelder and D. M. Delo, *Years of this Land: a Geographical History of the United States* (New York, 1943). By permission of the publishers, D. Appleton-Century Company, Inc.

in addition to their direct exports in payment for the goods received from the mother country.

There was one phase of this indirect trade which was so important and so lucrative that it deserves especial mention. This was the slave trade, and this in turn was based upon the manufacture of rum. The rum was carried to the coast of Africa where it was exchanged for slaves; these were sold in the West Indies where the demand for labor on the sugar plantations seemed insatiable. The profits from this triangular trade were received largely in the form of molasses —which again became the basis of another similar series of transactions—and of rum and sugar, currency and bills of exchange. These latter were quickly remitted to England. From the profits of this trade were built up the fortunes of smug merchants in Boston, Newport, Salem, and other New England towns. The accompanying illustration shows how greatly this trade was aided by the prevailing trade winds and ocean currents.

(2) The southern colonies traded directly with England, sending there their staples—tobacco, rice, indigo, naval stores —and buying supplies directly from English merchants. Since they had but little indirect trade, their exports served to pay for their imports, and the two remained in fairly steady equilibrium. The excess of exports over imports was absorbed, in part at least, in payment for ocean freights to British shipowners, for most of the carrying trade was done in British vessels; comparatively few of the ships in the great tobacco fleets were owned by southern planters. Another part of the surplus trade balance was absorbed in payments for the services of English "factors" or agents of the planters, who bought the tobacco or received the other staples on commission and frequently acted as purchasing agents for English goods ordered by the American resident planters. The relations between the American planters and the English merchants were much closer than similar relations were in other sections.

(3) The trade balance of the West Indies showed a striking disparity, but in exactly the opposite direction from that of the northern group of colonies. The explanation of the large excess of exports—almost three times the imports— is to be found in a number of circumstances. In the first place, many Englishmen owned estates in the West Indies and drew their profits from their investments. Or it might be that West Indian planters lived in London with their families and spent their income there; or they sent their sons to the English universities. In any case the products of the West Indian plantations were shipped to England and showed among the merchandise exports; the goods purchased with them, however, did not appear among the imports into the West Indies, for they were consumed in England instead of on the plantations, but the real effect was the same as though

English manufactures had been shipped to the West Indies. In the second place, a great deal of the trade with the West Indies was not carried on with England and consequently does not appear on the merchandise balance sheet with the mother country. Many of the exports were shipped in payment for supplies from the continental American colonies. In 1769 Pitkin[8] estimated that the value of these amounted to about £750,000, of which over £550,000 was from New England. These sums were paid partly in plantation products, and partly in currency or bills of exchange on London merchants. The currency and bills of exchange would then be used by Yankee traders to settle their indebtedness with the London merchants. Large sums were also paid to New England and New York shipowners each year for freight charges, as the greater part of the carrying trade was in the hands of northern traders. And finally, some £200,000 was paid out annually for slaves, an item which was not included in the statistics of merchandise imports.

There were thus plenty of offsetting invisible items to absorb the excess of merchandise exports and to effect an equilibrium between the two sides of the international balance sheet. It appears, however, that in the twenty years ending in 1775 the balance of trade ran against the continental colonies. This may be interpreted as meaning that the colonists were going into debt, or, what is more probable, that there was during these years a considerable investment of British capital in America.

Attitude of England to different sections. From the standpoint of the English government and merchants the continental American colonies were originally not so highly regarded as were the West Indian colonies, nor was New England so important to the mother country as the southern group. The northern colonists produced little that England did not possess, and along most lines competed with her fishermen or farmers or shipbuilders. But the South with its staples of tobacco, rice, indigo, and naval stores, and especially the West Indies with their sugar, molasses, and rum, furnished articles in very great demand, which could not be produced in the home country. The mercantilist attitude

[8] *Statistical View*, 20.

toward the colonies was forcibly expressed by Sir Josiah Child in his *Discourse on Trade*, written about 1680, who held that "New England is the most prejudicial Plantation to this Kingdom."

Since colonies were valued mainly for commercial purposes, the ideal colony was one which provided commodities that England did not produce and which she otherwise would have to buy from foreign countries; such a colony moreover would not compete with the industries of the mother country. Down to about the middle of the eighteenth century colonies were valued by England primarily as sources of raw materials and tropical foodstuffs, the sugar trade being held in especial regard. Judged by this standard, the West Indies were regarded as most valuable and the South was more highly esteemed than were the northern colonies.

After about 1745 England came to be less of an agricultural country and more industrial. With this shift in economic interests she changed her attitude toward the colonies and began to value them as markets for her manufactures. From this standpoint the West Indies, whose population was increasing slowly and was moreover composed largely of slaves, were obviously less valuable than the continental colonies, with their growing wealth and numbers. By reason of its climate, too, the North constituted a better market for the products of England's leading industry, woolens. This altered attitude found expression in the legislation which sought to secure the colonial market exclusively to the mother country and to effect an equilibrium between the two sides of the international balance sheet.

Chief ports and commodities. The varied and extensive character of colonial commerce will perhaps best be described by naming some of the chief ports and the nature of the cargoes which were carried. In New England Boston was of course the leading port, and its "long wharf" was the scene of a bustling activity which sent its shipping to all parts of America and Europe until it was closed by royal edict in 1774. Newport was next in importance, followed by such lesser towns as Salem, Providence, and New Haven. A fairly adequate picture of the trade from New England is furnished by the list of exports given by the author of *American*

Husbandry[9] at the end of this period. It will be seen that over half of the total consists of products of the fisheries, and that after these ranked forest products, such as masts, staves, boards, and ships, with potash, and a smaller amount of livestock and meat.

AVERAGE ANNUAL EXPORTS FROM NEW ENGLAND, 1763-1766	
Codfish, dried, 10,000 tons	£100,000
Whale and cod oil, 8,500 tons	127,500
Whalebone, mackerel, and shads	23,400
Products of the fisheries	£250,900
Ships, masts, naval stores, and potash	159,600
Agricultural products	74,500
Total	£485,000

The exports of the middle colonies were largely agricultural, none of the products of the fisheries being found there. Philadelphia was the leading port, considerably ahead of Boston, with New York a poor third, though the last-named port had a larger domestic trade than either of the other two. Since most of the products of the middle colonies were shipped from New York City or Philadelphia, it will be sufficient to list the exports from New York and Pennsylvania.[10] About two-thirds of the exports of these two provinces consisted of flour and biscuit, wheat and other grains, the other third being distributed among such varied items as meat, livestock, lumber, ships, pig iron, and other products.

AVERAGE ANNUAL EXPORTS FROM NEW YORK AND PENNSYLVANIA, 1763-1766	
Flour and biscuit, 600,000 barrels	£600,000
Wheat, 170,000 qtrs.	170,000
Other agricultural products	216,500
Products of cultivated lands	£986,500
Ships, lumber, and miscellaneous	210,500
Total	£1,197,000

The overwhelming importance of tobacco in the export trade of Virginia and Maryland is shown in the following

[9] Vol. 1, 59. Rearranged and classified.
[10] *Ibid.*, I, 124, 181.

table.[11] This was called a "true staple" by the author of *American Husbandry,* because it did not compete with the products of the mother country, and was accordingly highly approved. The methods of marketing tobacco were, however, cumbrous and expensive. Most of it was shipped in English vessels. These arrived in southern ports early each winter with cargoes of British goods ordered by the planters the previous spring, or sent by merchants to be traded for tobacco and other products, or to be sold on credit. These the captain delivered from wharf to wharf, at the same time making engagements for tobacco to be delivered as he returned down the river. Such a system of casual trading was bad both for the colonial planter, who was not sure of disposing of his crop, and for the English merchant who ran the risk of not selling his goods or of obtaining an insufficient return cargo. The remedy for these disadvantages was greater specialization at each end of the line.

AVERAGE ANNUAL EXPORTS FROM VIRGINIA AND MARYLAND, 1763-66	
Tobacco, 96,000 hogsheads	£768,000
Other agricultural products	127,000
Products of cultivated lands	£895,000
Deer and other skins	25,000
Ships and lumber	85,000
Iron in bars and pigs	35,000
Total	£1,040,000

Organization of foreign commerce. The casual tobacco trade of the seventeenth century developed into an organized traffic in the eighteenth. At the London end certain merchants began to specialize in American colonial trade, handling the sale of tobacco on commission, and shipping on order to the colonies cargoes of English merchandise, for which they often extended credit. These English merchants thus combined the functions of banker, selling agent, and commission man. At the other end of the line resident factors, acting as representatives of the British merchants, began to appear in the colonies. It was their business to purchase tobacco and other products or take them on consignment for

11 *Ibid.,* I, 256.

shipment to England, to collect debts, and to dispose of the cargoes sent to the colonies. These factors never became great merchants, such as developed in New England, for the profits of tobacco growing always tempted them to become planters, while the trade from wharf to wharf instead of in towns was not conducive to the growth of a mercantile class.

This marketing system produced complaints at each end of the line. The American tobacco grower grumbled at exorbitant commissions, scarcity of ships, high transportation and insurance rates, and low prices for his product. The English merchant, on the other hand, complained of the fluctuations in the price of tobacco and the irresponsibility of the planters, who ordered more than they could pay for, straining the merchant's credit, and themselves falling hopelessly into debt.[12]

In New England and the middle colonies the organization of commerce was more complicated. Owing to the scarcity of money and the difficulties of credit, most of the colonial trade was really barter. A Yankee skipper would sail with a cargo of dried and salt fish and home manufactures to a southern port where he would exchange his products for lumber,[13] rice, and meat. These he might carry to the West Indies, and in exchange would receive rum, molasses, and sugar, and perhaps ginger, logwood, indigo, and other tropical products. Freight rates on these goods were extremely high, running from 50 per cent on the initial cost of the less bulky items to 100 per cent on such things as corn and lumber. The larger vessels, of perhaps 400 tons, would proceed to London with their cargoes which they would trade for such merchandise as woodenware, pewter, iron pots, frying pans, and other manufactures, all articles in great demand in the colonies. Smaller vessels, such as the New England fishing smacks in the winter, did not undertake such long voyages, but would return north, stopping in at various ports to exchange their rum and sugar for rice, flour or bread, and iron.

[12] George Grenville, *The Regulations Lately Made Concerning the Colonies and the Taxes Imposed upon Them Considered* (London, 1763), 57.

[13] It should be noted that southern stores of red oak were preferred for sugar hogsheads and white oak for rum casks; New England supplied principally boards and scantlings to the West Indies.

Such trade was typical of the roundabout voyages which sometimes lasted two or three years, while the captain or the supercargo—the representative of the merchant—holding a sort of roving commission, wandered from port to port, buying, selling, bartering, or carrying freight, but always seeking for his cargo the market where he thought he could dispose of it to the best advantage. The cargo of such a vessel was frequently the property of a number of persons, the principal share belonging to a merchant, but various small lots representing "ventures" of the captain and crew or other persons. The merchant usually carried freight for other merchants as well as for himself. He performed varied services, now handled by specialists, such as collection, storage, transportation, insurance, and finance, and also acted as commission agent in disposing of cargoes for others. Taken as a group, the merchants constituted the wealthiest and most influential class in the northern colonies, and they ruled society and politics. For successful ventures the profits were enormous—50 per cent on fish and other products shipped to Europe, and 100 per cent on goods purchased in London with specie from the West Indian trade. Not until the rise of the new manufacturing class after about 1820 was their primacy disputed.

Smuggling, piracy, and privateering. In an age of much legislation but of rather lax enforcement of commercial regulations, it was inevitable that these should be frequently disregarded, especially when they ran counter to the self-interest of the traders. On the easily accessible coast of England smuggling was a recognized and lucrative industry, and much French wine and brandy was drunk, silk worn, and tobacco smoked which had not contributed to the king's customs. Colonial traders thought it no crime to evade laws which they considered an infringement on their rights, and carried on illicit but profitable trade with the Spanish, French, and Dutch West Indies; they trafficked in tobacco and other enumerated commodities directly with France and Holland, or landed their cargoes in England at places other than ports of entry.

The eighteenth century was a period of "salutary neglect" of the colonies, and it was not difficult to evade the Navigation Acts in collusion with complacent British customs officials. It was estimated that in 1700 one-third of the trade of Boston was in violation of the law. But even if this estimate is correct for Boston, it cannot be accepted as a true picture of colonial commerce as a whole, for south of New England the bulk of the trade was probably carried on in the regular way.

Piracy flourished along the southern coast, especially among the numerous islands of the Caribbean Sea. Here the prizes were greater, the possibility of escape and hiding better, and the policing of the waters less effective than elsewhere. Nettels [14] cites instances when single pirate ships brought in captured cargoes valued from £50,000 to £200,000, and states that the early supply of specie in the colonies was derived in large part from this source. From the days when Drake and Hawkins had seized the silver cargoes of peaceful Spanish galleons to the days when "Blackbeard" made his victims walk the plank, piracy had existed, and not altogether without encouragement from constituted authority. More than one governor closed his eyes to the visits of recognized pirate ships to colonial ports, for they sold their ill-gotten cargoes cheap and paid good prices for provisions and ships' stores. It has even been suggested that the lack of other economic opportunities in the Carolinas drove the settlers in those colonies into piracy until the introduction of rice and indigo and naval stores gave them a profitable industrial basis. In 1699 Parliament passed a stringent law against piracy, but it continued until about 1730, when legitimate trade became so important that it could no longer be tolerated.

Scarcely distinguishable from piracy, at times, was privateering. Today this is no longer permitted by international law, but in the seventeenth and eighteenth centuries it was the practice in times of war for governments to grant to private vessels "letters of marque and reprisal," which entitled them to prey upon the merchantmen of the enemy country. Since the prize money was shared in part among the officers and crew of the privateer, the gain was great and the risk comparatively small. During the frequent wars between

[14] C. P. Nettels, *Money Supply of the American Colonies before 1720* (Madison, 1934), 88.

England and her European rivals the colonists had abundant opportunity to engage in privateering.

All of these irregular commercial practices disturbed normal trade. Their magnitude is unknown, but it must have been considerable, and this fact reduces the validity of all colonial commercial statistics. In addition to these man-made interferences with legitimate trade, there were physical dangers. The shoals along the coast were not marked, channels were seldom charted, and the first lighthouse was not built until 1716; as a result of these factors wrecks were frequent and many ships were lost.

Communication. Means of communication were slow and cumbrous, and news traveled slowly. The first regular colonial newspaper was published in Boston in 1704, and others later in Philadelphia, Williamsburg, and Charleston, but their circulation was limited and in their place news-letters containing the most important items were circulated from hand to hand. Postal facilities were of the most primitive character; letters and valuable packages were usually carried by private messengers at high rates. Postage rates for a single letter ranged from eight to twenty-five cents, according to the distance, and the charges were paid by the recipient. Mails were both irregular and infrequent. An important advance was made when a general postal system was inaugurated by the second Continental Congress on July 27, 1775. Benjamin Franklin was placed at the head, and a line of posts were established from Falmouth (the present Portland), Maine, to Savannah, Georgia. This was gradually extended during the next few years and in 1789 was placed under the control of a postmaster general.

Even slower was foreign intercourse. At best government officials and merchants were able to exchange letters with English correspondents twice a year. Ships took six to twelve weeks to make a crossing and regularly scheduled sailings were almost unknown. Business was conducted at a slow pace which it is difficult for us to comprehend today.

Conclusion. Colonial trade was of first importance to the colonists, for it was the method by which they exchanged the surplus products of their particular localities for those of other climes or for the manufactured commodities of England and other industrially more advanced countries. For England also it was highly advantageous, for it provided the mother country with raw materials or articles of consumption for whose production she was not suited. The colonial trade constituted nearly a third of England's total commerce, which in 1700 amounted to about £12,000,000 and in 1770 to about £23,000,000. Much of this trade was carried on in colonial ships, which practically monopolized the intercolonial and coastwise traffic, and shared largely in that with Europe and Africa. Its development was interfered with but little by artificial restrictions imposed by England or by natural hindrances like piracy. Along no line did the independence, the energy, or the ingenuity of the colonists produce more striking results than in the field of commerce. That they should have resisted the efforts of the British government to alter the system built up by the labors of a century and a half of adventurous traders cannot be a matter of wonder.

CHAPTER VI

COLONIAL FINANCE

To carry on the commerce just described it was necessary to have ships and other means of transportation for moving the goods from the points of origin to the markets. But it was almost equally essential to possess a medium of exchange in the form of money and credit instruments to facilitate the transfer of ownership and the processes of purchase and sale. The apparent lack of these bothered the colonial producer and merchant and introduced many difficulties and disorders into colonial finance and business, although it is difficult to show that this lack distinctly retarded the economic progress of this period. The keynote of colonial monetary history is to be found in the constant complaints about the scarcity of money and the repeated efforts of the colonists to make up this scarcity by various expedients.

Metallic money. There were no gold or silver mines in the English colonies and consequently it was necessary to import all the specie for use there. But the colonists were for the most part people of small means and brought very little money along with them; and even if they did they soon discovered in their new settlements need for many other forms of capital more urgent than money, and speedily sent this back to England to lay out in such useful commodities as agricultural implements, plows, tools, household utensils, and manufactured goods. This was recognized by Governor Ward of Rhode Island, who wrote [1]: "And as the first settlers were not of the wealthiest sort, nor overstocked with servants, the greatest part of their money was unavoidably swallowed up in procuring provisions, clothing, and utensils for husbandry and labor, to subdue and cultivate the soil." Another contemporary writer stated that money from the West Indies

---

[1] *Records of Rhode Island*, V, 8, quoted by Bullock, *Monetary History of the United States* (New York, 1900), 3, note.

"seldom continues six months in the province before it is remitted to Europe." In other words, specie was exchanged, like any other commodity, for other goods which were deemed of greater utility. This was not understood by most of the colonists and they attributed the constant draining off of the metallic money from the colonies to the operation of the Navigation Acts, the machinations of the merchants, unfair treatment by the English, and any cause except the correct one.

The scarcity of coin was accentuated by at least three other factors. One was the sparseness of population and the isolation of households and communities which made exchange difficult and circulation of money slow, so that a given amount of specie was much less effective than the same sum would be today. Another was that the prevailing mercantilist notions on the balance of trade made other nations disinclined to give up their specie for colonial products. And finally, England found it impossible, even had she been so inclined, to provide the colonies with an adequate currency because of the disordered state of her own coinage, at least prior to the recoinage of 1696. Under these circumstances the colonists proceeded to employ various expedients to retain and supplement their scant supply of specie and to devise substitute forms of money.

Monetary legislation. The most obvious method of solving the problem, and one which has always been tried in similar circumstances in almost every country, was to prohibit the export of money. This was done by a Massachusetts law of 1654, which forbade the exportation of coin, except a sum of not over 20 shillings for traveling expenses, upon pain of forfeiture of the offender's whole estate. It was further required that a searcher for money be appointed in every port of entry to examine outgoing vessels. Such legislation was futile.

Other legislation grew out of the poor quality of the money available. Most of the coins in circulation were foreign ones, obtained in trade with the West Indies, which were well supplied with Spanish money. Each foreign coin had an accepted value in English money in the colonies and all accounts were kept in terms of pounds, shillings, and pence.

The chief foreign coin in use was the Spanish silver dollar, or piece of eight reals; the mint value of a full-bodied "piece of eight" was four and a half shillings (4s. 6d.). The various foreign coins differed considerably in weight and fineness, and the original mint errors were magnified by the universal practice of clipping and sweating, which was not difficult with the crude coins of that period. By the middle of the seventeenth century it was estimated that the coins in the colonies had lost one-fourth of their weight. Since English merchants received foreign coins only according to weight, the heavy ones were exported to England, and the light ones circulated at home, quite in accordance with Gresham's Law that "bad money drives out good money."

Partly as a result of the low metallic content of the coins circulating in the colonies, and partly, apparently, in order to attract more coin by a favorable estimation, the different colonies vied with each other in raising the valuation of the Spanish dollar. The rate was generally made 5s. for convenience, but in 1652 Massachusetts raised her valuation to slightly under 6s., and shortly after Virginia increased hers to over 6s.; New York went up to 6s. 9d. in 1676, and in 1707 Pennsylvania followed with a valuation of 7s. 6d. A further motive was the belief of the debtor class that this form of inflation would provide them with cheap money. That it was effective in enabling American debtors to pay English creditors at considerable reduction is evidenced by the constant complaints that emanated from England. The English government tried to introduce order into this chaos and in 1704 by royal proclamation of Queen Anne declared that the maximum colonial rating of a Spanish piece of eight should be 6s., or a third higher than the regular English rating, and that other coins should be valued in like proportion. Money so valued was known as "proclamation money." But already the price level in many of the colonies had risen in accordance with the higher ratings mentioned above. Enforcement of the law would have caused considerable losses and produced a marked deflation or fall in the general price level; consequently the proclamation was not well observed.

Colonial mints. Because of the scarcity and the disordered state of the scanty supply of money in circulation, which was made up of a heterogeneous collection of foreign coins without uniformity in denomination or weight or fineness, attempts were made three times to establish colonial mints. Those projected by Virginia (1645) and Maryland (1662) seem never to have got actually into operation, but in 1652 Massachusetts established a mint for the coinage of shillings, sixpenny, and three-penny pieces. In order to keep them in circulation they were made lighter than the equivalent English coins, containing only about three-quarters as much silver, but in spite of that they were exported. The "pine-tree" shillings issued by this mint, so-called because of the design stamped upon the face of the coins, were in general use throughout New England, but about 1688 the mint was closed by the English government as it was thought to run counter to the royal prerogative of coinage.

None of the attempts to provide the colonies with gold and silver coins was very successful. Prohibiting their export was futile, raising the local legal tender value was interfered with by Queen Anne's proclamation, and colonial mints were forbidden. It was necessary to find some other kind of money than specie, i.e. than gold or silver coins.

Barter. In order to carry on exchange without metallic money the colonists early resorted to direct barter, although the value of the articles exchanged was usually stated in terms of specie. Taxes were made payable in produce. Dewey states that the "term bills of students at Harvard College were for many years met by the payment of produce, livestock, meat and occasionally with various articles raked up from the family closets of student debtors. One student, later president of the College, in 1649 settled his bill with an 'old cow.'" [2] The itinerant cobbler and other wandering craftsmen as well as the peddlers were generally paid in produce. But the village store was the point at which most barter was effected. Here country products, like butter, cheese, eggs, and flax, or household manufactures like yarn, nails, etc., were received, set off against one another, and paid out. Near the frontier, trade with the Indians was likewise conducted on a barter basis. Since Indian families, for the most part, led a self-sufficient existence and did not specialize,

[2] D. R. Dewey, *Financial History of the United States* (New York, 1928), 19.

most tribes had not developed a medium of exchange of their own before the white man came.

Wampum. However, it was soon found that there was one article most Indians were willing to accept.

This was *wampum*, a name given to black and white beads made from the whorls of periwinkle shells in which holes were bored with stone drills, the beads being then worn as strings or embroidered on pieces of deerskin and worn in the form of girdles or belts as charms or ornaments. Wampum seems to have been first used in 1627 in New England, where it was found that the Indians would work for wampum and trade their furs for wampum but not for specie. It was usually used in the beaver trade, and as long as beaver had a market, wampum maintained a certain value; but this was always fluctuating and varied with the price of beaver.

These fluctuations are clearly evidenced by contemporary legislation; about 1630 Roger Williams wrote that wampum was quoted at about 3 beads for a penny; in 1637 Connecticut received it for taxes at the rate of 4 beads for a penny, and in 1641 Massachusetts made it legal tender at 6 beads for a penny. Wampum was at its height about 1646, but after that from a number of causes it began to decline in value. The price of beaver, with which it was closely connected, fell in England and as a result the price of wampum fell in the colonies. The white man, with steel drills, was able to manufacture the beads more rapidly than the Indians had done, and there was soon what one may call an overissue of this money. And counterfeiting began: the natural black beads were worth double the white ones, so the colonists began to dye the white beads.

By 1662 all the New England colonies had withdrawn the legal-tender quality from wampum, and ceased to receive it as lawful money, but this did not drive it out of circulation and it remained current in smaller transactions and in the interior for some time afterwards. It continued to circulate in remote districts of New England and as far south as the Potomac until the beginning of the eighteenth century. In spite of its disadvantages wampum served as a universal currency in the colonies for practically three-quarters of a century, and during most of that time was readily exchangeable for merchandise, labor, or taxes. Frequently there was no other currency available, and judgments of courts as well as taxes were made payable in this shell money. It circulated not only in New England, but the Dutch in New York had scarcely any other effective currency for smaller sums, and it was common in Pennsylvania and New Jersey.

Wampum illustrates the basic difference between barter and money. As long as only a few persons wanted wampum it was an article of barter. When everyone, even white men who had no thought of wearing the Indian decoration, became willing to accept wampum in trade because they could pass it on to others, it became money. This attribute of general acceptability is the basic quality of money. Wampum was not the only commodity that became money.

Commodity money. A wide variety of agricultural products was used as money by the colonists at one time or another, differing of course in the different sections, but in each case being the most universally used article in the community. Thus, in 1631, Massachusetts ordered that "corne shall pass for payment of all debts at the usual rate it is sold for, except money or beaver be expresly named." In 1640 wheat was made current at 6s. a bushel, rye and barley at 5s., and peas at 6s.; dried fish was also made a legal tender. Taxes might be paid in any of these articles, or in cattle.

It was soon discovered that when commodities which were not uniform in quality were used indiscriminately as money, taxes and other debts were often settled by the payment of the worst specimens. Hence in 1658 an order was issued that no man should attempt to discharge his taxes with "lank" cattle. This was another illustration of Gresham's Law that "bad money drives out good money," for debtors saved those specimens which were of most value to themselves and passed on to their creditors the poorest. Other disadvantages soon showed themselves. The cost of transporting produce paid in for taxes from different parts of the colony to Boston was about 10 per cent of the whole amount, and a further loss of 5 per cent was incurred through shrinkage and deterioration.

In the southern colonies resort was had to the use of the staple agricultural products of that region as substitutes for the scarce metallic money. Tobacco was used as currency in

Virginia for almost two centuries and in Maryland for a century and a half. It seems to have been used as a medium of exchange from about 1619, and in 1642 was virtually made legal tender by a law prohibiting the enforcement of contracts calling for metallic money, though this was repealed fourteen years later. Like wampum in New England, tobacco fluctuated greatly in value; as the production of tobacco increased, its value depreciated, and persons who had debts or wages payable to them in so many pounds of tobacco found themselves with a much smaller purchasing power.[3] Tobacco is, moreover, not a uniform product, and the poorer qualities were passed on to the creditors.

Constant attempts were made to limit the amount of tobacco (so as to prevent its depreciation), to keep it up to standard (so as to insure uniformity in quality), and in other ways to remedy the disadvantages to which it was subject. A great improvement was made in 1727 in Virginia, when tobacco notes were legalized; these were in the nature of certificates of deposit issued by official inspectors for tobacco deposited in government warehouses. Since this tobacco was graded, the evil of lack of uniformity was partially eliminated; in 1734 "crop notes" calling for particular casks of tobacco were introduced. The tobacco notes passed freely from hand to hand and formed a more convenient medium of exchange than the actual tobacco which they represented.

In South Carolina the scarcity of metallic money led to the adoption of rice as the chief medium of exchange. In 1719 the Assembly made rice receivable for taxes "to be delivered in good barrels upon the bay at Charleston." Rice went into circulation as money, however, chiefly in the form of rice orders or certificates, like those for tobacco in Virginia, at the rate of 30s. for one hundred pounds of rice. The rice orders were made legal tender for all purposes.

[3] Because of this fluctuating value, the Virginia legislature came into conflict with the British Crown. The salaries of the clergy had been fixed by the colonial legislature in so many pounds of tobacco, payable by the people, or taxpayers, to the clergy; this was later changed to a fixed money value of 2d. a pound, under the Twopenny Act of the Virginia legislature. When the price of tobacco went up, and the parsons still got only 2d. a pound, they complained, and the King vetoed the act, thus favoring the clergy and placing the burden of payment upon the tobacco growers. Known as the Parsons' Cause, this situation furnished Patrick Henry an occasion for denying the right of the King to veto colonial legislation.

Other commodities authorized and used as money in the colonies in the payment of public and private debts were wheat, oats, barley, peas, bacon, pork, beef, tallow, butter, cheese, fish, flax, wool, sugar, brandy, whisky, and even musket balls.[4]

Advantages and disadvantages of commodity money. The use of commodity money was attended with many inconveniences, some of which are suggested in a lively description by Mme. Knight of the methods of trade followed in New Haven in 1704.[5] Prices differed according to the kind of medium of exchange used, which were pay, money, pay as money, and trusting. Pay was grain, pork, beef, etc., at the prices set by the General Court that year; money was pieces of eight or Spanish reals, Boston shillings, silver coins, and wampum; pay as money was provisions at prices one-third cheaper than those set by the General Court; trust was the result of a bargain between merchant and buyer as to the time allowed for payment. "Now when the buyer comes to ask for a commodity, sometimes before the merchant answers that he has it he says, 'Is your pay ready?' Perhaps the chap's reply is 'yes.' 'What do you pay in?' says the merchant. The buyer having answered, then the price is set; as suppose he wants a sixpenny knife, in pay it is 12d, in pay as money 8d, and hard money its own price, viz., 6d." "It seems a very intricate way of trade and what Lex Mercatoria had not thought of," added Mme. Knight.

The use of these commodity moneys was unquestionably necessary and beneficial in the absence of a sufficient supply of metallic money. Their general adoption as a medium of exchange during the seventeenth century is an evidence both of the need and of the ingenuity of the colonists in finding substitutes for the expensive precious metals. Just as they used wooden pegs in the absence of iron nails or screws in building their houses and ships, so they used wampum or tobacco in place of gold and silver in exchange. In neither case was the substitute so convenient as the article substituted for, but it served until the economic development of the

[4] See list of articles used in North Carolina in Bogart and Thompson, *Readings*, 97.

[5] *Journal*, 53; quoted in A. B. Hart, *History told by Contemporaries* (4 vols., New York, 1897), II, 229.

country permitted something better. All these commodity moneys were subject to serious disadvantages, for they lacked most of the requisites of good money, such as durability, uniformity, portability, divisibility, and stability of value. They fluctuated in value, and the holders suffered loss in storing or hoarding them. Their unsatisfactory character consequently led to a resort to other expedients and substitutes for metallic moneys.

Foreign exchange. In foreign trade, especially with the British West Indies, extensive use was made of bills of exchange. When gold and silver were not readily available, or where direct barter was not possible, the colonial ship captain often accepted bills of exchange drawn on London merchants. With these he could readily purchase in the English market the supplies which he needed to take home. A draft or bill of exchange was an order drawn by some exporter in the colonies upon an English merchant to whom he had sold his goods but from whom he had not yet received payment, directing such merchant to pay to a third party a part or all of the amount owed. In this way a transfer of credit was effected without the expense of transmitting money. Bills of exchange were frequently drawn on Europe in all of the colonies, the rate of exchange differing from place to place and from time to time, according to the supply of bills or the demand for them[6]; they were commonly drawn at thirty days' sight. Interest rates ranged in the different colonies from 5 to 7 per cent. Goods were generally imported from Europe on eighteen months' credit, and sold in the colonies on twelve months' credit. The earlier commerce of the seventeenth century was carried on for the most part by the direct exchange of one commodity against another, but during the eighteenth century there was greater resort to money and to credit devices.

Paper money in Massachusetts. To meet the demands for a larger circulating medium for colonial trade, and also as a source of revenue for the treasury, paper money was early issued by the colonial legislatures. The first issue was made by Massachusetts in 1690, to pay the soldiers who had

[6] Testimony of Benjamin Franklin, before the House of Commons, 1776, in *Works* (Boston, 1840), II, 425.

returned unsuccessful and penniless from a military expedition against the French in Quebec. This was not only the origin of paper money in America, but also in the British Empire, and almost in the Christian world. These notes were limited to £40,000 in amount, but in spite of this they rapidly depreciated to about two-thirds of their face value, and the soldiers who were paid with them lost a third of their wages. To prevent this depreciation the plan was adopted the following year of retiring and destroying a certain number of bills each year, and in 1692 they were given legal-tender quality and made receivable for public dues at 5 per cent advance, and at the same time secured by the public taxes and other revenues. These measures were successful in keeping the paper on a par with specie for about twenty years, although the redeemed notes were usually promptly reissued. This first emission, thus secured, was really an issue of non-interest-bearing treasury notes or certificates of indebtedness, much like modern treasury warrants that are issued in anticipation of taxes. They passed from hand to hand, however, and served as currency.

This method was so successful that when a second expedition against Canada took place in 1709, a new issue of £30,000 was made to meet the expenses, together with £10,000 reissue of the first emission. This was too much, and from now on province bills began to depreciate; not only were they overissued, but the public soon lost confidence in them owing to the manner in which the period of redemption was postponed. This had been extended in 1704 to two years, in 1708 to three, in 1709 to four, and now it was again prolonged to five years in 1710, to six in 1711, and finally to thirteen years. By 1714 it was estimated that a total of £194,950 had been issued in Massachusetts. Province bills were now at a discount of 30 per cent, and as they depreciated they drove out the little metallic money still in circulation.[7] This is still another example of Gresham's Law.

[7] A Massachusetts pamphleteer, writing in 1720, said, "As to silver and gold, we never had much of it in the country; but we can very well remember, that before we had paper money, there was a sufficiency of it current in the country, and as the bills of credit came in and multiplied, the silver ceased and was gone; and of all men, you in Boston, especially merchants, should be silent as to that matter, for you have shipped it off and yet now complain of the want of it." J. B. Felt, *An Historical Account of Massachusetts Currency* (Boston, 1839), 74.

As prices rose in terms of the depreciated bills, the complaints about the scarcity of money grew louder and still greater pressure was brought to bear on the legislature to issue more money. Farmers and other producers who were in need of capital, and of course debtors, urged additional issues of the inexpensive money. Government expenses went up with rising prices. And nearly everyone was willing to agree that there was not enough money in circulation: after all, no individual had as much money as he wanted. It is noteworthy that the complaint of insufficient money in circulation is often loudest when money is actually most plentiful. The fact that prices rise proves money is plentiful, but because prices rise faster than wages and the average man's income does not buy as much as before, he believes that there is insufficient money in circulation.

Between 1715 and 1724 slightly over £200,000 was put into circulation. To prevent depreciation, laws were repeatedly enacted giving the bills the legal-tender quality and punishing counterfeiting with death. The legislation was unavailing, however, and the bills sank steadily in value, as is shown by the price of an ounce of silver in terms of this paper money: in 1700, 5s. would buy an ounce of silver; in 1710 it required 8s.; in 1719, 12s.; in 1730, 20s.; in 1740, 29s.; and in 1750, 60s. At this last quotation the bills were worth, in modern parlance, 8⅓ cents on the dollar.

It is not necessary to follow in detail the further history of issues in Massachusetts, except to say that, as the older issues depreciated, new forms of notes were put out in the hope that they at least might circulate at par. Between 1702 and 1750 there were only three years in which issues were not made; the major series were emitted in 1737, 1741, and 1744, at which time the successive series of bills were known as old tenor, middle tenor, new tenor firsts, and new tenor seconds. As each series had a different rate of depreciation the situation was little less than chaotic.

Paper money in other colonies. The history of colonial paper money was much the same in the other colonies as it was in Massachusetts. In all of them there were overissues, consequent depreciation in value of the bills, and a rise in prices of commodities in terms of these bills, followed by turmoil and disorder. The usual sequence in the history of emissions of paper money was, according to Horace White [8]: issue, driving of specie out of circulation, counterfeiting, wearing-out of bills, replacement of worn-out and counterfeited issues with new bills, postponement of time of redemption, depreciation, and finally in some cases repudiation. The royal governors, acting under instructions from the Crown, opposed the colonial issues and as a result were in constant disagreement with the assemblies and the people.

In New Hampshire, for instance, the legislature refused to vote appropriations for five years (1731–36) because the governor vetoed the acts authorizing issues of paper money. Conditions were probably the worst in Rhode Island, since the debtor class was in complete ascendancy and there was no check upon the issues; even the neighboring colonies complained of the depreciated Rhode Island paper money and legislated against it. In the three middle colonies conditions were never so bad, because of the stubborn resistance of the governors to emissions, and the value of the paper money was only about 30 to 40 per cent below sterling. The same thing was true of Delaware, Maryland, and Virginia, but in South Carolina the monetary situation was worse than in any of the colonies except Rhode Island. In 1719 the people of South Carolina deposed the proprietor's governor because he refused to assent to the issue of bills of credit. Georgia did not issue any until 1760.

Loan offices and land banks. Not all this inflation was caused by government bills of credit. Another variety of paper money was the loan-office bill or land-bank note which bore some resemblance to a modern bank note. The only significant difference between loan offices and land banks was that the loan offices were government institutions and the land banks were usually privately organized. They were not real banks but they were the nearest thing to a modern bank that existed in colonial times. While they did not receive deposits as modern banks do, they did lend money they had created, the loans usually being secured by real estate but sometimes by commodities.

The basic idea of issuing notes based on land or other

[8] *Money and Banking* (Boston, 1914), 85.

property appears to have originated in William Potter's book, *The Key of Wealth*, published in 1650.[9] This book fell into the hands of Governor Winthrop of Massachusetts and was eagerly read in the colonies, where the idea formed the basis of similar proposals for the next century. Private land banks were planned and tried on a small scale in Massachusetts during the last quarter of the seventeenth century. Barbados tried the scheme without success in 1706. An attempt in South Carolina in 1712 to finance an expedition against the Tuscarora Indians by establishing a public loan office was a dismal failure in practice but apparently a great success in theory, for in the next few years colony after colony experimented with the plan—Massachusetts in 1714, Rhode Island in 1715, and New Hampshire in 1717. Pennsylvania, which began in 1723, is generally conceded to have had the most success. Before the end of the colonial period every colony but Virginia had tried the scheme.

These colonial "banks" were pioneer experiments and had little to guide them in the experience of European institutions: the Bank of Stockholm, the first bank in Europe, was not established until 1616, and the Bank of England dates from only 1694. It is probable that the founders of the colonial banks and loan offices were acquainted with John Law's projects in France between 1716 and 1720, but these were scarcely to be regarded as models for a sound monetary and banking system.

The loan-office system appealed to the colonists on several scores. When, for example, £100,000 was ordered printed by the legislature for private loans, a farmer could go to his county loan office and mortgage his £200 farm up to half its value for a loan payable over a sixteen-year period. Interest was at 5 per cent, not at 8 per cent as on a private loan. Repayment of the principal took care of the retirement of the original issue of paper money, and the interest payments provided funds for running the government and thus reduced taxes or eliminated them entirely in some instances. Even the British government, ever skeptical of colonial paper-money projects, seems for a time to have had a slight preference for the loan-office system over bill-of-credit issues. On the

[9] *The Key of Wealth, or A new way for Improving of Trade* (London, 1650).

whole, because the loans were more self-liquidating, the loan-office issues were not characterized by the extremes of inflation that attended the issues of bills of credit. But even when well run, the loan-office system sometimes had a serious defect. Because the issues were retired in some colonies with fair regularity and because those colonies were expanding economies, the system gave rise to cycles of inflation and deflation. Prices rose soon after the loans were made; prices fell as the loans were repaid and the money retired. That produced a new clamor from debtors that money was scarce, and the result was that a new loan was authorized and the cycle repeated itself.

Probably the best-known land bank was the "Land Bank Manufactory Scheme" established in Massachusetts in 1739. The prospectus stated that it was a plan for emitting bills secured by real estate which were to serve as a medium of trade. Subscribers to a so-called stock of £150,000 paid a small subscription fee and agreed to borrow certain amounts in bills of the company. Each subscriber was to furnish satisfactory mortgage security for his loan, on which he was to pay interest at 3 per cent per annum; while the principal was to be repaid in twenty annual instalments. These payments might be made either in the notes of the company, which were described as "manufactory notes," or in produce of manufactured articles. Thus the mortgages might have been paid off by commodities, and if these were distributed among the subscribers, the notes would have been left afloat without any security. Notes to the amount of £49,250 were actually issued. About one thousand persons subscribed to the loans, including members of the legislature where the friends of the land bank were in the majority.

The scheme was vigorously opposed by Governor Belcher and the Council and by the wealthier merchants. About one hundred and fifty of the latter signed an agreement that they would not accept the notes in any transaction; and in order that the accusation should not be made that they were preventing the issuance of needed money, some of them organized a silver bank and issued their own notes, which they agreed to redeem in silver after fifteen years. These silver notes were hoarded in accordance with Gresham's Law, and

those of the Land Bank continued in circulation. The colony
was divided into two groups upon the matter and the dispute
threatened to cause a political and social revolution. The opponents of the Land Bank realized that the Massachusetts
Assembly would not suppress it; hence they turned to the
English government for assistance.

The Bubble Act. Parliament acceded to the demand that
it suppress the enterprise and extended the provisions of
the Bubble Act to the American colonies. This was an act
passed in England in 1720, after the failure of the disastrous South Sea bubble and similar speculations, to prevent
"business by joint stock companies without special authority
of statute." Under this act the Land Bank and similar
schemes would have been impossible in Great Britain, but
rulings by the Board of Trade and the attorney general had
held that such a bank was not illegal in New England.
Nevertheless Parliament specifically enacted in 1741 that the
Bubble Act did originally apply, had continued to apply, and
was then in full force in all the colonies.

This was clearly *ex post facto* legislation and was bitterly
resented by most of the colonists. By the terms of this law
every contract made by the Land Bank or any similar organization was rendered null and void, and all who had
participated in the schemes were made individually liable
to the holders of the notes. The holders demanded the redemption of the notes and most of them were redeemed, but
some of the subscribers either could not or would not pay
their loans; some were insolvent and others had left the
province. Many of those who had accepted the notes, as
well as the subscribers, suffered serious losses, and the cases
dragged on in the courts until 1768. Probably no other act
of Parliament aroused such resentment against the mother
country as did this anti-bank legislation, and it undoubtedly
helped to create a state of mind which led ultimately to revolution. John Adams stated in 1774 that it was more important
than the Stamp Act in creating opposition to British authority
in Massachusetts.

Evils of paper money. The disadvantages consequent upon
the use of paper money in the colonies were very serious and
real. Perhaps the most serious was the lack of control over

the amount of the issues. There was almost complete ignorance of the principles of money, and there was a confusion between money and capital in general. The colonists needed capital goods of every sort and thought to supply their needs by multiplying stamped pieces of paper. They were using capital faster than they could accumulate it, and could not always borrow from abroad all that they needed. The pressure was great to increase the amount of the paper issues and the legislatures yielded readily to the popular demand. It was an easy method also for raising funds needed by the provincial treasuries, and as they became accustomed to the use of paper money, the colonists insisted more and more upon the use of credit rather than taxation.

The debtor class undoubtedly urged further issues as a method of lightening their burdens, especially in the interior where specie was lacking and a defective system of taxation pressed heavily. Often the result was an enormous overissue, far beyond the monetary needs of the colonists, with a consequent depreciation in the value of each unit of the money, and a rise in prices calculated in terms of this depreciated unit. The effect of such a change in the value of money was to injure creditors and persons with relatively fixed incomes like ministers, artisans, laborers, etc., and to benefit debtors and producers of goods for sale. There was thus introduced into colonial politics an issue which divided the community into two groups [10] with opposing economic interests and which created bad feeling between debtors and creditors, royal governors and colonial legislators, the colonists and the Crown.

Defense of paper money. But in spite of all these disadvantages it must be recognized that the issue of paper money met a very real and acute need in the colonies, namely the lack of a sufficient quantity of metallic money to serve adequately as a medium of exchange. Commodity money was used during the seventeenth century, but it proved unsuited to the requirements of the expanding commerce of the eighteenth. For this the device of paper money was better adapted, and, had it not been abused, would have served the

[10] Horace White goes so far as to state that the emission of bills of credit by legislative assemblies which were controlled by the agrarian interests was the result of "a conspiracy of needy landowners against the rest of the community."—*Money and Banking* (Boston, 1914), 87.

colonists well as an economical and convenient substitute.
Even with all its abuses and disadvantages, it may have been
better than the system of barter which it replaced, and it
found defenders among some of the ablest men of the
colonial period. Thus Governor W. Burnet of New York, in
a report to the Board of Trade, defended the issue of bills
of credit as a method of anticipating tax receipts, and another
able colonial administrator, Thomas Pownall, once governor
of Massachusetts, argued in 1764 for the issue of paper
money to supply the lack of metallic money: [11]

"In Colonies, the essence of whose nature requires a progressive increase of settlements and trade, and yet who from
the balance of trade with the mother country being against
them, must suffer a constantly decreasing quantity of silver
money; *a certain quantity of paper money* is necessary. It
is necessary, in such circumstances, to the equal distribution
and general application of those benefits to the whole Colony; which benefits would otherwise become a monopoly to
the *monied merchant only:* it is prudent, and of good policy
in the mother country to permit it, as it is the surest means
of drawing the balance to the Colony trade and culture, to
its own profit."

Benjamin Franklin, certainly the most eminent man in all
the colonies, threw the weight of his authority in favor of
paper-money issues through loan offices in 1729 by the publication of his pamphlet, "A Modest Inquiry into the Nature
and Necessity of Paper Money." Thirty-seven years later, in
1766, he testified before the House of Commons as follows: [12]

"Pennsylvania, before it made any paper money, was totally stript of its gold and silver.... The difficulties for want
of cash were accordingly very great, the chief part of the
trade being carried on by the extremely inconvenient method
of barter; when, in 1723, paper money was first made there,
which gave new life to business, promoted greatly the settlement of new lands (by lending small sums to beginners on
easy interest, to be repaid by instalments), whereby the prov-

---

[11] *Administration of the British Colonies* (London, 1774), I, 194; in Bogart and
Thompson, *Readings,* 104.
[12] *Works* (Boston, 1840), II, 343.

ince has so greatly increased in inhabitants, that the exports from hence thither is now more than tenfold what it then was; and, by their trade with foreign colonies, they have been able to obtain great quantities of gold and silver, to remit hither in return for the manufactures of this country. New York and New Jersey have also increased greatly during the same period, with the use of paper money; so that it does not appear to be of the ruinous nature ascribed to it."

Prohibition of paper money. In spite of these and other arguments the weight of authority in England was against colonial paper money; the mercantile interests in London opposed it as interfering with trade and the payment of debts due them in specie. The Crown too always regarded these acts of the colonists with jealousy, since the power of coining money, and hence of issuing paper money, was a royal prerogative. In 1751, consequently, Parliament forbade the issue of bills of credit in the four New England colonies where conditions were the worst, though treasury notes in anticipation of taxes were allowed in case of war and fiscal emergencies. Finally, in 1764, it extended this prohibition to the remaining colonies.

Politically, this was probably an unwise move on England's part, for it became an important though little-emphasized cause of disaffection between the colonies and the mother country. However, from a purely economic viewpoint it was probably a wise decision although that opinion is not unanimously held. Historians and economists are still debating whether there was a shortage of money in colonial times, with the historians usually relying on contemporary testimony that there was too little money, and economists generally taking the view that money is after all a commodity and, since the colonists preferred to exchange it for other things, they could not expect to have both. The controversy really revolves around what is meant by money. Money is often defined as any generally acceptable medium of exchange. The colonists admittedly had little metallic money, the kind needed for international trade, because they preferred to exchange it for capital goods. But they had plenty of paper money; indeed, they had too much of that. The proof is that prices rose in every colony, which is another way of saying that the value of that money fell, and it fell because paper money was so plentiful. Without England's restraining hand the inflation would undoubtedly have been worse; indeed, it was worse after the colonies declared their independence.[13]

Financing colonial wars. The long colonial period representing half the history of our nation was punctuated by four major wars in which the colonists were asked to take part. The first of these was King William's War, 1689-97; the second was Queen Anne's War, 1702-13; the third was King George's War, 1744-48; and the last was the French and Indian War, 1754-63. The French and the Indians were the chief enemies in all four wars. And all of these wars had different names in Europe: the fact that the colonists thought of them as the King's war is significant, for it indicates an attitude that had important financial consequences. Until they were attacked or immediately threatened, colonial assemblies were not much interested in voting troops and funds for England's wars. The middle and southern colonies did little to aid Massachusetts in the first two colonial wars. Often the colonial legislatures would plead inability to assist the King in his war unless funds could be supplied on their own terms. Those terms, in the last two wars, were a relaxation of restrictions on paper-money issues.

Then, as now, there were only three basic ways of financing a war, namely, borrowing, taxation, and paper-money issues. There were no wealthy Fuggers or Rothschilds from whom to borrow in America and bond issues were unknown. The taxes to which the colonists were accustomed were light, and in some of the middle colonies where the profits of the loan-office systems paid government expenses, the people were used to only local levies. Since they were unwilling to submit to much taxation, the issuance of paper money was all that was left. As has been pointed out already, Massachusetts discovered that paper money could be used as a way of financing her part in King William's War, and paper money remained for a century the favored colonial means of financ-

---

[13] Of course inflation is a usual accompaniment of war and some allowance must be made for that. Even so, inflation was not nearly as bad in the French and Indian War as it was in the Revolution.

ing wars. By the middle of the eighteenth century some of the colonies had come to prefer the loan-office method to the issue of bills of credit because taxes did not have to be levied to retire the loan-office bills. However, the English firmly opposed this method after the Bubble Act was extended to the colonies in 1741. During the French and Indian War the Crown permitted bill-of-credit issues if the assemblies agreed to retire the bills within a five-year period. Sometimes that was the only condition under which assemblies would vote needed troops and funds, despite the facts that the troops might soon be needed for their own protection and that the English agreed to repay some of the money spent. Because of wartime emergencies and the new opportunities to issue paper money, considerable amounts were issued during the French and Indian War, and by the war's end the price level in several colonies was up about 50 per cent.

Following the French and Indian War a postwar depression was brought on by a number of factors. These included the departure of the British troops from many areas, the levy of new English taxes, the reduction of money in circulation through the collection of colonial taxes, and Parliament's 1764 prohibition of further issues of legal-tender money. Against this background Parliament imposed the notorious Stamp Tax, which affected and antagonized nearly everyone in the colonies. It started a train of events leading to the next war—the Revolution.

Conclusion. For one reason or another it is clear that the colonists were inadequately supplied with metallic money as a medium of exchange. The main causes for this were that the colonists were poor and had little money at best. Since they were situated in a new and undeveloped country they needed other forms of capital more, and consequently soon exchanged their specie, which is only one form of capital or a tool of exchange, for other forms. The adverse balance of trade with England, especially on the part of New England, drained the colonies of such coins as came into their hands and prevented the retention of a stock of gold and silver for use there as money; it was more needed to settle international accounts than it was wanted at home.

Because the supply of metallic money was inadequate

various substitutes had to be found. Wampum, commodity money, light-weight coins, and other methods were tried but the substitute that proved most popular was paper money. Basically there were two kinds of paper money, namely, bills of credit and loan-office or land-bank bills. The latter were less subject to inflation and preferred by the colonists but were first forbidden by Parliament. All these experiments must be regarded as pioneer efforts to solve perplexing monetary difficulties. The colonist attacked these as confidently and boldly as he did the other problems of the New World; undeterred by theory, he attempted to solve them empirically. Ignorant of the laws of money, he made mistakes—but this is scarcely to be wondered at.

The colonist favored the issue of paper money not merely to provide the necessary medium of exchange; he also relied upon it to relieve him of debt by raising the prices of his products and to supply the needed governmental revenues, and he thought thereby to escape taxation. The tendency toward inflation was inherent in the currency situation. Two factors kept it from being worse. One was the restraining hands of the British government, guided of course by the interests of the British merchants; the other was the steady growth of the colonial economy which was able to absorb some of the increased supplies of money.

CHAPTER VII

ENGLISH COLONIAL THEORY AND POLICY TO 1763

The Mercantile System. Between the sixteenth and the eighteenth centuries there developed in most European states a more or less coherent body of practices and policy which aimed at the development of national power. The set of measures by which this national power was to be developed has since then been given the name of the *mercantile system*, and it was under the influence of this system that not only England, but all European countries, regulated their trade and commerce during this period.

Mercantilism in England emphasized four points, which taken together would render the country rich, powerful, and practically self-sufficient. These may be briefly stated as follows. (1) To accumulate as large a store of the precious metals as possible, because these constituted the most valuable form of wealth and were especially important in time of war; but, since England had no mines, gold and silver could be obtained only by trade and consequently a favorable balance of trade, which would bring in these metals, was sought. (2) To build up a large merchant marine, so that the country would be independent of foreign shipping, a hardy race of sailors would be developed, and profits would be made by shipowners. (3) To protect and encourage agriculture in order to make the country self-sufficing in respect to food. (4) To stimulate domestic industry, both to provide employment and to make the country industrially self-sufficient. Later, the desirability of obtaining raw materials and the need of markets for English manufacturers were emphasized.

England was slow in applying these principles to her colonies, for she was occupied during the first half of the seventeenth century in acquiring, in more or less haphazard

fashion, what was later styled "a grand marine empire." Laws
had been passed to encourage and protect shipbuilding and
shipping, to develop fisheries, and to build up agriculture
and manufactures, but the legislation had been spasmodic
and without consistency or definiteness. By 1650, however,
a fairly clear notion had been developed as to the proper
economic functions of colonies, as they were then thought
of, and as to the methods by which these could be made to
contribute to the wealth and power of the mother country.

The doctrines of the mercantile system, applied to the
colonies, resulted in a policy by which their resources were
used to make England powerful. The emphasis was economic
rather than political. In this scheme the colonies were assigned a definite if subordinate place in an imperial plan,
supplying the raw materials for English manufactures and
a market for the finished goods; at the same time a large
exchange of commodities between the colonies and the mother
country would build up a profitable carrying trade for British ships. In carrying out this policy the colonies were required to send to England alone especially valuable goods
(the "enumerated" articles) but were not allowed to send
to England goods which would compete with home industries. They must buy their imports from the mother country;
consequently, manufactures in the colonies which would provide the colonists with goods which otherwise they would buy
from England must be prohibited. On the other hand, industries of value to the mother country must be built up in the
colonies. And most important of all, the carrying trade must
be confined to British ships. These regulations, taken together,
constituted a definite and comprehensive scheme of economic
imperialism, which seemed both logical and just to an Englishman of the seventeenth and eighteenth centuries.[1] The
aim was to create a self-sufficient commercial empire composed of mutually complementary economic parts. This point

[1] Perhaps the words *definite* and *logical* are too strong to apply to a series of acts
passed to meet particular conditions, for these were frequently haphazard and
unrelated. It is possible today to constitute out of these acts a coherent system, but
it is improbable that this was logically thought out and applied by the men who
enacted the legislation. In view of the confused political situation in England during
most of this time and the overshadowing importance of the struggle between Parliament and the Crown, it would moreover have been difficult to carry through a consistent policy.

of view is succinctly stated by an English publicist, writing about 1745:[2]

Aims of mercantilism. "Colonies ought never to forget what they owe to their mother country in return for the prosperity and riches they enjoy. Their gratitude in that respect, and the duty they owe, indispensably oblige them to be immediately dependent on their original parent, and to make their interest subservient thereunto. . . .

"From the end of the establishment of colonies, result two kinds of prohibitions. First, it is a law founded on the very nature of colonies, that they ought to have no culture or arts, wherein to rival the arts and culture of their parent country. For which reason, a colony, incapable of producing any other commodities than those produced by its mother country, would be more dangerous than useful; it would be proper to call home its inhabitants and give it up.

"Secondly, colonies can not in justice consume foreign commodities, with an equivalent for which their mother country consents to supply them; nor sell to foreigners such of their own commodities as their mother country consents to receive. Every infringement of these laws is a real, though too common, robbery of the mother country's labourers, workmen and seamen, in order to enrich the same classes of men belonging to rival nations, who will sooner or later take advantage of it against those very colonies.

"From these principles it follows, that colonies are designed for culture only, and that the navigation occasioned by that culture belongs to the seamen of the mother country."

The same idea was expressed even more bluntly by Sir Francis Bernard,[3] long governor of Massachusetts: "The two great objects of Great Britain in regard to the American trade must be: 1. to oblige her American subjects to take from Great Britain only, all the manufactures and European goods which she can supply them with; 2. to regulate the foreign trade of the Americans so that the profits thereof may finally center in Great Britain, or be applied to the improvement of her empire."

[2] Malachy Postlethwayt, *Britain's Commercial Interest Explained* (London, 1747), I, 107-8.
[3] *Select Letters on the Trade and Government of America* (London, 1764), 20.

The general principle then was that the colonies should be used for the benefit of the mother country, and is well expressed in Lord Sheffield's famous observation that "the only use and advantage of American colonies, or West-India Islands, is the monopoly of their consumption and the carriage of their produce." There was indeed a certain justification for this position since the colonies were, at least during the eighteenth century, a constant expense to England, and it seemed only fair, therefore, for the mother country to use their resources for her profit. The attitude of England in this regard was considered by Adam Smith "less illiberal" than that of other nations. No country in the eighteenth century allowed foreigners to carry on trade with its colonies; such was the policy of Spain, Holland, and France, as well as of England. This policy has usually been thought, however, to have injured the English colonies in America and to have imposed upon them heavy and unjust burdens, which eventually led to revolution. It will be worth while, therefore, to inquire somewhat carefully into the colonial policy of England prior to 1763, in so far as it affected the commercial and industrial development of the American colonies.

The regulation of the carrying trade. Encouragement of shipping had been provided for by legislation since the middle of the fourteenth century, but the definite commercial policy of England is usually held to date from the famous Navigation Act of 1651, passed by the Parliament of the Commonwealth under Cromwell. The merchant class, which had for the most part taken the side of Parliament against the King, now sought to obtain legislation in their favor. Much of the trade of England and of her colonies was at this time being carried on in Dutch ships, and it was desired both to cripple Holland and to build up English shipping by confining English trade to English vessels. The act required that all colonial exports to England were to be carried in ships owned and operated by Englishmen; and that European products were to be taken to England or to the colonies only in English vessels or in ships of the producing country or of the country of usual exportation. Since the word *English* was interpreted to include *colonial*, this act aimed to give a monopoly of the carrying trade between

England or the colonies and other countries to British (i.e., English and colonial) shipowners, for the purpose of building up British shipping.

The Navigation Act of 1660, in so far as it related to the carrying trade, simply strengthened these provisions. At first this act bore rather heavily upon the planters in Virginia and Maryland, since the scarcity of British ships caused the freight rates to go up, but the law was not strictly enforced and considerable tobacco continued to be carried in Dutch ships. This difficulty, however, was only temporary, for English and colonial ships were rapidly built and were soon able to take care of the colonial carrying trade; between 1660 and 1688 the merchant marine was doubled. On the other hand, this monopoly greatly stimulated the shipbuilding industry in the colonies and gave greater opportunity to the colonial carrying trade. It was indeed an advantage to the mother country to have New England vessels carry cargoes on the long voyages between England and the colonies, and especially to care for the American coastwise trade, for this set free English ships for the more profitable European commerce.

Shipbuilding. Shipbuilding soon became the most important industry in New England outside of farming and fishing. Colonial vessels soon began to be sold in England and to displace English vessels in the carrying trade; this called forth protests from English shipbuilders, which, however, were never heeded by Parliament. By 1775 it was estimated that one-third of the ships engaged in British trade were colonial-built. Certain branches of this trade were almost monopolized by New England vessels, for the shipping interests of England did not care to make a practice of carrying cargoes to places from which no return cargo was available. Consequently, a large part of the carrying trade between England and the northern colonies (whose chief products were excluded from the mother country), between the colonies and southern Europe, the intercolonial trade, and other minor trade routes, were relinquished to New England vessels. Colonial shipping was also helped by the growth of English naval power, which protected it from foreign enemies and from pirates, by the concentration of trade routes, and by the development of the English empire which opened up new ports in the rest of the world.

Regulation of colonial exports. The Navigation Act of 1660 was designed to make England the distributing point or entrepôt for certain colonial products. Certain "enumerated" commodities were not to be sent to continental Europe, but were first to be landed in a British port, from which they could be reshipped to the Continent after the payment of customs duties; [4] but they could not be exported directly from the colonies to any foreign country. By this act the English merchants were to be given the profits from handling these goods, English manufacturers were to have first opportunity of using valuable raw materials and supplies which could not be raised at home, and English artisans were to be given profitable employment. It was an arrangement which seemed to benefit everyone: manufacturers gained profits, workers received wages, merchants obtained more business, and shipowners had more voyages; and finally the government collected customs duties. Only the colonial producer was overlooked.

The original list of enumerated articles included seven colonial products: sugar, tobacco, raw cotton, indigo, ginger, fustic, and other dyewoods. It was considerably expanded during the eighteenth century by the addition of various other commodities: naval stores, such as tar, pitch, turpentine, hemp, masts, and yards (1704); molasses and rice (1706); copper ore, beaver skins, and other furs (1722); bar and pig iron, whale fins, hides, lumber, raw silk, and pot and pearl ashes (1764). The monopolization of rice and sugar to English markets became impolitic if not impossible as the production of these commodities in the colonies increased far beyond the power of consumption in England, and the laws were somewhat relaxed with regard to them. The shipment of rice was permitted after 1730, and of sugar after 1739, direct from the colonies to any part of Europe south of Cape Finisterre, on the northwest corner of Spain; as the countries to the south of this point were not manu-

[4] For exception in the case of tobacco see p. 152.

facturing countries England was less jealous of colonial trade with them.

The non-enumerated commodities could originally be sent to any part of the world, including England. No restrictions were placed by the Navigation Acts until 1766 upon the markets for commodities of this sort. Other legislation, however, such as English tariffs and early corn laws for the purpose of protecting English agriculture prohibited the importation of certain foodstuffs into England. After 1660, for instance, New England fish were entirely excluded from the English markets; other articles affected were wheat, corn, flour, and meat, all staple exports of the New England and middle colonies. Articles other than foodstuffs could, however, be sent to England, and, as a matter of fact, were shipped there in large quantities, for to them London offered the best market; such were iron, lumber, pot and pearl ashes, whale fins, and similar commodities.

Enumerated articles. Of the original group of seven enumerated commodities only one—tobacco—was a product of the American continental colonies; the rest were from the West Indies. But tobacco was so important to Virginia and Maryland, forming their great staple crop and constituting one-half of all colonial exports, that the whole principle of restriction may be justified or condemned by its effect on this one article. By the act of 1660 tobacco could be shipped only to England or to English colonies; in 1698 about one-third of the tobacco shipped to England was consumed there, the other two-thirds being exported to the continental nations, chiefly France, Holland, and other northern states, but by 1775 four-fifths of the colonial tobacco was re-exported. On such shipments a drawback of the import duty was allowed, but the additional freight and warehouse charges went into the pockets of English middlemen. On the other hand, the growing of tobacco in England and Ireland was prohibited after 1660, and heavier duties were imposed on Spanish and other tobacco, thus guaranteeing to the Virginia tobacco planter a monopoly of the English market. On the whole there was so nice a balance of gains and losses that so competent an authority as Beer[5] considers it doubtful whether

[5] G. L. Beer, *The Old Colonial System*, 1660-1754 (New York, 1912), II, 116.

Virginia would have welcomed complete free trade, with a removal of all restrictions and of all special privileges.

The inclusion of rice in the list of enumerated commodities in 1706 imposed a real hardship on the Carolina rice-growers by depriving them of the Spanish and Portuguese markets; that this was regarded as an injury is proved by the relaxation of the law in 1730 so as to permit the direct exportation of rice to any country south of Cape Finisterre. The restriction in 1704 of naval stores (i.e., tar, pitch, turpentine, hemp, masts, and bowsprits) to the English market was probably more than offset by the granting of bounties for their production. By the time the exportation of beaver skins was regulated in 1722, the fur trade was already passing from the American colonies to the French in Canada, but for a time the restriction was keenly felt by certain sections of the colonies.

Regulation of colonial imports. Having excluded foreign ships from the trade with the colonies and having required that certain colonial exports go through English ports, Parliament next undertook to regulate, through the Staple Act of 1663, the importation of European goods into the colonies. The law of 1663 prohibited the importation into the colonies of any commodities of the growth, production, or manufacture of Europe, unless from English ports and in British-built and manned shipping. The only articles excepted were salt for the fisheries, wine from Madeira and the Azores, and all sorts of provisions from Scotland and Ireland. The purpose of the act was to make England the "staple" or depot for all this trade and to give to English merchants and shippers the profits from handling all European goods that were sent to the colonies.

The colonists were not forbidden to import European goods; only they must go to England for them. This meant, for instance, that a New England vessel, after carrying a cargo of lumber to the Azores or fish to Spain, would be obliged to return empty (except for wine from the former or salt from the latter), or to make a roundabout trip and load in England for a return cargo on the way home. A little noticed act of 1736 forbade English and American shipbuilders to make sails of material manufactured outside the

British isles[6]; in this case therefore New England ship-owners were restricted to British products. The rigor of these restrictions was eased by the granting of drawbacks of duties upon most European goods re-exported from England to the colonies. But drawbacks were not given on iron and steel, cordage, and sailcloth, in order to afford protection to English manufacturers of these articles.

While English merchants and factors were thus afforded an opportunity of pocketing a middleman's profit and English manufacturers were assured a market for their products, the prices of such goods to the colonists seem to have been little if any higher as a consequence, since England was able to sell these articles at equal or lower prices than her competitors; it was, moreover, the natural place in which to purchase articles for consumption in the colonies.

The Molasses Act. Wholly shortsighted, however, was the restriction, by the imposition of prohibitive duties in the Molasses Act of 1733, upon the importation into the colonies of sugar, molasses, and rum from foreign plantations. It seems to have been passed for the double purpose of aiding the British planters in the West Indies, whose sugar trade was declining as a result of the competition of the foreign islands, and of hitting the French. But this law, if enforced, would have destroyed the extremely profitable trade carried on between the continental colonies and the foreign West Indies. Since France had a flourishing brandy industry at home which she wished to protect, she forbade the importation into France of rum from her colonies. Holland did the same because of her gin industry. It followed, therefore, that in the French and Dutch islands molasses, which had little use except as the raw material for the basis of rum manufacturing, was frequently thrown away as a waste product or sold at a much lower price than in the British West Indies. And it did not take the Yankee traders long to discover that they could obtain much better bargains in molasses from the foreign islands than from the British; from the latter the northern colonies bought only 7 per cent of the molasses

---

[6] P. Mantoux, *Industrial Revolution in the Eighteenth Century* (New York, 1929), 101, note 2.

which they used for the distillation of the rum which formed
the basis for the very lucrative three-cornered trade with
Africa.

The products of the northern colonies, moreover, were in
great demand in the French and Dutch West Indies, and the
fish of New England, the flour and bread of the middle colonies, and the cattle, horses, and especially lumber of both
sections, found a ready market in exchange for the sugar,
molasses, cotton, logwood, indigo, and other tropical products of the West Indian islands. The economic necessity for
this trade lay in the fact that the British West Indies offered
only a limited market for these products, while the agricultural production in the American continental colonies was
rapidly increasing. The French, Dutch, and Spanish islands,
on the other hand, were dependent upon these northern
supplies.

Complaints were forwarded by British sugar planters to
the home government, and the powerful West Indian lobby
in London appealed to Parliament for the protection of their
special interests. These groups insisted that the trade between
the continental colonies and the foreign sugar islands was
responsible for the decline of the sugar industry in the British
West Indies. To satisfy them, Parliament imposed by the
act of 1733 practically prohibitory duties on sugar and molasses imported into the continental colonies from the foreign
West Indies. Rum and spirits were to pay 9d. per gallon,
molasses and syrup 6d., and sugar 5s. per hundredweight.
Trade with the French and Dutch West Indies would have
been destroyed by this act, had it not been generally disregarded. Since the object of the act was to aid the maintenance of the declining British sugar industry, the American
colonies were sacrificed, not to the best interests of English
manufacturers and merchants who stood to lose by the act,
but to the greed of British West Indian planters.

The willingness of Parliament to grant such legislation is
interesting evidence of the high esteem in which they held
the sugar colonies as compared with New England, and of
the power of the sugar interests in London. In practice, however, the act remained a dead letter. More serious to the

continental colonies was the strict enforcement of the lower duties provided for in the Sugar Act of 1764, discussion of which, however, must be deferred to the next chapter.

Restrictions upon intercolonial trade. There was still one other branch of commerce which had remained open to the colonies and that was the trade with each other. The act of 1660 had not imposed any restraints upon the intercolonial trade, but certain irregularities in carrying out other provisions of the Navigation Acts had developed. Virginia planters, for instance, would send their tobacco to New England, whence it could easily be reshipped, perhaps by collusion with English customs officials, to the Continent, escaping the payment of English duties and underselling the English merchant. The law was also evaded by transferring the tobacco from colonial to Dutch vessels at sea. Since the colonial vessels which carried the tobacco to continental Europe would not dare seek a return cargo in England, and since they did not wish to return home empty, they generally brought back European goods direct from the Continent, thus disobeying the act of 1663 as well as that of 1660. Such direct trade, which did not pass through an English port, also occasioned various indirect losses: owners of English wharves lost the wharfage fees, stevedores lost employment in unloading and loading the vessels, merchants lost the profits from handling the goods, manufacturers lost the sale of their products, and the King lost the revenues.

In order to make these acts effective the colonial Duty Act of 1673 was passed, requiring that every vessel carrying exports of enumerated articles must either give a bond of £1000 to £2000 that the commodities would be landed in England, or a small export duty must be paid on them. The intention of Parliament seems to have been that the intercolonial trade must be carried on by way of England or pay export duties, but the ambiguous phraseology of the law gave a chance for diverse interpretations. The colonists were disposed to evade paying export duties on enumerated articles shipped to a colonial port. They also insisted that if they paid the export duty they had a right to ship the commodities from an intermediate colonial port to any foreign country, and the denial of this right was one of the chief grievances of

New England against the laws of trade.[7] Parliament, however, was determined that the export duties should be paid if the enumerated articles were shipped to another colony, and that a bond must also be given that they would be delivered in England or at an English plantation, unless consumed in that colony.

The Board of Trade. The administrative measure of 1696 enacted this view into statute, and provided the machinery for strict enforcement of the earlier acts. Not only were defects in administration remedied, but a system of registration for British vessels, whether owned in England or in the colonies, was established; a regular body of royal officers was substituted for the occasional collectors, commissioners, and others who had previously represented the interests of the home government in colonial affairs; and an elaborate system of admiralty courts was established. This was followed a few years later by a new set of instructions for the royal governors: in order to insure imperial control all governors not appointed directly by the King had to be approved by him; they had to take oath to enforce the Navigation Acts, and failure in this respect exposed them to heavy fines and loss of office. Moreover, all colonial laws at variance with the acts of trade were declared null and void. But perhaps the most effective piece of machinery was the establishment of a permanent Board of Trade and Plantations, which functioned until the very eve of the Revolution. In this body was centralized the supervision of colonial affairs. It was primarily concerned with the promotion of commerce, but it also supervised other branches of colonial administration and legislation.

The usefulness and power of the Board varied greatly, depending largely upon the personnel and the policy of the government. From 1696 to 1713 it sought vigorously to enforce the acts of trade and evoked loud complaints from colonial merchants; between 1713 and 1748, a period of peace for England, there followed the policy of "wise and salutary neglect," as Burke called it, when the colonies were

---

[7] Beer, *The Old Colonial System*, 1660-1754, II, 282. The other chief grievance arose from the act of 1663, which obliged vessels taking fish to the Mediterranean countries to return home via England.

permitted to develop almost untrammeled both politically and economically. The result was that the colonists developed trade and manufactures on their own account, and enjoyed an era of unprecedented prosperity.

Restrictions upon manufacturing. During the eighteenth century manufactures were developing in England, and as the colonies became more important the English manufacturers demanded not only protection at home against colonial competition, but also the monopoly of the colonial markets in which to dispose of their own products. Indeed, the prevention of manufactures in the colonies was an integral part of the imperial system and merely complemented the restrictions of the Navigation Acts; throughout this whole period Parliament watched most jealously every sign of the growth in the colonies of manufactures which might compete with home industries.

Three times Parliament took alarm and passed legislation restricting or prohibiting colonial manufactures. In 1699 the exportation of wool, yarn, and woolen cloth from the colonies "to any other of the said plantations, or to any other place whatsoever" was prohibited. Household manufacturing of woolen yarn and cloth for domestic use was not forbidden the colonial housewives, but the possible exportation of these articles in competition with the growing woolen industry of England was prevented. Some manufacture of cloth for sale had already been attempted in New England, New York, and Pennsylvania, as is evidenced by the reports of the colonial governors to the Board of Trade, and some homemade cloth was being exported to the southern colonies and to the West Indies [8]; the trade in these products was now stifled.

The second industry upon which Parliament cast a jealous eye was hat-making. In 1732 a Commission of Inquiry was ordered by the House of Commons to investigate manufactures in the colonies and they reported that "great quantities of hats" were being made in New England, partly from beaver skins. These skins being cheaply obtained in the Indian trade, the manufacture of beaver hats had become an industry of minor importance in New England, New York,

---

[8] See extracts showing the development of colonial manufactures in Bogart and Thompson, *Readings*, 60, 68.

and Pennsylvania, and some hats were being exported to the
West Indies, Spain, and Portugal. The Company of Felt-
makers became alarmed and successfully petitioned for protection against this competition, so that Parliament in 1732
prohibited the exportation of hats to a foreign country, to
England, or to another colony, and also limited the number
of apprentices to a master to two and required an apprenticeship of seven years.[9] The law was not strictly enforced and
some hats continued to be made in the colonies, although the
finer grades were imported from England.

The last restriction was more serious. The smelting of iron
and the manufacture of simple ironware, tools, and implements had been practiced in the colonies from an early date.[10]
The smiths and other ironworkers in England had petitioned
Parliament concerning this industry as early as 1717, but
nothing was done until 1750 when a law was passed which
had a twofold purpose: first, to encourage the smelting and
export of raw iron to England, and second, to prevent the
working up of the crude iron into manufactures in the colonies. The act provided, (1) that bar and pig iron might be
imported into the port of London free of duty (in 1757 this
was extended to any port in England), while foreign iron
was subjected to heavy import duties; and (2) that the erec-
tion in the colonies of slitting or rolling mills, plating forges,
tilt hammers, or steel furnaces should be prohibited.

England was importing annually some 20,000 tons of
Swedish and foreign iron and hoped by this act to stimulate
the production in the colonies of the raw material which she
needed for her developing iron manufactures. Iron ore was
smelted at this time by charcoal and the English forests had
been practically used up by the middle of the eighteenth
century so that the country was absolutely dependent upon
foreign supplies. Moreover, the development of iron manufactures in the colonies did not fit in with the colonial policy
of England.

The act permitted such establishments as were already in
operation to continue, but if new ones were constructed they

---

[9] This was simply an application to this industry in the colonies of legislation
long since familiar in England.
[10] See Chapter III.

were to be abated as nuisances under a penalty of £200. Apparently such things as kettles, salt pans, and other cast-iron products could still be made in the colonies since casting furnaces were not prohibited. The act was fairly well enforced, though slitting mills seem to have been operated in contravention of its provisions; had these been closed down even the making of nails, necessary for building, horse-shoeing, etc., and spikes, bars, and other shapes essential to shipbuilding would have been prevented. The colonies had reached a point in their industrial development when they could advantageously establish an iron industry, and this act was a severe blow, especially to New England. The exportation of bar and pig iron, on the other hand, increased slowly from about 2000 tons in 1745 to over 7000 tons in 1771, but as these were produced in Virginia and Maryland the irritation of the northern colonies was not mitigated by this fact.

The legislation prohibiting manufactures was the more irritating because the restrictive tariff and commercial policy of England, by shutting the English markets to the agricultural products of the northern colonies and by hindering their exchange in the West Indies, made it difficult for the colonists in the northern section to obtain the means with which to purchase English-manufactured commodities. The effect of these laws was, if anything, to stimulate manufactures in those colonies. In the southern colonies, whose staple products were not thus prevented from finding a profitable market, manufactures never gained a foothold.

Encouragement to industry. On the other hand, it should be noticed that along with the policy of restriction there went also the policy of encouragement. While manufactures were stifled, the production of raw materials was favored by an extensive system of bounties, from 1705 on, especially on hemp, masts, naval stores (tar, pitch, turpentine, and resin), and indigo (after 1748). One estimate makes the amount paid in bounties to the colonies more than £1,500,000. Other articles were favored by being admitted to England free of duty or at greatly reduced rates. Thus colonial lumber of all kinds, such as pipe, hogshead, and barrel staves, was placed

on the free list in 1723, when imported into England. Pig
and bar iron were admitted duty free after 1750 while
Swedish iron was held off by a heavy tariff. Since wood was
used for smelting at that time, and not coal, the colonies were
well adapted to the production of raw iron. Other articles,
as tobacco, molasses, raw silk, pot and pearl ashes, whale fins
and train oil, etc., were at different times admitted to England either free of duty, or at rates much lower than similar
articles from other countries, although the general rule was
that products from the colonies paid the same duties as similar articles from foreign countries.

Evasion of restrictions. The situation in the colonies and
the silent acquiescence of the colonists in this policy cannot
be fully understood unless we understand to how great an
extent the provisions were evaded. In the first place, the
laws were allowed to become dead letters or were not strictly
enforced by English officials. Except for the short periods
from 1696 to 1713, 1748-53, and 1763 on, when there was
comparatively strict execution of the laws, the policy of
"salutary neglect" of the colonies was adhered to by government officials. Indeed, there was often connivance of the
customs officers in the evasion of the laws. In the South there
was some illicit trade with the West Indies, and large
amounts went to countries other than England. Most of the
smuggling occurred in New England and the middle colonies,
where large quantities of wines, brandies, and other European goods, together with tea, coffee, spices, etc., from the
East Indies, were smuggled into the larger cities. But the
most extensive illicit trade was carried on with the foreign
West Indies. In 1700 one-third of the trade at Boston and
New York was said to be in violation of the law.

It must be remembered, however, that such contraband
trade was regarded in the colonies as perfectly justifiable in
view of the restrictive commercial legislation, and that some
of the most reputable men were engaged in it. On the coasts
of England itself, it is estimated that there were at this time
about 40,000 smugglers. The restrictive legislation, writes
J. T. Adams, made "a large section of the colonial population smugglers and law breakers by necessity, it lowered the

moral tone of the community and decreased the respect for law." Certain it is that the general practice of smuggling and the evasion of the laws made the restrictive legislation of England bear less heavily upon the colonists than it otherwise would have done. Indeed, had it not been for the profits from this illicit trade, the colonies would never have been able to pay for the enormous amount of British manufactures and European commodities annually imported from England; for the first half of the eighteenth century these amounted on the average to about £500,000 a year and were paid for only in part by the colonial products exported directly to England.

Conclusion. In general the commercial policy of England was designed to keep the colonies in the state of agricultural communities, which should supply raw materials to English manufacturers and furnish a market for their finished products. "Taken as a whole," writes a friendly critic [11] of the English policy, "the acts of trade may best be understood as application to the English empire of what is now called the protective principle, that is, the protection of English subjects against foreign competition. The empire was treated as an economic whole, so far as possible independent of the outside world, in which each part had its particular function to perform."

In appraising the Acts of Trade this theory must be kept in mind; it is not correct to judge them solely from the point of view of the colonists. The imperial ideal was, however, never realized in fact, for the colonies were so far removed from the mother country both in distance and in time required for communication that effective administrative control could not be established, and the colonies tended to develop an autonomous and independent economic life. There has been much controversy over the question of the effect of the English colonial policy upon the colonies, but a fair conclusion seems to be that on the whole the industrial and commercial development of the colonies was but slightly affected by the Acts of Trade, and that the colonists carried on those industries which were to them of the greatest advantage. Indeed, during this whole period, the colonies

[11] E. B. Greene, *The Foundations of American Nationality* (New York, 1922), 184.

grew steadily in population and wealth.[12] There were, however, points of friction in the application of colonial policy, opposition to which frequently found expression along political lines. The colonists were receiving a slow but steady education in theories of government and human rights, and these were emphasized when dissatisfaction with English colonial policy finally reached a head.

[12] The absence of serious disaffection before 1765 is emphasized by numerous authorities. Thus Parrington writes, "Of social unrest there was practically none," and Callender concludes, "The welfare of the colonists was not disregarded nor were their interests systematically sacrificed."

CHAPTER VIII

FROM REVOLUTION TO CONSTITUTION

Economic causes of the Revolution. A century and a half of discussion of the American Revolution has served only to emphasize the importance of the economic and social causes as compared with the political. The usual explanation of the conflict has been that it was an uprising of an oppressed people against the autocratic and unconstitutional acts of a stubborn king. But the causes of friction, as shown in the previous chapter, were more deep-seated and long-continued than this theory admits; they were bound up in the political relationship of the mother country and her maturing colonies, in the mercantile policy which governed their commercial relations, and in the conflicting interests of English merchants and manufacturers on the one hand and of the developing colonial commerce and industry on the other. In considering these causes, the discussion may well begin with the year 1763, for this may be taken as marking in a very real sense the beginning of the American Revolution.

In that year Great Britain concluded the Treaty of Paris after the successful termination of the Seven Years' War with France, or, as it was more frequently called in America, the French and Indian War. As a result of this struggle the British possessions had grown enormously, and the thirteen colonies now constituted but a small part of an unorganized and scattered empire. Strong colonial organization and administration were needed in place of the haphazard and unsystematic methods which had prevailed even under the Board of Trade. Closer integration and control were held to be essential, not only for purposes of administration, but also for defense against England's traditional enemies, France and Spain. It seemed only fair, moreover, that in the future the expenses of such wars as that just concluded with France, waged partly on behalf of the colonists, and of frontier conflicts with the Indians, should be borne, in part at least, by those benefited. Accordingly, a more vigorous policy of colonial taxation and control began to be enforced by successive English ministries.

To this program there were two insuperable obstacles—time and space. For a century and a half the colonies had been growing in size and power and economic development. They had, moreover, enjoyed a large measure of local self-government or home rule, in some respects greater than that exercised by Englishmen at home. As a result of their distance from the mother country the colonists learned to manage their own affairs and to care for their own economic interests to an extent not contemplated by the English colonial system. But the new imperial policy meant for the colonists unaccustomed tax burdens, the destruction of a lucrative trade, and serious restriction in the large measure of home rule which they had enjoyed. It was consequently resisted. By 1763 the policy of strict imperial control was an anachronism; it was instituted too late, and the time for it had passed. Delay made it impossible.

Not merely time, however, but also space worked against it. Even in favorable circumstances it took four months for a reply to be received by the Board of Trade to an inquiry sent to a colonial governor. With some exaggeration Adam Smith was able to say, "In everything except their foreign trade, the liberty of the English colonists to manage their own affairs their own way is complete."

It is clear today that, while the colonists usually got their way in internal affairs, it was not without considerable friction. The thousands of complaints and protests, vetoes and instructions which were recorded in the official papers of English and colonial authorities for controlling American commerce and industry, as well as political affairs, show how difficult imperial control was. There was a conflict between British mercantilism and the self-interest of the colonists.

Changes in the English colonial policy. (1) One of the first problems which presented itself was the disposition and *administration of the territory gained from the French*. As a temporary arrangement, to gain time for further study, the British government by the royal Proclamation of 1763 organized three new provinces out of the conquered territory on the continent. Westward expansion was forbidden and settlement was restricted to the seacoast.[1]

The purpose of the act was to protect the Indians and to prevent Indian wars, to restrict the fur trade, and to encourage the consumption of English manufactures by keeping the settlements on the seacoast and thus accessible to English commerce; but it was the first of the many blunders in the new imperial colonial policy, for it aroused profound discontent among the colonists, who rightly felt that their interests were being sacrificed to those of English manufacturers and of the Hudson's Bay Company. It is probable that this act contributed more than the Acts of Trade to the Revolution; it certainly did more to alienate the influential colony of Virginia.

(2) *Enforcement of the Acts of Trade.* The second step in the process of tightening the bonds on the colonies in the furtherance of a more efficient colonial administration was taken by the extension to all the colonies of a more rigorous enforcement of the Acts of Trade. The list of enumerated articles, which could be sent only to England, was extended in 1764 by the addition of such important colonial products as bar and pig iron, lumber, hides, whale fins, raw silk, and pot and pearl ashes. Two years later it was provided that non-enumerated exports could be sent only to England or Ireland or to countries south of Cape Finisterre.

(3) *Prohibition of paper money.* Another phase of the movement to enforce the British mercantilistic regulations was the extension to all the colonies of the prohibition of the issue of colonial bills of credit. This was simply the final stage in a process which had been going on since 1741, when Parliament had declared its authority over the matter. In 1751 it had prohibited legal-tender paper money in New England, and now the Currency Act of 1764 made the restriction general.

Most of the colonies had issued paper money during the war but had agreed to retire it within a few years. Parliament's prohibition blasted all hope of substituting new issues

---

[1] For an account of the reasons for this Proclamation as given by the Board of Trade, see Bogart and Thompson, *Readings*, 144-46.

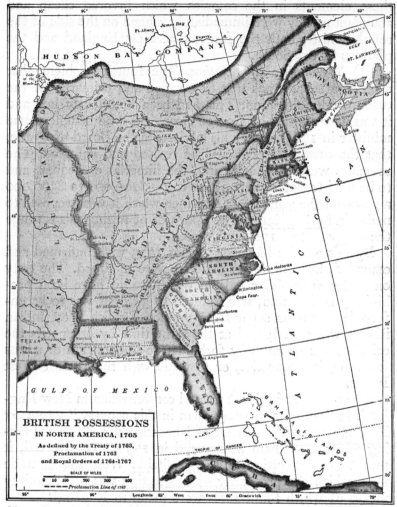

[From G. E. Howard, *Preliminaries of the Revolution*]

for old ones and forced a painful policy of deflation on the
colonies. These were already suffering from a postwar depression owing to the demobilization of their militia, the withdrawal of some English troops, and the reduction of
purchases of provisions and supplies. Those in debt or whose
business was overextended were denied the usual relief of
new issues of paper money. When revolution flamed out all

these elements in the colonies which favored cheap and abundant money were immediately ranged on the side of the revolutionists, both the farmers of New England and the planters of the South.

(4) *Tightening of taxation.* The fourth problem that claimed attention was that of taxation and primarily of the customs administration. This had been notoriously lax, and it was now decided by George Grenville, who became prime minister in 1763, and by his advisers in the Board of Trade, that the customs acts should be revised and enforced. The revenues were to be paid into the imperial exchequer, and to be used to defray part of the cost—£200,000 to £300,000 a year—of the army of 10,000 men which it was proposed to maintain in America. For the purpose of raising this revenue the Sugar Act of 1764 was passed.

By this act the Molasses Act of 1733 was confirmed and extended, but the duties under it were modified. The duty on molasses of 6d. a gallon, which would have been prohibitory if collected, was reduced to 3d., but was to be enforced; that upon sugar from the non-English West Indian islands was raised; and at the same time by other acts the colonists were absolutely forbidden to import rum or spirits from foreign countries, or to trade with the French West Indies.

The passage of this act created consternation in New England. It "caused a greater alarm in this country," wrote Sir Francis Bernard,[2] governor of Massachusetts, "than the taking of Fort William Henry did in 1757." If enforced, it meant the destruction of the profitable West Indian trade upon which the prosperity of this section was based and by means of which remittances were made to England.

Particularly irritating was the requirement that the sugar tax be paid in specie. By the Currency Act of 1764 the colonists had been forbidden to issue paper money; now the only method by which they could obtain specie was closed to them. The supply of paper money was reduced just at the time when the dwindling importations of Spanish coins made the use of specie impracticable. And yet they were required to provide specie for the tax.

[2] *Select Letters on the Trade and Government of America* (London, 1764), 9.

While the alarm and discontent were at their height came the news of the impending passage of the Stamp Act. The violence and extent of the opposition in the colonies created by this act were undoubtedly a surprise to the British government, for similar duties existed in England, but there were certain features about the Stamp Act which made it a better rallying point than the measures which had preceded it. The Sugar Act affected primarily the New England fishers, shippers, and rum-distillers, the Currency Act touched only a section of the population, and the prohibition of westward expansion checked merely the frontiersmen; but the Stamp Act struck at every class in all the colonies. Since it especially affected the printers and lawyers, it stirred into activity two particularly vociferous groups. But even more important from a political point of view was the fact that it was an "internal" tax. "External" taxes, that is, customs duties levied at the ports by Parliamentary act, were familiar, but here was an innovation. And it was an innovation that furnished a magnificent slogan—"no taxation without representation."

Non-importation agreements. Gradually the excitement grew, as the colonists came to realize more clearly the implications of the act. The Stamp Act Congress, which met in New York in October, 1765, passed resolutions protesting against the principles of the law. But more decisive than resolves or pamphlets was the complete nullification of the law through mob violence and terrorization. The stamps were destroyed, the stamp distributors were forced to resign, and on the day the taxes were to go into effect it was impossible to comply with the requirements. Newspapers were published, ships took out their clearance papers, and business proceeded without the use of stamped paper. Nullification was complete.

Even more effective, however, in forcing a repeal of the obnoxious measure was the non-importation agreement entered into by the merchants of New York, Massachusetts, Rhode Island, and Pennsylvania. They agreed not to import any goods from Great Britain; to countermand orders already given; not to remit their English debts; and to refuse to sell British goods sent on commission until the Stamp Act of 1765 should be repealed. At the same time the people generally agreed to abstain from the use of goods which were not of domestic manufacture, and in other ways to promote domestic manufactures as far as possible.

As a result of these agreements the demand for British goods fell off, merchants curtailed their shipments, and some English manufacturers were even compelled to close their mills. Exports from England to the thirteen colonies declined from £1,925,564 in 1764 to £1,580,324 in 1765. A serious depression occurred in England. In this state of things English merchants joined with colonial legislatures in demanding the repeal of the obnoxious measure which had caused all this distress. On this point Adam Smith wrote, "the expectation of a rupture with the colonies struck the people of Great Britain with more terror than they ever felt for a Spanish Armada or a French invasion," and "rendered the repeal of the Stamp Act, among the merchants at least, a popular measure." The pressure thus applied was successful and the Stamp Act was repealed in 1766.

Insistence on prerogatives of the Crown. But the British government, while yielding the stamp tax, insisted upon the principle and passed the Declaratory Act, asserting that Parliament had authority "to bind the colonies and people of America, subjects of the crown of Great Britain, in all cases whatsoever." A year later Parliament imposed some "external" taxes under the Townshend Acts. These placed import duties payable in the colonies on wine, oil, glass, paper, red and white lead, painters' colors, and tea. At the same time the customs administration was stiffened, writs of assistance were expressly authorized,[3] and a new customs board was established in America to administer the acts of trade.

These measures were recognized as only another form of taxation without representation and aroused fierce resentment throughout all the colonies. Systematic and official

[3] "The difficulty of enforcing was very great, for it was hard to seize the smuggled goods and harder still to convict the smuggler in the colonial courts. Search warrants were impracticable, because the legal manner of using them made the informer's name public, and the law was unable to protect him from the anger of a community fully in sympathy with the smugglers. The only feasible way to put down this unpatriotic trade was to resort to 'writs of assistance,' which would give the customs officers a right to search for smuggled goods in any house they pleased." C. H. Van Tyne, *The American Revolution, 1776-1783* (New York, 1905), 9.

resistance was directed against the unpopular acts. The first non-importation agreement had been so successful that in 1769 a second agreement was made by the merchants and the people in nine of the colonies to "boycott" English goods. Their purpose was to exert a pressure upon English exporting merchants which would cause the merchants to petition for the repeal of the objectionable acts, and in this they were successful. Exports from Great Britain to New England and the middle colonies fell off almost two-thirds; those to the southern colonies, which were economically more dependent upon England, remained almost constant.

This is shown in the following table: [4]

Exported from Great Britain to	1768	1769
New England	£430,807	£223,696
New York	490,674	75,931
Pennsylvania	441,830	204,979
Northern Colonies	£1,363,311	£504,606
Maryland and Virginia	£669,422	£714,944
North and South Carolina	300,925	327,084
Georgia	56,562	58,341
Southern Colonies	£1,026,909	£1,100,369

Once more the demand for the repeal of legislation which was ruining British trade, inciting resistance in the colonies, and not producing the anticipated revenue, compelled the ministry to yield and Parliament to repeal the offending measure. But again the right to tax the colonies was declared not to have been surrendered and the tax of 3d. a pound upon tea was retained as evidence of imperial authority. The repeal of the Townshend Acts was, however, accepted as a peace move and trade was at once resumed; by 1771 the imports had jumped to £4,200,000.

Depression. Another circumstance that rendered the colonists resentful of the changes in the British colonial policy was the economic depression that set in after the conclusion of the Seven Years' War. During this war both the commercial and farming classes had enjoyed unusual prosperity. The disbursements of specie by British quartermasters and the increased demand for supplies for the troops had tended

[4] D. Macpherson, *Annals of Commerce* (3 vols., London, 1805), III, 571.

to raise prices for colonial commodities, especially foodstuffs, and this had enriched the farmers. Other groups had waxed fat on army and navy contracts. But even more important as a source of profits was the illicit trade with the enemy. During the war the colonial merchants, sometimes with French or Dutch passports or even under flags of truce granted by American governors—the governor of Pennsylvania sold them for as little as £20 apiece—supplied the French forces in Canada with provisions and carried on a vigorous trade with the French West Indies. Considerable fortunes had been amassed by this unpatriotic but profitable commerce, and now this was to be largely destroyed by the enforcement of the Acts of Trade. The colonists were faced with the problem of reconversion from war to peace, but this was marked by a scarcity of currency, a slackening of trade, unpaid debts, and failure of important merchants. The result was a serious depression.

Other economic factors. Another feature that helps to explain the uncompromising resistance to the slight burden of taxation which the British government proposed to collect from the colonists was their comparative freedom from local taxation and their dislike of it. The colonists objected not merely to taxation without representation; they were unwilling to pay taxes at all. Governmental functions were but slightly developed in the unorganized and dispersed communities of the New World, and most needs, which today are met by governmental action, were then cared for by the individual.

A minor cause of friction was the frequent quarrels over quitrents and land tenure. Settlers who came to the colonies with the expectation of receiving free or for a low price a tract of land in absolute ownership were irritated to find that they could obtain land only on condition of paying an annual charge or quitrent or on some other semifeudal basis.

Subordination of colonial interests. Some writers[5] have attempted to show that the English colonial policy did not

---

[5] "The British rule which they threw off was not one of oppressors and tyrants which declaimers suppose, and the merit of the Americans was not that of oppressed men rising against tyrants, but rather of sensible young people getting rid of stupid and overweening guardians who misunderstood and misjudged them." Matthew Arnold, *Civilization in the United States* (New York, 1888), 116.

affect the colonies adversely, for there was a fairly even balance of burdens and favors. As proof they adduce the remarkable increase in the population and wealth of the colonies during the century and a half before the Revolution, and the fact that, after the Revolution, trade was carried on by the new nation with England just as it had been under the Acts of Trade. But the Revolution cannot be explained by a balancing of benefits and losses. The effects are sometimes of less importance than the motives. As Beer wrote, "It is more important to know what the people at the time *thought* the results were than exact estimates. The colonists thought the colonial policy was conceived in the interests of the mother country." Benjamin Franklin unerringly exposed the weakest feature of the colonial system when he pointed out the ease with which interested parties or private interests could obtain favorable legislation even if adverse to the colonies. Acts which might have been borne without a murmur, if clearly in the interest of the Empire, took on a very different aspect when they were seen to favor only a few individuals. There were enough such cases to discredit the whole system in the eyes of the colonists.

Tea as a test. Whether the Revolution might have been averted by a different policy on the part of the British government is a question which will probably never be answered definitely. At base it represented the refusal of a self-reliant and progressive people to permit their expanding energies to be restricted by any external authority. The American colonists wished a measure of autonomy, which was probably inconsistent with any real imperial control, but they differed among themselves as to the degree of home rule which they should demand. The more solid merchants wished freedom of trade, but the more radical minority soon gained control of the revolutionary movement and gave it a turn for political independence.

The control by the more conservative merchant-planter group was ended by the unfortunate effort on the part of the British government to help the British East India Company, which was on the verge of bankruptcy. In order to aid it in disposing of its huge stock of seventeen million pounds of tea, the Company was given a virtual monopoly of the sale of tea in America. It was permitted to ship tea directly to the colonies in its own vessels without paying the customary auction and English import duties. This arrangement destroyed the legitimate business of middlemen and importers, and it also struck a blow at the profitable illicit trade which had been carried on by smugglers. There was added therefore to the political dislike of taxation without representation the commercial resistance of those whose profitable trade was interfered with. It was John Hancock, the "prince of smugglers," who, in 1773, organized the Boston Tea Party, at which 342 chests of East India Company tea were thrown into Boston harbor.[6]

The Continental Congress. The answer of the English government to this outrage, as they regarded it, was the passage of the "intolerable acts." By these the port of Boston was closed until the town should pay for the tea, the charter of Massachusetts was annulled, its government brought more closely under royal control, and another act quartered upon the people the soldiers who were sent to enforce the acts. About this same time, but not for the same reason, the Quebec Act extended the boundaries of that province to the Ohio River. By this Quebec Act the territorial integrity of Virginia, with her claim to western lands, was attacked, and this colony was at once driven into camp with Massachusetts. The bond needed to draw the colonies together was furnished now by their common sympathy and fear, and the flame of rebellion spread rapidly along the whole seacoast. The other colonies immediately rallied to the support of the beleaguered city of Boston, and in various ways assisted her.

On a call from Massachusetts, inspired by Samuel Adams, delegates from all the colonies except Georgia met in Philadelphia in September, 1774. This first Continental Congress, which was dominated by the revolutionary element, drew up a Declaration of American Rights, in which they recited

---

[6] According to D. A. Wells, "The colonists were a nation of law breakers: nine-tenths of the colonial merchants were smugglers. One quarter of the whole number of the signers of the Declaration of Independence were bred to contraband trade. John Hancock was the prince of contraband traders, and with John Adams as his counsel, was on trial before the Admiralty Court in Boston at the exact hour of the shedding of blood at Lexington, to answer for half a million dollars' penalties alleged to have been by him incurred as a smuggler." Lalor's *Cyclopedia of Political Science* (3 vols., Chicago, 1881-84), I, 75.

their grievances, denied the right of Parliament to impose internal taxes, protested against the maintenance of a standing army in the colonies, and named other violations of their rights.

But even more important than this paper protest was the "continental association" which the radical group forced through and by which they agreed to cease intercourse with Great Britain until the "cruel and oppressive" acts of Parliament should be repealed. They unanimously resolved that after December 1st of that year "there should be no importation into British America from Great Britain or Ireland, or from any other place," of any goods, wares, or merchandise exported from Great Britain or Ireland; no molasses, syrups, coffee, or pimentos from the British West Indies; and no East India tea from any part of the world. All the colonies except Georgia adopted these resolutions and the boycott was more vigorously enforced and more generally observed than had been the case in the two earlier non-importation associations of 1765 and 1769. The following table of trade between Great Britain and the colonies shows a great decrease in imports, which shrank to a trickle in a single year; exports, on the other hand, increased.

TRADE BETWEEN GREAT BRITAIN AND THE COLONIES, 1774-75		
Year	Colonial Imports from Great Britain	Colonial Exports to Great Britain
1774	£2,590,437	£1,373,846
1775	196,162	1,920,750

This decline in trade had an immediate effect in Great Britain and the West Indies. English merchants and manufacturers appealed to Parliament to grant the demands of the colonists, as did the planters in the West Indies, who were greatly alarmed at the loss of their accustomed supplies.[7] But this time the King refused to yield and Parliament answered the resolutions of the Continental Congress by declaring Massachusetts to be in a state of siege, ordering additional troops to America, and later prohibiting New

[7] See petitions in G. S. Callender, *Selections from the Economic History of the United States,* 1760-1865 (Boston, 1909), 155-59.

England and subsequently the other colonies from trading with any part of the world except Great Britain and the British West Indies. But before this legislation went into effect the Revolution had begun.

The colonists now assumed control of their foreign relations as well as of their internal affairs, and brought to an end the policy of imperial control which Great Britain had been developing for a century and a half. After this the Declaration of Independence, on July 4, 1776, was only a formality; by this act the thirteen English colonies declared themselves the United States of America.

Agrarian changes. In its external aspects the Revolution was directed against Great Britain, but at the same time there occurred an internal movement in America against the feudal land system and privilege in other forms. "In nearly every colony prior to the Revolution," wrote Professor Turner, "struggles had been in progress between the party of privilege, chiefly the Eastern men of property allied with the English authorities, and the democratic classes, strongest in the West and the cities." [8] In general, the wealthy and conservative classes were Loyalists whereas the poor and middle classes were Patriots or revolutionists. The eventual victory of the latter, which was followed by the departure of many large landholding Loyalists, provided an opportunity to break up the great feudal estates which had been established in some of the colonies, and even before the war had proceeded far advantage was taken of this by the state legislatures. [9]

The movement toward the abolition of feudal privilege and more democratic landholding also found expression in the abolition of quitrents. Although these were small in amount and frequently evaded, the total annual payments just before the Revolution were nearly $100,000. These were now completely swept away, and their abolition removed a slight obstacle to the easy ownership of land. So too there disappeared the right of the King's surveyor to mark white pine trees with a broad arrow for use by the navy.

---

[8] F. J. Turner, *The Frontier in American History* (New York, 1921), 110.
[9] For details see Van Tyne, *The American Revolution*, 248, and Jameson, *The American Revolution Considered as a Social Movement* (Princeton, 1926), 51.

Two of the props of great estates had been primogeniture and entail, but within a decade after the outbreak of the Revolution entail had been practically abolished and in another five years primogeniture had disappeared; inheritance was thus made more democratic.

Financing the Revolution. The immediate task before the colonists was, however, not social reform nor territorial expansion, but the winning of the war. The written instrument of government known as the "Articles of Confederation"

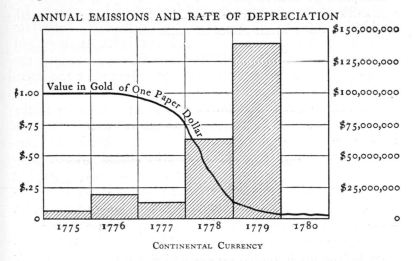

ANNUAL EMISSIONS AND RATE OF DEPRECIATION

CONTINENTAL CURRENCY

was submitted to Congress on July 12, 1776, but was not ratified by all the states until 1781. In the interval Congress exercised informal and unsanctioned powers. As a matter of fact, even after ratification, it possessed little power of its own and could only appeal to the states. Two things, however, it did on its own initiative; it authorized the organization of a Continental army, which was supplemented by the militia of the individual states; and it financed the war.

When war broke out, the colonies had neither arms nor ammunition, nor money wherewith to purchase them or to pay the soldiers. The first task that presented itself therefore was to provide the necessary financial resources; and this had to be done with discretion. In general there are only three methods open to a nation in time of war for raising revenue—these are the issue of treasury notes, taxation, or borrowing. The Continental Congress resorted to all three of these policies, but the first was their chief reliance and the one first used.

Paper money. It must be remembered that the Continental Congress was only an emergency body, with little authority and no compelling power for the collection of taxes, and therefore it had to resort to any device that, at the time, seemed capable of yielding revenue. Almost with the beginning of hostilities, in June, 1775, Congress authorized the first issue of paper money to the amount of $2,000,000. By November 29, 1779, Congress had authorized forty-two emissions to a total amount of $241,552,780. At this point Congress became alarmed at its own actions and limited the amount in circulation to $200,000,000. Meanwhile the states also were busy printing paper money.

Since the paper money issued was greatly in excess of the needs of the people for a medium of exchange, and the states failed to support their credit, the bills began after two years to depreciate rapidly, and prices of all commodities and services to rise correspondingly. "A wagon-load of money," it was said, "would scarcely purchase a wagon-load of provisions." "Not worth a continental" is even today a synonym for utter worthlessness.

Taxation. Congress had no power to impose taxes or to compel the states to contribute to the general expenses by taxes levied by themselves; it could only ask for money, but its requests were scantily honored. To many the demand for money by a distant Continental Congress was little more palatable than taxes levied by Parliament. Congress did, however, succeed in raising some small amounts by requisitions or assessments upon the states to be paid in specie or supplies.

Loans. More important were the loans which Congress was able to secure, both at home and abroad. Domestic loans were placed through loan-offices established in each state. With great difficulty some $11,585,000 (specie value) was obtained, owing largely to the exertions of Robert Morris, the so-called "Financier of the Revolution." Immediately after the Declaration of Independence commissioners were sent by Congress to France, Spain, and Holland to make commercial treaties and obtain financial assistance. Small subsidies were obtained from France and Spain in 1776; and beginning with the following year fairly regular and increasing sums were received from France. It may fairly be said that without the invaluable aid of France, by her loans as well as by her army and navy, the Revolution could not have been won.

The direct money cost of the Revolution, in specie, was estimated by Pitkin [10] at $135,000,000. Of this sum the Federal debt, as funded by Hamilton in 1789, represented $40,000,000, the foreign debt amounted to $11,700,000, and the state debts which were assumed by the central government made up $21,500,000, or together about one-half. The balance was met by taxation, repudiated paper money, and other means.

Industrial and commercial conditions during the Revolution. While the national treasury was practically bankrupt and Washington's army was suffering from lack of adequate food and clothing, the country as a whole was fairly prosperous. In so far as agriculture was self-sufficing it was little affected by the war, which did not disturb the ordinary farm routine outside of the areas of military operations. In the South the cessation of bounties for indigo and naval stores caused the decline of these artificial industries, but this was more than compensated by the enlarged markets and higher prices for tobacco and rice. After the first disorganization of commerce, blockade runners carried a steady stream of tobacco to northern Europe, and of rice to the Mediterranean countries; the latter industry was assisted by the invention in 1778 of a water mill for cleaning rice.

Manufactures felt the effect of the war more directly than did agriculture. The non-importation association cut off supplies of English manufactures even before the Revolution dried up the importations, and threw the Americans on their own resources. Spinning wheels, looms, and knitting needles were kept busy supplying the need for clothing, and quantities of woolen and linen cloth were produced in the North and of cotton in the South. A special stimulus was given to the iron industry by the unwonted demand for munitions and other war supplies.

[10] T. Pitkin, *Statistical View of Commerce of the U. S.* (New York, 1816), 25.

Although agriculture and manufactures prospered, another important industry—the fisheries—was almost destroyed. Along the coast of New England and off the Grand Banks the American fishing vessels were sunk by British naval ships and their operations prevented. The cessation of this industry crippled in turn the profitable trade with the West Indies and cut off the supplies of sugar and molasses. Rum began to decline as a beverage and in its place whisky was made from corn, rye, and other grains. The substitution of whisky for rum may be said to constitute one of the minor revolutions effected by the war.

Commerce and shipping were variously affected. The sale of ships to British traders of course came to an end, and traffic with the West Indies declined.

Territorial gains. The map on page 181 shows that as a result of the Revolution we acquired the Crown lands between the Appalachian Mountains and the Mississippi River. These were the lands which had been forbidden to us by the Proclamation of 1763. Our acquisition of them we owed to the efforts of a young Indian fighter named George Rogers Clark. Obtaining a commission from the governor of Virginia, he organized 150 men in 1778, floated down the Ohio River, and captured the old French posts now held by the English at Cahokia and Kaskaskia on the Mississippi and Vincennes on the Wabash. The Indian chiefs, impressed by Clark's daring, were persuaded to make peace. This exploit secured for Congress control of the whole Ohio Valley, so that when peace was made with Great Britain five years later, the treaty ratified this conquest by ceding to the United States all the British territory between the Great Lakes and Florida. The cession doubled the territory previously controlled by the thirteen states and made easier the westward expansion that took place in the next two generations.

Struggle with the mercantile system of Europe. In 1776, as stated above, the American ports were thrown open as far as possible to European trade, though British warships and privateers rendered such trade extremely hazardous. It was a period of perfect free trade on the American side. So it was not unnatural for the colonies, in their precarious situation, to invoke principles of generous treatment by other nations.

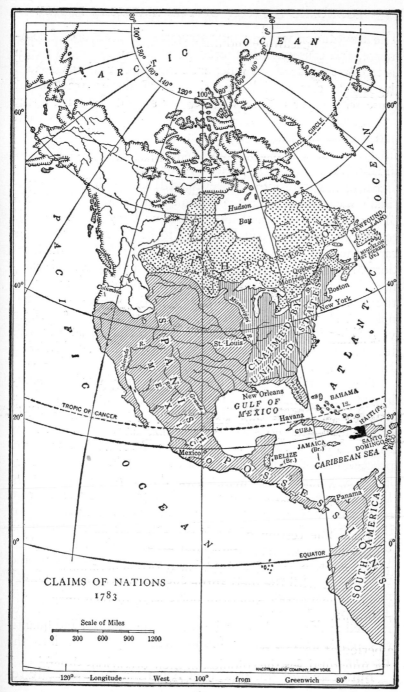

CLAIMS OF NATIONS
1783

Scale of Miles

| 0 | 300 | 600 | 900 | 1200 |

HAGSTROM MAP COMPANY, NEW YORK

120°   Longitude   West   100°   from   Greenwich   80°

The Revolution was in part a struggle for freedom of commerce, and consequently there was no desire to limit foreign intercourse; indeed, in independence the Americans beheld the key to commercial expansion. Accordingly, freedom of trade with other nations was eagerly sought for until about 1784. Indeed, Stanwood, an ardent protectionist, writes that, had the Constitution been drawn up in 1782, "it is not unlikely that it would have contained a prohibition of all laws in restraint of trade, foreign or domestic."

European statesmen, however, still clung to the mercantilistic ideas of commerce, and regarded the idea of freedom of trade as quixotic and impracticable. They wished to sell to us, but were not equally ready to buy from us or let us carry their produce. Pitt made a noble effort to obtain freedom of trade between the United States and the British colonies, but Parliament rejected this and proceeded to amend the navigation laws by admitting only British built and manned ships to the West Indies and subjecting American vessels in other British ports to heavy tonnage dues; by this legislation our ships were excluded from the British West Indian trade.

The loss of the West Indian trade was a particularly heavy blow to the United States, for even from early colonial times it had been a most valuable branch of our commerce. Fish, meat, flour, and lumber had been exported from the New England and middle colonies to the West Indies, with the proceeds from which goods had been purchased from England. Since these colonies had little to export directly to England, they could not have paid for their imports from that country without this trade. The economic prosperity of the United States therefore still depended in large part upon the triangular and other indirect trades into which the West Indies had been woven. The exclusion of our ships and products from the British West Indies would have been much more hurtful if the laws had not been so generally evaded. The trade with the Dutch and Danish islands, which remained open as in the past, increased enormously, and quantities of American goods found their way thence into the British islands.

But in spite of this treatment American trade speedily returned to the old channels as soon as peace was declared. Great Britain was, after all, the best place in which to buy manufactured goods and in which to sell American products. For this there were sound economic reasons. English merchants could best furnish the goods to which American purchasers were accustomed and which they wanted, and could furnish articles which were both superior and cheaper. They were almost the only ones able to furnish credit, and they gave longer credit than did those of other nations. And, finally, an American vessel found a better market for its cargo in England than in other ports, with the exception of certain articles.

Mediterranean trade. One other branch of the colonial trade still remained open to American shippers, and that was the trade with the Mediterranean countries of Europe. This had been very profitable during the colonial period. But when our vessels attempted to regain these markets after the Revolution, they were captured by the pirates of the Barbary States in northern Africa. The protection of the powerful British navy was now lacking, and the Congress of the Confederation was too weak to resist the pirates. Even after the Constitution was adopted, immunity from attack was obtained only by paying tribute, until we made successful war upon them in 1802.

The China trade. In lieu of the diminished West Indian and Mediterranean trade, Yankee skippers opened up bolder trade with China and the East Indies and with the Baltic. In 1784 the *Empress of China* sailed from Boston to the Orient, where it disposed of its cargo to good advantage in Canton. Two years later a group of Boston merchants conceived the idea of including the northwest coast of North America in this commerce, since furs could be obtained there and Canton was then one of the chief fur markets of the world, as the Chinese did not use coal and lacked wool for warm clothing. New England vessels were soon scouring the west coast of America and the South Sea islands. They brought varied cargoes to China, but the most valuable were furs, especially of fur seals and sea otters. For a time they carried enormous quantities and made enormous profits. "Sturgis in one voyage collected 6000 skins, purchasing 560 in half a day with goods worth a dollar and a half in Boston. The same skins sold for $40 apiece in the Canton market." [11] Another export much in demand was ginseng, an aromatic root supposed by the Chinese to promote fertility and the birth of boy children. Later, the vessels put in at Hawaii where they obtained sandalwood, which they sold in China at large profits. In return the Yankee skippers received tea, silks, nankeens, and China ware which were bartered in Europe or brought back to the United States. Early in the nineteenth century, however, this trade became less lucrative. Falling prices in the United States lessened the value of returning cargoes, the China market was becoming saturated, and the supplies of furs and sandalwood, on which this commerce was based, were becoming scarcer.

Economic depression. The first thought, with the declaration of peace, had been that great prosperity would now ensue, and a short period of speculation and commercial activity did actually occur. The American people were eager for English goods, of which they had been largely deprived during the war, while British manufacturers and merchants were equally eager to regain the markets which had been closed for so long. Since easy credit was generally given, American merchants overbought in the hope of disposing of their purchases at a good advance. During the year 1784 imports from Great Britain amounted to £3,679,467 and for 1785 to £2,308,023. That these were speculative purchases, far beyond the immediate needs of the people or their ability to pay for them, is evidenced by the unequal counterbalancing exports to Great Britain, which were £749,345 and £893,594 respectively for the same two years.

The buyers had expected to pay for these imports with domestic exports or with the profits of the West Indian and Mediterranean trade, as they had done in colonial days; but now these avenues were closed to them. Moreover, the economic situation in the United States was unfavorable to the production of large supplies of exportable commodities. American merchants incurred enormous debts to foreign exporters which they found themselves unable to pay; and domestic buyers were in a similar situation. The result was

[11] R. G. Cleland, *A History of California* (New York, 1923), 3.

a severe crisis, which affected almost every department of economic activity, and from which followed several important consequences.

Lack of money. The first effect was that the means of payment with which the merchants had settled for British goods or West Indian sugar and similar commodities during the colonial period were now lacking. Then the colonists had used the specie and bills of exchange which they obtained from the West Indies or southern Europe for products sold there to pay for the English manufactures, or they had exchanged goods against goods. Now that they could not avail themselves of either of these methods on any considerable scale they had to export their specie. It has been estimated that in the three years following the treaty of peace at least £1,260,000 in coin went to England.[12] But even this was insufficient to pay for all their purchases, and they remained heavily in debt to foreign merchants. In this emergency the state legislatures did two things.

In the first place, they passed stay laws or moratoria, suspending the right of creditors to collect debts for a certain period; and in the second place, seven of the states issued paper money to take the place of the vanishing specie. Only New Hampshire, Massachusetts, Connecticut, Delaware, Maryland, and Virginia, in which the wealthy merchants or the planters controlled the legislative bodies, were able to resist the demands of the farmers and debtor classes for cheap money.

Ruin of manufactures. Another result was the ruin of many of the struggling manufactures which had sprung up during the Revolution. The cheaper English manufactures, imported in large quantities and sold at auction at low prices or on long credit, brought the domestic concerns to bankruptcy; the workmen were thrown out of employment and the owners suffered serious loss. Some of these enterprises were of artificial growth and had been called into existence by the exigencies of the war; labor and capital had been diverted into them from agriculture or commerce, and now returned to those channels. Although there were no great

[12] A. C. McLaughlin, *The Confederation and the Constitution* (New York, 1905), 77.

factories then to close down, the distress was sufficiently serious to call forth protective tariff acts in New England and Pennsylvania.

Migration to the West. A third effect of the hard times was a great increase in emigration to the West. Beginning with about 1783 a steadily growing stream of soldiers with military scrip, debt-burdened farmers and artisans from the Atlantic seaboard, and adventurous pioneers combined to fill the western country with one of the most composite populations to be found in the United States; by 1790 there were about 200,000 people in the territory west of the Alleghenies.

Political discontent. A final result of the period of depression was to cause profound dissatisfaction with the Confederation. People have usually been prone to attribute economic adversity or prosperity to the government then in control of political affairs, and at this time there was a disposition to hold the form of government responsible for the economic difficulties under which the people were suffering. While it is true that this was weak and faulty, it is unlikely that any government, however powerful, could have saved the people from the consequences of their speculations. But the Congress of the Confederation could not even assist them. When the European states denied us freedom of trade, it could not engage in reprisals, as it did not have the power to regulate commerce nor to levy import duties; it could pass laws, but it must leave their enforcement to the states. Until 1789, therefore, the separate states undertook to regulate foreign commerce.

State tariffs. During the years 1780 to 1789, Pennsylvania enacted fifteen tariff acts; Virginia, twelve; Massachusetts, New York, and Maryland, each seven; Connecticut, six; and the other states a smaller number. To make matters worse, the states finally began to make commercial war upon one another, and to enact tariff laws which excluded one another's products. When New York placed high duties on British imports Connecticut and New Jersey thought to attract this trade by lowering theirs, and New York then retaliated against them by taxing their products when brought to New York City. To this New Jersey responded by a tax of £30 a month on the lighthouse which New York had erected at Sandy Hook, and the men of Connecticut agreed not to ship their products to the city. Boundary disputes added another cause of friction. The conflicting interests and jealousies of the states threatened to cause the complete disintegration of the Confederation.

The Constitution. It had now become evident that commercial relations with other nations could not be placed on a satisfactory basis by Congress so long as each state controlled its own action with regard to foreign trade. Unified action could never be obtained until Congress should be made supreme in foreign relations. Proposals to enlarge the powers of Congress, however, met with the obstinate objection of one or another of the states. But the commercial chaos was so bad that it brought its own cure.

In 1785 commissioners of Virginia and Maryland met to adjust differences over tariffs and the navigation of the Potomac River and Chesapeake Bay. Since the questions affected other states, also, Virginia invited all the states to send delegates to a commercial convention in Annapolis the following year "to consider how far an uniform system in their commercial relations may be necessary to their common interest." As some of the states were not represented at this meeting by delegates, another meeting was recommended to be held at Philadelphia in 1787. This was approved by Congress, and the constitutional convention, composed of delegates from all the states save Rhode Island and comprising most of the ablest men in the colonies, met in May of that year for its important work; by September it had framed the Constitution to take the place of the discredited Articles of Confederation.

Economic forces behind the Constitution. The movement for the Constitution was not unnaturally supported by those men of property and position who found their wealth threatened and their economic opportunities lessened under the Articles of Confederation. Holders of depreciated public securities, speculators in western lands, merchants and shipbuilders whose trade was adversely affected by the unfriendly commercial legislation of European nations, manufacturers who wished protection against stay laws and paper money— all these desired a strong central government to safeguard their interests. According to John Adams, "The Federal Constitution was the work of the commercial people in the seaport towns, of the slave-holding states, of the officers of the Revolutionary army, and the property holders everywhere."

It seems clear that the conservative party was in control of the convention and framed a document which abundantly safeguarded their property rights. The popular house was restrained by a system of checks and balances. Congress was given full power to raise revenue, to impose protective tariffs, and to regulate commerce. The states were forbidden to issue paper money, to make anything but gold or silver legal tender, or to make laws impairing the obligation of contracts. The debts of the Confederation were made an obligation upon the new government, and Congress was given power to raise and support military and naval forces, for the protection of the country against both foreign and domestic foes. In these provisions assurance was given that holders of public securities would be paid in full, the western frontier protected, foreign commerce regulated, manufactures fostered, and the financial excesses of the states prevented. The Constitution thus served to buttress the legal foundations of the system of individualism and private initiative which was being developed. It embodied the principles of modern competitive capitalistic industrialism.

Struggle over ratification. The struggle over the adoption of the Constitution was protracted and bitter, but the friends of the Constitution were, as Woodrow Wilson put it, "a strong and intelligent class, possessed of unity and informed by a conscious solidarity of material interest," and they finally succeeded in securing its adoption in 1789 by a narrow margin. An important factor leading to its aproval was the revival of prosperity, which began in 1787 and was in full swing during the next two years. Franklin, writing in 1787, declared that the country was "so prosperous that there was every reason for profound thanksgiving," and Washington a year later stated that "the people are emerging from the gulf of dissipation and debt into which they had precipitated themselves at the close of the war."

The cycle of speculation, crisis, hard times, and prosperity, beginning in 1783, culminated just in time to float the Constitution and the new government into power on a wave of prosperity. After the crisis of 1785 and 1786 the people had done the only two things possible to regain their prosperity; they had practiced economy and had worked hard. The importations of foreign manufactures and luxuries fell off decidedly, and many small domestic manufacturing establishments were started up. The first cotton factory in the United States was built at Beverly, Massachusetts, in 1787, and three years later Samuel Slater built his factory at Pawtucket, though they were crude affairs. They were followed soon after by others in Rhode Island, New York, and Pennsylvania.

Conclusion. Non-acquiescence in the enforcement by England of the commercial restrictions upon the colonies gave rise at once to the problem of the form which such resistance should take. After some vacillation the group favoring complete independence took the lead. When the Revolution finally occurred, the further problem arose as to how it should be financed. Peace in turn brought serious problems of domestic reorganization and of foreign commercial policy. It became evident that the "rope of sand" furnished by the Articles of Confederation was not sufficient to bind the thirteen states together and to solve these difficulties. As a result this was replaced by the Constitution, and a firm basis was laid for further economic as well as for political development.

Part II—The Westward Movement
1789-1860

CHAPTER IX

NEUTRALITY AND FOREIGN COMMERCE

Continental wars and the neutral trade. The same year that saw the establishment of our present form of government witnessed the French Revolution. In 1793 war broke out between France and England and spread until it finally involved all the nations of Europe. For over twenty years the best energies of the European peoples were devoted to destruction and warfare. These events made American shipowners, who throughout the struggle occupied a position of neutrality and at the same time possessed the only considerable neutral merchant fleet, the principal carriers of the trade between the warring nations and their colonies. Few ships except those of Englishmen or Americans were found on the high seas—the former because England was the undisputed mistress of the seas in contrast to her enemies, and the latter because of their neutral position.

After 1795 France abandoned the policy of maintaining her fleet on a footing of anything like equality with that of England and trusted to privateers to prey upon British shipping. French merchant vessels were left unprotected and their number declined until there was not a single merchantman flying the French flag to be found on the seas, while the fleet of Spain, ally of France, remained in port. And the effectiveness of the British merchant marine was reduced by the conversion of many ships to war purposes and by the attacks of French privateers. The chief effect of this was to throw into our hands the carrying-trade between France and her allies and their colonies. As a recent writer puts it, "While the great commercial nations were fighting one another for the carrying-trade of the world, America ran away with the bone over which they were quarreling."

Disregard of our rights. At the very beginning of this struggle, in 1793, President Washington issued a proclamation of neutrality. But, in their efforts to cripple each other's commerce, the belligerents paid little respect to the rights of neutrals. Each one sought not only to capture the enemy ships, but to prevent the carriage of supplies to the enemy in neutral ships. To give a color of legality to this, both Great Britain and France invoked the "Rule of War of 1756," according to which they held that a neutral could not engage in time of war in a carrying-trade which was closed to it in time of peace. Since the French West Indies had in theory been closed to our trade, Great Britain proceeded against such of our vessels as attempted to carry colonial produce from those islands to France or from France to her colonies. Moreover, according to the rather uncertain principles of international law, provisions were then claimed to be contraband of war, and in 1793 both the French and the British governments ordered the capture and condemnation of neutral vessels carrying grain and other foodstuffs to the enemy's ports. British naval vessels seized our ships, engaged in either of these kinds of trade, and took them into port where they were condemned and sold.

The United States government protested vigorously against these acts, contending that grain was not a contraband of war, and that even enemy property on board a neutral ship was not liable to seizure, since "free ships make free goods." In deference to these protests Great Britain yielded the first contention in 1794; as a matter of fact Great Britain needed American grain and did not wish this trade stopped. Since wheat and breadstuffs together made up our principal exports, their seizure would have been equally disastrous to us. On the second prohibition Great Britain would not budge and continued to capture American vessels which traded directly between the French West Indies and France. But this was easily overcome by having American vessels which traded with the French, Spanish, and Dutch West Indies carry the products to the United States and then re-export them from there to European ports. While none of the United States ports lay on the direct route between the West Indies or South America and Europe, the fact that the roundabout route was favored by the trade winds and Gulf Stream made the voyage but little longer in point of time. This is shown in the illustration on page 114. By calling at an American port, reshipping the goods, and taking out fresh papers showing that the cargo came from the United States, the danger from English naval vessels or privateers was removed from ships not carrying contraband of war; drawbacks of the import duties were of course allowed on all re-exports from the United States.

That this trade was profitable may be seen from the following table, in which the third column gives the figures for the re-export trade. This was extraordinarily lucrative between 1800 and 1810, constituting over half of our total exports; most of this trade was carried on during this time with the Spanish, Dutch, and French West Indies, or went direct to European ports. Imports received in return from these islands were also shipped to the continent.

FOREIGN TRADE OF THE UNITED STATES, 1790-1816
(in thousands)

1	2	3	4	5	6
Year	Domestic Exports	Exports of Foreign Origin (Re-exports)	Total Exports 2+3	Imports Kept for Home Use	Total Imports 3+5
1790	$19,666	$539	$20,205	$22,461	$23,000
1795	39,500	8,490	47,990	61,267	69,757
1800	31,841	39,130	70,971	52,122	91,252
1805	42,387	53,179	95,566	67,421	120,600
1807	48,700	59,643	108,343	78,856	138,599
1808	9,433	12,997	22,430	43,993	56,990
1810	42,366	24,391	66,757	61,009	85,400
1814	6,782	145	6,927	12,820	12,965
1816	64,782	17,138	81,920	129,964	147,102

As a result of these factors, the carrying-trade of American shipowners showed an enormous expansion during the period from 1793 to 1801. Even the commerce between Great Britain and the United States came to be carried more and more in American vessels; in 1790 our ships carried less than half of this trade, but in 1800 they were carrying 95 per

cent of it. Our exports grew from $20,000,000 to $71,000,-
000, while our total foreign trade increased from $43,000,-
000 to $162,000,000 for these two dates. After 1796 the
re-exports of foreign goods were practically equal to the exports of domestic origin, and in each of the years 1798–1800
and 1805–1808 the former exceeded the latter. It is evident
that the carriage of supplies for the belligerent nations of
Europe was responsible for a considerable proportion of the
carrying-trade. But there was also a large and growing demand for our own agricultural products on the part of the
two belligerents. Not only did the European wars withdraw
from productive labor large numbers of men and thus force
the belligerent nations to depend upon outside sources for
their needed supplies, but crop failures abroad increased the
demand for American foodstuffs.

The development of the carrying-trade received a temporary check during the Peace of Amiens (1802) which left
France, Holland, and the other European nations free to
carry on their own trade; but upon the renewal of the war
the following year our commerce again expanded until 1807,
when it was checked by the embargo. In this year our total
foreign trade amounted to $246,900,000; imports, $138,-
600,000; exports, $108,300,000, of which re-exports were
$60,000,000. The freight earnings of American vessels are
estimated to have averaged during this period about $32,-
500,000 per annum.

Under this stimulus the tonnage of American vessels engaged in foreign trade grew from 355,070 tons in 1790 to
1,089,876 in 1807. The merchant marine of the United
States surpassed that of any other nation except Great Britain.
Between these same two states the percentage of foreign
trade carried in American bottoms increased from 41 to 92
per cent. The shipbuilding industry entered upon a period
of prosperity: between the years 1798 and 1812 over 200,000
tons of American-built ships were sold to foreigners. Not
merely was the cost of building ships less in the United
States, but also that of operating them. Tench Coxe estimated in 1791 that an American ship could be built for about
$34 a ton, while a similar French-built ship cost from $55
to $60 a ton; and in 1805 a British Parliamentary committee

reported that the cost of a voyage for a vessel of 250 tons
sailing from England to America and back again was £513 for
the American vessel whereas it was £1083 for the English.[1]
The result was, as Pitkin says, "The increase of American
tonnage, during the period under review, has no parallel in
the commercial annals of the world." Sailors shared the
prosperity with shipbuilders and carriers; their wages rose
from $8 to $30 a month, and many foreign sailors, especially
Englishmen, became naturalized in order to take advantage
of this extraordinary demand. "Almost the whole carrying
trade of Europe was in their [American] hands," wrote Mc-
Master. "The merchant flag of every belligerent, save England, disappeared from the sea."

American vessels took advantage of this extraordinary opportunity to venture into hitherto unexplored fields. In 1798
an American vessel commenced trade with Argentina, and a
little later with Venezuela. The new decade saw our ships in
Brazil, and there began the phenomenal coffee trade which
was to make us the greatest consumers of coffee in the world.

American prosperity. But the effect of the Continental
wars was not confined to shipping and the carrying-trade.
A European market was created for the foodstuffs of the
United States. The belligerents were too busy fighting to
raise all the necessary food themselves, and moreover the
free export of grain from the Baltic regions, then the granary
of Europe, was prevented by Napoleon. The unprecedented
demand for the agricultural products of this country raised
their prices to extreme heights. Thus the price of flour at
Philadelphia averaged $9.12 a barrel from 1793 to 1807,
while for the nine years previous it had been only $5.41,
and for the nine years afterwards was $5.46. There was also
a growing demand for meat, for cotton and wool, and other
raw materials. The production and sale of these products
meant enormous profits for American farmers as well as shipowners, and was speedily reflected in the increased price of
lands. According to official valuations by the federal government, the price of lands advanced over $950,000,000 be-
tween 1799 and 1815.

Of course other factors were operative, such as the increase

[1] Bogart and Thompson, *Readings,* 205-6.

of population and the clearing of new lands, but no small part may be attributed to the profitableness of agriculture during the greater part of this period. From whatever aspect we look at the developments of this epoch, it is evident that the American farmer and shipowner were profiting largely at the expense of the European belligerents. Moreover, the profits obtained from these sources were used to develop our resources and improve agriculture still further.

Blows at neutral trade. The expansion of American commerce was seriously checked by the various English Orders in Council and Napoleon's decrees, which were directed against the neutral trade. As we had before especially profited by our position as neutrals, so now our prosperity was most disastrously affected. The war between Napoleon and Great Britain has been called the fight between the Elephant and the Whale; one was supreme on land and the other on the sea, and they could not come to grips. Since a military or naval determination was impossible, each resorted to economic warfare and tried to destroy the other's commerce. As each belligerent was being provisioned by the United States, a stoppage of this traffic by either would cripple the other. The English Orders in Council of August, 1804, had declared all French ports, from Ostend to the Seine, to be in a state of blockade; this was extended by the Order of May, 1806, to all the coast from the river Elbe to Brest.

While this was largely in the nature of a "paper blockade," it made neutral vessels trading with such ports liable to capture. The English government hoped in this way to deprive France of needed supplies from her colonies, and at the same time to stifle the alarming growth of the American carrying-trade. Napoleon, whom the battle of Jena had made master of the Continent, retorted with the Berlin decree of November, 1806, which declared the British islands in a state of blockade and forbade all trade with them; further, no vessel which had touched at an English port was to be permitted to enter any port of France.

This was quickly followed by other British Orders in Council during 1807, which declared all ports belonging to France or her colonies or allies to be in a state of blockade and stated that no neutral vessel could trade with them unless it first entered a British port, took out a British license to trade, and paid re-export duties. In answer to this, Napoleon issued the Milan decree, in December, 1807, which declared every ship sailing to or from Great Britain or her colonies to be good prize, and that every ship which submitted to the English orders was denationalized and liable to seizure. These decrees were directed against all neutral trade and were dictated by a desire not so much to harm it as to injure the antagonist who was profiting by this neutral trade. But the United States was the only neutral carrier of importance and naturally felt the full force of these acts. Privateers were licensed by England and France and their allies, and seized many a rich prize; less was done by ships of war. About 1600 American vessels and $60,000,000 worth of property were captured by French, English, and other privateers.

One branch of the neutral trade which Great Britain was determined to stop was that carried on between France and her colonies by American vessels. She therefore decided about 1805 to apply the doctrine of "continuous voyage" to products carried from the West Indies to the United States and then reshipped to France under the American flag. Such trade was treated as though it were carried on one continuous voyage and to it the Rule of War of 1756 was applied. Under this interpretation of the rule American vessels were stopped and searched and seized. America's trade was threatened with destruction and her rights as a neutral were entirely disregarded by these various acts. The desertion of her seamen especially angered England. The climax was reached when the American frigate *Chesapeake* was fired upon by the British man-of-war *Leopard* and four of her crew were impressed, of whom three were Americans.

Three courses were now open to Jefferson. He might let things go on as they were, trusting to diplomacy to obtain our rights; he might declare war against England or France or both; or he might refuse to trade with them. This last method had been effectively used in bringing England to terms before the Revolution, as Jefferson well knew. As a peaceful mode of retaliation for the injuries inflicted on

American commerce, a Non-Intercourse Act was now passed by Congress in 1806, directed against England and her colonies, which was to go in to effect in November, 1807. Before that time its operation had been postponed until December, and its repeal or non-enforcement was generally expected. Jefferson, who above all things desired peace, had also endeavored to conclude a treaty with England in 1806, but had not been able to secure a satisfactory adjustment of the matters in dispute. When, however, the news of these various indignities reached the United States, Jefferson recommended to Congress that an embargo be placed on American shipping or, as he expressed it, "an immediate inhibition of the departure of our ships from the ports of the United States."

The Embargo. The Embargo Act, passed December, 1807, prohibited American vessels from leaving the ports of the United States for those of any foreign power. Foreign vessels might depart from the United States only in ballast or with the cargo which was on board when the law was passed. American vessels might engage in the coasting trade, but in that case they must give bonds to twice the value of the ship and cargo that the cargo would be landed in the United States. Later acts placed the navy and the revenue cutters at the disposal of the executive and gave him almost despotic powers in dealing with both foreign and domestic trade.

This law acted like an overloaded gun, which shoots backward as well as forward. The effects of the embargo were immediate, and upon our shipping and foreign trade they were most disastrous; in a single year our exports fell from $108,300,000 in 1807 to $22,400,000 in 1808. "In the large shipping towns," wrote McMaster, "business of every kind fell off, and soon utterly ceased. The rope walks were deserted. The sailmakers were idle. The shipwrights and draymen had scarcely anything to do. Pitch and tar, hemp and flour, bacon, salt fish, and flaxseed became drugs upon the shippers' hands. But the greatest sufferers of all were the sailors." The same author estimated that 55,000 seamen were thrown out of employment, and that 100,000 mechanics and laborers were out of work for a year.

The classic example usually given of the effects of the

embargo is taken from the writings of John Lambert.[2] Describing his visit to New York City in November, 1807, he mentioned the immense trade with every part of the world and the activity of all lines of business. In April, 1808, he returned to the city, after the embargo had been in operation four months, and found the ships dismantled, the counting houses closed, and the merchants and their employees idle. "The coffee-houses near the waterside were almost deserted; the grass had begun to grow upon the wharves." Some mitigation of these losses was found in the expansion of the coasting trade, and in the diversion of capital and labor from commerce to manufactures.

The effects of the embargo were most severely felt in New England and New York, where foreign commerce was greatest, but even in the South and West they were harmful, and were felt by all who had depended upon foreign trade for marketing their products or obtaining supplies. The farmers, who had been buying land on credit and raising greater crops in expectation of the foreign demand, soon began to feel the results of lower agricultural prices, and many of them were forced into bankruptcy. This was true even of the producers of non-perishable commodities like tobacco, for the domestic demand did not absorb their production. Lumbermen and fishermen and finally merchants were injured by the stoppage of trade with the outside world. The jails were filled with debtors, 1300 men in New York City alone being thrown into prison for debt.

Equally important with the sailing of American vessels to belligerent ports, and therewith the export of American goods, was the prohibition of the importation of a selected list of British goods. It was thought that by denying England access to her best market she would be compelled to modify or repeal the odious Orders in Council. With considerable lapses, this policy, embodied in the acts of 1806, 1809, and 1811, controlled American import trade from 1806 to 1812. It was hoped that these forbidden articles might be obtained from other countries, but this was found impossible because of the British control of the sea. Some goods were smuggled

[2] *Travels through Canada and the United States of North America, in the Years 1806, 1807, 1808* (2nd ed., London, 1814), II, 62-65, 294-95.

into the United States and some were brought in legally
when the traffic was opened up at intervals, but on the whole
the cutting-off of foreign supplies gave a stimulus to domestic
manufactures, and household production was revived on a
wide scale. Albert Gallatin, the Secretary of the Treasury,
commented in 1809 on the extraordinary increase of household manufactures during the previous two years, and
thought it "probable that about two-thirds of the clothing,
including hosiery, and of the house and table linen, worn
and used by the inhabitants of the United States who do not
reside in cities, is the product of family manufactures."

Jefferson finally admitted that the embargo had failed to
influence English and French policies toward neutrals, and
yielded to the pressure for its abandonment; it was consequently repealed fifteen months after its enactment. In its
place was substituted the Non-Intercourse Act of 1809,
which removed the embargo upon American shipping and
instead adopted the policy of non-intercourse with Great
Britain and France. This was replaced in 1811 by another
act, which prohibited the entry into American ports of all
British ships and goods, but permitted American ships and
goods to go to Britain. None of these acts achieved the
sought-for goal, though as a result not merely had our commerce been seriously affected, but our treaty relations were
strained or broken.

The War of 1812. When the embargo gave way to non-
intercourse, American commerce quickly responded to the
opportunity, and in 1811 the tonnage engaged in the foreign
trade was 948,247 tons, a figure not equaled again until
1847. But the evils against which the embargo had been
directed continued unchecked; American seamen were still
impressed by British vessels, and renewed restrictions were
placed upon our neutral trade both by Napoleon and England. Partly as a result of these continued acts we finally
declared war against England in June, 1812. Owing to her
naval strength, our foreign commerce could now be carried
on only at great risk, and much of our shipping was destroyed. In three years we lost over 1400 merchant vessels
and fishing boats, and 1814 saw the tonnage engaged in
foreign trade reduced to 60,000 tons, the lowest point

reached since the year 1805. On the other hand, the five-hundred-odd American privateers which were commissioned by our government captured over 1300 British vessels.

The War of 1812 was a series of contradictions: the country itself was divided in its support, as commercial New England stubbornly opposed it, although the South and West approved. It is not necessary to describe the military events, which in themselves were inconclusive, but peace was not difficult to achieve in 1814. Although the treaty of peace settled definitely none of the questions for which we had gone to war, the conclusion of the struggle with Napoleon the following year put an end to the practices of which we had complained, such as impressment, the blockade, and other violations of neutral rights. The war was a phase of our commercial rivalry with Great Britain and brought out the irreconcilable views of the two nations as to the rights of neutrals contrasted with those of belligerents in time of war. It has sometimes been called the "second war of independence," for by it we successfully asserted our commercial independence. More important, however, than the military or political results were the effects which the war and the events of the long period leading up to it had upon the economic development of the country. The year 1815 may well be regarded as ushering in a new era along industrial, commercial, and financial lines.

Foreign commerce after the War of 1812. The effect of the war with England had been to reduce our foreign trade to its lowest levels: in 1814 the exports were only $6,927,000 and the imports $12,965,000. Immediately after the declaration of peace, however, the country was flooded with English goods which had accumulated during the closure of the European markets and which were now dumped on the American markets at low prices and on easy terms. Imports rose to $113,000,000 in 1815 and $147,000,000 in 1816; these were far in excess of the exports, which were only $52,000,000 and $82,000,000 for the same two years. Such a speculative expansion was abnormal and unhealthy and, as after the Revolution under similar circumstances, was followed by a crisis and depression, culminating in 1819. The unique and profitable re-export trade, which had enriched our shipowners and producers during the Napoleonic wars, now came to an end as European trade resumed its usual course and was carried in European vessels. American wheat and flour, which during the European wars had been in great demand abroad, were now virtually denied admission to Great Britain by the Corn Law of 1815, but their place as leading export was taken by cotton for which there was an insatiable foreign demand. On the whole, however, there was a steady decline in our foreign commerce from the high

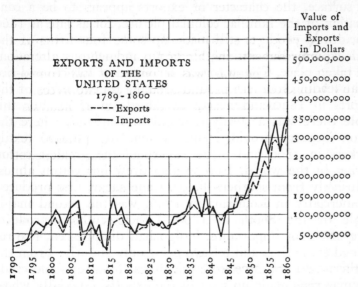

point of 1816 until about 1830; imports were held off by adverse tariff legislation and the development of our own manufactures, and exports were curtailed by the hostile protective legislation of European countries.

During the decade of the thirties there was another speculative upward swing in our imports, due to the large borrowing abroad and the investments of foreign capital in our internal improvements, and also to the reduction of tariff duties; exports increased, but not in the same proportion. By 1836 our foreign commerce amounted to over $300,-000,000, the highest figure yet reached. The panic of 1837 and the resulting depression reduced our foreign trade to $125,000,000 in 1843, but between 1847 and 1860, with the brief exception of the year 1857, in which a second panic occurred, the foreign trade of the United States reached the highest point it had ever attained. In 1861 our imports were $353,616,119, and our exports $333,576,057, or a total of $687,192,176. The general movements of our foreign trade are shown on the graph on the previous page.

Geographical distribution of commerce. A more detailed examination of our foreign trade during this period is necessary to appreciate the changes that were taking place. On the surface, the character of exports appears to be a continuation of the familiar colonial picture, for as late as 1860 agricultural products still made up some four-fifths of the total exports. But within this group momentous alterations had taken place. Cotton forged far ahead of tobacco and rice as the leading southern product, making up two-fifths of the exports in 1820 and nearly two-thirds in 1860. For this staple there was a steady demand in England, where the cotton industry provided employment for 450,000 textile workers in 1860 and made Liverpool the greatest cotton market in the world. Europe also drew her cotton almost exclusively from southern fields. Cane sugar, first produced commercially in Louisiana in 1796, was the second major staple of the South in 1860. Other southern products were of minor importance: indigo had disappeared, rice remained stationary, and tobacco grew only slightly. From the northern and middle states agricultural foodstuffs and crude raw materials made up most of the exports, especially wheat and flour, corn, wool, hides, naval stores, and furs. England was our best customer, taking most of our cotton and, after the repeal of the corn laws in 1846, an increasing amount of foodstuffs. The exports of wheat and flour, and of meat, of which the most important items were pork, bacon, and lard, expanded enormously in the 1840's and 1850's.

The "Products of the Sea" continued to figure significantly during most of this period, but markets for cod and mackerel fell off and by 1859 the whaling industry practically ended with the exhaustion of the whaling grounds and the discovery of petroleum.

Exports of manufactures showed a great relative increase during this period, but made up only one-eighth of all exports in 1860. Cotton goods and iron wares were the most important, but most of the items in this group were slightly processed raw materials.

Europe as a whole took over 77 per cent of our exports, the best customers being France, Germany, Holland, and Spain. The trade with the Orient showed considerable growth as British wars with China in 1840 and 1857 threw a part of that trade into our hands, but it always remained small in amount. The West Indian trade became of relatively less importance during this period but that with our North American neighbors increased. Commerce with Central and South America had not yet been developed, except with Brazil whose coffee was already entering our markets.

Of the imports, over half were manufactures ready for consumption, the most important of which were textiles—cottons, woolens, silks, and linens. Next came a variety of iron and steel products—especially rails for the railroads—mostly from England and western Europe, which altogether in 1860 supplied about 60 per cent of our foreign wares. The remainder, consisting largely of foodstuffs, came from North America, South America, and the Orient, in the order named.

Chief ports. New York became the leading port, both for imports and for exports, and occupied a pre-eminent and unassailable position. She passed Philadelphia by 1820, and cut deeply into the trade of her other rivals, Baltimore and Boston. Her success was due to the fact that she drew upon a rich field for exports by way of the Hudson River and later the Erie Canal, and, as the center of the greatest consuming area in the United States, furnished the best market for imports. The situation led to constant complaints from the South, which contributed so large a share of the exports and wished to see the foreign trade of its ports developed. But these aspirations were defeated, partly because of natural factors and partly by man's contrivance. Since first tobacco and later cotton were the country's leading exports, it might have been expected that southern ports would handle this commerce. But New York merchants managed to divert some of this trade to New York and to have it carried by northern ships. The greatest cotton export center was New Orleans and from this city much cotton went direct to Liverpool or Le Havre; but few vessels returned directly to southern ports. Since the South consumed only about one-tenth of the total imports, ships sailing directly to southern ports from Europe would have carried only partial cargoes. Consequently, the ships carrying cotton to Europe returned to New York with general freight and immigrants. Nearly all imports entered the country through northern ports, over two-thirds through New York City alone. From New York imported wares were distributed to the South by coastwise packet ships.

But much of the cotton exported from New Orleans did not go direct to Europe but was purchased by northern merchants and shipped by coastwise packets to New York, where it was reloaded on ocean-going vessels and sent on to its destination. The peculiar structure of southern economy hampered direct trade between that section and Europe. It proved impossible to revive the direct trade such as had existed during the colonial period between Great Britain and Charleston, and which had made the latter such an important colonial port. Professor Albion [3] considers that the diversion of the cotton trade via New York was both abnormal and impudent, but the fact remains that it did take this direction.

This diversion of the cotton trade finally took on such dimensions that the southerners became seriously alarmed. In a commercial convention held at Charleston in 1839 they urged southern shopkeepers to procure their imported goods through Charleston and other southern ports rather than by way of New York. "The direct trade," stated the convention report, "which was her own by every law of commerce and nature, and which should have grown and increased every year, grew less and less until it almost disappeared, being by this unpropitious policy transferred to the northern ports and people.... The importing merchants of the South became an almost extinct race, and her direct trade, once so great, flourishing and rich, dwindled down to insignificance." Other conventions, expressing similar demands, were held from time to time down to the eve of the Civil War, but nothing practical came out of the movement. It should be

[3] R. G. Albion, *The Rise of New York Port* (New York, 1939), 96.

noted, however, that an increasing proportion of the cotton shipped to northern ports, especially to Boston, was used for domestic manufactures and was not exported.

The balance of trade. For the period as a whole, from 1791 to 1860, the merchandise imports greatly exceeded the exports, the adverse balance for the period being $106 million. Only eleven of these seventy years showed a favorable balance. The large excess of imports was partially paid for by freight earnings of our merchant marine and, after 1848, by heavy shipments of gold, but the difference undoubtedly represented a steady investment of foreign and especially British capital in the United States. The following table shows the merchandise transactions:

EXPORTS AND IMPORTS OF MERCHANDISE, 1791-1860 * (in thousands of dollars)			
Yearly Average	Exports	Imports	Excess of Exports (+) or Imports (—)
1791-1800	$46,774	$59,185	— $12,411
1801-1810	74,532	92,766	— 18,234
1811-1820	58,989	80,812	— 21,823
1821-1830	69,421	72,949	— 3,528
1831-1840	103,550	119,520	— 15,970
1841-1850	122,620	121,123	+ 1,498
1851-1860	248,887	284,475	— 35,588

* Source: *The Statistical Abstract of the United States,* 1944-45 (Washington, 1945), 526.

The movements of gold and silver were not recorded before 1821, but a rough estimate indicates that the excess exports of the precious metals during this period amounted to about $300 million. Freight earnings of the American merchant marine amounted to about $500 million. If these two items be subtracted from the excess of merchandise imports, it would indicate foreign investments of some $260 million in 1860. That this calculation is not wide of the mark is shown by an estimate by James Guthrie, Secretary of the Treasury in 1853, that foreign holdings in the United States amounted to $223 million. Of these $111 million was in state bonds and $52 million in railroad stocks and bonds. Foreign capital was evidently largely instrumental in financing the program of internal improvements.

Organization of foreign commerce. The most important figure in the foreign commerce of this period, especially after 1815, was the commission merchant; he became more important than the merchant trading on his own account. In the United States the cotton and produce trade was largely in his hands and after 1815 the larger proportion of British manufactures. Cotton was usually marketed through an agent or factor, who handled it on a commission basis, charging about 2½ per cent for this service. The agent also advanced funds to the planter at an interest rate of 10 to 12 per cent, taking a mortgage on the growing crop as security. Finally, he purchased supplies for the planter, who was forced to pay credit prices for the goods he bought; thus he was charged 20 cents a pound for bacon, for which the cash price was 12 cents. Southerners claimed that for interest, commissions, insurance, and other charges northern agents got 40 cents out of every dollar paid for southern cotton.[4] Other staple products like tobacco, rice, sugar, grain, and provisions were also handled by commission merchants, but were not loaded with such heavy charges.

The marketing of British manufactures passed through various phases. Down to 1815 the British merchant sent goods to the United States on order to be sold on commission. Between 1815 and 1830 the British manufacturer, faced with overproduction at home, dumped his wares on the American market at low prices. A convenient mechanism for this purpose was the auction system, and this flourished for a decade and a half. After about 1830 the American merchant took over the business, giving orders for such supplies as were needed and selling them on a commission basis.

Such an expansion of foreign commerce called for a corresponding development of the credit system. It was the practice of merchants in the seaboard cities to sell to interior merchants on eight to ten months' credit; they therefore demanded long credit for the goods they bought. Great Britain, seeking a market for the products of her industrial revolution, extended credits to American importers running up to fifteen months. The American export trade, especially that of cotton, was also dependent on credit. The commission

---

[4] Albion, *op. cit.*, 96.

merchant stood in the middle of a long chain of credit transactions, which extended in both directions.

Commercial legislation and treaties. It will be remembered that when the Revolution began the new government attempted to combat the restrictive mercantilistic commercial policies of foreign nations and to introduce freedom of trade. Rebuffed in this effort, it next tried the policy of retaliation. There was a strong feeling against Great Britain because of her action in closing the West Indies to American ships, and both Madison and Jefferson were in favor of retaliatory measures. Congress, however, did not approve the plan of discrimination against the country with which most of our trade was being carried on—in 1790 nearly half of our exports went to Great Britain and her dominions, and we received from them over three-fourths of our imports—though Congress did establish discriminatory rates in favor of the American merchant marine. In order to promote the ocean-carrying trade a rebate of 10 per cent was allowed on all imports in American vessels, while special encouragement was given to the China trade by making the duties on tea brought direct from the Orient in American ships about one-half of those on tea carried in foreign vessels or in American vessels if brought from London. The shipbuilding industry was encouraged by confining registry under the American flag to vessels built in the United States; this provision remained in force until 1912.

The futility of discriminatory duties was soon apparent, for foreign countries usually retaliated with similar legislation against our vessels. Accordingly, in 1815 a different step was taken and reciprocal liberty of commerce was established. The act of 1815 repealed discriminating duties on the direct trade of any foreign nation which should abolish its retaliatory duties against us. In accordance with this generous offer, a commercial treaty with England of the same year provided that in the direct trade between Great Britain and the United States neither country should levy discriminating duties against the ships or commodities of the other. But Great Britain kept her West Indian ports closed to our vessels after the treaty as before, and we soon retaliated with new discriminating duties. American goods found their way into the British West Indies, however, by many a devious route, and cargoes landed on the neighboring French, Spanish, Danish, and Dutch islands were transshipped to the British ports with little additional cost. The rigor of official exclusion was mitigated by such evasion. In 1830 England agreed to open these ports and we removed many of the restrictions upon British commerce. As a result, our imports from the British West Indies increased from $1901 in that year to $2,965,585 in 1840.

Finally, in 1828, the President was authorized to suspend discriminations against vessels entering our ports from any country provided that country granted similar concessions to our ships. Treaties were accordingly negotiated which provided for "reciprocal liberty," with France in 1822, Prussia in 1828, and in subsequent years with Hamburg, Bremen, Lübeck, Norway and Sweden, Austria, Russia, Portugal, Holland, Belgium, and Switzerland. Commercial treaties were also signed with most of the Central and South American States.

Freedom of commerce with other nations on a basis of reciprocity had by 1830 been obtained by the United States. The old mercantilism was beginning to break down in Europe. The decade of the twenties saw the beginning of a more liberal policy in Great Britain, looking to the importation of cheap raw materials and the opening up of wider markets for her manufactures, and for both these ends a larger trade with this country was essential. And when, by the repeal of the Corn Laws in 1846 and of the Navigation Acts in 1849, British trade was thrown open, the United States applied to Great Britain the provisions of the act of 1828, which were already enjoyed by other nations.

American shipping from 1815 to 1860. Shipbuilding and shipping suffered all the vicissitudes which affected foreign commerce, and were subjected to some additional trials peculiar to themselves. The tonnage of vessels engaged in the foreign trade remained about the same between 1815 and 1840, with only slight temporary fluctuations, so that in the latter year the registered tonnage engaged in foreign trade was 763,800 tons, or only about 63,000 tons more than in 1815. Since the population was increasing, this really represented a relative falling off, from a per capita tonnage of 13.43 tons in 1810 to 4.25 tons in 1839. The capital of the country was being invested during this period in manufactures, internal improvements, and the development of our natural resources, all of which offered larger returns than the carriage of ocean freight. The high tariff too, which imposed duties on the materials needed for shipbuilding, considerably increased the cost of construction and equipment, and at the same time, by stimulating our domestic industries, diminished our dependence upon foreign supplies. About 1830, moreover, Great Britain began to increase its shipping, and to bid vigorously for the ocean carrying-trade.

But, while the tonnage of our foreign shipping showed a relative decline, its character was being improved. By 1818 the traffic across the Atlantic was deemed to be sufficient to support regular sailings, and between this date and 1838 lines of fast-sailing packet boats were established between New York in the United States, and Liverpool and London in England. The first of these lines was the Black Ball Line, which at first ran on a monthly schedule, later increased to weekly sailings as the scheme proved profitable. Soon other lines were added, the Red Star and the Blue Swallowtail. In 1824 a regular packet line was established between New York and Le Havre. Previous to this, vessels had sailed when and if cargoes were available, but these packet lines, specializing on passenger traffic and high-class freight, operated on regular schedules, making the transatlantic trip in eighteen to twenty days; *Dreadnaught*, the fastest of the packet ships, once made the trip from New York to England in 11½ days. In the building of wooden sailing vessels both the cost of materials—soft wood being used instead of hard, as abroad—and the skill of our shipbuilders gave us an advantage.

A new type of vessel was next developed, the magnificent sailing clipper, which proved superior to all others with which it came in competition. The first clipper ship, designed by John W. Griffiths in 1845, was built with sharp lines to give it the maximum speed, and with a long, narrow, overhanging prow from which the vessel gained its name. It was especially designed for the China trade and cut the sailing time between New York and Canton three weeks, but it was later, after the discovery of gold, diverted into the California trade. The record run of one of these clipper ships, *Lightning*, was 436 miles, the fastest day's run ever made by a sailing vessel, and rivaling that of many modern steamers. So superior in speed were they that, according to Levi Woodbury, an American vessel could make three trips between the United States and England while a broad-beamed British ship was making two. A radical change in rig and sail plan and the use of improved blocks and mechanical appliances reduced the number of seamen to two-thirds those required on a foreign ship. The high character of the masters also made the American vessels preferred by shippers. They carried what would today be called express freight, and mail.

Beginning with about 1840 a number of events combined to stimulate greatly the shipbuilding industry in the United States, and to give to American sailing vessels a leading place as ocean carriers in the world. In 1840 the British-China war diverted a large part of the China trade into American hands and led to the building of the China clippers. This foreign trade was increased by the revolutionary outbreaks in Europe in 1848, by the Crimean War of 1853 to 1856, and by the rebellion in India in 1857. The discovery of gold in California and Australia and the enormous emigration to those countries led to an unprecedented passenger traffic at fabulous rates, which, with the large immigration into the United States after 1846, gave immense profits to shipowners during these years. At the same time the lowering of the tariff in 1846 had reduced somewhat the cost of shipbuilding in the United States. As a result of this stimulus there was a great overproduction of ships: the tonnage engaged in foreign trade grew from 763,838 tons in 1840 to 2,494,894 tons in 1861, the highest figure for foreign tonnage that was reached in our history prior to World War I. Including the ships engaged in the domestic trade and the fisheries, our tonnage was one-third that of the world, and was practically equal to that of Great Britain.

The introduction of the iron steamship. During this very period of the supremacy of the American sailing vessels, a change was being effected in shipbuilding which was destined to revolutionize the ocean carrying-trade and lead to the eventual undoing of our foreign shipping. This was the substitution of steam for sails, and of iron for wooden hulls. Unfortunately for the American merchant marine, the excellence of the clipper ships blinded our naval architects to the importance of the changes and led to an unreasoning confidence in our wooden sailing vessels. The first successful steamboat was built by an American inventor, and the first steamship to cross the ocean was owned by an American shipowner, but it was left to British builders and merchants to make practical use of ocean steam navigation.

Great Britain immediately took the lead in the construction of iron steamers, while our shipbuilders, confident in their superiority, clung to the wooden ship. The industrial revolution had transformed the British iron and steel industry. The raw materials were conveniently located near the seacoast, iron plates could be cheaply manufactured, and marine engines had been further developed than in this country. In building wooden ships the United States had enjoyed all the advantages, but the tables were now turned. Nearly 25 per cent of the total tonnage of vessels built in Great Britain in 1853 were steamers, and a little more than 25 per cent were of iron.

In the United States, on the other hand, although 22 per cent of the total tonnage built consisted of steamers, hardly any were of iron. The vessel of the future was to be the iron or steel steamer, and by not changing the material used in the construction of their ships American shipbuilders gradually gave ground to Great Britain, who seized the opportunity of regaining her undisputed primacy on the seas. The British government encouraged the industry by subsidizing the steamship lines for mail service, beginning with the Cunard Line in 1838 and continuing down to the present time. Between 1845 and 1858 Congress granted subsidies to American steamship lines, of which the Collins Line between New York and Liverpool successfully competed with the Cunard Line, but opposition to the subsidy policy finally caused the withdrawal of this form of encouragement. Although our tonnage was increasing rapidly, in 1861 only 65 per cent of our foreign commerce was being carried in American bottoms, as against 92 per cent in 1807, and 83 per cent in 1840.

The coastwise trade. After the discriminating duties of 1789, but even more after the enactment of the law of 1793, which prohibited foreign vessels from taking part in the coasting trade, the number of vessels engaged in the domestic commerce of the United States increased rapidly. In 1793, the first year in which an accurate list of American shipping was obtained, the tonnage of vessels so engaged was 122,071 tons; in 1817 it was 500,000, and in 1840 it had grown to 1,000,000 tons, owing to the great expansion of the lake and river commerce. In the next twenty years the tonnage more than doubled again, amounting to 2,500,000 tons in 1860. Ever since 1820 the tonnage of vessels in the domestic trade had equalled that in foreign trade, and after 1860 it greatly exceeded the latter. It is impossible to say just how this traffic was divided between the coasting and inland trade, but each branch was expanding.

There was a profitable coastwise trade between northern and southern ports, carried on by northern vessels, which carried New England fish, manufactures, boots and shoes, dry goods, and other commodities to the South, to an amount of $100,000,000 a year. In return they brought back cargoes of southern staples, cotton, tobacco, and also foodstuffs, hay, and similar commodities, both for export and for domestic consumption. The falling-off of foreign commerce was amply compensated by the growth of domestic commerce, which provided business for American vessels.

Here was an illustration of the change in the outlook of American businessmen: they were turning their backs on the sea and looking to internal development. In local trade the sailing vessel was able to hold its own against the steamer. Opportunity for longer voyages was given when the rush to the California gold fields began; this was held to be coastwise trade and was consequently restricted to American vessels and brought in large, though temporary, profits. The building of the Chesapeake and Albemarle canal, which was completed in 1860, reduced the dangers of the perilous voyage around Cape Hatteras, and by so much aided the coasting trade.

Conclusion. There is danger, in a recital which emphasizes the effect of war, of commercial legislation, and of technical developments in shipbuilding, of losing sight of the fundamental basis of this growing foreign trade. This was to be found in part in the economic specialization of the United States in the great agricultural staples which entered into world trade, and in part in the fact that this country was in a stage of economic development different both from that of Europe and from that of the other countries with which we traded.

Our exports were still for the most part derived from the natural resources of a new country which were in constant demand by the countries of the Old World, while our imports reflected our increasing capacity to pay for the comforts and luxuries of a more developed civilization. This foreign trade represented in effect an exchange of our surplus agricultural wealth for the redundant manufactures of England and the specialized products of other countries. It was the growth in wealth and a higher standard of living that sent American ships to the Baltic and the Mediterranean, to the Far East, and to Central and South America.

CHAPTER X

THE WESTWARD MOVEMENT

Significance of the westward movement. From the beginning of our history the general movement of the population has always been westward, but the expression "westward movement" has a peculiar significance for the century beginning about 1767, for then began on a large scale the serious task of occupying and subduing the country west of the Alleghenies. Other peoples in their territorial expansion have had to meet and conquer rival nations. With the exception of the Indians, who often obstructed or diverted but never permanently hindered the westward expansion, the only serious obstacles at this time in the way of the Americans were the natural barriers and the inadequacy of the existing means of transportation.

In the United States the westward movement was the quiet, resistless, onward march, not of an invading army, but of peaceful settlers. For a century this continued, giving character to American life and a sturdiness and energy that were gained only by contact with primitive conditions and large opportunities. By this process the West was transformed from a rude and boisterous frontier to settled and prosperous communities, in much the same way that the economic and institutional development of Massachusetts and Virginia and the other colonies had been worked out. The growth of the West reacted upon the rest of the country, and the very nature of the people seems to have been changed by this great task of subduing a continent, gaining at once in initiative and vigor.

Beginning almost with the Revolution, and continuing with renewed energy after the embargo and the War of 1812, the people of the United States addressed themselves as a nation to the development of the internal resources. After 1808 capital and labor began to be diverted from commerce and shipping and invested in western lands and eastern manufactures; attention was now directed to domestic development rather than to foreign policy. The American people, who had hitherto faced the Atlantic Ocean and had been especially concerned with their relations to Europe, now turned their backs to the coast and devoted themselves to matters of internal policy and development. For the next ninety years the great work of the American people was that of opening up and developing the resources of the continent, and was surpassed in importance, if at all, only by the struggle for the preservation of the Union. This was the beginning of an economic revolution which gave color to and dominated our entire industrial and political history from that day almost to the end of the nineteenth century. The two aspects of this westward movement which first concern us are: (1) who got the western lands, and (2) how did the people get to those lands. Other factors in the westward movement will be taken up later.

The land cessions. By the Treaty of Peace of 1783 Great Britain ceded the western Crown lands to the United States. But immediately those states which had had previous claims to these lands by charter, by Indian treaties, or by conquest, began to urge these claims. The question of the western territory at once became a momentous problem for the Confederation. Virginia had already, in 1776, declared Kentucky to be a county, and two years later designated the country northwest of the Ohio River as a second county, while North Carolina laid claim to what is now Tennessee. Both states opened land offices for the sale of these lands, and made grants to their soldiers. Three other states—Massachusetts, Connecticut, and New York—contested the claims of Virginia to the territory north of the Ohio, and the first two also claimed lands in the unsettled portions of New York and Pennsylvania. Seven of the states claimed an extension of their western boundary lines; these were Massachusetts, Connecticut, New York, Virginia, North Carolina, South Carolina, and Georgia.

The other six members of the Confederation protested against the claims of these "landed states," and urged that the United States become the successor of the British Crown to the western lands, since these had been won by the united

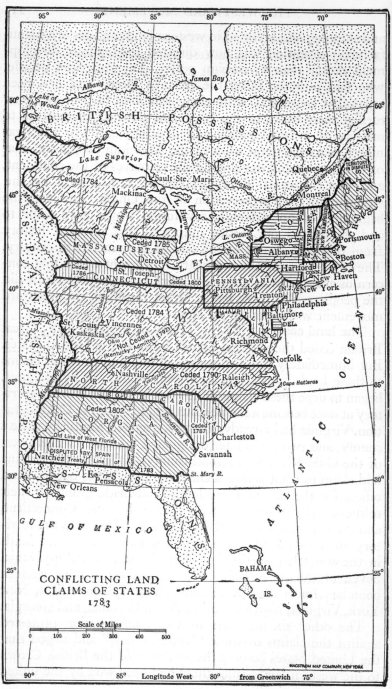

CONFLICTING LAND
CLAIMS OF STATES
1783

Scale of Miles

0   100   200   300   400   500

HAGSTROM MAP COMPANY, NEW YORK.

Longitude West   80°   from Greenwich   75°

forces and efforts of all the states. When the Articles of Confederation were submitted to the states for ratification, Maryland refused for three and a half years to ratify until the landed states should cede their claims to western lands to Congress to be used for the common good. In 1780 New York offered to cede its western claims to the central government without limitations and was followed by Virginia which, however, made large reservations in the present state of Ohio of military and bounty lands. The other claimant states slowly fell in line, but it was not until 1802 that Georgia, the last state to do so, surrendered her western claims.

One cannot study the problem of the western Crown lands surrendered by Great Britain in the Treaty of Paris without being impressed by the dangers which lurked in their unwise disposition and by the wisdom of the final settlement. The cessions prevented a succession of unhappy controversies among the states, inevitably arising from their conflicting claims, from boundary disputes, from difficulties of distant administration, and from other causes. They removed a serious cause of dissension between the two groups of landed and landless states, and, by creating a public domain, did much to give a material as well as a national basis to the new government. By these cessions the United States, which did not own a single acre of land in 1781, became possessed of an immense public domain of 488,248 square miles, which was larger than the area (341,752 square miles) of the thirteen original states.

The land ordinances. The next step was to provide for the administration of the public domain and for this purpose the three land ordinances of 1784, 1785, and 1787 were passed by the Congress of the Confederation. That of 1784 provided for the division of the western territory into states and for the treatment of the Indian claimants of the land; a treaty with the Indians the same year opened the southern part of this territory to occupation. The other provisions of this act were superseded by the more famous ordinance of 1787 before they could be put into effect.

The ordinance of 1785 provided for a system of rectangular surveys, according to which the land was to be divided into townships six miles square, and each township in turn was subdivided into lots of one mile square or 640 acres, numbered from 1 to 36.[1] The proceeds from the sale of lot number 16 in each township were reserved for the support of public schools, to which were later added those from lot number 36 in most of the states. Under this ordinance the government made its first land surveys, the so-called "seven ranges" in Ohio. Arrangements were also made for the establishment of offices where the land could be sold, the price being fixed at $1.00 an acre. This method of rectangular survey by townships fixed accurately the bounds of every parcel of land, permitted an accurate description, provided a simple, convenient, and cheap mode of registry and conveyance, and gave a safe title. In all these respects it marked a striking advance over the method of indiscriminate locations, tortuous and indefinite boundaries, and often conflicting titles of the southern states and of those parts of the country which did not adopt this system.[2]

The Ordinance of 1787 provided for the organization and government of the Northwest Territory. This was to be divided into not less than three nor more than five states which would be admitted into the Union when sufficiently populated. Thus it was determined· at the outset of our national existence that the newly settled districts were to become independent and co-ordinate commonwealths. They were not to be mere colonies to be exploited for the benefit of the older states. We had no intention of repeating the mistake England had made. In the meantime a territorial government was to be organized, which was highly centralized and required property qualifications for both voters and officeholders.

[1] An amusing comment upon this system of surveys is made by a French writer, E. Reclus (*The Earth*, 77) as follows:

"The country, which is thoroughly surveyed, is divided into townships of about six miles on each side, and subdivided into square miles, which are again separated into four parts. All these quadrilateral spaces are so accurately set that each of their sides faces one of the four cardinal points. The purchasers of large or small squares never allow themselves to deviate from the straight line; like true geometricians, they construct their roads, build their cabins, dig their ponds, and sow their turnips in the direction of the meridian or the equator. Thus the prairies now bear a strong resemblance to an immense chessboard. Even the railway engineers will hardly make up their minds to cross the lines of longitude in an oblique direction."

[2] A large amount of land in the southern states never came under this system, as it was not incorporated in the public domain; this was the case in Kentucky, Tennessee, and Texas, and in parts of Georgia, Florida, California, and other states.

The second section stated the general principles which were to govern the tenure, conveyance, and inheritance of property, which was to be as simple and democratic as possible; by it primogeniture was abolished. "The Ordinance," writes Professor T. N. Carver,[3] "has determined the form of land ownership throughout the entire West, and even the older states in which certain relics of a feudal tenure still survived have since remodelled their land laws after the pattern set by this Ordinance." Other clauses provided for religious freedom, political and civil liberty, education, a republican form of government, freedom of navigable waters, and a final one forbade slavery in the Northwest Territory. Many of the provisions of this famous Ordinance were later incorporated in the Federal Constitution.

Disposition of the public lands. It was not enough for the western territory to be acquired by the United States and for a system of government to be set up; it must be disposed of and put into the possession of occupiers who would use it. In the disposal of the public domain two distinct policies have been followed by the federal government. According to the first, which continued from 1785 to about 1820, it was held that the lands should be used and sold for the sake of revenue, to reduce taxes, and to pay off the public debt. Under the second, which has obtained from about 1820 to very recent times, the western lands were to be disposed of—sold or given away—to settlers and others for the sake of providing homes for the possessors and of developing the country.

Because a rapid disposal of the public lands and immediate revenue for the government were desired at first, it was provided in 1785 that the land be sold only in large quantities and at low prices; 640 acres was the minimum amount one person might purchase and the price was $1.00 an acre. But since large purchasers received considerable reductions, the revenue barely sufficed to pay costs of survey and registration. A few large sales were made under this act, all in the present state of Ohio; by 1800 these amounted to about 1,500,000 acres, or roughly 100,000 acres a year. The effect

3 "Historical Sketch of American Agriculture" in L. H. Bailey's *Cyclopedia of American Agriculture* (New York, 1909), IV, 48.

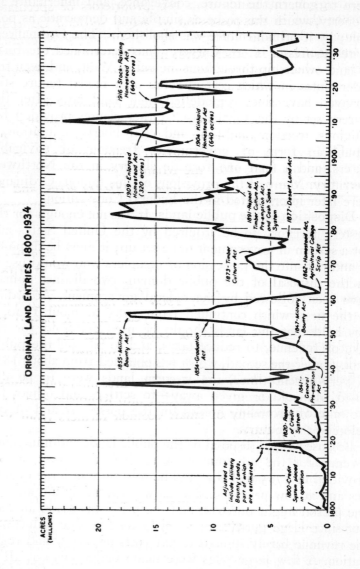

ORIGINAL LAND ENTRIES, 1800-1934

1800 - Credit System placed in operation

Adjusted to include Military Bounty Lands, part of which are estimated

1820 - Repeal of Credit System

1841 - General Pre-emption Act

1847 - Military Bounty Act

1854 - Graduation Act

1855 - Military Bounty Act

1862 - Homestead Act, Agricultural College Scrip Act

1873 - Timber Culture Act

1877 - Desert Land Act

1891 - Repeal of Timber Culture Act, and Cash Sales System

1904 - Kinkaid Homestead Act (640 acres)

1909 - Enlarged Homestead Act (320 acres)

1916 - Stock-Raising Homestead Act (640 acres)

ACRES (MILLIONS)

was not merely to retard the sales but to concentrate the holdings in the hands of a few proprietors or speculators rather than in the possession of actual settlers. Of course many settlers who ventured west despite these discouragements got land in other ways: many simply became "squatters"; others preferred to buy the state lands offered at lower prices in Kentucky and Tennessee; and still others bought from the various western land companies which had acquired large tracts in Ohio. These companies played a considerable role in our early westward movement. In 1787 the Ohio Company, a New England group, bought 1,500,000 acres, and not long after the Miami Company representing men from the middle states took 2,000,000 acres, and the Scioto Company 3,500,000 acres. These and other companies published glowing accounts of the soils and vegetation and soon emigration from all parts of the country began on a large scale. More than nine hundred boats were reported as floating down the Ohio during the latter part of 1787, carrying about 18,000 persons, 12,000 horses, cattle, and sheep, and 650 wagons. By 1800 the population of Ohio Territory was 55,000, and three years later it passed the 60,000 mark, thus permitting Ohio to enter the Union as the first state to be carved out of the Northwest Territory. Indiana followed in 1816 and Illinois in 1818.

Settlement of the Southwest. The first migration beyond the Allegheny Mountains was that into Kentucky and Tennessee and was chiefly of small yeomen farmers from Virginia. The real movement westward south of the Ohio did not take place until after the invention of the cotton gin and the spread of cotton culture. The apparently insatiable demand for this staple led to the opening up of land suitable to its growth and to rapid settlement. But this movement of population was very different from that which had taken place in the North. When the Southwest Territory was organized in 1790, all the provisions of the Ordinance of 1787 were made to apply to it by Congress, except the prohibition of slavery. Consequently when the march westward began to the cotton lands of the Piedmont region and to Alabama, Mississippi, and Missouri, most of the planters took their slaves with them. "In this newly developing cotton belt," writes Phillips,[4] "a pell-mell régime prevailed. In a scrambling scattered mass of many sorts of people, planters, slaves, farmers, poor whites, and frontiersmen nearly all were concerned with getting cotton lands."

Much of the land in the Southwest, especially in Georgia and the Carolinas, was sold to speculative land companies before those states had ceded their western claims to the United States, so that it was held in even larger tracts than the land north of the Ohio. The lands were usually sold to the highest bidders, and this gave an opportunity for the richer slave-owning planters to obtain the best cotton lands, for they were generally able to outbid the small yeomen farmers. The frontiersmen moved on to the ever-receding frontier, and the small farmers were pushed on to the pine barrens or back into the hills where the clay soil was not suited to the cultivation of cotton. The economy of these pioneer farmers was similar to that of the colonists and of their contemporaries in the Northwest.

Thus in both the Northwest and Southwest the early tendency was for land holdings to be concentrated all too much in the hands of a few proprietors and speculators. This somewhat slowed down the settlement of the West: Thomas Jefferson in 1803 estimated that it would be a thousand years before the region *east* of the Mississippi would be fully settled. The federal government's first land policy of selling land in large blocks only for cash made matters worse. Accordingly this policy was modified in 1800 to meet the demands of men of small means who wanted land. By 1812 Louisiana had enough settlers to enter the Union.

The credit system. The act of 1800 and subsequent acts permitted the sale of the land in minimum tracts of 320 acres, then later of 160 acres, on credit, at the fixed price of $2.00 an acre. Under this instalment system, by which only one-fourth of the purchase money had to be paid in cash, the remainder falling due in three annual payments, comparatively large sales were made, amounting in the next twenty years to about 18,000,000 acres. Many of the purchasers were speculators and many were venturesome settlers who

---

[4] U. B. Phillips, "Plantation and Frontier," in *A Documentary History of American Industrial Society* (Cleveland, 1910), I, 85.

assumed obligations beyond their ability to fulfill, especially during the hard times from 1808 to 1815.

It was possible for a settler to obtain a section of 640 acres for an initial payment of only $331 (including registration fees, etc., of $11), trusting to meet later payments from the proceeds of crops yet to be planted. For farmers in districts accessible to markets this was a fairly safe venture but in the Ohio country, which was fairly choked with its own produce, it invited disaster.

After 1815 the great rise in the price of cotton to 26 and 34 cents a pound led to still greater speculation in southwestern lands, the sales amounting to over five and a half million acres in the single year 1819. The fall in the price of cotton the following year and other causes led to another crash, and the arrears to the government on past due instalments for land purchases grew to $21,213,350. Numerous special relief acts had already been passed upon the demand of impecunious debtors, but in 1820 a general adjustment was made by allowing those indebted to the government to retain the proportion of land already paid for upon relinquishing the remainder to the United States. About 3,500,-000 acres reverted to the government under these acts. Perhaps three-fourths of the settlers who moved west before 1820, however, had not purchased their farms at the public land offices, but had settled in regions like Kentucky or Tennessee, which never came under the federal land system, or on land held under earlier titles, as in Ohio. These lands, as has been mentioned, could generally be had for less than the minimum price of the public lands.

The Act of 1820. The early policy of the government, that of land sales for the sake of revenue, gradually gave way to a system of land grants for actual settlement in small lots suitable for operation by a family. While this second policy was not always observed in practice—it was often difficult to prevent large speculative holdings—the government at least gave it loyal lip service. By the act of 1820 sale on credit was abandoned and the price cut to $1.25 an acre, while the minimum tract to be sold was set at 80 acres. In 1832 the minimum was again reduced, to 40 acres.

The system in use before 1820 had been denounced by

western men, who objected to the use of the public domain as a source of government revenue, to the high price of the land, and to the plan of instalment selling. Representatives of the eastern states, on the other hand, had resisted any change in these provisions, as they feared that land values in the East would be lowered if the public domain were opened up too rapidly, and that a reduction in the price of the land would drain off the population from the seaboard and cause a rise of wages in the manufacturing states. When the new system was introduced, it was found that no dire results followed; for the next ten years the sales of public land were very steady, averaging about 1,000,000 acres yearly.

The introduction of the steamboat into western waters, the extension of cotton culture throughout the Southwest, and the greater demand for agricultural produce owing to the industrial revolution and the growth in population, all led to a steady demand for land for actual cultivation and settlement. The possibility of using the public lands as an agency of social reform moreover, of providing homes for the workers, gradually dawned upon the workingmen, and they now began to demand, in their papers and conventions, that speculation stop and the public domain be made immediately available to the whole people. Land reform became an important issue in the platforms of organized labor, and during the years from 1825 to 1832 many schemes of a most questionable character were introduced into Congress, for disposing of the lands by sale or gift, for reducing the price to so little as 30 cents an acre, or for handing over the public lands to the states for them to dispose of.

The pre-emption system. One of the problems which presented itself from the beginning was the treatment of the "squatter." As the westward-moving population pressed on, it tended in its haste to pass beyond the surveyed lands and to settle in the wilds before they had been opened to settlement. The public domain was theoretically not open to settlement until it had been surveyed and was offered for sale through land offices which were opened at different places throughout the West. As a matter of fact the pioneers did not wait for government surveys, which lagged behind actual settlement, but "squatted" on the land. Here they built houses and made improvements, all of which they stood to lose when the land was offered for sale, for under the auction system established by the various land acts, anyone who wished was legally entitled to bid up the price of a particular piece of land as soon as the land office opened in that region. The temptation was sometimes too strong for the unscrupulous to resist and they bought up the cleared and improved land of the "squatters." In order to protect their interests, the squatters often organized claim committees. "It was not unusual," says Hibbard,[5] "for the members of this committee to carry guns and ropes and to indulge in remarks calculated to stimulate the claim-jumper in his tendency towards a speedy and amicable settlement." In such circumstances he rarely stood on his legal rights.

In order to abolish such questionable frontier institutions as these claim committees and at the same time give the premature settlers the protection they deserved, the pre-emption system was gradually developed. This did not amount to a free grant of land. It simply guaranteed to the settler a prior right to purchase, at the established price, the land upon which he had settled, without competition of any sort, in order that he might not lose the value of his improvements. The pre-emption system operated as a disguised credit system for the squatter, for it permitted him to defer payment for the land until he had improved it and could more easily meet the payment. The first pre-emption act was passed in 1801 to protect the settlers on the lands of the Miami Company, which had reverted to the government. Numerous other pre-emption acts were passed to care for special cases until 1830 when a general law was enacted, largely owing to the insistence of Senator Thomas H. Benton; this was continued each year until superseded by the permanent law of 1841.

Thus in about a half-century the attitude toward the squatter had been completely reversed. As the need for government revenues declined and the desirability of settling the western lands was more fully recognized, the squatter came to be regarded not as a lawbreaker but as a brave and self-sacrificing pioneer.

5 B. H. Hibbard, *History of Public Land Policies* (New York, 1924), 207.

Other public land acts. The planters and others who sought the distribution of the public domain in large tracts were continually in conflict with the widespread demand that public lands be sold or given in small tracts directly to the homeowner. While the reduction of the minimum tract to 80 acres in 1820 and to 40 acres in 1832 and the general pre-emption law did much to help the bona fide settler, it was still far from enough in the minds of many, including such social reformers as Horace Greeley and George Henry Evans. The latter once asserted that if all the public land in the country were divided into 160-acre homestead tracts there would be enough so that every family for the next thousand years could have one. The homestead idea was an appealing one and the battle for a homestead law was long drawn out. The first bill was introduced in Congress in 1846 by Andrew Johnson of Tennessee, later President. For the next sixteen years it was fought over intermittently, with southerners generally opposing the idea because they feared it would result in the peopling of the territories with anti-slavery farmers. Not until the southern states had seceded did a homestead bill become law. Even then it proved a disappointment, as will be told in a later chapter.

The forces seeking the distribution of land in large tracts were more successful. Southerners tended to favor the so-called Graduation Bill which became law in 1854. Under it land which had been on the market for years and was presumably inferior could be disposed of below the regular rate of $1.25 an acre at prices ranging from $1.00 an acre for land that had been available for ten years to 12½ cents an acre for land that had been available for thirty years. During the eight years of the life of this law some 25,000,000 acres —an area equal to the size of Ohio—were disposed of, mostly in the South to cotton planters and speculators at an average price of only 32 cents an acre. Indeed, during the twenty-year period before the outbreak of the Civil War, Congress generously—or imprudently—disposed of about 270,000,000 acres, three-quarters of it by gift. Some 65,-000,000 acres were granted to individuals; 105,000,000 were allotted to states for purposes other than internal improvements, of which the largest single gift was that in 1849 of all the "swamp and overflowed lands" within the limits of any state, and about 30,000,000 were granted to states and corporations for internal improvements. Only 70,000,000 acres were sold. Whatever one's views may be as to the wisdom of this disposition of the public domain, one must stand aghast at its recklessness.

It is unlikely that much of this land found its way directly into the hands of settlers. At least one speculator or middleman, often more, took his cut. But this is not to imply that western lands were dear: rather, they were not as cheap as a more equitable method of distribution could have made them. Despite these shortcomings, land in America was cheaper than almost anywhere else in the world and this, coupled with our political and religious freedom, made America a veritable utopia in the eyes of millions in other countries.

Effects of cheap land. It is almost impossible to exaggerate the influence which the vast western expanse of cheap land has had upon the economic history of the American people. In the latter days of the Confederation and the early days of the Republic it bound together the states by economic interests at a time when they otherwise might have drifted apart. It induced people from foreign lands, especially after 1820, to migrate here and thus helped solve our chronic problem of a shortage of labor. On the domestic scene it afforded an outlet for a growing population, which, instead of becoming denser, spent its force in taking up new territory. The problem of overpopulation—that bogey of early nineteenth-century England in the throes of the industrial revolution—had less meaning in a country where an increase of workers was generally the greatest need. Unemployment, the standard of living, and the rate of wages were improved by the existence of cheap land in the West; at least our scale of wages remained higher than those in England and other European nations. However, it would be a mistake to regard cheap land as a safety valve in times of depression, as is so often claimed. It takes but a moment's reflection to realize that cheap or even free land in Michigan or Wisconsin would be slight consolation to an unemployed weaver in say, Providence or Philadelphia. Not only would he lack the money to outfit and transport himself and his family 800 to 1000 miles westward and establish himself on a farm, but he would, in all likelihood, not know how to live on the frontier as the professional pioneer did. In general, the principal settlers in each new western state came from the state or states immediately east. There are very few recorded cases of people moving directly from the seacoast to the west, especially in depression times.[6]

Still other consequences of cheap land may be cited. As long as land was plentiful compared to labor and capital, it was not carefully used. "Soil butchery" characterized frontier farming throughout our history. Likewise cheap land was at least partly responsible for slavery. Free men preferred to work for themselves rather than for hire so that often the only dependable sort of labor in the South was slave labor. But slave labor was inefficient and wasteful, hence profitable only as long as land remained cheap and could be abandoned without serious loss when worn out. Cheap land made us backward in other respects, for in the generation after the Revolution cheap land attracted thousands westward and spread the population more thinly than in late colonial times when the people were hemmed in east of the Appalachians. Such dispersion meant fewer social contacts, a decline in culture and education among those who went west, less chance for specialization, and therefore lower standards of excellence for a time. Dispersion of the population necessitated more attention to transportation if outside markets were to be reached. Yet as long as cities were small and distant, expensive forms of transportation were not feasible. Fewer canals and railroads were built in the South and West: these sections depended on river steamboats. Finally, the hope held by every pioneer, and realized by many, that his land would rise in value, made nearly everyone a speculator to some degree. Improved land was one of the chief sources of cash for the pioneer. With nearly everyone speculation-minded, it is small wonder that the nation suffered several severe panics, those of 1819, 1837, and 1857 being the most significant.

Routes to the West. The western country was reached from the older states by four main routes which nature had

6 The California Gold Rush was the chief exception to this general rule.

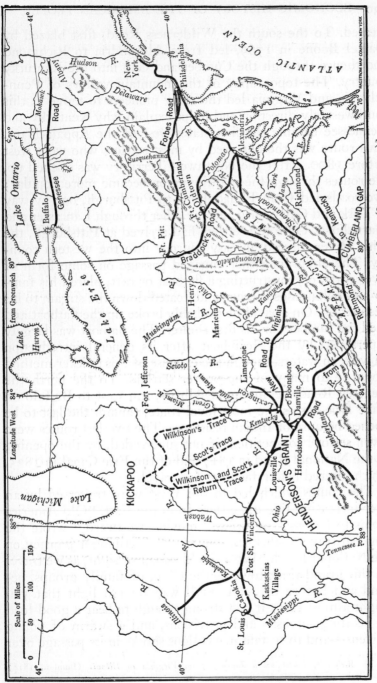

ROADS AND TRAILS INTO THE WESTERN TERRITORY

[From Gilbert Finlay's *A Topographical Description of the Western Territory of the United States* (London, 1792)]

created. To the south the Wilderness Road, first blazed by Daniel Boone in 1769, led from Alexandria to Richmond and thence through the Cumberland Gap into the Kentucky country. The topography of the mountain valleys of Pennsylvania and Virginia led the early pioneers to move in this southwesterly direction and helps explain why Kentucky and Tennessee became the first states west of the Appalachians. This route was the one used by most settlers who went west before 1800. After the Northwest Territory was opened up, the routes through the middle region became more popular; two roads led from Philadelphia to Pittsburgh, one by way of York and Gettysburg and the other through Lancaster and Harrisburg. Once the settlers had arrived at Pittsburgh, the Ohio River offered an easy journey into the western country. The emigrant either engaged passage on some form of river craft, or, constructing a flatboat or raft, placed his family and belongings thereon and floated down the stream to his destination. On arrival he probably broke up the flatboat and used the lumber for his first shelter. The flatboat was largely superseded by the steamboat after its general introduction on western waters, though the expense of this quicker method closed it to many of the poorer settlers. To the north the Genesee Road, beginning at Albany, ran west to Buffalo on Lake Erie across the most level route, though the last to be opened because of Indian resistance. The two last routes were given serious competition, if not superseded, by the opening of the National Road in 1817 and of the Erie Canal in 1825, which offered better facilities for travel.

The routes which led to the West were traversed by an ever-increasing tide of settlers from the East. "Old America seems to be breaking up and moving westward," wrote the English traveler Birkbeck[7] in 1817, describing a journey on the National Road. "We are seldom out of sight, as we travel on this grand track towards the Ohio, of family groups, behind and before us. . . . A small waggon (so light that you might almost carry it, yet strong enough to bear a good load of bedding, utensils and provisions, and a swarm of young citizens—and to sustain marvellous shocks in its passage over

---

[7] M. Birkbeck, *Notes on a Journey from Virginia to Illinois* (London, 1818), 25-26.

these rocky heights) with two small horses; sometimes a cow or two, comprises their all; excepting a little store of hard-earned cash for the land office of the district; where they may obtain a title for as many acres as they possess half-dollars, being one-fourth of the purchase-money. The wag-gon has a tilt, or cover, made of a sheet, or perhaps a blanket. ...A cart and single horse frequently affords the means of transfer, sometimes a horse and a packsaddle. Often the back of the poor pilgrim bears all his effects, and his wife follows, naked-footed, bending under the hopes of the family."

Three stages in settling the west. The process of settle-ment, carried on as it was by thousands of individuals and families, was spasmodic and irregular. In good times, as be-tween 1815 and 1819, or 1833 and 1837, the movement went on at an accelerated pace and when depression set in it slowed down. It was in the boom periods before major panics that organized territories gained the 60,000 population needed to join the Union as new states; thus Indiana, Mississippi, Illinois, and Alabama reached statehood in 1819 or before, and Michigan and Arkansas by 1837. The general features of the process of settlement have been well described by a contemporary writer: [8]

"Generally, in all the western settlements, three classes, like the waves of the ocean, have rolled one after the other. First comes the pioneer, who depends for the subsistence of his family chiefly upon the natural growth of vegetation, and the proceeds of hunting. His implements of agriculture are rude, chiefly of his own make, and his efforts directed mainly to a crop of corn and a 'truck patch.' ... A log cabin, and occasionally a stable and corn-crib, and a field of a dozen acres, the timber girdled or 'deadened,' and fenced, are enough for his occupancy. ... The pre-emption law enables him to dispose of his cabin and corn-field to the next class of emigrants; and, to employ his own figures, he ... 'clears out for the New Purchase' ... to work the same process over.

"The next class of emigrants purchase the lands, add field to field, clear out the roads, throw rough bridges over the streams, put up hewn log houses with glass windows and brick or stone chimneys, occasionally plant orchards, build

[8] J. M. Peck, *A New Guide for Emigrants to the West* (Boston, 1837), 119-21.

mills, school-houses, court-houses, etc., and exhibit the picture and forms of plain, frugal, civilized life.

"Another wave rolls on. The men of capital and enterprise come. The settler is ready to sell out and take advantage of the rise in property, push farther into the interior and become himself a man of capital and enterprise in turn. The small village rises to a spacious town or city; substantial edifices of brick, extensive fields, orchards, gardens, colleges, and churches are seen.

"A portion of the first two classes remain stationary amidst the general movement, improve their habits and condition, and rise in the scale of society."

South of the Ohio a corresponding movement was taking place, though different in character. The fur trader, the backwoodsman, and the small pioneer farmer were similar to their neighbors in the North, but the men of capital coming last were the slaveholders, whose plantations gradually took the place of the small pioneer farms in the richer cotton lands of the South.

The process of settlement. The location of the future home was frequently decided in advance by the purchase of a quarter section, or the land might be bought from the nearest land office after inspection, or the settler might simply "squat" on a desirable tract. In choosing this the color of soils, based on experience gained from many types, served as a dependable test of good land; black soils were generally the most fertile, and next to those came red. Vegetation, especially certain species of trees, was an even truer test than soil color; the nut-bearing trees were safe guides to good land, while cypress and scrub oak warned of poor soils.[9] In any case the site of the cabin would be determined by the presence of wood and of good springs of drinking water. The lack of these two factors prevented for a number of years the settlement of the prairie region in Indiana and Illinois, though the richer river bottoms gave rise to malaria and ague. To these the high death rate was usually attributed, but it was probably due as much to exposure to hardships, lack of a comfortable habitation, change of food, monotonous diet, and overwork, as to unhealthful location.

[9] A. B. Hulbert, *Soil* (New Haven, 1930), 70-72.

Having selected the site for his cabin, the pioneer cleared a piece of ground amid the forest and with the aid of his neighbors erected a log cabin. He next girdled the trees upon a tract for the next year's corn crop and cleared out the underbrush. The first crop was planted among the deadened trees. These were then cut down and burned, being brought together into huge piles by a "log-rolling," by the united efforts of the neighbors; if near enough to market the potashes could be sold for sufficient to cover the costs of clearing the land. With firewood at fifty cents a cord it did not pay to save the trees for fuel, especially since the ashes were a valuable fertilizer which would produce an increase in the next year's crop worth more than the value of the cord wood in the market. Some of the logs were split into rails and used to make the wasteful "worm-fences," by which four 40-acre fields in a quarter section would be fenced off.[10] Such a farm of 160 acres, fenced and partly plowed, with cabin and stables, would cost from $400 to $500.

The whole process of pioneering, especially in the early days before the introduction of the steamboat and the railroad, and even afterwards in the remoter districts, was distinctly reminiscent of colonial methods. Tools had improved, markets were nearer, and knowledge had increased, but the processes, where man confronted elemental nature, were the same as in the original colonies.

The men who carried on this work of pioneering were for the most part of American stock, but newly arrived immigrants also had a share in settling the Middle West. The Germans showed themselves best-suited to the task, followed by the Scotch-Irish and the English; those least well-fitted for the laborious work of transforming the wilderness into productive farms were the French.

Effects on the West. The most obvious result of the westward movement on the West was a great increase in the population of the western states, as can be seen from the accompanying table. The southwestern group showed a greater rate of expansion at first but fell behind after 1840, though the absolute increase was still large.

---

[10] The history of a pioneer farmer in the Middle West at this period is well illustrated in the early life of Abraham Lincoln.

POPULATION INCREASE IN THE WEST, 1800-1860		
Date	Northwest (O., Ind., Ill., Mich., Wis.)	Southwest (Ky., Tenn., Ala., Miss., and La.)
1800	50,000	350,000
1820	800,000	1,350,000
1840	3,000,000	3,000,000
1860	7,000,000	4,700,000

The westward movement also involved a shift of wealth from the seaboard states to the Mississippi Valley. It is difficult to estimate the value of the human capital which was transferred, though it must be estimated at many millions of dollars if the valuation of $1000 placed upon an adult immigrant by the United States immigration service be adopted. But each emigrant from the east also carried with him a certain amount of cash and of other wealth which in the course of time represented an enormous sum. This transfer was fortunately so gradual that it never impoverished the East, though it greatly aided in the development of the West.

Because the West was large and was opened rapidly, the population spread out over a wide territory in a thin layer; it rarely concentrated in compact masses. There were few cities in the West until the end of this period. Within two generations the pioneers had carried their settlements from the Appalachian range to the Pacific coast.[11] It is the occupation of the trans-Mississippi West in particular that now demands our attention.

The Louisiana Purchase. Between the Mississippi River and the Rocky Mountains lay a vast, rich, and little-explored territory known as Louisiana, which since 1762 had been a part of the already decadent Spanish Empire. A few thousand Americans, mostly fur trappers, were settled there by the 1790's, but we were chiefly interested in Louisiana because it controlled not one but both sides of the lower part of the Mississippi River. This was important because the river was the natural highway by which our western pioneers shipped their goods to market. In 1795, after considerable negotiation, Spain granted us the "right of deposit" at New Orleans, that is, the right to unload produce from the flat-

---

[11] See map on the following page.

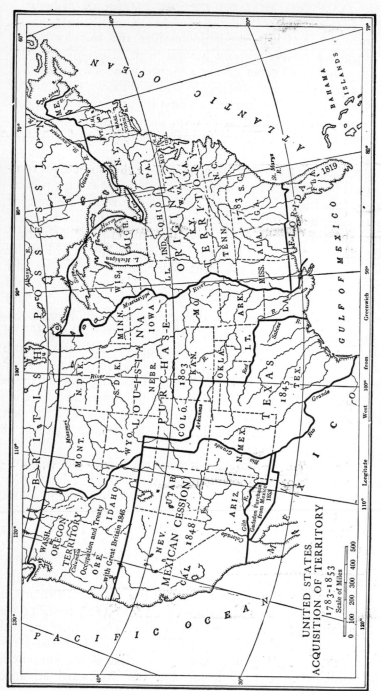

UNITED STATES
ACQUISITION OF TERRITORY
1783–1853

Scale of Miles

0 100 200 300 400 500

TERRITORIAL GROWTH OF THE UNITED STATES, 1783–1853

boats which had brought it down-river and to reload it on ocean-going vessels without having to pay customs duties to Spain. Then in October of 1802 the westerners were alarmed by the announcement that Spain had withdrawn the right of deposit. It was also learned about this time that Spain had secretly sold Louisiana to France, then ruled by Napoleon. All this stirred the western farmers to the point of threatening war.

President Jefferson realized not only the immediate commercial problem, but the long-run danger of having a powerful France instead of a weak Spain to our west. His first act was to dispatch James Monroe and others to France to negotiate for the purchase of New Orleans. In the meantime Napoleon's grandiose plans for building an American Empire had gone awry and he had also decided to renew his war with England. Fearing that what he had already done would drive us into an alliance with England or that England would seize Louisiana anyway, he determined to cash in on Louisiana as quickly as possible. His representative astonished Monroe and Livingston by offering to sell the whole Louisiana Territory, but they did not hesitate to exceed their instructions and bought it for $15,000,000. By this act there was added to the territory of the United States an area containing 828,000 square miles. With a few strokes of the pen our envoys more than doubled the size of their country, at a cost of three cents an acre.

In order to learn more about what we had bought the government sent out exploring expeditions under Meriwether Lewis and William Clark in 1804 and Zebulon Pike in 1806. These brought back much valuable information and one significant piece of misinformation. Pike reported that a "Great American Desert," quite unfit for tillage, began at the 95th meridian and extended half the width of the continent. Partly in this belief our government some years later ceded to various Indian tribes large areas beyond the 100th meridian (in Oklahoma, Kansas, and Nebraska). From 1825 to 1841 we had a fairly permanent Indian frontier. Then, as more and more traders and settlers travelling to the west coast reported that the plains were not as desertlike as was supposed, the Indians were routed out and our westward advance resumed. In the generation before the Civil War four out-posts of American civilization developed in the Far West—Texas, California, Oregon, and Utah—and were eventually gathered into the Union as new states. Let us look at each of them briefly.

Texas. The first one was Texas. In 1821 Moses Austin, a Connecticut Yankee, obtained from the government of Mexico a huge grant of land in the province of Texas on which to establish three hundred families; upon his death his son, Stephen F. Austin, carried out the project. Similar grants were made to other colonizing adventurers until most of southeastern Texas was parceled out amongst them. All advertised the rich new lands whose soil and climate were well suited to the growing of a variety of crops, such as cotton, corn, wheat, sugar, and tobacco, and whose pastures would support great herds of cattle. Settlers poured in from Kentucky, Tennessee, and Louisiana until by 1830 the province contained about 20,000 Americans as against some 3000 Mexicans of Spanish origin. Seeing too late the dangers of the alien invasion, the Mexican government tried to put an end to it, forbidding the importation of slaves, ordering the expulsion of squatters, and even tentatively abrogating the land contracts which had not been fulfilled. Against these measures the American settlers, led by Sam Houston, re-volted and in 1836 proclaimed the independence of Texas. The Texans soon after asked for admission to the American Union as a state. The slavery interests favored their admission, but the North objected, until speculators in Texas scrip and bonds won over enough votes to bring Texas into the Union in 1845.

A quarrel with Mexico soon occurred over the Texas boundary and war broke out in 1846. This war paved the way for our acquisition of two of the other western territories: California and Utah. The treaty of 1848, which ended the war, gave to the United States the area contained within the present states of California, Utah, New Mexico, Nevada, Arizona, and parts of Wyoming and Colorado—a domain greater than France and Germany together. Mexico received $15,000,000 and the cancellation of certain American claims for damages.

California. American interest in California developed gradually at first. By the 1820's whaling ships were stopping for food and other supplies, Yankee trading vessels had a lucrative hide trade, and a few fur traders had penetrated overland. The profits of the hide trade led to efforts to find a practical overland route to take the place of the long and dangerous voyage by way of Cape Horn, and in 1829 Ewing Young opened a trade route from Santa Fe. By the early 1840's pioneer farmers had begun to settle in the San Joaquin Valley and other favored spots in California. At the time of the outbreak of war with Mexico there were about 700 Americans and 7000 people of Spanish descent and 10,000 Indians in the area, but trade and industry centered in the hands of the Americans who were by far the most energetic element of the population. They promptly declared California an independent republic and then ran up the American flag.

The growth of California might still have been slow if gold had not been discovered in 1848 at Sutter's Mill near Sacramento. When the news got out, people began flocking to California from all over the nation, indeed all over the world, intent on quick and easy riches. They came by way of Cape Horn, through the steaming jungles of the narrow Panama isthmus, over Mexico, but mostly by caravan across the plains. A covered wagon expedition could leave Missouri near the first of May when the grass was up for the cattle to feed on, proceed at the rate of about 15 miles a day across the plains and mountains, being careful to follow the shallow western rivers wherever possible, and reach California by September before the early snows choked the high passes over the last barrier, the Sierra Nevadas. The trip was cheap in cash but a test of endurance, though the majority got through.

The settlement of California differed from that of most states in that the settlers came not from the region directly east but from all parts of the country and from all walks of life. Not many made fortunes digging gold—it has been estimated that all the gold mined would barely pay every digger the wages of an unskilled worker for his efforts. It was the merchants supplying the gold seekers who made the fortunes. Of course, those who reached California found it difficult to leave, so that the population jumped from 18,000 in 1846 to 90,000 in 1850, the year California became a state. Henceforth there was a lesser frontier slowly moving east to meet the larger frontier moving west. Overland trade between the two population centers grew and plans were laid for a transcontinental railroad. It was with this in mind that the Gadsden Purchase was made from Mexico for $10,000,000 in 1853. By this, a strip of land along the southern border of Arizona and New Mexico containing the best right of way into California was bought.

Oregon. Meanwhile the movement of frontier imperialism had reached Oregon. Shortly after the return of Lewis and Clark from their memorable journey, John Jacob Astor, a wealthy New York merchant, founded in 1811 the fur-trading post of Astoria on the Columbia River, but was forced by the British fur traders to abandon it. Later Daniel and Jason Lee carried on missionary work among the Indians in the Willamette Valley and Marcus Whitman did likewise among those living near the great bend in the Columbia River. Numerous letters home from missionaries in both areas did much to spread knowledge of the fine farm lands of the Far Northwest. Despite the extreme difficulties of overland travel to this region—for years no wagons could get through—first dozens, then hundreds, and finally thousands of emigrants from midwestern states found their way to Oregon in the early 1840's. By 1846 there were 10,000 Americans there. The demand grew that the United States take over all of Oregon, which up to that time we had owned jointly with Great Britain. In the campaign of 1844 the Democrats adopted the slogan of "Fifty-four forty or fight." A compromise was made by which the boundary between the United States and Canada was fixed at the 49th parallel. In 1859 Oregon became a state.

The Mormons in Utah. The Mormon state of Deseret was a settlement in whose founding religion played a large part. Indeed, this experiment bore many similarities to some of the early American colonies. The first half of the nineteenth century saw the birth of numerous new religious sects, one of these being founded by a practical mystic named

Joseph Smith who lived in upstate New York. He claimed
to have been entrusted with mysterious gold plates which
angels told him how to translate. On the basis of his trans-
lations the religion of the Latter Day Saints or Mormons
was founded about 1830. The Mormons were rarely popular in the various frontier regions where they tried to settle
in Ohio, Illinois, and Missouri, because they were different
and were considered arrogant. After several moves and the
loss of Smith by murder they decided to set up a colony in a
remote region where they would not be persecuted. An advance expedition picked a desert valley near Great Salt Lake,
made preparations, and then led out the main body of Mormons, some 1500 strong, in 1847. Because of the Gold Rush
of 1849 the Mormons were not destined to be undisturbed
for long. However, gold seekers headed west were willing to exchange valuable equipment from overloaded caravans for the fresh horses and simple supplies which they
desperately needed. Both sides gained from this.

The Mormons were well organized and industrious: they
irrigated the desert and made it green with their crops; their
leaders offered prizes to any who would discover coal and
iron, and soon coal and iron were found; advertisements were
sent east and to Europe promising assistance and work to
skilled workers in textiles, pottery, and other manufacturing.
This prospect of economic security and eternal salvation plus
reasonable help in reaching Utah attracted hundreds from
the eastern United States, England, and Scandinavia. By
1860 Utah had a thriving population of 40,000. To an unbiased observer the outstanding characteristic of the Mormon
settlement was the careful economic planning exhibited by
the leader, Brigham Young, not his collection of eighteen
wives. Polygamy was in fact practiced by a relatively small
number of Mormons. Approval of it however by the Mormon Church so scandalized the rest of the country that Utah
was not admitted to the Union until 1896, after polygamy
had been officially abolished.

Effects of the westward movement. The settlement of
the West had profound effects upon the economic, political,
and social development of the whole country. Some of the
economic problems have already been noted and others will

be discussed in subsequent chapters: these were the draining of the population from the East, with its resulting effect in keeping wages at a high level, the demand for better transportation between the sections, and the growing territorial division of labor among the South, the West, and the East, with its resulting sectionalism.

Important as these were, the *political* effects were more immediate and far-reaching. The aggressive and boisterous West introduced into American party politics new methods and new aims. The academic democracy of Jefferson was translated into leveling fact under Jackson, and property qualifications for voting and holding office were soon swept away. The new democracy felt the impact of the frontier, whose attitudes helped to shape national policy and legislation. The important issues of the time—internal improvements, the public lands, banking, and Indian affairs—were largely determined by western interests.

Finally, the westward movement had pronounced *social* effects. Inevitably it left its impress on the character and ambitions of the people. "A bold race," said Woodrow Wilson, "has derived inspiration from the size, the difficulty, the danger of the task. Expansion has meant nationalization; nationalization has meant strength and elevation of view." The national character was affected by the individualism, the passion for equality, and the love of freedom, the initiative, practicality, and democracy of the western people, and today shows these traits in marked degree. The migratoriness and wide dispersion of the people were less desirable features of a movement which on the whole bred qualities of strength and self-reliance.

CHAPTER XI

THE AGRICULTURAL REVOLUTION

The great colonizing movement which carried the frontier of settlement across the Alleghenies and on to the western plains had profound effects upon agriculture. It continued the exploitative methods which had characterized colonial agriculture, but it also introduced new conditions and new methods. The first half of the nineteenth century was above all a period of *transition*, when rapid changes were taking place, both in the new West and in the older sections of the country. Indeed, it may properly be called a period of agricultural *revolution*, so numerous and far-reaching were the changes that took place. It was a dynamic era of expansion and reorganization. It is therefore impossible to give a picture of agriculture which is typical of the whole country at any time, or even of any one section for the whole period. A truer view will be obtained if the changes are traced in turn in the different regions. Since the significant feature of this period was the development of prairie farming, it will be well to begin with the West.

Western settlement. West of the Appalachian mountain chain stretches the Prairie region, which extends from the western slope of these mountains to the Great Plains, and from the Great Lakes and Canadian border to the Gulf Plain on the south. It thus embraces all of the most fertile part of the Mississippi basin. Over most of this region was spread a thick fertile soil, free from stones and remarkably level. This region rose nowhere more than 2000 feet above sea level, and was mostly under 1000.[1] Heavily wooded plateaus sloped gently from the low mountains to the level plain, and in the river valleys the forest growth was also thick. Among these forested areas were treeless plains or natural clearings and west of Indiana stretched the open

[1] See physical map facing page 1.

prairie. Until about 1830 the pioneers settled chiefly in the wooded river valleys; settlement did not reach the prairie and prairie farming did not develop until after that date. There were thus two types of farming in the western country. The early settlers who crossed the Alleghenies engaged in the same type of woodland agriculture as that which had been followed by the colonists in the seventeenth and eighteenth centuries along the Atlantic coast; the later ones took up prairie farming.

Pioneering. It is scarcely necessary to describe again the pioneer processes of clearing the land by girdling, grubbing, log-rolling, and burning the trees, the construction of log houses, and the planting of corn and vegetables amid the standing trunks of the deadened trees. Here the pioneer repeated the agricultural experiences of the early settlements, but with less fumbling and experimentation. A well-understood technique had been developed along these lines, and, in spite of the hard work involved, the pioneer settler sought out the wooded tracts rather than the open spaces. Wood was essential for the construction of his house, for fuel, for fencing, and for making various farm implements and household utensils. And forests were highly important as shelter for game. The presence of a heavy growth of hardwood was moreover regarded as evidence of a good soil, while the absence of timber was thought to indicate a poor one. The emigrant evidenced his preference by the proverbial expression that he was going to "strike for the tall timber." The need of water both for drinking purposes and for transportation also dictated the selection of a site in the river valleys, which were always heavily forested. All these reasons led the pioneers who crossed the mountains and settled in the West to prefer the woodland and to avoid the clearings except for pasturage. It may seem strange that these pioneers should have preferred to spend years of toil clearing the woodland when open plains lay invitingly ready for the plow. But two centuries of accustomed methods, in which they had become highly proficient, were not lightly laid aside. This explains in part the long delay in occupying the open prairie region.

The early waves of settlement, as they pushed through

western New York and Pennsylvania to Ohio, Indiana, and Illinois, simply reproduced the typical frontier conditions of colonial days, with their primitive exploitative agriculture, lack of markets, rough life, and isolation. Since he was poor, the typical frontiersman had little capital, and since he had outdistanced the general movement of population he had few neighbors and only distant markets, if any. Agriculture was therefore extensive, that is, it involved the application of small amounts of capital and labor to large amounts of land. Indeed, it may be stated as a truism that the nearer to the frontier the settlers were, the more definitely were the agricultural practices of an extensive rather than an intensive character.

Another characteristic of this frontier period was the self-sufficiency of the typical pioneer farm. Without communication with convenient or profitable markets, the needs of the farm family determined the crops to be planted and the cattle to be raised. Farm production was limited by farm demand. There was little trade as yet, though a few products like whisky or cattle and hogs were sent to market, and such articles as salt and iron were obtained in exchange. It is difficult to say just when this pioneer period came to an end in any locality, but by 1830 frontier conditions were no longer typical of Ohio, and by 1850 they had passed beyond Indiana, Illinois, and southern Michigan.

Prairie farming. By 1830 most of the desirable woodland had been taken up and there remained only a choice between going farther west, in search of the favorite mixture of woodland and prairie, or of breaking away from the timber and engaging in pure prairie farming. About the same time several western states built canals connecting with the Great Lakes, thus obtaining an outlet to the ocean via New York's famous Erie Canal. These opened up the interior sections away from the rivers and gave access to the prairie region, and thus afforded convenient outlets to market for the produce of these hitherto inaccessible regions. Consequently, settlement now began on the open prairies.

On these treeless plains a new type of farming was developed, which was in sharp contrast to the pioneering in the wooded regions. "Here," wrote an English traveler, Stirling, "the pioneer is not the backwoodsman with his axe, but the 'prairie breaker' with his team and plough." Although there were no trees to cut down, there was a sod to break which was so tough that it yielded but slowly to the plow. Three, four, or even six yoke of oxen were required to draw the huge plow and turn the stubborn soil. The cost of breaking, if hired, was greater than that of the land itself,[2] and if done by the settler it was slow and laborious. Two or three seasons were necessary to decompose the sod thoroughly and render the soil loose enough to be turned by an ordinary plow, but even after the first plowing it was possible to plant seed in slits made in the sod with an ax and from this planting to obtain a crop of twenty to thirty bushels of "sod corn" to the acre, together with some potatoes. Even after the fields were readily cultivable, corn continued to be grown. In a predominantly subsistence economy it was preferred to wheat for several reasons: it was prolific and easily grown; it could be ground into meal by inexpensive grist mills—flour mills were costly; it could be used for human consumption in various forms, fed to the stock and converted into meat, or made into whisky.

An important and perplexing problem for the prairie farmer was fencing. As settlement was pushed out farther from the wooded districts the cost of wooden fences—which were only one cent per rail near the forests—became prohibitive; to fence forty acres with a rail fence in 1839 cost between $200 and $300. Sod, rail, picket, board, hedge, and lastly wire were tried, but all except hedge were too expensive. Professor J. B. Turner of Illinois College found, after many experiments, that osage orange made the best hedge fence and this was widely introduced throughout Illinois. Wire fencing came into use about 1850, but it was poor and expensive; not until strong wire was manufactured in large quantities at a low cost was the fence problem on the prairie farms solved.

Soil exploitation. The prevailing method of western farming was still soil exploitation. In spite of the criticisms of Europeans and of easterners, prairie farming followed the

---

[2] Land cost $1.25 per acre; breaking cost $3.00 per acre. Since few of the settlers had more than one yoke of oxen, it was usually necessary to hire this done.

same practices which had prevailed on the seaboard during the colonial period. This generally meant a one-crop system without fertilization or crop rotation—a process of soil mining. The usual practice of "earth butchery" is well described in the following account of farming in Missouri in 1849: [3]

"Farming here is conducted on the regular skinning system. ... There seems to be a continual struggle with each farmer to have longer strings of fence, bigger fields, and more ground in corn than his neighbor. The result of which struggle, in conjunction with the ease with which land is brought into cultivation in the prairie, convenient to timber, is that most of the farmers in this country *scratch* over a great deal of ground, but *cultivate* none. Instead, however, of endeavoring to extricate themselves from their difficulties in the most reasonable way possible, that of ceasing to enlarge their farms and growing grass seed until they are reduced to a manageable size, the cry is still more land, more corn. It is corn, corn, corn, nothing but corn. ... Take the state over and I have no idea that one farmer out of fifty has ever hauled a load of manure to his cornfields since he has been in the state. I have doubts, even, whether one in a hundred has ever done it."

As a result of these practices there was going on a steady depletion of the fertility of the soil. Soil erosion was an inevitable aftermath of this procedure. These evils might have been mitigated by more careful cultivation, but this was discouraged by the plentiful supply of new land. The factor most injurious to good agriculture was thought by an English observer [4] to be the occupation of too much land, which was poorly tilled. The farmer was told that if he would cultivate a smaller acreage more carefully he would realize the same returns and at the same time conserve the soil. But for this good advice the American farmer was not yet ready. The traditional practices of two centuries of wasteful extensive agriculture were too strongly ingrained.

Southern agriculture. Meanwhile an economic revolution was occurring in southern agriculture even more profound

---

[3] Quoted by Bidwell and Falconer, *History of Agriculture in the Northern United States, 1620-1860* (New York, 1941), 272.

[4] Frances Wright, *Views of Society and Manners in America* (London, 1822), 169.

and far-reaching than prairie farming in the West. It will be remembered that during the colonial period the staple crops in the South had been tobacco in Virginia and Maryland, naval stores and livestock in North Carolina, and rice and indigo in South Carolina. Very little cotton had been grown, owing to the greater profitableness of the other crops, but especially because of the difficulty and expensiveness of cleaning the cotton fiber of seed and impurities. But now the demand for cotton suddenly became great. Beginning about 1760 a remarkable series of inventions, especially in textile manufacturing, had completely revolutionized English industry. These inventions consisted in the application of machinery to spinning and weaving, immensely reducing the cost and increasing the output. The number of persons engaged in the spinning and weaving of cotton in England increased from 7900 in 1760 to 320,000 in 1787, and only the lack of a plentiful supply of cheap cotton prevented a still greater growth. The cotton from Egypt, India, and the Far East met the need inadequately and an insatiable market existed for additional supplies.

Sea-island or long-staple cotton was introduced from the Bahamas into the islands and lowlands of Georgia and South Carolina in 1786, and proved well adapted to conditions there, so that its production increased rapidly. Having a long staple to which the seeds adhered loosely it could be cleaned of its seed by a simple roller gin; but the area suitable for growing it was limited, and attention was next directed to the development of the short-staple or upland cotton which was grown on the interior lands. By 1789 the production of both varieties was estimated by Woodbury at 1,000,000 pounds; in 1790 at 1,500,000 pounds; and in 1791 at 2,000,000, practically all of it being the sea-island variety. The reason for the small production of short-staple cotton was the difficulty of cleaning the fiber by hand labor in sufficient quantities. According to Whitney a man could separate the seed by hand from only about one pound of lint of the short-staple variety, or about ten pounds of the sea-island cotton, in a day. If this difficulty could be overcome, a vast market lay open to the American cotton grower, which would be the more welcome because the tobacco crops were falling off by reason of the exhaustion of the soil, and the production and sale of indigo and naval stores had been adversely affected by the cessation of bounties from Great Britain. The stage was set for a vast expansion; the only obstacle was the difficulty of cleaning the fiber.

Invention of the cotton gin. In 1792 Eli Whitney was graduated from Yale College and soon after obtained a teaching position in South Carolina. On his way there he became acquainted with Mrs. Greene, the widow of Nathaniel Greene, the well-known commander in the South during the Revolution. His experiences can best be told by quoting a letter written by Whitney to his father in 1793:[5]

"I went from New York with the family of the late Major General Greene to Georgia. I went immediately with the family to their plantation about twelve miles from Savannah, with an expectation of spending four or five days and then proceed into Carolina to take the school as I have mentioned in former letters. During this time I heard much said of the extreme difficulty of ginning cotton, that is, separating it from its seeds. There were a number of very respectable gentlemen at Mrs. Greene's, who all agreed that if a machine could be invented which would gin cotton with expedition, it would be a great thing both to the Country and to the inventor. I involuntarily happened to be thinking on the subject and struck out a plan of a Machine in my mind, which I communicated to Miller (who is agent to the executors of General Greene and resides in the family, a man of respectability and property). He was pleased with the plan and said if I would pursue it and try an experiment to see if it would answer, he would bear the whole expense, I should lose nothing but my time, and if I succeeded, we would share the profits. . . . In about ten days I made a little model, for which I was offered, if I would give up all right and title to it, a Hundred Guineas ($511). I concluded to relinquish my school and turn my attention to perfecting the machine. I made one before I came away which required the labor of one man to turn it and with which one man will clean ten times as much cotton as he can in any other way before known, and also cleanse it much better than in the usual mode."

The machine in its first crude form consisted of a cylinder equipped with saw-teeth which pulled the lint through wire ribs, leaving the seeds behind, while a second cylinder, equipped with a brush, removed the lint from the saw-teeth. By this machine three hundred pounds of cotton could be cleaned by one person in a day, an amount which was later increased. Whitney and his partner Miller made the mistake of endeavoring to monopolize the production and sale of the gins, intending to set them up throughout the South and gin cotton for the planters at so much a pound. Within two years they had set up thirty gins in Georgia and South Carolina, but the

WHITNEY'S COTTON GIN

Until Whitney's invention the seeds had been removed from the cotton either by hand or by the roller mill. Now the cotton was forced by toothed cylinders through wire ribs, which separated the seeds from the lint. This greatly increased the amount of cotton which could be ginned and also reduced the cost of cleaning.

planters could not wait for such a valuable invention to be supplied so slowly and soon invaded their patents. South Carolina paid them $50,000 to secure the privilege of the gin for her citizens, and North Carolina about $12,000, most of which was soon spent in lawsuits defending the patents.

Increase in cotton production. The effects of the invention of the cotton gin were instant and far-reaching. Indeed it may safely be said that no other single invention in the history of the United States has so profoundly affected our economic history. Cotton almost immediately became the leading southern crop, and the most valuable single export of the United States. After the invention of the cotton gin,

American cotton, which had been dirty and poorly picked up to this time, became a popular and marketable commodity. Cotton culture spread steadily and rapidly throughout the South.

Production of cotton was greatly stimulated by the high prices which prevailed for a few years, the price reaching 44 cents a pound in 1799, owing to the increasing demand in England and at home. After this it declined to 19 cents in 1802, at about which point it remained for the next eight years; a decade later it was up to 26 cents again. The stimulus thus given to the extension of cotton culture may be judged when these prices are compared with the estimate of Woodbury that, where land and labor were cheap, 2 cents a pound for cotton in the seed, or 8 cents when cleaned, would pay expenses. As a result of these varied forces, production and export increased by leaps and bounds, as may be seen from the table below.

Average Annual Production and Exports of American Cotton, 1790-1860 *			
Years	Average Annual Production in the United States POUNDS	Average Annual Exports from the United States POUNDS	Average New York Prices for Middling-Uplands CENTS
1790	1,500,000	....	14.5
1796-1800	18,200,000	8,993,200	36.3
1806-1810	80,400,000	52,507,400	18.9
1816-1820	141,200,000	91,144,800	26.2
1826-1830	307,244,400	254,548,200	10.9
1836-1840	617,306,200	513,315,800	13.0
1846-1850	979,690,400	729,524,000	8.7
1856-1860	1,749,496,500	1,383,711,200	11.5

* The South in the Building of the Nation (Richmond, 1909), V, 211.

The first cotton was produced in Georgia and South Carolina, and until 1820 over half the cotton grown came from those two states. With the increase in demand, however, cotton culture spread into Virginia and North Carolina, and across the mountains into Tennessee. When the alluvial soils of Alabama and Mississippi were reached, a new impetus was given to the westward movement in the South. By 1850, cotton had taken almost complete possession of the lower Mississippi Valley, and by 1860 had reached the great central plain of Texas. As the center of cotton production moved westward, so the commercial cities which were built up on the cotton trade shifted and grew. Charleston and Savannah gave place to Memphis, Mobile, and New Orleans as centers of southern trade and wealth; during the decade 1850–1860 half the cotton crop passed through the port of New Orleans.

Agricultural methods in cotton growing. The agricultural methods employed during this period continued to be those which had been followed by pioneer farmers in colonial days and were a wasteful kind of extensive agriculture. The land was cleared for cotton, as it had been for tobacco and corn, by girdling the trees and then burning them as they decayed and fell. Before the fields were ready for cotton a few crops of Indian corn or wheat would often be gathered. The ground was prepared and cultivated in a very primitive fashion; but few agricultural implements were used and those only of the rudest and strongest kind, such as even the most careless slave could not break. Fertilizers were but rarely used, not even the cotton seeds being returned to the soil, while rotation of crops was unknown.

Although cotton is said to be the least exhaustive to the soil of the great staple crops of America, the single-crop system rapidly wore out the land. "Agriculture in the South," said John Taylor of Caroline, "does not consist so much in cultivating land as in killing it." The great abundance of land in proportion to population led to an exploitative agriculture, which reduced the fertility of the soil to such an extent that it was more profitable to abandon the exhausted land and take up a fresh piece. Partly responsible for the soil wastage was the employment of clumsy plows and other implements, of plowing up and down hillsides and permitting erosion, and of other bad agricultural practices. But even more important were the defects of slavery, tied as it was to a single-crop system of farming.

Other crops. Although cotton was the most important crop in the South, other agricultural staples were produced there during this period. Tobacco had been the leading crop during the colonial period and retained its pre-eminence as our chief agricultural export down to 1803, after which it sank rapidly in importance, owing to a variety of causes. Among these may be named the exhaustion of the old tobacco lands, the greater profitableness of cotton, the competition of Cuban and other foreign tobaccos, high import duties imposed by foreign countries, and the interference with the export trade by the French decrees and the English Orders in Council, as well as by the embargo and the War of 1812. The production of tobacco remained practically stationary until 1850, but during the next decade it more than doubled, owing to the opening up of new tobacco lands. Virginia, Maryland, and northern North Carolina, sometimes called the "Tobacco Kingdom," continued to be the leading tobacco district, but new areas of production were developed in Kentucky and Tennessee in the West, and in Connecticut and Massachusetts in the North.

Rice was still cultivated in the swamplands of South Carolina and Georgia, and between 1820 and 1850 its production was considerably increased, but after 1850 a decline set in. Confined to a small area of tide-swampland, which was used repeatedly for the same crop, the rice growers were forced to use fertilizers and to reclaim swamplands. They thus ranked among the best scientific farmers in the South.

Sugar cane was introduced from Santo Domingo and was first successfully refined in southern Louisiana in 1796 by Jean Étienne Boré. Commercial production of sugar rose until 1850, but during the next decade it too declined slightly. It may be noted that large-scale methods were employed in raising both these crops since they called for considerable investment in slaves and equipment. Tobacco, on the other hand, was best produced on a small scale, while cotton could be profitably grown by either method though the large-scale plantation finally proved most advantageous.

Development of commercial farming. It is dangerous to generalize for a territory so large as the South and during a period in which profound changes were taking place. Communities differed from each other, and within each community there were sharply contrasting economic groups. In the mountainous Appalachian region stretching from Maryland to Georgia were self-sufficing small farmers; cut off from markets by lack of transportation facilities, they lived in isolation and contributed little to southern agriculture. In the lower Piedmont section were found moderate-sized holdings where mixed farming—especially in wheat, corn, and live-stock—was carried on. West of the mountains Kentucky was famous for her fine horses and also led in the production of hemp and flax. Missouri was noted for her sturdy mules, but raised general crops, as did Tennessee.

In the pioneer stage of settlement the farm economy was practically self-sufficient, but as improved transportation opened up markets, there was strong pressure toward concentration on staples for which there was a steady demand. Commercial farming developed. The principle of land utilization for the most profitable crop led to concentration on certain staples; it was a case of territorial specialization. On the whole, therefore, the outstanding characteristic of southern agriculture came to be commercial farming, there being a heavy concentration in the lower South on cotton. It must not be supposed, however, that the cotton states raised nothing else. During seasons when work on the cotton fields was slack the slaves were engaged in planting and cultivating an equal acreage of corn. Swine, poultry, and some cattle were usually kept, sweet potatoes, peas, and beans were grown, and efforts were made to supply the major food requirements of the region. Such agricultural supplies as were lacking were drawn largely from the West.

Agriculture in the East. Agriculture in New England and the middle Atlantic states made little improvement for twenty-five years after the Revolution. Colonial methods still prevailed, and the distinguishing characteristic of the eastern farm, during this period, was its self-sufficiency. A step forward was made by the concentration of farmers upon the cultivation of the more profitable crops and the elimination of many which had long been under experiment. In New England and the middle states attempts had been made to grow lucerne (alfalfa), vetches, rape, spelt, spurry, poppies, madder, woad, and similar crops, but the discussions initiated by the agricultural societies showed most of them to be unprofitable and their culture was finally discontinued. The lack of progress in general and the failure to improve methods were attributed by contemporary critics to ignorance of the principles of scientific agriculture on the part of the farmers, to their conservatism, and to the cheapness of the land which made them use this agent wastefully while they economized labor. Although these factors all combined to hinder agricultural progress, the real cause of inefficient agriculture was the lack of markets for farm products.[6] As long as the farmers lacked markets they did not attempt to produce a surplus except for trading at the country store.

After about 1810, however, the character of agriculture was vitally affected by two changes which occurred at that time, namely, the development of manufacturing in the East and the improvement of transportation facilities with the West. These caused revolutions both in industry and in agriculture. The growth of manufactures and of factory towns affected especially New England, for it was near the water power of her small swift rivers that most of these enterprises were located. The rise of urban centers created a market for agricultural products which the local farmers could best supply, and commercial farming, that is, the production of agricultural commodities for sale rather than for family consumption, began to supplant the old self-sufficient economy. With this went greater specialization.

Far more revolutionary in their effects on eastern agriculture, however, were the improvements in transportation facilities, and especially those with the West. The building of improved roads, of steamboats, of the Erie Canal, of western canals, and of railroads brought western agricultural products to the eastern factory towns and to other markets for a fraction of their former cost, and exposed the eastern farmer after about 1830 to a new and sharp competition. Western wheat, pork, and wool could now be brought in at such prices as to discourage home production. Wool-growing and beef-fattening passed from New England to Ohio and the center of wheat production moved from New York to Illinois. On the other hand the areas of profitable specialization in market-gardening, fruit-raising, and dairying were rapidly widened by the new transportation agencies. The production of butter and cheese in New York, which had been confined to the southeastern part of the state, spread after 1825 to counties along the Erie Canal, and took the place of wheat farming. Dairying, based upon hay and pasture, dominated the agri-

[6] P. W. Bidwell, *Rural Economy of New England* (New Haven, 1916), 352.

culture of the East in 1860, the chief sources of income being whole milk, butter, and cheese. Orchard products also received greater attention. The period was one of transition and change, not merely in the newly developing West and South, but also in the older sections of the United States.

Livestock. The improvement of the common or so-called native cattle was a slow process and did not begin much before 1830. After this date representatives of all the important English breeds were imported, such as Herefords and Guernseys, and especially Durhams or shorthorns. These were crossed with the common cattle of the United States, resulting in a great improvement in size, early maturity, and quality of beef, and also in yield of milk. Some of these came to be known as the "beef breed" and others as the "milk breed."

Among the outstanding inventions which have contributed most to human progress that of breeding better types of plants and animals, and improving them by selection, has been one of the most important. Although the initial steps along both lines had been taken during the colonial era, they were carried forward more energetically and scientifically during this period and resulted in a great improvement in both crops and animal husbandry. The supply of human food was increased and bettered and some of the risk was removed from an essentially speculative business. This was of greater consequence than any other change that has occurred in our agricultural history.

The raising of dairy cows was at first carried on as part of the business of producing beef cattle and draft animals, but gradually attention began to be given to improving the breed of dairy cows, and after 1850 the development of a distinctively dairy type of cattle was sought. By 1860 most of the eastern herds had some improved blood in them, but in the West little progress had as yet been made. That improvement had begun is indicated by the increase in the amount of butter which it was calculated an ordinary cow would produce in a year; in Massachusetts it was estimated at 70 to 100 pounds in 1800, and at 150 pounds in 1850.[7] The increase in

---

[7] Bidwell and Falconer, *op. cit.*, 229, 431. The average for the whole United States was estimated in 1930 at about 200 pounds. In 1937 a famous cow at the University of Illinois College of Agriculture, "Illini Nellie," produced the equivalent in milk of 1500 pounds of butter.

productivity is explained by better management, shelter, and food, as well as by better breeding and selection.

The rise of manufactures and improvements in transportation facilities were bringing about revolutionary changes in the dairy industry, which altered both its regional distribution and its methods. Areas in the neighborhood of cities began to find it more profitable to ship to them their whole milk, whereas butter and cheese were manufactured in districts farther from the markets where they were produced by improved methods. Until 1850 all the butter and cheese were made on the farm, but in the next year the associated system of dairying, known as the American system, was inaugurated by the establishment of the cheese factory, of which twenty-one were built by 1861. New York was the leading dairying state in 1860, producing nearly half the cheese and nearly a quarter of the butter made in the whole country. Her Orange County butter was so superior that this name was adopted as a standard. It remained for a later period, however, to see butter-making taken over by factory methods.

Draft animals. Horses were kept by the well-to-do farmers, at the beginning of this period, "to go to mill, and to church, and for the convenience of the family," but for work on the farm oxen were preferred in the East and mules in the South. An interesting change was taking place, during this period, in the kind of animal power used on the farms in the North. So long as crude and heavy implements were used, such as the old bull-plow, the cart, and the clumsy wooden harrow, oxen were generally preferred, since they were powerful and docile, and could be slaughtered for food after their working days were over. With the introduction of light farm machinery, however, and the general speeding up which came with the railway, these slow and clumsy animals were displaced by horses, which were quicker and more intelligent.

The best draft horses were the Conestoga horses, which were supposed to be descended from some large Flemish horses which the Dutch had brought to New York; these later became famous for their speed and endurance in drawing the stagecoaches and heavy freight wagons between Philadelphia and Pittsburgh. A notable event was the importation into Ohio of the Percheron stallion "Louis Napoleon," from which dates a great improvement in the draft horse.

In the southern states particular attention was given to the raising of mules to supply the cotton plantations. The raising of mules for sale was pretty well confined to Kentucky and Missouri, and most of them found a ready market in the cotton plantations of the South; but some were raised in New Mexico and were driven east with caravans returning from Santa Fe.

Sheep farming. Sheep had been grown on most colonial farms for both mutton and wool, which was coarse but served as raw material for homespun clothing. The finest sheep in Europe were the Spanish merinos, whose exportation was forbidden without the King's permission. But in 1800 Napoleon invaded Spain and the royal flocks were dispersed. Large numbers were shipped to the United States and by 1810 it was estimated that 20,000 had been imported. Just at this time the embargo had cut off the importation of woolen cloth from England; consequently, general attention was directed in the United States to the raising of fine-wool sheep. A decade later Saxony sheep, which were more delicate but whose wool was still finer, were imported. Little success was made in building up pure-bred flocks, but the dispersion of these pure breeds led to the general improvement of the common or native animals.

Sheep husbandry was a highly speculative industry during this period. Incited by high prices for wool which were occasioned first by the restrictions of the embargo and the War of 1812 and later by the protective tariff, eastern farmers had rushed into the business almost to the exclusion of grain-growing and stock-raising. When prices of wool fell, cheaper areas of production were sought and a steady westward movement of sheep-raising and wool-growing took place.

Swine. In no class of domestic animals was there such striking improvement as in swine. Since they come to maturity so quickly, modifications in type are more easily made by selection and breeding than in the case of the more slowly maturing cattle or horses. In the East they were frequently raised in connection with dairying, being fed on skim milk, or near liquor distilleries where they were fed on the mash. After the building of the Erie Canal, western corn-fed pork displaced the eastern product, and hog-raising followed corn production in its westward movement. In the West, where

IMPROVEMENT OF THE HOG. I

The Southern pine-woods hog, which ranged wild in the woods at all seasons, developed fleetness of foot, coarse, large bones, and a thick, hard coat.

land was cheap and labor dear, little care was given to the feeding of hogs. Abundant and cheap food existed for them in the mast of the oak and beech forests, and in the corn which became their staple food after the forests were cleared. Before 1840 but little attention was given to the type of hog used for fattening, and the common hog was "of an ungainly type, with long legs and snout, a sharp back, of a roaming disposition, slow and expensive to fatten." [8] It was known as the "razorback," "prairie rooter," "alligator," and similar names. By 1860 this type had nearly disappeared and its place had been taken by improved breeds. As the numbers increased, pork-packing came to be an important industry, with Cincinnati the packing center until displaced, in 1861, by Chicago.

Laborsaving machinery. The real advance in western farming came

IMPROVEMENT OF THE HOG. II

The Western beech-nut hog shows an improvement, but was coarse, long-legged, large boned, slab-sided, and flab-eared.

after the introduction of laborsaving machines, which were peculiarly adapted for use on the broad, level, and practically stoneless stretches of land in the prairie region. Here was wrought a revolution as upsetting as that produced by the invention of the cotton gin in the South, though it took longer

[8] Bidwell and Falconer, *op. cit.*, 441.

to work out since it affected several crops and was brought about by numerous improvements in many implements. As late as 1830, writes Professor Carver, practically every part of the work of the farm except plowing, harrowing, and drawing loads, was done by hand, that is, with tools which were directed and moved by human muscles. "Small grain was sown broadcast, reaped with a cradle (which was a relatively new invention), and threshed with a flail, or trodden out by horses and oxen. Hay was mown with

IMPROVEMENT OF THE HOG.   III

The improved Suffolk shows the desirable qualities of a hog—small bones, short legs, round barrel, thin coat, ready fattening qualities, and sluggishness.

a scythe, and raked and pitched by hand. Corn was planted and covered by hand, and cultivated mainly with a hoe." With such primitive processes it took from seventy to eighty man-hours to produce one acre of wheat.

Many of these methods and implements showed no change since the times of the Greeks and the Romans. It is surprising that in a country where labor was relatively scarce and expensive improvement should have been delayed so long; but after 1830 progress was rapid. Agricultural machinery and improved implements were invented whose purpose was to save labor and to increase man's productivity rather than the product per acre of the land. By 1860 the farming industry had been revolutionized in every one of the processes just mentioned by the invention and introduction of labor-saving machinery whose motive power was non-human. No period of equal length in the history of agriculture has witnessed such a complete revolution.

The most important invention was that of the iron plow. The plow at the time of the Revolution was essentially of the same form as that of the ancients, with a clumsy frame and a wooden moldboard, covered more or less completely with scraps of sheet iron, a horseshoe, or a discarded hoe blade. The first suggestion of improvement was a cast-iron plow, patented in 1797 by Charles Newbold of New Jersey, who, after spending, as he alleged, his fortune of $30,000 in trying to get it into use, abandoned the attempt, the farmers declaring that iron plows poisoned the soil and prevented the growth of crops. Men like Jefferson and Webster studied the proper shape of the moldboard and directed attention to the need of improvement. It remained for Jethro Wood, of New York, to make the iron plow a practical implement. His improved plow, patented in 1814, was not cast in one piece, like Newbold's, but was made up of three castings joined together by interlocking pieces, so that if a part were broken it could be replaced. By 1830 the improved iron plow was in general use in the East, where it not only reduced the labor required, but promoted higher yields. The iron plow was, however, little better than a wooden one in the sticky western soils. Cast-iron cannot be given a smooth polish and such soils stuck to its pitted surface. This difficulty was solved by John Deere, a blacksmith, who in 1838 made a moldboard and share of sheet iron cut from old saws and bent to shape; a decade later he produced the first all-steel plow, which was a great success. These improved implements permitted a large saving in labor: the wooden plow required two men and four oxen to plow one acre a day; the cast-iron plow required one man and one yoke of oxen or team of horses; the steel plow was still more efficient.

The improvement of the plow, important as it was, would not have been so valuable had it stood alone; implements for further processes must also be provided. For the preparation of the seedbed the old triangular wooden-toothed harrow was supplanted by a hinged harrow with iron, and later with steel, teeth. Cultivating had been done by a hoe or by the shovel plow, but after 1830 specialized implements were introduced. Drill seeding was in general practice in the East by the early 1840's, and by 1860 it had spread to the Midwest. All these implements contributed to the production of larger crops and made the problem of the farmers just so much more acute at harvest time, when the crops must be gathered. Accordingly, inventors next began to work earnestly upon the making of machines for cutting hay and grain, threshing, and performing other processes in the work of harvesting.

Reaping. The substitution after 1803 of the cradle for the sickle, in reaping wheat and other small grains, was a great improvement.[9] The use of the sickle required a stooping position and was extremely fatiguing, so that a reaper could not harvest more than half an acre a day. The cradle scythe was a frame of wood with a row of long curved ribs projecting above and parallel to a broad scythe blade. It was much more efficient and less tiring to work than the sickle. Its great virtue lay in the fact that the cradle acted as a gathering rake and with every swing of the scythe deposited the grain in even piles which could be gathered up easily and quickly by the binders. But the cradle was still a hand tool and did not cut the grain any faster, though it facilitated binding. The average rate of binding was about three acres a day. What was needed was a machine for cutting grain which could be driven by animal power.

Gradually contributions were made by many minds until the successful reaper finally appeared. In the United States two men claimed the distinction of having invented the reaper —Obed Hussey, who obtained a patent in 1833, and Cyrus McCormick, who experimented with his machine even earlier but to whom a patent was issued only in 1834, though his reaper was not a complete success until further improvements were made in 1845. When the reaper was first invented it was thought that it could be used for cutting grass as well as grain, and little distinction was made between reaper and mower. The mowing machine, for hay alone, was, however, also being developed about the same time, the first patent having been granted to William Manning of New Jersey in 1831; but not until about 1854 was there a clear distinction between them.

The common use of the reaper began about 1845, and that of the mower a decade later. Their use was given a great impetus by the success of American machines at the World's Fair in London in 1851 and at the International Exposition at Paris four years later. At the first exhibition an American reaping machine won the medal by cutting a strip of wheat

[9] Bidwell and Falconer, *op. cit.*, 207, 212.

74 yards in length in 70 seconds. The triumph of the American reapers, said the official report at London, "marked a new era in agriculture." At the Paris Exposition a trial of mowing and reaping machines was made; and the trial of reapers had this result in a field of oats: A French machine cut an acre in 71 minutes; an English machine in 66 minutes; and an American machine in 22 minutes.

Mowing hay requires close cutting, which was not achieved by a reaper, so after about 1850 a distinction began to be made. Raking hay is more dependent on the weather than is mowing, so speed in this process is desirable. The horse rake was introduced about 1820 and soon supplanted the hand rake; it performed the work of eight to ten men. The first type was the revolving wooden rake, but by 1860 the sulky wire-tooth rake was rapidly coming into use.

Threshing. But there was another step in the handling of grain before the crop could be marketed, and that was threshing. Down to 1830 most of the grain in the United States was threshed by the wooden flail or trod out on the earthen threshing floor by oxen or horses. With the old-fashioned hand flail a man could thresh in a day from eight to sixteen bushels of grain, depending upon its condition. After it was threshed the grain was separated from the chaff by the crude method of tossing it in the air and letting the breeze blow the chaff away. An improvement came with the introduction of the fanning mill. Many efforts were made to construct a practical threshing machine which would do this work, and numerous machines were invented, some utilizing hand power and some horsepower. The best American machine was that invented by Hiram and John Pitt in 1836. Mechanical threshing rapidly displaced old methods and by 1860 had become the standard practice wherever wheat was grown on a commercial scale. One of these improved machines was entered in a trial of threshing machines at the Paris Exposition in 1855 and swept the field. Of the results a correspondent of the *New York Tribune* wrote: "Six men were set to threshing wheat with flails at the same moment that the different machines commenced operations, and the following were the results of an hour's work:

	Liters	*Bushels*
Six threshers with flails................	36	1.02
Belgian threshing machine...............	150	4.24
French threshing machine...............	250	7.07
English threshing machine.............	410	11.60
American threshing machine............	740	20.94

Effects of farm machinery. The application of machinery
to the work of harvesting marked an epoch in American
agriculture; there was now no practical limit to production
through inability to harvest the crop. In a new country like
the United States, where labor was still scarce and dear,
laborsaving machines were indispensable. The chief characteristics of the American machines were, as they still are,
lightness, simplicity, and cheapness, in all of which qualities
they excelled those of England and Europe.

The saving effected by the use of these improved implements was estimated in the census of 1860 as equal to more
than one-half the former cost of working. The man-hour
requirements in wheat production per acre were reduced from
75 before 1830 to about 35 in 1860. "By the improved plow,
labor equivalent to that of one horse in three is saved. By
means of drills two bushels of seed will go as far as three
bushels scattered broadcast, while the yield is increased six
to eight bushels per acre; the plants come up in rows and
may be tended by horse-hoes.... The reaping machine is a
saving of more than one-third the labor when it cuts and
rakes.... The threshing machine is a saving of two-thirds
on the old hand flail mode.... The saving in the labor of
handling hay in the field and barn by means of horserakes
and horse-hayforks is equal to one-half." But the real gain
to agriculture by the use of these machines cannot be measured merely by noting the increased area which could be
cultivated by a given labor force or by calculating the saving
in labor cost. The advantage consisted rather in the saving of
time, which permitted a large crop to be harvested at the
moment of maturity without loss through delay or exposure.
Except in the case of corn, grain must be harvested within
ten days after it matures or it falls to the ground or is spoiled.
In the West the amount of wheat a farmer raised was deter-

mined by the acreage he could effectively harvest. In 1860 the crops were so large that the entire labor force of the United States would probably have been insufficient to harvest them in season, if the methods of a generation previous had been used.

Scientific agriculture. Among the improvements which were made during this period two at least may be noted. One was the growing attention to rotation of crops and the other was a better appreciation of the value of fertilizer. In England a well-known crop system [10] had rotated turnips, barley, clover, wheat, but in the United States corn was substituted for turnips and served about as well the purposes of furnishing fodder for livestock and of conserving the soil. A widespread American system of rotation, developed in Pennsylvania, was corn, barley or oats, wheat, clover, which with modifications still forms the basis of farm management in many sections today. The other change was the greater use of fertilizers, though it must be said that this was done only in particular districts and was not yet a general practice among ordinary dirt farmers. Indeed, manure was at first regarded as a nuisance, and when too large a pile accumulated it was often said to be a problem whether to move the pile or the barn. Gradually, however, its value came to be appreciated and it was applied to the fields. Artificial fertilizers, such as guano, gypsum, lime, and marl were also used to increase the fertility or improve the soil qualities. Chemical fertilizers were introduced in the 1850's. But the full development of this phase of agriculture had to wait for the application of chemistry and physics to the soil.

The causes for the great advance in agriculture which characterized this period, in spite of the persistence of harmful practices, were several. First, there was the vast breadth of virgin lands, which permitted the use of only the best soils and secured extraordinary response to man's cultivation. In the second place was the high character of the farming class; "the men who tilled the soil here," wrote Francis A. Walker, "were the same kind of men, precisely, as those who filled the professions or engaged in commercial or mechanical pursuits. . . There was then no other

[10] Arthur Young, *The Farmer's Tour,* 1771, II, 156.

country in the world ... where equal mental activity and alertness have been applied to the soil as to trade and industry." A third set of causes comprised the great mechanical inventions, both in agricultural machinery and in transportation, which enormously increased man's ability to produce, harvest, and market the product of the country's expanding farms. In the fourth place, the various educational forces in operation during this period should be noted.

Educating the farmer. The formation of agricultural societies was an important step, for they awakened inquiry, disseminated knowledge, and paved the way for agricultural literature. The first of these was the Society for Promotion of Agriculture, founded in South Carolina in 1785; in the same year was established the Philadelphia Society, which included Franklin and Washington among its members. Washington corresponded with Arthur Young and Sir John Sinclair, leaders in the improvement of agriculture in England, and sought to introduce scientific principles developed there into America. But these early societies were composed of gentlemen farmers, who read learned papers at their meetings, and did not reach the ordinary dirt farmer. It remained for the nineteenth century to develop more practical organizations, whose aim was to act as a forum, to spread information as to innovations by successful farmers, and to encourage better agriculture by holding fairs and offering premiums.

The county fair was originated by Elkanah Watson in 1810 and was made permanent by the Berkshire Agricultural Society, organized to appeal to the average dirt farmer. The county fair differed from the older literary societies in that the aim was education through display of unusually fine crops or cattle or new methods for which prizes were given. By 1860 about 900 county societies were holding fairs. These agricultural fairs were extremely important in disseminating ideas and promoting rivalry, especially in connection with the new agricultural machinery. The plowing and reaping matches rivaled the Roman chariot races in interest and excitement, and served to introduce the machines to the farmers by actual demonstration and also to promote improvements by the manufacturers.

Agricultural journals were a product of the nineteenth century, the first one being *The American Farmer*, founded by John S. Skinner in Baltimore in 1819. American farmers at that time, however, were little given to reading and the early journals had hard sledding. The editor of *The American Farmer* complained in 1831 that "the farmers will neither take an agricultural paper, read it when given to them, nor believe in its contents if by chance they can hear it read." But, in spite of such pessimism, this pioneer was soon followed by a number of others, principally in the Middle West, of which only one, *Prairie Farmer* (Chicago, 1840), has continued publication to date. By 1860 there were about a hundred such papers in existence, with a combined circulation of some 250,000 subscribers. These papers did much to educate the farmers and to spread knowledge of the best practices; they were of even greater practical benefit than the county fairs.

Formal agricultural education belongs to the period after the Civil War, though Michigan State College of Agriculture was opened in 1857, followed by similar colleges in Maryland and Pennsylvania. The still tardier recognition that was accorded agriculture by the federal government is illustrated by the fact that not until 1862 was a Bureau of Agriculture established; between 1839 and 1862 the agricultural reports were printed in the annual report of the commissioner of patents. Agriculture was self-sufficient in more than one sense; farmers did not feel the need of governmental assistance in any form, and were rather skeptical of "book farming."

Conclusion. At the beginning of this period agriculture was for the most part simply self-sufficing, though in the case of some articles, like tobacco, for which there was an export demand, commercial farming had already developed. By 1860 the transition from a self-sufficient economy, in which a farmer produces practically all that he needs, to commercial agriculture, in which he specializes on a money crop and buys most of his supplies with the proceeds, had been generally accomplished. The change was not brought about, however, without some disturbance and friction, for habit, tradition, and ignorance held many farmers to known crops and to accustomed methods of production. But the new transportation agencies, the widening areas of production and of consumption, and better methods of marketing gradually brought about specialization and territorial division of agriculture. In the South cotton was the main crop, and the specialization in this provided a market for western foodstuffs and livestock, in which the West specialized. Eastern agriculture suffered from the competition of cheaper products from the newer lands, but this section made good the loss by developing manufactures, and by altering the character of its agriculture. These changes had been pretty thoroughly completed by 1860.

American farming was still characterized, at least in the newer regions, by the wasteful and exhaustive methods of cropping without fertilizing the land that had prevailed in colonial times. Such wasteful methods were caused partly by the fertility of the soil and the abundance of cheap land, and partly by the unsettled nature of farming and the unwillingness to sink capital in improvements. "It seldom happens," wrote De Tocqueville in 1840, "that an American farmer settles for good upon the land which he occupies; especially in districts of the far west he brings land into tillage in order to sell it again and not to farm it." So long as land was held only as a speculation, in order to sell again, farming could not be brought to a very high state of development. The American farmer of this period has been likened to a miner, who extracts wealth from the soil, but does not restore it. American agriculture has suffered from this fact down to the present time. For many of the farmers of that time, extensive agriculture was more economical than intensive, since capital and labor were scarce, whereas land was plentiful and could be used wastefully. In the East, however, methods had considerably improved by 1860.

CHAPTER XII

THE TRANSPORTATION REVOLUTION

Importance of transportation in the United States. At every period of our history the need for improved means of transportation has been pressing, but this was especially so after the westward movement carried the population beyond the Appalachian Mountains and away from the seacoast and easy water communication with markets. Transportation has been, from the first settlements, the essential condition of the opening up of the continent. As a cause of changes in our industrial and political organization, the extension of markets through betterments in transportation has been even more significant than have improvements in the technique of production.

The growth of cities, the concentration of industry, large-scale production, foreign trade, the development of modern economic and social life have been brought about by improvements in transportation. To the same factor is due the political success of a democratic government in the vast area of the United States, for the nation might have disintegrated had it not been closely bound together by economic ties and had not the growing distances been shrunk by quicker communication. The political necessity of interstate communication was emphasized by the Revolution and the separatist tendencies of the rapidly growing western territory.

The development of transportation in the United States advanced by stages, each of which marked an improvement over that which preceded. Down to the end of the eighteenth century land transportation was chiefly on horseback or by pack train on poor roads. The first improvement was the turnpikes, whose greatest development belonged to the period between 1790 and 1815. Before this movement had more than fairly gained headway, the steamboat was invented and introduced on our rivers and greatly stimulated the use of our natural waterways. At once it was perceived that if these could be joined by canals the country could be united by a network of waterways. This period may be said to have continued from 1815 to 1850. About the latter date railroad building, which had commenced twenty years before, set in on a considerable scale and railroads began to threaten the supremacy of water transportation; by 1860 they had begun to supersede it.

The turnpike period. The roads which existed in the United States at the close of the eighteenth century must have been poor even according to the low standards of that time, for not only English travelers, but also those of other nationalities and our own citizens, testified to the bad character of the highways. According to McMaster,[1] there were no bridges over the great rivers in 1784, roads were bad, and all journeys were made on horseback or in stagecoaches or boats. Weld,[2] writing of a journey from Baltimore to Washington in 1795, stated that "the roads are so exceedingly bad that a carriage will sometimes sink so deep as to defy the utmost exertions of the strongest horse to draw it forwards; and in some parts that would be otherwise totally impassable, causeways constructed of trees are thrown across the road; but these frequently break asunder and constantly expose a traveler to the most imminent danger. The bridges built across the creeks are equally perilous, being performed of a few loose boards that totter while a carriage passes over them." The construction and maintenance of these early roads were left to local authorities, who had neither interest in nor capacity for their development. Gradually, however, the demands of farmers for better transportation to markets, and of town dwellers for the cheapening of agricultural produce thereby made possible, together with the prospect of profits to inventors, led to improvement.

A long step forward was taken when turnpikes were built in place of the poorly constructed and disconnected local roads. These were built by private stock companies as continuous lines for through traffic, the cost being met by tolls

---

[1] J. B. McMaster, *History of the People of the United States* (7 vols., New York, 1883-1914), I, 44.

[2] Isaac Weld, *Travels Through the States of North America* (Philadelphia, 1800), 47. See also the accounts given in Bogart and Thompson, *Readings*, 240-243.

levied upon all who used them. The first one of importance was the Lancaster-Philadelphia turnpike, some 62 miles long, which was completed in 1794 at a cost of $7,500 a mile, and which connected a rich farming region and a growing city. The success of this road led to a craze for turnpike construction. In the next thirty years Pennsylvania chartered 86 companies which built 2200 miles of road. In New York 135 companies completed some 1500 miles by 1811, and in New England 180 companies had been chartered by 1810. The next step was to build toll bridges, which were financed in the same manner.

In spite of the great improvement in transportation effected by these new routes, the cost of moving freight on land was still very high, as compared with that by water. It cost about 33 per cent of the value of goods to convey them from Philadelphia to Kentucky by land, and only 4 to 4½ per cent from Illinois to New Orleans by water. On the average it cost about $10 a ton for every 100 miles to transport goods by land; articles which could not stand these rates, as flour and grain, were prevented from reaching a market unless they found an outlet by water. The freight per ton between Philadelphia and Pittsburgh by land was about $100, but from Philadelphia to Europe it was only $10. These rates included the tolls, which in many cases were extremely high; thus for a one-horse cart there was collected in New York .6 cent per mile, in Pennsylvania and Maryland 1.25 cents, and in New Jersey 3 cents.[3]

Government aid. These roads and turnpikes were for the most part constructed by private companies, though often with state aid, but now the federal government was urged to lend its assistance. In 1808 Albert Gallatin, the Secretary of the Treasury, made to Congress a report on roads, canals, harbors, and rivers, in which he proposed a comprehensive scheme of internal improvements by the federal government, to cost about $20,000,000. The net result of the ensuing agitation was the construction by the federal government of the Cumberland Road or "National Pike" from Cumberland, Maryland, to Vandalia, Illinois. The first

[3] B. H. Meyer (Ed.), *History of Transportation in the United States before 1860* (Washington, 1917), 68-70.

stretch to Wheeling, then in Virginia, was begun about 1811, and completed in 1817. The cost of the road to Wheeling was nearly $13,000 per mile. Further work carried it almost due west through Zanesville, Columbus, Indianapolis, and Vandalia, which was reached in 1838. This marked the end of the federal construction, for the last appropriation was made in that year, and the "Old Pike" petered out in a dirt road at this point.

[After Fite]

THE CUMBERLAND ROAD

Some idea of the wretched character of these early roads can be obtained from the specifications in the contract for building the extension through Ohio and Indiana in 1829: all stumps must be cleared from the middle 30 feet of the 80-foot road. This proved too expensive and it was modified to require that "all trees over 18 inches in diameter be cut not exceeding 15 inches from the surface" and be rounded and trimmed so as not to be an obstacle to carriages. On the remaining 50 feet the stumps were not to exceed one and one-half feet in height.[4]

Immediately upon its opening a flow of traffic swept over this great highway and it became the most important thoroughfare between East and West. The historian of this road states[5] that "As many as twenty four-horse coaches have been counted in line at one time on the road, and large, broad-wheeled wagons, covered with white canvas stretched over bows, laden with merchandise and drawn by six Conestoga horses, were visible all the day long at every point, and many times until late in the evening, besides innumerable caravans of horses, mules, cattle, hogs and sheep."

[4] S. Dunbar, *History of Travel in America* (4 vols., Indianapolis, 1917), II, 718.
[5] Thos. B. Searight, *The Old Pike* (Uniontown, Pa., 1894), 16.

Congress entered readily upon this policy of internal improvements, not merely for the economic purpose of obtaining better and cheaper transportation, but for political reasons also in order to unite the western country with the eastern; a minor consideration was the greater speed and safety of the mails.

Plank roads. Before discussing waterways and railroads, it is desirable to describe an improved form of road which seems to have been almost peculiarly American. This was the plank road. Introduced first in Canada in 1835, it soon spread to the United States, where it was declared "the most valuable improvement since McAdam's, and one superior to his in many localities." The method of laying a plank road was to embed parallel stringers in the earth about four feet apart, and across them to lay planks, eight feet long and three or four inches thick. Such a road cost about $1200 to $1500 a mile. Most of them were built by private companies, which charged tolls to the users. These roads were a great improvement over the old dirt roads and even over the macadamized turnpikes. They were called the "farmers' railroads," and as late as 1850 a writer in *De Bow's Review* advocated the building of plank roads rather than railroads on the ground that they were better, cheaper, and less complicated. Several thousand miles of these roads were built, especially in the West and South; here they proved of the greatest utility in opening up and developing the newer sections of the country which the railroads did not reach, but they went out of use as the latter were extended. They are not to be confused with the "corduroy" roads, made of logs thrown across the dirt roads and used to bridge swampy and wet places, which were commonly employed in the eighteenth and early nineteenth centuries. These latter were wretched makeshifts in a period of hasty and unscientific road making.

The steamboat period. Meanwhile efforts were being made to utilize better the navigable waters instead of building expensive land routes. As early as 1783 Oliver Evans began experimenting with the application of steam to the propulsion of wagons and boats, but not until 1804 did he successfully carry out his plans. Better claims for priority in successful steamboat building were advanced by John Fitch and James Rumsey, about the same time. Before the end of the century other successful experiments had been made by Nathan Read at Salem, by William Longstreet on the Savannah, by Elijah Ormsbee at Providence, by Samuel Morey on the Connecticut, and by John Stevens on the Hudson. Defects in the engines, in the size of the paddle wheels, and in other particulars prevented any of these inventions from becoming commercially profitable, and the honor of first making the steamboat a practical success was reserved

FULTON'S CLERMONT

When the *Clermont* started on her epoch-making trip up the Hudson in August, 1807, skeptical crowds lined the shore to see "Fulton's Folly." Fulton himself wrote: "The morning I left New York there were not perhaps thirty persons in the city who believed that the boat would even move one mile per hour, or be of the least utility; and, while we were putting off from the dock, . . . I heard a number of sarcastic remarks." While the speed was slow, the practicability of the steamboat had been successfully demonstrated and a new era in water transportation introduced.

for Robert Fulton. In August, 1807, he sailed the *Clermont* from New York to Albany, 150 miles, in 32 hours, and back in 30 hours.

When the *Clermont* started on her epoch-making trip up the Hudson, skeptical crowds lined the shore to see "Fulton's Folly." Fulton himself wrote: [6] "The morning I left New York there were not perhaps thirty persons in the city who believed that the boat would move even one mile per hour, or be of the least utility." The boat was 130 feet long, and was provided with side wheels 15 feet in diameter, with buckets 4 feet wide. Clumsy as the vessel was, it demonstrated the practicability of steam navigation, and secured

[6] See his letters in Bogart and Thompson, *Readings*, 250-51.

for its owners, Fulton and Livingston, a monopoly of the navigable water of New York State for twenty years.

Steamboats on western waters. Steamboats now began to be built for general use: the summer of 1809 saw one on Lake Champlain, another on the Raritan, and a third on the Delaware. Two years later the steamboat was introduced on the Ohio, and the era of steam as applied to water transportation had fairly begun. In the early days the long river journey down the Mississippi with no hope of a return cargo, the danger to the cargo by reason of the change to the hotter climate of the lower river, the likelihood of finding the market at New Orleans glutted, and finally the long sea voyage to a more distant market, made the shipment of produce down the Mississippi system a hazardous and often losing venture. These trips were made by flatboats or keelboats. The former were broken up at the journey's end and the lumber sold, but the keelboats could be propelled upstream with much labor. If the wind was right sails might be used; otherwise the boat must be poled or even towed by human muscle. Small wonder that the iron, salt, and molasses brought upstream in this laborious fashion were expensive and that the early western settlements were isolated. The steamboat promised relief from all these difficulties.

The *New Orleans,* built at Pittsburgh because of the lumber and iron manufactures established there, descended the Ohio and Mississippi in 1812, but was unable to return against the swift current of those rivers. Improvements were made, however, both in the shape of the hull, the character of the engine, and the paddle wheels, so that the *Enterprise,* the fourth of the western steamboats, was able in 1815 to make the trip upstream in flood water from New Orleans to Louisville in twenty-five days. Of this achievement Salmon P. Chase wrote [7] that it was "an event of more momentous consequences to the West than the issues of a thousand battles." The following year the *Washington,* built by Henry Shreve, with innovations in structure and engine, finally solved the riddle of the shallow, shifting western rivers. Instead of the usual clumsy low-pressure engine Shreve utilized

---

[7] *Statutes of Ohio and of the Northwest territory, adopted or enacted from 1788 to 1833, inclusive* (3 vols., Cincinnati, 1833-35), I, 11.

the small, light, but powerful high-pressure engine, which was placed on the deck and connected directly with the crank-shaft of the two side wheels.

With these events began the era of successful steam navigation of the Mississippi and its tributaries. Its full realization was delayed for a few years by the grant by Louisiana to Livingston and Fulton of a monopoly of navigation for steam vessels on the lower Mississippi, and by conflicts over patents covering the improvements made by various inventors. From 1811 to 1816, inclusive, only seven steamboats were built on western waters, but in the next year a suit was brought in the Louisiana courts to break this monopoly. Before this could be heard the Supreme Court had decided in the case of *Gibbons* v. *Ogden*, in 1824, that the waters of the Hudson, and hence of all other navigable rivers in the United States, were a heritage of the people and could not be monopolized by any state or individual.

Navigation was now made free to all, subject only to federal legislation, and a great impetus was given to the building of steamboats. The number on the western rivers increased rapidly, and it was estimated that there were 200 by 1829, 450 by 1842—the tonnage of which was greater than that of all the steamships in the British Empire—and over 1000 by 1860. So long as flatboats and barges were used, the trip downstream from Pittsburgh to New Orleans took a month, while the trip upstream against the current consumed four months. The steamboat made it in thirty days, and this reduction in time increased the number of trips.

Statistics give a very inadequate idea of the picturesque river steamboat phase of American transportation; it must be sought in such books as Mark Twain's *Life on the Mississippi*. Here are pictured the dangers from shoals and bars, from submerged trees, from boiler explosions, and other accidents, which in the early days destroyed two out of every five steamboats. Here, too, are portrayed the human types that were developed on the rivers—pilots, rivermen, gamblers, showboat players, and others. It was a bold, rough, crude, but romantic and vigorous stage of commercial evolution.

The Great Lakes also witnessed the advent of the steamboat during this period, the first one being built on Lake

Ontario in 1816; three years later the *Walk-in-the-Water*, the first steamer on Lake Erie, was launched. The building of the Erie and Ohio canals stimulated the lake trade, which, however, did not grow rapidly until about 1850, the tonnage on all the lakes increasing from 3500 in 1820 to 75,000 in 1840, and 470,000 in 1860. Lake cities like Cleveland and Detroit sprang into being and Chicago, with a population of 109,000 in 1860, already gave assurance of her later marvelous growth.

The great economic significance of the steamboat lay in the fact that it rendered available at once, without any expense of construction, a vast system of navigable waters, which permitted easy, cheap, and rapid transportation. This was of enormous importance to the new regions which had access to the rivers. But the farmers in western New York, in northern Ohio and Indiana, in Michigan, and other sections of the country which were not situated on navigable streams did not share these benefits and clamored insistently for better means of communication, especially with the East. In addition to the economic weakness there was also political danger in the situation. The country was divided into three strongly marked sections—the East, the South, and the West —and the economic bonds holding them together, especially those between the East and West, seemed at times almost inadequate to overcome the separatist tendencies which showed themselves from time to time.

The canal period. The first answer on a large scale to the demand for improved means of water communication was made by New York State in building the Erie Canal, connecting Lake Erie with the Hudson River. Gallatin named six canals which had been constructed prior to 1807 at a cost of over $10,000,000, but they had been short ones. Now began the construction of grand trunk canals, which connected important bodies of water and provided for through traffic. Of these the most successful was the Erie Canal. The actual work of building the canal began in 1817, and within eight years it was finished. The completion of the "big ditch" was celebrated with appropriate ceremonies at Buffalo, from which point a fleet of boats proceeded to New York, where their arrival was the signal for a fresh outburst of enthusiasm.

A flask of water from Lake Erie was poured into New York Bay, and the marriage of the inland waters with those of the ocean was declared to be consummated.[8] The cost of the canal was about $7,000,000, but the revenues from the tolls in the first nine years more than covered this sum; by 1841 the tolls amounted to $2,000,000 for the year.

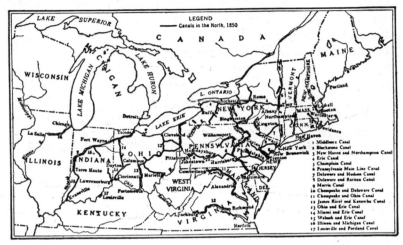

CANALS IN THE NORTH, 1850

Effects of the Erie Canal.

Still more important than the financial returns to the state were the economic advantages of the canal to the community at large. Wherever the canal touched a waterway a thriving town sprang up, as at Syracuse, Rochester, and Utica. Buffalo and Albany, the terminals, grew still more rapidly, and New York, the leading port of the United States, shot farther ahead of her rivals, Boston and Philadelphia. Branch canals were built connecting the main canal with Champlain, Ontario, and Seneca lakes, and these stimulated a vigorous trade. The number of vessels on Lake Champlain before the canal was opened was only 20, but a year later there were 218. Previous to the construction

---

[8] The question might be raised as to why the main canal was not run from Albany to Oswego on Lake Ontario, to which a branch canal was later built, instead of to Buffalo on Lake Erie. In answer it may be said that western New York offered a richer hinterland; that future traffic could more easily be diverted from the rival Montreal; and that the obstacle to western trade posed by Niagara Falls could be avoided.

of the canal the cost of transporting freight from Buffalo to New York City was $100 a ton, and the ordinary time of passage was twenty days; most of the wheat of western New York was consequently floated down the Susquehanna to Baltimore to avoid this long and expensive haul, while that from the central section went down the Delaware to Philadelphia. On the opening of the Erie Canal the cost of freighting from Buffalo to New York fell to $5.00 a ton and the time of transit was reduced to six days, thus diverting much of the western traffic to the new route.

PASSENGER PACKET AND FREIGHT BOATS, ERIE CANAL

On the slow, but easily moving canal packet boat, travel was decidedly more comfortable than in the jolting stage coach. Seated on the cabin roof the passengers exchanged views on the scenery or the topics of the day until the cry of "low bridge" drove them down. Berths were arranged along the sides within and partitioned off by curtains. An ordinary freight boat is also shown.

Nor were the effects confined to New York State alone; the entire western lake district had now obtained a new outlet for its produce and much that previously went down the Mississippi to New Orleans was shipped through Buffalo at greatly reduced rates. Freight rates between Ohio and the seaboard were steadily lowered until they were about one-tenth the former figures. The result was beneficial to the farmers, both as producers and as consumers. In 1824 corn was sold in Cincinnati for 8 cents a bushel, wheat for 25 cents, and flour for $1.25 a barrel; after the opening of the canal these commodities brought in double or treble to the western farmers, while at the same time the prices of those eastern manufactures which the farmers bought were lowered.

The building of the Erie Canal had established an economic bond between the East and the West, and had suddenly opened up a profitable trade between them. For

passenger travel, too, the canal packet boats proved very
popular; Horace Greeley stated, with journalistic exaggeration, that he traveled on the Erie Canal from Albany to
Buffalo, for "a cent and a half a mile, a mile and a half an
hour." Inadequate as these facilities were, they marked an
improvement over the jolting stagecoach. It is almost impossible to overemphasize the importance of the Erie Canal
and its far-reaching effects on the economic development of
that time. The change effected in transportation was much
more momentous than the early railroad building, for it
was more immediately revolutionary.

Other canals. The success of this undertaking led to a
mania for canal building and other "internal improvements,"
as they were called, which was greatest in Pennsylvania,
Massachusetts, Maryland, Virginia, Ohio, Indiana, and
Michigan. The diversion of the western commerce to New
York City threatened the prosperity of Philadelphia, Boston,
and Baltimore, and at once the states in which these cities
were situated began to plan works to compete with the Erie
Canal. Merchants of Philadelphia pointed out that it cost
them more to send goods by land 150 miles to central Pennsylvania than it did New Yorkers to send similar goods by
water 750 miles to central Ohio. Pennsylvania therefore
acted to assist her merchants and between 1826 and 1834
constructed between Philadelphia and Pittsburgh a remarkable and unique canal system, with a portage railway over the
the Alleghenies which conveyed the loaded canal boats without
transshipment of cargo. This cost more than the Erie Canal
—$10,000,000—and was not so successful as it tapped a less
productive region, but it saved to Philadelphia some of the
trade which otherwise would have gone to New York. Massachusetts appointed a commission to inquire into the possibility of cutting a canal from Boston to the Hudson River,
in order to divert some of the western trade which came
through the Erie Canal, instead of having it go down the
Hudson River. This was found to be impracticable, however, and Boston suffered a serious loss of trade until the
Boston and Albany Railroad made western connections in
1841. By the time Maryland was ready to act, railroads had
attracted favorable attention as an improved method of trans-

portation, and Baltimore was quick to seize upon this method of reaching the western territory by beginning the construction in 1828 of the first railroad, the Baltimore and Ohio.

It was in the western states, however, with their long distances, lack of roads, and great areas without access to natural waterways, that canals were of the greatest economic significance. The opening of the Erie Canal was accordingly the signal for similar improvements in several of these states. The most important projects were those to connect the lakes with the Ohio and Mississippi rivers, for by this means through communication with either New York City or New Orleans was obtained for all the interior country served by the canals. Ohio built two such canals, the Ohio and Erie Canal between Cleveland and Portsmouth, started in 1825 and completed in 1832, and the Miami and Erie Canal between Toledo and Cincinnati, started in 1833 and completed in 1845, both joining Lake Erie and the Ohio River. The heyday of these canals was between 1845 and 1857.

The effect of these canals in stimulating production as well as in diverting trade from its old routes was immediate; by 1835 there was shipped from Ohio to New York by canal and lake the equivalent of 543,815 bushels of wheat and 2,500,000 staves, and these shipments steadily grew in subsequent years. Until the opening of the Miami and Erie Canal the northwestern part of the state was almost a wilderness, and "before the completion of the canal in 1845 not a single bushel of grain nor a single barrel of pork was exported from this region; by 1846 over 125,000 barrels of flour and almost 2,000,000 bushels of grain were sent through the canal to the northern market." [9]

Not merely was the land opened up, but the products of the forests and the mines also found a market. At the same time the western farmer was enabled to obtain better prices for his goods: products, which before had glutted the local market, could now be sent to distant points where they were in greater demand. "The cash value of wheat," wrote the Ohio canal commissioners, "which forms a principal staple for exportation, has been advanced in the vicinity of the canals

---

[9] E. L. Bogart, *Internal Improvements and State Debt in Ohio* (New York, 1924), 86.

nearly one hundred per cent, while many articles of importation, comprising some of the most important necessaries of life, have been much reduced in price." The Ohio settler could now sell his grain and livestock at higher prices and purchase his axes, plows, and other implements and manufactured goods for a fraction of what he had formerly paid. These facts had a powerful effect in stimulating the settlement of the West, which was now assured profitable markets and communication with the seaboard.

The other western states soon followed the example of Ohio. Indiana constructed the Wabash and Erie (1832–43), which ran from Evansville on the Ohio River to the Ohio state line near Defiance where it joined the Miami and Erie Canal and so found an outlet to Lake Erie at Toledo. This state also built the White Water Canal. Illinois, still largely a wilderness, built the Illinois and Michigan Canal (1836–48), and Wisconsin and Michigan projected plans far beyond their needs or financial ability. The total canal mileage in the United States was 3700 in 1850, when building ceased. The southern states undertook far less in the way of canal building as they were well supplied with navigable streams, but instead put their money into state banks which were to supply to the expanding cotton industry the credit needed to buy land and slaves.

Internal improvements by the states. When the demand for internal improvements became urgent, the people turned to the states for assistance in carrying out the plans. The reasons for invoking state aid were several. In the first place, as we have seen, the federal government, which had undertaken willingly enough the work of improving the means of communication, had been estopped from continuing it by constitutional objections. But private capital was not equal to the task of carrying out such large enterprises as were now being planned. Even if it existed in large enough amount, which was doubtful, the projects were too large and the returns too remote to warrant an individual's risking his whole capital. While these works of public improvement might have been entrusted to corporations, there was the feeling, in addition to a distrust of corporate management, that many improvements should be made that might not be commercially profitable, and that the state alone could undertake these. As a matter of fact, few of the canals earned any profits. Moreover, the state had perpetual life and, with its high credit, could borrow the necessary capital on much better terms than could private individuals. It seemed eminently fitting, therefore, that the state governments should undertake the work of internal improvements. But there were some additional forces which should be mentioned, which explain the willingness of the state legislatures to enter upon this work.

The people of the whole country, particularly of the West, were insistent upon having improvements of every sort, and especially better means of transportation. Most of the state constitutions adopted during this period contained either directions or permissions to the legislature "to encourage internal improvements within the state." The federal government, though it had withdrawn from the work directly, gave assistance to the states in land and money: it donated a percentage of all sales of public lands to the states for this purpose and distributed among them the surplus revenue of the federal government in 1837. Counties and municipalities and even individuals gave donations of land and money, and clamored for local improvements. Finally, the success of the Erie Canal, the commercial rivalry of the Atlantic ports, the easy method of obtaining money by borrowing instead of by taxation, and the speculative fever of the period, led the legislatures to embark on enterprises far beyond the needs or means of the people at that time.

The magnitude of the work of internal improvements undertaken by the states may perhaps best be shown by the increase in state indebtedness. Up to 1820 the states had incurred practically no liabilities, but beginning with that year their debts began to grow: in 1820 these were almost $13,000,000; in 1830, over $26,000,000; and in 1835, over $66,000,000. During the next five years they trebled, reaching $170,000,000 in 1838, and $200,000,000 in 1840. Practically all this money went into internal improvements—roads, canals, railroads, and banks.

It is evident that this enormous expenditure of funds meant a large investment of capital. But where were these huge sums to be obtained? Little capital indeed was raised by taxation; practically all was borrowed, half at home, and half of it from foreign capitalists. The extent to which foreign capital was being invested in the United States, and domestic capital and labor were being applied to the work of developing the West, is well illustrated by the state of our foreign trade. During the decade 1830 to 1840 the merchandise imports exceeded the exports by about $160,-000,000, while in spite of our agricultural pre-eminence we imported over 5½ million bushels of wheat during the same period. In other words, we were so engrossed in the work of internal improvements that we did not even take the time or the labor to raise all our own food. The high credit then enjoyed by the American states, which had been greatly enhanced by the payment of the national debt in 1833, enabled them to borrow these enormous sums abroad, and especially in England, where capital had been accumulating, at comparatively moderate rates of interest. Ex-President Jackson in 1839 estimated that $200,000,000 was due from states and corporations to creditors in Europe, on which the annual interest charge was about $12,000,000.

The crisis of 1837 halted the work of internal improvements. As soon as the bubble of speculation and high prices was pricked, it was clear that many of the enterprises were premature and unnecessary. Most of them were extravagantly, if not corruptly, managed, while hundreds of thousands of dollars had been sunk in absolutely useless undertakings. When the debts, so easily contracted, began to press, several of the states suspended payments. Mississippi and Florida took advantage of a legal technicality to repudiate their loans; Arkansas, which had received only 25 per cent of the face value of the bonds sold, refused to pay; Michigan scaled her debt down from a little over $4,000,000 to about $2,000,000, claiming damages in having been paid worthless bank notes for her bonds; while five other states— New York, Pennsylvania, Maryland, Indiana, and Illinois —after a difficult struggle, managed to pay in full or in large part. The demand on the part of foreign creditors for payment, together with the unwillingness on the part of the other states to be branded with the defaulting states as "repudiators," led to a movement, which culminated in 1842, to have the federal government assume all the state debts, as had been done in 1790; but nothing came of the agitation.

The works already built were sold by most of the states, and these now withdrew from the business of supplying railroads and canals; New York, Ohio, and Illinois alone of the states retained all their public works. The changed attitude of the people regarding the advisability of state enterprises found expression in the inclusion of provisions in practically all the state constitutions adopted after this period, prohibiting the use of state funds or credit for internal improvements. Having failed in the business once, the states were to be debarred from further attempts along the same line. Accordingly, when the development of railroads increased at this time, the successive withdrawal of the federal government and the failure of the state governments in this work of internal improvement left the work of railroad construction to the enterprise of private individuals and corporations. These proceeded more cautiously after the panic, and made a better record for their investors than the states had for the taxpayers; they were fortunate, too, in taking over the task of building railroads after the costly experimental stage had been passed.

The railroad period. The early history of railroads in the United States is closely connected with the commercial rivalry of the seaboard cities in the race for western markets. Baltimore had taken the lead with the opening of the National Road in 1817, but New York had completely outdistanced her with the Erie Canal in 1825, and Philadelphia had maintained second place. Baltimore and even more Boston were debarred by geography from reaching the West by canal, and they therefore turned eagerly to the railroad as a means of regaining their lost trade.

The first railroad in the United States was the Baltimore and Ohio, begun in 1828 and opened for traffic on a short stretch in 1830, although the Quincy tramway, used for transporting stone to the Bunker Hill monument, and a couple of gravity roads in the coal regions of Pennsylvania, had anticipated it shortly. Horsepower and sails were used at first as a motive power on the Baltimore and Ohio, and not until after eighteen months of experimentation was steam finally decided upon. For the next two decades the development of railroads advanced rather slowly, for the early builders had many problems to solve and their work proceeded by trial and error. These early roads were built out from the centers of population, especially near Philadelphia, New York, Boston, and Baltimore, in order to reach as large a tributary territory as possible. By 1840 the railway mileage of the country had reached 2818 miles, but most of the roads were disconnected short lines, similar to the early electric railways. The Charleston and Hamburg railroad, which was 137 miles in length, was the longest line under one management in the world when it was opened for traffic in 1830.

The construction of these early roads was necessarily experimental and mistakes were frequently made, some of which proved very costly to the investors. The first rails were wooden beams, placed lengthwise or end to end, and bolted to granite or wooden piles. To protect the wooden rails from wear, a strap of iron was nailed on the upper surface, but this had an unfortunate habit of coming loose and curling up at the end; trains were frequently derailed by such a "snake - head." An important improvement was the substitution of iron rails for this transitional type, which began in the United States about 1844. This permitted heavier loads and greater speed, both of which were made necessary by the existence in the United States of bulky, heavy freight and long hauls.

English locomotives were imported at first, but when they were found to be too heavy and otherwise unsuited to American conditions, American engineers began to build their own. The first steam locomotive in this country, of which there is a reliable record, which carried people on a track, was built by John Stevens at Hoboken in 1820, but this was purely experimental. The first American-built locomotive used practically was the *Best Friend*, which was put in operation on the Charleston and Hamburg railroad in 1830. The same year Peter Cooper's engine, *Tom Thumb*, was introduced on the Baltimore and Ohio, which now turned definitely to steam as a motive power. In 1831 the principle of the swivel truck was applied to both passenger cars and locomotives, so that they could round curves more easily. A decade passed before locomotives were fitted with cabs.

Train of 1832. Reproduced at World's Fair, 1893.

Original methods attended also the construction of railway cars. At first stagecoach bodies were placed on flanged wheels, but gradually the American type of passenger car, with end doors and a central aisle, was developed. Different gauges were adopted by the various roads, ranging from four feet, three inches on the Delaware and Hudson to six feet on the Erie. This lack of uniformity necessitated transshipment of freight, since cars could not pass from one road to the other. As the through freight and passenger business developed, it became necessary to agree upon a uniform gauge, and in the fifties the "standard" gauge of four feet, eight and one-half inches began to be adopted; but there were still eleven different ones in 1861.

Owing to causes already enumerated, railroad building was left in the hands of private individuals or corporations, especially the latter. For these novel, untried, and risky enterprises the corporation with limited liability was well adapted, and the financing of the railroads was materially aided by the development of this form of business organization. Indeed, it may be said that without the corporation it would have been impossible for private capital to have financed the building of the railroads. In 1845 there were not half a dozen men in the United States who were worth more than $2,000,000, but the Baltimore and Ohio cost $20,000,000, the New York Central $25,000,000, the Pennsylvania $25,000,000, and the Erie $30,000,000. To obtain these sums it was necessary to pool the savings of many do-

mestic investors, and to offer attractive securities to foreign
lenders. For these purposes the bonds and stocks of private
corporations were admirably suited. To make the charters of
these companies more attractive banking privileges or exclusive monopoly were often granted.

In spite of these favors difficulty was at first experienced
in obtaining capital, owing to ignorance, prejudice, and the
opposition of vested interests. Opposition took various forms:
doctors warned of danger of concussion of the brain from
traveling at a speed of 15 to 20 miles an hour; farmers were
told that the sparks from the engines would set their hay and
buildings on fire; and that the noise would prevent the cows
from giving milk; officials refused to permit meetings to
promote railroads to be held in public buildings; and ministers condemned them as a device of the devil "to lead
immortal souls down to hell." These are illustrated by an
incident related by Senator Oliver H. Smith of Indiana.[10]
His opponent in the campaign of 1826 avowed himself in
favor of the newfangled device, saying, "'I tell you, fellow
citizens, that in England they run the cars 30 miles an hour,
and they will yet be run at a higher speed in America.'
This was enough.... An old fellow standing by me bawled
out: 'You are crazy, or do you think we are all fools; a man
could not live a moment at that speed.' The day was mine."

But more difficult to overcome than popular distrust was
the hostility of vested interests, such as the turnpike and
bridge companies, stage lines, canals, ferries, and innkeepers.
In New York, where the Erie Canal was a state enterprise
and competition was not desired, the legislature prohibited
any railroad from carrying freight; in 1844 the law was
amended to permit the carriage of freight when the canal
was closed, but not until 1851 were the railroads freed from
these restrictions. In spite of opposition, however, capital was
subscribed and the roads were built; American and foreign
capital was adequate for the task and by 1860 over $1,250,-
000,000 had been invested in railroads.

State aid to railroads. Although the railroads were built
primarily by private capital, and the states did not engage
directly in the construction of railroads, they gave valuable

[10] *Early Indiana Trails; and Sketches* (Cincinnati, 1858), 80.

assistance by subscriptions to stocks, loans of state credit, and guarantee of railroad securities. Every region and community was anxious to obtain the benefit of railroad connections and clamored for their encouragement. Ohio in 1837 authorized "a loan of credit by the State of Ohio to Railroad Companies," amounting to one-third of the capital, provided the other two-thirds had been otherwise subscribed, while Indiana went still further in permitting railroad corporations to issue

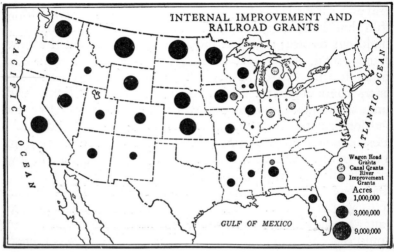

[From Hibbard, *History of Public Land Policies*, p. 268. Period, 1823-89]

paper money to pay for labor or material. The national government was also called upon for assistance, which it refused to give directly but found a way to bestow by making lavish land grants to the states, which were promptly passed on to the railroads. The first of these land grants was a gift by the federal government to the states of Illinois, Mississippi, and Alabama of alternate sections six miles on each side of the proposed Illinois Central Railroad from Chicago to Mobile. Similar gifts were made to Michigan, Wisconsin, Iowa, Missouri, Arkansas, Louisiana, and Florida. By 1861 there had been granted for internal improvements, mostly railroads, over 30,000,000 acres.

Although these methods succeeded in stimulating railroad building they prevented any orderly development in accordance with actual needs and resulted in speculation and extravagance. Railroads were built hastily and cheaply, in advance of traffic demands, in order to obtain the land grants, and then were sold to their stronger competitors or went into bankruptcy. Many financiers paid more attention to railroad securities than to solid construction or efficient service, and by stock manipulation and other shady practices lined their own pockets at the expense of the stockholders. Men who had constructed roads with their own capital could not fail to object to being forced into ruinous competition with these bankrupt roads, but the undeveloped West clamored for transportation facilities at any cost or by any method. The rampant individualism of the times was not restrained by social or long-view considerations, and each district and generation sought to realize its own immediate aims without regard to the future.

Railroad building. As a result of the demands of commerce and of the public encouragement thus given, the railway net spread rapidly through the United States. For a while railroads were regarded primarily as feeders to the lakes and rivers, or as connecting links between the lakes and the Atlantic seaboard, but gradually they developed a serious rivalry to the older transportation agencies. The carriage of coal over the Reading Railroad in competition with the Schuylkill Canal, and of flour over the New York Central in competition with the Erie Canal, showed the economic possibilities of the railway in the solution of the problems of cheap freight movements. In 1840 there were only 2818 miles of railroad as against 1076 miles of canal, but during the decade 1840–50 building was rapid, especially in New England and the middle states, and by 1850 there were 9021 miles of railroad in the country. In the next decade the middle and south Atlantic states developed their transportation systems on much the same lines as they exist at present, while the then western states, between the Alleghenies and the Mississippi, entered upon an era of rapid construction. Through lines were now projected by farsighted railway promoters in order to reach the mid-continental traffic. New York was connected with Chicago in 1853, and the following year the Mississippi was reached. In 1855 St.

Louis was given through rail connections with New York, and the building of lines into the Northwest was begun, one of which reached the Missouri River in 1858.

It must not be thought, however, that the South sat idly by while this development was taking place in the North. In 1845 a convention was held at Memphis to discuss the building of through railroads from Savannah, Charleston, Wilmington, and Richmond on the coast to New Orleans, Vicksburg, and Memphis on the Mississippi River and to Nashville on the Cumberland. But, in spite of grandiose plans, Chattanooga, on the Tennessee River, was the western-most point in 1850, when it was connected with Atlanta.[11] Ten years later the Mississippi River had been touched at Memphis and Vicksburg, but the connections at these points were poor. The western trade was lost by the South, which was now more isolated than ever. The total railroad mileage of the country in 1860 was 30,626, or more than three times what it had been ten years before.

Economic effects of the railroads. The economic results flowing from this introduction of a quicker transportation agency and from its rapid spread throughout the eastern half of the United States were startling in range and intensity. While in 1830 it was thought that canals would always be preferred to railroads, by 1860 the latter had completely demonstrated their superiority. This was not achieved without a struggle, for the railroad was considered by many as undemocratic and monopolistic in contrast to the open road and even the canal. Engineering and geography were on the side of the railroad, however, and once the railway net was connected its superiority was clearly shown.[12]

The turnpikes and canals had simply followed natural geographical routes of travel. They had made communication easier than it had been by the common roads, and had greatly increased the traffic between the different sections of the country. The canals had supplemented the rivers and

---

[11] B. H. Meyer (Ed.), *History of Transportation in the United States before 1860* (Washington, 1917), Plate 5.

[12] For an account of the competitive struggle between canal and railroad see E. L. Bogart, *Internal Improvements and State Debt in Ohio* (New York, 1924), 92-104. See also the discussion of the relative merits of canals and railroads in Bogart and Thompson, *Readings*, 396-403.

connected these with the lakes, and together they furnished a splendid system of transportation, but the main current of trade was still north and south; something better was needed if the growing West was to be brought into close touch with the East. It remained for the railways to break down the old sectional barriers and to divert the industrial development of the country into new channels. They were built east and west, they crossed the mountains and united parts of the country hitherto separated. With the introduction of the railway the country entered upon an entirely new phase of development.

A new sectional alignment was now created, which joined East and West, but isolated the South. Railroads were followed by banking and credit accommodations which strengthened the bonds of common interest. The South, on the other hand, was swinging away from the center of American economic life and finding in England the best market for her cotton and for the purchase of cheap manufactures. Thus transportation contributed to the sectionalism which led to the Civil War.

But the railroad did more than emancipate transportation from topography; it also released commerce from the limitations of climate. Water traffic had depended on the seasons, and winter had stopped canal and river traffic in the North as completely as it did agriculture. When commerce ceased, industry slackened, labor was thrown out of employment, and capital lay idle. The greatest benefit conferred by the railroad was, probably, continuity of service, though directness and speed were also important; compared with water routes, transportation by rail was more expensive, but this disadvantage was more than offset by the other three advantages. In the transportation of the growing commerce railroads became constantly more important, steadily encroaching on the canal and river trade until in the late fifties rail transportation took the lead; in 1860 it was estimated that the railroads carried two-thirds of the total internal trade. The railways were both a cause and an effect. It is a well-known principle that specialization is limited by the extent of the market. Improved transportation broadened the market and rendered possible the territorial specialization which made the East the center of manufacturing, the West the producer of foodstuffs, and the South the source primarily of cotton. But this very specialization created exchange and generated new traffic for the railroads and called for their extension. All branches profited.

The influence of the railroads in developing the West, in building up its population, and in moving its produce was enormous. "The railway," exclaimed the English traveler Stirling in 1857, "is the soul of western civilization." About 1850, Henry C. Carey wrote: "Twelve years ago the fare of a passenger from Chicago, Illinois (by lake and rail to New York City), 1500 miles, was $74.50. It is now but $17. ... Twelve years since the cost of transporting a bushel of wheat from Chicago to New York was so great as effectually to keep the grain of that country out of the market. Now a bushel of wheat is transported the whole distance, 1500 miles, for 27 cents. A barrel of flour can be transported from Chicago to New York for 80 cents."

This quotation indicates the changes that were taking place in rates, which were downward during the whole of this period, both for passengers and freight. Gradually, too, freight classification was introduced and bulky or heavy but less valuable commodities like wheat and coal were carried at lower rates than those charged for light, valuable products. At first the railroads had been inclined to leave the carriage of the former to the waterways, but as experience demonstrated that lower rates would attract this traffic in such volume that it would more than pay its way, there was a lowering of such charges. This was the much-misunderstood principle of charging what the traffic will bear.

Other transportation agencies. Brief mention may be made of other minor transportation facilities. To care for the rapidly growing urban population, the omnibus, a modification of the stagecoach, was introduced in the thirties, and two decades later horse-drawn street cars appeared, running on sunken rails. To meet the demands of regions not yet reached by the railroad, and especially to provide connection with California after the gold discoveries, stagecoach lines sprang up. By 1860 there were three through lines to San Francisco —one from New Orleans and two from St. Louis—carrying passengers and mail. Although this trip could be made in twenty-five days, speedier service was desired for letters and in 1860 the Pony Express was established which, by relays of horseback riders, got through in ten days. A unique experiment to solve the problem of transportation across the "Great American Desert" was the introduction of camels by Jefferson Davis, while Secretary of War. All these agencies, except those in the cities, were finally supplanted by the railroad.

Improved means of communication. Step by step with the development of better transportation facilities went improvements in means of communication. Probably the most important event of this whole period, after the invention of the steamboat, was the invention of the electric telegraph. Although Professor Joseph Henry of Princeton College had successfully conducted tests with the magnetic telegraph, the honor of making a practical success of it belongs to Samuel F. B. Morse. As early as 1832 he was experimenting with a plan of telegraphic communication, and after vainly endeavoring to interest private capitalists he exhibited his invention in 1838 to congressional committees in the hope of obtaining government aid; in 1843 Congress voted him an appropriation of $30,000 to establish a line between Washington and Baltimore, which was put into successful operation in June, 1844. Its practicability assured, there was now no difficulty in persuading men of capital of its usefulness, and a rapid expansion set in. By 1860 about 50,000 miles of telegraph had been built in the United States, connecting all the important cities of the Union; the system was extended to San Francisco the following year.

The postal system was also improved and extended during this period. The speed and safety of the service were of course intimately linked up with the development of the transportation agencies; with their improvement the time of carriage was steadily reduced. At the same time charges were lowered. During the earlier part of this period postage was calculated according to the distance carried and the number of sheets, and was paid by the recipient of the letter. Thus, the act of 1816 charged 6 cents for a letter of a single sheet carried not more than 30 miles; for more than 400 miles it was 25 cents. If the letter was composed of two sheets, the charge was doubled, etc. In 1845 the rates were reduced and simplified, being made 5 cents for a letter not exceeding one-half ounce for a distance of 300 miles, and 10 cents beyond that distance. In 1850 a flat rate was introduced for all letters, but not until 1863 was the charge reduced to 3 cents. Postage stamps were not authorized until 1847. Along with these changes went an enormous expansion of service. Between 1791 and 1859 the number of post offices increased from 89 to 27,977 and the annual service miles from 846,468 to 86,308,402.

The number of newspapers expanded rapidly during this period, owing to mechanical improvements in the printing press—the cylinder press was first operated in 1847—and in the manufacture of paper, as well as to the spread of education. In 1860 there were nearly 400 daily newspapers issued in the United States and no less than 3,266 daily, weekly, bi-weekly, and monthly papers, aggregating some 10,000,000 copies. The influence of the improved postal service, of the telegraph, and of the cheap and democratic newspaper can scarcely be overestimated. Their effect upon the intellectual development of the people can hardly have been less than that of the steamboat and the railroad upon their industrial and commercial expansion.

Conclusion. Improvement in means of transportation was the paramount condition to closer political integration at this time and to better economic development. Adequate facilities were necessary to connect the different sections of the rapidly growing nation and to afford to every region an outlet to suitable markets. Problems of engineering, of finance, and of politics had to be solved in furnishing these facilities. In solving them, successive systems were tried and then partially discarded in favor of better ones.

CHAPTER XIII

EXPANSION OF DOMESTIC COMMERCE AND EXCHANGE

Early commerce. Commerce, or the exchange of goods, is based upon regional differences in climate, natural resources, or production, which give to each section a relative superiority in the production of particular goods. There is little exchange between districts that are similar in location and products. This is well illustrated by conditions in the colonial period, when the liveliest trade was carried on between the New World with its stores of natural resources and the Old World with its manufactured goods. Each region specialized in those products in which it enjoyed the greatest advantages. And in the New World specialized trade, based upon climatic differences and diversity of products, developed between the colder northern colonies and those farther south, especially the West Indies. This mutually advantageous trade was rudely interrupted by the Revolution, one result of which was to cut off a part of the West Indian trade, and after the end of the Napoleonic wars this was nearly denied to us. At the same time transatlantic markets were partially closed to our products and we were thrown back on our own resources. A new emphasis was thus placed upon domestic or internal trade, which was, moreover, assuming a new importance.

The key to the expanding and ramifying domestic commerce of this period is to be found in the extension of the market. At first internal trade was slight and confined to limited areas, for sources of production, whether agricultural or manufacturing, were dispersed and operated in small units, and markets were consequently small and local. The interior markets were small because most of the people settled there were producing the same things and did not carry on exchanges among themselves to any considerable extent. The very similarity of occupations made these internal markets petty. Before trade could become important in our national life, industry would have to take on larger dimensions and broader markets would have to be opened. The first step in this development was the westward movement of the population which dispersed the people over an immense area, both north of the Ohio and to the southwest. The commercial significance of this movement lay not so much in the increase in population as in the opening up and settlement of new regions, whose products and wants were different from those of the older states east of the Alleghenies. These latter had grown in numbers, wealth, and culture during the previous two hundred years and represented a more advanced stage of economic development than the raw pioneer settlements on the Ohio or in the cotton lands to the south. In these differences was to be found the economic basis for domestic trade.

The spread of settlement and the growth of population tended to enlarge the market about any center of production, and this process was accelerated by the increase in wealth and the rising standard of living. But a limit was set by the high cost of transportation. This tended to the dispersion of industry and the growth of many small centers each with its own local market.

There were thus two contradictory forces in operation. The spread of settlement created new sources of production and new consumers' markets and tended to enlarge the scope of internal trade; but the high cost of transportation had the effect of confining the trade of each new section within narrow limits. Improvements in transportation and cheapening of costs, however, in turn widened the markets and permitted a more distant flow of goods. The process was like that of making a chain by adding link after link, until finally the whole country was bound together by a network of commercial interchanges.

The domestic commerce of the country had from the beginning certain well-defined currents, which give the key to the commercial history of this period. There was first the East-West trade, which underwent great changes as the pack horse was supplanted by the canal boat and steamer, and these in turn by the railroad. The second branch was the West-South trade, which remained throughout this period a river traffic. The third was the East-South trade, which was largely carried on along the coast. And finally there was the overland trade to the Far West.

East-West trade. At the beginning of this period most of the surplus products of the East were agricultural, and these sought a market in the seaport towns where they were exchanged for imported manufactures. Philadelphia, New York, Boston, and Baltimore were important collection points for meat, grain, flour, lumber, and fish, mostly for export, and from them were distributed imported manufactured wares of various sorts. As the population moved west, the sources of agricultural supplies became more scattered and more numerous. These interior producing areas, mostly agricultural, could not consume their own output and hence sought outlets on the seaboard or abroad. At the same time, domestic manufactures developed in the East which steadily became more adequate to meet home demands. Agricultural products were more and more drawn from the West, which specialized in these articles just as the East was concentrating on manufacturing. Between the two sections a thriving trade developed.

The industrial workers in the growing factory towns consumed in considerable part the foodstuffs and other agricultural products which had previously gone abroad and for them exchanged domestic textiles, iron wares of various sorts, and other manufactured goods. This trade steadily lengthened as the frontier receded, reaching the western parts of the Atlantic states at the beginning of this period and the Mississippi Valley and beyond by 1860.

So long as goods were moved by pack horse and wagon distant internal commerce was held down to the minimum. A few products, like furs, hides, and ginseng, which could stand the high charges of land transportation, were carried east, while hogs, cattle, and horses could be driven over the mountains since they conveyed themselves to market at a minimum cost. Baltimore and Philadelphia were the markets for western livestock, which was slaughtered there and formed the basis for further trade in provisions and in hides for the leather industry of New England. It was estimated that 100,000 hogs were driven east yearly from Kentucky alone. Drygoods, firearms, small metal articles, and other light and valuable commodities were sent back in return over the mountains by wagon.

The Erie Canal. The building of the Erie Canal had as momentous an effect upon the East-West trade as the introduction of the steamboat on the western rivers had upon the North-South traffic. For the first decade most of the east-bound traffic of the Erie Canal originated within the state of New York itself, but after the building of the trunk canals in the western states had provided continuous water passage from the growing West to the Atlantic seaboard the commerce between the East and West assumed importance. Much of the western produce, which had formerly gone down the Mississippi, now sought a market on the seaboard. Wheat was first shipped from Ohio in 1835, but six years later it was moving east by lake and canal from Indiana, Illinois, Michigan, and even Wisconsin. Grain and flour were the principal articles transported eastward, but large quantities of pork, bacon, and other provisions were also shipped. The westbound shipments consisted of manufactured goods, such as drygoods, boots and shoes, hardware, nails, machinery, paper, cordage, bagging, earthenware, articles of tin and copper, medicines, drugs, sugar, and coffee, tea, fish, salt, and general merchandise.

Along with the movement of freight, and largely as a cause of it, there went a reduction of cost. Thus in 1818 it cost $5.56 per hundredweight to freight goods from New York to Louisville, but when the Erie Canal was opened rates from New York to Columbus, a comparable distance, fell to $2.50 per hundredweight.

Another effect was to hasten the settlement of the West, into which a perfect stream of settlers passed. Commercial cities sprang up at strategic points along these routes. New York City, already the nation's leading port, leaped farther ahead of its rivals and attained a pre-eminence which it has never since lost. Buffalo, the chief point of transshipment between the canal and the lakes, did an enormous business and grew rapidly in population; by 1860 it was the second city in the state with a population of 80,000. Cleveland, at the head of the Ohio and Erie Canal, handled a growing trade in general agricultural produce; Toledo, the terminus of the Miami and Erie Canal and of the Indiana system, was primarily a grain port; Detroit added to her early trade in furs a later one in grain and lumber. But Chicago, strategically situated at the end of Lake Michigan, showed the most phenomenal growth; boasting barely 100 settlers in 1829 when it was laid out, by 1860 it had a population of 109,000. It was the largest primary grain market in the United States, its receipts exceeding those of all the other grain markets combined; it also handled other agricultural products such as flour, lumber, meat products, and similar items.

Effects of the railroads. The trade between the East and the West, which had been given an impetus in the thirties, was enormously stimulated by the railroads in the fifties. In this decade rail connection was made with the Mississippi and Missouri rivers and through routes between the Mississippi Valley and the Atlantic seaboard were established. The north central states increased greatly their shipments of grain, for there developed a growing European as well as eastern demand, especially in England because of the repeal of the British corn laws in 1846. The definite shift in economic interests in the eastern states from agriculture to manufacturing created a home market not only for foodstuffs but also for agricultural and mineral raw materials. The products sent east from the western states by rail were not very different from those already enumerated as going by the Great Lakes and the Erie Canal, though the volume was larger: livestock, flour, and grain were the most important items. The westbound shipments consisted of manufactured goods, such as drygoods, boots and shoes, hardware, nails, machinery, paper, and articles of tin and copper, medicines, drugs, and general merchandise. The value of the shipments going west in 1860 exceeded those received from the West by $100,000,000 a year. The excess represented in small part investment by easterners in western lands and enterprises, but primarily it was the method by which the West received payment for the various supplies and services it sold to the South, as will be shown later.[1]

West-South trade. The early trade of the newly developing West was for the most part not with the East, but with the South. Water furnished the easiest and cheapest avenue of transportation and nearly all of the produce of the western river settlements that found its way to market was sent down the Mississippi by flatboat to St. Louis or New Orleans. But there was little demand in those cities prior to 1816 for agricultural products, and most of these had to be reshipped to the Atlantic seaboard, the West Indies, or Europe. In that year the total value of the river produce received at New Orleans was only $8,773,000. The shipments were at first raw agricultural products like corn, hay, and livestock, then articles like pork, bacon, lard, flour, whisky, and others that required some process of treatment, and finally simple manufactured articles, such as bagging, rope, lead, candles, glass, nails, and iron. They tell the story as well of the industrial advance in the Ohio and upper Mississippi valleys as of the growing commerce between the sections.

Most of the crude craft that floated down the rivers to New Orleans were sold there, while the crews took passage for some eastern port or found their way back home on foot. Until the revolution effected by the steamboat, the West showed little commercial development; a growing population found easy subsistence on a fertile soil, but it had as yet little in the way of surplus products to sell and no important markets.

Changes in the Mississippi trade. The steamboat changed both the character and the extent of the river trade. Its greater speed increased the number of trips, lessened the time, and reduced the rates. But the greatest advantage lay not in the reduction of time or cost, but in the expansion of the market. The products of the farms could now be disposed of in distant markets where prices were higher, while goods received in exchange could be obtained more cheaply. The value of the commerce carried on the rivers expanded greatly, the value of the produce received at New Orleans

[1] See under East-South trade, p. 302.

increasing from $5,000,000 in 1807 to about $50,000,000 in
1840, and $185,000,000 in 1860. Including the intermediate
trade and the passenger traffic, the total commerce of the
western rivers was probably over $300,000,000 at the last-
named date.

Meantime changes were going on in the character of the
river trade. It is true that the Mississippi trade continued to
increase and the shipments directed to New Orleans reached
their highest point in 1860, but this was due to the expanding commerce of the lower Mississippi Valley. The receipts
at New Orleans of typically western produce showed a great
decline. Their place was taken by produce raised around St.
Louis, which was now being settled by immigrants, especially
Germans.

The return commerce upstream also changed in character.
There was a lively trade in supplying the needs of planters
in Louisiana, Mississippi, and Alabama with agricultural
produce which had been brought downstream, and with
manufactures and imported goods which came from the East
or abroad, for all of which New Orleans was the great distributing point. The regions north of these states bought their
coffee, sugar, molasses, and West Indian fruits from New
Orleans, but obtained their eastern manufactures and other
supplies more directly by rail, except sometimes heavy iron
articles which could still be shipped more cheaply by the
longer all-water route. Other factors, too, were important
in diverting this trade even before the Civil War brought it
to a practical end.

The trade of the upper Mississippi Valley, roughly as far
south as St. Louis, had always labored under handicaps which
became positive detriments when rail routes to the East were
opened. Transportation by river was dangerous on account
of the obstructions to navigation, in the form of sand bars,
snags, and low water. In the winter the upper Mississippi
was closed by ice. But the physical handicaps were aggravated by the primitive and expensive methods used in handling commodities, especially grain; the steam elevators,
warehouses, and loading machinery which were making Chicago the greatest primary grain market in the country, were
utterly lacking in New Orleans. As a result of all these fac-

tors the traffic on the upper Mississippi fell off greatly in the 1850's.

St. Louis occupied a strategic position and profited rather than lost by the shifts in the currents of trade. At first a river city only, she participated in the river traffic both upstream and down. When rail connection was effected with the East in 1855, she obtained her share of that. St. Louis was the point of concentration for the agricultural produce of much of Illinois, Iowa, Kentucky, and Missouri, and was a point of distribution of eastern manufactured goods and of the semi-tropical products from the South. Through all, she was a point of departure for the westbound overland trade. St. Louis was also the principal depot of the fur trade and handled more furs than any other American city.

East-South trade. Still another current of trade was that between the East—or North—and the South, and this, like the other two currents already described, flowed mainly in one direction. The principal products of the South, at least those which entered the markets for exchange purposes, were the staples, cotton, tobacco, sugar. The chief market for these was Europe, especially England with her great textile mills, which took over half the cotton crop. A much smaller proportion went to New England. The foreign trade was triangular, based on southern ports, Europe, and New York. Otherwise ships carrying cotton to Europe would have returned only partially loaded. The reason for this was that the South bought so largely of the West and met its debts to that section indirectly with the proceeds from its exports.

In the trade just described the older states in the South, as Virginia, Maryland, and Delaware, and perhaps North Carolina, seemed to have no share. In two ways, however, they contributed to the stream of domestic commerce and shared in the profits of this trade. Between these states and the northern ports there existed a profitable coastwise trade, carried on by northern vessels, which conveyed New England fish, drygoods, boots and shoes, furniture, and other manufactures to the South to an amount of over $100,000,000 a year. In return they took back cargoes of southern staples, cotton, tobacco, and also foodstuffs, hay and other agricultural commodities, both for export and for domestic consumption. To the lower South these states sent their surplus slaves, who in time became very much more valuable in the cotton fields than on the worn-out tobacco lands.

Territorial division of occupations. Until the development of adequate transportation facilities permitted the interchange of products among different regions, a self-sufficient family economy prevailed, which gradually widened into a neighborhood economy. A national commercial organization was possible only after the building of railroads. But a national commerce involved sectional specialization and interdependence.

The previous paragraphs have described such a sectional or territorial division of labor, according to which the South produced those staple crops for which it was best suited (mainly for export), the West raised foodstuffs and other agricultural supplies, and the East devoted itself to manufactures and commerce. This territorial division of occupations through concentration on specialized lines of production in the three great sections of the United States permitted each to employ its facilities to the best advantage and to exchange its surplus products with those of the other sections. The trade in each case, however, was a somewhat one-sided one and did not at first lead to close economic interdependence; the East sold more to the West than it bought from it, the West sold largely in excess of its purchases to the South, and the South exported three-fourths of its crop to England but bought most of its manufactures from the East. This involved the use of credit on an extended scale and the payment by each section of its debts to the others by means of bills of exchange and other credit devices, drawn against the debtor.

There was thus again a circular trade that moved like the reversed hands of a clock, similar to the triangular trade which during the colonial period was carried on among the northern colonies, the West Indies, and England.[2] Toward the end of this period, however, the triangular pattern was sadly disarranged, for the rail connections tended to divert much of the western produce to the East rather than to the South.

[2] See page 113.

Trans-Mississippi trade. The final branch of internal trade which developed during this period owed its existence neither to the steamboat nor to the railways; this was the commerce of the plains carried on west of the Mississippi. The explorations of Lewis and Clark revealed the opportunities of this western country and fur traders soon pushed west from St. Louis as far as the Rocky Mountains. Other traders ventured into the far Southwest, and by 1840 practically all the western fur-bearing country was being exploited. The value of the furs received annually at St. Louis was about $529,000 and at New Orleans about $480,000.

But the fur traders were only the forerunners of established commercial intercourse. After Mexico had won its independence in 1821, trade with the old Spanish town of Santa Fe was opened and the Santa Fe trail was beaten into a broad pathway of commerce. Caravans carrying cottons, silks, china, glass, and hardware, so well-packed that they survived the jolting roads, traveled the 700 miles from St. Louis to Santa Fe in five or six weeks. Their arrival was the great event of the year, and they were quickly disposed of at a profit of about 40 per cent. The return trip, with lighter cargoes of specie and furs, was made more speedily. The trade declined after 1843, when Santa Anna, fearful of political complications, placed an embargo on the traffic.

After the settlement of the Mormons in Utah the Salt Lake Trail saw a new line of western trade, and still later the mining camps in Colorado and other states called for supplies of goods which were freighted there by wagon. The discovery of gold in California gave a new stimulus to far western migration, but most of the supplies for these distant camps were conveyed by ocean-going vessels rather than across the plains. By 1860 the merchandise shipped west of the Missouri River was valued at $10,500,000. Kansas City was the center of most of this trade, but other towns like Leavenworth, Atchison, St. Joseph, and Omaha were springing up. The development of these western trade routes was full of romance and danger, but the real settlement of this country had to wait for the extension of the railroads after 1860.

While this commercial specialization was largely economic,

the political factors that favored this development must not be overlooked. The influence of the tariff, in shutting out foreign products, in part at least, reserved this growing domestic market for home producers. Much more important was the guarantee by the Constitution of general freedom of trade from one end of the United States to the other. The experience with hostile and retaliatory tariffs among the different states during the period of the colonies and of the Confederation had shown the dangers that lurked in such a system, and all political barriers to interstate commerce were swept away in 1789. This was an enormous boon. Only slightly less important was the grant of free navigation of all navigable rivers, though this was not in fact realized until 1824. But by then the political and physical foundations for the expansion of our internal commerce were firmly laid. Its growth from this time on corresponds with the economic development of the people.

Importance of the domestic trade. The internal commerce of the country steadily became more important than the foreign trade during this period. The relation between these two branches is indicated by a statement of Secretary R. J. Walker, in his treasury report for 1847–48: "The value of our products exceeds three thousand millions of dollars.... Of this $3,000,000,000 only about $150,000,000 are exported abroad, leaving $2,850,000,000 at home, of which at least $500,000,000 are annually interchanged between the several states of the Union." In an estimate for 1851–52, Andrews[3] put the amount of the internal trade at a much higher figure; he calculated that the total domestic commerce amounted to $1,461,000,000. By 1860 it must have been well over $1,500,000,000.

Marketing methods. Thus far the materials of domestic trade, the currents along which it flowed, and the markets have been described. Marketing methods have generally been neglected by writers on this period, and have indeed only recently engaged the attention of economists. At first there was little distinction between production and marketing; the

[3] I. D. Andrews, *Report on ... Trade of the Great Lakes and Rivers* (Washington, 1853), 905 He divided this commerce as follows: lake $157 million; canal, $594 million; railroad, $540 million. No mention is made of river traffic, which is undoubtedly combined with that by canal.

producer marketed his own wares. Farmers took their surplus foodstuffs to the country store where they exchanged them for imported wares or goods produced in the cities, or disposed of lumber, hides, wood ashes, and similar agricultural raw materials to local craftsmen. Or, if they were too far removed from a town, they drove their cattle and hogs or conveyed their grain to the nearest market, or loaded their produce on a New England coasting vessel or an Ohio flatboat and peddled it from wharf to wharf. Connecticut clockmakers interrupted their shop operations when they had completed a small stock of wares and peddled them through the country on pack horses. This primitive commercial organization disappeared with the introduction of steam navigation and the opening up of more distant markets through the improvement of waterways, and especially with the development of railways.

These wider and more distant markets could not be reached by the producer and it now became necessary to employ middlemen who devoted their whole time to the business of marketing. The functions of production and marketing were sharply distinguished and a division of labor between the two groups was introduced. It should be noted, however, that these changes took place gradually and that different sections of the country represented every stage from pioneer self-sufficing communities to highly complex systems of intersectional exchanges.

Wholesale trade. The commission or factor system had been, during the colonial period, the usual method through which were marketed tobacco, flour, fish, lumber, and other staple commodities. This system, widened to fit the enlarged markets and furnished with ampler capital, now assumed the function of distribution. The commission merchants received goods of all sorts on consignment from outsiders—importers, domestic manufacturers, or agricultural producers—and sold them to wholesalers or retailers. They differed from the merchants proper, who actually acquired title to the goods which they bought and sold, inasmuch as they acted solely as middlemen, but they handled much of the business of this period, not only in the seaports, but also in the most distant parts of the West and South.

The functions of these commission merchants were many
and varied and they performed numerous services which were
later turned over to other specialists. Thus, in addition to
buying and selling, they often stored goods, arranged for
shipping and insurance, and extended credit by collecting
and remitting payments, and endorsing and collecting on
bills of exchange. Since most of the internal trade of the
United States was conducted on credit, these banking services
were very important. For these they charged commissions
ranging from one-half of 1 per cent to 2½ per cent. And,
last of all, the commission merchants gave advice, based on
their wide knowledge of the market, to manufacturers as to
what they should produce. Usually they confined themselves
to a related group of commodities, such as hardware or leather
goods, on which they became authorities.

As the territorial division of the country developed sections
producing commodities for national and even international
markets, a more elaborate marketing organization grew up.
This was made necessary as the length of time and distance
in space between production and consumption grew greater.
An excellent illustration is furnished by the trade in agricultural products. In the agricultural West, where grain and
livestock were raised, primary markets, such as Buffalo and
Chicago, were established to which farmers from the neighborhood brought their products. Those living at a distance
sold to local dealers, who assembled small lots and shipped
them to the primary markets.

In similar fashion cotton was shipped by small growers to
interior gathering points, where it was sold to factors who
had frequently advanced money to the farmer on the security
of his cotton crop. Large planters often shipped their cotton
directly to the seaboard markets. The marketing of southern
cotton and other staples was almost entirely in the hands of
northern merchants and factors. Representatives of Yankee
concerns, provided with adequate capital to make loans,
swarmed into southern ports, where they absorbed the major
part of the business. These facts constituted a constant grievance on the part of southerners, but they were an integral
feature of the territorial and functional division of occupations which was developing in the United States. Not merely

did northern factors handle the cotton and tobacco, but they supplied the South with manufactures and other wares, of which some originated in the North and the rest were imported through northern ports and distributed southward by the coastwise trade.

Toward the end of this period a high degree of specialization had developed, especially in the primary markets. Specialized wheat middlemen, cotton factors, and others handled the leading agricultural products, and trading in these tended to be centralized in organized exchanges. The Chicago Board of Trade, which provided a market for wheat, corn, oats, and other grains, was organized in 1848, and a similar one in St. Louis in 1854. New York established the Produce Exchange in 1850. Trading in these centers was given a fillip in the fifties by grading wheat, based on weight, and by buying and selling futures. Manufacturers' products, such as rails and rolling stock to railroads, were sold directly to the consumer, but most commercial products were handled by middlemen, who sold them to the wholesalers. According to the census there were 2881 commission houses in 1840 and 3952 commission merchants in 1860. While these figures are not quite comparable, they suggest a considerable increase.

The emergence of the wholesale merchant occurred early in such large trading cities on the Atlantic seaboard as New York, Boston, Philadelphia, and Baltimore, but in the forties and fifties he appeared also in inland centers as large-scale trade developed there. New Orleans, Pittsburgh, Cincinnati, Louisville, and St. Louis were the principal trade centers of the Ohio and Mississippi valleys. This system was the chief method by which New England textile manufacturers and boot and shoe makers disposed of their products, and was found in every other organized industry.

The wholesale merchant, says Killough,[4] "was one of the largest and financially strongest business units in America. He assembled a great variety of goods from specialized and scattered manufacturers, and dispersed them in convenient quantities to retailers even more numerous and more scattered than the manufacturers. The wholesaler purchased

[4] H. B. Killough, *The Economics of Marketing* (New York, 1933), 165.

goods outright from the manufacturers, stored them, and resold them to the dealer. Early in the nineteenth century manufacturing capital was scarce and manufacturing technique was not easily acquired. The manufacturer was content to sell to the wholesaler and on occasions to receive financial assistance from him."

As trade developed, local retail merchants began the practice of visiting the wholesale trade centers to make their annual or semi-annual purchases. Lavish entertainment put them in a proper frame of mind. Increasing competition, however, led the wholesalers in the thirties to send out traveling men or "mercantile drummers" to visit the retailers in their home towns, and to sell them merchandise upon the basis of a sample and a description. There were about 1000 of these men in 1860. The traveling salesman held a position of considerable responsibility, for upon his judgment rested the determination of the credit that might be granted the retailer. The credit granted usually ran from six to twelve months and was adjusted to that granted by him to his customers. Not until 1841 was the first credit rating agency established and it was many years before this information was generally available.

The auction system intruded into this fairly well-ordered system in 1815, as already described. Although originated for the prompt sale of imported British manufactures, it was soon applied to domestic wares. Semi-annual markets were held in Boston for the sale of American manufactures, especially cloth and shoes; sales amounted to as much as $2,000,-000 for a single session. Similar markets were held monthly in Philadelphia. Auctions were frequent in New York and were held occasionally in the South. It was claimed that this method depressed prices and bitter opposition soon developed on the part of those adversely affected, but it served to distribute the goods to a wide circle of buyers. The auction system reached its highest point about 1830 and thereafter declined, though it was still in use in 1860.

Credit and money. Still another method may be mentioned by which eastern merchants disposed of their wares—that of establishing branches in the western and southern territory. Such branches would give settled connections and promote trade. This was particularly true when goods had to be bartered, for only a few western dealers or eastern manufacturers commanded ready money.

Describing conditions in Ohio, an early English traveler[5] asserted that "the entire business of these waters is conducted without the use of money. . . . To these places persons come from Baltimore and Philadelphia with British goods, which they exchange for local produce; charging on their articles at least 300 per cent and allowing the farmer and artisan but very low terms on theirs. . . . The storekeepers make two annual collections of these commodities; send them down the river to New Orleans; and there receive an immense profit in Spanish dollars, or bills on Philadelphia at short date. . . . This is productive of distressing incidents to small farmers who supply the market with provisions; for whatever they have to sell, whether trivial or important, they receive in return nothing but an order on a store for the value in goods. . . . The words *buy* and *sell* are nearly unknown here; in business nothing is heard but the word *trade*. 'Will you trade your watch, gun, pistols, horses, etc., for corn, pigs, cattle, Indian meal, etc.' But you must anticipate all this from the absence of money."

Since it took so long to complete transactions of this sort, long credits were customary, of from nine to twelve months. Collections were generally slow, a widely accepted maxim being to the effect that in hard times it was unwise to push one's debtor too hard. And since the balance of trade usually ran against both the West and South the specie was drained off to the East, just as during the colonial period it had been drained off to England in payment for commodities more urgently needed.

Retail trade. The description of marketing methods just given was confined for the most part to wholesale distribution, but the retail trade showed some interesting developments. The sale of goods direct to consumers was carried on by importers, peddlers, marketmen in the public markets, craftsmen, and manufacturers, but retailing proper was conducted in stores or shops. The federal excise tax of 1813 required retailers to obtain licenses, and the following year

[5] Thomas Ashe, *Travels in America, performed in 1806* (London. 1808), 51-53.

46,021 were issued. Twenty-five years later the census counted 57,575 retail stores with a total capital of $250,302,-000, or an average for each store of $4350.[6] Outside the larger cities these establishments must have carried on a very modest business. Over half of them were located in the five states of New York, Pennsylvania, Virginia, Ohio, and Mississippi. There was one store for each 300 inhabitants.

Of these stores the most typical, and indeed in many localities the only one, was the general store. The general store seems to have developed from the trading post. In sparsely settled communities the trade was able to support only one store, but this had to carry a general assortment of goods to meet the varied demands. In spite of the great variety the stock was usually small. The function of such a general store was largely that of intermediary in a system of barter, which was rendered necessary by the scarcity of money.

By the fifties the produce collected by the general store was usually shipped to a produce merchant in one of the commercial cities. Some articles, however—the so-called "cash articles"—were sold only for money; such were tea, coffee, leather, iron, powder, lead, and such things as the merchant himself had to purchase with cash. A few articles were accepted in trade at their cash value, such as linen, cloth, feathers, beeswax, and furs, which were in general demand and easy to transport; but most country produce was taken at a heavy discount.

The general store was more than a place of retail trade; it was also a social institution. This aspect is well described by a competent writer.[7]

"The general store is perhaps the most typical American development in merchandising institutions, since very few like it are to be found anywhere else in the world. The old-time general store distributed drygoods, hardware, groceries, drugs, and even liquors. It was frequently the location of the post-office, and served as the village social center for the men. The old box stove, the rickety chair or two, the nearby barrels, and the sawdust spit box, were the almost universal

---

[6] This was the only attempt on the part of the Census Bureau to collect data on this subject until the census of 1930.

[7] P. H. Nystrom, *The Economics of Retailing* (New York, 1919), 23.

furnishings that equipped it for its social services. Here politics, religion, and neighbors were discussed. It may not be too much to say that here the tariff question, the government bank, internal improvements, foreign policies, and other important government matters were ultimately settled. Certainly statesmen had to reckon with the forces of public opinion generated and cultivated around the stove of the country store. With all its inefficiency, its wasteful methods, and its shortcomings as a retail establishment, it must be said that it successfully served its day as probably no other type of institution could. Many general stores still exist and will for years to come. But with increasing density of population and a rising standard of living, the general store as such must give way to other types of retailing institutions."

Peddling. Another method of distributing manufactured wares and miscellaneous merchandise was the rather primitive system of peddling. Yankee traders were engaged in this business during the colonial period, peddling socks, mittens, and woodenware with French Canadians on the north, or fish and household manufactures among the tobacco and rice plantations on the south. An interesting account of the manner in which Connecticut tinware was later distributed has been left by Timothy Dwight,[8] who afterwards became President of Yale College:

"For many years after tinned plates were manufactured in this place [Berlin, Connecticut] into culinary vessels, the only method used by the pedlars for conveying them to distant towns for sale was by means of a horse and two baskets, ballanced on his back. After the war, carts and waggons were used for this purpose, and have from that time to the present been the only means of conveyance which have been adopted.

"The manner in which this ware is disposed of puts to flight all calculation. A young man is furnished by the proprietor with a horse, and a cart covered with a box, containing as many tin vessels as the horse can conveniently draw. . . . Each of them walks, and rides, alternately, through this vast distance, till he reaches Richmond, Newbern, Charleston, or Savannah. . . . Every inhabited part of the United States is visited by these men. I have seen them on the peninsula of

[8] *Travels in New England and New York* (London, 1823), II, 43-44.

Cape Cod, and in the neighborhood of Lake Erie; distant from each other more than six hundred miles. They make their way to Detroit, four hundred miles farther; to Canada; to Kentucky; and, if I mistake not, to New Orleans and St. Louis."

These peddlers of tinware were not individual traders, but were employed by a few capitalist producers in Connecticut. Supply stations were set up at strategic places from which regular routes spread out in every direction. The tin business was comparatively short-lived, but the peddlers then turned to brass wares—buttons, kettles, lamps, and similar useful articles. They also sold the famous Connecticut wooden clocks and later brass ones, whose interchangeable parts were stamped out by machine and which sold for the astoundingly low price of $6.00. Still later they added silver-plated forks and spoons to their list. These early peddlers constituted a useful link between localized producers and scattered consumers. Opposition of settled storekeepers and improved means of transportation finally brought this picturesque system of distribution to a practical end.

A unique and typically American variation of this process of peddling was found in the West, where it was conducted by river boats rather than by horse-drawn carts. This trade usually was carried on during the summer, the goods were stored in Pittsburgh over the winter, and the following spring were sent down the river on trading boats, which stopped at the towns on the banks to sell the articles. In a country so remote from supplies and so sparsely populated by a purely agricultural population, which could not visit the city markets, these trading boats contributed greatly to the convenience of life by bringing to each farmer's door those small necessities which it would have been troublesome and expensive to have procured otherwise. A picture of this trade is given by Levi Woodbury, Secretary of the Treasury, who made a trip down the Mississippi in 1833:

"At every village we find from ten to twelve flat-bottom boats, which besides corn on the ear, pork, bacon, flour, whiskey, cattle and fowls, have a great assortment of notions from Cincinnati and elsewhere. Among these are corn brooms, cabinet furniture, cider, plows, apples, cordage, etc. They remain in one place until all is sold out, if the demand be brisk; if not, they move farther down. After all is sold out they dispose of their boat, and return with the crews by the steamers to their homes."

In course of time, as the plantations grew larger, this method of peddling from wharf to wharf declined. The planters engaged agents at New Orleans to sell their cotton and to purchase supplies, which were shipped upstream by steamer. After about 1846 there was a gradual decrease in the number of flatboats, and by 1860 they had ceased to be a factor in the river trade and were no longer listed among the arrivals at New Orleans. The high price of lumber made their further use impracticable.

One other phase of commerce may be mentioned—accounting. Although today it is so important, in the period before 1860 it was still in a very primitive stage. The best bookkeeping in this period, as judged by the textbooks of the day and such old business records as have been preserved, was limited to very simple double entry. It was occupied mainly with keeping accounts with personal debtors and creditors for goods and loans. Very little was done in the direction of analyzing the merchandise into lines or departments. Profits were calculated in a single merchandise account and from separate "accounts in company" (i.e., consignment ventures in temporary association with others). There was little or no analytical subdivision of expense such as plays so important a part in modern managerial accounting. And, of course, accounting for manufacturing (cost accounting) had not yet been developed.[9]

Conclusion. Trade was the focus of a number of movements that were taking place during this period. Foremost in importance were the improvements in transportation and communication, which permitted an enormous expansion of trade. But these alone were not sufficient to explain the expansion, for there must be producers at one end and consumers at the other. Production of agricultural products was stimulated by the settlement of new land and improvements in agricultural techniques, and of manufactured goods by new

[9] We are indebted for this information to Professor A. C. Littleton, of the University of Illinois.

inventions and reduction in costs and prices. There was thus fed into the stream of commerce a torrent of new and cheaper products. But consumers for these were found in the swelling population. As the people spread out over the land, the chain lengthened by which goods of various sections were exchanged. The growth of great cities was made possible whose importance rested primarily on the outreaching wholesale trade.

All these changes called for improved marketing facilities and better organization. A division of functions was introduced in this field, and the structure of commerce took on its present form. Wholesale and retail trade were differentiated and each assumed its rightful position. Peddling and other temporary forms all but disappeared. By these methods American products were conveniently distributed to all parts of the country. The dispersed and unorganized local centers were gradually knit into a national marketing system, with adequate commercial machinery. Banking and credit institutions grew in response to commercial needs, insurance companies came into being, the express business was born to meet a new demand, the introduction of the telegraph made possible instant communication to distant trading centers, and in many ways commerce adjusted itself to the requirements of a growing and changing industrial structure.

CHAPTER XIV

MONEY, BANKING, AND FINANCE

The American dollar. Necessary as were improved means of transportation for conveying the wares of commerce, they were no more important than a safe and adequate system of currency to act as a medium of exchange. The discredited Continental currency had ceased to circulate and that issued by the states was greatly depreciated, while the metallic money in circulation was insufficient in amount and was made up of English, French, Spanish, and Portuguese coins of varying denominations and value. Indeed, inadequate control of the currency by the central government and popular distrust of paper money was one of the rocks on which the Articles of Confederation had foundered. To safeguard against a future repetition of paper-money inflation the Constitution provided that "No State shall...emit bills of credit, make anything but gold and silver coin a tender in payment of debts," and gave to Congress the power to coin money and regulate its value. Congress had no specific authority to issue paper money and until the Civil War the federal government regarded itself as forbidden to do so.

It fell to the lot of Alexander Hamilton, the youthful Secretary of the Treasury, to lay the plans for the improved currency system. Jefferson had already suggested a decimal system of coinage with the dollar as the monetary unit and Hamilton accepted this. The choice of the dollar is not surprising because for a long time the most common coin in circulation had been the Spanish silver dollar, despite the fact that accounts were kept in terms of pounds, shillings, and pence. Hamilton also chose a bimetallic standard which was the best system then known. Under it the value of the dollar was equal to a certain weight of gold or another certain weight of silver. The complications this was to cause were not foreseen. The weight of the silver dollar was fixed at 371.25

316

grains of pure silver and that of the gold dollar at 24.75 grains of pure gold, which made the ratio between the two 15 to 1, that is, the silver dollar weighed fifteen times as much as the gold dollar. This was the essence of the Mint Act passed by Congress in 1792.

A nation's bimetallic standard will not work if other nations disagree with it upon the relative value of gold and silver. This fact was not understood. Other nations in their coinage laws placed a higher value on gold compared to silver (15½ to 1) than we did. Consequently, when the mint began operations in Philadelphia in 1794, little gold was brought to it to be coined, since gold was undervalued in this country and was worth more as bullion to be shipped abroad than as coin here. But some silver was coined, most of the metal presented for this purpose being the imported foreign coins, as no silver mines had yet been opened up in the United States. Copper coins for small change also were minted. Our silver dollars circulated freely, not only at home but also in the West Indies on a parity with the Spanish milled dollars, although the latter were about 2 per cent heavier than the American coins. It did not take the Yankee traders long to discover that a neat profit could be made by taking American dollars to the West Indies, bringing back Spanish dollars, having them coined at the mint, and repeating the process. When Jefferson learned of this exportation in 1806, he peremptorily closed the mint to the coinage of silver dollars, and from that date until 1836 no silver coins of a higher denomination than the 50-cent piece were minted. This left the metallic currency still a composite mass of foreign coins, fractional silver, and copper. In practice the country was on a haphazard silver standard although legally we still had a bimetallic standard. During the first third of the century nothing more was done to solve the currency difficulties except that every few years Congress extended the period in which foreign silver coins would be accepted as legal tender. As late as the early 1850's a few foreign coins still circulated.

The gold standard begins. About 1834 circumstances conspired to alter our monetary standard. Although still legally on bimetallism, in practice we shifted from a silver to a gold standard. There were several motives for the change. President Jackson had a high esteem for hard money and was opposed to having the country so dependent on bank notes and on the Second Bank of the United States. The East preferred gold to silver and there was considerable speculative activity in Congress in behalf of some newly discovered gold mines in North Carolina and Georgia. When Congress reduced the weight of the gold dollar from 24.75 grains of pure gold to 23.2 grains, it made the silver dollar 16 times the weight of the gold dollar and so committed the country to a mint ratio of 16 to 1. That had the opposite effect from the previous mint ratio. Now gold was overvalued and silver was undervalued. Congress knew what it was doing this time and expected Gresham's Law to operate and drive the undervalued silver out of circulation. Actually, the silver disappeared slowly since many of the coins were underweight from clipping and long wear. Thus bimetallism nearly worked between 1834 and 1849. But after the Gold Rush of 1849 began the flood of newly mined and already overvalued gold caused silver coins rapidly to disappear. Up to this time the half dollars, quarters, and dimes had contained exact fractions of the amount of silver in a silver dollar; consequently, the same causes that led to the withdrawal from circulation of silver dollars removed also the fractional silver coins.

The lack of subsidiary silver to make change was such a serious disadvantage to retail trade that Congress passed a subsidiary coinage law in 1853, debasing the fractional coins by decreasing the amount of pure silver in each to keep them in circulation. The mint bought the necessary bullion and minted the debased fractional silver coins. The silver dollar was now the only silver coin for which the right of free coinage still existed, i.e., the right of anyone to bring the metal in unlimited quantities to the mint to be coined. Few were coined, however, since it usually required about $1.03 worth of silver to make a silver dollar. On the other hand, the silver subsidiary coins remained in circulation since there was only 97 cents worth of silver in a dollar of them. Gold coins of course circulated freely. The country was thus on a gold standard in practice although legally, because of the unused

right of free coinage of one coin, the silver dollar, our standard was still bimetallism.

Banking. The amount of metallic money in circulation in
1800 has been estimated at about $3.00 per capita, which was
clearly insufficient for the monetary needs of the country.
Thus, despite the clauses in the Constitution outlawing legal-
tender paper money the most common kind of money in circulation throughout this period was paper money, namely
bank notes without the legal-tender quality.

It was in this period that modern banking began in America, although it had been known in Europe for a hundred
and fifty years. A bank is expected to perform three basic
functions: first, it accepts money on deposit; second, it makes
loans to customers; and third, it makes most of those loans
in the form of its own credit. This last point requires fuller
explanation, for it is the essence of banking. Banks have
two ways of loaning credit, either by printing and lending
bank notes or by granting customers deposits against which the
customers may write checks. The bank-note method was developed first and during most of this pre-Civil War period
was the more widely used. While an individual would hardly
dare to do business and pay his bills by handing out his own
I.O.U.'s to circulate through the community, banks do just
this and thereby make their profits. From the bank the individual borrows bank notes which are simply the bank's
demand I.O.U.'s, and with these he pays his bills. The bank
is paid interest for substituting its superior credit for the
individual's inferior, or less well-known, credit. Back of the
bank notes are the general credit of the bank, some specie
reserve, but chiefly the customers' promissory notes. Of
course, if the public becomes suspicious that the bank is un-
sound and starts a "run" on it, demanding specie for bank
notes, the bank could probably not redeem them all promptly
and in full. In the early days of banking the penalty for this
was a sharp decline in prestige; later it was bankruptcy. But
the banker knew this situation would not arise if he was careful to make good loans and not too many of them. He thus
tried to steer a middle course between safety and profit, that
is, to keep enough reserve so that all likely demands for specie

could be met, yet he printed and loaned enough bank notes so that he could receive considerable interest income from loans. The more bank notes he had out, the greater the profit, but also the greater the danger. Early banks had to learn by experience how many notes could be issued on a given specie reserve. Often the lure of profits tempted them to issue too many notes. The history of early American banking centers on this problem more than on any other.

The first real bank in the United States was the Bank of North America, founded by Robert Morris in Philadelphia in 1781 to finance the closing years of the Revolutionary War. Its specie reserve was derived from a loan made to us by France. The second and third banks were the Bank of Massachusetts and the Bank of New York, both founded in 1784. By 1800 there were 26 state banks in the country, 88 by 1811, and some 1600 by 1860. State banks were banks receiving their charters from the government of the state in which they were located. All these banks were commercial banks too, not land banks such as existed in colonial times. Nor were they central banks, which are bankers' banks whose function it is to assist commercial banks rather than individuals, to direct general banking policy, and to serve the federal government. We had, however, two central banks in this period.

First Bank of the United States. Our first central bank was the First Bank of the United States, founded in Philadelphia in 1791 largely by the efforts of Alexander Hamilton. It also acted as a commercial bank. Its capital of $10,000,000, subscribed within two hours after the books were open, made it by far the biggest business institution in the country and aroused the suspicions and fears of many democratically-minded people. This distrust was increased by the fact that the federal government both chartered the Bank and subscribed for one-fifth of its stock, thus making it almost a government institution. Partly for this reason its charter ran for only twenty years, at which time it was to come before Congress for renewal. Its specie reserve of $2,000,000 was probably a third to a half of all the specie in the country. The Bank was of great service to the treasury department, but more important were its services to the people in providing a safe credit currency and in furnishing banking facilities for commercial transactions through its eight branches.

Unfortunately for the Bank and also for the people its public services were not fully appreciated. This was a period of war prosperity in which our commerce grew enormously and our agriculture was greatly stimulated. Each year saw more state banks chartered and heard more cries of anguish at the strictness of the rules enforced by the Bank. As fiscal agent for the federal government the Bank was custodian of import duties and other tax monies. By refusing to accept the notes of non-specie paying banks it also became the regulator of the currency. But it thereby incurred the enmity of all slovenly and fraudulent banks and sometimes even of better-grade banks. Their opportunity for profit was lessened by the necessity of standing ready at all times to redeem an accumulation of their own banknotes that might be presented by the Bank. When the question of renewing the Bank's charter came up, many state banks brought pressure on Congress to oppose recharter.

There was also fear of the malignant influence exerted by the large amount of foreign capital invested in the Bank—no less than $7,000,000—and of the "money power" concentrated there. "This institution," wrote Jefferson, "is one of the most deadly hostility existing against the principles and form of our Constitution.... What an obstruction could not this Bank of the United States, with all its branch banks, be in time of war? It might dictate to us the peace we should accept, or withdraw its aid. Ought we then to give further growth to an institution so powerful and so hostile?" Consequently the affairs of the Bank were wound up, and the field was left to the state banks.

State banks, 1811–1816. The dissolution of the First Bank caused the withdrawal of $10,000,000 in bank notes and the export of a large amount of specie which had been invested by Europeans in its stock. There was thus a vacuum in the currency of the country which needed to be filled, and this the state banks hastened to supply. Between 1811 and 1816 the number of these institutions grew from 88 to 246. They did not, however, limit themselves to the normal needs of trade, but issued their notes in excessive quantities. No longer was there a central bank to serve as a policeman among them. Many of these banks were organized with almost no restrictions, for the state legislatures which chartered them had little experience to guide them; and the bank managers knew little of the principles of sound banking. The demand for capital on the part of the mercantile community was strong; the loose credit system of selling public lands in the West led to demands for bank loans in that section; and the financial disorganization and monetary needs of the government and people during the War of 1812 were additional factors leading to overexpansion.

When Washington, D. C., was captured by the British in 1814 all banks except those in New England, which had been conservatively managed, suspended specie payments, that is, they ceased to redeem their notes in specie on demand. Relieved of all responsibility, the state banks now increased their issues still more recklessly, a step encouraged by the action of the government in accepting bank notes in payment of public dues. Add to all this the fact that there was as yet no widespread system of publicity or of knowledge as to the condition of banks or the state of the currency, and it can scarcely be a matter of wonder that some inflation ensued. The marvel is that there was not more.

Between 1812 and 1817 the bank-note circulation rose from $45,000,000 to $100,000,000, most of the increase taking place in the West. The country was now again upon a paper-money basis. Many of the old evils reappeared; overissue, depreciation, and inequality in value. The notes of the New York banks were 10 per cent below par, those of Washington and Baltimore 22 per cent, while in the West some of them fell as low as 50 per cent below par. But, bad as it was, the people were compelled to use this depreciated and fluctuating currency or resort to barter, since there was no other currency to take its place.

Second Bank of the United States. By this time the public had come to appreciate the services once performed by the First Bank and so in 1816 the Second Bank of the United States was established. Two reasons were advanced for its organization at this time: (1) it would afford assistance to the treasury, which was financially embarrassed on account of the war; (2) it would act as a regulator of the currency. The Bank was chartered in 1816 for twenty years, with a capital of $35,000,000 of which one-fifth was subscribed by the federal government. The circulation was limited to the amount of the capital, and notes were made payable in specie on demand and were receivable in all payments to the United States. It was expected that the circulating notes of the Bank, being redeemable in specie on demand, would compel the state banks to resume specie payments or would drive the depreciated state bank notes out of circulation.

Unfortunately, however, the Bank itself was very badly managed for the first three years of its existence: only a part of the specie reserve was paid in, the notes were overissued, and loans were made on insufficient security. It consequently contributed to the evils of speculation and reckless banking which characterized this period, instead of reforming them. In 1819 the Bank was almost bankrupt, and was saved from ruin only by the appointment of a new president, Langdon Cheves, and a thorough reorganization. A severe contraction of circulation and loans followed, but, while this saved the Bank, it helped bring on the financial storm which had been brewing during the years of speculation.

This broke in the crisis of 1819, which was the first general crisis in the United States. Its causes were complex, and bad banking was only one. In addition may be mentioned the speculation in western lands, the rapid commercial expansion, and the unstable position of the manufacturing industries, which had grown abnormally during the embargo and the war and had afterwards been exposed to foreign competition. At the same time the state banks contracted their note circulation from $100,000,000 in 1817 to $45,000,000 in 1819, and thus reduced the credit facilities at the very time they were in most demand. But nothing could have saved these overexpanded institutions. "In 1817–1818 forty banks of issue had been chartered in Kentucky, and Tennessee and Ohio hastened to adopt the same alluring expedient. The banks issued money without stint and loaned to speculators on easy terms.... Then suddenly, in 1819, the National Bank presented an accumulation of notes for redemption; the state banks, unable to meet their obligations, were forced to suspend specie payment, and the boom collapsed." [1] Nor was this an unusual case. In every part of the country, specie payments were generally suspended, prices fell disastrously, failures occurred, industries stopped, and many laborers were thrown out of work. A period of readjustment ensued, which continued in some parts of the country for three or four years.

The career of the Bank during the next few years was uneventful. It increased its circulation, and as these notes passed at par, the state banks were compelled, on pain of having their notes refused, to limit their issues and maintain specie payments. The Bank brought pressure upon them by steadily presenting to them for redemption notes which were paid into it from day to day, and it thus acted as a "regulator of the currency," just as the First Bank had done. But this fact made it very unpopular in the South and West, where the inflation was greatest and where public opinion did not support such action. Several of the states attempted to tax out of existence the branches which were established within their borders,[2] but from this they were debarred by the adverse decisions of Chief Justice John Marshall in *McCulloch v. Maryland* (1819) and *Osborn v. United States Bank* (1824), in which he declared such taxes unconstitutional, on the ground that no state might destroy any agency of the federal government which the Constitution permitted it to establish.

From now on for some years the country had a comparative rest from currency troubles. Each state and community was solving its own difficulties as best it could, but the secrecy attending banking operations made correction of abuses difficult. In the South and West the demand for plentiful money and for capital—which was confused with money—was paramount, and few precautions were taken to prevent overissue. In mitigation of this demand for bank money it must be remembered that the balance of trade with the East was steadily unfavorable and that the metallic money was drained off to meet the large purchases of manufactured goods which the West bought, in payment for land purchases, in specula-

---

[1] K. Coman, *Industrial History of the United States* (rev. ed., New York, 1910), 201.

[2] See E. L. Bogart, "Taxation of the Second United States Bank by Ohio," in *American Historical Review*, vol. XVII (1911-12), 312-21.

tive profits to eastern owners, and for other purposes. The situation of this section was not unlike that of the colonies in their trade relations with England. In each case the loss of specie was not understood but was attributed to the machinations of a distrusted money power. In the West at this period, as in the colonies a hundred years earlier, there was need for an inexpensive and convenient medium of exchange, and again, as then, resort was had to a form of paper money, this time bank notes.

Although the Bank was an object of dislike in parts of the country, there seems to be no evidence to show that it was badly managed. Opposition to the Bank was, however, brought to a head by President Jackson, who was strongly opposed to a central bank, which he regarded as a dangerous monopoly. The unseasonable political activity of the Bank only confirmed this view in the mind of one who regarded political opponents as enemies of the commonwealth. There were many persons also who were opposed to all bank-note issues, as they desired to see specie in circulation. The question of rechartering the Bank was made an issue in the presidential election of 1832, and as this resulted overwhelmingly in favor of Jackson, the Bank was refused a recharter and its affairs were wound up. This brought to an end the policy of regulating the credit bank-note currency of the country by means of a great central bank. In its place came the policy of permitting the unmanaged state banks to furnish the necessary credit money, and of having the government keep its own funds and make use only of specie. In this way, it was thought, the use of a large amount of coin in the country would be enforced, and the undue expansion of bank-note issues would be restricted. This policy, however, was not put into practice for some years.

Speculation. With the failure of the Second Bank to secure a recharter the way was open again for an expansion of their bank notes by the state banks, and these quickly availed themselves of the opportunity. Internal improvements by the states had been growing in popularity since the success of the Erie Canal across upstate New York. One did not have to be a great financier to realize that in regions served by a new canal crops could be sent to market more cheaply and supplies could be brought in more easily and this would attract more settlers and raise the value of land. Whoever owned the land would then make a generous profit. Of course money was needed to purchase these lands and, consequently, many banks were hastily organized to secure the enormous profits to be made from loans to speculators. Government funds, now deposited in politically favored state banks known as "pet" banks, made possible even greater credit expansion than would have been probable under the Second Bank. This only added further fuel to the fires of speculative enthusiasm. The accompanying table shows how the boom developed.

EXPANSION OF BANK CREDIT, 1829-60

(*In millions of dollars*)

Year	Number of Banks	Capital	Loans	Bank Notes	Specie
1829	329	110.2	137.0	48.2	14.9
1834	506	200.0	324.1	94.8	
1836	718	251.9	457.5	140.3	44.0*
1837	788	290.8	525.1	149.2	38.0
1843	691	228.9	254.5	58.6	33.5
1847	715	203.1	310.3	105.5	35.1
1853	750	207.9	408.9	146.1	47.1
1857	1416	370.8	684.5	214.8	58.3
1860	1562	421.9	691.9	207.1	83.6

* 1835

Banks granted loans readily on the security of government land, and borrowers used these loans to purchase their land from the land agents. The purchase money was often redeposited by the land agents in the same bank, where it again served as the basis of another loan for the purchase of more land. From an average of less than $2,000,000 a year before 1830 the receipts to the federal government from the sale of public lands rose to $25,000,000 in 1836. So unprecedented were these sales that the expression, "doing a land-office business," became synonymous with great commercial activity or merchandising success.

Prices rose, not only of land, but also of commodities: the price of cotton moved up from 6 to 8 cents a pound and then to 20 cents in 1835. Great profits in cotton and grain stimulated further speculation in land. It was a period when men's imaginations were stirred, and the prospects of the future were mortgaged to a reckless extent. Michael Chevalier, a noted French economist who visited the United States in 1834, was astonished by the speculations. "Everybody is speculating," he wrote,[3] "and everything has become an object of speculations. The most daring enterprises find encouragement; all projects find subscribers.... The principal objects of speculation are those subjects which chiefly occupy the calculating minds of the Americans, that is to say, cotton, land, city and town lots, banks and railroads."

The panic of 1837. The mad dance of speculation was brought to an abrupt close by the panic of 1837. The immediate occasion of the crisis was the so-called specie circular of the Treasury Department of July 11, 1836; this was an order to the government agents for the sale of public lands, that they should thereafter take in payment only specie; the notes of specie-paying banks, if signed by the Treasurer of the United States, would also be accepted. A check was thereby placed upon land speculation which cramped the operations of the western banks, whose situation was made more serious by the failure of American crops in 1835 and 1837. The failure of important business houses in England at the end of 1836 caused a lessening in the demand for cotton, while at the same time these brought pressure for the repayment of loans made in the United States. Cotton fell from 20 cents a pound to 10; several of the greatest cotton factors in New Orleans failed, and southern planters and banks were involved in the crash of the prevailing credit system. In May the banks of New York City suspended specie payments, followed soon by every bank in the country. Over 600 banks failed, the discredited bank notes depreciated in value, and prices shrank to a hard-money level. When foreign investors asked for the repayment of their loans, some of the states repudiated their bonds and others delayed their interest payments. Several of the western states declared a moratorium on private debts. A period of liquidation and readjustment ensued, which was followed by a severe depression lasting five or six years. The bank-note circulation was rapidly contracted from $149,000,000 in 1837 to $58,000,000 in 1843, while the sales of public land steadily fell off

[3] *Society, Manners, and Politics in the United States* (1834), 305.

from the high-water mark of 20,000,000 acres in 1836 until they reached about 1,000,000 acres in 1841.

Dark decades of banking, 1833-63. Now that the federal government had entirely withdrawn from the banking field, banking regulation was left to the states. A few discharged this responsibility well but the majority did poorly. In general, the seaboard states had the better banking systems; the western states, which had less experience and perhaps greater temptations, had the worst banks. The thirty years before the Civil War saw many stupid mistakes made, the worst being the practices leading to the panic of 1837 just described, but the period also saw valuable experiments tried.

Difficulties arose largely from the temptation constantly before bankers to lend more bank notes than their specie reserve could safely support (see table on page 326). Not only was this profitable, but the banker often felt that he was benefiting the citizens of his community and the community itself by providing funds for the purchase of needed equipment. He got genuine appreciation for his favors whether they were bestowed for wise or unwise ventures. Furthermore, there were few laws fixing adequate specie reserves to guide him or to justify his refusal of a loan.

Bankers resorted to various devices to keep the public from drawing on their scanty supplies of specie. White relates that in the South and West generally "anybody coming from a distance to draw specie from a bank incurred the odium of the community." It meant fewer loans could be made to local citizens. In such cases the bank would often pay in the most inconvenient coin possible and take hours to count it. Occasionally such an out-of-town visitor would even be threatened with a coat of tar and feathers by aroused citizens. A Georgia bank required every person presenting bank notes for redemption to take an oath in the bank before a justice of the peace, the cashier, and five bank directors that he was the owner of the notes and not cashing them for someone else. Needless to say, it was almost impossible to bring these seven persons together at once.

It was but a short step from this device to "wildcat" banking, so called because these banks made loans from their branch offices in town but redeemed notes only at their head office, located, if at all, in a remote place inhabited only by wildcats. Michigan was especially famous for these. It was there also that a single box of specie was once made to do service for one bank after another, being rushed ahead of the bank commissioners in their tour of inspection. In another case the box of specie had only a thin layer of coins on top, while beneath were glass and nails. Banking in those days of few regulations was characterized by tricks of this sort ranging from understandable but "artful dodges" to downright frauds. The resulting depreciation and lack of uniformity of note issues produced a confused currency system and augmented the normal hazards of business. "A country merchant," says Dewey, "might receive and pay out a thousand kind of notes, some good, some doubtful, some presumably bad, and this condition grew worse as the circle of business activity was enlarged with the construction of railroads." At one time as many as 5400 different kinds of spurious or counterfeit notes were recorded as being in circulation, and every merchant and bank teller was compelled to keep at his elbow a Bank-Note Reporter and Counterfeit Detector. Not until the establishment of the National Banking System in 1863 were these evils brought to an end.

Another banking difficulty of the period arose from the fact that the state banks were small single units, no one of which was large enough to provide for itself a proper diversification of risks; being unrelated to one another there was no method by which reserves could be pooled or the strong banks come to the aid of the weak. The success of the Suffolk system in Massachusetts (1819–56) and of the Safety Fund system in New York (1829–66) lay in the fact that each of these provided for the association of banks for certain purposes. This was likewise true of the state-operated systems in Ohio and Indiana. After the end of the Second Bank this association was not accomplished again on a national scale until the establishment of the Federal Reserve System in 1913. This banking by single units has been a major reason for the terrific number of bank failures throughout our banking history.

A third difficulty was that we had the wrong kind of bank for the type of business being done. The banks in the West were organized as commercial banks and commercial banks should, as far as possible, concentrate on short-term commercial loans. Repeatedly this has been demonstrated in financial history. But our western commercial banks were trying to serve agricultural communities to which they made long-term loans, often for land speculation or with land as the security. In these circumstances their assets lacked the essential quality of liquidity—they could not be readily turned into cash. Many banks had good assets but these were "frozen." Yet the penalty for inability to redeem bank notes was bankruptcy. Today a sharp distinction is made between agricultural credit banks and commercial banks; then the attempt to combine their diverse functions led all too often to failure.

Finally, and perhaps most important, was the fact that the debtor agricultural classes, both southern planters and western farmers in need of capital, and many other borrowers in the eastern financial markets too, saw that their interests were best served by easy money, and there is little doubt that they deliberately favored an inflation policy. By one means or another they wished to get more money into circulation. The banks owned and operated by the states illustrate this. These are not to be confused with the ordinary state-chartered bank. It is true that the Constitution had forbidden the states to emit bills of credit, but these state-owned and -operated banks were corporations established in the name of the state by the legislature, which chose their president and directors. They were authorized to issue notes, make loans, and carry on other banking functions. Did their notes come under the constitutional prohibition? The state of Kentucky had created such a bank in 1820, and the Supreme Court at a preliminary hearing, under the leadership of Marshall, held the Kentucky act void. But when the case was finally decided in 1837 before a full court, it was declared that the issuance of notes by a state-owned and -operated bank, even though the state was the sole stockholder, was not unconstitutional. This opened the door to the southern and western states to issue what was practically fiat money, and the agrarian groups took full advantage of the opportunity. Some of the worst excesses were perpetrated by these state-operated banks.

Sound banking systems. Some banks in this period were very well managed. There were even good state-operated banks, in Ohio and Indiana. The large New England banks were sound. Probably the best banking system was found in Louisiana. The Louisiana state law of 1842 required all banks to hold a specie reserve equal to one-third of their liabilities and to keep the other two-thirds covered by customers' promissory notes and drafts due within ninety days. Bank directors were liable for losses resulting from loans and investments made contrary to law, and the state provided effective supervision of the banks. Some of these provisions foreshadowed reforms found in our present Federal Reserve System. It was the popular preference for these reliable Louisiana notes that is presumed to have given the name "Dixie" to the South. Some of the New Orleans banks printed one side of their notes in French, the $10-note having DIX in large letters across it. River traders and boat captains heading south with merchandise were wont to remark that they were going to get a lot of "dixies," and thus that part of the South got the name of Dixie Land which was gradually applied to the whole South and popularized by a song hit just before the Civil War.

Another banking reform, known as "free" banking, was tried with varying degrees of success in about 15 states. There were frequent complaints that the only persons who could get a bank charter were the rich with the right political connection and some cash to spare their sponsors in the legislature. This was undemocratic, to say the least. Once established, the banker occupied a position of privilege and power in the community and could make or break many a business venture. This, too, was undemocratic. To cure this evil the state of New York passed the Free Banking Act in 1838 making it possible for anyone with the necessary funds to start a bank. He simply turned his cash into acceptable state or federal government bonds which he deposited with the comptroller of banks in exchange for bank notes. He was now ready to do business. If he made wise loans, he got interest on them and on his bonds and was a successful banker. If he made unwise loans, he soon went bankrupt and his bonds were forfeited to redeem the bank notes which were by now in the hands of the general public. Thus the plan had the dubious but democratic merit of giving anyone with capital a chance to be a banker and yet of protecting innocent noteholders from his mistakes. The basic principles of this plan were incorporated in the National Banking Act of 1863 which will be discussed in a later chapter.

Panic of 1857. Banking grew by fits and starts. Each boom produced a bumper crop of new banks and rapid expansion of credit; each panic saw the weak banks weeded out and credit contracted. This was true of the 1819 and 1837 crises already discussed and it was true of the panic of 1857. After the crisis of 1837 and the resulting depression, the number of banks and their business, as indicated by their loans and circulation, remained fairly steady for a decade (see table on page 326). By 1843, however, courage returned and business resumed its normal course. Banks responded to the demands made upon them for accommodation and gradually expanded their loans and circulation. Between 1853 and 1857 the number of banks doubled and the credit expansion became extremely rapid, as is indicated in the following graph: The credit expansion was stimulated by the enormous additions to the gold supply from California and Australia and also by the unusual demand for our products resulting from the famines in Ireland and the areas affected by the Crimean War. Rising prices increased the speculative optimism. The decade of the 1850's was also a period of railroad building, coal- and iron-mining developments in Pennsylvania, and industrial growth. There was an overinvestment of fixed capital and an overbuilding of railroads—some $1,250,000,-000 of railroad securities were marketed between 1850 and 1860, a stupendous sum for that era. In August, 1857, the Ohio Life Insurance and Trust Company, which had $5,000,000 tied up in railroad loans, and whose New York agent had defaulted, failed with large liabilities to eastern institutions. This was sufficient to topple over the house of cards. A panic followed in New York City, and most of the banks were forced to suspend specie payments. Many of the western railroads went into bankruptcy, as did numerous other speculative enterprises. In 1857 there were almost five thousand failures. It was the financial institutions and finan-

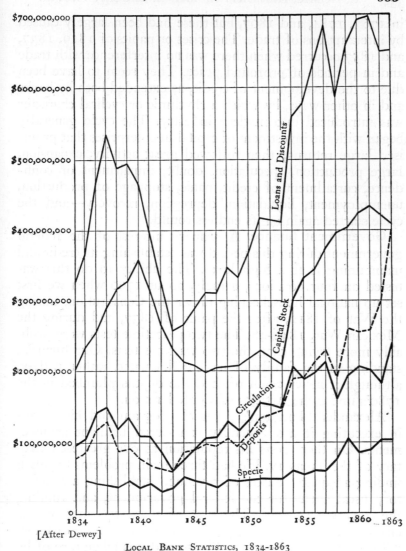

[After Dewey]

LOCAL BANK STATISTICS, 1834-1863

cial centers that were most affected, however. The country as a whole quickly recovered from the effects of this panic and by the end of the decade showed no trace of its results.

The panics that appeared during this period were a new phenomenon in American economic life. There had been commercial depressions during the colonial period and later, as in 1763, 1784, and 1807, but these had been largely caused by interruptions of trade. The crises or panics of 1819, 1837, and 1857 occurred when there was no interference with trade and in periods of profound peace. They seem to have been due to the development of credit, as extended both by banks and in other ways, by which a rhythmic or cyclical character was introduced into modern industry. The cycle generally began with the investment of capital in enterprises that promised large returns; then followed great activity, expansion, large production, speculation, doubt, impairment of confidence, curtailment of credit, panic, stoppage of production, unemployment, liquidation, depression, recovery—and the cycle started again on its endless round.

Government finance. A primary interest of the federal government during this period was establishing its credit and maintaining it at a high level. The ability to do this was tested on four occasions, namely, about 1790 when we first set up national housekeeping under the Constitution, during the War of 1812, after the panic of 1837, and during the Mexican War, 1846-48. The two peacetime tests were probably more trying than the two wartime tests. Our financial standing in the family of nations fluctuated rather widely, although it never again reached the depths plumbed in the 1780's under the Articles of Confederation.

Alexander Hamilton's financial program and his success in executing it are generally considered brilliant achievements. On them rests his reputation as our greatest Secretary of the Treasury. He had three main problems to solve: finding adequate sources of revenue, establishing a satisfactory fiscal agent for the federal government, and funding the government debt. The first of these was met by the enactment of a tariff act and later by the imposition of internal revenue or excise taxes. The second was taken care of by founding the First Bank of the United States which has already been described. It not only loaned the government over $6,000,000 in the difficult years after its founding, but also collected, transferred, paid out, and generally cared for government funds, which are functions of a fiscal agent.

The third problem, funding the public debt, was more complex. During the war and the unsettled period of the

Confederation Congress had borrowed abroad, borrowed at home, issued quantities of paper money, and called upon the states to use their credit, all to win the common struggle against England. Nearly all these debts were still outstanding, most of them at a heavy discount. As long as that condition continued, our credit or ability to borrow any more would be very poor indeed. If another emergency should arise, it might result in a calamity. Hamilton proposed to reorganize this complex mass of debts and set up a program for paying off our creditors, some at a discount and some in full, depending on the kind of debt held. There was little question as to the desirability of paying off the foreign debt of $11,700,000, or the domestic debt of $40,000,000, but the proposal that the federal government assume the debts incurred by the several states—$21,500,000—met with considerable opposition. In the first place, the southern states, which had paid their debts, objected to helping pay northern state debts, too. In general, the industrial and commercial interests, as well as those who saw a chance for profit by speculating in public securities, were united in support of the funding program, including assumption of state debts, while against them were ranged the farmers and planters, the artisans and mechanics upon whom would fall much of the taxation needed to pay off this indebtedness. Only through a political bargain between Hamilton and Jefferson, by which the national capital was to be located on the Potomac, were sufficient votes finally obtained to carry the measures through Congress. Altogether some $70,000,000 worth of debts were funded, including about $600,000 for Continental paper dollars at one cent each. As Hamilton had prophesied, this action improved the nation's credit immeasurably, and also, as he had planned, it had the result of consolidating popular support of the federal government. Holders of the new government bonds now had a direct personal stake in the success of the new central government.

Despite a drastic reduction in the national debt before the War of 1812, the nation was not financially prepared for that war. The First Bank had just been liquidated; an able Secretary of the Treasury, Albert Gallatin, was under political fire and about to resign; New England was unsympathetic to the war and contributed little toward waging it; the army and navy were not ready although hostilities had been threatening for years; and, finally, Congress was unwilling to impose adequate taxes. The war was financed largely by means of loans, although some non-legal-tender treasury notes were put in circulation. If the conflict had been more serious or prolonged, our finances and general credit might have fallen into a very bad state indeed. Even as it was, specie payments were suspended for over two years after the burning of Washington in 1814, prices rose about 40 per cent, and government bonds had to be offered at more than 20 per cent discount at times. However, the situation rapidly improved with the coming of peace and especially after the founding of the Second Bank in 1816.

In the years that followed the national debt was gradually reduced until by January of 1835 it was entirely paid off. That rare and happy event in the financial history of nations caused considerable concern to Congress. Unless the tariff was further lowered, against the wishes of industrial sections, tax money would pour into the treasury and either drain cash from commercial centers or excite the avarice of many congressmen seeking some special benefits for their districts. In the end Congress elected to leave the surplus on deposit with the states. However, before the third quarterly payment was made, the panic of 1837 took place and deficits instead of surpluses worried the treasury. To make matters worse, several states defaulted on bonds they had issued to pay for internal improvements. Close to half of the bonds were in the hands of foreign investors who had bought them from the English investment house of Baring Brothers and others. The defaults reflected not merely on the states but on the Barings and on the United States. Many persons, including the Barings, expected the federal government to assume the debts of the states as had been done in 1790. When that did not happen again and the treasury sought to borrow money elsewhere abroad, the Paris member of the famous Rothschild family told our treasury agent, "You may tell your government that you have seen the man who is at the head of the finances of Europe, and that he has told you that they cannot borrow a dollar, not a dollar." [4] Nevertheless, the state debts were not assumed and the federal government was in time able to restore its credit and by the latter 1840's Europeans were again investing large amounts here.

Meanwhile order had to be restored to the treasury's system of collections and disbursements. When the panic of 1837 broke, millions of dollars had been "frozen" in the "pet" banks that were government depositories after 1834. To prevent a repetition of this the founding of a Third Bank was urged. When it did not materialize, the so-called independent or subtreasury system was established, at first temporarily in 1840 and then permanently in 1846. According to this the government was to separate itself completely from the banks, and was neither to establish a central bank nor to make use of the state banks. It would not use them as fiscal agents nor deposit government revenues with them; nor would it receive bank notes in payments to itself. The government was to establish subtreasuries, which should collect all the revenue in specie, and make all disbursements in cash through its own officials. Although not as versatile and effective an institution as the First or Second Banks, the independent treasury system prevented losses to the government and gave to the treasury better control of its funds than it had possessed before. It was established in time to help with the financing of the Mexican War.

The Mexican War cost the country about $65,000,000 but was actually little strain on the nation's credit. Bonds were sold at a premium and paid for in specie in contrast to the War of 1812 when they were sold at a discount for paper money. The general price level hardly fluttered. The reason for the better showing lay not so much in improved methods of financing, for both wars were financed chiefly by borrowing, but in the greater economic strength of the country and the relative ease of the victory. Not until the Civil War were the nation's finances to be severely tested again.

Conclusion. The main thread which runs through the financial history of this period is the continued effort of the people of the United States to provide themselves with the

[4] C. Lewis, *op. cit.*, 28.

necessary media of exchange. In the solution of this problem the federal government lent its aid directly by establishing a mint and twice by chartering a central bank, and indirectly by instituting the independent treasury system. It endeavored in these ways to regulate the money supply and to furnish the people with a uniform national metallic currency and with a safe credit money. The people, especially in the less developed sections, were frequently impatient with these restraints and sought to organize banking institutions which would provide them with cheaper and more plentiful money. These experiments were attended with mistakes and sometimes led directly to serious panics, but they were the mistakes of an impulsive and untutored child rather than the results of wilful misbehavior. By the end of the period, the principles of sound currency and good banking were better understood, and in the older sections of the country were being embodied in practice.

CHAPTER XV

THE INDUSTRIAL REVOLUTION

Manufactures to 1808. The course of industrial development was but little affected by the events that immediately preceded and led up to the Revolution. During its progress the production of various articles was greatly stimulated by the urgent demand for war supplies, by the interruption of foreign commerce, and by the high prices of a paper-money regime. Especially was this true of the iron and steel industry, of textiles, and of other articles of necessity, such as paper, gunpowder, glass, and pottery. The cutting off of foreign supplies stimulated household industries primarily, for the factory had not yet been developed. These household industries expanded and contracted quickly and silently in response to changes in demand, but their growth at this time indicates no significant trend to manufactures nor movement away from other occupations. This is shown by the prompt disappearance of many of these infant industries when peace was declared, since they could not compete with the flood of cheap manufactured goods that poured into the country from Great Britain.

Political independence had been achieved, but industrially the people of the United States were almost as dependent upon Great Britain as they had been during the colonial period. After the Revolution, as before, they continued to devote themselves to agriculture and commerce; this event, important as it is in political history, marks no such definite turning point in our industrial development. Manufacturing was confined for the most part to village crafts and household industries, which were to be found widely diffused, and gave no hint of the future development of the factory system with power-driven machinery. At this time the most important household manufactures were of flax, and quantities of linen were made in New England homes and trafficked throughout the then western country. Hosiery, lace, edging, and other knit goods were made in families and sold to merchants or bartered with peddlers for other manufactures. Nail-making was still partly a fireside industry.

The industrial revolution. Early in the nineteenth century there began in this country such fundamental changes in methods of manufacturing that they have since been called the industrial revolution. To most of us the phrase means the coming of the factory with its machine methods of production and the factory towns with their poorly paid and ill-housed workers weary from long hours of monotonous toil. Thus the industrial revolution connotes social as well as mechanical change. As it progressed, a growing portion of the population depended on industry rather than on agriculture or commerce for their livelihood. But while the industrial revolution brought profound changes in the lives of thousands it did not bring about these changes suddenly, as the word revolution suggests. The shift from manufacturing in the home to manufacturing in a factory was really more of an evolution. How it took place in the shoe and the textile industry will be described shortly. First, however, we need to know the conditions that produced an industrial revolution.

Economic conditions in the United States at the start of the nineteenth century were ripe for an industrial revolution. Labor was no longer as scarce as it had been in colonial times, yet it was still sufficiently expensive for laborsaving devices to be very profitable. We were not handicapped by very cheap labor, which is what has stifled interest in machinery in the Orient and delayed the industrial revolution there. The rapidly growing population and improving means of transportation provided adequate markets for larger-scale production. Capital was available as a result of a hundred and fifty years of success in commerce, and the nation was endowed with timber, coal, iron, water power, and other resources, all in reasonably close proximity to one another and to the markets. All that was needed was a resourceful and energetic people—to discover and realize the possibilities of these factors. The people were here; all waited upon the proper occasion.

For a time circumstances conspired not only to postpone the development of factories but even to discourage household industries. Beginning in 1793 war broke out between France and England, and extended until it involved practically all the nations of western Europe. Between 1793 and 1807 we were the leading neutral nation, and gained greatly by our position. Enormous profits were being made from the sale of our agricultural produce to the belligerents and from the carriage of our commodities and of the colonial products of those nations whose ships England had driven from the seas. Capital and labor were diverted from household manufacturing and applied to the more profitable lines of farming and shipping; this is illustrated by the growth of American merchant shipping between 1789 and 1810 from 202,000 tons to 1,425,000 tons, all built in the United States. For our exports we received in exchange not merely the factory-made goods of England, but also low-grade handmade cotton fabrics from India and China and Russia and Holland. It was cheaper to buy imported goods than to manufacture them at home.

Looking back over this period twenty years later, Albert Gallatin, the Secretary of the Treasury, explained the slow growth of domestic manufactures in the United States by the following reasons: the abundance of land, the high price of labor, the scarcity of capital, the greater profitableness of agriculture and commerce during the continental wars, and the continuance of old habits.

So slow was the growth of manufactures that in 1800, ten years after the establishment of the first cotton mill by Samuel Slater, there were only eight cotton factories in the country. Indeed, Great Britain supplied us with such a large proportion of our manufactured goods that when in 1806 it was proposed to cease intercourse with her, such a plan was pronounced impossible, and we read of Secretary of War Henry Dearborn, after the embargo, asking that it be suspended in order that woolen blankets might be imported for the Indians, since these could not be produced in the United States. "China, glass, pottery, hardware, cutlery, edged tools, blankets, woolen cloths, linen, cotton prints," says McMaster, "and a hundred other articles of daily use came from Great Britain in such quantity that the value of each year's imports amounted to $35,000,000." English and French outrages against our neutral shipping, however, grew worse and required retaliation. The resulting break in our commercial relations with England provided the opportunity needed for domestic manufacturing to develop.

The United States as an industrial nation. The year 1808 may be taken as a convenient line of demarcation to distinguish the period of industrial dependence of the United States upon European countries from that of industrial self-sufficiency and diversified internal development. With the passage of the Embargo Act, the Non-Intercourse Act, and finally with the outbreak of the War of 1812, foreign trade was greatly hindered if not destroyed, and the country was thrown back on its own resources. Domestic production was greatly stimulated by this period of restriction, and establishments for the manufacture of cotton and woolen goods, iron, glass, hardware, and other articles sprang up with mushroom rapidity all over the country.

The conduct of the War of 1812, moreover, tended to stimulate manufactures. The purchase by the government of large quantities of uniform articles[1] favored the factory rather than the scattered household industries. Writing of this period, Warden reported:[2] "The immense capital which had been employed in commerce, previously to the restrictions, was transferred to manufactures; and workshops, mills and machinery for the fabrication of commodities, were erected, as if by enchantment." The manufactures prospered, and the profits from them offset in part the losses from the cessation of commerce.

---

[1] The manufacture of firearms is a good illustration of this. In 1798 Eli Whitney applied the principle of interchangeable parts, which had already been used in France, to the manufacture of guns. He obtained a contract with the federal government to manufacture some 10,000 muskets by a plan which he said would "make the same parts of different guns, as the locks for example, as much like each other, as the successive impressions of a copper plate engraving." For each part he made a mold, so that the castings of any gun were interchangeable with the same parts of any other gun. Whitney was very successful, recouping the fortune he had lost in the cotton gin, and the interchangeable system was introduced generally into government armories and private establishments for the manufacture of firearms. So identified did this method become with our best practice that the system of interchangeable parts was known in Europe as "the American method."

[2] D. B. Warden, *Statistical, Political, and Historical Account of the United States* (Edinburgh, 1819), III.

The evolution of a shoe factory. Factories of course did not spring from nowhere, mushroom fashion. The factory is but the last of several stages in the transfer of manufacturing from home to factory. Although the factory first appeared in the production of cotton textiles, the clearest picture of the rise of the factory system is to be found in the shoe industry.[3] Familiarity with that will help in understanding the developments in other industries and so it will be discussed first even though it did not all happen first. There were four stages in the development of the shoe industry.

The home stage. In colonial New England, and in later frontier areas too, shoes were generally made in the home. Under frontier conditions the father of the household was of necessity a jack-of-all-trades. His shoemaking equipment was simple—a knife, an awl, needles, and several lasts or foot forms. On an autumn evening, when the season for going barefoot was about ended, he would take the foot measurements of one of his sons, choose from his supply of lasts the one nearest the proper size, cut the leather he had tanned himself, and make the boy a pair of shoes. The shoes were crude and might pinch the lad's toes or he might seem to take several steps before starting to walk, but they got his feet off the cold hard ground. If someone in the community developed skill at shoemaking, the neighbors were glad to let him make their shoes in exchange for some other service. But if a man were to put in all his time making shoes, he would soon run out of orders if he stayed in one small village. Hence the early shoemaker became an itinerant craftsman, moving from village to village, boarding at the homes of his customers and accepting food, clothing or other produce in exchange for his services. Since he made better-fitting shoes and brought gossip from other villages and stories of adventure from the outside world, his arrival was always welcomed. But in time the shoemaker tired of the wandering life and yearned to settle down in a community large enough to support him most of the year. At this point the home stage ended and the handicraft stage began.

---

[3] Most of the material in the next few pages is based on Blanche Hazard's *The Organization of the Boot and Shoe Industry in Massachusetts Before 1875* (Cambridge, 1921). A shorter version is in the February, 1913, *Quarterly Journal of Economics.*

2. *The handicraft stage.* The chief characteristic of the handicraft stage was that the shoemaker still met his customer face to face, but now it was in the shoemaker's shop, for the customer came to him. Most shoes were made on order —called "bespoke work"—and the shoemaker usually supplied the leather. Occasionally a customer died or failed for some reason to take the shoes he had ordered, and sometimes business was dull and the shoemaker made up a batch of average-sized shoes to have on hand. These he could sell from his shop, or he might trade them to the local general store in exchange for groceries or other supplies, or he might even take them to a larger town and dispose of them to a merchant there. It is at this point, when the shoemaker ceased to deal directly with his customer, that the handicraft stage ended and the domestic stage began.

3. *The domestic stage.* In the domestic stage the middleman appeared. Usually he had been a shoemaker himself but sometimes, like Ephraim Lincoln of Braintree, he was a local storekeeper. Whoever he was, he left orders with various shoemakers throughout the countryside, supplied them with leather, picked up the shoes periodically and sold them in town or even shipped them to points as far distant as New Orleans or the West Indies. This system of distribution and collection was known as "putting out." Most of the shoes were still plain in appearance—lefts and rights were made only on special order before the 1850's. Shoes were often displayed in a general store in a barrel from which the customer picked out two of about the proper size. In fact shoemaking standards declined during the domestic stage because the shoemaker no longer dealt directly with his customer. Instead his chief interest was the income he received—the more shoes he made the more pay he got and the middleman would generally take them as fast as he could make them. To fatten their incomes some of the less scrupulous shoemakers cut the leather that was furnished them wastefully and disposed of the leftover pieces to traveling scrap-leather dealers. And to speed up production the shoemaker taught members of his family to perform some of the simpler tasks while he did the more difficult ones.

This idea appealed to the middleman too. In order to avoid paying master-craftsman rates and to eliminate the scrap-leather racket, the middleman set up his own central shop where he cut his own leather and then portioned it out to workers to do the "fitting"—the work on the uppers—and then to bring it back to the central shop, from which it was again distributed to the "makers" along with the proper number of rough-cut soles and the right amount of thread to assemble the shoe. Yet this involved much lost motion, wide variation in the quality of work done, shoe parts left a long time in the hands of slow workers, and other inconveniences. Delays became especially exasperating when hundreds of crates of shoes were being prepared for shipment to California or Australia in the early 1850's. It was this urgent need to save time and gain efficiency that resulted in the final concentration of shoemaking in one building. Here, too, machines could be used most profitably, for they could be kept in almost constant operation. Thus the domestic stage ended and the factory stage began. Probably the first shoe factory was founded at Lynn, Massachusetts, shortly before the Civil War.

The factory stage. Whether the article produced is shoes, textiles, or something else, the factory system has certain well-defined characteristics. By the factory system is meant the concentration of all the processes of manufacture in a factory, involving their withdrawal from the household and shop where they had previously been carried on; it involves also the use of specialized machines, driven by non-human power, and the organization of the workers under skilled management, for stipulated wages and fixed hours, with production for the general market and not upon order.

The evolution of the factory system has been going on ever since the eighteenth century and is still in process. In general, the older and more populous parts of the country reached the factory stage first. Shoemaking remained in the handicraft and domestic stages in the Middle West for some time after the factory stage was reached in New England. Of course not all industries have passed through every stage outlined above; ironmaking did not, for example. On the other hand, even today these preliminary stages may be found in occupations not yet ready for the factory system. In most homes the mother is still the "jill-of-all-trades" so far as food preparation is concerned; we can all remember itinerant scissors grinders, who still exist in many sections, and are familiar with tailors who do custom work; and in big cities cheap dresses are still being "put out" for completion just as in the domestic stage in shoemaking. The products that reached the factory stage first were those which could be easily standardized, hence made by machine methods, and for which there was a large and fairly steady demand. Cotton cloth came first, both here and in England.

Cotton textiles. Textile fabrics can be made out of almost any fibers, but only five have had any significance in the United States; these are cotton, wool, flax, hemp, and silk, and of these only cotton will be described here. Fibers are transformed into fabrics by four processes: (1) Preparation, which consists of cleaning and straightening the fibers and forming them into a ribbon or roll of loose parallel fibers for spinning. This operation was usually performed by passing two parallel cards over one another by hand; the cards were furnished with metal teeth which combed out the fibers. (2) Spinning draws out and twists the loose roll into a firm thread or yarn. (3) Weaving interlaces the threads into a fabric. (4) Finishing embraces such processes as bleaching, dyeing, fulling, pressing, and otherwise preparing the crude fabric for final use. Until the time of the Revolution all of these processes were performed by hand. Most women had to devote many hours of their life to this tedious household duty. Probably that is why people wore less clothing and patched their clothing more in the eighteenth century than in the nineteenth. When a way was found to relieve the housewife of this chore, she speedily accepted it.

It was in cotton cloth that most rapid progress was made in the machine manufacturing of textiles. The invention of the cotton gin by Eli Whitney in 1793 was most important in the cleaning of cotton, and shortly before 1790 cylinders revolving against rollers were substituted for hand cards. Spinning machinery, based on the English inventions of Hargreaves and Arkwright, was also introduced about the same time and somewhat later the power loom for weaving was adapted to American usage. All these inventions, except the cotton gin, were of foreign origin, but were improved upon by American inventors. As they were introduced, hand methods gave way to machines, and the industry began to move from the home to the factory.

Credit is usually given the English immigrant, Samuel Slater, for establishing the first successful factory in this country at Pawtucket, Rhode Island, in 1790. Only cotton yarn was made in the factory itself and it was "put out" for cleaning, weaving, and dyeing. Soon orders were being received from as far away as New York and Boston, but the company could be no more specific about delivery than to promise it sometime during the winter. As business grew, Slater, in conjunction with various partners, established mills in other towns, partly because the local labor supply was inadequate, partly to gain a wider market. By 1801 the firm was selling in Baltimore and by 1812 in Buffalo, but it was now encountering stiff competition from other new mills. The number of mills in the country grew from 8 in 1800, all in New England, with about 20,000 spindles, to 269 in 1810 with 87,000 spindles, and to 130,000 spindles in 1815. Consumption of raw cotton by domestic manufactures showed the same expansion, increasing from 500 bales [4] in 1800 to 10,000 bales in 1810 and 90,000 bales in 1815.

Further developments in cotton textiles. In 1814 Francis C. Lowell brought the various processes of spinning and weaving under one roof in his factory at Waltham, Massachusetts, which has therefore been called "the first complete factory in the world." Up to this time only the spinning was done by machinery, while the weaving was "put out" in homes, where it was done on hand looms. Lowell introduced a power loom which he "invented" upon his return from an inspection tour of English factories where somewhat similar looms were already in use. By 1822 the business of the company was too large for the water power available at Waltham and a new mill was established at Pawtucket Falls on the Merrimac River and the new village was named Lowell. By the time of the Civil War this had become the second largest city in Massachusetts.

[4] A bale contained 300 pounds at this period.

The fall in the price of cotton cloth after factory weaving began was remarkable. "In 1815, when cotton cloth was still woven chiefly by hand—the family weaver finishing only four yards of cloth a day—the price of ordinary cloths for sheeting was forty cents a yard. In 1822 it had fallen to twenty-two cents, and in 1829 to four and one-half cents." In 1860, by which time the factory system had completely abolished household manufacture, and when the power loom was in full operation, the price was reduced to 2 cents a yard as a result of machine methods. The increased productiveness of labor through machinery was the cause of this great reduction in cost. "A hand-wheel spinner spun about 4 skeins of yarn a day. In 1815 a mill spinner could attend 90 spindles, producing daily 180 skeins. Ten years later each operative served more spindles and each spindle produced 5 skeins of yarn. Within another decade a single spinner operated nearly 200 spindles, and each of these produced a still larger product."[5]

From the beginning the cotton industry led all other manufactures in the amount of capital invested, the number of persons employed, and the value of the product. In 1830 the United States was second only to England in the amount of cotton consumed, and exceeded only by England and France in the number of spindles. The typical factory was, however, a small plant and the average unit had only 1500 spindles. The industry was early localized in the New England states, especially Massachusetts, three-fourths of all the cotton goods produced in 1840 being turned out by New England mills. The advantages of this section for manufacturing were close settlement, a population apt with machinery, many easily developed water-power sites, and an active commerce; and so great were these that they overcame the disadvantages of lack of most of the raw materials that entered into its varied manufactures. Between 1840 and 1860 the number of spindles more than doubled, the cotton industry growing nearly twice as fast as the population. Part of this enlarging output of textile mills represented a transfer from the home to the factory rather than an absolute growth of production. An effort was made to in-

[5] V. S. Clark, *op. cit.*, I, 432.

troduce cotton manufactures in the South, but the absence of a large local demand, the lack of skilled operatives, and the greater profitableness of cotton-growing prevented its development. In 1860 the total number of spindles in the South was only 290,000, or three-fourths of those in the single city of Lowell. The development in the West was even more backward. By this time cotton manufacture had reached a high stage of development. Six-sevenths of the cotton goods consumed in this country was made here, only the finer grades being imported.

The progress of cotton manufactures is shown statistically in the following table.

Year	Number of establishments	Capital	Number of employees	Number of spindles in factories	Raw cotton consumed (pounds)	Value of manufactured product
		COTTON MANUFACTURES, 1830-1860				
1830	795	$40,614,984	62,157	1,246,503	77,757,316	$26,000,000
1840	1240	51,102,259	72,119	2,284,631	118,500,000	46,350,453
1850	1074	76,032,578	94,956	3,634,000	272,527,000	65,501,687
1860	1091	98,585,269	122,028	5,235,727	422,704,975	115,681,774

The iron and steel industries. The use of metals, and especially of iron, has by common consent come to be considered the best measure of a nation's industrial progress. Judged by this standard, the United States advanced rapidly during the half century ending with 1860, for the output of iron multiplied nearly twentyfold, while the population only quadrupled. Beginning with 1790 American ironmasters enjoyed considerable prosperity, which was enhanced from 1807 to 1814, when importations were cut off and a great increase in production and manufacture of iron took place.

To understand the progress made in the iron industry in this period a few simple facts about iron- and steelmaking are essential. The difference between iron and steel is a chemical one of carbon content. Indeed, there are three forms which iron may take: cast iron, wrought iron, and steel. Cast iron has a high carbon content and is easiest to make but is brittle. Wrought iron or bar iron has no carbon in it, the carbon having been pounded or burnt out by a further processing of cast iron. It is malleable but is soft and wears out easily. Steel stands between cast iron and wrought iron in the matter of carbon content. It is more malleable and durable than wrought iron. But for centuries the process of making steel was not only time-consuming but required great skill to attain the proper amount of carbon in the metal. Only an expert cook could tell from the appearance of his "iron brew" when he had steel. Steel was therefore so costly that it could be used only in small amounts for special purposes. Obviously whoever discovered a cheap and quick method of making steel would make himself a fortune and would advance the industrial revolution greatly.

There are two basic steps in the manufacture of wrought iron or steel. First, the iron ore must be smelted in a blast furnace. The ingredients for this step are fuel, iron ore, and limestone to serve as a flux and carry off the impurities. When heated the lighter limestone and impurities ("slag") float on top like cream and the heavier molten iron settles to the bottom of the furnace. When the plug in the furnace is drawn out the iron flows into prepared channels and molds lined with sand. The appearance of the customary molds and main channel resembles pigs suckling a sow, hence the name pig iron for the product of the blast furnace. Of course the molten metal can be directed into any sort of shape desired, but it is still only cast iron at this stage. The second basic step is refining the iron in order to get rid of the excess carbon to obtain wrought iron or steel. The early method of making wrought iron was to heat the pigs in a furnace and then hammer them out on an anvil; this operation often required several reheatings. And of course there was always the third step of making the finished iron or steel implement for which the forging steps were only preparatory.

There was progress in all these stages of iron- and steel-making in the period before the Civil War. First let us look at the smelting or blast-furnace stage in which pig iron is produced. As long as pig iron was smelted with charcoal, the iron furnaces were necessarily small because a heavy load of ore would pack the light charcoal so tightly that the furnace would not draw. The small furnaces produced only two to four tons a day, and they had to be abandoned when the local wood supply was exhausted. For both these reasons the cost of producing pig iron remained high. Meanwhile the English had cut their costs by using coke, the hot-air blast, and other improved techniques and were able to ship iron and iron products to this country, much to the distress of our iron industry which loudly demanded a protective tariff. But about 1840 the smelting of iron in this country was revolutionized by the substitution of anthracite coal for charcoal, and by 1860 record furnace runs had risen to over 50 tons a day. This greatly improved the competitive position of our iron industry.

Progress was also made in methods of producing wrought iron. In 1817 the puddling and rolling process, invented in England thirty years earlier, was first introduced into this country at Plumstock in western Pennsylvania. By this method the molten iron was first puddled or stirred to expel the carbon, then passed through a squeezer to expel the cinder, and finally rolled into bars. This process and the use of anthracite as fuel came just in time to supply the vast demand created by the building of the railroads. Until 1845 there were practically no facilities for manufacturing the rails needed for the rapidly expanding railroads, and they were mostly imported from England. With the making of the first heavy rails in this country in 1845 there began a new era in iron rolling, which up to this time had produced chiefly bars for making nails. By 1850 there were sixteen rail mills in existence with an annual output of 100,000 tons; by 1860 their number had doubled.

Finally, not long before the Civil War, two inventors, William Kelly of Kentucky and Henry Bessemer of England, independently and almost simultaneously discovered a quick and cheap way of making steel. The process was amazingly simple. Molten iron was placed in a pear-shaped receptacle called a converter and a blast of air was blown through the hot metal. Sparks flew as oxygen united with carbon and burned. Then a chemical known as spiegeleisen which contained a known amount of carbon was added to the carbon-free iron in the converter to make it into steel.

Because of patent disputes between Kelly and Bessemer the new process was not used to any extent in this country until after the war.[6]

As for the manufacture of finished articles of iron, the United States early took the lead from all nations in the application of automatic machinery to metalworking. By combining this with the system of interchangeable parts, what was essentially a new system of manufacture was developed. Machines for cutting nails and making card-teeth for carding cotton, invented before 1790, were followed by others for making tacks, screws, spikes, bolts, rivets, files, chains, and pins. An equally striking illustration of the ingenuity of American producers is furnished by the manufacture of brass clocks, the parts of which were stamped out by machinery and which for cheapness and excellence were without rivals.

Localization of industries. The distribution of miscellaneous manufactures was fairly general throughout the country, every state being represented; New York, Pennsylvania, Massachusetts, and Ohio led in the value of output, in the order given. But there was already apparent a tendency to localization of particular manufactures in sections favorable to that industry. Thus New England ranked first as the seat of the textile industries, cottons being concentrated in Massachusetts and calicoes in Rhode Island. Bonnets and straw goods and boots and shoes were also strongly localized in Massachusetts, and hardware and rubber goods in Connecticut. The center of the iron industry shifted to Pennsylvania in 1810 and that state's importance in the industry was further enhanced when anthracite coal from the eastern counties replaced charcoal for smelting purposes. By the Civil War over half of all the iron produced and manufactured in the country came from Pennsylvania. Ohio ranked second. A few other cases of strong localization existed, primarily owing to the presence of supplies of raw material —such as turpentine in North Carolina, lard in Ohio, and lead in Wisconsin—but the great territorial division of in-

---

[6] Bessemer's converter was invented slightly earlier and was better than Kelly's, but Kelly had the exclusive rights to the spiegeleisen patents in the United States. In 1866 the two contestants wearied of fruitless litigation and combined.

dustry did not occur until after 1860 when the transportation systems were more fully developed.

New kinds of power. As the factories grew in number, size, and complexity, important changes took place in their machinery. Iron frameworks replaced those of hickory and oak, mineral oils supplanted animal and vegetable oils for lubrication because they could stand higher temperatures, coal supplanted charcoal, making possible larger blast furnaces, and human or animal power gave way to water power and that in turn to steam power. The power in Slater's first cotton mill was supplied by a Negro boy trotting on a treadmill. Many early mills were powered by float wheels which could be easily built because they required no dams or expensive equipment. But as the demand for more output developed, dams were constructed so that the more efficient overshot, undershot, or pitch-back mills could be used. At first engineering skill permitted only the damming of small streams and some of these, like the Blackstone River, were crowded with mill sites, but in time larger streams were harnessed. Beginning about 1840, as a result of the efforts of General Charles James, the more forward-looking textile mill owners began to replace water power with steam engines, which would run despite flood, drought, or freeze. The problem now was to find the coal and a way to transport it cheaply. Whenever this could be solved, as in the neighborhood of Philadelphia and New York, where canals connected with the Pennsylvania coal fields, steam quickly replaced water power. The fact that the water power there had been poor anyway was a further incentive to making the transition.

Sources of capital. All this industrial growth could not have occurred without a growing supply of capital. Capital has been defined as produced goods intended for further production, and by that is meant reapers, dynamos, sewing machines, spindles; in fact, tools and equipment of all kinds. During the nineteenth century the cost of producing a bushel of wheat declined about 80 per cent, chiefly through the use of machinery. Likewise the cost of producing steel, making cloth, preparing meat, and of pursuing countless other industrial activities was reduced primarily by the aid of machines and to a smaller degree by the increased skill of labor. Put improved tools in the hands of the worker and he becomes much more productive. Before the invention of the cotton gin it took one worker ten hours to separate the seeds from a pound and a half of cotton lint; a century later a worker operating an improved machine could gin from 1500 to 7500 pounds of lint in ten hours. Improved machinery has been a distinguishing feature of the industrial revolution and the chief cause of our steadily rising standard of living.

Capital, economists agree, is the result of saving but it is a mistake to assume that most of early industry's capital was derived from myriads of small personal savings. Even in the twentieth century most people normally spend all they get; this was probably even truer in the nineteenth century. Evidence on this point is scarce but what there is suggests that a hundred years ago, when the industrial revolution was beginning in this country, the small factory owner provided much of the capital himself. In forty years Samuel Slater accumulated $690,000 by plowing back some or all of the profits into his textile business. Lowell and his brother-in-law diverted to textile manufacturing the savings they had originally made in commerce. Two or more men as partners could usually supply and accumulate capital more rapidly than one; and as the corporation developed it proved even more effective than a partnership.

The rise of the corporation. The industrial revolution led to the widespread use of the corporate form of organization. J. S. Davis has estimated that there were only 335 corporations before 1800, two-thirds of them (200) being new turnpike companies or some other type of business "affected with public interest." An evil and monopolistic connotation had been attached to the corporation in the public mind ever since the South Sea Bubble episode of 1720, and democratic legislators were loath to grant corporate charters to private enterprises. Gradually, as the usefulness of corporations was realized, suspicions abated and restrictions were relaxed. By 1860 several states had general incorporation laws for certain types of business, which meant that a company no longer had to secure its charter in the form of a special law. Many of the charters now lacked the once popular clause limiting the life of the corporation. Probably the most important change was the withdrawal of the earlier imposition of unlimited—as in the partnership—triple, double, or proportional liability of the stockholders in favor of simple limited liability. This enabled corporations to draw capital from more investors since the participants shared in the profits but were protected against losing more than the value of their stock. The corporation was an artificial person, and when its funds were exhausted creditors could recover no more from the stockholders. As an artificial person the corporation could stand or bring suit in a court of law; moreover, it did not die with the death or retirement of a member. The corporate device, with these features protecting the businessman and the investor, was of invaluable assistance to the expanding business unit.

The textile companies located at Lowell were among the first industries to make use of the corporate device. In fact, for a time, the words "Lowell corporations" had the same rather ominous ring that the words "big business" often have today. Yet these companies were not large by modern standards. The Merrimac Company, one of the biggest, had only 390 stockholders and a capitalization of $2,500,000 in 1845. Following the panic of 1837, when the state governments ceased financing internal improvements, railroads turned to the corporate device to gain capital. By the Civil War it was being extensively used by textile, iron, and other manufacturing concerns, by railroads, by insurance companies, and by banks.

Investment agencies. Another significant source of capital was England and the Continent. Down to 1845 England supplied nearly all our iron rails and loaned us the money to buy them. By 1838 Europeans had close to $200,000,000 invested here, much of it in state bonds that had been issued to finance internal improvements. Large firms importing drygoods, investment houses like Baring Brothers of London, and the Second Bank of the United States were some of the channels through which these securities reached the English investors. It is said that on a single trip in 1836 the cashier of the Second Bank took $30,000,000 of American securities to London. Englishmen were tempted by the profit possibilities of canals and railroads in this growing nation and by the higher rates of interest. By 1860 some $400,000,000 of foreign money was invested here. Despite some disgraceful defaults in the late 1830's the average nineteenth-century English investor got his money back and a generous return on his American investments.[7]

In America bonds and stocks were sold in coffeehouses and later by brokerage firms and large commercial banks. The market consisted of a few wealthy persons, several large insurance companies, a growing number of banks, and numerous merchants and manufacturers. Not until the Civil War period was there a serious attempt to sell securities to small investors and those sold were government bonds. Stock exchanges or markets for the resale of securities already in circulation also began in this period.[8]

As a consequence of all these developments, the evolution of the corporation and of investment banking, the birth of stock exchanges, and the growing interest of foreign investors in this country, capital grew rapidly before the Civil War. Census figures for capital invested in manufactures alone indicate a growth from $50,000,000 in 1820 to $250,000,000 in 1840 and $1,000,000,000 in 1860.

The patent system. Another factor in promoting the industrial development of this period was the inventive genius of the people, which in turn was stimulated by the American patent system. Provision was first made by Congress in 1790 for giving to inventors the exclusive right to their discoveries by the passage of a law said to have been inspired by Jefferson. The number of inventions grew steadily, from an average of 31 per annum in the decade ending in 1800 to 2500 in the decade ending in 1860. The revolutionary improvements in farm implements have already been described; even more

---

[7] C. Lewis, *op cit.*, 167-68.

[8] The New York Stock Exchange dates its informal origin from 1792, but was not formally organized and housed until 1817. Government bonds, stocks of the United States banks, and state-sponsored internal improvement projects were the principal securities traded: the first railroad stock to appear on the exchange was that of the Mohawk and Hudson Railroad in 1830, and the first industrial shares were of the New York Gas and Light Company in 1831. By 1857 as many as 70,000 shares were traded on a record day. The stock exchanges encouraged security investment and thereby capital formation by making it easy for a person to turn his investments into cash on short notice.

spectacular were the new inventions of this period in the manufacturing industries. The magnetic telegraph, invented in 1835, was first practically applied by S. F. B. Morse in 1844, and in 1846 Elias Howe patented the sewing machine —two of the most important inventions of the half century. The sewing machine revolutionized the craft of the housewife, transferred the clothing industry to the factory, and was soon applied to the making of shoes, hats, harness, and similar articles. The period 1840–60 was one of great technological advance, the like of which did not occur again until the electrical inventions in the 1880's.

Most of the inventions for which patents were issued during this period consisted of laborsaving devices, the application of machinery to industrial processes, and new processes which simplified methods and reduced cost. But the inventions of this period were not merely of new machinery; they were largely of a utilitarian character and included many of the improvements which have raised the general standard of comfort in this country. "They related to improvements in looms for producing figured fabrics; to airheating stoves, cooking stoves, musical instruments, firearms, sewing machines, printing presses, boot and shoe machinery, rubber goods, floor cloths, and thousands of other inventions tending to raise and improve the standard of living of the people."

The manufacture of American edge tools began; the invention of planing machines revolutionized woodworking; in 1842 the Nasmyth steam hammer was invented, and in 1847 the cylinder printing press. Piece by piece, in response to industrial needs, the mechanical appliances were being perfected which made possible the enormous production of the complete factory system and its operation under skilled and centralized direction.

The tariff. Manufacturing was also influenced by tariffs. In those days the tariff was one of the few ways in which government policies directly affected business, and therefore the tariff received relatively more attention than it does today. A tariff is an import duty—the Constitution forbids export duties. It is imposed by act of Congress signed by the President—the Constitution forbids states to impose tariffs. In general, tariffs are enacted for one or the other of two purposes, either to raise revenue or to protect the country's industries from foreign competition. The same tariff often does both, although it cannot do both satisfactorily, for the two purposes are contradictory. A really protective tariff will carry such high duties that foreign goods cannot enter and consequently no revenue will be produced; and a true revenue tariff will place import duties only on articles not produced at home, in order to obtain as much revenue as possible. American tariffs were primarily revenue tariffs until about 1816. As can be seen on the accompanying table, the average level of duties rose steadily from 1789 to 1828, and thereafter, with one exception (1842), declined steadily until the Civil War.

AVERAGE LEVEL OF DUTIES UNDER TARIFF ACTS, 1789-1861

Year	Name of Tariff (if any)	Average duty
1789		5 per cent
1816		20
1818		25
1824		40
1828	Tariff of abominations	44
1832		40
1833	Compromise tariff	Gradual reduction to 20 per cent
1842		40
1846	Walker tariff	35
1857		30
1861	Morrill tariff	35

Probably the chief protection to American industry was afforded not by the tariff at all but by the severance of commercial relations with England between 1807 and 1814 because of the embargo and non-intercourse acts and the War of 1812. In general, the chief articles affected by the tariff were cotton and woolen textiles, wool and hemp, and iron and iron products. Proof that the tariff on many articles was not protective is seen in the fact that 80 to 95 per cent of the federal revenues came from import duties in this period. More important, however, than the degree of protection enjoyed by various products were the attitudes of different sections of the country toward the tariff.

Sectional attitudes toward the tariff. Except in 1816 when hatred of England was uppermost the South vigorously opposed the tariff. Since the South specialized in raising cotton, tobacco, and sugar, and brought in its manufactured goods, a tariff forced it either to pay duties on imported English manufactured goods or to buy higher-priced and sometimes inferior-quality American manufactures. Neither choice was pleasing, for both had the effect of reducing the real income obtained from the sale of cotton, tobacco, and sugar abroad. Perhaps the degree of prosperity also had something to do with the southern attitude toward the tariff. South Carolina usually led the opposition. When depression settled on that state because her lands were wearing out and because competition from new cotton areas in the rich Gulf states was being felt, South Carolinians fastened on the tariff as the scapegoat for their economic difficulties. As one historian has since described the situation, "In 1816 the average price of middling uplands in New York was nearly thirty cents, and South Carolina's leaders favored the tariff; in 1820 it was seventeen cents, and the South saw in the protective system a grievance; in 1824 it was fourteen and three-quarters cents, and the South Carolinians denounced the tariff as unconstitutional. When the woolens bill was agitated in 1827, cotton had fallen to but little more than nine cents, and the radicals of the section threatened civil war." [9] Some historians believe that southern hostility to the tariff was a more important cause of the Civil War than the slavery question.

The attitude of New England toward the tariff was fairly evenly divided, the manufacturing sections favoring the tariff and the commercial cities opposing it. The merchants saw clearly enough that protective tariffs lessened international trade and thereby lessened the demand for shipping and other mercantile services. The industrialized middle states of New York, New Jersey, and Pennsylvania consistently supported the tariff.

The viewpoint of the West toward the tariff varied. Producers of wool in the Northwest and of hemp in Kentucky demanded protection. And the West was strongly influenced by Henry Clay's "American System" for about twenty years after 1824. Clay proposed the development of a "home

[9] F. J. Turner, *Rise of the New West* (New York, 1906), 325.

market" by the combination of federally supported internal improvements—roads and canals—and the tariff. The internal improvements were to enable the West to ship its produce east to sell for tariff-protected American manufactures. By the 1840's the appeal of this program had worn off and the West joined the South in support of lower duties until the Republicans offered a homestead act in 1860 as an inducement for western support of the tariff.

Economic significance of the tariff. The influence of the tariff on the development of manufactures in the United States is complicated by so many other factors that it is difficult to establish causal relationships. Manufactures were prostrated so completely by the excessive importations of British merchandise in 1815 and 1816 that the tariff act of the latter year was a minor factor in the general situation. The recovery which followed after the crisis of 1819 was due less to the tariff acts of 1818, 1824, 1828, and 1832 than to the normal revival of industrial activity; indeed, the political agitation of the tariff was a retarding influence by creating business uncertainty. The tariff act of 1833, though it provided for lower duties, introduced a settled tariff policy and permitted a steady development. The prosperity which followed the protective tariff of 1842 was due in any event after the long depression resulting from the panic of 1837, and was even greater under the revenue tariff of 1846. And finally the panic of 1857, which some writers have ascribed to the tariff act of that year, was really brought about by the undue credit expansion, too rapid railroad building, speculation in western lands, and doubtful industrial enterprises. The negative conclusion seems justified that the protective tariff was not an important cause in the growth of manufactures, as a whole, though some of them profited greatly by the protection granted them during the difficult years of infancy. It should not be overlooked, however, that the consumers paid a price, and in some cases a high one, for the benefits conferred upon the protected industries.

The three economic revolutions. The development of manufactures was at all times limited by the state of transportation which largely determined the size of the market.

The turnpike, canal, steamboat, and railway reduced the time and the cost involved in assembling materials, fuel, and laborers at some convenient point and in distributing the finished products. The industrial revolution could not have taken place if there had not been a transportation revolution simultaneously. It is noteworthy that Samuel Slater was a heavy subscriber for turnpike stock because he believed good roads were "a necessary appendage to the manufacturing interest," and that the proprietors of textile mills on the Merrimack contributed a bonus of $100,000 to the building of a road from Lowell to Boston.[10] As transportation improved there was a tendency toward the concentration of manufactures at the most favorable locations, and industrial cities grew up like Fall River, Paterson, Rochester, Cincinnati, and Pittsburgh. But the people who worked in the mills and offices in these cities had to be fed. Improved transportation was therefore needed to bring in the surplus farm products from many parts of the country. When farmers began producing for more than their own needs, the improved and more efficient equipment had a stronger appeal to them. These lightened their labors and increased their buying power for the cities' manufactures. Thus the agricultural revolution fitted into the picture, too. None of the three economic revolutions could have occurred without the other two and no one came first—they all occurred together —they had to.

[10] V. S. Clark, *op. cit.*, I, 353.

CHAPTER XVI

POPULATION AND LABOR

Growth of the population. In accordance with the section of the Constitution providing for a decennial enumeration of the inhabitants of the United States for the purpose of apportioning representatives and direct taxes the first census was taken in 1790. This was not merely the first in this country, but was the first periodic census in any nation, for not until 1801 did England and France make provision for similar statistical inquiries, and other countries did so still later. The census of 1790 recorded a population of 3,930,000, which was almost evenly divided between the North and the South. Most of the people (about 69 per cent) were native whites of English descent, for there had been little immigration since the beginning of the Revolution; but there was an admixture of various other white racial elements (about 12 per cent) and about a fifth of the population (19 per cent) were Negroes, most of whom were to be found in the South.

The majority of the people still lived along the Atlantic seaboard, although the movement to the West was already beginning which was to drain the East of part of its population. At this time Virginia was the most populous state, followed by Pennsylvania, North Carolina, Massachusetts, and New York. Manufactures had not yet developed sufficiently to bring about the great population increase in the industrial states which was to follow the introduction of the factory system, and consequently the agricultural and commercial states held the lead. The rural communities were largely self-sufficing, supplying their wants by farming and by household industries. In the seaboard cities there was considerable commerce, but inadequate means of transportation prevented foreign wares from penetrating far inland. The largest city in the country in 1790, Philadelphia, had a

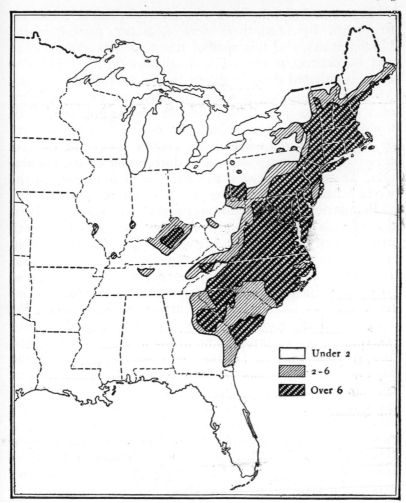

POPULATION PER SQUARE MILE, 1790

population of only 42,444, while New York, which ranked
second, had 33,131, followed by Boston (18,028), Charleston (16,359), and Baltimore (13,503); no other city had
over 8000 inhabitants and only 3.3 per cent of the people
lived in towns of 8000 or more.[1]

During the next seventy years the population grew steadily
and rapidly, increasing each decade almost 35 per cent,

[1] *Abstract of the Fifteenth Census of the United States* (Washington, 1933), 23.

which is equal to a doubling of the population every twenty-five years. By 1820 there were 9,600,000 persons in the United States, and this number rose to 17,000,000 in 1840 and 31,000,000 in 1860. The distribution of the population at three selected dates is shown in the accompanying maps. Most of this increase was due to the natural excess of births over deaths, as immigration did not become important until toward the end of the period. Not merely was the rapidity of the growth remarkable, but certain significant changes occurred in the composition and distribution of the population. These changes were the increase in immigration, the westward movement, and the growth of cities.

Population changes: immigration. No official immigration records were kept until 1820, but estimates have been made which indicate that between 1789 and 1820 about 234,000 aliens arrived in this country or about 7700 a year. It is not surprising that the movement should have been so small, for numerous factors conspired to hamper it. The interruption of normal relations during the Revolution, the long period of depression which followed it, the European wars which gave employment at home, our own embargo and War of 1812 and the panic of 1819, as well as the expense and hazards of the ocean voyage all tended to discourage immigration. After 1820, however, a period of good times set in—interrupted only by the panic of 1837 and the resulting depression—and this, combined with a number of bad conditions in Europe, brought an ever-swelling tide of immigrants to the United States. During the twenties immigration was small, but in the thirties the industrial depression in England sent overseas a larger emigration, bringing the number up to 100,000 in 1842. But the first great wave occurred after 1845, owing to the potato famine in Ireland in 1846, which drove a million and a quarter destitute Irish to this country in ten years, and to similar famines and the political disturbances in Europe in 1848, which resulted in a large exodus of Germans and others. At the same time the United States offered extraordinary attractions: the demand for labor at high wages, the availability of cheap land, and the discovery of gold in California in 1848, together with the cheapening and quickening of ocean transportation

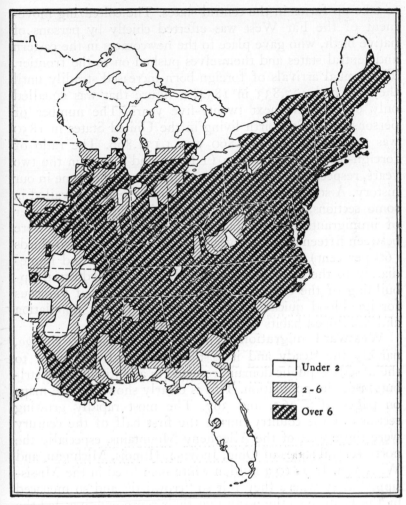

	Under 2
	2 - 6
	Over 6

POPULATION PER SQUARE MILE, 1840

through the introduction of ocean steamers—all these factors stimulated a large population movement toward this favored land.

Of the immigrants landing during this period over half came from Great Britain and Ireland and nearly a third from Germany. The Irish furnished much of the unskilled labor for the works of internal improvement or settled in the eastern cities, while the Germans and the English tended to take up farms in the central states. The colonizing movement of the Far West was effected chiefly by persons of native birth, who gave place to the newcomers in the eastern and central states and themselves pushed on to the frontier. The annual arrivals of foreign-born increased steadily until they reached 427,833 in 1854, a figure that was equalled only once in the next twenty-five years. The number of persons of foreign birth living in the United States in 1850 was 2,240,535, and in 1860 was 4,131,866. The ratio of foreign-born to native-born (1 to 10 and 1 to 8 in the two years, respectively), was greater than in any other time in our history. A strong spirit of hostility to foreigners prevailed in some sections.[2] Equally significant with the large number of immigrants was the fact that two-thirds of them were between fifteen and forty years of age and almost two-thirds (60 per cent) were males, thus adding greatly and immediately to the labor force, and aiding in the industrial upbuilding of the country. Such a large infusion of vigorous foreign blood quickened the movement of the population and developed habits of change and enterprise.

Westward migration. The second important change, namely the steady and irresistible westward movement to the unsettled public domain, resulted in a continuous redistribution of the population. This is clearly shown by the maps on pages 363, 365, and 367. The most rapidly growing sections of the country during the first half of the century were those west of the Allegheny Mountains, especially the north central states of Ohio, Indiana, Illinois, Michigan, and Wisconsin. In 1810 a million white men lived in the Mississippi Valley where they felt so "crowded" and so menaced by the English to the north that their representatives led the agitation for war with England with the idea of conquering Canada. The census of 1850 showed that almost half (45 per cent) of the population lived west of the Allegheny Mountains. After 1850 the states west of the Mississippi

---

[2] In the 1850's a strong third party, the American or Know-Nothing Party, developed which held that immigration and Catholicism menaced our country. In the 1856 campaign the party urged that only native Americans be allowed to hold political office and that twenty-one years' residence in this country be a prerequisite to citizenship. The party's candidate for the presidency, ex-President Millard Fillmore, polled over 20 per cent of all the votes cast for that office and carried Maryland.

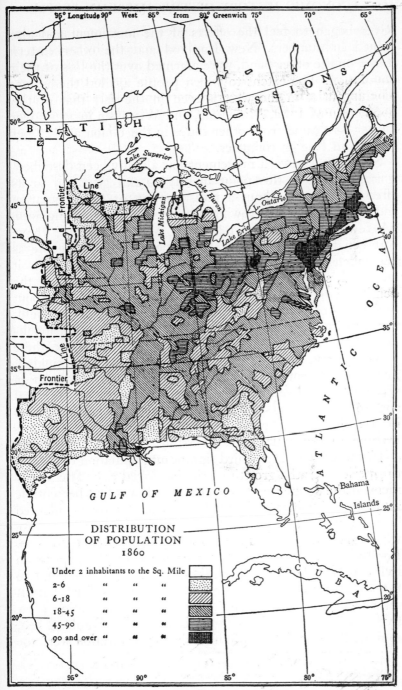

DISTRIBUTION
OF POPULATION
1860

Under 2 inhabitants to the Sq. Mile
2-6   "   "   "
6-18   "   "   "
18-45   "   "   "
45-90   "   "   "
90 and over "   "   "

River began to feel the effects of the movement and also gained in numbers. New England and the other eastern states, on the other hand, were alarmed over the loss of their population. The extent to which people availed themselves of this outlet in the west is seen in the fact that of the population of Iowa, Minnesota, and Wisconsin in 1860 over 43 per cent came from other states in the Union and 27 per cent from foreign countries.

Since the westward movement has already been described, it is sufficient at this point merely to call attention to its effect in bringing about a redistribution of the population and in spreading the growing numbers over a widening area. "A few clear-headed men," wrote Miss Martineau, "have foreseen the evil of so great a dispersion of the people as has taken place."[3] The population spread faster than it increased, so that with each acquisition of new territory the density of the population per square mile decreased. "About two-thirds of the inhabitants of America," stated Wakefield, "pass the greater part of their lives in comparative loneliness."[4] As a result of the lack of social intercourse these pioneers sank, or were thought to be in danger of sinking, into a state of semi-barbarism. The diffusion of the population was also considered to retard the accumulation of capital and to affect adversely the development of manufactures in the older states until improved transportation facilities made the newer settlements accessible.

Urban growth. The third significant population change of this period was the growth of the industrial city. The movement of the population to the city, which was first perceptible in the twenties, became marked after 1840. This is evidenced by the number of cities with a population of 8000 or more, which grew from 5 in 1790, to 44 in 1840, to 141 in 1860. For the same three dates the percentage of the population living under these urban conditions increased from 3.3 to 8.5 to 16.1. The distribution of these cities for 1840 is shown on the map on page 369. The city population grew five times as fast as that of the country as a whole. Then, as now, the chief causes of this urban concentration were the

---

[3] Harriet Martineau, *Society in America* (2 vols., New York, 1834-36), II, 67.
[4] Wakefield, *England and America* (London, 1834), 199.

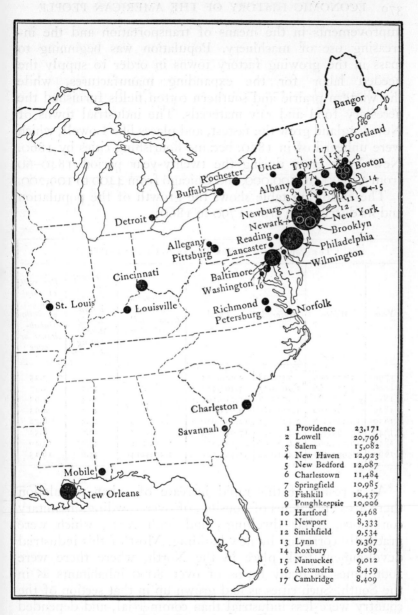

URBAN CONCENTRATION, 1840

improvements in the means of transportation and the increasing use of machinery. Population was beginning to mass in the growing factory towns in order to supply the needed labor for the expanding manufactures, while the western prairie and southern cotton fields furnished the necessary food and raw materials. The industrial towns of New England grew the fastest, and places like Lowell, which were unheard of in 1820, became flourishing cities by 1860. New York grew during the twenty-year period 1840–60 from 300,000 to 800,000, and Chicago from 4400 to 109,200.

The following table shows the growth of the population and its distribution from 1790 to 1860:

		THE POPULATION OF THE UNITED STATES, 1790-1860				
Year	White	Colored	Total	Immigration during decade ending with year	Per cent of growth of population during decade ending with year	Per cent of total in towns of 8000 inhabitants or over
1790	3,172,006	757,208	3,929,214			3.35
1800	4,306,446	1,002,037	5,308,483		35.1	3.97
1810	5,862,083	1,377,808	7,239,891	about 234,000	36.4	4.93
1820	7,862,166	1,771,656	9,633,822		33.1	4.93
1830	10,537,378	2,328,642	12,866,020	143,439	33.5	6.72
1840	14,195,805	2,873,648	17,059,453	599,125	32.7	8.52
1850	19,553,068	3,638,808	23,191,876	1,713,251	35.9	12.49
1860	26,991,491	4,441,830	31,443,321	2,598,214	35.6	16.13

As a result of this rapid increase of urban population there arose problems of housing, of overcrowding, insanitary conditions, cellar dwellings, and high rents, which were gradually corrected by new building. Most of this industrial development took place in the North, where there were four times as many towns of over 8000 inhabitants as in the South. Such cities as had grown up in that section of the country were less industrial than commercial, and depended for their prosperity upon the cotton, tobacco, and sugar trade rather than upon textile or iron manufacturing. Cotton presses and warehouses, not factories and foundries, filled the business sections and gave employment to labor. In the decade

1850–60 the movement to the cities slackened perceptibly, owing to the gold discoveries and the rush to the Far West. Not until 1880 did the drift cityward proceed again as rapidly as it had between 1840 and 1865.

Changing industrial organization. Because this period of urban growth and industrial change witnessed the coming of both the factory and the trade union, the conclusion is often reached that the factory produced the trade union. This is not strictly true. While the factory system eventually stimulated unionism, the first unions came before the factory system. The women and children who were the principal operatives in the first factories were unsuitable material for unions and no serious attempt was made to organize them. The reasons for the first unions may be found in the loss of independence suffered by the industrial worker and this began when the middleman intervened between the craftsman and his customer. That occurred in the domestic stage, which was the step just preceding the factory stage.

The clear-cut distinction between employer and employee has not always existed. It is hard today to realize this fact or to understand the frequent complaints made in the nineteenth century against the wage system. We accept it as inevitable but for our forefathers it was a new and often distasteful experience. Before undertaking to discuss the labor movement it therefore will be necessary to trace the changes in industrial organization which gave rise to the wage system.

During the colonial period many articles were produced in the home, and in these household industries there was no possibility of price or wage struggles, for the producers and consumers were identical. Even the itinerant artisan, working up the raw material belonging to his customer in the home of the latter, was at little disadvantage, since labor was still so scarce that his wages remained high. When population became denser, the handicraftsman set up his own shop, where he worked up his own material on order from his customers, who were his neighbors. In the language of the day his product was a "bespoke" product. In this custom-order stage of industry the three functions of merchant, master, and journeyman were united in the same person, and the only things which threatened his returns were the poor quality of his own work or the competition of other handicraftsmen.

The next stage came when the master workman began to employ journeymen, and also to make goods in advance of orders for sale in his shop to transient visitors, in addition to the custom-made articles. The journeyman now occupied a less stable position, for he no longer owned the raw material or the shop, although he still retained his hand tools. Owing, however, to the restricted area of the market the relations between master and journeyman remained harmonious; they worked side by side and were not sharply differentiated either by earnings or social position. Conflicts over wages or hours were consequently infrequent. This retail shop stage prevailed in the shoe industry in Philadelphia in 1789.[5]

The next step was revolutionary for the worker. Improvements in transportation began to widen the market, and some of the more wealthy and enterprising merchants sought orders in the newly developing markets of the West and South. By 1800 trade was carried on by Philadelphia merchants as far west as Pittsburgh and Cincinnati and as far south as Charleston and New Orleans. With the widening of markets and sale to distant customers it became necessary to extend long-time credit, and this required capital. New banking facilities came into being and a new credit system which favored the larger producer. Under these conditions there developed a new type of merchant who took over the wholesale business made possible by the wider markets, with the recently added warehouse and commission business. The former master became a small contractor, employing one to a dozen journeymen, and sold his product to this merchant wholesaler instead of to his customers.

Meanwhile the merchant seeking orders and selling to retailers in the distant markets of the South and West encountered competition from other centers of manufacture and was forced to offer his goods at as low a price as possible. He could no longer afford to pay as high wages to the craftsmen

---

[5] J. R. Commons, and others, *A Documentary History of American Industrial Society,* (Cleveland, 1910), III, 30.

whom he hired or into whose hands he "put out" the raw materials to be made up. The attempt of the merchants in this domestic or wholesale order stage to reduce wages so that they could meet distant competition was the beginning of the conflict between capital and labor. Efforts were also made to lower costs of production by employing less skilled labor, or by the use of machinery which was eagerly sought from England or invented at home. The journeymen organized to resist these attempts to reduce their wages. The "working rules" they sought to impose on their employers not only set minimum rates, but limited the number of unskilled workers or "apprentices" who might be hired in the shop or locality. In effect they wanted what we now call the "closed shop" in order to keep the supply of their services scarce and their wages up.

Early labor organizations. The first continuous organization of labor in the United States for the purpose of maintaining or advancing wages was that of the shoemakers of Philadelphia, organized in 1792.[6] There had been sporadic outbursts and strikes during the colonial period, but these were temporary and no permanent organization had been effected. The shoemakers organized again in Philadelphia in 1794, as the first society had disappeared, and in the same year the printers of New York founded the Typographical Society. Between 1800 and 1820 the shoemakers and printers had more or less continuous organizations in Philadelphia, New York, Baltimore, Boston, Pittsburgh, Albany, Washington, and New Orleans. Strikes were conducted from time to time by carpenters, tailors, and sailors, but these workers seem not to have had any permanent unions. Their organizations came into existence to meet a particular evil, and disappeared when they had remedied it or were defeated. The period to 1820 may fairly be called the "dormant period" in the history of the American labor movement.

But the new forces of competition, resulting from the improvement of transportation and the widening of the markets, began in the twenties to rouse the workers to more aggressive action. They resisted the encroachments upon their

---

[6] John R. Commons, and others. *History of Labour in the United States,* (2 vols., New York, 1918), I, 108.

earnings and standards of living. Strikes became more frequent and stable organizations were effected in numerous trades, such as among the hatters, tailors, carpenters, painters, stonecutters, weavers, sailors, and cabinetmakers. The period from 1820 to 1840 is therefore called by Professor Commons the "awakening period" of the American labor movement.

Then, as now, the chief issues were wages and hours. In periods of rising prices especially, such as between 1835 and 1837, workers struck for higher wages. And against the farmer's "sun to sun" workday the city mechanic raised the standard "six to six." Successful strikes in Philadelphia in 1835 initiated a movement that culminated in President Van Buren's famous ten-hour order in 1840 for all public establishments. Most of the unions were still local in character and short-lived. The workers did not realize the need for a continuing organization and generally broke up after their strike was won or lost. An additional reason for doing so was that their existence was illegal. There was always the danger that the common laws against conspiracy and combination would be applied against the unions. It was a conspiracy if the workers struck to obtain wages higher than those set by law or long-established custom. It was an illegal combination if the union was monopolistic and restrained trade. In 1836 an employers' association obtained a conviction in court against twenty striking tailors and had them thrown into jail for the crime of jointly refusing to work. Laborers were debarred in several instances from combining to raise their wages or improve their working conditions until the Massachusetts Supreme Court in 1842 decided in *Commonwealth* v. *Hunt* that unions were legal.

Political demands of labor. The workingman also made considerable impression by his political activities. Andrew Jackson's party drew its support from the eastern working classes as well as from the western pioneers. In this period the removal of strict property qualifications for voters gave the common man a real voice in government for the first time. He quickly determined to make use of this privilege. For example, in Philadelphia in 1827 the Mechanics' Union of Trade Associations was founded and out of it grew a local

Workingmen's party. It also published the *Mechanics' Free Press* through which the public was informed of the social and industrial reforms the workingman desired. The workingman, it should be explained, was chiefly the skilled worker, for the unskilled worker remained inarticulate and unorganized.

Free schools, supported by taxes, were the first demand of enfranchised labor. Professor Carlton [7] has shown that the movement for tax-supported schools was derived, not from great humanitarian leaders like Horace Mann, but from the growing class of wage earners. The extent of the need is indicated by an estimate of 1833 that over 1,000,000 children between the ages of five and fifteen (one in every four) were not in any school. Tax-supported schools date from this period, although it was not until 1846 that the first state law was passed limiting the hours of children in factories. New Hampshire set it at ten for children under fifteen. Another political demand by labor in the latter 1820's was the abolition of imprisonment for debt. The laws on this subject were particularly harsh; for indebtedness in even the smallest sum a man could be thrown into prison and kept there until his debt and the prison charges were paid. In 1829 it was estimated that about 75,000 persons were annually imprisoned for debt in the United States. The workingman as a wage earner, on the other hand, often failed to get the full wages due him. He was paid at irregular intervals, often in store orders or in depreciated bank notes, and if not paid at all was unable to secure his dues by a mechanic's lien on the product of his labor. Other issues that appeared in the workingmen's party platforms were equal taxation, a less expensive system of legal procedure, no legislation on religion, direct election to all offices, a district system of elections, opposition to banks and other chartered monopolies, and abolition of the compulsory militia system.

Labor in two types of factory. Meanwhile the factory system, which had been introduced in the textile industry at Waltham, was spreading into other forms of industry, especially branches of wood and metal manufactures. Those industries which permitted the mechanical production of

[7] F. T. Carlton, *Education and Industrial Evolution* (New York, 1908), 33.

uniform and interchangeable parts were the first to adopt power-driven automatic machinery with its resulting systematization of processes and administration of labor. Shortly before the Civil War the factory system dominated the making of firearms, agricultural implements, sewing machines, musical instruments, clocks and watches, as well as textiles. The handicraft system, with its methods of apprenticeship, hand tools, and personal skill of the workman, which characterized industry at the beginning of this period and which still characterized most of the mechanic arts, was giving way to the factory system with its power-driven machines, use of unskilled labor, and a mobile and changing labor supply. The economy of factory production, which increased the output of labor enormously over the old hand methods—sometimes as much as 50 to 1—was extremely advantageous in a new country.

The factories, however, were not uniform in organization or in their effects. Two types must be distinguished which may be illustrated by the Waltham or Lowell type and the Fall River type in the textile industries.

The Waltham system of factory organization, which was also adopted at Lowell, Lawrence, Manchester, and generally throughout Massachusetts and New Hampshire, depended more on automatic machinery and less on operative strength or skill. These factories used throstle spindles and employed women both as spinners and weavers. To attract the young women needed in the factories of the Waltham type, it was necessary to assure them of respectable surroundings, and the companies therefore found it advisable to establish boarding houses and to control the conditions of life as well as of work. The conditions at Lowell, the most famous of these early factory towns, were described as follows by Chevalier, a French traveler, in 1836:

"The cotton manufacture alone employs six thousand persons in Lowell; of this number nearly five thousand are young women from seventeen to twenty-four years of age, the daughters of farmers from the different New England states.... The manufacturing companies exercise the most careful supervision over these girls. I have already said that, twelve years ago, Lowell did not exist; when, therefore, the manufactories were set up, it also became necessary to provide lodging for the operatives, and each company has built for this purpose a number of houses within its own limits, to be used exclusively as boarding houses for them. Here they are under the care of the mistress of the house, who is paid by the company at the rate of one dollar and a quarter a week for each boarder, that sum being stopped out of the weekly wages of the girls. These housekeepers, who are generally widows, are each responsible for the conduct of her boarders, and they are themselves subject to the control and supervision of the company, in the management of their little communities. Each company has its rules and regulations."

The rules thus alluded to required of the operatives industry, temperance, attendance at religious services, neatness, punctuality, and early hours.

During the thirties there was a steady migration of farmers' daughters to the rapidly growing factory towns of Lowell, Lawrence, Manchester and other industrial centers. In the cotton mills of New England and the middle states two-thirds of the employees in 1831 were women.

The Fall River type, on the other hand, following English precedent, used mule spindles and employed men spinners with young children as helpers; the labor force was recruited from the local population who lived in their own homes or in company tenements. This type prevailed throughout Rhode Island, New York, Pennsylvania, New Jersey, and Maryland. Writing of the Fall River type, the editor of the *Voice of Industry* exclaimed in 1846, "I have seen no factory tyranny in Lowell, nor anywhere else in New England, which would compare with that existing in Rhode Island." And a communication in the *Mechanics' Free Press* of 1830 pictures the following conditions in Philadelphia factories:[8]

"It is a well known fact, that the principal part of the help in cotton factories consists of boys and girls, we may safely say from six to seventeen years of age, who are confined to steady employment during the longest days in the year, from daylight until dark, allowing, at the outside, one hour and a

[8] Quoted in J. R. Commons, and others, *A Documentary History of American Industrial Society* (10 vols., Cleveland, 1919), V, 61.

half per day for meals. In consequence of this close confinement, it renders it entirely impossible for the parents of such children to obtain for them any education or knowledge, save that of working that machine, and that too with a small sum, that is hardly sufficient to support nature. . . . We are confident that not more than one-sixth of the boys and girls employed in such factories are capable of reading or writing their own name."

On the whole, the result was a higher standard of labor conditions in large New England textile towns where the Waltham type of factories existed than in the areas where small village mills or city factories were organized on the Fall River model. The distinction between these two factory types must be kept in mind when reading contemporary descriptions of the factory system in America. Few labor organizations appeared in either type of factory, for neither the Lowell girls nor the Fall River children were suitable material for unions.

In the forties, when the first great wave of immigration into the United States occurred, immigrants began to find employment in numbers. The effect of their competition was soon felt and as early as 1846 labor leaders complained that alien operatives were preferred by Rhode Island millowners because under the state constitution they could not vote and were more submissive than native Americans; consequently Irish and British operatives soon constituted a majority of the mill population in Fall River. In factory towns of the Waltham type the farmers' daughters who lived close at hand had to be supplemented by girls recruited from northern New England. Then, as more work was required of them and their pay was reduced, immigrants began to take their places, too.

The humanitarian movements. The continued spread of the factory system with its harsh discipline, monotonous work, and dismal living conditions drew fire from two groups. One was the humanitarians—they would be called "pinks" today—who sought some more pleasing substitute for the factory system. They received relatively little support from the workingmen in whose behalf they were striving. The other group was the skilled workers who, for the most part, accepted the factory system but sought to protect themselves from its worst effects.

The decade of the forties has been called the "hot-air" period of American history—"the golden age of the talk-fest, the lyceum, the brotherhood of man." It was a period of philosophizing about human rights and of social and economic reforms along a great number of lines.[9] Perhaps the most significant and far-reaching of these was *Fourierism*, or *Association* as it was more often called. Charles Fourier was a French writer, who, before his death in 1837, elaborated a scheme of industrial organization on the basis of associated activity. Social harmony was the keynote of his system: people should group themselves in congenial industrial associations called *phalanxes*, each of which should contain about 1500 persons. They should live in a great central building, in which labor should be carried on co-operatively; each member should choose his occupation according to inclination, and vary it as soon as it became tiresome; the less attractive kinds of work should be the best paid. According to this scheme, labor was to be made both dignified and attractive, and, since everyone in the phalanx would work, it would also obtain a larger reward than under the existing competitive regime.

This scheme of social reorganization was presented to the people of the United States by Albert Brisbane in a book published in 1840. A wave of socialism swept over the country. Immediate efforts were made to put these ideals into practice, and phalanxes or industrial groups were established by the dozen. Of these Brook Farm was the most famous; it was organized on a farm near Boston and numbered among its members such well-known men as George Ripley, William Channing, Horace Greeley, and Wendell Phillips. All these experiments failed and gradually the Associationists began to pay more attention to particular remedies for particular evils, such as land reform and the organization of

---

[9] "The columns of advertisements in a newspaper might announce for Monday night a meeting of the anti-slavery society; Tuesday night, the temperance society; Wednesday night, the graham bread society; Thursday night, a phrenological lecture; Friday night, an address against capital punishment; Saturday night, the 'Association for Universal Reform.' "—J. R. Commons, and others, *A Documentary History of American Industrial Society* (Cleveland, 1910), VII, 19.

labor, or were diverted into the anti-slavery movement. Agrarianism was another reform movement that illustrates the efforts of labor to escape from such evils as the wage system with its alleged exploitation of workers. As set forth by Thomas Skidmore in 1829, this asserted that all the evils of society were caused by the unequal distribution of property, and that reform could be achieved only by its equal division. Thus stated the doctrine made little impression, but fifteen years later George H. Evans applied the idea to the public domain, which he insisted should be given to the landless. Such a plan, he thought, would afford an escape to the dissatisfied workers for a thousand years. Agrarianism, with political action, rather than Association, he urged as the best method of protest against existing economic evils.

Somewhat more practical and certainly having more appeal to the worker was another movement, an attempt to introduce co-operation as a substitute for strikes. For a period of four or five years beginning with 1847 experiments in productive co-operation were carried on by the iron moulders in Cincinnati, the tailors in Boston and New York, the puddlers of Pittsburgh, the printers of Philadelphia, and other industrial groups, but they all failed. More successful was consumers' or distributive co-operation, of which the best example was the New England Workingmen's Association, which maintained itself from 1845 to 1858.

These more or less unusual schemes all had one major characteristic and it was a conservative, not a radical, characteristic. All of them sought to bring back the "good old days," to restore to the workingman the freedom he had once enjoyed when he owned his own tools and farm, worked for himself, quit when he wanted, and was not beholden to some factory owner for his livelihood. They were a protest against the industrial revolution because it "took the workman from the land and crowded him into the towns. It took the loom from his cottage and placed it in the factory. It took the tool from his hand and harnessed it to a shaft. It robbed him of his personal skill and joined his arm of flesh to an arm of iron. It reduced him from a craftsman to a specialist, from a maker of shoes to a mere stitcher of soles. It took from him, at a single blow, his interest in the workmanship of his task, his ownership of the tools, his garden, his wholesome environment, and even his family. All were swallowed by the black maw of the ugly new mill town."[10]

Labor organization after 1850. But the efforts and exhortations of the social reformers were unavailing: the forces which produced the factory system swept on irresistibly. In the 1850's the energies of the humanitarians were diverted into the anti-slavery struggles and the workingmen were left alone to work out their own salvation. Gradually there emerged out of this chaos of experiments and reforms a "pure and simple" trade union movement which Professor Commons dates from about 1853.

The skilled trades settled down to the practical task of getting more pay for themselves by means of permanent and exclusive organizations. A new type of union was established, which steered clear of all programs of social and political reform and confined its activities to improving conditions in the trade. "Its main weapon was the strike; its aim, to establish a minimum wage for the trade and to maintain it by means of a closed shop." Down to about 1850 employers had frequently been included in the membership of unions along with the workers, but by the end of this year scarcely a union admitted them.

Collective agreements began to be made between unions and employers, which fixed wages, hours, and other conditions of employment, and by 1854 this method had partly supplanted the system of dealing with employees as individuals. Specific problems were attacked in these agreements, such as the regulation of apprenticeship, minimum wages, time and method of wage payment, strike benefits, joint employment offices, and other matters. Unfortunately the panic of 1857 shattered most of the organizations attempting these reforms, and it remained for the more permanent unions of a generation later to carry them out. Labor organization during this period was still confined for the most part to the formation of small local unions; the first national union, that of the printers, was not established until 1850 and by the time of the Civil War only five trades had national organizations.

[10] S. J. Orth, *Armies of Labor* (New Haven, 1919), 8.

Hours and wages. Two of the best measurements of the effectiveness of organized labor and of the material gains realized by the working classes are the decline in hours of work and the increase in wages received. The farm custom of working from sunrise to sunset or even longer was carried over into the early factories. Hours of labor in the 1820's were, according to modern standards, extraordinarily long. The early movement for shorter hours had been successfully carried through by mechanics, artisans, and other workers outside the factory, but now operatives in these establishments demanded relief.

An estimate of the time worked in factories, which may be considered representative of conditions throughout this period, was made in 1839 by James Montgomery,[11] superintendent of a factory in Maine. According to his account, the day's work at Lowell varied from 11 hours and 24 minutes in December to 13 hours and 31 minutes in April, the average for the year being 12 hours and 13 minutes per day. In many, and perhaps the majority, of the middle and southern states, he wrote, the average was even higher, being about 13¾ hours per day in summer and an average of about 12½ hours per day throughout the year. A year later President Van Buren set ten hours as a day's work in governmental establishments, and this was followed rather tardily by state legislation. In 1850 the average working day, according to the Aldrich report, was 11½ hours and in 1860 it was 11 hours. This represented a considerable reduction since the beginning of the century. The employing class was practically a unit in opposing the reduction of hours of labor.

Wages varied so from time to time and from one occupation to another that it is difficult to generalize on this subject, but an analysis of the different classes of labor reveals certain tendencies. (1) Unskilled labor was always in demand and commanded wages perhaps 50 per cent higher than in Great Britain and not far below those of skilled mechanics. The main reason for this was the presence of cheap land which gave the worker an alternative although not in the way that is usually assumed. Wages had to be high enough to persuade

---

11 *Practical Detail of the Cotton Manufacture of the United States* (Glasgow, 1840), 173-74.

the farmer's sons to work in the village or town rather than go west as independent farmers. But it should be emphasized: the farm boy had the choice, not the factory worker. The latter was too poor, too far from cheap land, too inexperienced in frontier living to have any choice. (2) Expert artisans and mechanics were scarce relative to the increasing demand. The large returns in agriculture and commerce at the beginning of this period kept capable persons from entering manufacturing in large numbers. Most of the experienced operatives came from abroad, in spite of prohibitory legislation, and they received high pay. The wages of a skilled mechanic varied from about $1.00 a day at the beginning of this period to about $2.00 at the end. (3) The third group was factory labor, which was recruited chiefly from the women of the farms and villages. They usually undertook this work as a temporary service, the average period of employment in the New England mills being between four and five years. Children were also employed, and later immigrants, but none of these classes was organized and the effect of their competition was depressive.

The chief force which kept their wages from falling to the European level was the rapid growth of the factory system, which was able to absorb the labor supply flowing from the household into the factory, as well as the pressure of a higher standard of living in this country and the opportunity of engaging in other pursuits. The wages of factory workers were miserably low, however, those of a woman operative ranging from about $1.00 a week in 1791 to $3.00 a week in 1860. Male workers received about $1.00 a week more than women. The wages of all of these groups were from one-third to one-half higher than those of the corresponding classes in England, and the tendency of nominal wages, omitting temporary depressions, was steadily upward.

Real wages. The movement of wages alone, however, unrelated to prices, means little, and it is therefore necessary to inquire what prices were. "The cost of living in general was low," writes Professor Jennings,[12] "as would be surmised from the wages. Morris Birkbeck referred to the opportuni-

[12] W. W. Jennings, *A History of Economic Progress in the United States* (New York, 1926), 303.

ties enjoyed in the West in 1817, where the best board could be obtained for $2.00 a week and the traveling expenses for man and horse were only a dollar a day. Board in the East was also low. Harvard students paid only $1.75 a week in 1820.... In most of the older eastern states in 1850 board was less than $2.00 a week. In 1854, according to Charles Richard Weld, the 'young ladies' of Lowell paid only $6.00 a month for board and lodging, while they earned $3.50 each week." This was in good times; in times of depression and unemployment, or in periods of rapidly rising prices due to inflation of the currency, even the low prices were beyond the reach of the poor and their sufferings were great. Indeed, according to Professor Commons,[13] the great labor movements of this country are closely related to the fluctuations of prices.

The years 1807, 1819, 1837, and 1857 were years of panic and ushered in periods of depression of varying length, during which wages fell and unemployment increased. The most serious of these was the panic of 1837; during the seven-year depression which followed, wages were generally reduced. The rise in prices which began in 1843 at first had the effect of increasing the cost of living to the working classes, but the wide industrial expansion which characterized this period made employment general and ultimately led to improved conditions. Wages rose between 1840 and 1860, and while prices also increased, they did not do so in the same proportion. According to the Aldrich report, if wages and prices in 1840 be stated as 100, relative wages in 1860 were 121.2 and relative prices 101.5, indicating a 20 per cent improvement in the economic status of workingmen. It seems to be unquestioned that the American workingman could and did purchase more with his earnings in 1860 than was possible in 1800 or 1840.

This growth of real wages, in the face of the rapid growth of population, was thought by Professor Bowen[14] to be a unique phenomenon. "I attribute the result, therefore," he wrote, "to American institutions more than to the fact that

---

[13] *A Documentary History of American Industrial Society*, (Cleveland, 1910), V, 19. See also chart on p. 1 of the same volume.
[14] Francis Bowen, *American Political Economy* (New York, 1870), 181.

America is still a new country, and is rich in fertile and yet unoccupied land. The mobility of society, the wider distribution of property, the absence of caste ... account for the phenomenon." But the chief reason for higher real wages was the better equipment which enabled labor to produce more.

Summary. One of the most serious obstacles to the introduction of manufactures in a new country is the scarcity and expensiveness of labor; this was mentioned by Alexander Hamilton and other early writers. During this period population doubled every twenty-five years and immigrants poured in between 1840 and 1860 with the result that industry progressed and complaints of labor scarcity became less frequent. The appearance of merchant capitalists and permanent laboring classes created an obvious conflict of interest between employer and employee. Trade unions and employers' associations resulted. Even before the factory came, skilled workers formed unions to resist wage reductions or to limit the hiring of unskilled workers to do their jobs. Unions before the Civil War were usually local, short-lived, and made up of skilled workers only. The women, children, and foreign labor in the factories were not union material and improvements in factory conditions were slow. And the reform movements of the 1840's, which were calculated to abolish the new wage system on which the industrial revolution depended, were futile. However, labor got benefits from its political activities in the Jacksonian period. Among these benefits were the beginning of free schools, abolition of imprisonment for debt, and mechanic's lien laws. The legality of unions was recognized by the courts in 1842. Unions, American institutions, and better capital equipment were largely responsible for the shortening of the workday from about 13 to 11 hours between 1820 and 1860 and a 20 per cent increase in real wages between 1840 and 1860. The presence of cheap land kept wages higher here than abroad by giving farmers' sons the choice of going west or to the cities. It offered no outlet to unemployed poverty-stricken industrial workers on the eastern seaboard.

CHAPTER XVII

THE ECONOMICS OF SLAVERY

The development of the South. While the country as a whole made marvelous progress during this period, the benefits were confined largely to the North and West. The great advances in manufactures, in agricultural improvements, and in commerce scarcely affected the South. Although the population was almost evenly divided between the North and the South in 1790, by 1860 nearly two-thirds of the population and a still greater proportion of the wealth of the country were in the northern states. In 1860 the population of the North was 19,100,000 as against 12,300,000 in the South. Of the $3.7 billion of wealth recorded by the census as having been produced in 1859, over $2.8 billion, or 75 per cent, came from northern farms and factories. By far the greater part of the manufacturing and mining industries of the country were situated in the North. In fact, the South had lagged far behind in the industrial advance of the previous half century. A southern writer, Trenholm, made the following statement on this point: "The whirl and rush of this progress encompassed the South on every side.... Yet alone in all the world she stood unmoved by it; in government, in society, in employment, in labor, the states of the South, in 1860, were substantially what they had been in 1810, when the abolition of the slave-trade had impressed upon their development the last modification of form of which it seemed susceptible." The reason for the industrial backwardness of this section was the existence there of Negro slavery, and to a fuller discussion of this institution as a system of labor we must now turn.

Decline of slavery. After the Revolution, Negro slavery declined not only in the North, but in the South as well. Vermont abolished it in 1777, as did Massachusetts in 1780, and in the same year Pennsylvania provided for gradual emancipation. New Hampshire followed in 1783, and in the next year Rhode Island and Connecticut. By the Ordinance of 1787 Congress prohibited slavery in the Northwest Territory, and in 1799 New York declared that all children born thereafter of slaves in that state should be free, as did New Jersey in 1804. By the latter date all the states north of Delaware had in one way or another outlawed slavery. Even in the South, except in the pestilential rice swamps of South Carolina and Georgia, the economic disadvantages of slave labor were so apparent that many prominent southerners favored its early abolition. Jefferson was opposed to it and feelingly remarked, "I tremble for my country when I reflect that God is just." Washington wrote in 1774, "Were it not then that I am principled against selling negroes, as you would do cattle at a market, I would not in twelve months hence be possessed of a single one as a slave"; and again in 1786 he said, "I never mean, unless some particular circumstance should compel me to it, to possess another slave by purchase, it being among my first wishes to see some plan adopted by which slavery in this country may be abolished by law."

A decade later Delaware, Maryland, Virginia, North Carolina, and South Carolina had all forbidden the importation of slaves, leaving only Georgia open to the slave trade. Even from Georgia came the statement by a representative in the fifth Congress: "Not a man in Georgia but wishes there were no slaves; they are a curse to the country." The fall in the price of slaves was another indication of the unprofitableness of slave labor: in 1790 the best hands could be bought for $100 each. It seemed as if the contingency might arise which was predicted by John Randolph of Roanoke, that, instead of the slave running away from his master, the master would run away from his slave.

Invention of the cotton gin. Before these fair hopes of the abolition of slavery could be realized, an event occurred which created a revolution as profound and far-reaching in southern agriculture as was worked by the new machinery in northern industry. This was the invention of the cotton gin in 1793. The introduction of sea-island cotton in 1786 was an important event, but its production was limited to the seacoast, while the upland or short-staple cotton, whose profitable use in manufacturing the cotton gin made possible, could be grown almost anywhere in the South. The new power-driven machinery in the textile mills of Great Britain and later in New England, by cheapening the costs of manufacturing, opened up vast areas of demand, while the cotton gin for the first time permitted the marketing of raw cotton at a price low enough to meet the demand with a cheap material. The result was a rapid and enormous growth of cotton production, which disrupted the old southern economy based in part on the staples tobacco and rice and in part on a self-sufficient farm practice, and gave new life to the institution of slavery. The planters of the old regime had developed a patriarchal mode of life, with much of social charm and culture, and, except in the rice districts, had treated their slaves with consideration. But now the opportunity of large wealth opened new prospects for everyone who could avail himself of it, and made slavery a commercial rather than a feudal institution.

When the cotton gin made it possible to grow the short-fibered variety at a profit, the white yeomen farmers, who had been thrust out of the rich tobacco lowlands by the planter class and had lived a backwoods life in the upland pine barrens, seized eagerly upon the growing of cotton as a means of escape from their poverty. The Piedmont region, from Maryland to eastern Georgia, was occupied by a large though scattered population of farmers who were as well suited to raising cotton as they were to growing grain and livestock. The invention of the cotton gin and the spread of cotton culture at first benefited this group primarily, and they made large profits from the sale of their cotton at high prices. Many of the yeomen farmers used their suddenly acquired wealth to purchase slaves and themselves became planters. The large slaveholders, too, eagerly seized the opportunity afforded by a new crop to employ their slaves in its production, for the former staple southern crops, rice and indigo, were declining in importance, and the tobacco lands had long been showing signs of exhaustion. The huge profits to be made in growing cotton unleashed forces of competition and exploitation "akin in spirit," as Beard remarks,[1] "to the dynamic and acquisitive capitalism of the industrial world."

[1] C. A. Beard, *Rise of American Civilization* (New York, 1927), I, 654.

Revival of slavery. Under the impetus of these forces, cotton culture, and with it slavery, gradually spread westward until in 1860 it occupied the whole of the lower South as far as Texas. At the time of Whitney's invention cotton was raised only in Georgia and South Carolina; thence it spread to North Carolina and Virginia, but until 1810 it was confined to the Atlantic seaboard. The next year a beginning was made in Tennessee and Louisiana, and during the next decade Alabama and Mississippi began to attract attention; for the following ten years a perfect stream of settlers poured into this fertile district. By 1821 the four last-mentioned states raised one-third of the cotton grown in the United States, by 1831 nearly one-half, and by 1834 over two-thirds. The production of sugar was also increasing in Louisiana at this time, and was proving very profitable. The profits from cotton growing in a new country were extraordinarily large, and in 1835 were reported to Harriet Martineau, in Alabama, as about 35 per cent per annum. How such profits could be made is told by another traveler, Postel,[2] who visited plantations along the lower Mississippi in the latter 1820's:

"A cotton plantation may now be established by means of a capital of 10,000 dollars, 3000 dollars for the purchase of 1500 or 2000 acres of land, on the banks of the Mississippi from Baton Rouge up to the Walnut-hills, on both sides of the river, or what is still preferable, on the banks of the Red river. Ten slaves at 5000 dollars leaves 2000 for the first year's current expenses. The beginner will not find it difficult to clear fifty acres in the first twelve months; and to raise from twenty-five acres, thirty bales of cotton, the produce of which will, with the crop of corn from the remaining twenty-five acres, keep him for the first year, the cotton alone being worth 1500 dollars, independently of the corn. The following year he may raise sixty bales, giving an income of 3000 dollars, every slave thereby yielding about 300 dollars; proceeding thus in a manner which in a few years more will render his income equal to his original capital."

Hand in hand with this extension of cotton territory and of production went the growth in the number of slaves. The

---

[2] *The Americans As They Are.* Quoted from G. S. Callender, *Selections from the Economic History of the United States* (New York, 1909), 650.

total number of slaves increased from about 700,000 in 1790 to nearly 4,000,000 in 1860. Furnishing as it did the labor for this profitable crop, slavery was now firmly established on an economic foundation. So far as the South was concerned the whole gain from the expansion of cotton culture went to build up and extend the system of slavery. Slavery became increasingly localized in the South; in 1820 only about 20,000 out of approximately 1,500,000 slaves lived north of the Mason and Dixon line, and in 1840 only 1129 out of some 2,500,000 were to be found there.

Advantages of slave labor. The economic conditions existing in the South at this time favored the use of slave labor. Edward Wakefield,[3] the Australian colonizer, once pointed out that "labor has never been employed on any considerable scale, with constancy and in combination, except by one or other of two means; either by hiring, or by slavery of some kind. . . . Slave labor is on the whole much more costly than the labor of hired freemen; and slavery is also full of moral and political evils, from which the method of hired labor is exempt. Slavery, therefore, is not preferred to the method of hiring: the method of hiring would be preferred if there were a choice; but when slavery is adopted, there is no choice: it is adopted because at the time and under the circumstances there is no other way of getting laborers to work with constancy and in combination. What, then, are the circumstances under which this happens? It happens wherever population is scanty in proportion to land." It appeared in ancient times when the Greeks, and later the Romans, acquired vast new territories. The serfdom of the Middle Ages was for all of Europe what it was until recent years for Russia, "a kind of slavery required by the small proportion of people to land." Slavery was used by the few Spaniards who conquered and held Spanish America in the sixteenth century; it appeared in the form of convict labor in Australia in the nineteenth century; and it was revived by the Nazis in the 1940's when their armies overran virtually all of Europe's lands.

Negro slavery was extensively used in our South in the nineteenth century because there was an inadequate supply of white wage laborers, since the yeomen farmers preferred

---

[3] Quoted from G. S. Callender, *op. cit.*, 742-43.

their independence and immigrants avoided the South because of the existence there of slavery. The cotton planter therefore assured himself a permanent and controllable labor supply by buying it. And in so doing he argued that he served himself better than if he had hired wage workers. He could determine in advance the size and character of his labor force. He had nothing to fear from strikes or labor troubles, though he had to guard against accidents, sickness, and shirking.

The peculiar institutions of the South—slavery and the plantation system—may therefore be regarded as adaptations to conditions of time and place and circumstance. Originally, it may be argued, they possessed a certain fitness, but like feudalism they became rigid and anachronistic and had to yield to other institutions—free labor, industrialism, and political democracy—with which they came into conflict. It was this rigidity that held back the South.

Disadvantages of slave labor. The slave was used as an instrument of production, and was regarded in much the same light as an animate machine. But the analogy broke down, because the slave had a mind and a will of his own, which affected the output. There was a fundamental difference between free labor and slave labor. In the case of the free farmer the full returns of his efforts belonged to the worker; the motive to exertion was self-interest instead of compulsion or fear, and consequently diligence and application were exercised. Slavery, on the other hand, was essentially a system of forced labor; and since the worker did not reap the reward of his toil he was not interested in the results. The slave had no motive to improve methods of production, to increase the output, to preserve the fertility of the soil, or to economize in the use of equipment. If he showed superior capacity he would only increase his labors without increasing his reward. "His ambition is the reverse of that of the free man; he seeks to descend in the scale of industry, rather than to ascend."

"The economical defects of slave labor," wrote Cairnes,[4] "may be summed up under the three following heads: it is given reluctantly; it is unskilful; it is wanting in versatility." Since his labor was forced, the slave gave it reluctantly; he put as little strength and earnestness into his work as was

[4] J. E. Cairnes, *The Slave Power* (London, 1863), 43.

compatible with safety from flogging. Olmsted concluded that slaves were hardly one-half as efficient as free laborers, though such a sweeping generalization needs to be qualified for many individual Negroes, for the kind of work performed, and according to the time and place. This disinclination to work, and the frequent shamming it led to, necessitated the use of overseers, which tended to offset the cheapness of the slave labor. Another characteristic was its ignorance, clumsiness, and wastefulness, though under the systematic direction of whites these disadvantages were moderated. In general only the heaviest and simplest tools could be used; improved implements and machinery and fine livestock could not be entrusted to the slaves. The inefficiency of Negro slave labor as compared with the responsible and intelligent white free labor of the North was thus greatly augmented. As it was impossible to introduce improvements in methods of agriculture or complicated laborsaving devices into the South, this section of the country tended continually to fall farther behind the rest of the nation in the relative production of wealth. Finally, the lack of interest, of elasticity, and of versatility of Negro slave labor confined the southern states to a few staple agricultural crops, and entirely prevented any diversification of industry or the rise of manufactures. The difficulty of teaching a Negro slave anything was so great that when he had once been trained to a particular occupation there was every inducement to confine him to that for life. Under slavery, therefore, there could be no variety of production. That the Negro, at best only a generation or two removed from African barbarism, should have remained below the industrial standard of the white man, with his centuries of discipline, was natural. When to this incapacity were added the defects of the system of slavery, one cannot feel surprised at the inferiority of Negro slave labor.

Another defect of slavery was to be found in the composition of the labor force. Under a system of free labor the employer could exercise a certain choice and could reject or discharge those who fell short of his standard. The slaveowner, on the other hand, had to make shift with such material as the slave traders brought his way, or as was born on his plantation. His problem was to get out of such a general run of slaves the maximum of energy and skill. But the average planter possessed neither the ability nor the resolution necessary to attain the best results.

Economic cost of slave labor to the South. The disadvantages of slavery were not confined to the character of the labor alone. A defect of another kind was the difficulty a young man of small means experienced in getting a start in a slave district. Land was cheap, but to purchase the necessary labor force necessitated a large investment of capital—more even than was required for the land and buildings and livestock. It was difficult for any one to become a planter unless he had inherited slaves or had wealth. There was therefore a tendency to monopoly in the hands of the large planters. A farmer in the Northwest could expand his operations with very much less savings. Even in the case of wealthy planters the necessity of locking up a large amount of capital in slaves probably held the labor force down to a point below its most economical expansion.

The most serious economic weakness of the system of slavery was to be found in the retardation or prevention of the accumulation of capital. By capital is meant instruments of production, the result of past labor, which are applied to future production, such as machines, tools, agricultural implements, factories, railroads, ships, banks, stores, merchandise, and a hundred other items. In its concrete forms capital is the chief means of economic progress. But the South was always starved for capital for industrial and commercial purposes and was compelled to borrow from the North. Northern capital carried on southern commerce, built southern railroads, and financed southern banks. Why did this scarcity of free capital exist in the South in spite of the wealth produced there each year?

The only persons who could save large amounts of capital were the planters, and they used their incomes in other ways. In the first place, they adopted a luxurious and expensive style of living, spending lavishly at home, making visits to fashionable resorts in the North or in Europe, sending their sons to college, and in other ways consuming their wealth instead of saving it. In the second place, what they did save was invested in land and slaves. The circle of investment, as described by a southern journal, was "making more cotton to buy more Negroes to raise more cotton to buy more Negroes." The capital of the South was absorbed in land and slaves; and as a consequence manufactures, commercial enterprises, adequate transportation systems, and other appurtenances of an advanced civilization were lacking.

The economic cost of slave labor to the planter. That slavery involved an economic loss to the nation and also to the South as a whole is evident. Was it profitable to the slave-owner? The average plantation owner believed that the chief economic advantage of slavery lay in the fact that he obtained the whole fruit of the slave's toil, in return for which he had to make only a small outlay for maintenance. How far the small running expenses offset the returns from slave labor was the economic problem involved in the system of slavery. The items involved in the yearly cost of a slave to his master were many, including interest on capital invested in him (would it have yielded more elsewhere?), taxation, depreciation, insurance against death or flight, medical attention, cost of maintenance (food, clothing, lodging), and the hire of an overseer. Yet the total of all these was not large.

Let us assume 8 per cent interest on a $500 slave—a generous price for the average slave during most of this period (see page 395). That will give $40. Taxation was a minor expense. Depreciation or the fact that a slave was a liability in old age, not to mention in early childhood, and insurance against death and flight, may be considered balanced by the fact that the slave population was increasing nearly as rapidly as the white and that all children born of slaves belonged to the master. Thus the slaveowner's principal was appreciating in value. As for maintenance, the chief item was food. The diet of the slaves was coarse but wholesome; cornmeal, with molasses, and generally bacon, were the staples. The custom of permitting each slave family to cultivate a piece of ground for its own use was very general; vegetables and other produce could therefore be added to the otherwise monotonous dietary. A report to the Secretary of the Treasury from forty-six sugar planters in Louisiana gave the cost of feeding and clothing an able-bodied slave as $30 a year. An Alabama planter estimated that food, clothing, medical attention, and taxes for each slave on his plantation averaged $34.70.[5] In general the clothing was of the coarsest, and the cabins, while rude, were probably as good as the inmates could appreciate. Finally, add to this the cost of an overseer earning $500 a year and able to supervise 25 to 50 Negro slaves and the total cost per slave will be roughly $80–90 a year. A Louisiana planter with 50 slaves estimated that they averaged $112 worth of cotton and a South Carolina planter calculated that his slaves produced $104 if cotton was at 8 cents and $130 if cotton was at 10 cents a pound. Where the land was fertile, as in the Black Belt of upper Mississippi and Alabama or along the Yazoo River, slavery was unquestionably profitable. Planters there were willing to pay good prices for Negroes brought from Virginia and from the older eastern states where the lands were worn out and unable to support slavery. Certainly one fact seems incompatible with the frequent assertion that slavery was generally unprofitable and that is that over a period of two generations before the Civil War the price of cotton tended downward while the price of slaves tended upward (see accompanying table). It seems unlikely that such a trend would have persisted if the planters had found slavery unprofitable.

PRICES OF COTTON AND SLAVES *			
Year	Cotton per lb. at New Orleans	Prime field hands in Norfolk, Va.	Prime field hands in New Orleans
1802	14.7 cents	$400	$600
1811	8.9 "	450	850
1822	11.5 "	500	700
1833	11.2 "	550	1050
1840	9.1 "	750	1000
1847	7.0 "	650	860
1855	9.1 "	950	1350

* Cotton prices are from L. C. Gray, *History of Agriculture in the Southern United States to 1860* (New York, 1941), II, 1027. Slave prices are from U. B. Phillips, *American Negro Slavery* (New York, 1918), 370. According to Gray (p. 665) the average price of all slaves was 40 to 50 per cent of the price for prime field hands.

The literature on slavery is full of statements to the effect that slave labor was more costly than free labor. The evidence in support of this is strong, but the many critics of slavery who

[5] R. T. Smith, "Was Slavery Unprofitable in the Anti-bellum South?" *Agricultural History*, XX, 63.

have relied on this argument have ignored the fact that free white labor was often not to be had. Furthermore any comparison between slave labor and free labor is misleading because many of the defects of slavery were due to the fact that the slave was a Negro as well as a bondman. The real problem involved was that of the relative efficiency of slave and free Negro labor. If the institution of slavery was the root of the difficulty, one would expect to find Negro labor more productive after the Civil War. For a long time he was less productive, and the process of educating him and increasing his efficiency was slow and laborious.

Conditions necessary for slavery to succeed. Although slavery was economically and morally harmful to the South as a whole and was not profitable to individuals in some sections, it was quite successful in other sections under favoring conditions. Some of the more important of these favoring conditions were that: (1) crops were chosen in whose production slaves could be profitably employed; (2) the plantation system was used; (3) plenty of new land was available; (4) there was an adequate supply of slave labor; and (5) other regions could be relied upon to provide the food, clothing, manufactures, and other necessities which the plantation required. The extent to which parts of the South met these conditions will be discussed in more detail.

Staple crops. Slaves were employed in the commercial production of cotton, sugar, tobacco, and rice. Large amounts of corn and hay were also grown for local use. Of all these crops cotton combined most perfectly the conditions necessary to an economical use of slave labor. Cotton culture was very simple, requiring few tools and only routine work on the part of the worker. The planning, direction, and management were carried on by the skilled plantation owners or their overseers. Furthermore, it gave employment for practically every month in the year, and to every member of the family, so that there was no unused labor. This is shown on the graph opposite. During the few slack periods the slaves' energies were turned to corn which needed most attention at just those seasons. Moreover, cotton permitted the organization of labor on a large scale; a single slave could not cultivate more than 9 or 10 acres and often not that (as compared to 20 or 30 acres in the case of wheat); [6] slaves raising cotton could be compactly massed and better watched and directed than in the case of the small cereal crops. Such crops as sugar and rice also, because they required expensive vats or dams, were satisfactorily cultivated on a large scale. The cultivation of these crops entrenched slavery and caused its rapid extension up to the 1850's. About that time it reached its climatic bounds within the continental United States. (See map.) In fact, Webster in favoring the Compromise of 1850 pointed out that the spread of slavery was limited by nature, since the crops for which it was suited could be grown only within a well-defined area.

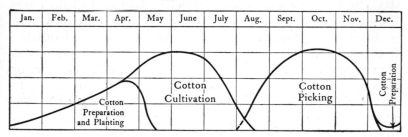

Jan.	Feb.	Mar.	Apr.	May	June	July	Aug.	Sept.	Oct.	Nov.	Dec.

SEASONAL DISTRIBUTION OF MAN LABOR ON COTTON

Five counties in central Alabama

Tobacco was produced on plantations, too, but it was most profitably raised by the small planter working alongside a few slaves. Both crop and slaves required constant detailed attention which could not safely be delegated to others. Partly for this reason and partly because the lands were wearing out, thousands of slaves were transferred by sale from the northern tobacco kingdom to the southern cotton kingdom. It is interesting to note that others were rented out by their masters to work in the tobacco factories: some 13,000 were so engaged in Richmond and nearby cities in 1860. Many of these slaves were allowed to make their own living arrangements in town.[7] Slavery was decaying in Virginia.

Plantation system. If staple crops were to be grown, the plantation system was generally superior to the small farm.

[6] L. C. Gray, *History of Agriculture in the Southern United States to 1860* (New York, 1941), II, 708. But he could also handle about 5 or 6 acres of corn.

[7] P. C. Roberts, *The Tobacco Kingdom* (Durham, 1938), 197, 203.

As indicated above, the chief reason for this was the opportunity to apply the principles of organization and combination to a high degree. On the better-managed plantations the work was carefully planned and practically executed. Provision was made for a certain division of labor and the slaves were humanely treated.[8] Instructions drawn up by owners prescribing the management of the plantation, show enlightened views and the application of scientific methods.[9] By 1822 the large plantation system with slave labor was taking the lead and by 1840 it had largely displaced the small planter who was working with free labor. The character of slavery had meantime changed from the patriarchal serfdom of colonial days to a well-organized industrial system upon which was founded the economy of the South.

The organization of work on the plantation varied from district to district and even within a region. The task system was prevalent on most of the large plantations, whether of rice or cotton, in eastern Georgia and South Carolina. According to this each hand had a definite amount of work assigned to him according to his ability, and when this was done he was through for the day. The gang system was used on the large cotton plantations of Alabama and Mississippi and the sugar plantations of Louisiana. In this a capable slave acted as driver, urging the working slaves to their tasks and holding them to a good pace by word and whip. The smaller and less enlightened owners had no system, but simply set the slaves to work and got as much out of them as they could. On the large plantations the management was generally left to an overseer, which was unfortunate, for good overseers were scarce. Since his success was measured by his ability to produce a large crop, the overseer drove the slaves harder and exploited the land worse than the owner. Absenteeism of the owner was not frequent, since the planter's life was regarded as an ideal one. But the planters felt a contempt for labor, were often unenterprising and lazy, and did not develop their estates. Although the agriculture of the South was inferior to that of the North because of the incapacity of these

[8] For a good illustration see Susan D. Smedes, *Memorials of a Southern Planter*, (Baltimore, 1887), 47-69, quoted in G. S. Callender, *op. cit.*, 641-46.

[9] See examples in U. B. Phillips, *Plantation and Frontier* (Cleveland, 1910), I, 112-15, quoted in Bogart and Thompson, *Readings*, 582-90.

men, the fact remains that southern planters were generally more successful than southern small farmers. Approximately 90 per cent of the cotton was raised by slaves and the planters owned the majority of the slaves. The typical slave owner had five to ten slaves.

Abundance of new land. The plantation system and slavery grew in importance as long as there was an abundance of new land. If land anywhere became scarce and dear, slavery tended to disappear. Intensive and scientific methods of farming were seldom possible under the indifferent and wasteful slave system. Consequently, the colonial method was continued, of cropping a tract of land until it was exhausted and then moving on to a fresh piece. Such a system of "mining the soil" required practically unlimited quantities of unoccupied and fertile lands suitable for cotton culture. In this need for new lands for cotton growing is to be found an explanation of the rapid westward movement of the slave plantation system, of the unceasing efforts on the part of the slave interests to widen our boundaries by the inclusion of Texas, Mexico, and the lands to the Southwest, and of the extraordinary Ostend Manifesto of 1854 designed to wrest Cuba from Spain. This one-crop economy involved at once an enormous waste of natural resources and a rapid exhaustion of the soil. In every southern state there were enormous tracts of reserved and of abandoned cotton lands; in fact, the uncultivated land far exceeded the cultivated. The following table [10] shows the differences in this respect among the different parts of the country:

LAND IN FREE AND SLAVE STATES, 1860			
	Free States and Territories	*Border States (Ill., Md., Ky., and Mo.)*	*Slave States*
Improved land, acres..........	88,730,678	17,547,885	56,832,157
Unimproved land, acres........	72,983,311	27,474,315	143,644,192
Total quantity, acres......	161,713,989	45,022,200	200,476,349
Cash value.................	$4,091,818,132	$702,518,382	$1,850,708,493
Average value per acre........	$25.30	$15.60	$9.25

[10] E. C. Seaman, *Essays on the Progress of Nations* (2d Series, 1868, N. Y.), II, 572.

An illustration of why and how planters moved west is found in Susan Dabney Smedes' story of the transfer of her father's plantation from Virginia to Mississippi about 1835.[11]

"Thomas Dabney went through a large part of Alabama, Louisiana and Mississippi looking at the country before deciding on a body of land in Hinds County, Mississippi. He succeeded in purchasing four thousand acres from half a dozen small farmers.... The journey was made with. so much care and forethought that not a case of serious illness occurred on the route. The white families were quartered at night, if practicable, in the houses that they found along the way. Tents were provided for the Negroes. The master himself, during the entire journey, did not sleep under a roof. The weather was perfect: no heavy rains fell during the two months.... It was Thomas's plan in the management of this large estate to bring under cultivation a certain portion of new land every year. His rule was to clear one hundred acres each season. The cotton-plant delights in a virgin soil, and he counted on making a bale and a half of cotton to the acre on all new ground. This was, of course, above the average. In the hill country a planter thinks himself well rewarded for his labor by an average yield of half a bale to the acre. Thomas one year made six hundred bales on six hundred acres, but that was an exceptional season."

Mrs. Smedes' account illustrates several developments we have been discussing, such as the abandonment of less productive land in Virginia, the economic attraction of rich land in the deeper South, the buying out of small farmers by the money planters from the East, the movement of slaves to a region where they could be used more profitably on fertile virgin soil, and the one-crop system.

But such a one-crop system carried in itself the seeds of its own destruction. An industry based on slave labor whose profits were obtained by mining and selling the fertility of the soil could not endure after the supply of available land was all in use and intensive culture became necessary. St. George Tucker believed that slavery would tend to become economically moribund when the density of population reached 66 per square mile. The exhaustion of the soil had once nearly

---

[11] S. D. Smedes. *Memorials of a Southern Planter* (New York, 1890), 47, 49, 64.

destroyed tobacco growing in Virginia and Maryland, and before 1860 had begun to affect the older cotton regions. Opinion differs as to whether that stage had been reached in the more newly opened sections of the deep South. Early writers like Von Holst collected considerable evidence to show that slavery was already becoming unprofitable before the Civil War put an end to it. However, more recent researches seem to support the view that "the plantation system had utilized only a small fraction of the available land area" and that railways were opening up new fertile areas. Consequently, "far from being a decrepit institution, the economic motives for the continuance of slavery, from the standpoint of the employer, were never so strong as in the years just preceding the Civil War." [12]

Adequate supply of slave labor. A fourth condition upon which depended the success of slavery was an adequate supply of slaves. The increased demand for slaves to be used as hands in the cotton fields led at first to an extension of the slave trade and to fresh importations from Africa. Although the separate states had forbidden the traffic, the profits were so enormous as to encourage the growth of a vast illicit business. Finally, in December, 1803, South Carolina, influenced no doubt by the great gains to be secured, repealed all prohibitory laws and threw open her ports to the slave trade. Charleston became the most important slave mart in the United States, and grew rapidly in wealth and importance; in size it was the fourth largest city and seemed destined for a brilliant future. New England traders carried on a large share of the traffic, and slave ships were fitted out in Boston and New York; the voyages were usually made under the flag of a foreign nation. From 1804 to 1807 inclusive, 202 cargoes of Negro slaves were taken into Charleston; of these, 8488 Negroes were sold for account of persons living in Rhode Island, Massachusetts, and Connecticut. In the latter year the constitutional restriction upon federal interference expired, and on March 2, 1807, Congress by law prohibited the importation of slaves. The act was disregarded, however, as the punishment was insufficient—illegally imported slaves if captured were sold for the benefit of the state in which

[12] L. C. Gray, *op. cit.*, I, 476.

they were being bought—and a considerable illicit trade continued. In 1820 the traffic was made piracy, with the death penalty.

The restriction of the slave trade, together with the growing demand for slave labor, forced up the price of slaves, which by 1815 was $250 a head. This demand was met by the sale of the surplus slaves from the exhausted tobacco plantations of the border states; they were sent to the cotton regions by the tens of thousands. Notice in the table on page 395 how much higher slave prices were in New Orleans than in Norfolk. This tempted the owners either to sell them or move with them to the growing cotton regions, as Thomas Dabney did. A vigorous internal slave trade developed between the older states of Maryland, Virginia, and the Carolinas on the one hand and the cotton-growing states on the other. Olmsted calculated that the importation of slaves into seven of the cotton states in the lower South during the decade 1850–60 averaged about 25,000 annually; Collins estimated the transfer of slaves from selling states to buying states at about 20,000 a year for the four decades, 1820–1860. This aspect of slavery undoubtedly created the most suffering by breaking up families.

But the growing need for cotton and the movement of population into the rich bottom lands of the Mississippi and its tributaries led to a demand for labor which could not be met even by this internal traffic or by the natural increase of the slaves on the cotton plantations. A movement in Congress to reopen the slave trade met with failure. An illicit slave trade accordingly sprang up between Africa and the West Indies or Texas, whence slaves were smuggled into the southern states. The increased price of slaves (prime field hands reached $1800 in the later 1850's), owing to the risk attached to the business and to the demand in the cotton fields, proved an irresistible attraction to American capital and much was invested in the business. Probably 50,000 slaves a year were imported.

Reliance on other regions for supplies. The final prerequisite to the profitableness of cotton growing by slave labor was the possibility of concentration on this staple crop through the purchase of supplies of food and livestock from the West and of manufactured goods from the Northeast or from abroad. In other words, the territorial division of labor already described made possible the specialization of the labor of slaves upon tasks in which they were most efficient and stimulated their withdrawal from less profitable lines. From the growing states of the Northwest corn, flour, bacon, hams, lard, livestock, hay, with a hundred other articles of minor importance, were floated down the Ohio and Mississippi rivers and found a ready market in the southern states. An estimate of 1845, given by Ingle, was that in twenty years southern planters had spent $900,000,000 in neighboring states for mules, horses, implements, and clothing, an expenditure made necessary because they were devoting their labor and land to the production of staple crops. From the Northeast came the equally large amounts of manufactured commodities.

It thus became possible for the planters of the lower South to direct the larger part of their labor force and capital into the one channel, the production of cotton. De Bow estimated in 1850 that of the 3,177,000 slaves then in the South, 1,800,000 were engaged in cotton culture. In 1820 the production of cotton had equaled 109 pounds to each slave; by 1853 it was 395 pounds per slave. These figures do not indicate the increasing efficiency of slave labor; they show rather its concentration upon one staple crop. In the decade 1850–60 the per capita production in the southern states of every important cereal product, of cattle, and even of the products peculiar to the slave states, as flax, rice, and sugar, fell off absolutely, while in the production of tobacco the increase was relatively less than in the northern states. In the case of cotton alone was there a relative as well as an absolute gain; it more than trebled in the twenty-year period, 1840–60, increasing from 1,500,000 to 5,300,000 bales. These facts show a great concentration of slave labor upon cotton growing.

It must not be concluded, however, that all the land and labor was devoted to commercial farming in the form of cotton growing. Wide areas, where it was impracticable to raise commercial staples, were farmed on the self-sufficing principle. Some of the farmers, who were favorably located, furnished supplies to the commercial planters. In those districts, however, which were less well-situated by reason of geographic isolation, poor soil, or rough topography, the farmer tended to be almost as wholly self-sufficing as his colonial forebears had been. Such a farmer raised his own corn and hogs and carried on household industries during all of this period.

Effect of slavery on cotton production. Cotton was almost completely dependent on slavery. Southern writers before the Civil War insisted that the prosperity of the South was bound up in the "peculiar institution," and that to destroy slavery was to ruin southern industry. As a matter of fact, nearly nine-tenths of the cotton was raised by slave labor. By 1850 it may fairly be admitted that the question of free versus slave labor was no longer a debatable one. The existence of slavery and the plantation system long ago had driven out the supply of white yeomen labor which might have done the work of raising cotton, and the plantation owners were unable to make use of any other than slave labor. When the gin was invented cotton was generally raised by white farmers. As its culture spread out to the richer lands of Alabama and Mississippi, the large plantation with slave labor competed successfully with the small farm and finally supplanted it. That cotton depended on slavery is further shown by the concentration of slaves in the cotton-growing states. In 1840 over two-thirds of the slave population were in the ten cotton-producing states, while in 1860 nearly three-fourths were to be found there.

Reliance of the cotton planters on slavery increased their risks from a business point of view. The equilibrium between the supply and demand of cotton was made unstable. Since the planter's capital was all invested in slaves and cotton lands, he found it practically impossible to decrease his production in times of oversupply and low prices, and equally difficult to increase it rapidly when prices rose. The returns from cotton growing were thus extremely uncertain and speculative.

From the point of view of markets there was another disadvantage in a slave society. Since the slaves lived on a low subsistence minimum and were not paid wages they did not

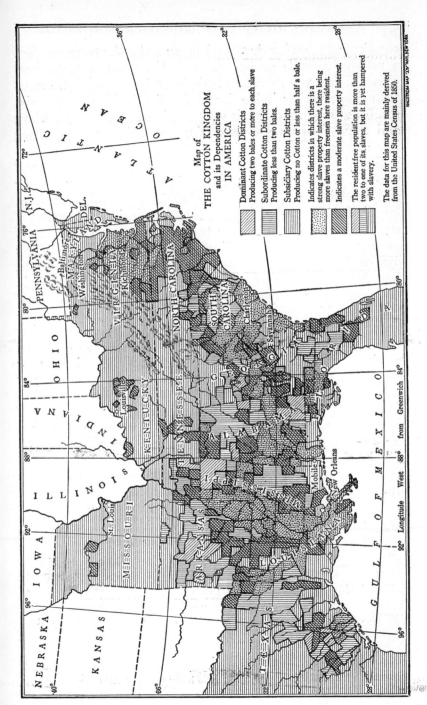

Map of
THE COTTON KINGDOM
and its Dependencies
IN AMERICA

Dominant Cotton Districts
Producing two bales or more to each slave

Subordinate Cotton Districts
Producing less than two bales.

Subsidiary Cotton Districts
Producing no Cotton or less than half a bale.

Indicates districts in which there is a
strong slave property interest, there being
more slaves than freemen here resident.

Indicates a moderate slave property interest.

The resident free population is more than
two to one of its slaves, but it is yet hampered
with slavery.

The data for this map are mainly derived
from the United States Census of 1850.

405

constitute a good market. And because the slaveowners were a relatively small group they could not absorb large purchases. There was therefore little incentive to establish manufacturing or other industries in the South. The commercial staples were compelled to seek foreign or northern outlets, and those farmers not producing staples were thrust back into a primitive self-sufficing economy.

Social effects of slavery. "The essential evil of slavery," wrote J. G. Brooks, "was that the Negro as slave gave shape and direction to *the whole industrial life* and, therefore, largely to the political life."[13] Southern society was strongly stratified, being divided into three broad groups, the slaveowners, the non-slave-owning white, and the slaves. The ownership of the slaves was concentrated in a very few hands, less than 5 per cent of a population of 8,000,000 whites in the southern states owning the 3,950,000 slaves in the United States in 1860. A distinction should be made, however, between the large planters and the small owners of a few slaves. The former group was more powerful and influenced southern politics and society out of all proportion to its numerical strength. Out of the total number of 347,525 slaveholders in 1850 just half (173,200) owned more than five slaves, while only about one-quarter (92,000) owned more than ten each. The owners of a few slaves were in a different class from the rich planters; they frequently worked side by side with their slaves in the fields and did not insist vigorously on either racial or social distinctions.[14] The slaveowners were thus a very heterogeneous class.

The non-slave-owning whites fell into three groups. The first of these consisted of the professional classes, merchants, and even clergymen, who, while not holding slaves themselves, were identified economically and socially with the planter class and sympathized with them in their attitude toward slavery. The second group was made up of yeomen farmers who owned and cultivated their own farms. Forced off the best land by the plantation system, they retreated to the less fertile soil or to the mountainous regions. Bitterly

---

[13] *As Others See Us* (New York, 1908), 296.
[14] *Cf.* G. S. Callender, *op. cit.*, 783. In 1860 it was estimated that there were 384,753 slaveholders.

hostile to slavery, if Hinton Helper, the famous southern anti-slavery propagandist, can be taken as a fair type, they formed a large and distinct element in southern society. It must not be thought that slavery occupied the whole of the land south of the Mason and Dixon line. There were vast stretches of territory in which slavery either did not exist at all or only to a limited extent. Slavery was profitable only where it could be used to grow the staple crops of cotton,

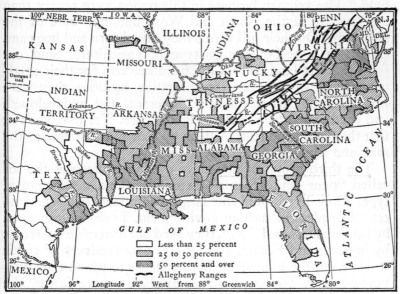

[From Beard and Beard's *History of the United States*.
By permission of The Macmillan Company, publishers.]

DISTRIBUTION OF SLAVES IN THE SOUTHERN STATES

sugar, tobacco, and rice, and was not able to entrench itself except where one or more of these crops could be profitably grown.

"A glance at the map," wrote Professor Shaler,[15] "will show that the Appalachian system of mountains widens as we go southward from Pennsylvania, until it occupies nearly one-fifth of the Southern States, extending southward so as to include half of Virginia and North Carolina, a considerable part of western South Carolina, much of Georgia, Ten-

[15] N. S. Shaler, *Nature and Man in America* (New York, 1910), 208.

nessee, and Kentucky, and a part of Alabama. In this section the character of the soil and form of the surface, and the nature of the climate, make the land unsuited for the extended culture of either tobacco or cotton. The result was that slavery never firmly established itself as an economic institution in any part of this vast territory. Here and there in the more fertile valleys a few slaves were employed; but there were counties in this area where a slave was never held." The yeomen farmers in this region were poorer than the farmers of the North and West, but they were of the same type. On their hill farms they raised corn and hogs and carried on a self-sustaining type of agriculture. Shut out from the best land and cut off from markets for their produce by lack of adequate transportation facilities, they were for the most part uneducated, ignorant, and undeveloped, and condemned to a backwoods existence. Yet they showed that they had good stuff in them by four years' service as the rank and file of the Confederate army.

The third group of non-slave-owning whites was the so-called "poor whites," small in numbers and degenerate in type. They lived amid the large plantations, but found no economic place in such an environment. Looked down upon by both planters and slaves, they eked out miserable existences by hunting and fishing, and by acting as receivers of goods stolen from the plantations by the slaves to whom they purveyed liquor. The worst effects of slavery were felt by the yeomen farmers and the poor whites, for they had to compete with the cheap labor of slaves. Quite aside from the question of whether the existence of slavery caused labor to be looked down upon, there is no doubt that the competition of unpaid slave labor lessened the opportunities of free white labor and cheapened the prices of goods which they produced. The effect of slavery was to make and keep these white workers poor.

At the bottom of the scale stood the Negroes, free and slave. Of the former there were few because the southerner disliked and feared the free Negro. His legal, economic, and social condition was miserable in the extreme; he was an outcast in a slave society. The slaves were differentiated into house servants, mechanics, artisans, etc., and field hands. The former were the pick of the Negroes with not infrequently a strain of white blood in their veins. Here was revealed the moral weakness of slavery. According to the census of 1860 mulattoes numbered 520,000, or 12 per cent of the Negroes.

Treatment of slaves. The worst aspect of slavery was to be seen on the slave markets where the slave dealers auctioned off their human chattels. To the credit of the South be it said that the slave dealer was usually a social outcast.

Slaves were most likely to be mistreated on the large plantations where they were driven and herded in gangs under the direction of overseers. House servants and slaves owned in small numbers were usually treated with humanity and even consideration. The possession of unlimited power by irresponsible masters must sometimes have led to the abuse of this power and to inhuman conduct, though this was restrained by neighborhood opinion and by economic self-interest. Flogging necessarily accompanied the system of slave labor, but chiefly as a punishment for some crime or misdeed and not as a regular method of driving the Negroes to work harder. Day-to-day and year-to-year relationships on such a basis could not hope to succeed. Indeed, unbiased visitors to plantations were continually impressed by the extreme patience shown by the southerners in their dealing with the Negro slaves. Many planters showed a genuine concern for their well-being and instructed their overseers in the amount of food, clothing, medical attention and other care that should be allotted them.[16] It was not merely humane but good business to keep the Negroes reasonably content. Usually each Negro family was allowed a garden patch on which to raise additional food for themselves. On some plantations they were allowed to sell from this patch. Religious instruction was encouraged but education was frowned upon. At Christmastime a general holiday was usually declared which often lasted a week or more. By long experience southerners learned how to handle the Negro patiently but firmly to good advantage. Only expert handling can explain the astounding loyalty shown by the slaves to those masters when they were away in the Confederate armies and the plantations were left in charge of the women and the aged.

[16] Bogart and Thompson, *Readings*, 582-90.

Conclusion. Slavery, on the eve of extinction by reason of the exhaustion of the tobacco lands, was given a new lease on life by the invention of the cotton gin. Although cotton was first grown by white yeomen farmers the pressure to expand production rapidly led to the use of Negro slaves for this purpose. The plantation system was organized to use slave labor on a large scale in growing cotton, sugar, and other southern staples, and showed itself efficient and profitable. Its success was based on the continued existence of abundant cheap land and an adequate supply of slave labor. By the 1850's the price of slaves had risen sharply and the outer climatic bounds of cotton culture had been reached, so that slavery was commencing to decay in the older regions although still thriving in the newer ones. Abolition of slavery probably would have been brought about in time—perhaps a half century or more—by the operation of purely economic forces, but before this process could work itself out the question was settled by war. The profits of cotton growing by slave labor enriched a few, but the majority of the southern white population did not share in this wealth, and the tasks of the slaves were not lightened thereby. There was a strong concentration upon a few staple agricultural crops, and manufactures and mining were undeveloped. The southern states were rich in natural resources, deposits of coal and iron, timber and water power, but these remained almost absolutely unexploited prior to 1860. It was impossible to carry on these industries with slave labor, and so long as slavery existed, neither free labor nor capital could be attracted to them. The South therefore lagged behind the rest of the country in the production of wealth. Of the real and personal property in the country in 1857, $10,957,000,000 was credited to the northern states as against $5,202,000,000 to the South. Industrially and commercially this section remained stagnant, and not until war had abolished slavery was it ready for the splendid industrial advance upon which it afterward entered.

CHAPTER XVIII
SOCIAL PROGRESS TO 1860

THE object of the varied economic activities described in the preceding chapters was after all to give the people a living and if possible to raise the standard of comfort. A standard of living or of comfort differs greatly from time to time and among different groups at the same time. It is conditioned by the stage of technological progress, by the knowledge and use of the natural resources, and by the abilities of the people. "The luxuries of one generation," it has been said, "become the comforts of the second generation, and the necessities of the third." So it was during this period. The standard that was attained during the colonial period and again by 1860 must be judged by the possibilities of those times and must not be compared too closely with the standards of today. Not merely economic, but also social, political, cultural, and even religious conditions may be included under this concept. The progress along these various lines will be briefly described.

Class distinctions. We must disabuse ourselves of the idea that social equality prevailed in the colonies or that the ideal of democracy was realized. The social structure of the New World reproduced most, if not all, of the inequalities of contemporary England and Europe. The dominant class was made up of rich merchants and the professional groups in New England, of traders and great landed proprietors in the Middle colonies, and of planters in the South. This class maintained its position of power by property and religious restrictions on voting and office holding, so that only a small proportion had the right of suffrage or office. The institutions of entail, which made it impossible for the owner of land to sell or give it away, and of primogeniture, which provided that the oldest son should inherit the estate, perpetuated wealthy families. Class distinctions were rigidly enforced in dress, in titles, and even in seating worshippers in church.

Members of the superior classes were addressed as "Mr." or "Gent."; those lower in the scale were saluted as "Goodman" or "Goodwife"; while the common man was known by his first name only.

Next in order below the dominant class stood the farmers, owners of small freeholds. This group formed the bulk of the population in New England and the Middle colonies and the back country of the Southern colonies. They were industrious and ambitious, though often illiterate, and throughout the colonial period steadily pushed their way up toward greater power and improved standards of living.

The third layer of the social order was made up of free artisans and laborers. As population increased and towns grew there appeared a class of free artisans who worked for hire. This class included carpenters, masons, tilers, millwrights, wheelwrights, ship carpenters, thatchers, and many others. The proportion of free laborers differed in the various colonies, but was always greatest in New England, where slavery had the slightest foothold and where industry was most diversified. This group was somewhat more restless than the farmers, and was progressive and often radical.

Below the level of legal freedom stood two other groups— the indentured servants and the slaves. It is not necessary to describe them further at this point, except to note that, during the period of their bondage, they were excluded from the enjoyment of even such rights as the free laborers exercised.

From what has just been said it is evident that the social structure of the colonies failed to realize the ideal of political, social, or economic equality. But society in the New World, removed from artificial trammels and exposed to new conditions, tended to break down class distinctions and afforded to able and industrious members of any group an opportunity to improve their position. The full realization of political democracy and of substantial economic equality had to wait, however, until a later period.

The distinctions just described tended to disappear after the Revolution with the suppression of some of the legal props, such as primogeniture and entail, and the replacing of the former Tory landed gentry by a more pushing commercial group. Differences in birth, in education, and in wealth still found expression in dress and manners, but the rigid class barriers of the earlier period were swept away. It was possible for any young man of ability to rise from the lowliest to the highest position, both in political life and in economic affairs. Two examples may be cited to illustrate the point— the rise of the poor North Carolina mountain boy, Andrew Jackson, to the presidency of the United States, and of the poor and illiterate New York youth, Cornelius Vanderbilt, to a position of unexampled wealth and power. Except for the Negro slaves there were no closed castes, either of aristocracy, of middle-class farmers and shopkeepers, or of poorer artisans and the growing group of factory workers.

With the opening up of new opportunities in land speculation, in trade, in manufacturing, and in finance, however, a new emphasis was placed upon the possession of capital. The old colonial leadership, based upon birth, education, and land, was now transferred to a rising moneyed class in the North and to a powerful slavocracy in the South. Political power passed from the colonial Tories to the democratic masses, particularly of the developing West.

Certain lines of cleavage, economic rather than social, were revealing themselves during this period with increasing distinctness. The first of these was the struggle between the dynamic industrialism of the North and the static slave system of the South. The other line of cleavage was between capitalists and wage earners. During the colonial period man had carried on a struggle with elemental nature and had succeeded in utilizing, in ever greater measure, her resources and forces for the satisfaction of his needs. Now, however, steam and water power were substituted for human muscle, and machines run by power took the place of hand tools. Capital became increasingly important, not only in manufacturing and the mechanic arts, but also in transportation, marketing, finance, and even agriculture. But capital required labor to utilize it, and labor depended on capitalists for employment. Beginning in the 1830's a struggle developed between the capitalist owners of the new instruments of production and the wage earners, now shorn of their hand tools and of their skills as hand workers. Upon what terms and for what wages should the laborers accept employment? The answer to this question must be sought in the history of the labor movement and of labor legislation; but it was not settled by 1860. Before the workingman could obtain economic freedom, his equality before the law must be established.

The acquisition of civil rights. The three-quarters of a century ending in 1860 was essentially a period of pioneering, and of pioneering not merely into the lands west of the Appalachian Mountains, but in other fields of human endeavor. Behind the unceasing efforts to subdue nature and to turn the resources of a rich environment to the satisfaction of men's needs there lay a passionate belief in equality on the part of the common people. Although this was given clear expression in the Declaration of Independence it had little practical application at first. The traditions of the past, the time-honored distinctions between learned and unlearned, between rich and poor, and the lack of organization and articulateness on the part of the masses prevented its realization.

The first breach in the crust of custom was made by the extension of the suffrage. At the time of the adoption of the Constitution perhaps one person in twenty was a voter. The decade of the twenties, however, swept away most of the old property and religious limitations upon the right of universal manhood suffrage, and a little later removed those on office holding. A new weapon was thus placed in the hands of the working class in their struggle for the realization of human rights. The fight was a long one, however, and bitterly contested at every step of the way.

A particularly flagrant denial of human liberty, as it seems to us today, and against which society earliest reacted, was imprisonment for debt. For a debt as small as a cent a debtor could be seized and thrown into jail, there to remain until the debt and prison charges were paid in full. No provision was made for furniture, for bedding, or for food; these must be provided by relatives or friends.[1] Although Pennsylvania after 1794 furnished fuel, blankets, and an allowance of seven cents a day for food, no further change was made in the debtors' prisons for another twenty years. In 1817 New

---

[1] For a graphic description of the terrible conditions in the prisons, see J. B. McMaster, *History of the People of the United States* (New York, 1885), I, 98-102.

York forbade the imprisonment of debtors for sums less than $25; New Hampshire followed the next year with $13.33, and Vermont a year later with $15. This led the way, and state after state followed with similar legislation. The waste and injustice of the system was well illustrated by a report of the keeper of the debtors' prison in Philadelphia in 1828. During that year there had been confined 1085 persons, whose debts amounted to $25,409; the creditors had recovered $295, and the cost to the community of supporting the prison and the debtors was $285,000. Against such an indictment the system could not survive, and imprisonment for debt, unless fraudulent, was gradually abolished by all the states. This was followed in the next decade by the actual exemption of wages and tools from seizure for the wage earners' debts. Thus the rights of persons were declared to be superior to the rights of property.

Not only was the workingman treated harshly as a debtor, but as creditor he lacked the protection of the law. He was frequently paid in truck, in store orders, or in depreciated bank notes. And if not paid at all he could collect only by the expensive method of bringing suit before a court of law. Lien laws protected the master, but not the wage earner. If a contractor failed, the man who had supplied the raw materials had first claim and the workmen might lose the wages due them. In 1829 the Workingmen's party in New York demanded a lien law to protect laborers, which was granted by the legislature. This was the beginning of a movement to compel employers to pay their workers regularly in cash and before all other creditors. By 1860 practically all the states had passed mechanic's lien laws.

Rights of women. In all this advance women had shared, but very unequally. Their position in 1800 was practically the same as that of their grandmothers in the colonial period. The home was considered their rightful domain and to it they were expected to restrict themselves. Women were assigned a place in the social organization distinctly inferior to men, intellectually, politically, economically, and legally. Institutions of higher learning were closed to women until Oberlin College, founded in 1833, opened its doors to them. The right of suffrage was denied them during the whole of this period, as it was to slaves. Business and the professions were regarded as the exclusive domain of men, but breaches were gradually made in the citadel of privilege. In 1849 the first medical diploma was granted to a woman and in 1853 for the first time a woman was ordained as a (Congregational) minister. The movement for legal equality had begun even before this. Married women demanded the right to acquire and to hold property and to be exempt from their husbands' debts. Mississippi was the first state to recognize this claim, in 1839; New York, Pennsylvania, Indiana, and Texas took similar action in 1848, followed two years later by California and Wisconsin.

The first women's-rights convention in the history of the world was held in 1848, at which a declaration of woman's independence was drawn up. In this it was asserted that "all men and women are created equal," and the demand was made for equality with the men before the law, in educational and economic opportunities, and in the suffrage. More might have been accomplished along these lines had not the struggle over slavery diverted the interest of the feminist leaders into the anti-slavery movement.

In curious contradiction to the denial of civil equality to women was the high social position accorded them. In no country was greater deference shown them, even in the more primitive communities, a phenomenon universally noted by European travelers.

Food. Game and fish were plentiful in all the colonies. "No man need starve," said Franklin, "who could bait a hook or pull a trigger." Indeed, the abundance of fish probably saved the lives of the earliest settlers at Jamestown and at Plymouth. Fish filled the waters to such an extent that one writer testified, "I myself at the turning of the tyde have seen such multitudes of sea bass that it seemed to me one might goe over their backs dri-shod." From the Indians the colonists learned the trick of catching the fish in weirs. Game was so abundant that venison was esteemed less than mutton, and farm laborers are said to have stipulated that salmon should be served only once a week. Domestic cattle and swine were soon introduced and multiplied rapidly, adding another supply of meat. For winter use this was salted, pickled in saltpeter and brine, or smoked.

Of the grains, Indian corn or maize was the most important and was served in a variety of forms, already described. Other vegetable foods were pumpkins, squashes, potatoes (especially sweet), cabbages, parsnips, turnips, and carrots, such as could be stored for winter use in root cellars. Berries grew wild in profusion, and these were soon supplemented by tame varieties. Apples, pears, peaches, and quinces seem to have been favorites among the fruits; one writer speaks of the "gallant orchards" to be seen on every farm.

At the time when America was settled water was not drunk freely in Europe, for bad sanitary and drainage conditions contaminated the supplies and made them unsafe for human use. The English people consequently slaked their thirst with ale, the Dutch with beer, and the French and the Spanish with light wines. But the early colonists could not obtain these beverages and were forced to drink water, which to their surprise agreed with them and improved their health. It did not take the colonists long, however, to produce Old World drinks, and soon distilled and fermented liquors were being made everywhere, especially beer among the Dutch and rum in New England and New York. Light wines and "home-brew" were made from persimmons, peaches, blackberries, elderberries, birch bark, and other roots, berries, and fruits. Cider was a universal beverage. Among non-alcoholic drinks, chocolate was a favorite, though coffee was used; tea was introduced about 1714 and by the time of the Revolution was very popular. It was then boycotted, and we later became the greatest nation of coffee drinkers in the world. Milk was a staple article of food, and was plentiful and cheap, but butter was not common. Wild honey and maple sugar were the principal articles for sweetening, though molasses was used by the poorer people. In the eighteenth century a fairly plentiful supply of cane sugar was obtained from the West Indies.

One must not be misled by this long enumeration of foods into thinking that the common man's table groaned under the weight of many varied dishes. It is true that the dinners of the wealthy might consist of an abundance of meat, vegetables, preserves and jellies, pies and puddings, with several kinds of wine, but this was certainly not typical. The diet of the people in general was simple and plain, though bountiful. Among the farmers, who raised most of their own food, breakfast would probably consist of porridge and milk; dinner of a hotchpotch of corn and kidney beans stewed in a

A CORNER OF A COLONIAL KITCHEN

If you visit the Paul Revere House in Boston you will see this kitchen with its old furniture. The spinning wheel was to be found in every colonial farm house. So important a part did spinning play in the home life, that an unmarried woman was known as a "spinster" from her chief occupation. Cooking was done over the open fire, which was also the sole source of heat in winter.

great pot with a slice of salt beef, pork, or venison, topped off with a piece of pumpkin pie or stewed fruit; for supper the children might have hasty pudding with milk or pumpkin stewed in milk, while the parents would enjoy a slice of cold pork, brown bread, and a mug of cider or beer. The fare of the workingman was still simpler; we read that many of them did not taste meat oftener than once a week.

Cooking was done over the open fire and consequently there was a predominance of stewed and roast dishes, which were prepared in iron pots or brass kettles; roasting was done on a spit. Food was served on wooden trenchers and pewter plates; only on the tables of the rich was silver to be seen. A steel knife and a pewter spoon were the only utensils in common use; forks were uncommon until the eighteenth century, the first one in the colonies being imported by Governor Winthrop in 1633. Drinking vessels were pewter cans, wooden tankards, gourds, or coconut shells. China was not introduced in quantity until after the opening up of a direct trade with China after the Revolution.

By 1860 improvements had been made along all these lines, but one feature, which practically all European travelers noted during this period, was the monotony and lack of balance in the diet. "The national taste," wrote one observer, "certainly runs on pork, salt fish, and tough poultry. Two favorite condiments are cranberry jelly and tomato sauce. They form a part of every dinner." Indian corn was the national crop and this appeared on the table three times a day. Corn was eaten as such in various dishes, but more frequently in the form of salt pork, into which it was transformed by being fed to the hogs. Accordingly, the main diet was salt pork, Indian corn in one form or another, and heavy pastries, washed down by strong coffee or stronger liquor. William Cobbett thought drinking was the national disease. In colonial times rum was the favorite alcoholic beverage, but when trade with the West Indies was interrupted by the Revolution, whisky took its place. Cider was consumed in vast quantities, and home-brewed wines were general. Only the wealthy could afford imported wines. "A pint of rum or whisky to a pound of pork" was a measure that was commonly applied for the supply of workmen. Drinking was universal and excessive, with serious effects on health and family finances.

Milk, curiously enough, was but sparingly consumed. In 1853 the estimated per capita consumption in New York City was only one to one and one-half pints a day.[2] Judged by modern dietary standards the main flaw in the American diet of this period was the large consumption of meat and the small use of the so-called "protective" foods—milk, fresh

[2] E. W. Martin, *The Standard of Living in 1860* (Chicago, 1942), 51.

fruits, and leafy vegetables. But the vigorous outdoor life of most of the people, with plenty of fresh air, partially offset these faults. Another lack was the absence of artificial refrigeration. A household refrigerator was invented in 1803 by Thomas Moore, but the high cost of ice prevented its general use. About 1827, however, Nathaniel Wyatts invented an ice-cutter which greatly reduced the cost of harvesting ice and the refrigerator became more popular. This had the double advantage of preventing bacterial action and of protecting perishable foods and made possible a greater use of fresh fruits and vegetables.

Food supplies in the cities were improving and the monotonous diet of the rural districts was being modified by the increasing importations of sugar and exotic fruits, and by larger supplies of fresh vegetables. On the frontier a rude abundance of the necessaries of life was everywhere to be found, and a generous hospitality was remarked by travelers as a characteristic of the people. Breadstuffs—wheat and corn —were plentiful and cheap. Game was abundant and cattle and hogs multiplied rapidly and foraged for themselves in the woods, so that animal food was a usual article of diet. The settler's garden furnished him all the vegetables necessary for his table, with little attention on his part; there was usually a superfluity of potatoes, squashes, melons, and other common vegetables. Tomatoes, curiously enough, were grown as ornamental shrubs under the name of "love apples," but were not eaten until about 1830, as they were generally supposed to be poisonous. Apples, peaches, pears, and other fruits were fairly plentiful.

Houses and furnishings. The first shelters were of the rudest and flimsiest construction, hardly worthy to be called houses. "Our houses and churches," wrote the Virginia Assembly, "were so mean and poor . . . that they could not stand above one or two yeares." Some of the poor families made cave dwellings, with one chamber half underground on the side of a hill, roofed with rushes, bark, and sod. With the introduction of sawmills, houses were built of hewn logs and boards, which now became very cheap. Log cabins of the now familiar American type seem not to have been built before 1640, when they were introduced by the Swedes, but were not adopted by the English until the eighteenth century. With the increase in wealth and the growth of an artisan class better houses came to be constructed, and differences, comparable with the class distinctions already noted, began to appear.

During the seventeenth century the wealthy merchant class of the North and the planters of the South built frame houses with shingled roofs, usually of one story with a loft and containing not more than six to eight rooms. The great stone chimney, providing for two or three open fireplaces, was placed in the center. The eighteenth century saw the construction of larger and more solid structures of brick: after about 1720 the introduction of the Georgian style produced the type of architecture which we call colonial. Outstanding examples of these early types, still preserved, are the House of the Seven Gables in Salem, Massachusetts, the Van Cortlandt mansion in New York City, and Washington's home in Mount Vernon. The furnishings of such homes were generally obtained from abroad, especially in the case of the wealthy merchants of the Middle colonies and the planters of the South.

Less pretentious were the houses of the farmers. In the seventeenth century the familiar type was a one-story lean-to, with a long sloping rear roof, but in the eighteenth century this gave place to a clapboarded frame house of full two stories. They were, however, generally unpainted. At first there was a serious lack of glass and the few windows were covered with oiled paper, but this condition was steadily remedied. There was no plumbing, even in the houses of the wealthy; the sanitary arrangements were therefore of the simplest character. Tubs for bathing were unknown. The furniture was homemade or fashioned by a local cabinet-maker, but was substantial.

The homes of the workers were poor and rude. After about 1700, in newly settled regions, log houses were the usual type. The chinks between the logs were filled with mud and moss and plastered over with clay. The floor was at first of earth, and later of hewn logs or unplaned boards. The furniture was equally primitive, consisting of a bunk fastened against the wall, three-legged stools, and a table made by setting up a long slab from a tree trunk on four legs.

The problem of heating the houses during the winter, especially in the severe climate of the North, was a serious one during the whole of the colonial period. The great open fireplace, found in all homes, met the difficulty very inadequately. Most of the heat went up the chimney, and people complained that, while their faces burned, their backs froze. Chimney seats, built along the sides of the fireplaces, were preferred places. Cotton Mather and Judge Samuel Sewall wrote of the ink freezing in their pens as they composed by the chimney side, and of the sap at the end of the long logs on the fire freezing while the center of the log was consumed by the flames. "Bundling," to keep warm and to save fuel, was a not infrequent custom in colonial New England. A great improvement was introduced by the Germans in Philadelphia who built iron stoves in the wall, and another step forward was made through the invention by that universal genius, Benjamin Franklin, in 1742, of the Franklin heater, which could be set in the fireplace. This fairly revolutionized the heating of colonial houses, both of the poor and of the wealthy.

Another problem was that of providing artificial light after darkness fell. A partial solution, which also solved the lack of heat, was to go to bed soon after sundown. The earliest colonists burned great pine knots on a flat stone in the corner of the fireplace, but they exuded tar and smoke and gave a poor light. Candles were early made of tallow and similar materials, but these afforded only a flickering light, and were unsatisfactory in many ways. With the development of whaling, spermaceti candles came into general use and marked a great improvement in lighting. The whaling industry, therefore, came to be of primary importance. Lighting by candle was, however, very expensive. The president of Harvard College calculated in 1761 that the cost of a single tallow candle for five hours every evening was about $8 a month, while that of a spermaceti candle was double. The smoky lamps of the seventeenth century, similar to ancient Roman lamps, with a loose wick floating in a shallow saucer filled with tallow, grease, or oil, were supplanted in the eighteenth century by glass lamps of modern style which burned whale oil. Fire was obtained by flint, steel, and tinder, concerning which a saying ran, "If you had good luck, you could get a light in half an hour."

The home of an unskilled laborer in 1784 is described by McMaster as follows: "In the low and dingy rooms which he calls his home were wanting many articles of adornment and of use now to be found in the dwellings of the poorest of his class. Sand sprinkled on the floor did duty as a carpet. There was no glass on his table, there was no china in his cupboard, there were no prints on his wall. What a stove was he did not know, coal he had never seen, matches he had never heard of. Over a fire of fragments of boxes and barrels, which he lit with the sparks struck from a flint, or with live coals brought from a neighbor's hearth, his wife cooked up a rude meal and served it in pewter dishes."

The next seventy-five years saw a change in practically every one of the items just mentioned. About 1815 coal began to be used in the home, iron ranges were substituted for the open fireplace for cooking, and iron stoves were set up in other rooms. Tinware became the favorite kitchenware in place of the heavy iron pots and brass kettles, while glass and china replaced pewter on the table. Gas was introduced for street lighting in Boston in 1822, and in other cities soon afterward, and made its way more slowly into the homes. Light in the rural districts was still provided by candles and increasingly by improved lamps, burning either whale oil or some inferior substitute like lard oil, turpentine, or other product. Coal oil was introduced in the 1850's, as the price of whale oil kept rising. Shortly after this, all these illuminants were displaced by kerosene made from petroleum.

Wells and cisterns, from which most drinking water was obtained, were endangered by contamination of leaky privy vaults, and the rivers were polluted by sewage. Water closets were to be found only in the cities. The major public health problems were the disposal of the contents of privies, which sometimes overflowed, and of garbage. The latter was partially cared for by wandering pigs and dogs acting as scavengers.

This period also saw the distribution of an ample supply of pure water in the growing cities by way of municipal water mains consisting of wooden pipes. The construction in 1842 of the Croton aqueduct, which brought water to New York City from a watershed 50 miles distant, was hailed as an engineering triumph. The first omnibus line was established in New York in 1828, and two decades later efficient fire departments began to be organized in place of the volunteer companies in the larger cities. Thus, step by step, the basis was laid for a more comfortable and safer existence for the increasing urban population.

Many of these improvements, however, were enjoyed only by the well-to-do. The rapid growth of cities in the decade of the forties, as a result of the expansion of manufactures, outran the housing facilities and resulted in thoroughly unwholesome conditions. The chief of police in New York reported in 1850 that a thirtieth of the people were living in underground cellars, and attributed the high rate of mortality to the "overcrowded and filthy state" in which the population lived. And the Massachusetts Labor Bureau described the tenement houses of Boston as "hovels reeking with damp and mold...with putrid cesspools and uncleaned drains."

In the rural districts, and especially in the developing West, living conditions did not differ so radically from those of the colonial period. But the rapid growth of domestic manufactures, the improvements in transportation, and the reduction in the costs of distribution brought to the farmer's door a growing stream of useful commodities which lightened his toil and raised his scale of living.

Clothing. During the colonial period striking contrasts existed in the dress of the rich and the poor, which were the more insistently prescribed by legislation and usage since they gave visible evidence of the class distinctions already described. "The gentleman was permitted to adorn himself with articles of dress forbidden to the goodman; the goodman wore others which were withheld from the day laborer or the servant." [3] And yet the frequent trials before the courts gave evidence less of the enforcement of these rules

[3] T. J. Wertenbaker, *The First Americans*, 1687-1690 (New York, 1929), 73.

than of the steady pressure from below to break them down. The well-to-do merchant or the wealthy planter might display his gold-laced hat, powdered wig, colored coat, and silken hose. But such garments were ill-suited to farmers or artisans, and these groups wore clothing dictated by convenience and economy as well as by law.

The homespun suits of the farmers were made of wool, which was grown and made into cloth on the colonial farm. Wool, however, was too expensive for everyday use and leather garments were common. The Massachusetts Bay Company gave to the settlers at Salem, among other things, "two suits of doublet and hose of leather lined with oiled skin." Leather trousers and aprons were common and were kept pliable by being oiled and greased. Clothing was also made of linen, of canvas, and of "linsey-woolsey" (a mixture of linen and wool), but very little use was made of cotton as this was too expensive until after the invention of Whitney's cotton gin in 1793; silk was reserved for the dominant class. Woolen stockings and heavy cowhide boots and shoes, often with wooden heels, completed the costume of the working-man. Indentured servants wore similar clothing, though of poorer quality, but the slaves of the South frequently wore only a breechcloth in the summer.

The invention of the cotton gin led to a great reduction in the price of cotton textiles, which in turn resulted in their substitution for leather and linen garments and in smaller degree for woolens. This promoted better health, for cotton goods could be washed more frequently and kept clean. It led also to an extraordinary increase in the yardage of cloth which a well-dressed woman felt compelled to wear. Aided by bustles, cushions, the puffing given by six or eight petticoats, and other devices to make the skirt flare in a fashionable bell shape, the "average dress of 1855 required some thirty yards of material, while the petticoats and other garments underneath brought the total close to a hundred yards." [4]

Men's clothing also showed changes during this period. Long trousers gradually replaced the knee breeches of colonial days; these were made of woolen cloth. Ready-made

[4] R. G. Albion, *The Rise of New York Port* (New York, 1939), 55. See also Appendix, 417.

clothing appeared in the 1830's and began to displace custom-made garments. For this change the newly-invented sewing machine was responsible. About this time a change took place also in children's wearing apparel; previously their clothes had been modeled upon their elders' but now somewhat more sensible types were adopted and manufactured with the help of patterns. Yet other changes were the appearance of crooked shoes—lefts and rights—in the 1850's, the sale of suspenders, rubber boots and mackintoshes after the discovery of vulcanization in 1839, and the observable decline in the price of silk goods, which, however, still remained a luxury. The working classes of course could not afford many of these clothes except for "Sunday, go-to-meeting" purposes, and wore chiefly jeans, ginghams, and calicoes.

Health. Information on the subject of health was scanty during this period, for vital statistics had not yet been developed. Scientific medicine and the principles of hygiene had made little progress since the colonial period. The greatest advance was achieved in the discovery of anesthesia. First applied in dentistry in the 1840's it was soon used successfully in surgical operations, usually in the form of ether. "Within a few years," wrote the Beards, "practitioners in the United States had done more for the relief of human pain and suffering than all the soothsayers and shamans of ten thousand preceding generations." [5]

Medical schools increased, but most young doctors, after a year or two at such a school, gained their practical knowledge in the offices of older practitioners. Home remedies, such as boneset, sage tea, sarsaparilla, and other herbs, were used for most illnesses, and only when these failed was a physician called in. Quacks abounded and patent medicines were in general use. Until about 1850 bloodletting was regarded as the most efficacious treatment for most ills. The most dreaded and usual diseases were pulmonary consumption among adults and "canker rash" or scarlatina among children. Some of the maladies were the result of bad working and living conditions; contagious diseases spread through ignorance of methods of combatting them. As a result of poor diet and bad

[5] C. A. and M. R. Beard, *The Rise of American Civilization* (New York, 1927), I, 744.

cooking, dyspepsia was common; cold houses produced rheumatism; and in the swampy regions and river bottoms malaria and fever were prevalent. The backward state of medical science was revealed by the Civil War when half of all the deaths for both belligerents resulted from typhoid fever and pneumonia. Antiseptic surgery had not yet been developed and trained nurses were unknown, but Clara Barton and other spirited women of both North and South showed the usefulness of such aids to the doctors. The expectation of life at birth was estimated at about 35 years in 1789 [6] and, according to Massachusetts life tables, was less than 40 years in 1850.[7] This was a very slight improvement for sixty years in such a favorable environment. The high death rate (varying from 200 per 1000 in Providence in 1857 to 40 in New York), and low life expectancy were largely the results of the lack of observance of ordinary sanitary precautions and of personal uncleanliness. Under such conditions epidemics spread easily and rapidly.

Education. In estimating the well-being of the people it is not sufficient to note how fully the needs for food, clothing, and shelter were met; we must also note their education, recreation, and general state of culture. In the colonies there existed wide differences among the various groups, with all the advantages on the side of the wealthy.

The common school found its highest development in New England. Here the compact settlements made it possible to gather pupils together in sufficient numbers to employ a teacher, while the clergy insisted upon education. Massachusetts led the way in 1647 with a law requiring every town with fifty or more householders to establish an elementary school, and those of one hundred householders a grammar school as well.[8] Although the act was not fully enforced, it set a standard. The primary schools, often called dame schools because the teacher was usually a woman, taught spelling, reading, and the catechism. Having mastered these

6 W. S. Thompson and P. K. Whelpton, *Population Trends in the United States* (New York, 1933).

7 L. I. Dublin and A. J. Lotka, *Length of Life: a Study of the Life Table* (New York, 1936), 63.

8 The religious basis of this step is evidenced by the quaint preamble to the law: "It being one chief object of the old deluder Satan to keep men from the knowledge of the Scriptures . . . it is therefore ordered," etc.

the pupil was ready for the grammar school, where he began the study of Latin. To New England belongs also the distinction of establishing the first college in the British colonies,[9] Harvard College being opened in 1638 in Cambridge, Massachusetts. Other northern colonies followed this example rather slowly. Not until 1693 did New Jersey authorize towns to levy taxes for the support of schools; Rhode Island and New Hampshire were almost entirely without schools until 1701, and as late as 1756 the schools of New York were declared to be "of the lowest order." Since school attendance was not compulsory, the children went only when they could conveniently be spared from work.

In the southern colonies the separation of plantations and consequent wide dispersion of the population made it impossible to establish effective school systems. The boast of Governor William Berkeley in 1671 that there were no free schools in Virginia was not true, for when he wrote there were two such schools in that colony. There were also quite a few Old Field schools, so called because they were established on the abandoned tobacco fields; the clergyman or the wife of the planter usually presided and taught reading, writing, and the catechism. They were, however, scattered, small, and inefficient. In such circumstances it is not surprising to find illiteracy common among the white adults. Of 12,445 men who attached their names to deeds between 1641 and 1711 in Virginia, 5006 or 40 per cent were forced to make their mark, while of 3066 women 2310 or 75 per cent did the same. Grammar schools also existed, and in 1697 William and Mary College was opened, but it was for many years little better than a grammar school. Southern planters who wished their sons to enjoy a college education employed tutors or sent them to England.

In judging the state of education in the colonies it must be remembered that America constituted the western fringe of population, and that the country was isolated from the intellectual movements in Europe. There was, moreover, no leisure class who could study and carry on research.

[9] The National University of Mexico was founded in 1553 in Mexico City by the Spaniards.

Most of the writing was done by the clergy on theological topics. The schools were almost a monopoly of the wealthy and the colleges were even more so. For the mass of the people education was obtained, not from books, but from practical experience on the farm, the sea, or in the shop. Vocational training was given by the system of apprenticeship. A boy preparing for a skilled craft, usually that of his father, was apprenticed to a master craftsman at the age of twelve to fifteen years until he was twenty-one. Generally, too, it was stipulated that he be taught to read and write and receive moral instruction. The colonial boy was for the most part schooled in the arts of the farmer and the woodsman; though he might make his mark instead of writing his name he knew how to care for a farm, handle an ax, or shoot a gun. The many demands of a pioneer life trained the minds as well as the hands of the settlers. They developed habits of industry, thrift, and initiative, but their life was hard and they were apt to have a narrow outlook and to be provincial and superstitious. In no domain was the effect of environment so noticeable as in the field of education.

The movement for universal free elementary education made slow headway. Jefferson proposed in 1779 that Virginia be divided into districts, in each of which a school should be supported by taxation, open to the children of all citizens, free of tuition for the first three years, but this suggestion was not adopted. The wide dispersion of an agricultural population, the opposition of the propertied class to a system of popular education for the masses, the lack of political power of the workers until the suffrage was obtained, and other factors delayed for half a century the full realization of the Jeffersonian ideal. Yet the pressure was too strong to be entirely ignored, and some forward steps were taken.

In addition to pauper and parochial schools of the colonial period three new types were introduced after the Revolution. The Sunday school, for the purpose of giving working children instruction in reading and the Church catechism, was imported from England into Philadelphia in 1791. The churches, objecting to secular instruction on

Sundays, soon took these over and made them agencies for religious education. A second type of elementary school, also borrowed from England, was the Lancastrian or monitorial school, in which competent older pupils transmitted to the younger ones information that they had learned by rote from the teachers. Introduced into New York in 1809 it quickly spread to every state in the Union, and was even adopted as a method of teacher training in some. It had the merit of being cheap, it provided mass training, and it was a step toward the ideal of universal free education. A third type, of less importance, was the infant school for poor children who were too young for the monitorial school. This became the primary school of a later day.

A vital force in the movement toward free popular education was the demand of enfranchised labor for free schools other than the charitable or "ragged schools" which had come down from colonial days. The Workingmen's party of the late twenties and thirties placed first among its demands a free public school system supported by taxation and non-sectarian in its control. This demand was soon sponsored by the major political parties and was given vitality by the Jacksonian program of destroying monopoly and privilege in every form—in education as well as in banking and manufacturing.

In the thirties and forties the movement for free public schools took on new vigor, especially in the newly created western states. Here there were no vested interests in the form of private schools or academies, sectarian control of the churches was weaker, and the people were more convinced of the need for education as a basis for the successful management of democratic political institutions. The honor of leadership belongs to Michigan, which in 1827 laid the foundation for a system of free public schools and in 1837 created a state university. The eastern states made slower headway against the vested interests and prejudices of an older society, and in the South there were no state-wide systems of public schools in operation up to 1860. Taking the country as a whole, however, there were nearly 100,000 elementary schools in existence at this date.

For the learning of trades apprenticeship was the only

method. As machinery began to be introduced and standardized articles were produced in factories, craftsmanship lost its importance and more reliance came to be placed on general intelligence and ingenuity. However great the shortcomings of formal education may have been, the Americans were learning valuable lessons in the school of experience, using new methods and new tools to solve the varied problems of a changing environment.

THE FIRST AMERICAN HIGH SCHOOL

This drawing shows the Boston Public Latin School as it appeared at the close of the seventeenth century. The one room was fairly large, and on the second floor were quarters for the schoolmaster and an assistant or non-resident pupils.

The education of the children of the workingman usually ended with the elementary school. But for the children of the more prosperous middle class something more was demanded. The narrow Latin grammar schools did not fill the need for a liberal and vocational training, such as befitted the requirements of an increasingly commercial and industrial country. The need was met by the establishment of academies, founded under private or local auspices, free from sectarian control and with a broad curriculum of studies. To these academies flocked the sons and daughters of merchants and farmers who could not hope to go to college, but who wished a liberal education of our present-day high-school level. By 1860 more than 6000 academies were in existence. In addition to these between three and four hundred high schools had been established.

At the top of the system of education stood the college. Some of these had been founded during the colonial period, but now a new impetus was given to the movement. To the 9 colleges of colonial days there were added about 35 more by 1820; by 1860 almost 250 institutions of college level had been founded, of which 17 were state institutions. The narrow curricula of the colonial period were gradually broadened, but the students were drawn almost exclusively from the more well-to-do classes. In addition to these colleges there were about 50 theological seminaries, nearly the same number of medical schools, and a third as many law schools.[10] An observation of de Tocqueville gives a fair statement of the situation: "If an observant stranger only singles out the learned, he will be astonished to find how rare they are; but if he courts the important, the American people will appear to be the most enlightened community in the world."

Recreation. The seventeenth century was one of pioneering and unremitting toil. All the energies of the settlers were absorbed in the strenuous tasks of clearing the forests, building homes, producing food and clothing, and developing profitable industries. Life was primitive and hard and as a result there was little time or energy to devote to the arts or to play. The outlook on life was, moreover, colored by the prevailing English middle-class ideas of the period, which we are accustomed to call Puritan but which were found equally in the Southern colonies. Alike both in the North and in the South was to be found legislation against idleness, drunkenness, Sabbath breaking, dicing and card playing, and "excess in apparell." But as time went on life developed along such different lines in the two sections that by the end of the seventeenth century Southern planters had quite forgotten their early scruples and sought pleasure unabashed in racing, hunting, dancing, card playing, cock-fighting, and other sports. In New England pleasure seeking

[10] James M. Phillips. *The United States and Cuba* (London, 1857), 215.

was regarded with suspicion, and card games, dice, stage playing, and mixed dancing were frowned upon. Yet even the Puritans had their diversions, such as shooting matches, lectures, military training days, wrestling matches, and running races.

By the eighteenth century the growth in population and wealth and the increased security began to have their effect on social as well as on economic activities. "The pioneering period is past," said Franklin, "and the time has come to think of other things than merely subduing the wilderness." After the middle of the eighteenth century a distinct American culture began to show itself. Clubs were formed for social and intellectual purposes; from one of these latter came the American Philosophical Society, founded by Franklin in 1747. Weekly newspapers existed in six of the colonies in 1763. Painting, music, and the drama obtained a foothold toward the end of this period. Most of this culture was based on English models, but the environment of the New World was impressing upon it a stamp that was increasingly American.

As in other lines, so even in matters of recreation and culture there was an uneven distribution of their benefits. Most of the things mentioned could be enjoyed only, or chiefly, by the wealthy and the educated. The farmer, the artisan, and the workingman had little share in the higher artistic forms of recreation. They sought their pleasures in such community sports as "bees," house-raisings, spinning matches, and the like, on which occasions games of physical prowess, feasting, and drinking were their chief diversions. Human pleasures are, however, largely a matter of contrast, and any change from hard work, sweetened with human companionships, undoubtedly yielded satisfactions that may not be measured by comparison with the relaxations of the twentieth century.

Until the opening of the nineteenth century Americans had scarcely begun to amuse themselves. Most of the people lived in the country and the diversions were such as cost little and fitted into the daily lives of the people. Timothy Dwight, a minister and later president of Yale College, wrote as follows of New England:

"The principal amusements of the inhabitants are visiting, dancing, music, conversation, walking, riding, sailing, shooting at a mark, draughts, chess, and unhappily in some of the larger towns cards and dramatic exhibitions. A considerable amusement is also furnished in many places by the examinations and exhibitions of the superior schools; and a more considerable one by the public exhibitions of colleges. Our countrymen also fish and hunt. Journeys taken for pleasure are very numerous, and are a favorite object. Boys and young men play at foot-ball, cricket, quoits, and at many other sports of an athletic cast, and in the winter are particularly fond of skating. Riding in a sleigh, or sledge, is also a favorite diversion in New England."

Such amusements may have satisfied Puritan New England, but in other sections of the country different diversions were sought. Outside of New England horse racing was the most general sport, especially in the South. Trotting races began to rival the old running races in popularity, and new breeds of horses were developed to meet the demand. The traveling circus brought relaxation to thousands of lonely farm families, debarred from the city theater or similar entertainment. The supreme showman of this period was P. T. Barnum, whose numerous hoaxes delighted the people, but who also furnished high-class entertainment, as in the case of the Swedish singer, Jenny Lind.

In the newer and rural districts the men preferred rougher sports, like bear-hunting or fighting, wrestling, running matches, and other feats of strength. By the end of this period the more brutal forms of sport, like bearbaiting, cockfighting, and gouging had been outlawed by public opinion. Few men in America had much leisure for amusements as such, and these were usually fitted into a program of work, as a house- or barn-raising. For the young people there were quilting parties, husking bees, and similar events. Camp meetings furnished relaxation and excitement as well as religious conviction of sin. Fishing and hunting were everywhere popular.

Distribution of wealth. During the colonial period there was a considerable increase of wealth. Homes had been constructed and furnished, land cleared and brought under cultivation, towns had grown up at strategic points, ships had been built and articles produced to fill them with salable cargoes, and industries had been established. To handle this growing business wealthy merchants had come into existence in the North, while in the South the system of slavery tended to concentrate capital in the hands of the planters. The leveling poverty of the seventeenth century was replaced in the eighteenth century by increased wealth more unequally divided. Some groups, as the slaves and the convicts, did not share at all in the improved conditions; the lot of the common laborer was bettered little if at all and even the skilled artisan did no more than hold his own. The self-sufficing farmer had an assured existence and undoubtedly enjoyed many of the benefits that came with increased population and closer social relationships. But the dominant groups prospered in much larger measure than any of the others just mentioned.

Any judgment of colonial conditions, of class distinctions, and of the distribution of wealth must always be qualified by the important fact that these lines of cleavage were not fixed and permanent. Only the Negro slave had a fixed position, for which even freedom offered little improvement. In the South, in the seventeenth century, when most of the labor was performed by indentured servants, the class distinctions were slight, and the servant, upon the expiration of his term of service, became a farmer or an artisan. Many of them rose to positions of wealth and distinction. In the eighteenth century, when slavery had been fastened upon the South, there was less opportunity for the man of small means, and classes tended to become fixed.

In the North the commercial development of the eighteenth century opened up many new opportunities. Few of the wealthy merchants inherited their fortunes; they earned them. The artisan might become a shopkeeper and then a merchant; the sailor-fisherman might embark upon foreign trade; the farmer become a large landowner. And, above all, the children of these groups could enter upon any profession or business for which they had a liking. The door of opportunity was open. Classes there were, but the membership of these classes fluctuated and was constantly being recruited from below. This is the most significant fact to be considered in estimating the progress of the people of the colonial period.

It is difficult to generalize about conditions in the United States during the first half of the nineteenth century, for they differed widely from time to time and from place to place. Certain broad distinctions may, however, be made. Wages and the general level of comfort tended to become higher as one moved westward from the Atlantic seaboard, and they were higher in the North than in the South. Writing in 1836 Chevalier commented on "the appearance of general ease of the people of this country," and at the close of the period a competent English observer wrote of the absence of pauperism in the United States and the universal appearance of respectability. Wages were, however, generally reduced as a result of the panic of 1837 and the seven-year long depression which followed. They rose between 1840 and 1860, and, while prices also increased, they did not do so in the same proportion. These broad generalizations are apt, however, to be misleading for they leave out of account unemployment and the tragic results of fluctuations in the business cycle which bore with undue severity on the working class. During periods of rising prices and prosperity the increased cost of living tended to absorb the gains from higher wages, while during periods of falling prices and business depression the decrease in cost of living was offset by unemployment. The skilled handicraftsman suffered from the increasing competition of machinery, and all labor on the Atlantic seaboard felt the depressing effect of immigration. On the whole the living conditions and the real wages of labor were better in 1860 than they had been in 1800, but the claim of labor for a proportionate share in the increased wealth of the nation was far from being realized.

Wealth was increasing in the eastern cities, but a group of propertyless factory workers had also appeared there. The tendency was toward greater inequality in the distribution of wealth. It has been estimated that there were fourteen millionaires in New York City in 1846 and twenty in 1855. The contrast between city and country grew greater, as wealth came to be concentrated more largely in the growing industrial and commercial cities. But here even the less well-to-do shared in the benefits of central sewage, improved water supplies, better lighting, and other improvements. ·

Conclusion. The energies of the American people were absorbed primarily in material tasks during this period, but they were not neglectful of cultural, educational, and recreational needs. The extent to which these should be developed, especially if they seemed to interfere with necessary economic improvements, always presented a problem. The great advance in this period was in the clearer recognition of human rights rather than in the development of culture or of leisure and its enjoyment.

Part III—Industrialization
1860-1914

CHAPTER XIX

AGRICULTURAL EXPANSION

ONE of the most striking features of American agriculture during the period from 1860 to 1914 was the lack of equilibrium between supply and demand and the frequent and painful readjustments rendered necessary thereby. Production outran the capacity of domestic and even of foreign markets to absorb the agricultural surplus at profitable prices. As a result, prices were generally low and farmers were discontented. In seeking for explanations of their troubles they directed their attention to railroad rates, marketing practices, the supply of money, and anything except the real cause. Other problems of land utilization, of shifting areas of production, and of changing agricultural techniques made this a period of constant readjustment and political and economic experimentation.

The appropriation of the public domain. More than half the area of the country—1,048,000,000 out of 1,920,000,000 acres—still remained in the public domain in 1860. Beginning with the Homestead Act of 1862 the government adopted the policy of giving away the land in free farms to settlers in place of the early policy of attempting to obtain some revenue from its sale.

The fundamental principle of the act was the grant of a free homestead not exceeding 160 acres to the actual settler; after five years' residence the title passed, without charge, to the "homesteader." This was the logical outcome of the pre-emption system and was the accepted policy of the government in disposing of the public lands down to 1935, when it was discontinued. The acquisition of a farm home, especially for those with little capital, was thus, in theory at least, made easy and profitable.

During the decades following 1860 the principle of the Homestead Act was liberalized and extended. In 1870 veterans of the Civil War were permitted to count their term of service against the five years' residence which was required of homesteaders. In this decade, also, a series of acts was passed which were designed to facilitate the process of alienation of the public domain. The Pre-emption Act, which was not repealed until 1891, permitted a homesteader to purchase an additional 160 acres at the minimum price of $1.25 an acre. The Timber Culture Act of 1873, the Desert Land Act of 1877, the Timber and Stone Act of 1878, and the Stock-Raising Act of 1909, all liberalized residence or purchase requirements and enlarged the size of the tract that might be acquired.

The purpose of these various acts was to create a land-owning, home-owning class of independent farmers. Under pressure from land speculators and from the mining, cattle, and lumber interests, however, features were introduced which partially nullified the good intentions of the acts. The most hurtful was the privilege of commutation, by which a homesteader was permitted after six months of filing his claim to obtain title by paying $1.25 to $2.50 an acre for it; in 1891 the commutation requirement was raised to fourteen months. For the first two decades little use seems to have been made of this privilege, and practically all the homesteaders acquired their land by residence. After 1880, however, the picture changed. More people were taking up land, the railroads were opening up new regions, the cattle industry was flowing over the Great Plains, and the price of land was going up. Many homesteaders, therefore, took advantage of the commutation privilege, bought their lands as soon as possible and sold them at a profit.

Although the liberal land policy ushered in by the Homestead Act was hailed at the time as a socially constructive and democratic method of promoting landownership and of settling the western states, its wisdom has been seriously questioned by later generations. In the first place the original intention of the acts, to place the land in the hands of independent owners, was in fact frustrated by the fraudulent evasion of the law. Mining and lumber companies, cattle graziers, and speculators took advantage of the commutation clause in the Homestead Act and of the Pre-emption law to acquire lands. They filed claims for the maximum allotments through each employee or through dummy homesteaders, and after six months took over the land from them by paying the fixed price. Such practices were attended by false swearing and not infrequently with the connivance of local land officers.

In the second place the grant of 160 acres was entirely too small for much of the public domain that was brought under the Homestead Act. A farm of this size suited the climate of the humid regions and the farm technique of the period, but it did not fit the semiarid and arid regions where most of the public domain was situated. Many luckless homesteaders, enticed to the dry public lands by the lure of a free gift, found they could not make a living on it. They plowed up land that should have remained in grass and tried to raise crops that failed in two out of three years. Later acts increased the size of the land grant in these arid areas, so that stock raising could be carried on profitably. Larger tracts were also necessary for lumbering operations.

In the third place land settlement was unduly stimulated, land was brought under cultivation more rapidly than it was needed, wasteful methods of farming were encouraged, the market was glutted with unwanted crops, agricultural prices were depressed, and the value of land in the older sections of the country was decreased. It is significant that the very regions in which homesteads were most largely taken up were those in which distress was subsequently most acute and in which discontent was most general. A slower movement and a more gradual settlement of the new land in response to market demand would have avoided some of the later difficulties of the American farmer.

Not all of the blame can, however, be placed on the Homestead Act, for much of the land put under the plow by early settlers was purchased from the railroads. It was more economical for a settler to purchase a farm from a land-grant railroad, which would convey his produce to the market, than to homestead a tract 20 to 40 miles from a railroad to and from which he must haul everything over bad roads. The government was in a way responsible for this, for the law set individual grants in the railroad grant areas at only 80 acres. A settler who wished a sizable farm had therefore to go far afield or buy his land from a speculator, from the states to which grants had been made, or from a railroad. But it is a mistake to picture the railroads as mere speculating land-grabbers, for they carried on colonization schemes with educational features which were of benefit to the settlers as well as to the railroads.[1]

The following table shows the disposition of the public lands.

DISPOSITION OF THE PUBLIC LANDS*			
Perfected homestead entries		Federal grants to states and corporations for railroads	
PERIOD	ACRES	PERIOD	ACRES
1868-1891	52,000,000	1850-1923	129,000,000
1892-1912	76,000,000		
1913-1944	120,000,000		

* *Statistical Abstract of the United States,* 1944-45, 949, and B. H. Hibbard, *A History of the Public Land Policies* (New York, 1924), 264, 396-98. This does not include lands obtained under the Pre-emption Act, Desert Land Act, Timber and Stone Act, etc., nor cash sales.

Settlement of the public domain. The movement of the population into the territory thus opened up proceeded at a pace that made the earlier westward movement seem slow indeed. During the decade 1860–70 the movement barely got under way, for only 500,000 acres were added to the farm area. The next three decades witnessed the most remarkable migration that history has ever recorded. In the single decade 1870–80 over 190,000,000 acres, or a territory equal in extent to Great Britain and France combined, were added to the cultivated area of the United States. The settlement of the wheat and corn belts resulted in a great increase in the production of grain, which was facilitated by the introduction of the new agricultural machinery. Wil-

[1] See P. W. Gates, *The Illinois Central and Its Colonization Work* (Cambridge, 1932), and R. C. Overton, *Burlington West; a Colonization History of the Burlington Railroad* (Cambridge, 1941).

liam H. Seward is said to have stated that "the harvester pushed the frontier westward at the rate of thirty miles a year."

After 1880, when three new transcontinental railroads were making new areas accessible, the westward movement went on still more rapidly. In the twenty-year period, 1880–1900, there were added to the farm area over 303,000,000 acres, or a territory equal to the rest of Western Europe, with the exception of Spain. By this time the frontier had disappeared and the predominance of agriculture in American economic life had come to an end. Between 1900 and 1910 there was an addition to the land in farms of only 40,000,000 acres, an area, however, more than equal to Spain. The number of farms increased between 1860 and 1910 from 2,044,077 to 6,361,502; in other words, more than twice as many farmers were settled in these fifty years as in the previous three hundred years of American history. Probably most of the tillable land taken up under the Homestead Act went into the possession of small holders, although there were a few large estates.

The settlers. The men who settled those western farms were for the most part native Americans. The disbanding of the army set free thousands of young men accustomed to an active outdoor life, and the liberal provisions of the Homestead Act attracted them to the free lands of the West. These people were, for the most part, without capital and they were therefore forced to pioneer. A proposal to grant each homesteader a government loan of $500 to equip his farm was introduced into the House of Representatives in 1878, but was not passed. These pioneers built log or sod houses or frame shanties, plowed a small tract of land, and gradually expanded their operations. Within a lifetime they became prosperous farmers.

Foreign immigrants supplemented this stream of native Americans. The opening of new land to settlement stimulated immigration to such an extent that during the twenty years, 1860–1880, some 5,500,000 persons came to the United States, of whom a large proportion settled in the Middle West. Of these immigrant settlers the Germans came first, fairly flooding Wisconsin and besprinkling the Middle West in general. A little later the Scandinavian elements settled Minnesota and the Dakotas, finding in those states climatic conditions similar to those in their European homes. By the nineties the source of immigration had changed from northern Europe to southern Europe, and the later arrivals preferred to settle in the eastern cities rather than to become farmers. The immigrant farmers impressed certain features upon American agriculture, such as the dairying and cheese making of southern Wisconsin, and also upon social institutions and political thinking which are clearly discernible in these sections today.

New methods. Pioneering on the Great Plains was very different from that of the settlers in the wooded tracts between the Atlantic coast and the Missouri River. This new district stretched roughly from the Red River to Canada and from about the 98th meridian to the Rocky Mountains. The absence of trees, the deficient rainfall, the presence of hostile Indians, and the cattle industry combined to introduce marked changes in the methods of pioneering and of living. In the presence of new conditions, old traditions were scrapped and social institutions modified. In the open plains of Kansas, Nebraska, and the Dakotas, pioneers lived in sod houses. Fuel was scarce, consisting of hay or buffalo chips; water was to be had only by digging deep wells. The introduction of windmills, which became common in the late seventies, was a great boon. The general use of barbed wire, first sold in 1874, permitted homesteaders to fence in their holdings and increased the conflict between them and the ranchers.

This combination of land and labor needed only the assistance of capital to become productive. This capital took two forms, namely, that used by the farmer himself to stock and implement his farm, and that invested by society in railroads and transportation facilities by which his products could be carried to markets and other supplies furnished to him. The second of these will be treated in a later chapter. Of the first, the most important form, at least in the grain states, was agricultural machinery, and to this we may now turn.

Agricultural machinery. The relative scarcity of labor, as contrasted with the enormous tasks to be performed, compelled the farmers to make use of laborsaving machinery, as indeed they had done ever since 1830. But now it was introduced on a still more extensive scale. Machinery having to do with the preparation of the land, as the plow; with planting, as grain drills and corn planters; and with cultivation, as harrows, had been carried a long way toward perfection before 1860, but the great improvements after that date centered about the reaper and thresher. The climate in the grain states required a prompt harvesting when the grain was ripe; accordingly the limit upon production was set by the possibility of gathering the crop rather than of planting or of tilling it.

The invention of the reaper has already been described, but the early machine merely cut the grain; it was necessary for a man to rake the piles of cut grain off the machine and for still other men to gather and bind it. The final step was the invention of the self-binder. After experiments with wire failed, John Francis Appleby, of Wisconsin, invented the twine binder in 1878. This permitted one man to do as much as eight men had done before. "It was the twine binder," wrote Professor Carver,[2] "more than any other machine or implement that enabled the country to increase its production of grain, especially wheat, during this period. The per capita production of the country as a whole increased from about 5.6 bushels in 1860 to 9.2 bushels in 1880." In the latter year the census reported that "probably four-fifths of all the wheat grown in the United States is cut by machine." Finally, the perfecting of a combined harvester and thresher about 1885, and a general substitution of steam and later of gasoline for horsepower to run threshing machines, permitted the grain to be cut and threshed, cleaned, sacked, and weighed without the intervention of human hands.

These big and expensive machines tended to promote large-scale farming, for they could be used economically only on farms of considerable size. Consequently there was a movement for larger farms in those areas where these machines

[2] T. N. Carver, *Principles of Rural Economics* (Boston, 1911), 99.

PRODUCTIVITY IN AGRICULTURE
(PER MAN HOUR)

PICTOGRAPH CORPORATION

1830 (HAND METHODS)

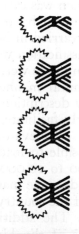

1896 (EARLY MACHINES)

1942 (MODERN MACHINES)

Each symbol represents 40 lbs. of wheat produced

From Hacker, Modley, Taylor, THE UNITED STATES: A GRAPHIC HISTORY, Modern Age Books, Inc.

were in use, though this was offset by co-operative use of the more expensive ones. Most of the threshing was done by machines that traveled from farm to farm.

Other machines were invented for planting and cultivating. Plows, harrows, and grain drills were improved and specialized; an advance in the last was the check rower, which planted the crop in rows at right angles, thus permitting cross cultivation. Haying was relieved of much backbreaking work by the introduction of sulky rakes, tedders, loaders, and balers. Even in the South the cotton seed planter, fertilizer, and other specialized tools were introduced, and the cotton gin was greatly improved.

Hardly less important than the invention of agricultural machinery were the improvements in the methods of transporting and handling the grain. As long as it remained in the farmer's hands the grain was carried entirely by hand in bags or sacks and was moved by teams. After it left the farm it was handled and carried in bulk by steam power. A system of grading and classification was established by which all specific lots of a certain grade were dealt with together in bulk, in the most economical manner. This made possible the marketing of grain by description instead of by delivery of a specific lot, and greatly facilitated dealings on the produce exchanges. The use of elevators for transferring or storing grain made it possible to load vessels from the elevators at the rate of 8000 to 10,000 bushels an hour. The use of such unique methods alone made it possible to handle the growing grain trade of the country.

Increased production. The addition of vast acreage to the improved farm lands of the United States, and their efficient utilization with the aid of improved agricultural machinery, resulted in a rapid and great expansion of production. The most spectacular increase was made in grain, for this was facilitated most of all by machinery. In the fifty-year period, 1860-1910, the production of barley increased tenfold, reflecting the development of the brewing industries; that of oats sixfold, most of which went to feed the multiplying horses; that of wheat fourfold, which served for human consumption, either at home or abroad; that of corn trebled, keeping pace with the expansion of beef and hog production. All this was far in excess of the growth of population during this period.

It is difficult to say how much of this increased production was due to machinery and how much to the larger acreage under cultivation, to better methods of cultivation, to the use of fertilizers, better seeds, crop rotation, and other factors. During the greater part of this period most of the gain came from opening up new land, especially in Minnesota, the Dakotas, Nebraska, Kansas, Texas, and Oklahoma.

An interesting investigation, made some years ago by the Department of Labor, tried to determine the contribution of machinery. A single illustration will suffice: to produce 20 bushels of wheat required 61 hours in 1830 and 3 hours in 1896, and at the same time the cost was reduced from $4.00 to $1.12 a bushel. It would have been impossible to plant, cultivate, and harvest the crops of 1910 without the aid of machinery. At the same time the crops obtained were of better quality, for hay, corn, and small grains could be harvested quickly without injury or waste, while the work of threshing wheat or ginning cotton was done in cleaner fashion.

Demand for farm products. Production is usually carried on in response to economic demand, but in the United States during this period the lure of a free farm rather than the profits to be derived from the sale of its produce was the determining factor that led to the settlement and cultivation of the land. If agriculture had been in the self-sufficing stage it is conceivable, though not probable, that each homesteader might have practiced subsistence farming and consumed what he produced. But the homesteader needed livestock, farm equipment, clothing, and other supplies for which he must pay cash, or its equivalent in the yield from his farm. He therefore carried on commercial farming, that is, he grew cash crops for the market, and by this fact he entered into the complex and interdependent economy of national and international exchange. His position became dependent upon market and price fluctuations which affected his profits even more than the weather did his production.

This expansion of production brought about the partial disorganization of agriculture in the eastern states and dissatisfaction in the West itself. So eager were the settlers to acquire land on such favorable terms that the taking up of farms proceeded more rapidly than was justified by the economic demand for the products they raised. There was thus a great overproduction, especially of wheat and cotton, and prices were greatly depressed. In many cases, perhaps the majority, crops were grown at a loss, the rise in the value of the land, originally cheap, being counted as the real reward. But "overproduction" is meaningless except in relation to cost and demand. It is therefore necessary to ascertain if possible whether the demand for American agricultural products was keeping pace with the output.

The demand for these products was domestic and foreign. It is difficult to determine accurately the domestic requirements for American farm products during this period, but the growth of population furnishes a rough measure. The accompanying graph shows that crop production proceeded

POPULATION AND AGRICULTURE, 1870–1930

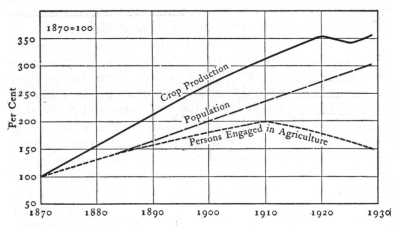

much more rapidly than population. Assuming that production was adequate to home needs in 1870 and that no marked changes in consumption habits had occurred in the interval, the conclusion seems justified that the production of agricultural foodstuffs and raw materials was in excess of the domestic needs.

The foreign demand was more capricious and its fluctuations affected adversely our export crops. The exportation of breadstuffs from the United States had already begun before the Civil War, but during that struggle it grew enormously, partly because of the cutting off of the southern market and partly because of a series of crop failures in Europe. For a time after the Civil War there continued to be an eager demand in Europe for our products, especially wheat and cotton, and it seemed that a satisfactory outlet for the surplus over domestic requirements had been found. The exports of wheat increased up to about 1885, but after that remained relatively stationary until World War I. The reasons for this lack of growth were several: after 1871 Europe enjoyed a long period of peace and developed and protected her own agriculture by high tariff duties; other producing areas closer at hand, like southern Russia, were penetrated by railways and sent their products to this market. In the case of cotton the opening of the Suez Canal in 1869 brought Indian cotton closer to European textile mills and increased the competition of that staple. The price fell disastrously, and in spite of—or because of—a great increase in exports the cotton grower actually received fewer dollars for greater amounts.

Agricultural discontent. Another result of the large agricultural surplus and the accompanying disastrous fall in prices was a general growing discontent among the farmers. Prices of agricultural products in general declined from 1866 to about 1897; the general price level fell from 132 to 46.5, but farm prices declined even more, to 39.6. All prices then rose more or less rapidly to 1910; in the case of many products there was a period of stability from 1910 to 1914. The demand for staple agricultural foodstuffs does not expand rapidly because of the limited capacity of the human stomach, and is therefore inelastic; the demand for cotton expanded, but supply outran it. Consequently, the larger production could be sold only at lower prices. Between 1867 and 1878 the gold price of corn fell from 57 cents a bushel to 32 cents, that of wheat from $1.45 to 78 cents a bushel, while that of cotton fell from 30 cents a pound (in 1866) to 8 cents; in 1894 the prices of the three articles were, respectively, 41 cents, 67 cents, and 7 cents. If currency prices were taken, the decline would be much greater. Many of the farmers who had bought land or equipment while prices were high, perhaps giving a mortgage on their farms, were now faced by ruin and the loss of their land.

The increase in mortgage indebtedness, it was stated, was greater than the increase of income derived from agriculture; in Kansas 60 per cent of the taxed acreage was under mortgage in 1890, in Nebraska 55 per cent, and in Iowa 47 per cent. Corn was so cheap that it was burned for fuel in many places, and wheat was left unharvested or fed to the stock. It must not be forgotten that many of these farmers hoped to profit by the rise in value of their land as well as from the sale of their produce. Seeking for the cause of their misfortunes they fastened the blame on the currency legislation, the bankers, the railroads and other monopolies, the tariff, taxation, and other factors which seemed to them to be responsible for their plight.

After the Civil War, Congress pursued a policy of currency contraction which meant a fall in prices from the dizzy heights of the war inflation. Since the farmer was a producer and a debtor he was adversely affected by lower prices and believed that one cure for his economic ills would be a renewed inflation of the currency and higher prices. Needing capital to equip and stock his farm if not to buy it, the farmer was accustomed to borrow from the banks or from eastern capitalists; as prices of his products fell he was frequently unable to meet the interest payments and had his mortgages foreclosed. Interest rates were high; those in one typical western state averaged 9.4 per cent in 1870; the length of the average mortgage was less than three years; and, finally, 90 per cent of the mortgages were held by non-residents.[3]

The bankers and the capitalists constituted for the farmer a vague "money power" which he distrusted and hated. Even if he succeeded in holding onto his land and in meeting his obligations the western farmer was convinced that the profits on his grain and other products were absorbed by high railroad charges or by middlemen who stood between him and the consumer. He therefore demanded lower railroad rates and a reduction of handling charges. He saw that the tariff

[3] C. M. Thompson and F. M. Jones, *Economic Development of the United States* (New York, 1939), 281.

raised the prices of articles he bought, but did not help obtain a better market for the things he sold. And finally he felt aggrieved because of the high and unequal taxes and the waste and corruption in government circles.

The economic position of the farmer, who was a small-scale producer of perishable commodities, which he could not long withhold from the market, was a weak one. Even if his products could stand storage, in the hope of better prices, he was frequently compelled to sell at whatever price he could obtain to meet taxes and interest charges. Confronted with stronger and better-informed buyers and shippers, he had a feeling of helplessness which led him to combine with his fellow farmers and demand redress against his real and sometimes fancied wrongs.

The Granger movement was the dissatisfied farmers' first organized effort to remedy these various ills by independent political action. This astonishing society had its origin in the formation by O. H. Kelly in 1867 of the "Patrons of Husbandry," which had for its primary purpose the improvement of farming and of the social and economic position of farmers. By 1874 it had nearly 15,000 local granges and claimed 1,500,000 members. As a means to economic betterment it sought to eliminate some of the middlemen's high charges by co-operative buying and selling, and to reduce railroad charges by obtaining legislation prescribing lower rates.[4] After 1876 the Grange declined as rapidly as it had grown, largely owing to the failure of ill-advised co-operative enterprises; by 1890 it had only 100,000 members.

The next step was the formation in 1876 of the Greenback Party, which demanded a repeal of the specie resumption act, the abolition of bank notes, and the substitution therefor of legal-tender paper money issued directly by the government. Many of the farmers were attracted to this movement, which promised higher prices by inflating the currency; they believed with Solon Chase of Maine, who cried, "Inflate the currency, and you raise the price of my steers and at the same time pay the public debt." Checked by the resumption of specie payments in 1879 the Greenback Party steadily lost ground and disappeared after the election of 1884. Many of

4 See Chap. XXIII for a fuller discussion.

its members joined the free silver movement, which promised some inflation of the currency and therefore attracted them.

Another organization which made a strong appeal to western farmers was the Peoples' Party. Formed by the amalgamation of the Farmers' Alliance with several other organizations it nominated a candidate for the presidency as a third party in 1892 and obtained 22 votes in the electoral college. The platform demanded a national currency of greenbacks, free and unlimited coinage of silver, a graduated income tax, postal savings banks, government ownership of monopolies, and other reforms, but it met with only temporary success and disintegrated after 1896. Populism was an exhibition of the old pioneer ideals coupled with insistence upon federal aid in realizing them.

The next year saw the end of the long period of agricultural depression and from then on the farmers' skies began to brighten somewhat. The general price level rose steadily, but the prices of agricultural products advanced still more. The great surplus of farm products which had exerted such a depressing influence on prices was absorbed in increasing measure by the rapid growth of the population, so that by 1900 the domestic food requirements nearly equaled the capacity of the country, under existing methods, to produce the needed food supply. For the first decade and a half of the twentieth century American farmers enjoyed one of the most prosperous periods in their history. Our agricultural exports declined until 1914; since we had less to spare for our neighbors in other parts of the world, the exports of wheat, corn, meat, dairy products, and other foodstuffs all fell off. Domestic production and domestic consumption were now finally in equilibrium on a higher standard of living. On the other hand, the increasing demand for agricultural produce could no longer be so easily supplied as formerly by merely extending the cultivated area westward. The practical exhaustion of the supply of good arable land in our public domain closed that avenue for agricultural enterprise.

Regional specialization. Another readjustment which created problems for American farmers during this period was the constant shifting of areas of production. There was going on an experimental process of land utilization, which

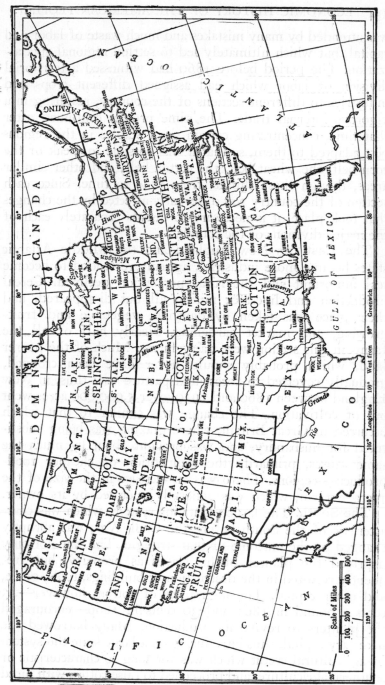

REGIONAL DISTRIBUTION OF PRODUCTS IN THE UNITED STATES

was attended by many mistakes and much waste of labor and capital, but which ultimately led to settled regional specialization. The period before 1860 had witnessed a territorial division of labor which had assigned different crops and industries to different sections of the country, resulting in a vigorous internal trade. The same process continued after that time, concentrating certain great staples in the regions best adapted to them, so that it was possible to speak of the corn belt, the wheat belt, the cotton belt, and other similar areas, though these shifted from time to time. Since each section of the country was differently affected by the changes that took place, it is necessary to discuss separately each of the major divisions of the country.

The East. As New England and the Middle Atlantic states became more industrial, agriculture tended to become less important and the rural population declined. Cereal production and livestock raising all but disappeared, and their place was taken by dairying, vegetable and fruit-growing, and market gardening. Nearly half of all the farms in this section were dairy farms. Much of the poorer land, which probably should never have been cropped, gradually reverted to forest and pasture use: thus, in New England between 1860 and 1910, over 5,000,000 acres went out of cultivation. The change was similar to that which occurred in Great Britain, where grazing was being substituted for husbandry, and was brought about by much the same causes, primarily the competition of cheaper food-producing regions. There was an increase in the size of the average farm, which was generally operated by its owner.

The South. The large plantation system, which was characteristic of the South before the Civil War, was abruptly changed by the outcome of that struggle. The war not only deprived the planter of his slaves as property, but frequently resulted in the destruction of buildings, tools, cattle, and other capital. The high price of cotton, however—43 cents a pound in 1865 and 30 cents in 1866—encouraged the planters to revive its production. Many borrowed the necessary capital, thus introducing on a large scale the system of agricultural credit which was for long so characteristic of southern agriculture, and proceeded to raise cotton with hired labor. This had two unfortunate results: (1) there was a revival of the old one-crop plantation system, with its concentration on cotton; (2) there was an overproduction of cotton, accompanied by a fall in the price.

The planters who undertook the growing of cotton were at once confronted with a serious labor problem. How could they induce the freedmen to work? At first they adopted the wage system in vogue wherever men were hired to work —a weekly wage for a specified number of hours of labor. The wage system which was thus inaugurated was, however, found to be utterly unsatisfactory, as the freedmen were quite irresponsible. The so-called "standing wage" system was next devised, according to which the Negroes were paid their wages monthly, semi-annually, or even annually, in order to keep them at their tasks. But the payment of all or a part of their earnings was a signal for wholesale desertion by the freedmen, who resented the control of the planters and had not yet learned habits of voluntary industry.

An era of small farms followed the failure of the large plantation system under free Negro labor, and the large landholdings were broken up to suit small purchasers. Many of the white yeomen and a few Negroes purchased farms of 10 to 12 acres, and proceeded to raise cotton on their own account. In Mississippi, for example, there were only 412 farms of less than 10 acres in 1867, but 10,003 in 1870.

Since the Negroes would not work for wages and were unable to purchase land, an effort was next made to have them farm the cotton lands on shares, and this "cropping" system soon became the all but universal method. The system of cash rents was never widespread. Under share cropping the Negro tenant had more independence but crops became smaller because he worked fewer hours and with less intelligence. Not until 1879 did the cotton crop (2404 million pounds) pass the yield (2155 million pounds) of 1860, the last uninterrupted year of production under slavery.

A characteristic feature of cotton growing in the South for a generation after the war was the system of agricultural credit. The white yeoman farmers and the Negro tenants were alike without working capital and were compelled to borrow money or to buy the needed food supplies, seed, and tools on credit, giving a mortgage or lien on the growing crop as security. The lender was usually the merchant and country storekeeper, who was personally familiar with the small borrower and who could, moreover, exercise constant supervision over the crop.

While economically necessary at first as a means of securing the needed capital, this practice of agricultural credit soon resulted in a system of peonage of the debtor farmer to the merchant who became his creditor, under which the debtor was kept almost in a state of serfdom, working for his creditor until his debts were paid. All supplies must be purchased through the creditor, and the crops must be sold through him, on both of which transactions lucrative commissions were charged in addition to frequently usurious rates of interest. The local landlord or merchant, moreover, often owned the cotton gin, and since all cotton had to be ginned before being sent to market, he was in a position to prevent the tenant from bootlegging the cotton.

This system had certain undesirable effects. Since cotton was the most marketable crop and would always sell for cash, the lender insisted that the farmer concentrate his efforts upon cotton growing. His cry for cotton, and more cotton, led to a constant increase in the acreage and production of this staple, in the face of an almost steady decline in the price. In the second place, since the farmer was compelled to buy all his supplies from the lender's store, he was discouraged from growing his own corn or bacon since this would diminish his purchases. There was a steady decrease in the production of corn and wheat between 1865 and 1890 in all the southern states except Texas. As Hammond put it, "The raising of corn would not only give a less marketable crop in to the hands of the merchant, but it would eventually lose him his customers, for the raising of his own supplies would release the farmer from the necessity of doing business on a credit basis." Diversification of farming and even rotation of crops were thus prevented in the South. The system of tenant farming thus developed was even more ruinous to the soil than the old plantation system had been, for the tenants had neither the opportunity nor the interest in maintaining its fertility.

By 1879 cotton growing had practically recovered from the losses of the Civil War and the injuries of reconstruction, and production never again fell below the record of 1860. Prices also began to improve by the beginning of the twentieth century, due to the increasing demand for the staple on the part of the expanding textile manufactures. The high price of cotton during the next few years was of great importance in lifting the cotton planter out of the slough of debt and dependence upon store credit. The crop lien almost disappeared, deposits in the banks increased, and the farmers enlarged their purchases of farm machinery and fertilizer.

The Middle West. The rapid settlement of the Middle West and the consequent expansion of grain production have already been described. Involved in these developments was a steady westward movement of agriculture, which transferred the center of production of most of the staples from the East to the Middle or Far West. This transition was the most marked characteristic of the West throughout the larger part of this period. By 1890, however, practically all the arable land in the Mississippi Valley had been occupied, and thereafter agriculture tended to adjust itself to more settled conditions and to assume what may prove to be its permanent form. The migrating staples settled down in comparatively fixed habitats.

The center of wheat production had moved from Massachusetts in colonial times to central New York in the 1830's and by 1860 to Illinois. The wheat grown during this long period had been soft winter wheat. But when this was introduced into Kansas and Nebraska, the severe winters and scanty rainfall caused frequent crop failures. A revolution was effected in wheat growing by the introduction in 1873 of hard winter wheat from the Crimea and twenty-five years later of a variety of spring wheat resistant to cold and drought. The former was raised principally in Kansas and neighboring states, and the latter in Wisconsin, Minnesota, and the Dakotas.

Corn has always been our most important cereal crop, representing about three-quarters of the total world production and over half of all the cereals grown in the United States. Since it can be grown nearly everywhere, it has never shown the high degree of regional localization exhibited by some other products. It is nevertheless possible to point to the corn belt, which was taking form during this period. In 1860 the three leading states were Illinois, Ohio, and Missouri, but by 1910 the center of corn production had moved farther westward and Iowa, Illinois, and Indiana constituted the leading trinity of this cereal.

The raising of beef cattle, hogs, and poultry, based for the most part upon the use of corn, also developed in this section. There was a strong concentration of this industry in Iowa, Illinois, Missouri, Indiana, and Nebraska, and it was in these states that the great slaughterhouses and meat-packing establishments were found, notably in the cities of Chicago, Kansas City, and Omaha.

The process of converting this livestock into food for human consumption began its marvelous growth during this period. The introduction of the refrigerator car, which made its first shipment of dressed beef in 1869 from Chicago to New York, gave a wonderful impetus to the slaughtering and meat-packing industries. The total value of the products in the slaughtering and meat-packing industries grew enormously, from $29,000,000 in 1860 to $3,435,000,000 in 1914, at which time it was the nation's leading industry.

The dairy industry, which is quite distinct from the livestock industry, followed the westward movement of the great staple crops, though this clung more closely to the great centers of population. In 1860 dairying was carried on primarily in the eastern states, with New York as the leader and Ohio as the western outpost, but by 1910 the center of the industry was in the Middle West. Agricultural colleges and cow-testing associations gave considerable impetus to improving the milk production of dairy cattle by good breeding and improved feeding practices. The demand for year-round supplies of fluid milk for cities together with the introduction of the silo increased the winter supply of milk. After its introduction in 1860 production of condensed milk and later evaporated milk increased rapidly. The center of the dairy industry moved to the surplus milk producing areas of the corn belt with Wisconsin the leading dairy state, Minnesota second, and New York third.

The dairy industry was also revolutionized by the introduction of factory methods in the making of butter and cheese. Cheese making developed rapidly under the factory system during the sixties and seventies, and by 1880 more than four-fifths of the cheese produced in the United States was made in factories. There were natural limits to the expansion of the industry, due in part to the relatively small domestic consumption of cheese, and in part to the lack of a foreign demand for the American product.

After 1880 buttermaking displaced cheese making as the leading dairy industry. At that time most of the butter was still made on the farms, but a great stimulus to the development of factory methods in buttermaking was given by the invention of the Babcock test for determining the butterfat of milk, and of the centrifugal cream separator for extracting cream without having to "set" the milk and wait for the cream to rise. Still more important as an explanation of the development of the butter industry was the expanding demand on the part of the American people, who are great bread eaters, and who, unlike the French and the Italians, eat butter on their bread. The American dairy industry therefore specialized in buttermaking rather than in cheese making, in contrast to European countries. Butter is also a great stabilizer in milk production, for when milk is very plentiful and prices are apt to fall, it can be made into butter which can be stored almost indefinitely. When milk is scarce the butter is taken from the refrigeration plants and all the milk can be consumed as such.

The Far West. West of the 100th meridian to the Rocky Mountains stretches a region where the rainfall is insufficient for ordinary agriculture, being less than 20 inches a year. Here the chief industry is grazing. Cattle raising has always been a frontier industry in the United States, keeping somewhat in advance of pioneer farming, whether in the colonial forests of North Carolina, later in the Middle West, or since 1860 on the ranches of the Far West. The so-called "native" cattle, probably the descendants of Spanish cattle brought over to Mexico by Cortés, had multiplied rapidly in the Southwest, and after the Civil War an outlet for them was sought in the North. Texas cattle had been driven to the corn lands of Illinois as early as 1857, but the movement was checked by the war. In 1866 the long drives to the north began again, but this time to the northern ranges on the public domain. It had been accidentally discovered the previous year that the dried buffalo grass on these semi-arid plains provided excellent winter forage for cattle. Texas cattle driven north and fattened on the open ranges gained more rapidly in weight than if they remained in Texas, and moreover the beef was of better quality. The cattlemen, meanwhile, had simply utilized the unappropriated public domain for their purpose without formality of grant or lease, until they had come to regard the vast unfenced area of semi-arid plain from Texas to Canada as their special domain.

By 1870 well-defined cattle trails had been marked out over which an average of nearly 300,000 cattle were driven northward annually from the breeding grounds of Texas. A territorial division of labor resulted, by which Texas became the breeding ground and northern ranges matured and prepared the steers for market. This was the cattle kingdom, where men on horseback managed vast herds, and differed greatly from stock farming farther east. During the next fifteen years the range and ranch industry spread over the great plains of the West. Between 1866 and 1884, according to Joseph Nimmo, 5,250,000 cattle were driven northward from Texas.

After 1885 the importance of the cattle trail began to decline, as a result of several factors. Homesteading farmers invaded the open ranges and fenced in their farms with barbed wire, and, although the cattlemen resisted the "nesters" their advance could not be stayed. The railroads were built into the heart of the cattle country and transported the cattle direct to market or to the corn-growing regions where they were fattened. Minor causes were the quarantine laws against Texas cattle, and the terrible winters of 1886 and 1887 which almost destroyed the herds. The enclosed cattle range now replaced the open range. In the meantime the introduction of the Scotch Shorthorns and later of Herefords brought about a meatier type of beef cattle that fattened at an earlier age and produced more desirable meat. The demand for smaller cuts and meat with less fat, owing to the growth of city and apartment-house life and the decreasing average size of American families, led to the marketing of beef steers at lighter weights and finally to the production of baby beeves on the corn-belt farms. The best ranges were put under fence, and range cattle wintered to a large extent on alfalfa. On the poorer ranges sheep gradually replaced beef cattle.

With the passing of the long cattle drives and the great ranches on the free range of the unfenced public domain, a picturesque feature of the American frontier disappeared. The spread of the range and ranch cattle industry over the Great Plains during the fifteen years from 1866 to 1880 was a striking development in the kaleidoscopic changes of American agriculture during this period. But the romantic aspects of the annual roundups, the branding of the young steers, and the picturesque cowboys have been given more attention in history and fiction than their economic importance justified. It was a transient episode which was brought to an end by the inexorable pressure of homesteading farmers.

Farming in the arid region. Between the 100th meridian and the Rocky Mountains lie some 300,000,000 acres of fertile soil, where the scanty rainfall—from 10 to 20 inches per annum—makes agriculture extremely precarious. The vast extent of this region is made apparent on the map on page 462. With the extension of the population and the taking up of all the arable public lands in the moist regions, the problem of reclaiming the arid plains of the western states began to attract attention.

The first experiments were made with irrigation, both public and private, but these were not altogether satisfactory, while the costs were enormous. In the debatable strip of land between the arid and the moist regions, known as the semi-arid district, another method of agriculture was introduced. This was dry farming, so-called. By disking and plowing the land after the harvest, and then after each rain, keeping down the weeds, and tilling during alternate summers without planting a crop, evaporation is prevented and the moisture from two years is stored in the ground and utilized for one crop. Dry farming made available for agriculture some millions of acres which had seemed hopelessly arid. But the terrific erosion of the soil which resulted when the protective grass was removed,[5] showed that a bad mistake in land utilization was made when this land was put under the plow.

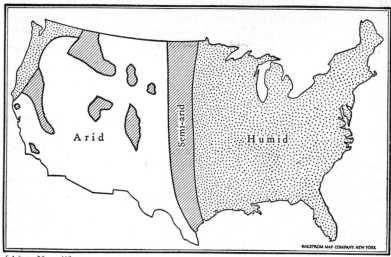

[After Newell]

HUMID, SEMI-ARID, AND ARID REGIONS OF THE UNITED STATES

Farm tenancy. Democratic landownership had always been the boast of the American republic, and it was assumed that the Homestead Act had provided every settler with a farm of his own. It was something of a shock therefore when, in 1880, the statistics of farm ownership were for the first time published in the census and it was revealed that one-quarter (25.5 per cent) of the farms were in the hands of tenants. After that the proportion grew steadily, to 28.4 per cent in 1890, 35.3 in 1900 and 37.9 in 1910, and alarm was expressed that our democratic conditions of landownership were giving way to a system of peasant tenantry, like that in Europe.

A more optimistic interpretation has, however, been made, and the presence of the tenant class has been viewed as an intermediate step in the agricultural ladder. This was probably true of most of this period, but not of the next one. Tenancy indicated the endeavor of ambitious farm laborers and

---

[5] In May, 1934, a dust storm swept up nearly half a billion tons of soil from the states of Nebraska and South Dakota and scattered it over the eastern states and even on vessels far out in the Atlantic.

persons of small means to make themselves independent rather than the fall of unsuccessful owners to the rank of tenants. This was shown by the steady growth in the number of farm owners, more rapid even than the increase in the agricultural population. Most of the tenant-farmers were, after all, to be found in the South, where the abolition of slavery had let loose a flood of necessitous Negroes or impecunious whites, who could become only wage earners or tenants. Since the former owners were unable to re-establish their plantations with paid labor, these were broken up and rented to small cash or share tenants.

The division of the plantations of the South and of the "bonanza" farms of the West showed the extension of the small farm system rather than the decline of ownership; a large proportion of the tenant farms in 1900 were under 20 acres. A study of the ages of operating owners, tenants, and laborers strengthens this conclusion. Almost 90 per cent of the farm laborers were under 35 years of age, 67 per cent of the tenants were under 45, while nearly 60 per cent of the owners were over 45 years of age. There was thus, with advancing age, a steady rise from the condition of laborer to tenant and finally to that of owner. Nor did the existence of mortgage indebtedness warrant any gloomy foreboding; taken in connection with the other facts it may be held to represent the struggle of the former tenant to purchase an equity in the land he tilled, or of the small owner to provide himself with the necessary capital for improvements.

Farm laborers constituted nearly half the agricultural labor force, making up almost 48 per cent of those engaged in agricultural pursuits in 1880, and remaining on this level until 1910. The agricultural wage earners were divided about equally between a permanent resident group, most of whom probably expected eventually to become independent farmers, and a class of temporary seasonal workers, such as the harvest hands in the western wheat fields, gatherers of fruit in California, of vegetables in New York, and of cranberries in Massachusetts.

Agricultural research. The year 1862 was an important one in the annals of American agriculture, for not merely was the Homestead Act passed, but the Department of Agriculture was established and the Morrill Act was made law; not until 1889, however, was the head of the Department admitted to the Cabinet. The Department was directed "to acquire and diffuse among the people of the United States useful information on subjects connected with agriculture in the most general and comprehensive sense of the word, and to procure, propagate, and distribute among the people new and valuable seeds." In pursuance of this latter object the bureau of plant industry sent men to every quarter of the globe to search for new plants and to determine whether they were practicable and desirable for introduction into the United States. During the single year 1904, for instance, nearly 1500 new kinds of seeds and plants were introduced into this country, including species especially adapted to the arid regions. Other bureaus were gradually established which performed equally valuable service, such as those of forestry, weather, entomology, animal industry, chemistry, and the more recent bureaus of agricultural economics and of markets.

The Morrill Act established in each state a "land-grant" college to teach "such branches of learning as are related to agriculture and the mechanic arts." For the endowment of these institutions each state was given a grant of 30,000 acres of public land for each Senator and Representative in Congress; by later acts an annual income of $50,000 was granted as a federal subsidy. From this beginning sprang most of the colleges of agriculture and of engineering in the state universities, which were generously supported by additional state appropriations. It was soon discovered, however, that book learning alone did not make dirt farmers, so in 1887 Congress provided for the establishment of agricultural experiment stations. There had been state stations before this, the first having been established in Connecticut in 1875, but now they were co-ordinated, their number increased, and their activities enlarged. By them science was applied to agricultural problems, experiments carried on, and the results disseminated among the farmers. Their influence was far-reaching, and became important. It was estimated that the North Dakota station added to the wealth of that state $10,000,000 a year for a decade by the better development of cereals. Most of these stations were situated at the agricultural colleges, which were soon to be found in every state and territory in the Union.

Conclusion. In no branch of enterprise were adjustments so numerous and drastic as in agriculture between 1860 and 1914. The American farmer since colonial days had been and for the most part still was a "cheap land" farmer, who economized labor but used land prodigally, always ready to desert old lands for new. This process continued until practically all the easily available land in the country was taken up. With the cessation of free homesteading on the public domain, however, there came to be increasing resort to careful and exact farming. The necessity for more intensive cultivation involved changes in agricultural practice and methods, and the transition was not easily made by those trained under laxer conditions. The unduly rapid development of new land brought to the front problems of marketing, which were aggravated by technical changes in agricultural methods, shifts in areas of production, price fluctuations, and other factors, some of which lay quite outside the control of the individual farmer. Restless under conditions of falling prices and of change he sought relief by various methods, some political and others non-political, but none very effective.

CHAPTER XX

THE RISE OF LARGE-SCALE MANUFACTURING

The growth of manufactures. The factory system had already obtained a firm foothold in the United States before 1850, but its great expansion came after that date. "Until about 1850," stated the census report,[1] "the bulk of general manufacturing done in the United States was carried on in the shop and the household, by the labor of the family or individual proprietors, with apprentice assistants, as contrasted with the present system of factory labor, compensated by wages, and assisted by power." But during the decade ending with 1860 the country made the most remarkable industrial progress in its history. The textile and iron industries grew two-thirds. We probably already led all other nations in the use of interchangeable mechanism and in the application of automatic machinery to the production of standardized parts. This development already long begun was greatly stimulated in the North by the events of the Civil War, and the country's manufactures emerged from that struggle with expanded plant capacity and strengthened resources. This war did not, like that of 1812, call into being new industries or radically change prevailing methods of production, but it intensified certain tendencies already in operation.

The most striking feature in the industrial development of the United States has been the enormous growth of manufactures, both absolutely and relatively to other branches of industry. Between 1850 and 1910 the population of the country quadrupled, and the products of agriculture trebled in value; but in the same period manufactures showed an increase of seven times in the number of wage earners and of twenty times in the value of the product. The growth of manufactures as a whole is shown in the following statistical

[1] Twelfth Census (1900), Vol. VII, liii.

table, though the remarkable diversity of industries and increase in the volume of products are not revealed by the statistics of value:

Year	Number of establishments	Average number of wage earners	Wages	Cost of materials used	Value of products
GROWTH OF MANUFACTURES, 1849-1909 *(Values in millions of dollars)*					
1849	123,025	957,059	$236.7	$555.1	$1,019.1
1859	140,433	1,311,246	378.9	1,031.6	1,885.9
1869	252,148	2,053,996	620.5	1,990.7	3,385.9
1879	253,852	2,732,595	947.9	3,396.8	5,369.6
1889	355,405	4,251,535	1,891.2	5,162.0	9,372.4
1899	512,191	5,306,143	2,320.9	7,343.6	13,000.1
1899*	204,750	4,501,909	1,892.6	6,385.9	11,032.9
1909*	264,826	6,262,242	3,205.5	11,783.2	19,945.2

* The statistics of manufactures from 1849 to 1899 covered the neighborhood, hand, and building industries, as well as the factory industries; since then they have been confined to factory industries. For 1899 figures compiled on both bases are given. 1943 *Statistical Abstract.*

Down to 1880 agriculture was the principal source of income in the United States, but each succeeding census report showed larger values of manufactured articles than of agricultural products. This transition of the United States from a predominantly agricultural nation to a predominantly industrial one, which was completed in this period, was the most outstanding fact to be noted. In 1820 five-sixths (83.1 per cent) of the population was engaged in agriculture and one-sixth in manufacture, trade, transportation, and professional vocations; in 1910 the two groups were one-third (33.0 per cent) and two-thirds. At the same time the United States outstripped her European rivals in the volume of her manufactured products; from fourth place in 1860 she achieved first place by 1894, and before World War I produced as much as her three nearest competitors—Great Britain, France, and Germany—combined.

Demand. This remarkable expansion in manufactures resulted from the demands of an extending and insatiable market. The sheer growth of population required ever larger quantities of goods to meet needs. The workers and capitalists responsible for the increased production, when paid, became a market for still more goods. New demands were also quickened, if not called into being, by new methods of advertising and salesmanship, so that the market constantly expanded. As a result of these forces, important new industries were created, such as the manufacture of plumbing, telephones, bicycles, and many other semi-luxuries. Per capita national income more than doubled between 1860 and 1910. Thus there developed a steady if slow improvement in the well-being of the American worker and a consequent increase in his purchasing power.

Equally important was the industrial demand of the construction and other industries. The growing population must be housed, water and other utilities must be provided for the developing cities, rails and rolling stock must be manufactured for the spreading railroad net, and factories must be built and equipped with machinery. In a word, the production of the material equipment of an increasingly mechanized civilization constituted a need whose satisfaction called into being manufactures on a scale hitherto undreamed of.

RANK OF LEADING INDUSTRIES IN 1860 AND 1914
(*Value in millions*)

Rank	1860 Industry	Value of Products	1914 Industry	Value of Products
1	Flour and meal	$248.5	Slaughtering and meat packing	$1,652
2	Cotton goods	115.7	Iron and steel	919
3	Lumber, planed and sawed	104.9	Flour and gristmill products	878
4	Boots and shoes	91.8	Foundry and machine-shop products	867
5	Iron founding and machinery	88.6	Lumber	715

Foreign demands for our manufactured goods increased tenfold between 1850 and 1900. By 1910 we were exporting nearly as much manufactured goods as we had produced altogether in 1850. While foreign demands for our manufactures were only a small fraction of domestic demands (7 per cent in 1900), our exports of manufactured goods were large compared to those of most nations. Foreign manufacturers were increasingly worried by the competition of our products.

And the foreign demand for certain of our manufactures, like iron and steel, was very important to those particular industries.

Factors in growth. But demand is only one side of the equation; on the other side is supply. American manufacturers during this period showed increasing ability to meet the expanding demands of the domestic market. In this they were aided by numerous favorable conditions, of which the most important factor was probably the abundance and richness of *natural resources*. The basic raw materials for practically every branch of manufacturing industry were to be found within the country. This wealth of natural resources determined in large measure the nature and methods of our leading manufacturing industries, for the most important ones remained, during most of the period, those which carried the raw materials through a few comparatively simple processes. A reference to the table on page 467 shows that the cost of materials used has always made up a large part of the value of the finished products as compared with the changes wrought by the manufacturing process itself.

The close dependence of our leading manufactures upon our primary resources, especially in the early period, is clearly brought out by the table on page 468. In 1860 the first four groups were based upon our agricultural and forest wealth; in 1914 those dependent upon our mineral wealth, which was now being exploited on a grand scale, were in front. Not until after World War I was first rank taken by what may be called a pure manufacture (automobiles), that is, one in which the value of the final product is due primarily to the working up of the raw material into finished forms rather than to the original value of the materials.

The *labor* supply was a most important factor in the growth of industry, for upon its quantity and quality depended the effective use of the raw materials and capital. A growing though never adequate supply was furnished by the natural increase of the population, to which was added immigration. While the population grew from 31,443,000 in 1860 to 91,972,000 in 1910, the immigration increased from an annual average of 259,800 for the decade ending in 1860 to 879,600 for the decade ending in 1910. But the statistics of growth do not tell the whole story, for over half the immigrants were in the productive age-groups between 15 and 45, and therefore were available at once for work.

More important even than the number of workers was their quality, and in this respect the United States has been fortunate. The native-born labor possessed the characteristic American qualities of energy, initiative, adaptability, inventiveness, mechanical knack, and similar traits. The foreign-born contributed their strength as unskilled workers, and as skilled artisans and mechanics they brought to their tasks the careful training, habits of obedience, and knowledge of tools and processes which they learned under the apprentice system of the Old World. American industry profited from these contributions.

Another factor contributing to our industrial progress was the supplies of *capital* which were available for the development of new manufacturing industries or for the expansion of old ones. Some of our capital, especially in the first half of the period, came from direct investments or loans on the part of citizens of Great Britain, and to some extent of France, Germany, and Belgium; but most of it was furnished from the earnings of the businesses themselves or from the savings of the rich. Capital may take the form of buildings, of equipment, of new machines, or of cash ("liquid" capital).[2] The characteristic feature of American manufacturing has been the use of laborsaving machinery; this form of capital increased after 1860 more rapidly than the number of the wage earners or the value of the products. In 1850 each worker used $555 worth of capital; but in 1910 each wage earner used $2800 worth of capital. In other words, the relative scarcity of labor, compared with the demand for goods, was made up by a resort to the use of laborsaving machinery, and the expansion of our manufactures was attended by an increase in the number of machines rather than in man power.

Manufacturers in the United States have always been willing to introduce laborsaving devices and to experiment with new mechanical appliances, while the *inventive genius* of the people has been directed into industrial lines as in no other country. The explanation of this widespread use of improved

2 See p. 72.

machine methods and of invention must be sought first of all in the relative scarcity of labor when compared with the gigantic tasks to be performed in the development of a continent. In the second place, the American people seem to possess a mechanical skill and inventive genius, the result both of inheritance and environment. American manufacturers are moreover possessed of a certain venturesome open-mindedness, which gives any new device or method a fair trial. But most of all their profitable introduction has been made possible by the enormous domestic market, which can absorb large amounts of uniform standardized articles, and by the character of the raw materials which must be worked up.

In no branch of mechanical improvements has the genius of the American inventor shown itself more strikingly than in the development of the system of interchangeable parts. Its greatest application probably took place in the sewing machine, but it revolutionized the manufacture also of guns, locomotives and railroad machinery, watches, clocks, and agricultural machinery. Equally important was the standardization of machinery and parts. In the manufacture of screws or iron beams, for example, certain dimensions and sizes, which were best adapted for general use, were selected as standard sizes, and these were then turned out in large quantities by automatic machinery. Odd sizes and special designs could generally be obtained only by special order. In this manner cheapness and rapidity in filling an order were secured, while a broken part could be obtained from any firm making or handling the standard sizes. Such a system was not possible until measuring instruments of exceeding accuracy had been invented, but after this was done it spread rapidly.

An important factor in the development of inventions in any country is the *patent system*, and that of the United States has been undeniably effective in stimulating the inventive genius of its people. One of the unexpected results of the Civil War was the impulse given to the invention and use of machines designed to economize human labor; from 4363 patents in 1860—the high-water mark up to that time—the number rapidly grew to 8874 in 1866. Writing in 1865, Peto, a keen English observer, remarked, "Mechanical contrivances of every sort are produced to supply the want of human hands.

Thus we find America producing a machine even to peel apples; another to beat eggs; a third to clean knives; a fourth to wring clothes;—in fact, human hands have scarcely been engaged in any employment in which some cheap and efficient labor-saving machine does not now to some extent replace them." [3]

The number of patents grew to 37,421 in 1909, which was the largest number ever recorded for a single year up to that time. While not all of these applied to the art of manufacturing, they influenced its growth and called into existence a number of new manufacturing industries. The improvements in the telephone, the invention of the typewriter and typesetting machines, of the cash register and of the recording adding machine, of various medicines and serums, of the steel-frame building, electric lighting, and the gasoline engine serve to suggest some of the numerous points at which the people's lives are affected by the inventions patented during the last generation. Many extensive industries were built up on the basis of patents, or old ones were completely revolutionized; such were the iron and steel, textile, and railway industries, the manufacture of sewing machines, rubber goods, wood pulp, photography, and typesetting and electrotyping. But the American inventor did not merely modify the methods of making old things; in many instances he produced absolutely new commodities and devised original ways of manufacturing them.

Power is the fundamental factor in modern industry, for only by its aid can laborsaving machinery and inventions be made available. Consequently, the progress of manufactures in a country and its rank in the scale of present-day civilization can be measured better by the amount of power that is utilized than by the number of workmen employed or even the volume of goods produced. Tested by this standard the United States made great advances during this period. Statistics of amount of power used in industry were collected for the first time in 1870, when it was shown that 2,346,000 horsepower was being employed in manufactures, of which about half was generated by water and the other half by steam (coal). By 1900 the number of horsepower had grown

---

[3] S. M. Peto, _Resources and Prospects of America_ (London, 1866), 100.

to 11,300,000, and by 1914 had further increased to 22,291,000.

The widespread system of cheap _transportation_ was another important factor in the development of manufactures in the United States. The rivers were utilized only to a slight extent, in striking contrast to the busy streams of Europe, but the traffic on the Great Lakes reached enormous proportions. The cheap transportation afforded by these inland seas brought

the iron ore of northern Michigan and Minnesota to meet the coal of southern Ohio, Indiana, and Illinois at a series of iron and steel cities, of which the most important were Cleveland, Gary, and South Chicago. The coastwise shipping also developed, but the railroads were the main arteries of commerce throughout the whole United States. It is significant that the average revenue per ton mile on railroads fell over 60 per cent between 1867 and 1900. Cheapening transportation widened or extended the market for many products. All this made possible mass production methods in which each worker specialized on the manufacture of only one small part of the finished product. Regional specialization too was encouraged.

Closely connected with this was the *freedom* from restriction of *interstate commerce*, guaranteed by the Constitution. "The mainland of the United States," said a 1900 census report, "is the largest area in the civilized world which is thus unrestricted by customs duties, excise taxes, or national prejudice, and its population possesses, because of its great collective wealth, a larger consuming capacity than that of any other nation." The large market within the country permitted the production and sale of immense quantities of standard goods, and hence encouraged large-scale methods, the use of expensive and highly specialized machinery, and a territorial division of labor. Free trade within the United States afforded the American manufacturer an unparalleled opportunity; the rewards for the successful enterprisers were so munificent that they attracted the best talents into industry, and these constantly improved the technical processes and the organization of manufacturing.

Finally, the *tariff* with increasing severity excluded foreign competition, and reserved this large domestic market largely for home producers. Protection to particular industries stimulated their growth, but as a single explanation of the phenomenal industrial growth and present pre-eminence of the United States, protection alone is inadequate. Unless other conditions are favorable, a patent law or a protective tariff will not cause permanent manufactures to develop.

The really dynamic factor was to be found neither in legislation nor even in the presence of rich natural resources, but rather in the *ability* of America's industrial leaders. Few will dispute the genius of Andrew Carnegie in the domain of steel; of John D. Rockefeller in oil refining; of Philip D. Armour in slaughtering and meat packing; of Thomas Edison and George M. Westinghouse in the electrical industries; of J. P. Morgan in finance; or of Cornelius Vanderbilt in railroading. Probably any other modern generation of Americans would have produced similar captains of industry if given like opportunities, but this particular generation did so beyond any serious doubt. Great organizers and administrators, these men caught a glimpse of the imperial opportunities offered by the expanding American market. The prizes for successful achievement were enormous.

Concentration of manufacturing in large establishments. Manufactures showed a striking concentration, especially along certain lines, into a relatively smaller number of establishments. This tendency had been in evidence even before the Civil War, but was greatly accelerated during the last two decades of the nineteenth century and has shown no abatement in the twentieth. If the product was one for which there was a great demand and which could be readily standardized, or if it was one requiring large amounts of equipment to produce, such as in many of the metal industries, concentration into a few large industries was likely to be the result. It was most marked in the case of the iron and steel industry, cotton manufactures, and leather goods, but was noticeable also in the manufacture of agricultural implements, boots and shoes, carpets, glass, paper, shipbuilding, slaughtering and meat packing, and tobacco. A few industries essentially local in their nature showed no such tendency, such as flour and gristmills, cheese and butter factories, millinery, picture framing, etc., but with few exceptions it was the prevailing characteristic of American manufactures. The extent to which this large-scale production proceeded is shown concisely in the following table.

SIZE OF AVERAGE MANUFACTURING ESTABLISHMENT*			
Date	Average product of each establishment	Average capital of each establishment	Aver. no. of employees of each establishment
1849	$8,280	$4,330	7.7
1859	13,420	7,190	9.3
1869	16,780	6,720	8.1
1879	21,100	10,960	10.6
1889	28,070	19,020	13.8
1899	54,969	43,360	20.5
1909	76,993	68,687	24.6

* *Statistical Abstract of the United States,* 1939 (Washington, 1940), 772.

Although this table shows a remarkable growth in the size of the average establishment, it does not reveal the enormous concentration which took place in the industries especially suited to large-scale production. Thus in the iron and steel industry, although the number of establishments actually declined from 808 in 1869 to 654 in 1909, the average number of employees per establishment increased from 197 to 426, the capital from $161,000 to $2,282,000, and the value of the products from $275,000 to $2,119,000, showing an astounding growth in the size of the typical plant. Manufacturing began to be organized and carried on by the great captains of industry, small independent producers began to disappear, and laborers to be marshaled in bodies of a thousand men or more.

Advantages of large-scale production. This concentration of manufactures in large establishments was caused by certain distinct advantages enjoyed by large-scale production. Foremost among these are the economies which are possible in the great industry. The operation of a business on a large scale permits the minute division of labor, the introduction of expensive and complicated machinery and its constant use, the employment of more skilled management and superintendence, the utilization of by-products, and the economical purchase of raw materials and marketing of the finished product. In the large plant a high degree of specialization of labor is possible, and the division of labor is carried to the limit. The modern factory requires a large investment in expensive machinery; from the table above it will be seen that while the average number of employees per establishment grew over threefold between 1849 and 1909, the average investment of capital increased about fourteen times and the product over nine times. This indicates that the tendency in manufacturing was toward machine production.

In a large establishment every machine is utilized to the utmost, there is no needless duplication of machinery such as would occur for several small plants, while expensive machines to carry on relatively small processes can be profitably installed. In experimenting with and inventing new machinery and methods the large establishment also has an advantage. Indeed, it may be stated as a general principle that industries in which machinery can be used with advantage constitute the group of large-scale industries, and that those in which the conditions are not favorable to the use of machines will remain small.

The large-scale industry is possible, however, only if the market is a wide one. The large and constantly expanding domestic market in the United States has made possible the introduction of economical methods and the application of laborsaving devices and improved appliances. But these methods are economical only if there is a large output. "The condition of cheap manufacture is running full," said Carnegie out of his abundant experience. Continuous operation, however, requires abundant and steady supplies of raw materials and an adequate market in which to dispose of the output. Both of these have been guaranteed in the United States by the development of cheap transportation which has widened the market area. Until the construction of adequate transportation facilities, the average business establishments in the United States were essentially local in their nature, supplying a comparatively narrow market and using a small capital. With the rapid extension of the railway system after the Civil War, it became possible to expand operations over a wider territory, to localize and concentrate manufactures, and to use larger masses of capital in a single establishment. With the widening of the market there went therefore an expansion in the size of the business unit.

Sources of capital. Enormous amounts of capital were required by the expanding industries. Where was it obtained? Adequate statistical studies on capital formation in this period have yet to be made, but Carl Snyder and others who have made this subject their specialty believe that the bulk of the capital was derived from industry itself. Most individuals spent all they earned. The rich saved (sometimes not so much by self-denial as because it required too much effort to spend all they had) and thereby made important contributions to our capital supply. But industry was in the best position to provide its own capital. It is a long-established principle for good corporate management to distribute the annual profits on the basis of "a dollar for dividends and a dollar for betterments." Additional funds for long-term investments were obtained from various new institutions that grew in importance during the nineteenth century. Life insurance company assets grew from $4 million in 1850 to nearly $5000 million in 1914; deposits in savings banks rose from an estimated $150 million in 1860 to $8500 million in 1913, and assets of building and loan associations increased from $625 million in 1895 to $1358 million in 1914. All of these encouraged thrift, stimulated capital accumulation, and invested large portions of their funds in the business growth of the country.

The corporation. The corporate device was well suited to mobilize the savings which industry attracted and accumulated. Businessmen favored it because it enabled them to control the savings of others and yet in case of bankruptcy it protected their own personal property. The limited liability feature of the corporation was the key to its popularity. Because of it the investor knew that the maximum he could lose was the amount he had paid for his stock. As the century progressed the corporation grew in importance and handled an increasingly large percentage of the nation's business. A Twentieth Century Fund study shows that by 1904 manufacturing corporations, while only a third as numerous as individually owned businesses or partnerships, turned out 73.7 per cent of the products. Ten years later the figure had risen to 83.2 per cent. Without the convenience and security afforded by the corporation it is certain that industry would not have grown as big or as fast.[4] For large-scale operations the partnership was as outmoded as the spinning wheel or the wooden sailing vessel.

Another development favorable to the corporation was the protection against sudden or local prejudices which the courts provided by their interpretation of the federal Constitution. The first clause of the Fourteenth Amendment provided, "nor shall any State deprive any person of life, liberty or property without due process of law." Intended originally, in 1867, to protect Negro enjoyment of civil rights, it was within a few years employed to protect corporations against discriminatory legislation. Ex-Senator Roscoe Conkling of New York claimed before the Supreme Court in 1882 that the framers of the amendment intended such protection from the outset, but this conspiracy theory is now largely discredited. In both this and the similar clause of the Fifth Amendment, which

---

[4] Like any good idea the corporate device was subject to abuse. By the eighties corporation charters of almost any description could be had for a price in Delaware, Maine, and New Jersey. The custom of "interstate comity," by which any state treated the institutions of other states as it treated its own, encouraged many companies to seek their charters at the hands of the most liberal state, and virtually assured a situation where the state with the most lax incorporating practices would set the standard for the nation. See pages 492 and 502.

restricts federal legislation, the word "person" was interpreted to include a corporation, which is an artificial person; the word "property" was translated to include income, and the phrase "without due process of law" to mean "unreasonably" in layman's language. Thus the two amendments forbade either the state or federal governments to deprive any corporation of its income in a manner that was "unreasonable" in the opinion of a majority of the judges. Such protection of capital undoubtedly encouraged its accumulation.

The geography of manufacturing. At the beginning of this period the manufactures of the United States were confined chiefly to that part of the country north of the Potomac and Ohio rivers and east of the Mississippi, and were especially dense in southern New England, southern New York, New Jersey, and eastern Pennsylvania. This predominance of the northeastern section of the country may be accounted for on historic and economic grounds which have already been described; but at the same time there were asserting themselves other industrial tendencies which are less obvious but no less interesting. These were the localization of industries in particular states and cities, the specialization of certain localities, and the shifting of industrial centers.

The tendency toward localization has been apparent ever since the beginning of colonial manufactures, and not merely in this country but in other places as well. While sometimes it seems as though the choice of a location for a young industry were purely a matter of chance, it will generally be found to have been determined by economic causes. The principal factors affecting the establishment of industries are nearness to raw materials, markets, power, and a good supply of labor; climate was formerly important, as were local supplies of capital. In exceptional cases the initiative of the founder of an industry or the momentum of an early start seemed to be the only explanation. Once begun the localization of industries tended to become constantly greater and was overcome only by potent counterforces.

The very forces which made for localization tended also to cause the migration of industries when these advantages showed themselves more strongly in other localities. Thus the manufacture of agricultural implements advanced from

New York to Ohio and Illinois, following the retreating hardwood forests and the agricultural markets. The flour-milling interests shifted from Rochester, New York, to Chicago, and finally to Minneapolis. Slaughtering and meat packing, which had its beginning in Cincinnati about 1818, moved gradually westward to Chicago and Omaha, following the opening up of new grazing and fattening regions for cattle and swine. Sometimes a change of process or of the materials used in producing a commodity affects its location. As long as rags were the chief material in the manufacture of paper, the principal paper mills were located near cotton factories as Holyoke, Massachusetts, or near large cities, as Philadelphia; but when wood pulp became the chief raw material, the industry shifted to Maine, northern New York, and Wisconsin. In the cotton industry a striking change took place; by 1910 over half the raw cotton was being manufactured in the South. The reason for the shift was to take advantage of the cheaper labor supplies there rather than to be nearer the source of raw material which is light and valuable enough to stand long shipment.

Industries have been more nomadic in the United States than in Europe because of the opening up of new sources of raw materials and the settlement of unoccupied territory. The movement of manufactures has been steadily westward, the center of manufacturing having moved from the neighborhood of Harrisburg, Pennsylvania, in 1850 to a point west of Columbus, Ohio, in 1910. In a broad way the tendency was for a growing proportion of agricultural machinery and farm implements, of building and construction materials, of wood manufactures, especially furniture, of foods and drinks, of railway supplies, and of the iron and steel industry, including automobiles, to concentrate in the Middle West. The finer manufactures, especially those calling for highly specialized skills, remained largely fixed in the East. The smaller proportion of the nation's output contributed by this section is due less to its decline than to the expansion of the shares of the West and the South.

Industrial development of the South. A most significant change was the industrial awakening of the South. Although cotton growing was for a generation after the Civil War the

chief interest of that section, manufacturing began to develop
about 1880. The value of all its manufactured goods increased from $338,792,000 in 1879 to $2,637,117,000 in
1909, or about eightfold; but an even greater development
took place in cotton manufactures. In 1859 the southern cotton mills produced an output representing 10 per cent of the
total product of cotton goods for the whole country; by 1909
this had grown to 40 per cent. More than half the cotton
spindles in the country were located in the South. Important
new industries were built up on the utilization of cotton seed
and other by-products. The iron industry also made great
strides: in North Carolina, Tennessee, and especially in Alabama, abundant supplies of coal, iron, and limestone lay so
near one another that pig iron could be made more cheaply
there than anywhere else in America, and probably in the
world. The production of southern pig iron increased from
397,000 tons in 1879 to 2,500,000 tons in 1909, or about 10
per cent of the country's production; and great iron foundries, steel plants, rolling and rail mills sprang up at Birming-
ham and elsewhere with marvelous rapidity.

In 1901 vast deposits of petroleum were discovered in
Texas, furnishing a cheap fuel and illuminant. The unrivaled
water power resources of the southern Appalachians were
utilized for the development of hydroelectric power. The
splendid forests of hard pine and other timber throughout the
South were reached, cut, and sold during this period, and
the mineral wealth was located and developed. Manufactures
in the southern states had to depend largely on the labor of the
native white population; the Negroes did not show the persistence necessary for factory labor, and the foreigners who
migrated to that section preferred to work on farms or to run
stores rather than to work in factories. Child labor was largely
employed, and the industrial transition brought up economic
problems which were burning questions in New England in
the middle of the nineteenth century and in old England at
the beginning of the century.

The iron and steel industry. The progress of manufacturing may best be traced by noting the development of the
most typical industries, and for this purpose the iron and
steel and textile industries may be selected, not only because

they rank high in importance but especially because they exemplify pre-eminently the use of laborsaving machinery and of mass production, both of which are characteristic of American manufactures.

The manufacture of iron and steel is the nation's key industry, by which the progress of other branches is determined. The great expansion of manufactures since 1860 and of production on a large scale is due to the use of power and the improvement of machinery, both of which are based on the use of metals. The iron and steel industry provides other industries with machines, tools, and equipment of various sorts. Thus in 1910 the census enumerated 346 products of the iron and steel industry, of which 98 were for direct consumption and 248 were machines or articles for use in other industries. Among the sixteen great groups of American manufactures, iron and steel and their products ranked third in 1914, with 6326 establishments and products valued at $2,137,113,000. The development of the manufacture of crude iron and steel alone is shown in the following table:

COMPARATIVE SUMMARY OF THE CRUDE IRON AND STEEL INDUSTRY, 1859-1909*

Year	Number of establishments	Number of wage earners	Capital (in thousands)	Cost of materials (in thousands)	Value of products (in thousands)	Tons of products
1859†	402	22,014	$23,343	$19,242	$36,537	509,084
1869	808	77,555	121,772	135,526	207,208	3,263,585
1879	792	140,798	209,904	191,271	296,557	6,486,733
1889	719	171,181	414,044	327,272	478,687	16,264,478
1899	669	222,607	590,530	522,431	804,034	29,507,860
1909	654	278,505	1,492,316	978,139	1,377,152	75,019,765

* U. S. Census Reports, Manufacturing.
† Iron forged, rolled, and wrought.

There are two stages in the conversion of the iron ore into commercial steel products: (1) the reduction of the iron ore to pig iron, which is done in a blast furnace; and (2) the conversion of the iron into steel, which was usually done by either the Bessemer or the open-hearth process.[5] The further working up of the steel into highly finished products, like machines

[5] A description of these processes is given in E. L. Bogart and C. E. Landon, *Modern Industry* (New York, rev. ed. 1936), Chap. 31.

or cutlery, belongs to other branches of iron and steel manufacture and will not be discussed here.

(1) In 1859 the blast furnaces of the United States produced 821,000 tons of pig iron, which grew to 27,304,000
tons in 1909. This great development was caused by a remarkable expansion in demand and by improvements in blast-
furnace construction and practice and was accompanied by a
westward movement of the industry. When the Civil War
broke out, more than half the iron made in the country was
produced with anthracite coal, the center of this industry being eastern Pennsylvania; charcoal iron, produced in the eastern states and in Kentucky, Michigan, and Wisconsin, was
twice as important as that smelted by bituminous coal and
coke. Most bituminous coal could not be used for smelting
purposes but had to be reduced to coke. Coke is partially
burned coal just as charcoal is partially burned wood. Not all
bituminous coal makes good coke: the best in this period came
from Connellsville, about 40 miles from Pittsburgh. Extensive development of this deposit began about 1860: by 1875
coke surpassed anthracite as the leading fuel for smelting
iron. During this period most of the coke was made in beehive ovens, a wasteful process since the gases containing valuable by-products were lost [6]; but in the nineties, by-product
coke ovens began to be built, and by the end of the period
they turned out 27 per cent of the coke in the United States.
In 1875 the introduction of the Whitewell hot-blast stove
reduced the fuel consumption and enabled a much hotter
temperature to be attained. At the same time improvements
in the construction of blast furnaces and the use of the regenerative gas furnace permitted much greater production, so
that the average weekly furnace output was eight times as
great in 1900 as it had been in 1877.

By 1890 the United States passed Great Britain as a producer of pig iron, and in 1914 produced about one-third of
the world's supply or as much as Great Britain and Germany
combined. In the meantime there was a steady movement of

---

[6] In beehive ovens a ton of coal yielded about a quarter of a ton of coke at a cost
of $1.15 and a serious smoke nuisance for the neighborhood. In by-product ovens,
by contrast, nearly three-quarters of a ton of coke was recovered, not to mention
hundreds of by-products like tar, ammonia, and gas, whose value often exceeded that
of the coke. The trouble was that the by-product ovens were costly to build.

production westward, as the Lake Superior ores began to be exploited. The ranges in upper Michigan and Wisconsin were opened in the seventies, and a decade later the soft and very rich ores of Minnesota began to be dug out by steam shovels.

(2) As it comes from the blast furnace, pig iron does not possess the strength or ductility which is needed for commercial use, because of the presence in it of carbon, phosphorus, and other elements. It is therefore made into steel by processes which get rid of all impurities and give the metal the desired qualities. Before the Civil War steel was so expensive that it was used only for fine cutlery and similar purposes for which cost was not important. Then in 1855 the Bessemer process of making steel was discovered and in 1864 the first Bessemer steel was made in the United States. In 1860 scarcely any of the pig iron produced in the United States was converted into steel; by 1900 four-fifths was so converted. Steel rails completely supplanted iron ones, and a thousand new uses of steel for the construction of office buildings, bridges, cars, wire and wire nails, structural metalwork, hardware, and other products greatly increased the demand.

About 1890 the basic open-hearth process of converting pig iron into steel began to be generally used. This consisted of recooking the molten iron in a large receptacle with a base lining of limestone. The new process had several advantages. It permitted the use of iron having more impurities than the Bessemer process could eliminate. It could handle larger amounts of metal at one time. And it permitted more accurate control of the iron brew so that faults were less likely to occur in the steel. There had been frequent complaints of Bessemer rails on the last score. All these factors led to the gradual displacement of Bessemer steel by open-hearth steel until in 1908 more steel was made by this method than any other.

Although machinery for the manufacture of iron and steel was expensive and the processes were complicated, the achievements of the industry were cited by Andrew Carnegie as one of the wonders of the world. "Two pounds of ironstone mined upon Lake Superior and transported nine hundred miles to Pittsburgh; one pound and one-half of coal, mined and manufactured into coke and transported to Pittsburgh; one-half pound of lime, mined and transported to Pittsburgh; a small amount of manganese ore mined in Virginia and brought to Pittsburgh—and these four pounds of material manufactured into one pound of steel, for which the consumer pays one cent." Compared with this complicated and scientific operation, the deeds of the pyramid builders take their place as a lower order of achievement.

The steel industry showed a striking concentration into huge establishments of great producing capacity. Thus the average daily capacity of a Bessemer converter grew from 5 tons in 1880 to 15 in 1900 and that of an open-hearth furnace for the same dates from 10 to 50 tons. Not only did the size of the single establishment grow, but the number of hitherto separate industries combined under one organization was greatly enlarged: iron and coal mines, railways and steamers, coke ovens and blast furnaces, steel plants and machine shops, were all brought together under a single head, as in the case of the United States Steel Corporation. This was known as vertical combination or integration of industry and was becoming characteristic of the very biggest industries of this era.

The textile industries. The combined textile industry ranked second in 1914 among the sixteen great groups of manufactures in the United States, with a total product of $3,444,810,000. The growth of the textile fabric industry alone, which includes the manufacture of cotton, woolen and worsted, hosiery, and knit goods, and silk, together with dyeing and finishing, is shown in the table below.

TEXTILE FABRIC INDUSTRY, 1859-1909*				
Year	Number of establishments	Number of wage earners	Capital	Value of products
1859	3027	194,082	$150,080,852	$214,740,614
1869	4790	274,943	297,694,243	520,386,764
1879	4018	384,251	412,721,496	532,673,488
1889	4276	517,237	767,705,310	759,262,283
1899	4312	661,451	1,042,997,577	931,494,566
1899	4099	631,979	982,559,000	886,882,000
1909	4825	834,087	1,717,795,000	1,591,736,000

* *U. S. Census Reports, Manufacturing.* See note to table on page 467.

Of the different branches of the textile industry, the manufacture of cotton goods ranked first in importance ($677,-000,000 in 1914). Almost destroyed during the Civil War by the cutting off of the supplies of raw cotton, whereby two-thirds of the spindles in the country were rendered idle, it quickly recovered after that event. Great improvements were made in all departments of the cotton industry; steam ginneries were substituted for the older ones run by horse or mule power, and cottonseed began to be used for oil and fertilizer. The main improvements, however, took place in the processes of manufacture itself. New England not only maintained, but improved her position as the center of the cotton-spinning industry, and Fall River displaced Lowell as the "spindle city" because of the substitution of steam for water power. "The twenty years ending with 1893," records Clark,[7] "cover the period of greatest expansion that the cotton industry has ever experienced."

The rapid expansion favored the adoption of new machinery and methods, which went on so rapidly that progressive factories were completely revolutionized at least once a generation. Among the improvements were the revolving flat card, which reduced waste, saved time, and enabled a poorer staple to be profitably carded, and combing machines. In the nineties the Northrop loom was perfected, which had devices to fill exhausted shuttles, and to stop the loom if a thread broke. As a result, the number of looms that a weaver could attend increased from eight to eighty-four and the quality of the cloth was better. In the next decade the automatic loom was adapted to colored goods and the output was still further increased. These improvements were adopted faster in the South where new mills were being built and where automatic machines were more highly prized than in the North. Inexperienced southern workers could easily be taught to attend them, whereas they could only with difficulty be taught to run machines that required greater skill. The New England factories concentrated on finer fabrics and left the production of the coarser weaves to the South.

The most significant event of this period was the industrial revolution effected in the South as the result of the develop-

[7] *Op. cit.*, II, 384.

ment in that section of cotton manufacturing, a strong impetus to which seems to have been given by the Atlanta Cotton Exposition in 1881. Technically and economically this development reproduced many of the features which characterized the growth of the same industry in New England fifty years earlier. Most of the southern mills were located in the Carolinas and Georgia.

This same period witnessed a slower growth in the woolen industry, though this branch ranks second in the textile manufactures. Of this group the manufacture of carpets was carried farthest by American inventors, who made the United States the greatest carpet-producing nation in the world. One of the striking features of the recent development of the textile industries was the rapid growth of the manufacture of hosiery and knit goods, which was revolutionized by the application of automatic power machinery. The most phenomenal advance, however, was seen in silk manufactures, although it drew its raw materials entirely from abroad.

Conclusion. The period following the Civil War produced businesses larger than had ever been known before. Such big business was made possible by remarkable transportation improvements which widened markets, by such technical improvements as the manufacture of cheap steel for machinery, improved oil for lubricants, and numerous advances in power production, by the richness of this country's natural resources, by a growing labor supply, by effective mobilization of capital at home and abroad, by the inventive genius of the people which our patent system encouraged, by tariff protection from foreign competition at this critical time and yet freedom of access to the wide domestic market, and by the enterprise of our industrial leaders.

CHAPTER XXI

THE TRUST MOVEMENT

Laissez-faire. One of the purposes of studying history is to gain a perspective on the progress of human events. During the last thousand years, man has been trying to decide whether he prefers to live in a free or a regulated type of economy. Each type has its advantages, each is subject to abuse, and each has been tried several times. Every age has its own name for the two economies. In the Middle Ages the Church and the nobles gave us an economic and political order known as the feudal system. This collapsed about the time of the Renaissance and the Reformation. But the new nations which developed soon recognized the importance of economic strength and self-sufficiency. Such realization produced mercantilism, or the government-regulated economy which the English imposed on our forefathers. Excessive regulation and corruption brought on the collapse of mercantilism and it was gradually supplanted by *laissez-faire* ("let things alone"). This is the economic philosophy that the best government is the one that governs least. The economist, Adam Smith, preached this doctrine in 1776, explaining that when individuals were free to apply their capital and labor without government interference they would act in a way which would do both them and society the most good. *Laissez-faire* reached its peak in the United States in the generation following the Civil War. As we shall see, the freedom allowed under *laissez-faire* was abused and the pendulum swung in the other direction. Our generation has grown up under an economy that is more and more closely regulated by the government. It is interesting today to speculate what the forces will be that may some day drive us toward a freer economy again.

Laissez-faire is the object of our interest at this point. The last third of the nineteenth century was a period of unbridled individualism in which the fullest scope was given to initiative and enterprise, while the size of the market permitted the development of industries to maximum size. The American manufacturer, railway magnate, and business-man were animated not merely by a desire to make money, but also to gain power, and to do big things. Such men used competition to crush their rivals as well as to win markets, to hold down wages as well as to reduce prices. Their methods were often ruthless, frequently tainted by fraud, and only slightly restrained by fear of illegality or social disapproval.

Legislation was favorable to big business. Railroad land grants, protective tariffs, non-interference on the part of government, the liberal judicial interpretation of the common law concerning restraint of trade, and the protection to property rights behind the bulwarks of the Fifth and Four-teenth Amendments to the Constitution—all these gave advantages upon which industrial leaders were quick to seize. Political conditions were particularly bad for almost two decades after the Civil War, and business dominated politics and in some cases even the judiciary, in the furtherance of its plans. The public, absorbed in its private affairs and sharing in the generally prevailing prosperity, was apathetic and uninformed and uttered no effective protest. The stage was set for the appearance of "trusts."

Trusts. The word "trust" has two meanings. The narrow meaning will be explained later but since it has limited usage it will not be employed in this book. The broad meaning of trust is an industrial monopoly operating over a wide market if not the whole nation.[1] Thus a huge banking house was not a trust, a public utility empire was not a trust, a strong trade union was not a trust (although sometimes prosecuted under the anti-trust laws), and a local building supplies monopoly was not a trust.

More is needed than a favorable stage to explain the trust movement. The stage had been set in previous ages without producing trusts. In fact, much of it had been wait-ing all during the nineteenth century. Why did trusts appear in such numbers at this particular time is the ques-tion. There are two major explanations and several minor

[1] This is the conception of a trust used by Eliot Jones, *The Trust Problem* (New York, 1924).

ones. It is of course assumed that the business leaders of any age would strive for the profits and the power that go with monopoly: that was not a motive or a cause peculiar to this generation.

In the first place trusts or nationwide monopolies were impossible before there was a nationwide transportation network capable of delivering cheaply in one region goods made in another. Plenty of local monopolies, from gristmills and salt mines to brass pools, had existed in earlier periods. But intersectional and nationwide monopolies had to wait for the building of trunk-line railroads. It is significant that the appearance of trusts coincides roughly with the coming of the transcontinental railroads, although it is incorrect to imply that the west-coast trade had to be secured before a business could be considered a trust.

Another reason for the appearance of trusts in this period was the sharp increase in fixed costs in industry. Economists divide costs into two categories, variable and fixed costs. They are also known sometimes as operating and overhead costs. In the iron and steel industry, to take an illustration, the variable costs were labor, raw materials, and fuel. These costs would vary with plant output, that is, if the company was busy it would use more ore and fuel and hire more men; and if times were dull, less ore and fuel would be used and men would be laid off. The fixed costs were property taxes, wages of management, obsolescence; but primarily interest on funds invested in plant equipment. Fixed costs would be the same whether the plant operated at full or fractional capacity. Before the industrial revolution, and even in its early stages, the bulk of the costs were variable. As markets widened and as increasing specialization made possible the use of more machinery, and as the machines became more complex and expensive, fixed costs became a greater portion of total costs. This stimulated cutthroat competition. It is easy to see why.

Unit costs were much less when the plant operated at full capacity, for the fixed costs were spread over a larger output. Thus, as cheap transportation made it possible for companies to sell farther afield and to invade one another's markets, the competition that followed took a price-cutting form. Since no one company could long afford to operate at fractional capacity while its competitor operated at full capacity, and since large investments were at stake, the competition was often very bitter. The result of such competition was generally combination and often monopoly. One or the other of two things was likely to happen. Either one company would defeat and take over its rivals, or most of the competing concerns would tire of their costly battle and join forces.[2] The burden of the testimony by businessmen before the Industrial Commission in 1899 was that a strong impelling force to industrial combination was "competition so vigorous that profits of nearly all competing establishments were destroyed."[3] The combining companies anticipated not only greater profits from more stable costs, but also fewer marketing problems which multiplied greatly with fluctuating prices. Stable prices can do much to reduce business risks.

When big business concerns decided to combine to exploit the public rather than fight one another, the public was not in a good position to defend itself. The public was often uninformed and disorganized. It was difficult to find substitutes for some monopolized products like kerosene, steel, sugar, and tobacco. Although new competitors were sometimes attracted to the scene by the profits being made, this relief was not dependable because of the vast amount of capital needed to set up in business, not to mention the hostility of the already entrenched monopoly. Imports of foreign products might have alleviated the public's distress but that avenue was closed by our high tariffs. H. O. Havemeyer, president of the sugar trust, admitted, "the mother of all trusts is the customs tariff." A national monopoly is obviously easier to obtain than a world monopoly in any product. Big business, through generous campaign contributions, sometimes to both parties' candidates, saw to it that tariffs were kept high. The years after the Dingley tariff (1897), the highest in our history, saw more trusts formed than ever before.

---

[2] Industries with large fixed costs, like the steel industry, for example, tended toward monopoly for the same reason that railroads and public utilities are often regarded as "natural monopolies."

[3] Preliminary Report of the Industrial Commission (Washington, 1900), 9.

The evolution of the corporation during the nineteenth century, moreover, made possible not only big business but also trusts. While less than one-third (28.3 per cent) of the industrial establishments in the United States in 1914 were corporate in form, these turned out five-sixths (83.2 per cent) of the goods manufactured. Far more flexible than the partnership, the corporate device enabled a few business leaders to assume control of an industry. They were in a position to make quick decisions, take over potential competitors, and lop off losing ventures with a minimum of effort. When corporate charters were first sought early in the century, legislatures were fearful that corporations would become monopolies. But, as we have seen, the corporation was a highly useful aid to the growth of business, especially industry. Not until the end of the century were the fears of monopoly justified to any degree. Even then the misuse of the corporation might have been avoided in part if companies engaged in interstate commerce had been required to seek federal instead of state charters. Instead each state granted charters and through the practice of "interstate comity" gave recognition to out-of-state corporations. A state with lax corporation laws could do great harm to its neighbors. In 1889, at a time when public outcry against the trusts was causing several state legislatures to pass anti-trust laws, New Jersey revised her corporation law to permit corporations to acquire the property or stock of other corporations, thus assisting monopolies to evade restrictive legislation aimed at them. According to Lincoln Steffens, when the New York legislature threatened to investigate the sugar trust, a law was rushed through the New Jersey legislature in eighteen hours' time forbidding any New Jersey court to maintain an action against the stockholders or directors of a New Jersey corporation if the action was started because of the laws of another state. Moreover, this shameful act was advertised to induce corporations to incorporate in New Jersey.[4]

Other factors which stimulated the formation of trusts at this time were the perfection of the telephone and the prospect of underwriters' profits for promotional services. The telephone was known as the "little mother" of trusts

[4] L. Steffens, "New Jersey: A Traitor State," *McClure's Magazine* (May, 1905).

because it made possible quick and unrecorded "deals." The promoters or underwriters of trusts worth millions of dollars were generously rewarded for their efforts. The promoters of the American Can Company, the tin can trust, made a profit of $17,000,000, while those who arranged the formation of the United States Steel Company made a profit of $62,000,000. These promoters were generally paid in stock, often watered common stock, but the trusts' prospective monopoly profits made the market value of such stock high.

Methods of combination. Under the pressure of these economic forces the movement toward industrial reorganization began. Various devices had been resorted to for the purpose of restricting competition, even before the Civil War, but beginning about 1865 more conscious and stronger efforts were put forth. The first were simple *agreements* among competing producers to fix prices or to limit output, like those of the anthracite coal mines and the salt producers. This was the typical form of combination from 1865 to 1875, but the agreements were extremely loose and constantly broken by the members under the temptation of higher profits. A more formal and complex combination was the *pool*, which was the leading form of organization between 1875 and 1895. It was the favorite form of agreement among the railroads until it was forbidden by the Interstate Commerce Act of 1887, but it was used also by industrial groups such as the steel-rail pool, the powder pool, the tobacco pool, and others. An industrial pool was a combination of independent businesses which sought to control prices by limiting the output, dividing the market, or pooling the profits. It, too, did not stand up under the temptation of higher profits, and its agreements could not be enforced in a law court because it was a conspiracy in restraint of trade under the common law.

Before this form had run its course, a stronger form of organization, involving more complete control over the member organizations, was devised by one of John D. Rockefeller's lawyers. This was the *trustee device* or trust in the original, narrow, now rarely used sense of the term. The first and the model of all later ones was secretly organized in 1879 as the Standard Oil Company, consisting of an earlier company of this name and some of its strongest competitors. According to this scheme a board of nine trustees was selected to whom the stockholders surrendered their stock, receiving in return trust certificates; the trustees then operated all the plants in harmony and divided the profits among the holders of the trust certificates. The success of this new-style combination led to the formation of similar arrangements in the manufacture of whisky, sugar, lead, cottonseed oil, starch, etc. Hostile legislation and adverse decisions of the courts forced the trusts to change their form in the early nineties. The trusts were dissolved, but in legal form only, for the combinations continued.

Between 1890 and 1904 the prevailing form of combination was the holding company, of which there were two types. During the first ten years the *property-holding company* was the more common type. This sometimes took the form of a merger, on other occasions it was effected by the sale of property by one company to another, or finally it might take place through the exchange of property for stock in the expanding concern. The American Tobacco Company of 1890 and the American Sugar Refining Company of 1891 were property-owning holding companies. After 1900 the prevailing type was the *security-holding company*; this is a corporation organized to hold a controlling interest in the capital and therefore the management of hitherto competing business units, but which does not itself conduct any business. The closing years of the nineteenth century witnessed a wholesale reorganization of manufacturing, transportation, and mercantile enterprises under this new form. The security-holding company was made possible by the deliberate amendment by New Jersey of its corporation law in 1889, followed by similar modifications by Delaware and Maine, to permit this form of combination. All that was necessary in order to transform a trust into such a holding company was to obtain a charter of incorporation from one of these charter-granting states and to exchange the trust certificates for stock in the new company.

After 1904 the vigorous enforcement of federal and state

anti-trust laws in turn rendered the holding company form of organization precarious and led to another style of combination, looser than the trusts and holding companies which it succeeded. This was control through *interlocking directorates*. The device is almost self-explanatory: the same men serve on the boards of directors of several companies with the result that each company knows what the other is doing and all follow a fairly uniform policy and may even charge the same prices. The same ends were achieved also by the establishment of statistical associations and *open price associations*, for the ostensible purpose of exchanging information as to production, sales, prices, and other matters.

This brief survey shows a determined and persistent effort on the part of American enterprises to exercise increasing control over the processes of production and marketing. The growth of large-scale production and the concentration of manufactures in single large establishments was primarily a phenomenon of the nineteenth century, while central-office management is a product of the twentieth. The methods by which it was achieved differed from time to time in response to new needs, the genius of individual organizers, and the pressure of public opinion. Though the legal form changed in chameleonlike fashion, the essential purpose in the combination movement persisted with little variation.

From an economic point of view, as distinguished from the mere legal forms which have been described, two types of combination may be differentiated. The "horizontal" or trade combination, which unites competing organizations in the same trade, and the "vertical" or industry combination which unites successive stages of an industry from the beginning to the end. Most of the pools, trusts, and other combinations already described were of the former type. The latter effected an integration of many industries which represented different steps in the transformation of raw materials into finished goods. Striking examples were found in the United States Steel Corporation, which brought under one ownership and management ore mines, ships, railroads, blast furnaces, rolling mills, and other plants; and in the tobacco industry, where the growing and curing of tobacco, the manufacture of snuff, chewing tobacco, cigars, and cigarettes, to say nothing of machinery, tinfoil and cans, and finally the retailing of the finished product were combined.

The peak of the trust movement. The combination movement began on a large scale in 1898 and ran at fever heat during the next five years. Up to 1897 most of the combinations had been railroads, but thereafter industrial combinations became increasingly numerous. Promoters and speculators took advantage of the eagerness of the investing public to purchase industrial securities and floated many questionable enterprises. Over $6000 million worth of securities was marketed by the new industrial trusts before the movement spent itself. By 1903, however, it came to an end; the collapse of the shipbuilding trust revealed some of the evils of fraudulent trust financiering, and the decline of the stocks of most of the new companies disillusioned the investor and brought about a general reaction in public sentiment.

Many exaggerated estimates have been made of the extent of this movement, but the most trustworthy count at the time it was made was probably that of the census of 1900, from which pools and simple expansion of existing businesses were excluded. One hundred and eighty-five industrial combinations were reported, comprising less than one-half of 1 per cent of the establishments in the country, but owning 15 per cent of the capital, employing 8 per cent of the employees, and turning out 14 per cent of the manufactured products in the United States. The greatest combinations had taken place in the iron and steel industry, which alone produced nearly one-third of the gross value of the products of all industrial combinations.

After the publication of this conservative report, other combinations were effected which greatly changed these figures. In 1904 it was estimated that 318 industrial trusts with a capital of $7,246,000,000 and representing consolidations of nearly 5300 distinct plants existed in the United States; of this capital over one-third was controlled by seven great organizations. While these figures are far from trustworthy, they at least serve to indicate roughly the extent to which combinations of various sorts entered into our national industrial life. Seager estimated that "making full allowance for industrial combinations in the mining field, it appears that by 1904 the trust controlled fully two-fifths of the manufacturing capital of the country." [5] They controlled more or less successfully the production of tobacco, petroleum, sugar, linseed oil, iron and steel, copper, shipbuilding, beef, starch, flour, cottonseed oil, candy, chewing gum, candles, salt, ice, glucose, crackers, matches, whisky, anthracite coal, fertilizers, tin cans, farming tools, locomotives, writing paper, school furniture, sewer pipe, glassware, rubber goods, buttons, leather, electrical supplies, and other products.

Trust characteristics. Not every type of industry lent itself to monopoly control. There was never a cotton-goods trust or a bread trust, since it would have required little capital to set up competing plants. A wire nail pool was short-lived for this very reason and the attempt to monopolize cigar making was unsuccessful. Neither was there a gravel trust because of the cost of transportation as well as the commonness of the product. Trusts were usually most successful in articles that could be standardized, that required much specialized equipment for cheap large-scale production, and that could stand shipment considerable distances.

Every successful trust held a near monopoly control of some one stage of production. The Standard Oil Company controlled refineries and later pipelines, leaving much of the risk of well operation to others; the sugar trust possessed a majority of the refineries in the industry; and the shoe machinery trust had patents on the machines which it leased instead of sold, at the same time requiring its customers to use only its machines. Yet despite the tight grip of some of these trusts, competition continually crept in, especially when a trust was making sizable profits. The history of many of them show a steadily declining percentage of control, interrupted occasionally when the trust bought up a competitor. The sugar trust controlled 67 per cent of production in 1900, dropped to 55 per cent in 1903, but then raised it to 58 per cent in 1904 by acquiring several

[5] H. R. Seager and L. Gulick, *Trust and Corporation Problems* (New York, 1929), 61.

beet-sugar refineries, after which control fell steadily to 42 per cent in 1910.

The steel trust. Perhaps the best way to understand trusts is to look into the history of one of them.[6] As late as the early 1890's the steel business was highly competitive. Few companies were "integrated," i.e., few had their own iron mines, ore-carrying fleets, railroads, coal mines, etc. The strongest and most efficiently run steel company of the time was Carnegie Steel headed by that genial but canny Scotsman, Andrew Carnegie. Carnegie Steel made semi-finished steel such as rails, plates, bars, and the like. These were sold chiefly to other steel companies which in turn manufactured tin plate, wire, tubes or pipes, sheet steel, and other more finished steel products. During the 1890's numerous combinations and trusts were formed among these specialized companies. There appeared in rapid succession a tin-plate trust, a wire trust, a tube trust, and a sheet-steel trust.

Toward the turn of the century Carnegie began to talk of retiring. He gave a group of Chicago promoters a ninety-day million-dollar option to buy him out for $158 million, one-third to be paid in cash. When the promoters were unable to raise the money on time Carnegie coolly pocketed the million. Next he discussed selling out to the Rockefeller interests for $250 million, but this did not materialize either. Meanwhile some of Carnegie's rivals and customers were investing considerable sums in expanding their operations. All seemed to be acting on Rockefeller's maxim of "pay profit to nobody." Some of the specialized steel trusts were preparing to build their own mills to supply them with semi-finished steel. Carnegie watched and waited until all were deeply involved and then set on foot operations of his own calculated to create panic in their minds. He started to build his own tube, wire, and other specialized mills. If carried through, all these operations would have enlarged the steel-producing capacity of the nation far beyond its needs. Bitter competition would have ensued and the financial losses would have been tremendous. Carnegie had vast

---

[6] Much of this material is drawn from John Moody, *Masters of Capital* (New Haven, 1921), Chap. 5, and from Eliot Jones, *The Trust Problem* (New York, 1924), Chap. 9.

amounts of capital and could carry out his threats to build and could probably outlast the others in a price war. It was not safe to believe he was bluffing. He had to be bought off.

Andrew Carnegie finally agreed to sell out for $447 million, which was approximately three times his offer to the Chicago promoters some months earlier. But the damage that Carnegie could do to his steel rivals on a grand scale, other steel companies could do on a somewhat smaller scale to those who had bought out the Carnegie interests. It was necessary to bring most of the big steel companies and specialized steel trusts into one gigantic trust. Each of the steel tycoons had to be induced to join more or less at his own price. J. P. Morgan and Company made all the arrangements and received a profit of $62 million for their services.

This trust which Morgan founded in 1901 was the United States Steel Company. A security holding company, it was capitalized at $1,403 millions, roughly one-third in bonds, one-third in preferred stock, and one-third in common stock. Because of the inflated prices which had been paid Carnegie and the others for their plants, all the common stock and about half the preferred stock was "water." In other words, securities supposedly worth $1,403 million had only about $682 million of assets behind them. Only the prospect of generous earnings from those assets could maintain the market value of all that watered stock. However, since the United States Steel Company controlled over 66 per cent of the steel production of the nation, it was in an excellent position to set prices and wage ruthless war on any independent company that threatened to undercut. It could thus make enough profit to pay dividends on all its securities. The chairman of the board of directors of United States Steel was Judge Elbert H. Gary. For several years, at regular annual dinners, he set forth his company's basic policies in suave after-dinner addresses. The little millionaires who headed the independent steel companies came and listened attentively to what the head of the billion-dollar corporation had to say. Although Gary was careful to tell them that they were under no obligation to conform, still, most of them saw fit to do so. It was not only the most discreet course of action but also the most profitable one. By 1910 the independents had grown more than United States Steel had. The big company's control had slipped from 66 per cent to 55 per cent. However, United States Steel had earned 12 per cent a year on the average of its capitalization. That included much watered stock and some as yet undeveloped iron mines. Reasonable dividends were paid to the stockholders, but most of these huge profits were plowed right back into the business so that by 1910 the company's assets had increased from $682 million to almost $1,200 million. All the water had been squeezed out of the preferred stock and about half of it from the common stock.

Such great profits were achieved by setting high and unvarying prices for steel products. Steel rails afford an example of this. Between 1867 and 1900 the price of steel rails fluctuated continually owing to competition for the business during most of those years. Between 1896 and 1898 the price varied from $28 a ton to $17 a ton, but even at the lower prices two of the major producers, Carnegie Steel and Illinois Steel, made a profit. After the United States Steel Company began operations in 1901 the price went to $28 a ton and remained there without change for ten years.

If there were any economies from combination and integration in the business of making steel rails the buyers of them, the railroads, did not share in the benefits. This was bound to have its effects on railroad rates and hence on transportation costs for shippers and therefore on the prices of all products shipped by rail. It added only a fraction of a cent to the costs of most products but it was an unjustified additional cost. Moreover, if many trusts resorted to similar practices, the cost of living would be bound to rise and the standard of living for the masses of people would decline. All this would occur so that a few might become millionaires.

Advantages and disadvantages of combinations. Many of the advantages claimed for industrial combinations and trusts are due as much to large-scale production as to combination, and may be enjoyed by producers not within the combination. The following are the chief economies of production effected by combination: (1) only the best-located and most efficiently equipped plants are operated, as in the former whisky trust; (2) obsolete machinery is scrapped and only the best is used, thus applying the latest inventions and utilizing patents; (3) the best ideas in the combining plants are exchanged, and the efficiency of all raised to the level of the best, as in the sugar and tobacco trusts; (4) by engaging in the manufacture of several different articles, the risks are better distributed, as in the case of the tobacco trust; (5) by-products are utilized; (6) the best managerial talent and organizing ability are obtained.

The peculiar economies obtained by combinations lay, however, rather in the savings in marketing than in production, and these may be summarized as follows: (7) better bargaining power exists in the purchase of raw materials; (8) there is better command over capital and credit facilities; (9) the cost of advertising, of traveling salesmen, and of other items which figure largely in a strongly competitive business, may be materially reduced under combination; (10) saving in cross freights is effected in the case of those trusts which have plants located in various parts of the country, and which can fill orders from the nearest plant.

Insofar as the industrial combination secured economies of production and marketing which would not otherwise have been effected, it was justified as an efficient mode of organization. Savings of this nature as a result of large-scale methods, were, however, not new, but characterized the manufacturing industries of the United States after the middle of the nineteenth century and contributed largely to the concentration of industry. The aim of industrial combinations was rather to obtain a monopoly position and to control prices. When they effected economies, they did not lower the prices of their products to the public in proportion—witness the oil and the tobacco trusts—and in some cases they even raised prices—witness the steel and the sugar trusts.

Another serious indictment against industrial combinations and trusts was that they used unfair methods. Among these may be mentioned the practice of crushing smaller competitors by local price cutting, by the establishment of bogus independent concerns, and by the sale of certain brands at a loss; refusal to sell to dealers unless these obligated themselves not to sell products of competitors; the receipt of rebates and discriminating favors from the railroads; and other unfair practices to strangle competition. Even more serious was the legislative corruption by means of which "big business" contrived to obtain valuable rights and privileges, immunity from attack, or special favors. These abuses tended to disappear under the increasing regulation of our lawmaking bodies and of the courts, and by reason of a higher standard of business ethics in industry itself.

Trust legislation. Under the common law monopoly was a crime punishable by fine and imprisonment, and agreements in restraint of trade, carried so far as to be unreasonable, were held to be illegal and unenforceable. There arose a popular demand, however, for more positive legislation against monopoly and combination. In 1887 Congress passed the Act to Regulate Commerce, prohibiting pools among railways, and in 1890 the Sherman Anti-trust Act, which provided that "every contract, combination in the form of a trust or otherwise, or conspiracy, in restraint of trade or commerce among the several states, or with foreign nations, is hereby declared illegal." These two acts marked the culmination of a decade of persistent agitation against combination, especially on the part of the railroads. The beginning of the twentieth century witnessed an even more remarkable public protest, this time against the trusts. An era of "muckraking," as it was characterized by President Theodore Roosevelt, revealed many flagrant abuses and resulted in further federal legislation.

At the same time there began the enactment of anti-trust legislation by the states; thirty-two states and two territories in all passed such laws, and in seventeen states anti-trust provisions were inserted in the state constitutions. These enactments were very severe, but before they could be fairly tested in the courts, they were deprived of all power to control the growing trusts by the lax policy of the three "charter-granting" states, New Jersey (until 1913), Delaware, and Maine, which not only failed to pass any anti-trust legislation, but greatly relaxed their existing statutes. Ninety-five per cent of the trusts were accordingly incorporated in these states,[7] and as a corporation can be deprived of its charter only for violation of the laws of the state in which it is incorporated, the other states were practically helpless.

Defects in the federal acts soon became apparent. Railroads avoided giving full testimony to the Interstate Commerce Commission until 1896; in 1897 the Supreme Court ruled that the commission lacked power to prescribe rates, and the teeth of the commission were drawn in other ways. Much of the force of the Sherman Anti-trust Act was destroyed when the Department of Justice lost its first important case through poor preparation of the brief. Prosecution of the sugar trust was set aside on the ground that purchase of the E. C. Knight Company refineries, which gave the trust 98 per cent control of the industry, was merely a contract for acquisition of a manufacturing plant within a state and "bore no relation to commerce between the States." The first successful prosecutions of trusts took place in 1898 and 1899 when the Trans-Missouri Freight Association, and the Addyston Pipe and Steel Company, both pools, were ordered to dissolve. The decision in 1904 against the Northern Securities Company, a securities-holding company controlling two parallel transcontinental railroads, demonstrated that security-holding companies were not immune to anti-trust prosecution. Defects in the federal laws were partially remedied by the Elkins Act of 1903, which facilitated prosecutions under the Interstate Commerce Act, and by the creation of the Federal Bureau of Corporations with power to make "diligent investigation into the organization, conduct, and management" of corporations engaged in interstate commerce (railroads excepted).

Under President Theodore Roosevelt, moreover, the federal government made a vigorous effort to apply existing legislation to the evils of monopoly and combination. Within the decade 1901 to 1911, 81 suits were brought and prosecutions instituted by the Department of Justice under the Sherman Anti-trust Act. By the latter year, however, the early

[7] Early in the nineties a company known as the Corporation Trust Company of New Jersey was founded, which made it a business to handle, for a modest fee, the procedure of incorporating any concern and to serve as official main office. This company displayed at its Jersey City main office in 1905 the signs of approximately 1500 large corporations.

crusading spirit was beginning to ebb and in the decisions against the Standard Oil Company and the American Tobacco Company the Supreme Court laid down in an obiter dictum its famous "rule of reason" regarding trust prosecutions. In order to be illegal a combination now had to act in *"unreasonable* restraint of trade," and the following year in the case of *U. S.* v. *St. Louis Terminal Railway Association* the Court went a step further and added that a combination that was illegal because of unreasonable restraint of trade might achieve legality by modifying its by-laws. Since the Sherman Anti-trust Act did not contain the adjective "unreasonable" the Court's obiter dictum has often been pointed to as a case of judicial legislation, a usurpation by the Court of a Congressional function. It should be observed, however, that the rule of reason was a principle of long standing in law.

It was becoming obvious that further and more specific anti-trust legislation was needed to supplement the loosely phrased and variously interpreted Sherman Anti-trust Act. Under the sponsorship of President Woodrow Wilson, who demanded a "new freedom" from monopoly, two important pieces of legislation were passed by Congress in 1914.

A Federal Trade Commission was created to administer the anti-trust laws and to prevent unfair methods of competition. The commission was to determine whether unfair practices were being used, and if so to order their cessation; final enforcement of such an order rested with the federal courts.

The other measure, the Clayton Anti-trust Act, also defined specifically certain unfair practices, such as discrimination in prices among different purchasers and exclusive or tying contracts which prevent purchasers of goods from dealing in competing goods, all of which were declared unlawful. The act also prohibited the acquisition by one corporation of stock in another where the tendency would be "substantially to lessen competition." Interlocking directorates, the connection of railways with construction companies, and similar practices were also restricted.

The purpose of anti-trust legislation and of the court decisions based thereon was to destroy monopoly and to restore competition. It is evident that the anti-trust movement rested on the theory that competition was beneficial and that individualism and *laissez-faire* were the best methods by which social well-being could be achieved. Both theory and practice contained serious flaws. (1) It was not clearly perceived that railroads and some large industries, like steel, were burdened with high fixed costs and must operate continuously to live, that competition from overbuilding or during a depression would bring on combination or receivership, that receivership would not cause the plant to be scrapped but only reorganized, and that some working agreement must eventually result which meant combination. (2) If competition was desirable, then the tariff, recognized by some as the "mother of trusts," should be greatly reduced, but Congress was reluctant to take this step. (3) If monopoly was so undesirable, then a greater penalty was needed than a "fine not exceeding five thousand dollars" or "imprisonment not exceeding one year" or both if the court saw fit. Such a penalty was a mere slap on the wrist and hardly calculated to deter anyone from trying to make millions of dollars. Only once did the courts scare any of the big combinations. This was in 1907 when District Judge Kenesaw M. Landis tried to fine the Standard Oil Company of Indiana $29,240,000 for its hundreds of offenses against the anti-rebate law. His decree was reversed by the next higher court. And (4) if trusts were evil, particular care should have been taken to see that they were effectively dissolved; but here the course of action was very muddled. In the Standard Oil Company dissolution the court merely ordered that the stock of the subsidiary companies be distributed pro rata among the stockholders of the parent company. This meant that those who had been prominent in running the trust were later prominent in running the presumably competing successor companies; in other words, the holding company was dissolved and an interlocking directorate established in its place by court order. In the dissolution of the American Tobacco Company stock was so distributed among three companies by brands that each enjoyed a monopoly in a distinct sales territory.

Summary. The last third of the nineteenth century saw *laissez-faire* reach its peak and then decline. One reason for the decline was that business competition was becoming more and more junglelike in character. Only the big and the ruthless or the very cunning could survive. The prize for which all were striving was monopoly profits. Nationwide industrial monopolies or "trusts" appeared at this time not only because there was nothing to stop them but also because there was much to encourage them. Cheap transportation via railroads and steamships had widened markets; mechanical advances made possible the use of costly machinery and these so increased fixed costs that cutthroat competition was stimulated; tariff laws kept out competing foreign goods, and corporation laws simplified the problem of absorbing competitors. Trusts first took the form of pools; then the trustee device was used; this was followed by the two types of holding company, property and security, and these were succeeded by the interlocking directorate. As fast as laws were passed against one form, another was discovered and put to use. Of course not all businesses could be readily monopolized. Most suitable were those using much expensive capital; hence there were steel, oil, and cigarette trusts, but not bread, cigar, or textile trusts. The greatest period of trust formation was between 1898 and 1903.

If the trusts had employed fair means of competition and had passed on to the public most of the economies they realized from combination, they might have been tolerated. They did neither: they often raised their prices. The public realized that the business game needed more rules. At first the states and then the federal government passed legislation to curb the trusts. But the anti-trust legislation was largely ineffective until Theodore Roosevelt's administration. Even then the dissolution of the trusts was so poorly executed that often nothing more was accomplished than the substitution of an interlocking directorate or a series of regional monopolies. Furthermore, Congress seemed unwilling to recognize that high tariffs and anti-trust laws were incompatible or that in some cases a regulated monopoly might be preferable to unenforceable competition. Because of these oversights the trust problem was not solved a generation ago and is still far from solution today.

CHAPTER XXII

POPULATION, IMMIGRATION, AND LABOR

The growth of population. For two hundred years, from 1660 to 1860, the population of this country doubled every quarter of a century. After the Civil War the rate of growth began to slow down and between 1860 and 1910 the population only tripled, from 31,000,000 to 92,000,000, instead of quadrupling. This slower growth may be explained in part by the fact that the country was filling up, but even more by the fact that our standard of living was rising. People who have a high standard of living or who seek to raise their standard of living generally have small families. The birth rate fell steadily from an annual average of 37 per 1000 in 1871-75 to one of 26 in 1912. The average size of the American family in 1860 was probably about six; in 1890 it was just under five, and in 1910 it was 4.5.

The growth of population would have been reduced even more if great strides in medicine and sanitation had not cut the death rate from 19.8 per 1000 in 1880 to 13.6 in 1912.

A third significant change was the rate of growth of the native white population. It steadily declined until it fell below that of the foreign born; that is to say, of the additions to the population through immigration. Francis A. Walker, superintendent of the tenth census, reached the conclusion that in the long run immigration had not increased the population of the United States, but had merely "replaced native by foreign stock."

On the other hand, it may be noted, in the fourth place, that the increase of the Negroes was not so rapid as that of the white population; between 1860 and 1910 the whites tripled and the Negroes doubled in number.

Still a fifth change which was beginning to make itself apparent was the aging of the population owing to the declining birth rate. If it had not been for the great increase in immigration—most immigrants were between the ages of 15 and 44—this would have been more pronounced. In 1860 about half the population was under 20 years of age, only about 14 per cent were over 45 and persons over 65 were rare. By 1910 half the population was under 25; about one-fifth were over 45 and the percentage over 65 had doubled. While these shifts did not have very significant economic effects at the time, they foreshadowed important ones in the next generation.

THE POPULATION OF THE UNITED STATES, 1860-1910*						
Date	White	Negro	Total	Immigration during decade ending with year	Percentage of growth of population during decade ending with year	Percentage of total in towns of 8000 inhabitants or over
1860	26,991,491	4,441,830	31,443,321	2,598,214	35.6	16.1
1870	34,337,292	5,392,192	39,818,449	2,314,824	26.6	20.9
1880	43,402,970	6,580,793	50,155,783	2,812,191	26.0	22.6
1890	55,166,184	7,903,572	63,069,756	5,246,613	24.9	29.2
1900	66,990,788	8,833,994	76,303,387	3,844,359	20.7	32.9
1910	81,736,957	9,827,763	91,972,266	8,796,308	21.0	38.7

* The column labeled "Total" contains a small number of Indians, Japanese, Chinese, and others who are not comprised in either of the two preceding columns. The population for 1870 is the corrected figure given in the census of 1910, as the census of 1870 was erroneous.

The changes thus far enumerated have to do with the growth and composition of the population, but other movements and regroupings were taking place. The geographical shift from East to West was continuing and caused the western states and particularly those on the Pacific coast to grow more rapidly than those to the east or south. The population of the Rocky Mountain and Pacific coast states was ten times as great in 1910 as it had been in 1860. But perhaps the most striking shift in the distribution of population came about through the growth of large cities, which absorbed the major portion of the immigrants and in some states even occasioned a decrease in the rural population. The number of towns and cities over 8000 increased from 5000 to 35,000 and three cities passed the million mark. While the movement from country to city was nationwide in scope, it proceeded most rapidly in the industrial states.

The immigration problem. The industrial problems of this period were greatly affected by the rapidity of immigration. During the Civil War immigration declined, but soon after the war, it was renewed with increased vigor. The need for laborers was great in every line of industry and many western states established immigration bureaus to encourage foreigners to come and settle with them. The flow was temporarily checked by the crisis of 1873 and the resulting depression, but in 1882 it reached the huge number of 789,000, a figure not equaled for twenty years thereafter. An all-time record was set again in 1907 with 1,285,000 arrivals. The incoming tide of labor rose and fell, as the westward movement had done fifty years earlier, in correspondence with periods of prosperity and depression. This is shown in the graph on page 510.

In general the immigrants were attracted to this country by higher wages and the hope of raising their living standards. Up to about 1880 nine-tenths of the immigrants were from Germany, Ireland, Great Britain, Canada, and the Scandinavian countries. They are frequently described as the "old immigration." During the next generation the character of immigration changed, large numbers coming from Austria-Hungary, Russia, Poland, Italy, and the Balkans. They are often referred to as the "new immigration."

There were several reasons for this change. As long as transportation costs were high, most of the immigrants came from the near-side or west coast of Europe. However, as transportation cheapened and as steamship companies undertook extensive advertising campaigns, more people came from eastern and southern Europe. Once started the flow grew in intensity, for the first comers wrote home and encouraged others to follow. The higher American wage scales were even more attractive to the peoples of eastern and southern Europe than to those of northern and western Europe whose living standards had improved and were more comparable to those of America. Furthermore the Anglo-Saxon and Teutonic

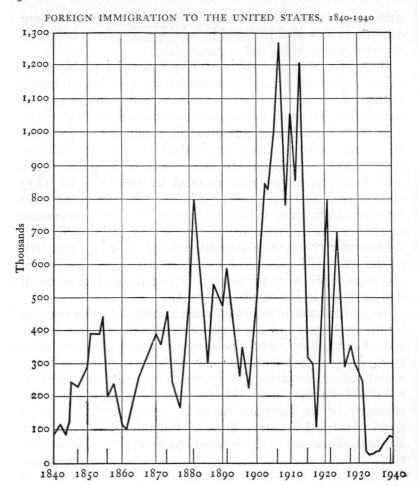

FOREIGN IMMIGRATION TO THE UNITED STATES, 1840-1940

The short vertical lines at the bottom indicate a panic preceded by prosperity and followed by depression. The major panics occurred in 1847, 1857, 1873, 1884, 1893, 1907, 1914, 1921, 1929, 1938.

peoples felt superior to the Slavic and Latin peoples and disliked having to compete with them. Their higher living standards, moreover, made it hard for them to do so successfully. Hence the "old immigration" declined in importance and was supplanted by the "new immigration."

Just as the "old immigration" had comprised, in part at least, the unskilled laborers and had taken the lower places in the industrial system while the native workers moved up into higher ones, so now the "new immigration" took the heavy and unskilled jobs and the children of the "old immigration" moved up to better paid jobs.

Between 1881 and 1914 about 16,000,000 immigrants entered this country and stayed. Nearly 75 per cent of them were males and over 80 per cent were between the ages of 14 and 45. Most of the cost of raising them had been paid for and they were arriving in the most productive years of their lives. They came to a country that was making rapid progress industrially and that needed ever larger supplies of reasonably priced unskilled labor to man its expanding mines and factories. It is obviously difficult to measure with any accuracy how important this immigration was to our economic development. Dr. Farr, an English government statistician writing in 1877, calculated that every emigrant leaving England represented a loss of $875, and Thorold Rogers in 1888 valued European immigration to America at the somewhat higher rate of $500,000,000 a year. If these admittedly rough estimates are accepted, then the immigrants who came between 1881 and 1914 were worth between $14 billion and $16 billion to this country. That is seven to eight times the value of the Negro slaves freed as a result of the Civil War.

However, this enormous immigration had its disadvantages as well as its advantages. While the new immigrants were probably just as hard-working, thrifty, and intelligent as the old immigrants had been, one-third of them were illiterate and they were unfamiliar with democratic government. Their racial and social background was different and their standard of living decidedly lower. Many of them were mere sojourners and expected to return to the land of their birth with their savings after a stay in this country. These differences led to a racial stratification which complicated the trade union movement by making common action more difficult. On all these counts they were therefore more difficult to amalgamate with the native population, and their presence created new problems.

Restrictive legislation. The earliest laws regulating immigration were passed by the states of New York, Massachusetts, and California, but these were declared unconstitutional in 1876. The first restrictive federal legislation was an act passed in 1882 limiting Chinese immigration for ten years; two years later the restriction was made absolute. In 1882 also a law was passed forbidding the landing of convicts, idiots, lunatics, and persons liable to become public charges, and requiring their return at the expense of the ship which brought them here. In 1885, under pressure from the Knights of Labor, the importation of contract labor was forbidden. There were marked similarities between the colonial system of indentured servitude and the nineteenth-century system of contract labor, but the more crowded condition of the labor market, the disapearance of cheap land, and the vigorous voice of organized labor now altered the public's outlook. The feeling grew in labor circles that the presence in the United States of a large supply of low-priced labor with low standards of living had checked increases in wages and had exercised a depressing influence upon the higher wages and standard of living of the American laborer. Labor therefore asked for protection against these low-standard laborers. However, the problems created by the new immigrant labor were only a few among many labor problems, for the labor scene was rapidly changing in character.

The growth of a wage-earning class. So long as the United States remained primarily an agricultural country in which most of the workers were independent farm owners, the number of persons working for wages remained small. After 1860, however, the development of manufacturing, of mining, and of lumbering, the growth of large-scale production, the use of automatic machinery, the concentration of industry, and the immigration of large numbers of unskilled, capital-less laborers all tended to augment a wage-earning class. The early ideal of having every worker become ultimately the owner of a farm or the manager of his own business passed away, and the existence of a distinct wage-earning class, that is, of persons who would always work for wages, came to be recognized as a permanent feature of American society. This can clearly be seen in the attitude of the twentieth-century college student whose chief interest on graduation is who will give him a job. A few generations ago most young men expected to make their own jobs, not to depend on some other person's capital and initiative to provide one.

By 1910 the number of persons employed in manufacturing almost equaled those in agriculture and during the next decade exceeded them. The composition of this labor force has varied slightly from time to time, but for the most part has been made up of men. As might be expected in an industrially developed country like the United States, most of the people in the productive age groups were at work. Over 90 per cent of the men between the ages of sixteen and sixty were engaged in some gainful occupation.

The proportion of women between these ages, recorded by the census as wage earners, was much smaller, since most of them stayed at home as housekeepers. The year 1850, when these statistics were first gathered, recorded the largest percentage of women in the manufacturing industries, but this was due to the inclusion of household manufactures in this group. During the next quarter century the development of industries that required heavy manual labor and physical strength, such as the iron and steel industry, called for men, and there was a relative decline in the number of women employed. In the last quarter of the nineteenth century, however, other industries grew up in which women were preferred, and there was a relative gain of women over men, a movement which continued at accelerated speed in the twentieth century. Proportionately more women were employed in 1910 than in 1860, over 25 per cent of all the workers in gainful occupations at the later date being women as contrasted with about 10 per cent at the earlier. Domestic and personal service still claimed the largest number, though the tendency was away from these traditional occupations to factory and office work. Retail selling also attracted a large and increasing number of women wage earners. In several other industries where special rapidity or lightness of touch were required the women outnumbered the men, as in typing and telephoning, the manufacture of cotton goods, hosiery, hats and caps, gloves, rubber goods, millinery, umbrellas, and similar lines.

Prior to 1870 no statistics were gathered in the United

States of the number of children engaged in gainful occupations; the census of that year showed that 740,000 children between ten and fifteen years of age were thus employed, of whom 115,000 were in manufacturing establishments. During the next decade the number increased sharply, the census of 1880 showing a total of 1,100,000 children in all occupations. Approximately one out of every six children between ten and fourteen years of age was a wage earner. The disclosure of such an undesirable development called forth restrictive legislation in most of the states, and during the next decade the number of children engaged in manufactures declined 33 per cent. But the number increased again in the next ten years, even beyond the figures of 1880, owing especially to the development of the cotton-manufacturing industry in the southern states, where but little factory legislation existed as yet. In 1910 the total number of children at work reached 2,000,000, or about the same proportion as in 1880. This was the high-water mark; thereafter the number and percentages declined. Responsible for this, in large measure, was the raising of the age for school atttendance.

Industrial changes and labor organization. These census statistics, so carefully collected and analyzed, give the essential facts as to our industrial growth, but they do not present causes or explain why things happened as they did. For this it is necessary to examine more closely the structure of industrial society at different times during this period. After 1860 the labor movement was profoundly affected by the changes which occurred in industrial organization.

The first of these changes was the nationalization of the market through improvements in transportation, so that local areas of competition were widened to embrace half a continent and more, and competition was both increased and intensified. Not only did the railway net grow in size, but east and west trunk lines were built and consolidated into great systems, so that transportation became quicker and cheaper and touched more points The worker was now exposed to sharper competition and his bargaining power was lessened. The competition in the same market of products from widely scattered localities tended to reduce prices and this exerted a depressing influence upon wages. At the same time labor became more mobile, and migratory out-of-town journeymen competed with local mechanics.

Another change was the shift from a handicraft to a machine basis and the consequent division of labor, which broke up the old established trades and made possible the employment of unskilled workers. The growth of factories tended to concentrate the workers in larger masses in cities, and large-scale industry tended to group them under one roof and management. Here they exchanged ideas, found common needs and grievances, and combined more easily in organizations, while an aggressive labor press educated them and presented their claims to the world.

The passing of the small industry and the coming of the great corporation substituted for the personal contact of master and man the impersonal relationship of capital and labor. Wealthy owners sitting aloof in distant offices or stockholders chiefly concerned with dividends had little interest in the problems and complaints of the factory worker. And on the other hand, the worker who no longer owned his own tools, who made only a small part of the finished article, and who rarely saw a customer, often took less pride in his work. His thoughts came to center increasingly on his pay envelope,

The middleman was growing in importance in the seventies and eighties. As more machinery was used and factory problems became more complex, the manufacturer was forced to concentrate on production and leave the marketing of the ever-growing output, which must rapidly be turned into money, to a specialist in that field, namely the wholesale jobber. This middleman came to be the dominant figure in industry. By playing off the competing manufacturers against one another he produced cutthroat competition, low prices, and low profits. The manufacturer tried to recoup himself by reducing wages, and the worker found his bargaining power threatened by all the technical and industrial changes which marked this period.

All these changes bore most heavily upon the trades in which machinery was most generally used, such as the iron and steel workers, machinists, molders, coopers, shoemakers, and typesetters, and it was these men who led the labor movement which accompanied the industrialization of the country.

National unions. The nationalization of the market gave birth not only to the national monopoly or trust but also to the national union. In the first place, in a big market the poorly organized and underpaid worker was a constant threat to the better-paid workers. Furthermore, local unions could not hope to deal with large monopolies: they also had to be large to gain recognition and bargain successfully. During the decade ending with 1873 twenty-four national unions were organized in an endeavor to meet the depressing effects of nationwide competition by a corresponding widening of the scope of the trade unions. Among these national organizations, founded at this time, were the locomotive engineers, the first of the great railroad unions, the iron molders, machinists and blacksmiths, miners, and shoemakers. The total membership of the national unions in 1873 was probably about 300,000.

It was not enough to organize national unions in the separate trades; the next step was to bring these together in a single body. This was done by the founding in 1866 under the leadership of W. H. Sylvis of the National Labor Union, a weak federation of local, state, and national organizations. The measures urged by this body show the problems confronting labor at this time and the economic philosophy of the workingmen, which had changed but little in the last generation. The first convention in 1866 devoted its attention to securing an eight-hour law, partly to relieve the unemployment which was serious at the war's close, but even more as a means toward obtaining a wage increase. Numerous eight-hour leagues were formed, Congress responded in 1868 with an eight-hour law for federal employees, and six states passed laws, but without adequate provision for enforcement. Attention was also directed to co-operation as a method of self-help and of escape from the wage system and the rigorous discipline of industrialism. Finally, the espousal of "greenbackism" by the National Labor Union gave the labor movement a new turn which led it into politics. In none of these efforts did the union achieve much success and when the panic of 1873 struck, the national trade unions began to disintegrate and the gains of the eight-hour movement were swept away. The demands of labor up to this time had been primarily political, in that they called for legislation. The improvement of working conditions by strikes and boycotts was tried by the next great national union, the Knights of Labor.

The Knights of Labor. Organized in 1869 as a secret society by Uriah Stephens, a Philadelphia garment cutter, the Knights of Labor grew slowly at first. Considerable uneasiness was caused when the appearance in public places of strange hieroglyphics, including five stars standing for the union's name, would bring hundreds of workmen together. Although intended to protect the men against employer persecution, the mystery exposed the organization to misrepresentation and did more harm than good, so that in 1878 the element of secrecy was dropped. Thereafter membership grew rapidly, reaching 100,000 in 1885. Finally the union forced that shrewd financier, Jay Gould, to treat with it in order to avert strikes on the Wabash and the Missouri Pacific railroads. The effect of the victory was electrifying: membership skyrocketed to 730,000 by the following year, making the Knights the most imposing labor union the country had ever known.[1]

The ideals of the Knights were very high. They looked forward to the end of the wage system, but they were not socialists; rather they hoped to establish a new social order by means of co-operation and political action for the benefit of the workers. They wished "to secure to the workers the full enjoyment of the wealth they create, sufficient leisure in which to develop their intellectual, moral, and social faculties, all of the benefits, recreation, and pleasures of association." To obtain these they demanded, among other things, the establishment of bureaus of labor statistics, reservation of public lands for actual settlers, the repeal of unequal laws, a weekly payday, mechanic's lien laws, abolition of the contract system of labor on public works, substitution of arbitration for strikes, prohibition of the employment of children under fourteen years of age, the eight-hour day, etc.; but the cardinal principles remained always union, education, and producers' co-operation.

[1] S. Perlman, *A History of Trade Unionism in the United States* (New York, 1922), 273. This book gives an excellent sketch of these changes.

The Knights sought to realize the ideal of "one big union" and aimed to bring into one organization all productive labor, using the strength of the skilled to improve the condition of the unskilled, and mobilizing the unskilled so that their competition would not hurt the skilled. Most of the authority rested at the top of the organization. The lowest unit was the local assembly, usually made up of about a dozen workers largely of one trade. Next came the District Assembly in which numerous trades were represented and which had complete authority over its locals. Above it was the General Assembly, "the highest tribunal," and when it was not in session its power rested in the hands of the General Executive Board headed by a Grand Master Workman. After 1878 Terence V. Powderly, an ardent idealist, succeeded Stephens to this office and held it almost continuously until 1893, by which time the Knights had lost their importance in the labor world.

The reasons for the rapid decline after 1886 are numerous and include such mistakes as dabbling in politics and abusing the boycott, but the chief ones may be summed up under four heads.

(1) Despite their early professed abhorrence of strikes the Knights engaged in a number of large ones for which they were quite unprepared. This of course hurt them in the workers' eyes. Considerable blame for this falls upon the organization's officers, who often lacked a settled policy and showed poor judgment in exercising their large powers. Certainly the ease with which they called one sympathetic strike after another with little regard to the strategic importance of the groups selected did more harm than good.

(2) The Knights' uncompromising attitude and sometimes violent methods lost them public support. The sabotage connected with the Southwestern railroad strike in 1886 made an impression on the public mind second only to that of the destructive railroad strike of 1877, and this was merely the most outstanding of many Knights' strikes at this time. On top of that came the bomb-throwing episode in Haymarket Square, Chicago, during a renewed eight-hour movement. Although it was not known who was responsible for the missile, eight anarchists were arrested for inciting the outrage, and when one proved to be a Knight and his local assembly

would not expel him, many persons condemned the whole Order.

(3) Many failures occurred in the co-operative enterprises of the Order. According to Perlman some 200 co-operative ventures were undertaken, chiefly in cooperage, shoemaking, and mining, the best-known being a coal mine at Cannelburg, Indiana. The average investment was $10,000 and the financial losses were heavy. In the days of Robert Owen, when small workshops and independent artisans were the rule, co-operation appeared to be a possibility, but after the Civil War, when large-scale production and expensive machinery called for huge investments of capital and centralized control, producers' co-operation was a naïve anachronism and was doomed to failure.

(4) Most important was the breakdown of the feeling of solidarity among the different types of members. The mixed assemblies possessed little in common, and the vague ideals of brotherhood were not powerful enough to bind workers from diverse industries into a unified body for action. In fact, between the skilled and unskilled there developed at times a positive animosity because the skilled workers realized that they were strategically more important in winning a strike than the replaceable unskilled workers and consequently resented sharing the gains if the strike was successful or were bitter if it failed. Add to this the success of the compact craft unions outside the Order in winning their strikes, and it becomes apparent why after 1886 the skilled workers in both industrial and craft unions drifted more and more into the ranks of the new American Federation of Labor.

American Federation of Labor. This organization officially dates its founding in 1881 with a membership of 48,000, but during the first five years of its existence it was weak and ineffective and did not function vigorously until its reorganization in 1886. About twenty-five trades were represented at this time, including carpenters and joiners, cigar makers, furniture makers, iron molders, miners and mine laborers, and typesetters. The Federation grew to 200,000 in 1889—at which time the declining Knights claimed about an equal number—expanded to 550,000 in 1900 and to 2,000,000 in 1914. Much of the Federation's success must be attributed to the astute leadership of Samuel Gompers, an English-born immigrant of Dutch-Jewish descent and a cigar maker by trade, who was president from 1886 to his death in 1924, with the exception of one year.

The chief purposes of the Federation were to unite the various unions for mutual assistance, to obtain legislation favorable to the interests of the working classes, to use every possible means to remedy abuses from which workers suffered and to improve their working conditions. In carrying out this program the Federation maintained that the strike, the boycott, and the unfair list were justifiable and necessary methods in achieving its ends. It consistently attempted to raise the standard of living by shorter hours, higher wages, and better working conditions. It is noteworthy that the Federation had no long-range program of establishing cooperatives and abolishing the wage system. Gompers prided himself on being a realist, disapproved of political entanglements, avoided the sympathetic strike, and was generally conservative. He believed that the betterment of labor's conditions by short stages, as opportunities arose, would be more lasting.

The organization of the Federation differed markedly from that of the Knights. The lowest unit was the local union, whose members were all of one trade, say cigar making; then all the cigar-making locals were organized into one national union, and finally the American Federation of Labor united all the nationals. The system was modeled on our own government, with each national union playing the part of a state. It is true that there were central and state organizations, but they were of secondary importance and often temporary. The Federation was thus merely a loose grouping of practically self-governing national or local unions, which were largely independent of one another. The members of one affiliated union might strike and those of another might continue at work in the same plant. Only matters of general interest came before the Federation's officers. Thus authority was highly decentralized and the Federation was held together largely by the recognition of each union's independence plus the assurance that the Federation would admit no rival union of the same trade.

At first the unions making up the American Federation of Labor contained the skilled members of a particular craft or trade, and largely neglected the unskilled. But as machine methods destroyed the value of special skill or the need of training for a particular craft, and as industrial combinations brought together under one management various branches of an industry, the power and importance of the older type of self-sufficient or separate trade union was threatened. Some of the unions within the A. F. of L., while not yet approving the idea of "one big union," sought to organize all workers in their industries; such were the coal miners, the brewery workers, and others. With the dawn of the twentieth century, therefore, a tendency showed itself for a new type of organization, comparable with the integration of various industries in a vertical trust, to develop in the field of labor. An outstanding example of the new type of union, called the industrial union, is the Industrial Workers of the World (I. W. W.).

The Industrial Workers of the World. This union was founded in 1905 under the leadership of Eugene V. Debs and Daniel DeLeon, two socialists, and William D. ("Big Bill") Haywood of the radical Western Federation of Miners, and was noted from the outset for its violent methods. Never enjoying a large regular membership because of the poverty of its supporters, it began with 14,000, rarely exceeded 50,000 at any one time, and had issued a total of only 300,000 cards by 1916. Its leaders believed in direct action and were opposed to arbitration, collective bargaining, trade agreements, or seeking aid from existing parties: their terms were unconditional surrender. They advocated a great general strike which would paralyze society and would cease only when control of the means of production had been turned over to the workers. Meanwhile they practiced sabotage—destruction of property as well as loafing on the job—initiated boycotts, and conducted strikes. Internal dissensions weakened the I. W. W. at an early date and its unpatriotic sentiments and methods wrecked it during World War I. Although never the serious rival to the A. F. of L. that the Knights of Labor had been or the recent and more moderate Congress of Industrial Organizations was to be, the I. W. W. proved a useful stimulus. It mobilized and directed the strikes of unskilled workers in lumber camps in the Northwest, of migratory laborers on the wheat fields of the West, of miners in the Great Lakes and Rocky Mountains, and of textile workers in eastern mill towns. The A. F. of L. realized their neglect of this stratum of labor and took some action to remedy the oversight. Thus the chief contribution of the radical organization was the attention it brought the unskilled, but even here success was short-lived because the I. W. W. leaders refused to enter into trade agreements, and soon after their departure the gains were usually lost.

Summary. All these unions may be classified as to structure or as to aims, and there are three sorts in each classification, according to Professor Berman.[2] With regard to structure there is: (1) the labor union which takes in all skills, whether butcher, baker, or candlestick maker, and all degrees thereof —the Knights of Labor is an example; (2) the industrial union which seeks to organize all the workers in a given industry—the Western Federation of Miners and the I. W. W. are examples; and (3) the craft or trade union which limits itself to a single occupation like cigar maker—many of the unions in the A. F. of L. are examples. Then with regard to aim there are also three kinds: (1) the welfare union which has high ideals of social welfare—the Knights of Labor falls in this category because of its desire to abolish the wage system and to provide self-employment through co-operatives; (2) the revolutionary union with its hope of violently revamping the social order—the I. W. W. was of this sort; and (3) the business union, which seeks to benefit its own members by securing shorter hours, more pay, and better working conditions as opportunities arise—obviously the A. F. of L. unions fall in this category.

Certain truths concerning organized labor in this period stand out. No union which opposed the wage system lasted, and the organization enjoying the greatest success, the A. F. of L., always accepted the wage system. Attempts to organize the unskilled usually failed, but unions were now able to survive major business depressions. They were also

---

[2] W. E. Spahr and others, *Economic Principles and Problems* (New York, 1936), II, 277-78.

becoming national in organization and scope. The period of most rapid and enduring union growth coincided with the great period of business consolidations—both labor and capital moved in the direction of monopoly at the same time. Probably only 3 to 5 per cent of the working population was unionized in 1900 and about 10 per cent in 1910. Besides the giant A. F. of L. and the colorful Industrial Workers of the World there were the four railroad brotherhoods, a large bricklayers' union, and two textile unions which were beginning to grow rapidly just before World War I, and, of course, numerous smaller independent organizations.

Industrial disturbances. Although trade unions in the United States have never been formed purely, or even primarily, as strike organizations, this method of enforcing their demands was soon resorted to as they became conscious of their strength. Yet as late as 1874 an American writer could say: "Strikes in this country have not been very serious nor long protracted." Indeed, according to the only available statistics, up to 1867 there were only three years in which more than ten strikes had occurred; after that time, however, only one year showed a smaller number than ten.

The railroad strikes of 1877 were the first important exhibition of the growing power of labor, and directed public attention forcibly to the industrial problems involved. In that year strikes occurred on the Baltimore and Ohio, the Pennsylvania, and other railroads, which by reason of their magnitude and their far-reaching effects have become historic. Reductions had been made in the wages of the employees to offset the decline in business after the panic of 1873, the tonnage and length of freight trains had been increased, and various other causes for dissatisfaction on the part of the employees had occurred, which finally led to widespread strikes on a number of lines, but especially on the two systems named. Violence was used, property destroyed, and armed conflicts resulting in considerable loss of life took place between the strikers and troops who were called out to maintain order. The country awoke to the fact that our growing industrialism had brought with it serious problems as well as increased wealth.

Strikes became more prominent in the United States as the system of capitalistic industry developed. The high-water mark of the nineteenth century was reached during the "Great Upheaval" in 1886 when the Knights of Labor engaged in numerous violent ones.

The Pullman Strike of 1894 was probably the most significant strike of the entire period because it was the first major strike suppressed by means of the injunction. The Pullman Palace Car Company built an apparently model town outside Chicago, but the workers claimed that the landscaping was an advertising stunt and that rents were higher and accommodations poorer than in a near-by town to which they dared not move lest they lose their jobs. This was a depression period and, although wages had been cut, rents had not, so that the men often received but $1.00 to $6.00 cash for two weeks' work. Despite company hostility several locals of the American Railway Union were organized, and when three of the committee who had presented the men's grievances to company officials were discharged, the men struck. Other affiliated unions followed in sympathy and refused to handle Pullman cars, but this support was balanced by the aid brought to the Pullman company by the General Managers' Association, representing twenty-four railroads serving the Chicago area. As the strike spread, hoodlums seized the opportunity to rob, pillage, and burn property. President Cleveland called out federal troops to protect the mails and the General Managers' Association got a sweeping anti-labor injunction restraining the American Railway Union from interfering with the mails, with interstate commerce, or with the business of the twenty-four railroads. Unable to comply, the Union's officers were arrested and the strike was soon broken. Labor learned two lessons: that the government would suppress revolutionary outbursts, and that the injunction was a formidable weapon in the hands of employers.

Toward the end of this period labor unions became more conservative in the use of the strike. As they grew in strength, their organization improved and they came under the control of more far-sighted leaders. In the most strongly organized trades strikes were relatively fewer, but these were more apt to be successful than those in weakly organized industries. The most prolific cause of strikes was naturally the demand for increase of wages; next to this came the question of hours.

The injunction. In the generation following the Pullman Strike the injunction became one of the most devastating weapons at the disposal of the employers. An injunction is a court order to refrain from causing damages which cannot be made good afterward, or to perform some act by way of correction. It is a preventive order and stands in contrast to a damage suit which is for injuries already suffered. Courts sometimes took the attitude that the employer had a right to carry on business without interruptions that might interfere with his ability to fill orders. They then enjoined boycotting, picketing, and striking because of the loss of income or other property damage caused. How sweeping the injunction was depended considerably on the social philosophy of the judge. Failure to heed an injunction was contempt of court: President Eugene Debs of the American Railway Union served a six months' jail sentence for this after the Pullman Strike. Another notable example of the use of the injunction was the Buck Stove and Range Company dispute in which the American Federation of Labor was enjoined from placing this company on its "We Don't Patronize List." Samuel Gompers ignored the order, was cited for contempt of court, and escaped only after eight years of litigation. A type of injunction particularly obnoxious to labor was the blanket injunction which applied not only to the persons addressed but to anyone who heard about it. Labor's attempts to outlaw the use of the injunction were unsuccessful, but they did secure the passage of other favorable legislation.

Labor legislation. It has come to be recognized that labor is not a mere commodity to be bought and sold on the market like other commodities, and consequently that the wage contract differs from ordinary price contracts in several respects. The latter are between property owners and concern insensate things for the most part. The former is a bargain which involves not only wages, but also conditions of work, hours, speed, safety, with possibilities of fatigue, accident, disease, and even death. Since these are matters which affect the well-being of society itself, the state asserts the right to legislate regarding them. This enlightened view is, however, comparatively recent, for little significant labor legislation to protect labor and guarantee its rights appeared before 1882.

Much of the first labor legislation was designed to protect the weaker members of the wage-earning class from exploitation. In 1866 Massachusetts, which was one of the first states touched by the industrial revolution, took the lead in this direction by the passage of an eight-hour law for children under fourteen years of age. Other laws followed, fixing the hours of labor for women and for young persons under eighteen years of age at sixty per week, and providing for factory inspection and the safeguarding of dangerous machinery. Similar legislation was enacted in other states, directed for the most part to protecting the interests of the weaker members of the industrial body; but the efficient administration of the laws followed their enactment rather tardily.

Not until the beginning of the twentieth century was any really effective legislation enacted for the protection of children at work in factories. In 1903 Illinois passed a pioneer child-labor law forbidding the employment of children under fourteen in factories and requiring that they remain in school until that age. The example of Illinois was promptly followed by other states. By 1909 all but six states had some kind of law restricting the employment of children in factories, although in 1914 only nine states had met the reasonable requirements of the National Child Labor Committee. And no federal law had been passed.

Protective legislation for women workers paralleled that for children. New Hampshire is usually credited with the passage of the first legislation of this kind in the ten-hour law of 1846, but the first really effective act was a similar law by Massachusetts in 1874. By the close of the century a number of other states had followed this example. Many of these early laws, however, were declared unconstitutional on the ground that they interfered with the right of freedom of contract.

Of legislation in favor of adult male workers there was practically no sign until the end of the nineteenth century. The redress of their grievances was left to them to obtain by their own efforts. In this fact lies the keynote of the history of labor during this period, and one of the causes for the organization of labor. The very qualities that made the American worker such an efficient producer disinclined him to rely upon the government to improve his condition, but led him to trust rather to his own efforts for self-help. Government interference was accordingly not invoked to regulate the freedom of the wage contract or of employment, which was regarded as a constitutional right; but legislative protection was extended to the working classes by factory legislation and inspection, and by laws regulating child labor, hours, and conditions of labor. Down to 1900 about half the states had passed factory acts. These laws generally provided for sanitary conditions and sufficient air space; for the health and safety of the employees against fire, unhealthfulness of the work, and danger from machinery; and for other forms of protection to the life, well-being, and morality of the employees. Legislation for the control of industrial accidents also became more general and the employer was gradually required to assume greater liability for accidents. This last was a much-needed reform and needs further explanation.

Under the common law as it had developed in the nineteenth century, an employee had an infinitesimal chance of recovering damages from his employer. The employer had three chief defenses: (1) that the employee knew the dangers of the occupation and assumed the risks when he took the job; (2) that the employee himself was at least partly responsible for the accident; and (3) that a fellow worker had been responsible. Moreover, if the employee died, his widow might be told that the right of action expired with her husband. But even assuming the employee got past all these and several more defenses, it would require a long, expensive lawsuit at the end of which his lawyer's fees might devour most of the damages. The first attacks on this system were made by the states: Georgia in 1856 and Iowa in 1862 abolished the fellow-servant rule for railroad accidents, Colorado was the first to eliminate the defense altogether, and by 1910, twenty-three states and the national government had laws covering employers' liability. Finally, in 1912 the Supreme Court upheld a federal statute making railroads engaged in interstate commerce liable for accident to employees. It seems highly unjust to ask a single employee to bear the costs, economic as well as physical, for an injury he may well have been unable to prevent: far better is it to assess the employer and let him pass it on to the customer as one of the costs of the industry.

Labor and the courts. Under the American system of jurisprudence, according to which the courts pass upon the constitutionality of legislation, many of the statutes designed to protect the workers in their struggle for higher standards or better conditions were declared unconstitutional. Only gradually and by determined effort did labor achieve the advances recorded in the preceding paragraphs. Not only were the judges more conservative than the legislators, who readily responded to the demands of the people, but they expounded an individualistic legal philosophy and an economic doctrine of free competition. The Fifth and again the Fourteenth Amendments of the Constitution declared that no one could be "deprived of life, liberty, or property without due process of law," and the courts, basing their decisions on these provisions, annulled many labor laws as an infringement of liberty, a confiscation of property, an abridgment of the freedom of contract, or as class legislation.

Down to the end of the nineteenth century the courts usually held unconstitutional laws fixing the hours of labor for men, and sometimes even for women, on the ground that they interfered with freedom of contract. Beginning about 1898, however, a new stage in the development of public opinion and judicial decisions on this subject set in, which Professor Commons calls the public-benefit period of labor legislation. The health of the producer was now held by the courts to be a public benefit and laws passed to protect him were approved. This protective legislation was sustained by the exercise of that elastic power of the state known as the "police power," which enabled the state to limit or even to destroy private rights of property and contract in the interest of the public welfare. Labor legislation accordingly covered almost every phase of the labor contract.

Whether labor obtained more from the legislatures and courts or from organizing and striking is a debatable question, although the evidence for this period suggests that the unions accomplished more.

Wages and hours. One of the claims of organized labor is that as a result of its efforts wages have been raised.

Whether this is true or not, it can hardly be disputed that during the entire history of the country the general tendency of real wages has been upward. By real wages is meant what the worker can buy in goods or services for the money wages he receives. If part of his pay is, say, room and board, those, too, are part of his real wages. Only real wages need concern us. According to Professor Hansen,[3] who has made a study of real wages between 1860 and 1923, the chief gains were made between 1860 and 1890. Real wages rose 68 per cent, and this was despite a 33 per cent drop during the Civil War inflation. After 1873 money wages declined fairly steadily but prices fell even more, so that the workers' real wages increased. Between 1890 and 1913 money wages rose about one-third, but so did prices, with the result that real wages were not noticeably better at the end of that twenty-three-year period. Of course real wages of different occupations varied. For example, the unskilled suffered more in poor times than the skilled workers. Teachers made the greatest advances and were followed by farm laborers, salaried and clerical workers in manufacturing and transportation, and building trades workers, in that order. The gains of teachers and farm laborers were long overdue as both had been poorly paid in the previous generations. Wage earners in manufactures, public utilities, and railroads, coal miners, postal employees, and unskilled laborers about held their own; and government employees, other than in post offices, and ministers were distinctly worse off, especially the former. On the whole, the position of the wage earner, provided always that he had work, was much better in 1914 than in 1860.

During the same period the hours of labor were materially shortened. In 1860 the average working day was 11 hours, in 1890 it was 10 hours and by 1914 it was 9 hours. Of course, not all occupations gained equally in this regard. Workers in the building trades enjoyed a shorter than average workday, for example, while men in the steel industry worked longer than average hours.

Labor in the South. Still another problem was presented by the labor situation in the South. The efforts to organize

[3] A. H. Hansen, "Factors Affecting the Trend of Real Wages," *American Economic Review* (March, 1925), XV, 32.

the freedmen as wage earners after the Civil War and the failure of that system have already been described. It became evident that the freedmen did not understand how to use their liberty, and that the best solution of the problem would be to give the Negroes engaged in agriculture an interest in the crop and make them at least partly responsible for the consequences of their idleness. To secure this result the share system, or "cropping system," was extended throughout the greater part of the South. While this system secured better results than the preceding wage system in stimulating the interest of the Negro, it led to a more rapid deterioration of the land.

As the industries of the South became more diversified, the Negro seemed to lack the energy and intelligence to occupy the new positions. Vigorous efforts, led by Booker T. Washington, were made in the South to educate the Negro along lines of industrial efficiency and to make him a more reliable and competent worker. Encouraging as were the results, it was manifest that any such work of improvement must be slow and laborious. Toward the end of this period there was a considerable influx into the southern states of immigrants, notably Italians, who supplied an increasing share of the labor needed in the industrial regeneration of that section, and even competed with the Negro in the cotton fields. The native white population supplied most of the labor required by the new cotton factories, steel mills, etc., in which, owing to the lack of restrictive factory legislation, many of the abuses attendant upon the early growth of the factory system elsewhere were being reproduced.

Conclusion. In spite of difficulties in obtaining complete recognition of unionism from the employers, of halting legislation, and sometimes of hostile judicial decisions, labor made steady and, in the latter part of the period, rapid progress in raising its standards and improving its conditions both of work and of living. Some of these have already been described, but further evidence is readily obtainable. The material progress of the people can be gauged fairly accurately by their consumption of certain semi-luxuries like tea, coffee, sugar, tobacco, etc., all of which showed a steady increase. Thus in the United States between 1871 and 1903 inclusive, the per capita consumption of coffee increased from 7.91 to 10.79 pounds, that of sugar from 36.2 to 71.1 pounds, that of tobacco from 4.00 to 4.91 pounds, and that of wheat and flour from 4.69 to 5.81 bushels. Other articles of convenience or even luxury, unknown at the earlier date, were now generally purchased by the workers, such as household appliances, plumbing, central heating, and other things. When to these statistical evidences of well-being are added such items as improved houses, better and more frequently renewed clothing, more thorough education, and more abundant leisure, it is evident that a great advance in the lot of the worker had taken place since 1860.

CHAPTER XXIII

COMPETITION IN TRANSPORTATION AND COMMUNICATION

Railroad building. Cheap and rapid systems of transportation have been a necessity over the enormous distances of the American continent, and the railroad has therefore attained here an importance greater than in any other country in the world. The great need of the country in 1860 was adequate transportation facilities, which were considered to be the key to economic progress, for only as they were built could the undeveloped West be opened up. The building of the great trunk lines and of the transcontinental railroads, which linked together the various sections of the United States by a unified transportation system, was the most important economic achievement of this period. In no country has the growth of railroads so directly affected the life of the people or the development of staple industries. Their building led to agricultural expansion, to foreign trade in grain, to the growth of domestic markets for manufactures, to rapid immigration and settlement, to large-scale production, and to urban concentration. Railroads were both a cause and an effect, but always a necessity.

The transcontinental railroads and government aid. One of the most significant and dramatic railroad events of this period was the completion of the first transcontinental line and the launching of others. This matter had been under discussion in Congress for years, and in 1853 a survey of the most practicable route was authorized. But the southern states wanted a southern route and the northern states wished a northern one, so nothing was done until the withdrawal of southern members from Congress gave the northerners a free hand. Events now made such a road, moreover, a military and political necessity. One of the military plans of the Confederate states was to invade Colorado and California from Texas in order to seize the mines and obtain a supply of the precious metals. If the North were to meet this threat it must have railroad connections. Accordingly, in 1862 Congress passed an act, amended in 1864, to aid in the construction of a railroad to the Pacific. These acts gave to the Union Pacific, which was built from Omaha to a point near Ogden, Utah, some 12,000,000 acres of land, and to the Central Pacific, which was built eastward from Sacramento to connect with the Union Pacific, about 10,000,000 acres. In addition to the grants of land the two roads were given government loans, secured by a second mortgage, in amounts varying from $16,000 a mile on the level plains to $48,000 for the mountainous stretches; in all they obtained over $27,000,000. The junction of these roads was effected on May 10, 1869, at Promontory Point, Utah, where Leland Stanford drove the last spike, made of California gold. The blows of the sledge were carried by telegraph to all parts of the country, and the event was celebrated as the climax of railroad achievement.

A way had now been found, it seemed, by which needed railroads could be built with federal aid. In view of the prevailing individualistic philosophy, government ownership and operation were impossible, and there were constitutional scruples against subscriptions to railroad stocks by the federal government. But in the public domain lay the largess which could fill the treasuries of the companies and aid them to build roads which, in the nature of things, must for some time remain unremunerative. Lavish grants were accordingly made.

The pattern for such grants had been set in 1850, when the state of Illinois transferred to the Illinois Central alternate sections of land in blocks extending six miles on either side of the railroad—land which had previously been given to the state for this purpose by the federal government. Since the transcontinental roads ran for the most part through the territories, Congress made direct grants of land to them in those areas. The Northern Pacific, chartered in 1864, was allotted the largest total grant, some 39,000,000 acres. The Southern Pacific, with its grant of twenty alternate sections per mile of road built through the states and forty sections in the territories, obtained the richest gift. The Atchison,

Topeka and Santa Fe and the Texas and Pacific also received land grants. Between 1850, when the federal government inaugurated its policy of land grants to railroads, and 1871, when it discontinued it, more than 158,000,000 acres were placed at the disposal of railroad corporations by the federal government. Not all of the land thus granted was actually obtained by the railroads, as they did not fulfill the conditions of the grants by actual construction, but about 129,000,000 acres were eventually allotted to the land-grant roads by the federal government.

Grants of land were also made directly by the states, amounting to 55,000,000 acres. States, counties, cities, and towns, unless restrained by constitutional prohibition, vied with each other in giving tax exemption, extending credit, subscribing for stock, guaranteeing railroad bonds, or donating money. Many minor political units bonded themselves for these purposes and were left with a heavy burden of debt when, as sometimes happened, the projected roads were not built. Most of the railroads were constructed under state charters, which always granted the right of eminent domain and sometimes other concessions.

The effects of government aid were varied. So far as the federal government was concerned, it suffered a slight monetary loss of $6,000,000 when the loans made to the transcontinental roads were repaid, but it profited enormously from a provision that these roads were to carry United States troops at one-half the regular fare. By the time this was finally abrogated in December, 1945, it was estimated that the government had saved approximately $900 million. The policy of land grants opened the door to corruption and fraud, both of which unhappily characterized both Congress and the General Land Office. The policy also induced speculative building, the reward for which was the grants of land rather than the returns from traffic. Whether the railroads profited from these grants cannot be answered by a general statement. Some lines, like the Illinois Central which developed a system of colonization, or the Southern Pacific on whose land oil was found, undoubtedly profited. For other railroads the case is not so clear. But whether they profited or not, their building was hastened and the development of the country was quickened. The further question as to whether the price paid for the rapidity of growth was too high is debatable. If Poor's estimate is correct that a population of 850 for each mile of line was necessary for profitable operation, then the West was overbuilt for at least a generation.

Private capital. But grants of land, which were not received until after the roads were built, would not pay contractors, laborers, and suppliers of material. For this purpose money was needed, and this was obtained from private capital. The early railroads had been constructed chiefly with the proceeds from the sale of stock. The first issue of mortgage bonds covering railroad property was offered in New York in 1849,[1] but that was exceptional. When, however, the roads began to be built beyond the limits of settlement investors demanded a mortgage rather than a share in the equity. Money was therefore obtained by the sale of bonds, mostly to eastern capitalists, but some to British, and, to a less degree, to German and other foreign investors. "Until the panic of 1873," wrote Ripley, "European investors bought our railway securities eagerly." It was estimated that one-third of the railroad mortgage indebtedness was held abroad. The heavy bonded indebtedness involved in this method of raising funds resulted later in frequent financial disaster to the railroads and in loss to the investors. Common stocks usually represented so much water in the railroad capitalization, based on the hope of future profits, and were given as a bonus with the bonds; but sometimes contractors accepted them at an enormous discount in part payment of their services. Most of the capital was thus supplied by private individuals.

Railroad expansion. The Civil War checked railroad building in the South, where much of the track and rolling stock was destroyed, but gave an impetus to that in the North. For the country as a whole the operated mileage almost doubled—from 30,626 in 1860 to 52,922 in 1870. Railroad extension was again interrupted by the crisis of 1873, which was in large measure caused by the too-rapid railroad construction and the intense speculation attending it, but by 1878

---

[1] *Poor's Manual of the Railroads of the United States* (New York, 1900), lv.

it began to revive, and the end of the decade saw the mileage again nearly doubled—brought up to 93,262 miles in the United States.

The ten-year period 1880–90 witnessed the greatest expansion of the railroad net that had as yet taken place: from 93,262 miles in 1880 to 156,414 in 1890, or the building of 63,000 miles of railroad in a single decade. By 1890 the country seemed to be pretty well supplied with railroad facilities, and after that construction was less rapid. The crisis of 1893 and the resulting depression again retarded railroad growth and forced the railroads not merely to curtail new building, but to practice the most rigid economies. Nevertheless, by 1900 the railroad net contained 193,345 miles. This was more than the combined mileage of Europe and nearly half that of the world.

The period of rapid railroad construction came to an end with the birth of the twentieth century; since that time there has been a slower growth. Between 1900 and 1916 the railroad net grew to 259,705 miles of line (the highest point in our history) or an average of about 4200 a year.

Track and equipment. Improvements in track and equipment kept pace with the growth in mileage, and made the railroad system of 1914 a much more efficient instrument of commerce than was that of 1860. Two features of American transportation differentiated railroads in this country from those in Europe, and impressed upon them certain distinctive characteristics. These were the nature of the traffic and the great distances between areas of production and markets. Over three-quarters of the freight tonnage consisted of heavy, bulky articles, such as coal, gravel, iron, lumber, grain, livestock, and petroleum. It is evident that heavier rails, bridges, and cars were needed here than in areas where the traffic consisted of light general merchandise. Even more necessary before such goods could be moved profitably were speed in transportation and low rates. Consequently, development in American railroads since 1860 was in all these directions.

Railroad service. The transportation service of the railroads comprises the movement of freight, the carriage of persons, and the transmission of express and mail matter. Of these the freight service is much the most important, for the exchange of goods increases with the expansion of production and the territorial division of labor.

Various improvements were made along all lines. Among these may be mentioned the establishment in 1883 of four time zones in each of which a "standard" time was observed, the division of the country into districts for purposes of freight classification, and the interchange of freight cars by different lines. Since much of the freight transported was handled in large quantities and hauled long distances, the tendency was to build larger freight cars.

As the capacity of the railroads to care for the increasing traffic, and also the size of the units handled, grew, the terminal facilities for handling freight, especially ore and grain, were greatly improved. Electric cranes, elevators, and other laborsaving devices for handling these commodities in bulk were introduced at terminal stations to an increasing extent, and corresponding economies in loading and unloading the cars were effected. Refrigerator cars were developed in the sixties and fast freight lines were established to bring perishable commodities quickly to market.

Pullman sleeping cars, dining cars, and parlor cars were introduced after 1860 and were constantly improved. By the beginning of the twentieth century the passenger on a fast through train on an American railroad could probably travel more luxuriously than in any other country in the world. At the same time greater safety was assured the traveling public by the introduction of the block signal system, and of automatic train brakes and couplers.

The first of these to be perfected was the system of block signals, the New Haven lines leading the way with an automatic electric system in 1866, but their general introduction was very slow. George Westinghouse, a brilliant inventor, experimented with the air brake from 1866 on and in 1872 produced his first automatic air brake, which was constantly improved until 1907. Before this it had been necessary for brakemen to apply the brakes on each car separately, which involved running along the tops of the cars and often resulted in accidents. Now the engineer could set the brakes for the whole train and stop it quickly. Another dangerous operation, that of uniting cars by the old link and pin coupler, which required the brakeman to stand between the cars while coupling and then jump quickly out of the way, was finally corrected by the appearance of the automatic coupler in 1889; the adoption of this was made compulsory on all railroads in 1893, and by the end of the century it was in general use.

Rates. These various improvements made it possible for the railroads to transport the increasing number of passengers and volume of freight at lower rates and thus to benefit both producers and consumers. The decline in rates was brought about by the competition among the railroads themselves, by the competition of the railroads with water routes, and finally by the competition among various productive centers in different parts of the country. Freight rates declined more rapidly than passenger fares, especially for the through traffic; this was made possible largely by the various improvements in the equipment and management of railroads just described. The average freight rate per ton-mile was 1.93 cents (gold) in 1867; fifteen years later it was 1.24 cents, and in 1916 it was 0.73 cent. The extent of this reduction is more clearly brought out by comparing the rates on wheat from Chicago to New York City, which are shown in the table below.

AVERAGE ANNUAL RATES ON WHEAT FROM CHICAGO TO NEW YORK CITY			
Year	Wheat (average rates per bushel in cents)		
	By lake and canal	By lake and rail	By all rail
1868	22.8	29.0	42.6
1880	12.3	15.7	19.9
1890	5.8	8.5	14.3
1900	4.4	5.1	9.9
1910	5.1	6.6	9.6

The effect of these low rates was soon seen in the development of the West, the shifting of cereal production entirely from New England and largely from the north Atlantic states to the central and northwestern states, and the diversion of traffic from the lake and canal routes to the railroads. So long as railroad rates were high, the major part of the agricultural products and other bulky heavy freight was transported by water—lake and canal—to New York City.

In 1873 the railroads transported only about 30 per cent of this kind of freight; but when the all-rail rates began to decline, more of this traffic was moved by the quicker route. In 1876 the railroads carried 52 per cent of all the agricultural produce but by 1900 they carried 95 per cent of all the freight that moved from west to east.

While the competition of rival roads for freight traffic was resulting in the steady reduction of freight rates, in the passenger service competition led rather to improvements in accommodations, speed, and safety. Passenger fares were not reduced to the same extent as freight rates, since lower fares do not stimulate travel in the same degree that lower rates stimulate freight traffic. In 1871 the average fare per passenger mile was 2.63 cents (gold); by 1882 it was 2.43 cents, by 1900 it was 2.00 cents, and in 1910 it was 1.94 cents. Freight rates on the average were considerably lower and passenger fares somewhat higher than those in European countries.

Express and mail. The third form of railroad service is the transmission of express and mail matter. The express business, that is, the carrying of small and valuable packages which require little room and pay heavy rates, had passed out of the hands of the railroad companies into those of express companies, organized for this purpose, as early as 1845. So profitable was the business that by 1868 there were 3000 express companies and agents in the United States. By the end of the century competition and consolidation had reduced the number to some half a dozen companies, which controlled practically the entire business. Abuses crept into the system and the express companies were accordingly brought under the control of the Interstate Commerce Commission by the Hepburn Act of 1906.

The transportation of the mails is a distinct department of railroad service, separate from those already described. As the railroad net spread over the country, the stagecoach, the pony express, and other forms of mail transportation gave way to the railroad.

Early railroad abuses. In the process of the rapid extension of railroad facilities numerous abuses sprang up, which were probably unavoidable under the conditions which existed, but were nevertheless serious and created many new problems. In the first place, there was a too-rapid expansion and consequent overbuilding of railroads. The system of government land grants was in part responsible for this, since it substituted for the economic incentive of railroad earnings the artificial stimulus of a political bonus. To this must be added the speculative enthusiasm of the times and the willingness of investors to risk their capital in the undeveloped West. Railroads were therefore built in advance of paying traffic and often into unsettled regions. This overinvestment of capital in fixed forms in advance of the economic need or of the possibility of earning adequate returns led to numerous crises during this period, the panics of 1873, 1884, and 1893 being primarily ascribable to this cause.

It also led to intense and ruinous competition among the railroads to obtain the small amount of traffic that developed and to divert it from their rivals. Heavy fixed costs bred cutthroat competition. Unused capacity of the overbuilt railroads was responsible for insufferable practices and abuses. Competition was, however, the cornerstone of the prevailing economic philosophy, and the policy of *laissez faire* was generally held, so that little was done to correct abuses by legislation or public regulation. Unfortunately, the abuses which arose under a régime of unlimited competition were not checked by a high code of business morality. It was a pioneer stage of development in which strong men, practically untrammeled by restraining legislation or public disapproval, performed extraordinary feats of railroad construction, but by methods which today would not be tolerated. It was "an era of ruthlessness, of personal selfishness, of corruption, of disregard of private rights, of contempt for law and legislatures, and yet of vast and beneficial achievement." [2] Under such conditions abuses developed in the construction, financing, and operation of the early roads, some of which may be described.

Some of the worst of the early frauds were practiced by means of construction companies. These companies were organized to take over the work of construction at so much a mile, and thus relieve the railroad company of the risk;

[2] B. J. Hendrick, *The Age of Big Business* (New Haven, 1919), 23.

they were usually paid with land and railroad securities. On the surface, such an arrangement was legitimate and useful, as it served to distribute the risks incident to a rather hazardous venture according to the principle of limited liability. But in effect it opened the way to scandals of national proportions. To build the Union Pacific a construction company was formed, to which was given the French name of *Crédit Mobilier*, the stockholders of which were also leading stockholders and directors of the railroad; in their latter capacity they voted themselves in their former capacity unduly profitable contracts, thus reaping enormous profits as builders, but defrauding both the government and the innocent investors in the railroad. Bribery was used among Congressmen and in the exposure which followed in 1872 many a promising political career was brought to a sudden end.[3] The profits possible by such methods were also exemplified by the case of the Central Pacific, the cost of building which was estimated at $58,000,000, but for which a construction company was paid $120,000,000.

The disclosure of such reckless waste of funds aroused the anger of those who had contributed to the financial support of the railroads. In order to obtain transportation facilities many states, counties, and towns had made grants of land, loans of money, or subscriptions to stock; and these contributions had to be paid out of taxes. Ripley estimated that the railroads received financial aid amounting to about $700,000,000. Individual farmers and merchants were persuaded to buy stock in a railroad in order to insure its coming through their territory, but the profits seldom reached the ordinary stockholder. Irregular financial methods were also exemplified in the wrecking of the Erie Railroad by Jay

---

[3] George F. Hoar's severe indictment of the period may be quoted in this connection. On May 6, 1876, he made this statement in the Senate:

"My own public life has been a very brief and unimportant one, extending little beyond the duration of a single term of senatorial office. But in that brief period I have seen five judges of a high court of the United States driven from office by threats of impeachment for corruption or maladministration ... I have seen in the state in the Union foremost in power and wealth four judges of her courts impeached for corruption, and the political administration of her chief city become a disgrace and a by-word throughout the world ... When the greatest railroad of the world, binding together the continent and uniting the two great seas which wash our shores, was finished, I have seen our national triumph and exaltation turned to bitterness and shame by the unanimous reports of three committees of Congress—two of the House and one here—that every step of that mighty enterprise had been taken in fraud."

Gould and his associates, a particularly deplorable feature of which was the corruption of the state judiciary. "The system was, indeed," wrote a railroad president, "fairly honeycombed with jobbery and corruption."[4] In all fairness, however, against the railroad manipulators and wreckers must be placed the honest and capable railroad men, such as John Murray Forbes, who developed roads in the Middle West, Charles Francis Adams, who brought order into the tangled affairs of the Union Pacific, and James J. Hill, who built the Great Northern, and many others.

But the abuses did not stop with the construction and financing of the railroads; the evils connected with their operation were even more serious. Rates were high, though perhaps not unduly so in view of the large costs and light traffic. But the charges against the railroads most frequently reiterated concerned the practice of granting discriminating rates. High freight rates were reduced by the fierce competition, but this very competition increased the amount of discrimination, which favored certain individuals or localities at the expense of others. It was easier to steal some of the existing traffic from one's rivals than to develop new traffic, and to accomplish this various devices were used. Of these, the least defensible were personal discriminations, which were special favors granted by a railroad to certain individuals or corporations in order to obtain their business by diverting it from rival roads. An extreme case was the granting to the Standard Oil Company by the Cincinnati and Marietta Railroad in 1885 of a rate of 10 cents per barrel on shipments between two points, while charging the independent shippers 35 cents; and the railroad moreover turned over to the Standard 25 cents of the rate collected from the independents. The Standard Oil Company and other trusts owed their successes in large measure to their ability to obtain such concessions.

Personal discriminations were granted by means of secret rates and rebates; by paying exorbitant rentals for private cars; by commissions for obtaining freight; by underbilling and underclassification; by excessive allowances for the use of terminals owned by shippers; and in other ways. Although

---

[4] Charles Francis Adams, Jr., *Railroads: their Origin and Problems* (New York, 1878), 126.

these were forbidden by the Act to Regulate Commerce of 1887, the receivers of the Baltimore and Ohio Railroad testified before the Industrial Commission in 1898 that more than 50 per cent of the traffic, at least on certain lines, was still carried at discriminatory rates.

Discriminations between places, while objectionable, are not secret and are therefore less reprehensible than personal discriminations. Localities in which there was water or railroad competition were usually given lower rates than noncompetitive points; indeed, the rates were sometimes raised at the latter points in order to recoup the low rates at the former. A single illustration may be given. It was testified before a Senate Committee in 1905 that the rate on cotton goods from New York City to San Francisco was $1.00 per hundred pounds, while from New York City to Denver it was $2.00.[5]

Hostility to railroads. The abuses of the railroads might have been endured, but other factors were at work to arouse discontent and to direct this against the transportation agencies. It has already been pointed out that the settlement of the West was proceeding very rapidly during the sixties and was leading to a relative overproduction of grain. Owing to this fact, and also in a less degree to the contraction of the currency, prices were depressed and the agricultural surplus would frequently not bring sufficient on the market to pay the costs of transportation. The discouraged and embittered farmers, who discussed their troubles in the meetings of the Grange, organized in 1867, soon came to the conclusion that the railroads were responsible for their evil plight. The railroads, which in the sixties were "pioneers of prosperity," became in the seventies "tools of extortion in the hands of capitalists." Since some two-fifths of the total cost of construction of the railroads had been met by grants of land, subsidies, loans of credit, etc., the farmers argued that the roads were a public trust to be used for the benefit of the shippers and not for the exploitation of the very people who helped to build them. Other groups now united with the farmers in demanding legislation to correct the worst abuses, and in the early seventies the Granger movement, which was

[5] Eliot Jones, *Principles of Railway Transportation* (New York, 1924), 106.

especially strong in the Middle West, lent its weight to the protest.

Illinois led the movement in 1870 by the enactment of legislation establishing maximum rates for passengers, forbidding extortions and discriminations in freight rates, and creating a railroad and warehouse commission with large powers. That state also declared grain elevators to be public warehouses and established maximum charges for their use in 1871. The constitutionality of this law was protested by the railroads. In his opinion upholding this law Chief Justice Waite said: "Property does become clothed with a public interest when used in a manner to make it of public consequence, and affect the community at large. When, therefore, one devotes his property to a use in which the public has an interest, he, in effect, grants to the public an interest in that use, and must submit to be controlled by the public for the common good."

This example was followed by other states in the West and South—Iowa, Wisconsin, Minnesota, Georgia, California, and others. The so-called Granger legislation of this period was extreme and was either repealed or modified in a few years, but it was notable as the first effective demand of the shippers that the railroads be treated as public-service corporations and not as mere private enterprises for the enriching of their promoters or owners. To the farmers of the West adequate transportation facilities and fair rates were an essential condition of prosperity, and these they endeavored to obtain by the means under their control.

Beginning with the seventies, two main movements in railroad transportation may be noted, one the effort of the railroads themselves to avoid the consequences of ruinous competition, and the other the effort of the government to bring the railroads under public control. Each of these may be traced in turn.

Railroads are natural monopolies. Although it was first thought that competition was the best regulator of rates, experience has shown that such is not the case. The reason is that railroads have such heavy overhead cost. Vast amounts must be spent to build a roadbed and the expensive terminals and to buy costly equipment. The interest on this investment is constant and large and must be met whether traffic is light or heavy. Operating costs, such as for fuel, are relatively small. Thus once it is built a railroad's expenses do not grow proportionately with an increase in traffic; if more business can be obtained at the same rates it will yield larger profits, for the overhead cost is divided among a greater amount of traffic. There is thus strong pressure to obtain new business, and where this was limited, as it was in the western states during the seventies and eighties, competition among the rival railroads became intense, rebates were often offered, especially to big customers, and rates were sometimes forced down to ruinous levels. Then one of two results was likely to occur. One railroad would defeat or buy out the other and thereby gain a monopoly, or the two would tire of warring with each other and agree on rates and division of traffic and that would amount to a monopoly also. In either case the public would be the loser, not only because it had to deal with a monopoly, but also because it had to pay rates high enough to support two fully equipped roads when one would have been sufficient. Thus certain businesses like railroads, street-car companies, power companies, telephone companies, and others have come to be regarded as "natural monopolies." They can be handled best by giving them a monopoly to start with and then regulating their rates through government-appointed commissions. However, it took a long time to learn this lesson and in the meantime the public encouraged competition and the railroads evaded it.

Consolidation. One method of escape from the evils of competition was combination, and this has gone on in the United States since the fifties. The first phase of this to attract public attention was the combination of end-to-end lines. As long as the traffic was local the lines remained short and disconnected; not until after 1850 was a length of 500 miles attained by any one railroad. During the decade 1850–60 many consolidations of short links into connected roads were made, and this process continued during the next decade, notably in the case of the Pennsylvania and of the New York Central and Hudson River railroads. Under the leadership of such able railroad men as Thomas A. Scott and Cornelius Vanderbilt the connecting railroads were welded into great trunk lines. The growth of the western grain trade and of other long-distance traffic made through shipments desirable and brought about an era of consolidation.

The formation of great trunk lines, while reducing the number of competitors, increased the intensity of competition, especially for the through traffic between the central west and the Atlantic seaboard. A series of ruinous rate wars was initiated by the efforts of the competing roads to divert as much of their rivals' business to themselves as possible. In 1868 the rate from New York City to Chicago was $1.88 per hundred pounds on first-class goods and 82 cents per hundred pounds on fourth-class goods; during the rate war of 1876 these fell to 15 and 10 cents, respectively, while passenger fares were cut to $7.00 and cattle were carried for $1.00 a carload.

Pooling. Since combination among these competing trunk lines was out of the question, escape from such ruinous competition was sought by making agreements which usually took the form of pools, according to which the whole traffic or earnings were divided among the erstwhile competitors on some prearranged basis. Pooling, which began in 1870, was the leading characteristic of railroad development during the decade following. The pooling agreements introduced a certain element of stability into the relations among the railroads, and by the middle of the eighties practically every large railroad was a member of one or more pooling organizations. In 1887 the Act to Regulate Commerce forbade "any contract, agreement, or combination ... for the pooling of freight of different competing railroads."

This prohibition was met by the reorganization of the various traffic associations, without the pooling clause, "for the purpose of facilitating the transaction and exchange of business with each other"; in this way they still co-operated. These traffic associations, while technically avoiding pooling, regulated rates and punished offending members. In 1897 and 1898 the Supreme Court decided in two important cases —those against the Trans-Missouri Freight Association and the Joint Traffic Association—that rate agreements violated the Sherman Anti-trust Act of 1890, which prohibited "every contract, combination in the form of a trust or otherwise, or conspiracy, in restraint of trade or commerce," and that they were therefore illegal.

Railroad combination. As pools and rate agreements were now both forbidden, the railroads were compelled to devise a new method of regulating their relations or to return to unrestricted competition. The first and most noticeable result was the combination of hitherto independent and competing lines and the absorption of the smaller roads by the large systems. Beginning with 1898, the combination of railroads proceeded rapidly until the whole country came to be divided among less than a dozen great railroad systems. It was now possible for these groups of capitalists to prevent competition without resort to pools or traffic associations; this was by the so-called "community of interest." An investigation in 1905 disclosed the fact that a majority of the boards of directors of practically all the railroads east of the Mississippi River could be drawn from a list of thirty-nine persons. By making representatives of one group members of the boards of directors of other groups, a community of interest and management was established which secured the harmonious co-operation of the various lines. Usually there was a community of ownership also, the owners of one group of roads being financially interested in the other rival roads.

The next step in the combination of railroads was the attempt to bring together under one management parallel and competing systems. Thus the Northern Pacific and the Great Northern railroads were jointly operated by the Hill and Morgan interests; E. H. Harriman, owner of the Union Pacific, attempted to gain control of one of the rival roads to the north, and a compromise resulted in the formation of the famous Northern Securities Company, a holding corporation. Harriman also acquired the Southern Pacific and other lines, and J. P. Morgan planned a monopoly of all New England transportation lines.

This movement to closer combination met its first obstacle in adverse court decisions. In 1904 the Supreme Court in the Northern Securities case declared the control of so many transcontinental railroads by one group illegal; in 1912 it ordered the Union Pacific to dispose of its Southern Pacific stock; and in 1914 the New Haven combination was also broken up. Congress took the next step against railroad combinations by enacting legislation for the purpose of restoring competition. The Panama Canal Act of 1912 provided that after 1914 railroads should not control water transportation lines operating through the canal or in other cases where competition might exist. And in 1914 the Clayton Anti-trust Act forbade one carrier to own stock in another when the effect would be to lessen competition between them. It was evidently the purpose of these laws to enforce competition by legislative edict.

Meanwhile efforts were being made in Congress to obtain federal regulation. In response to agrarian demands and decisions of the Supreme Court holding that states could not legislate concerning interstate commerce, Congress finally was forced to act in 1887.

The Act to Regulate Commerce. This act provided that all charges must be reasonable and just, prohibited discrimination, prohibited a greater charge for a short haul than for a long haul, forbade pooling, required publicity of rates, and provided for a commission of five persons (since increased to eleven), to which should be entrusted the investigation of alleged violations of the act. The Interstate Commerce Commission, appointed by the President by virtue of this act, collected statistics, and sat as a tribunal to hear complaints and render decisions upon cases brought before it, but the enforcement of its decisions was obtained through the courts, to which the railroads could appeal from the commission. For a few years the commission functioned satisfactorily, but soon the opposition of the railroad officials and adverse decisions of the Supreme Court reduced it to a mere bureau of statistics.

By 1897 judicial interpretation had left the commission with little more than the power to make reports and issue protests.

Further regulation. The early years of the twentieth century, it will be recalled, were marked by a strong movement toward combination, both industrial and railroad. Fear began to be expressed lest railroad monopoly lead to trusts and monopoly in manufacture, and gradually Congress proceeded to build up again the shattered edifice of government regulation and control. Some of the difficulties in the federal regulation of interstate commerce were removed by the Elkins Act in 1903, which defined more clearly unfair discrimination and rebating, and expedited the trial of railroads against which charges were brought. It failed, however, to provide any machinery for compelling railroads to reduce unreasonably high rates, and applied only to personal discriminations. The Hepburn Act of 1906 went farther than any previous legislation in enlarging the powers of the Interstate Commerce Commission, and definitely extended the principle of detailed government supervision, which had been previously exercised only in the case of the national banks, over the common carriers of the country—express, sleeping car, and pipeline companies, switching and terminal facilities—as well as over the railroads themselves. It forbade the granting of free passes, prohibited railroads from carrying their own products to market, strengthened the law against rebates, and placed private car lines, etc., under the control of the commission. Most important, it provided that the Commission should "determine and prescribe what will be the just and reasonable rate"; the final control over rates was, however, left with the courts.

In 1910 the Mann-Elkins Act carried government regulation another step forward. All the telegraph, telephone, and cable companies were now brought under the control of the Interstate Commerce Commission. An important provision of the act was that which gave to the commission power to suspend all proposed increases in rates until it could hold hearings and determine their reasonableness. Further legislation in 1913 ordered the commission to report the physical valuation of all property of common carriers as a basis for rate-making, and provided for voluntary settlement of railroad disputes. In 1916 the government passed an eight-hour law for railroad employees engaged in interstate traffic. "And thus," wrote John Moody,[6] "after fifty years of incessant struggle with the public, was the mighty railroad

6 *The Railroad Builders* (New Haven, 1920), 238.

monster humbled. It had lost power to regulate the two items which represent the existence of a business—its income and its outgo."

Summary. The first problem laid upon the transportation system during this period was that of providing adequate facilities for carrying the rapidly increasing commerce of the country. The response was overgenerous, leading to excessive building, ruinous competition, and the development of undesirable railway practices. The railroads endeavored to correct some of these evils by combination in one form or another, but while these helped the investors they did not protect the shippers. In response to their demands the government instituted a policy of regulation, but the effectiveness of this was seriously impaired by judicial interpretation, much as labor legislation had been. The Supreme Court, basing its decisions upon the Fifth and Fourteenth Amendments, became the citadel of privilege and vested interests and steadfastly resisted agrarian assaults. Provisions incorporated in the Constitution to protect personal liberty now became the bulwark of property rights.

By 1900 the country was fairly well supplied with railroad facilities. The urgent problem was now no longer how to get needed transportation, but rather how to obtain the proper relations between the railroads and the shippers on the one hand, and between the railroads and the government on the other. The questions of rates and of regulation were therefore the paramount problems before the people in these years.

Electric railways. The first effective competitor which the steam railroad faced on land was the interurban electric railway. This was first developed in the cities and grew out of the effort to solve the problem of urban transportation. Here were repeated some of the unsavory practices which had by now largely disappeared from the railroad field. By controlling the city councils or boards of aldermen the electric railway companies obtained perpetual or long-term franchises, built inferior lines, and unloaded them on gullible investors. By 1907, however, these methods were brought to an end and some of the malefactors were put in jail.

The growth of electric railways outside cities belongs

almost entirely to the period after 1895 and reached its highest development in the central states of Illinois and Ohio, and in New York, Pennsylvania, California, Michigan, and Indiana. Almost 17,000 miles of electric lines existed in 1902, which by 1917 (the year of greatest development) had grown to 44,677; of these over 18,000 were interurban. Down to that date their chief task had been the transportation of passengers in thickly settled districts.

The interurban trolley lines possessed certain advantages over steam railroads which made them popular: owing to the fact that no locomotives were necessary, the cars could be sent off one at a time and hence frequent service was possible; comparatively high speed, with frequent stops, was another advantage; fares were much lower because of the greater economy of construction and operation. The convenience of the trolley greatly increased the amount of travel in the districts through which they were built, and contributed largely to the interchange of business between the cities and the small towns and farms. The interurban electric lines had a distinct socializing effect upon farm life, breaking down its isolation, introducing higher standards, and broadening the horizon of the country dwellers. They afforded a profitable outlet, by means of the express and freight trolley, for the produce of the farm, brought the superior school facilities of the town within reach of the country home, and rendered the urban markets and shops easily accessible.

Road transportation. Under the impact of the bicycle and the automobile there was a revival of road building, reminiscent of the turnpike era of almost a century earlier. The early development had been halted by the building of canals and railroads, which were greatly preferred to the slower routes. For three-quarters of a century labor and capital were devoted to the construction of these rather than to roads, which lagged behind. The two-wheeled velocipede of the late sixties was followed by the high bicycle in the seventies, and finally in the eighties by the "safety" with two low wheels and a chain drive. These were very popular and by the end of the century over 1,000,000 bicycles were being produced annually. The bicyclists soon demanded better roads and about 1890 a "good roads" movement was begun. Commencing with New Jersey in 1891 this quickly spread to other states, especially in the East, and culminated in the formation in 1910 of the American Association for Highway Improvement.

This movement was reinforced by the appearance of the automobile. Although Oliver Evans propelled a vehicle by steam through the streets of Philadelphia in 1804, it was not until 1892 that the first practical automobile with internal combustion engine was produced in the United States by Charles E. Duryea. After a decade of experimentation and improvement it entered upon the amazing career of expansion and development which soon gave it first rank among the manufactures of the country. The automobile makers were fortunate in having a metalworking industry, a petroleum industry, and a steel industry already in operation, which greatly facilitated their task. The automobilists were as little content with the old dirt roads as were the bicyclists, and demanded better facilities. By 1914 stretches of concrete and of brick roads had been laid, and a beginning was being made with the construction of "black-top" roads, made by applying a surface of tar on the macadam roads. Highway improvement proceeded *pari passu* with the betterment of the automobile, but the great expansion came in the next period.

Inland water transportation. A less effective competition was offered the railroads by the rivers and canals, in spite of excellent facilities along these lines. The United States is marvelously blessed by nature with a system of long navigable rivers. The Mississippi River with its tributaries drains over 1,000,000 square miles of territory in the very heart of the most fertile region of the country, and cities more than 1000 miles inland have direct water communication with the seaboard. Altogether it is estimated that there are 26,000 miles of navigable rivers in the United States— counting as navigable those waters whose minimum depth throughout the year is three feet—while the shore line of the Great Lakes extends for at least 1500 miles more. In spite of the provision by nature of this admirable system of internal waterways, there has been a continuous decline in their use and a steady diversion of traffic from them to the railroads.

The high-water mark of river steamboat traffic was reached in 1879 when the jetties at the mouth of the Mississippi were opened to commerce. In that year over 1,000,000 tons of lower Mississippi traffic were received at or shipped from St. Louis; after that date it steadily declined and in 1905 was only 141,000 tons. The receipts at New Orleans of western produce—flour, pork, and lard—were only just sufficient for domestic consumption, while no wheat at all was received. Even cotton, of which over 1,000,000 bales were received at New Orleans in 1880 and which formed the staple of the lower Mississippi traffic, fell off as the years went by.

By 1914 it was estimated that the rivers carried less than 4 per cent as much freight as did the railroads. Almost the only traffic remaining on the rivers was that in cheap, bulky commodities, such as coal, stone, sand, lumber, and wood, with some cotton on the lower Mississippi. Instead of the picturesque river steamer, immortalized by Mark Twain, the typical freight carrier to be met on the river was a string of coal barges towed by a powerful tug. The Mississippi River and its tributaries, however, ranked next to the Great Lakes as avenues of internal trade by water.

The decline in the utilization of the canals was even greater. Although by 1880, according to the census report of that year, almost 4500 miles of canals had been built in the United States at a cost of $214,000,000, over 2000 miles had been abandoned and the traffic over the remainder was declining. The Erie Canal was the only artificial waterway which after the Civil War still carried any considerable amount of traffic. As late as 1868 practically all the grain arriving at New York City came by the water route, but after 1873 it began to be diverted to the railroads. The diversion of traffic was so serious that in 1882 the canal tolls of the Erie Canal were abolished; but this was not sufficient to check the decline in canal traffic which by 1900 fell to 5 per cent of the entire freight movement across New York State. Beginning in 1903 the Erie Canal—rechristened the New York State Barge Canal—was widened and deepened at an expense of about $200,000,000, in order to hold the vanishing business; but the increase in traffic did not justify the outlay. The other old canals, which had not been improved or deepened, became utterly valueless except to a few manufacturing plants which utilized the water or to occasional pleasure boats.

A few artificial ship channels, which are connecting links between important bodies of navigable water, showed, on the other hand, a notable development. Thus the St. Marys Falls Canal between Lake Superior and the lower lakes, an indispensable link in the Great Lakes system, carried a constantly growing traffic. By 1914 it had become the greatest internal waterway in the world, with five times as many ships as passed through the Suez Canal and a traffic tonnage equal to nearly 40 per cent of that of the entire railroad system of the United States. The Panama Canal, connecting the Atlantic and Pacific oceans, was completed in 1914 at a total cost of $365,000,000, and promised to cause a shifting of trade routes.

The reasons for the lessened utilization of the rivers and canals may be briefly stated. The tidal rivers on the Atlantic coast and the Columbia River on the Pacific afford wide and deep channels and are used in connection with the coastwise traffic. But the rivers in the interior of the country are for the most part fluctuating in depth and frequently without sufficient water in summer for efficient navigation. Even the larger streams, like the Mississippi and the Ohio, present difficulties from low water, shifting sand bars, swift currents, floods, ice on the upper reaches in the winter, and other navigation obstacles. Equally responsible for the loss of traffic was the backwardness of equipment, whether of landing stages and loading appliances or of boats, and poor business methods. The canals, which were of inestimable service before the days of the railroads, were not improved, with the exception of the New York State Barge Canal, to meet the demands of commerce, and sank into almost complete disuse. The movement of internal commerce became increasingly east and west, whereas the rivers flowed in a southerly direction; and the trunk and transcontinental roads were therefore not only better laid out for this traffic but ran through many places inaccessible to rivers or canals. The shifts in the location of the producing areas of raw materials and of manufactured articles altered the direction of traffic. The greater speed of the railroads also commended them to shippers in an age when delay meant inconvenience or loss.

In contrast with the river and canal traffic, that on the Great Lakes showed a great increase. Statistics covering the movement of freight upon the whole lake system were not collected until 1889, when it amounted to 25,267,000 tons; by 1910 it was 85,000,000 tons. These "unsalted seas" afford a deep and practically unbroken channel of trade for 1000 miles, providing cheap transportation like that of ocean carriers for the heavy and bulky commodities produced in the areas they serve. This branch of inland water transportation alone maintained itself against railroad competition, though the traffic was confined chiefly to coal, iron ore, lumber, and grain.

One other branch of the domestic water transportation of the United States may be mentioned—the coastwise trade. This has been restricted since 1817 to vessels flying the American flag and was therefore not exposed to the competition of foreign-owned vessels, though the railroad proved itself a serious competitor between many points. Between 1860 and 1880 the number of vessels engaged in the coastwise trade remained almost stationary, but by 1900 it had practically doubled; and in the next decade showed an even greater rate of increase. Coal, lumber, cotton, and similar bulky commodities constituted the chief items of coastwise commerce. The tonnage engaged in the coastwise trade was larger than that engaged in foreign trade, and was second only to the total tonnage of Great Britain.

Means of communication. New and rapid means of communication are vital factors in our modern industrial society, and their development during this period kept pace with the industrial and commercial growth in other directions. Almost as necessary as an adequate system of transportation for carrying on domestic and foreign trade are means of communication by which businessmen can inform themselves of industrial conditions and can direct distant enterprises. Only with the help of rapid communication can large enterprises be managed from a central office, which must keep in touch constantly with every subordinate part. Indeed, without the telegraph and telephone the great manufacturing enterprises and railroads could not have been brought together in unified concerns. By their aid producers, manufacturers, and merchants may be constantly informed as to trade conditions, price changes, and other factors which might affect their actions. Thus a drought in India, too-heavy rains in Argentina, a bumper crop in Canada, would all be telegraphed at once to Chicago or Liverpool and be reflected in the price of wheat on those markets. Competition is made world-wide and local price differences tend to be eliminated.

The postal service of the country expanded during this period even more rapidly than population or industry. It is difficult to find an accurate measure of the growth of the post office, but the sale of postage stamps is as significant as any other: the number issued increased from 216 million in 1860 to 9000 million in 1910. Various improvements in the mail service increased its efficiency; such as free city delivery (1863), postal money orders (1864), the sorting of mail on mail cars *en route* (1864); postal cards were first issued in 1873, special delivery letters were authorized in 1885, free rural delivery in 1896, motor vehicle service in the larger cities in 1914, and air mail in 1918. At the same time postage rates on first-class mail were reduced from 3 cents per half-ounce, as established in 1850, to 2 cents an ounce by federal act in 1883. The facilities of the post office were greatly extended by its entrance into the fields of banking and express service, though both were bitterly fought by the interests affected. A postal savings system was introduced in 1910 to provide small savers, and especially immigrants, a place for the deposit of their savings without risk of loss; the rate of interest on deposits was purposely fixed at the low rate of 2 per cent per annum so as not to compete with savings banks. In 1912 the parcel post system was added.

The telegraph, like the railroad, was stimulated by the Civil War, and by 1862 a telegraph line had been stretched across the continent. The expansion of this service was greatly aided by numerous inventions; a tremendous impetus was given by the invention in 1872 of duplex telegraphy. Soon two messages were being sent each way simultaneously, and finally came multiplex telegraphy, all of which greatly increased the capacity of the physical plant and decreased the cost of sending messages. The importance of the telegraph is only partially indicated by the number of messages sent, which increased from 8,000,000 in 1869 to about 100,000,000 in 1910. American ingenuity also applied telegraphy to various other uses, such as fire-alarm boxes, stock tickers, district messenger service, etc. The first commercially successful Atlantic cable was laid in 1866 by Cyrus W. Field, although an earlier one had been in operation a few months in 1858. At the end of the century cables crossed both the Atlantic and the Pacific oceans and afforded quick communication with every part of the globe. By 1914, however, the development of radiotelegraphy and of radiotelephony was already threatening their importance.

Of more general use for short distances was the telephone, which was invented in 1876 almost simultaneously by Alexander Graham Bell and Asa Gray. Its use made slow progress until Theodore N. Vail brought his organizing genius to the company that was formed to exploit it. After some changes of name and form there emerged in 1885 the American Telephone and Telegraph Company. By 1914 there were over 10,000,000 telephones in use in the United States. In course of time the service was extended over longer distances; in 1892 a line was opened between New York and Chicago, and in 1915 between New York and San Francisco.

All these improvements in the means of transportation and communication facilitated the gathering of news and the distribution of newspapers and magazines. The newspapers in the United States increased from about 400 in 1860 to 23,000 in 1911, but the subscription lists grew much faster. The wide distribution and low price—thanks to the advertising—of reading material in this country had a marked effect on our social and political development as well as on our economic progress.

Conclusion. The effects of improved transportation on modern industrial society stand out more clearly if we contrast our present railroad age with the pre-railroad period. Improved agencies made transportation more regular and certain, cheaper, safer, and quicker. The greater cheapness and speed enlarged the areas of production and distribution, and made possible the grouping and feeding of large numbers of people in cities, the assembling of materials there for large-scale manufacturing establishments, and the distribution of their products over world-wide markets. The costs of food and manufactured articles were greatly reduced to consumers, both by direct savings in transportation and indirectly through the economies resulting from regional specialization and division of labor. With the enlargement of areas of production and distribution, moreover, supplies became more regular, shortages tended to disappear, and business became stabilized. All these results followed the improvement in methods of transportation in the United States.

Although most of this chapter has been devoted to the subject of railroads, it is evident that all the various agencies described had their parts to play in moving the immense traffic of the United States. In the movement of freight the railroad cut deeply into the services of rivers and canals, and less so into that of the Great Lakes. In the carriage of passengers, however, the railroad was already yielding ground to the automobile, and still other changes seemed to be imminent. The same change and adaptation was taking place in means of communcation. A study of the past may well make us open-minded as to the future.

CHAPTER XXIV

SPECIALIZATION IN DOMESTIC AND FOREIGN COMMERCE

Domestic commerce. It is evident, from the great growth of the means of transportation, that a vast internal commerce was developing in the United States during this period. Although the volume of this traffic has never been accurately measured, as is done in the case of the imports of foreign goods which enter our harbors, a rough estimate would place the total movement of freight in 1860 at about 50 million tons, and in 1914 at about 2000 million. In the first part of this period the railroads and the inland waterways divided the traffic fairly equally, though there was a large but unknown movement by wagon. By 1900 the pipelines had been built and were carrying large quantities of petroleum, and by 1914 motor-driven trucks were beginning to bid for the traffic. Probably in no period of our history has the extension of the market proceeded so rapidly as it did at this time. The value of all this trade may be estimated at $3500 million in 1860 and $30,000 million in 1914.

This increase in the internal trade of the country was occasioned by the growing localization of sources of supply and of specialization in agriculture and manufacturing which was taking place, and was facilitated by improvements in methods of transportation and in the mechanism of exchange. In a community where each family produced its own food and other necessities, few exchanges were made, but as each individual and locality came to specialize in a single line of production, the business of effecting exchanges of these specialized products became increasingly important. Marketing organization was also influenced by the changes that were taking place and became more complicated.

In 1860, as has already been pointed out,[1] there was a large though declining trade between the West and the South and a rapidly growing exchange of goods between the East and the West. The Civil War interrupted the first of these and stimulated the second, and after that struggle the poverty of the South reduced the relative volume of trade with that section. The building of the trunk lines of railroad from the Atlantic seaboard to Chicago and St. Louis, and later the completion of the transcontinental lines to the Pacific, opened up new areas of agricultural production, of mining, and of lumbering, and gave to eastern manufacturers plentiful supplies of raw materials and markets for their finished products.

This territorial specialization was greatly facilitated by the extension of transportation facilities and the steady reduction in costs, which widened the areas of production and the markets. There was a tendency for markets to become national in scope, even the frontier agricultural communities being drawn into the net by improvements in transportation. In 1860 a commodity like wheat could not stand the expense of transportation by rail for more than a few hundred miles, and long-distance freight traffic was largely confined to finished goods and the more valuable raw products such as cotton. As charges were reduced, however, it became profitable to ship all kinds of grain and livestock, heavy minerals, lumber, and similar cheap and bulky articles, which now became accessible to distant consumers. This growing tendency to move less valuable kinds of products is well illustrated by a comparison of the amounts and values at different dates, given in the first paragraph of this chapter.

Routes of trade. Shifts in the routes of trade occurred in conformity with the changing sources of supply and with the growth of new centers of manufacturing and distribution. The commerce down the Mississippi increased to 1880 and then declined, partly owing to the diversion of traffic from the slower water route to the railroad, but primarily because of the movement of grain-producing areas into the West and Northwest and of cotton growing into Texas, which could not be reached by the river route. Grain began to move in large volume by the Great Lakes route, especially after

[1] See Chap. XIII, p. 300.

the settlement of the spring wheat section in the Northwest in the early seventies and still later after the development of Canadian wheat farms just across the border. More important was the movement of coal to the upper Lake region and of iron ore in the opposite direction. For the movement of these heavy commodities in bulk this long uninterrupted water route was unrivaled, and this commerce showed steady development. The major railroad routes in the United States also connected areas of dissimilar economic interest and thus facilitated the exchange of different commodities. The manufacturing states of the Northeast were joined with the cotton, tobacco, and lumber districts of the South and with the grain regions of the Middle West, which in turn were in touch with the petroleum and livestock districts of the Southwest and the mineral, lumber, and fruit regions of the Far West.

Each of these great specialized areas originated large amounts of traffic and received other distant commodities in exchange. These producing areas are shown on the map on page 455. The movement of trade no longer took place, as it had done in colonial days and again in the 1830's, along the lines of a triangle and in one direction on each line; instead the country was now crisscrossed by hundreds of lines of traffic which flowed in every direction.

Organization of wholesale marketing. In order to care for this expanding commerce specialized middlemen became increasingly important and the marketing function was more sharply differentiated from production. Already at the time of the Civil War trade organization was fairly complex and goods passed through many hands in their transfer from producer to consumer. Wholesale houses, jobbers, and commission men assisted in moving goods from areas of production to those of consumption and in distributing them to the markets. The organization differed according to the kind of commodity. Agricultural raw materials were raised on many widely scattered farms and these had to be assembled in larger lots. Consequently, they passed through many hands. Foodstuffs usually followed a more direct route from producer to wholesaler. Minerals, like coal and iron, whose production was concentrated, were frequently sold by the mineowner direct to the manufacturer, without the help of middlemen. As time went on, great centers of trade grew up in the large commercial cities, which gathered the surplus products of the neighboring areas and distributed them to manufacturers and consumers. Wholesale trade tended to concentrate in these primary markets and to reach out in both directions. Commercial practices differed for almost every line of industry, but, for purposes of illustration, the trade in manufactured goods may be accepted as fairly typical.

Most classes of manufactured goods were sold by the producers to brokers, jobbers, or commission men and were distributed by them to wholesalers; or in some lines the manufacturer dealt directly with the wholesaler. The latter maintained continuous stocks of particular lines of merchandise sold directly to the retailer, who in turn sold to the consumer. The jobber bought odd lots of merchandise known as "jobs" from the manufacturer. Both these groups assumed the risks of sale and of market fluctuations, but received any speculative profits from price changes. The broker was usually found in an industry like the canned and preserved food trade of today, where the manufacture was highly specialized and often protected by brands; he assembled different lines and placed these at the disposal of the wholesaler. The commission merchant was simply the agent of the manufacturer and was paid a percentage of the sales effected by him.

In a period when manufacturing establishments were small and widely scattered, it was difficult for the manufacturers to deal directly with the wholesaler and still more so to establish direct connections with the retailer; in these circumstances middlemen performed a useful and necessary function. As the business units grew larger, however, and improvements were made both in transportation facilities and in means of communication, changes in trade organization were introduced looking to the elimination of the middleman. The chief factors making for a simplification of the process of distribution were the development of mass production, the standardization of goods, the growth of national advertising, and the efforts of manufacturers and dealers to gain immediate access to the consumer.

Four types of organization may be distinguished: (1) The

manufacturer sold to a jobber, commission agent, or broker, who sold to a wholesaler, by whom the goods were sold to the retailer and by him to the consumer. As marketing methods improved there was a tendency to dispense with the middleman who stood between the manufacturer and the wholesaler. In some lines he was largely eliminated.

(2) The manufacturer sold to the wholesaler, the wholesaler to the retailer, and the retailer to the consumer. In this case the wholesaler occupied a strategic position and the question was not infrequently raised as to the value of his services. A spirited defense is furnished by Killough:[2]

"The wholesaler performed indispensable services for the dealer; he was equally important to the existence of many struggling manufacturers. The wholesaler had a definite clientele of more or less permanent customers with whom trade connections were maintained. He provided the manufacturer with a force of trained salesmen who handled so many lines that they could afford to call regularly upon the smallest dealer in the smallest towns. The wholesaler assumed the risk of credit extensions to dealers, stored the merchandise as fast as it came from the factory and, as already stated, granted, on occasions, financial assistance to the manufacturer whose limited funds were tied up in machinery and tools, raw materials and semi-finished goods. The wholesaler also provided the manufacturer with market information to be used as a guide in production. In fact, the orders advanced by wholesalers often served as requisitions for manufacturing. Thus the wholesaler originally assumed much of the price risk and furnished much of the foresight that more recently has been shifted in large measure to manufacturers."

(3) The manufacturer sold direct to the retailer. Some large companies, like the Standard Oil and the Pittsburgh Glass, adopted this method of direct sales, but on the whole this method was more characteristic of the next period.

(4) The manufacturer might sell direct to the consumer; this was sometimes done by mail, as in the case of clothing, or by canvassers, as in the case of aluminum kitchen utensils or books.

[2] Hugh Killough, *The Economics of Marketing* (New York, 1933), 166.

Produce exchanges. The most highly organized and sensitive market was the produce exchange. As a place where commodities could be bought and sold in large quantities, the produce exchange developed about the middle of the nineteenth century. In addition to the New York, Chicago, and St. Louis produce exchanges, which had been organized before the Civil War, there were now established the New Orleans Cotton Exchange (1872), the New York Cotton Exchange (1878), the Minneapolis Chamber of Commerce (1881), and the New York Coffee Exchange (1882). Although dealing in different commodities, the various exchanges had the common purpose of providing auction markets for their members, who established the prices and volume of trade of these products by bidding. The choice of commodities and the successful operation of these exchanges was determined by the progress in developing grades and standards, so that various lots could be sold by name with an assurance that they were equivalent, a method which was facilitated by the use of warehouse receipts. Trading on a large scale was also made easier by the development of warehousing or storing, and for some products by the advance of cold-storage through the improvement of refrigerating processes. Most of the smaller exchanges were "spot" or "cash" markets, but the larger ones dealt also in "futures." The purchase or sale of a commodity for delivery at a future date, when properly conducted, has a stabilizing effect on prices, and offers a form of insurance against losses from price fluctuations. Unfortunately, it also opened the way to speculative manipulation and unfair practices which brought the whole system of dealing in futures under suspicion. Speculators sometimes tried to "corner" the market.

Organization of retail distribution. At the beginning of this period the retailer was wholly dependent upon the wholesaler for his supplies of merchandise, for he could not possibly have assembled his varied stock directly or have obtained credit from scattered manufacturers with whom he lacked contact. Retail trade responded to changes in population shifts and improvements in transportation in much the same way that wholesale trade did. The growing specialization of areas of production and of individuals within each area, and the growth of cities, tended to lessen the importance of the old general store, though this did not disappear. The country peddler, who had contributed so usefully to the distribution of goods during the earlier period, retired to remote districts. The marketing organization of the rural sections was linked up more closely with the larger trading centers, and in these there was growing specialization. The retail trade of the cities was also profoundly affected by the economic movements that were taking place and altered its character and distributive agencies. These changes were quite as important and as significant as those which were occurring in the wholesale field.

The period after the Civil War, from about 1865 to 1896, was one of falling prices. If a retailer kept his goods on his shelves for any length of time he might have to sell them for less than the cost price. He was therefore under pressure to sell his merchandise as rapidly as possible. He sought to carry a smaller and better-assorted stock and to turn this over more frequently. In this he was aided by the traveling salesman. Styles began to change more rapidly, especially of clothing, and new inventions placed entirely novel articles on the market. Many things formerly made in the home were taken over by the factories and appeared for sale in retail stores. Such were ready-made clothing, factory shoes, baker's bread, creamery butter, and canned goods.

Under the pressure of these forces the old general store gave way to more economical and efficient methods of retailing. Four types developed: (1) the specialty store, (2) the department store, (3) the mail-order store, and (4) the chain store.

(1) The specialty store resulted from a splitting off of one line from the conglomeration of the general store and concentration on this. It was a species of specialization by which better goods and a wider choice could be offered the buying public by a merchant who understood this particular business better than the proprietor of a general store could. Specialization was made possible by the concentration of population and the growth of wealth, as well as by the extension of the trading area which brought in purchasers from a distance. In the larger cities specialty stores dealing in

expensive luxuries were to be found side by side with general department stores.

(2) But a counter movement set in with the development of the department store, which brought together under one roof varied lines. This differed from the old general store, however, in that each department was in charge of a specialist; it was really a combination of specialty shops brought together for the convenience of customers. The department store seems to have been first introduced into the United States[3] in 1861 by A. T. Stewart in New York City, though the Jordan Marsh Company in Boston is credited by some with the honor of priority. Other pioneers were Gimbel Brothers in Milwaukee, R. H. Macy in New York, Marshall Field in Chicago, and John Wanamaker in Philadelphia. The one-price policy, traditionally assumed to have been introduced by A. T. Stewart, had been in use in some stores since the 1820's, but was now more generally adopted. With this were soon combined other improvements, such as marking prices of goods in plain figures, selling at one price to all customers, giving a money-back guarantee, and in some cases selling for cash only. Other stores followed this example and the department store became a typical American institution. The idea underlying the department store was the bringing together under one roof of the usual "shopping lines"—dry goods, ready-made clothing, furniture, jewelry, etc.—so that the shopper, usually a woman, might satisfy all her wants without leaving the building. The advantages of such a store were economies in buying—as it could frequently purchase direct from the producer—in operation, and in financing; but it lacked the personal relationship of the small retail store.

(3) The mail-order house dates from the establishment of Montgomery Ward and Company of Chicago in 1872. The principle upon which it was based was to buy direct from the manufacturer and sell direct to the consumer; it thus combined the functions of the wholesaler with those of the retailer. It substituted a catalog for salesmen and made

---

[3] Department stores were established in Paris in the 1830's and in Berlin in the 1840's.—E. L. Bogart, *Economic History of Europe*, 1760-1939 (New York, 1942), 132, 135.

a direct appeal to the consumer on the basis of low prices. A great impetus was given to this type of store by the establishment of the parcel post in 1912.

(4) The chain store represented another effort to simplify the distributive organization and to reduce costs; it aimed to obtain the buying advantages of the department store or the mail-order house and the selling advantages of the small retail store, and relied mostly upon convenience and emergency goods. Chain stores were established as early as 1859 by the Great Atlantic and Pacific Tea Company, which sold groceries; by 1914 this company had over 3000 stores. Other chain stores were organized to sell groceries, tobacco, drugs, candy, hardware, dry goods, clothing, hats, shoes, and other lines. The chain store was made most familiar to the public in the form of five-and-ten-cent stores, the first of which was started by F. W. Woolworth in 1879.

Growth of foreign trade. The development and transformation of the domestic commerce of the United States could not take place without corresponding changes in our commerce with the rest of the world. The advance of this country from fourth place among the commercial nations of the world in 1860 to second rank in 1900 and to first place today is simply another evidence of the industrial expansion which was taking place in the United States. The following table shows briefly the growth of the foreign trade.

Year ending June 30	Exports of merchandise	Imports of merchandise	Excess of exports over imports	Percentages which agricultural products formed of total exports	Percentages which finished manufactures formed of total exports
1860	333.5	353.6	20.1*	81	11
1870	392.7	435.9	43.2*	79	15
1880	835.6	667.9	177.7	83	11
1890	857.8	789.3	68.5	75	16
1900	1,394.5	849.9	544.6	62	24
1910	1,744.9	1,556.9	188.0	52	29
1914	2,364.5	1,893.9	470.6	40	31

FOREIGN TRADE OF THE UNITED STATES, 1860-1914
(*In millions of dollars*)

* Excess of imports over exports. *Statistical Abstract of the United States*, 1941, 526.

The Civil War interrupted the steady growth of our foreign trade, for although exports from northern fields and factories increased, they were not enough to offset the blockade of cotton. After the war there was a conscious policy of developing the internal resources of the country by the Homestead Act, the construction of the transcontinental railroads, and the building up of domestic industries by a high protective tariff, as a result of which interest was diverted from foreign trade. A certain expansion was inevitable as the result of our industrial development, but on the whole the table given above shows only a slow growth until the end of the nineteenth century.

With the opening of the twentieth century the foreign trade of the United States experienced a great expansion. The causes of this were varied. The Spanish-American War in 1898 stirred the pride and imagination of the American people and broke down provincial barriers. The great development of our internal resources and of our manufacturing industries was by now furnishing a surplus of products above what the domestic market would absorb at prevailing prices; and the great industrial combinations were seeking an outlet for this surplus in foreign markets. In 1900 and 1901 a veritable panic was occasioned among European manufacturers by the so-called "American invasion" of those years. The foreign trade of the United States expanded rapidly, but steadily, during the period from 1900 to 1914, both exports and imports increasing about $1000 million, with the relations between the two sides of the international balance sheet remaining about the same. The increase was due in part to a rise in the general price level.

Exports. The United States in 1860 was still thinly settled, and one-half the population was engaged in agriculture, cattle raising, lumbering, mining, and other extractive industries. Compared with the industrial states of Europe, which together were nearly equal in area to the United States, this country was only in the extractive stage of industry. This is clearly indicated by the nature of the leading exports in 1860. Cotton made up nearly two-thirds of the total, but tobacco and naval stores also contributed to the southern exports; from the North, wheat, flour, and provisions were important. So long as cheap or free land and an open frontier continued in the United States, agricultural products constituted the mainstay of this traffic, to which mineral products were added in the last two decades.

The changes going on in industry during this period, the opening up of new areas of grain production and of cattle raising, the location and exploitation of iron and copper mines and of petroleum deposits, and the cutting of the southern pine forests, all laid the basis for a growing export trade. By 1914 the six leading exports in the order of their importance were raw cotton, machinery, petroleum and its products, copper and its manufactures, wheat and flour, iron and steel mill products. It will be seen that most of these were still derived from the fields, forests, and mines rather than from the factories.

Down to about 1900, then, the growth of foreign trade reflected primarily the expansion of agriculture and the extractive industries. But the export of these commodities would not have been possible had there not been waiting markets in the industrialized states of Europe, eager to avail themselves of our food and raw materials. Comparative costs of production determined the particular items that entered our export trade and the markets in which they were sold. Foreign tariffs held off some of them, but the cheapening of transportation and of handling and improvements in marketing organization tended to widen the markets for our goods.

The characteristic feature of our export trade during the early part of the twentieth century was the growing volume of exports of manufactures. In 1860 this group, including only manufactures ready for consumption, was less than 11 per cent; by 1914 it was 31 per cent. It seemed clear that the country had at last reached a stage in its economic development where it could compete on equal terms with the industrially older nations of Europe. Of the seven raw materials which are the most needed in manufacturing—coal, iron, petroleum, copper, wood, cotton, and wool—the United States was the largest producer of all but the last and was therefore admirably equipped for manufacturing a great variety of commodities. The shift in exports marked not only the close of an agricultural era, but even more impressively it testified to the emergence of an industrial era. During this period foreign trade entered also somewhat more fully into our economic life. Thus, in 1860, exports amounted to only slightly over $10 per capita, but by 1914 they were $23; similarly, imports rose from $11 to $19 per capita for the same two dates. But foreign trade was still less important to us than it was to the industrial countries of Europe which were all smaller in extent and more dependent on outside contacts.

At the beginning of the twentieth century some of the important manufactures exported were iron and steel products such as tools, sewing machines, locomotives, and typewriters, manufactures of copper such as electrical apparatus, petroleum, the products of wood, the coarse cotton textiles, agricultural implements, crude chemicals, leather goods, paraffin, and paper. Most of these were based upon a plentiful supply of raw materials and on mass production in large quantities, in which the United States excelled, especially in the iron and steel industry. But early in the twentieth century we won recognition as machine builders and as manufacturers of many practical appliances in the factory, the office, and the home. Our growing pre-eminence in this field was due to a variety of causes, among which may be mentioned the cheapness of raw materials, a liberal patent law, the genius of men like Westinghouse and Edison, and a general skill in the use of machinery. American industry produced certain manufactured articles which were peculiar to the United States and which had to be bought here by foreign nations if they were to be had at all. Among these may be listed sewing machines, typewriters, cash registers, adding machines, office fixtures, fountain pens, alarm clocks, elevators, agricultural machinery, and many other articles. On the whole, manufacturers were as yet surprisingly independent of foreign outlets; the growing domestic market absorbed most of their products.

Imports. Before the Civil War the principal group of imports had always been manufactured goods, which in 1850 constituted over 70 per cent of the value of all imports and in 1860 over 63 per cent. These were followed by tropical products. This is clearly shown in the following list of the leading imports into the United States in 1860: wool manufactures, cotton manufactures, sugar, coffee, hides and skins, and wool. During the next seventy-five years the importance of the group of foreign manufactures steadily declined, as American industries grew and high protective tariffs closed the door to European wares. The need of raw and semi-raw materials for use in American factories and mills caused an increase in the imports of crude materials, such as rubber, hides and skins, raw silk, wool, vegetable fibers (flax, hemp, jute, sisal, etc.), and long-staple cotton. By 1914 this group had taken the leading place among the imports, constituting 34 per cent of all.

The twentieth century saw a great increase of wealth in the United States and caused a growth in the demand for luxuries and tropical foodstuffs. The people of this country were the greatest sugar eaters and coffee drinkers in the world, and consumed enormous quantities of other exotic products. The chief expansion, however, continued in the group of manufacturers' materials, especially in imports of hides and skins for the expanding boot and shoe industry and of raw silk to meet the apparently insatiable demand for silk dresses, underwear, stockings, etc. In 1914 the leading imports in order of their value were hides and skins, coffee, sugar, raw silk, crude rubber, and cotton manufactures.

Balance of trade. It is not enough to state the exports and imports; to obtain a true picture the relation between them, the balance of trade, must be given. Down to 1874 the balance was usually "unfavorable"; that is, merchandise imports were greater than merchandise exports. As in most new countries, the people of the United States were purchasing more than they sold, running heavily into debt for supplies of capital and manufactured goods. Much of the capital needed to build the transcontinental railroads and develop western lands came from England and other European countries during this period. Between 1874 and 1914 the balance was "favorable" in all years but three; that is, the exports exceeded the imports. It must be emphasized that exports do not represent surplus goods; they are means of payment for imports and also for services rendered us by other nations. The excess of exports was small, averaging $400,000,000 or $500,000,000 a year, and was just about enough to pay the "invisible" items on the international balance sheet, which were running against us. These included such costs as interest on foreign capital invested in this country, expenditures of American travelers abroad, immigrants' remittances, payments to foreign shipowners for carrying our freight, insurance, and similar expenses. Each of these items was increasing during this period: foreigners were steadily buying our securities so that we were paying larger sums in interest, more tourists went abroad and spent more money, the swelling tide of immigrants sent back ever greater amounts to relatives in the Old World, and foreign ships carried a larger proportion of our foreign trade and exacted more in freight charges.

Nations with which we traded. Two outstanding facts should be noted with respect to our foreign markets—first, the continuing importance of Europe during the latter half of the nineteenth century both as customer for our exports and source of supply of our imports; and second, the development of new markets after 1898. In 1860 Europe received 77 per cent of our export trade and in 1914 still took 63 per cent, although there were slight fluctuations in the intervening years. The importance of the European market was greatest in the eighties when our exports of grain were at their peak and we found there an outlet for our surplus breadstuffs, cotton, meat products, beef cattle, leaf tobacco, lumber, petroleum, and copper. Great Britain was our best customer. Trade with our neighbors in North America accounted for about half the balance, while the other half was scattered throughout the rest of the world.

The sources of our imports were not quite so concentrated as were the markets for our exports, though Europe provided us with 60 per cent in 1860 and 47 per cent in 1914. As the proportion received from Europe fell off, the loss was made up by a relative as well as an absolute increase from South America and Asia, whose products—raw materials and tropical or sub-tropical foodstuffs—were not so generally held off by competing American industries and prohibitive tariffs. The development of a higher standard of living among our own people, moreover, increased the demand for such semi-luxuries as coffee, sugar, and similar items.

As a result of the shifts in foreign trade or of changes in domestic industry, the importance of various ports was altered. New Orleans, which held first place in 1860 by reason of its cotton exports, fell to third place as the relative importance of cotton declined and its production moved westward. New York was always the leading port for imports and in 1914 led also for exports. The Pacific and Great Lake ports shared in the general advance.

The merchant marine. To carry on this growing commerce it was necessary to develop a complex mechanism of foreign trade, and step by step this was produced in order to meet the changing needs. We have already seen the response within the country, in the building of railroads, the improvement of inland waterways, the construction of harbors, lighthouses, docks, loading and unloading facilities, to care for our internal commerce. But upon the ocean also bigger and swifter steamships were needed, which could carry greater cargoes at cheaper rates. Gradually, too, ocean cables, radiotelegraphy, international banking and credit facilities, and all the intricate mechanism of modern international trade were created in response to economic demand. Not all of these could be provided simultaneously by American capital, and in the case of ocean shipping we came to depend more and more upon space in foreign ships.

The era of the clipper ship had brought the tonnage of our merchant ships engaged in the foreign trade up to 2,496,894 in 1861, the highest point ever reached up to that time. During the Civil War almost a third of our vessels were sold to foreigners, others were destroyed by Confederate cruisers or were sold to the government for conversion into transports and cruisers. Congress refused to readmit to American registry vessels sold abroad, and our shipbuilders were unable to make up the loss. The heavy war taxes which had been imposed upon hulls of vessels and marine engines were repealed in 1868, but the duties on cordage, copper, and iron still remained. These disadvantages made it impossible to compete with British and foreign shipbuilders in the construction of iron steamships, and with the decline of the wooden sailing vessel the ocean carrying-trade passed almost entirely into foreign hands. Between 1865 and 1870 we had made a slight gain, even with our wooden sailing vessels, which did not have to give up valuable cargo space to coal, as did steamers on long voyages; but in the latter year the opening of the Suez Canal gave the advantage to steamers in the trade with the Orient by permitting them to recoal *en route,* and inflicted the last blow on our struggling merchant marine. In spite of the great expansion of our foreign trade the number of American vessels engaged in this service steadily declined until in 1898 the tonnage reached 726,213, the lowest figure since 1839. At the same time the proportion of our foreign trade carried in American vessels fell from 66.5 per cent in 1860 to 8.2 per cent in 1901, which was the lowest point reached.

The explanation of this steady decline in the American merchant marine is to be found not in a lack of patriotism on the part of American shipbuilders or shippers, but in the larger profits to be obtained from other branches of industry. This was a period of rapid railroad building, of the exploitation of our mineral and forest resources, and of the development of large-scale manufactures. The greatest returns were to be had by the investment of American capital in these lines, and the ocean carrying-trade was consequently handed over to other nations which lacked similar opportunities for internal development. The cost of building ships here was much higher than it was abroad and American builders were discouraged by vacillations in our shipping policy. On the other hand, foreign ships were heavily subsidized, they were organized in powerful international shipping trusts, and they were bigger and more economical. A large amount of American capital was invested in foreign shipping, especially in the 1890's—perhaps as much as in our own.

When, after 1900, our export trade began to take on larger dimensions certain disadvantages showed themselves in this situation. In many cases direct service between American ports and foreign markets, especially in South America and the Far East, did not exist, and it was necessary to ship goods via German or British ports. American exporters were thus placed at a disadvantage in their competition with exporters of those nations upon whose ships we depended.

In the period between 1900 and 1914 a slight gain was made, and in the latter year the tonnage of ships under American registry engaged in foreign trade was 1,076,152. Some efforts had been made in Congress to encourage shipping, such as the proposals to pass subsidy laws and the granting in the 1913 tariff law of a 5 per cent discount of duties on goods imported in American vessels. The subsidy bills were not passed, however, and the 5 per cent discrimination was disallowed by the Supreme Court. In 1912 foreign-built vessels under five years of age, owned by citizens of the United States, were admitted to American registry and permitted to sail under the American flag; at the same time materials used in the construction and equipment of ships were admitted free of duty. In spite of this permission few foreign-built ships were brought under American registry during the next two years, and few American ships were built.

Domestic shipping. The coastwise, Great Lakes, and river traffic was reserved wholly for American vessels, and foreign ships were excluded from it. The growth of these therefore reflected our economic development and the success of domestic vessels in competing with the railroads for the traffic. Taken as a whole, the shipping engaged in domestic trade increased from 2,800,000 gross tons in 1860 to 6,850,000 gross tons in 1914. Somewhat over half was engaged in the coastwise trade, conveying coal and fishery products from Baltimore, coal from Philadelphia, lumber, ice, and stone from New England, and lumber along the Pacific coast; the water shipments of cotton from New Orleans, once important, fell off after 1870. The bulk of the Great Lakes traffic, too, consisted of heavy, cheap, and bulky commodities—coal moving west and iron ore and wheat east. The tonnage of vessels on the Great Lakes grew from 467,000 gross tons in 1860 to 2,740,000 gross tons in 1914. The river traffic, on the other hand, showed a steady decline during this period.

Commercial policy of the United States: the tariff. In the United States the tariff has generally been held to be a matter of domestic concern for raising revenue and providing protection to home manufactures and labor rather than a question of foreign trade involving international relations. The internal aspect, the effect of the tariff on our factories and farms, has been kept in view almost to the exclusion of the external or international aspect. In the making, the tariff is a domestic issue, but in its effects and repercussions it is truly international, for it influences directly the inflow of goods and indirectly their outflow, and may affect our political relations with other nations. The tariff has so many aspects that it might with equal propriety be discussed from an industrial, a financial, or a commercial point of view, but it seems most logical in this period to treat it from the standpoint of commercial policy. It must be said, however, that the tariff appeared on the stage after 1860 in the innocent rôle of a revenue measure, as it had at its debut in 1789.

The panic of 1857 had been followed by a series of deficits in the federal treasury, owing to the falling off of import duties, and in 1861 Congress passed the Morrill Act, which restored the rates of 1846. The outbreak of the Civil War revolutionized the traditional revenue system of the federal government, which had depended on import duties and the sale of public lands. But the Homestead Act deprived the treasury of the latter source of revenue and the former was quite inadequate.

At first Congress relied largely on selling bonds and issuing paper money, but it soon became evident that taxation would have to be used more vigorously to raise the needed funds with which to meet the expanding costs of the war. The first vigorous resort to taxation was made in 1862 when two measures were passed, the first of which established a comprehensive system of excise taxation or internal revenue duties, and the other greatly expanded the tariff, both increasing the number of articles taxed and raising the rates. But the climax was reached in the revenue measures of 1864. The internal revenue act of that year created twenty-two new kinds of taxes, which seemed to have been selected, as David A. Wells put it, on the principle of the Irishman at Donnybrook Fair: "Wherever you see a head, hit it; whenever you see a commodity, tax it." The tariff act, passed at the same time, greatly extended the system of import duties, enumerating 1450 separate articles and raising the average rate to 47 per cent.

After the war the need for financial reorganization was evident. The internal revenue taxes, which were vexatious and burdensome, were gradually reduced, until in 1872 there remained only a skeleton of the former confused mass.

It would have been consistent to reduce the tariff duties which had been raised to offset these internal revenue taxes, but the pressure from interested manufacturers was too strong, and the tariff remained practically unchanged. The high duties brought in surplus revenues, however, of $100,000,000 a year, and finally in 1870 the first step was taken to lower the tariff. A general 10 per cent reduction was accordingly made in the tariff in 1872. After the panic of 1873 and the resulting deficit in federal revenues this "horizontal" reduction was easily repealed in 1875 and the previous rates restored.

No further changes were made in the tariff until 1883. For twenty years, therefore, the war tariff remained practically unaltered. Manufacturers who prospered under the high protection thus granted proved strong enough to resist any efforts at tariff reform, and the system of protection which then grew up became a permanent part of our commercial policy.

The revival of prosperity about 1878 again caused a great increase in imports and a corresponding increase in customs revenues. Although most of the remaining excise taxes were repealed, the effect on the growing revenues was slight. A tariff commission, appointed by President Arthur in 1882, recommended a "substantial reduction of tariff duties" of from 20 to 25 per cent. Congress, however, in which the protectionist element was powerful and well organized, refused to sanction such a radical change and in the tariff act of 1883 made an average reduction of only 5 per cent. Three years later President Cleveland declared the existing tariff to be a "vicious, inequitable, and illogical source of unnecessary taxation," and urged its revision in order to reduce the cost of living and to provide free raw materials.

The elections of 1888 resulted in a victory for the Republican party, which construed it as an endorsement of their policy of high protection. This was now advocated, not, as Hamilton had argued and Clay and Garfield had agreed, as a temporary aid to young industries, but as a permanent commercial policy. Commercial isolation rather than industrial maturity was the goal of the new policy. The McKinley Act of 1890 was accordingly passed, increasing the general level of duties up to an average of 49.5 per cent.

The higher rates of the new tariff were soon reflected in higher prices of commodities and a violent political reaction took place which swept the Democrats into control again. In 1894 they passed the Wilson Act, but this fell far short of their campaign promises, owing to the high protectionist views of the Senate, and the Democratic ideal of free raw materials was only partially carried out. The average level of this tariff was 20 per cent below that of 1890.

The panic of 1893 and the long ensuing depression were characteristically attributed to the Democrats by the people, who are always inclined to hold the political parties responsible for economic conditions. The panic was the culmination of a long period of speculation and overinvestment of fixed capital in railroads and other enterprises which did not yield prompt returns, though its immediate cause was the unsatisfactory currency situation. But the business uncertainty caused by the frequent tariff changes undoubtedly contributed to the prevailing economic disorder. As a result of these combined causes the Republicans were returned to power in 1896, and the following year they once more revised the tariff by the passage of the Dingley Act, which raised the general average of duties to 57 per cent, the highest ever attained in our history.

For a decade the tariff dropped into the background as other issues crowded to the front, such as trust regulation, conservation, etc. But a conviction was steadily gaining ground among the tariff reformers that the tariff was largely responsible for the growth of large combinations—"the mother of all trusts is the customs tariff," declared H. O. Havemeyer, himself president of the sugar trust—and for the rise in prices and the consequent advance in the cost of living. The Payne-Aldrich Act of 1909, passed by a Republican Congress, was designed to meet these criticisms, but it reduced the general level of duties inadequately.

The failure of the Payne-Aldrich tariff to revise the rates farther downward, especially in those schedules which protected the trusts, caused general dissatisfaction and was a factor in the formation of the Progressive party in 1912. Popular disapproval was sharply registered in that year by the election of a Democratic President and Congress, which the following year passed the Underwood Tariff Act. This represented the most complete reversal of tariff policy since the movement to high protection in the sixties, though it was by no means a free trade measure, the average rate of duties being about 30 per cent.

Date	Name	Rate Level	Purpose
		TARIFF ACTS, 1861–1913	
1861	Morrill Act	35	Larger revenues to meet deficits
1862		37	Larger revenues for war
1864	War tariff	47	Revenues for war and to offset excise taxes
1872		10% reduction	To reduce the surplus
1875		rates restored	To meet deficits
1883		42	To reduce the surplus
1890	McKinley	49.5	Protection to industry
1894	Wilson	39.9	Free raw materials
1897	Dingley	57	Protection to industry
1909	Payne-Aldrich	40	Reduction of duties
1913	Underwood	30	Further reduction of duties

The accompanying table shows the various tariff acts of this period. The frequency of change is exceeded only by the extreme oscillations in rates. For domestic business as well as for foreign trade such vacillation in policy was distinctly harmful. An effort to remove the tariff from the political stage was made in 1916 by the appointment of a Tariff Commission of six members. Its functions were purely investigational and advisory, but its personnel was such as to command respect.

Commercial policy of the United States: reciprocity. The international commercial relations of the United States have been very different from those of most European nations, whose tariffs are usually the result of bargaining and higgling and are consequently different for different nations. Insisting on our own right to raise our protective duties to any height we pleased we have not been concerned with the level of foreign tariffs, but we have insisted upon equality of treatment. With the development of our agricultural and mineral resources and the growth of large-scale manufacturing, which greatly expanded our exports, the belief gained ground that the tariff might be used as an instrument to open markets for our products as well as to encourage domestic production.

In 1889 a Pan-American Congress, consisting of delegates from seventeen of the Central and South American countries, met in Washington, and as a step to closer commercial union recommended reciprocity treaties. A clause was accordingly added to the McKinley Act, giving the President power to impose by proclamation certain duties on sugar, molasses, coffee, tea, and hides (which were on the free list), if he considered that any country exporting these commodities to the United States was levying on the agricultural or other products of the United States duties which in his judgment were "reciprocally unjust and unreasonable." Reciprocal trade agreements were made with most of the Central American states and West Indian islands. In most of these cases the United States obtained material concessions in return for a mere promise to retain the enumerated articles on the free list. The Wilson tariff practically destroyed the system of reciprocity by reimposing duties on sugar since reciprocity depended on the freedom of sugar, and after 1894 only the treaty with Hawaii remained in force.

The principle of reciprocity was reaffirmed in the Dingley Act of 1897, but along different lines and in weaker fashion, but the repeal of this act in 1909 again ended this experiment. A reciprocity agreement with Canada was passed in 1911, but was rejected by the Canadians. Certain bargaining powers were granted to the President by the Underwood Tariff Act of 1913, but President Wilson made no use of them. No further attempts were made during this period to negotiate reciprocal commercial treaties with other nations.

CHAPTER XXV

MONEY AND BANKING

Monetary problems. As our economy became more commercialized and industrialized, nearly everyone became a specialist of some kind. Except on the frontier and in a few other remote places the self-sufficient household disappeared. Specialists must trade and to facilitate trade a reliable money or medium of exchange is needed. Likewise specialized merchants and manufacturers need extra amounts of working capital from time to time to pay for raw materials, labor, fuel, or stocks of goods. To provide such capital is the proper function of commercial banks. In doing this the banks also contribute to the money supply. Indeed, bank notes and demand deposits (which may be spent by writing checks) were our chief money during much of the nineteenth century. Banks actually have provided most of our money, not the government.

The second half of the century saw great improvements in our monetary system and in our banking system. Banking standards were improved and bank notes were made trustworthy. Following the Civil War several major attempts to inflate the currency were narrowly averted, but the significant fact is that they were averted. The monetary experiences of the Civil War in both North and South demonstrated clearly that if money is issued in excess, prices will rise. People learned that if prices rose, creditors suffered and debtors gained. And they knew that prices would rise unevenly, which meant that the wage earner and salaried man would lose. As a consequence of this knowledge there was strong opposition to the inflationary movements of the period. On the other hand, farmers and debtors knew that they had much to gain from rising prices and that they were suffering from the falling prices which prevailed during the generation between 1865 and 1896. They therefore demanded that more money be put into circulation. The monetary history of this period is basically the story of the conflict of creditor and debtor classes, just as the monetary history of colonial times had been, only this time the creditors were in the East instead of in England.

Causes of inflation. Inflation, as the term is used here, is virtually synonymous with rising prices. Rising prices are usually caused by the overissuance of money. Money was issued for three basic reasons during this period. First was the desire on the part of Congress to lighten the burden of taxation. Sometimes the reasons advanced to defend such additional issues were absurd. For example, a long-forgotten senator from Wisconsin who favored the original issue of greenbacks at the outset of the Civil War said, "There is no probability that a currency based upon the resources of a great nation...will depreciate 50 per cent or even 5 per cent. No such paper ever did depreciate, and none such, I venture to predict, ever will." [1]

Second, more money was demanded and issued to stabilize a falling price level. We had a declining price level during most of the thirty years following the Civil War largely because the business needs of the nation were expanding more rapidly than the currency supply. A larger supply of money in circulation was needed to correct this situation. This is what the Greenbackers and the Free Silverites wanted, but it was not all that they wanted. They wanted prices not only to stop falling but to start rising.

Third, those who lacked capital have often mistakenly blamed their difficulties on a shortage of money and demanded that more be issued. This has generally been true of frontier sections from colonial times down through the nineteenth century. Always, the cry of "there is not enough money in circulation" has been hard to combat, since almost any individual would admit that he did not have enough money. Human wants being insatiable, there never will be enough to buy all the equipment and "necessities" everyone wants.

Obviously the motives for advocating more money have been mixed. Greenbackers and Free Silverites wanted not only

[1] Senator T. C. Howe, *Congressional Globe*, February 12, 1862, 763. Cited in E. W. Kemmerer, *Kemmerer on Money* (Philadelphia, 1934), 63.

to stop the downward spiral of prices which hurt them but also to ease the problem of acquiring capital.

Two movements to increase the money supply stand out in the two generations between the beginning of the Civil War and the beginning of World War I; one of them sought to increase the supply of paper money, notably greenbacks, and the other sought to make money plentiful by the unlimited coinage of silver. Both grew out of financial dislocations caused by the Civil War, and to understand them the financial conduct of the war must be examined first.

Financing the Civil War. The Civil War, or, as it is called in the South, the War Between the States, began with the firing on Fort Sumter, April 12, 1861. In the North it was generally believed that the war would be of short duration and consequently slight resort was had to taxation.[2] The government counted on borrowing most of the money needed. During the first year $8.52 was borrowed by the treasury for every $1.00 collected in taxes, and even after four years the ratio was not better than three to one. The final record showed $667 million collected in taxes as against $2621 million obtained through loans. At an early date more pressing needs for cash were felt than could be satisfied by loans and so $50 million was issued in demand treasury notes in denominations as low as $5.00. They were receivable for public dues and designed to circulate as money. It was these notes and the misfortunes of war that caused the suspension of specie payments on December 30, 1861. Subsequent needs for cash led, in February, 1862, to the issuance of $150 million worth of United States notes, $50 million being used to retire the demand treasury notes. The new notes were known some-

---

[2] The Confederacy was still more handicapped in raising revenue: taxation was unpopular, the population was sparse, the central government had little authority except in levying customs duties, which the northern blockade quickly rendered illusory, and other taxes levied were inadequate and slow in their yield. Loans were made at home and abroad, but there was only a limited market for the bonds of a rebel government and the returns from this source were insufficient.

Of metallic money there was only a small supply in the South, and specie payments were suspended there soon after the war began. With half the population and a third of the wealth of the North, the South put out $1,000,000,000 of fiat paper money or twice as much as the North issued. In addition, the separate Southern states issued their own notes, and even cities and counties, railroads, and finally private persons put in circulation notes or tickets which passed as money. The procedure was reminiscent of the financing of the Revolutionary War and the runaway inflation that eventually took place was likewise similar.

times as "greenbacks" because they were the first to be printed
with green ink, and at other times as "legal tenders" because
they were the first legal-tender notes put out since the adoption of the Constitution. A second issue of $150 million occurred in July, 1862, and a third of similar amount in March,

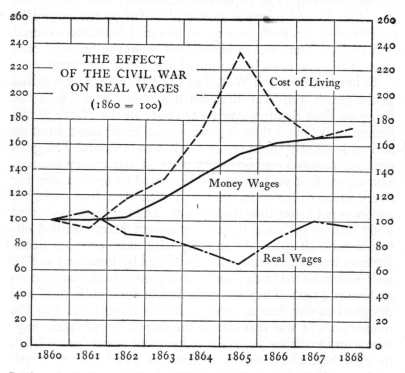

THE EFFECT
OF THE CIVIL WAR
ON REAL WAGES
(1860 = 100)

Cost of Living

Money Wages

Real Wages

Based on A. H. Hansen's "Factors Affecting the Trend of Real Wages," *American Economic Review* (March, 1925), XV, 32.

Real wages are obtained by dividing the cost of living into money wages: real wages
are thus 100 if cost of living and money wages remain identical. Wage earners are
losing ground only if real wages fall below 100.

1863, making a total of $450 million authorized, or approximately one-seventh of the cost of the war to the North.

The successive issues of greenbacks caused the circulation
per capita to rise about 71 per cent. With money more plentiful and circulating over a smaller nation and with consumers'
goods less plentiful because of wartime needs, it is not surprising that the general price level began rising. Grave in-

justice was done to some classes while others prospered undeservedly. Wage earners suffered because the cost of living rose more rapidly than wages. The graph on page 584 shows how real wages declined but does not relate personal episodes of family sacrifices in food, clothing, and many things formerly looked upon as necessities. Lowering one's standard of living is a painful process. The losers were chiefly persons whose salaries were on a contract basis and revised only at long intervals. A second injustice was the fact that debtors could pay their creditors in money that would purchase less than the dollars originally loaned—a farmer could repay his mortgage in 1864 through the sale of about half as much wheat, corn, or pork as would have been required in 1861 when, possibly, he borrowed the money. Persons with savings accounts or money invested in bonds saw the purchasing power of their savings dwindle as prices climbed. And third, some businessmen made exorbitant profits at the expense of their customers as prices rose far above original cost and kept rising so that profits were made on replacements, too. The liability of failing firms declined sharply from $178 million in 1861 to $8.6 million in 1864, which suggests that nearly everyone was making money. Professor W. C. Mitchell has estimated that the use of greenbacks increased the cost of the war to the government by $589 million, largely because the rise in prices caused a greater expenditure and hence a greater public debt burden than if metallic money had been used. In other words, even from the government's viewpoint the paper-money method was no saving in the long run.

   The Greenback movement. Various injustices produced by the greenback inflation, coupled with the desire of western farmer and debtor groups and certain labor elements for more money in circulation or more capital, as some thought, produced what was known as the Greenback movement after the war. Government bond issues specifically called for payment of interest in gold; some bonds promised that the principal would likewise be paid in gold. All of them had been sold with the general understanding that both payments would be in gold; indeed, there can be little doubt that this expectation furthered the sale of the bonds. The bonds had been bought with greenbacks and their retirement in gold after the war assured the holders of a handsome profit. Profits are the reward of those who take risks, but many were quick to point to the unpatriotic nature of profit made at the expense of one's government in distress and to urge that at least some of the bonds be retired with greenbacks. This was the "Ohio Idea," prominent in the presidential campaign of 1868 and voiced in the phrase, "The same currency for the bond holder and the plowholder." If adopted this would probably have put more greenbacks into circulation.

Secretary of the Treasury McCulloch had different ideas about the greenbacks. At the close of hostilities he said that the greenbacks "ought not to remain in force one day longer than shall be necessary to enable the people to prepare for a return to the constitutional currency." Congress supported this view and the currency was contracted with a view to an early resumption of specie payments. By February, 1868, the greenbacks in circulation had been reduced from the 1865 peak of $431 million to $356 million, and the price of a gold dollar in terms of greenbacks had fallen sharply. But so had other prices.

Vigorous opposition to further greenback retirements developed. Continuation, it was claimed, would hurt the debtor class, depress business, cause unemployment, and lessen government revenues. For nine years inflationists and deflationists argued with each other, but in the end specie payments were resumed January 1, 1879, and the circulation of greenbacks was fixed at $346 million—the amount outstanding on that day—where it has remained ever since. The good name of the American dollar was preserved.

Resumption with a smaller gold dollar, devalued to correspond to the higher price level, would probably have been a more sensible compromise but was not urged. Such an attempt would at least have helped eliminate some of the evils of deflation. As it was, the nation suffered first from inflation and then from deflation. No doubt some people gained in one and lost in the other, but there is little likelihood that their gains and losses balanced, and of course many gained in both or lost in both.

The Free Silver movement. The resumption of specie payments, the return of prosperity in the late seventies and the stigma of radicalism that attached to the Greenback party led to the decline of the Greenback movement. Meanwhile, another cheap money program was appearing and, since it involved the precious metal—silver—with which inflation was not associated, it gained wider support. The new rallying cry, "free coinage of silver at 16 to 1" needs explanation. The nation had been on a bimetallic standard from 1792 to 1861 (when specie payments were abandoned); that is, anyone was permitted to bring any amount of gold or silver to the mint to be coined into dollars. That was free coinage. Since 1834 the silver dollar, containing 371.25 grains of pure silver, weighed about 16 times as much as the gold dollar of 23.2 grains of pure gold. That was 16 to 1. The government's assumption that gold was 16 times as valuable as silver did not square with the facts, however; it underestimated the value of silver slightly so that people were discouraged from bringing silver to the mint to be coined, and this was particularly true after the gold rush of 1849 threw enormous quantities of gold on the market. In 1853 the government reduced the silver content of all silver coins except the dollar and withdrew the free coinage privilege of all but the dollar. Then in 1873 the privilege of free coinage of the silver dollar was also removed.

Charges subsequently were made that British and eastern seaboard capitalists had succeeded in a midnight plot to adopt the single gold standard and hurt the debtor interests. The law demonetizing the silver dollar consequently was called the "crime of '73." There is no reputable support for this belief; the evidence shows that the act was considered in five sessions of Congress, read repeatedly, debated at length, and was merely a recognition of the fact that the silver dollar had long been out of circulation. It was the fall in the price of silver, caused by abandonment of free coinage of silver in several nations, and more efficient methods of mining silver in this country, that led to the cry of anguish over the new law. Now it would have been worth while to bring silver to the mint to be coined, but it was no longer possible. Exactly how the silver miners gained the assistance of the western and southern farmers is not clear, but most certainly the depression and low prices in 1873 for wheat, cotton, and other farm produce, coupled with widespread resentment against eastern mortgage holders, railroad magnates, and others, made the conspiracy theory easy to believe. By 1877 "free silver" was a national issue. At this time 371.25 grains of pure silver, enough to become a dollar if free coinage existed, was worth about 90 cents.

In 1878 the House of Representatives passed a bill restoring bimetallism, but the Senate amended it to provide for the coinage of two to four million dollars of silver a month. This was the Bland-Allison Act, supported by the West and South and opposed by the Northeast. The law was a disappointment for most of the twelve years it was in operation, for a number of reasons. Successive Secretaries of the Treasury limited silver purchases to the minimum. The silver dollars did not circulate readily until the idea of substituting one-dollar certificates for each silver dollar was devised in 1886. The silver money did not raise the price level as had been hoped. Although the total circulation of money per capita rose from a postwar low of $15.32 in 1878 to $22.82 in 1890, the price level fell slightly. The industrial development of the country was proceeding during this period at an unprecedented rate and it would appear that the addition to our money supply in the form of silver did not even keep pace with our growing monetary needs. This was despite the fact that the larger currency supply was further supplemented by deposit currency circulating through the growing use of checks.

The silver advocates could never forget that the Bland-Allison Act was a compromise and that the supposed "crime of '73" remained to be righted. By 1890 they were strong enough to obtain more favorable action in Congress, although they were still unable to secure a free coinage act. Trading on their support of a tariff law, they obtained the passage of the Sherman Silver Act, which provided that the Secretary of the Treasury should buy 4,500,000 ounces of silver each month, an amount equal to the total output of the country at the time and about twice that required by the 1878 law. Payment was to be made in legal-tender treasury notes and the Secretary was directed to "redeem such notes in gold or silver coin, at his discretion." A reminder was added, however, that it was "the established policy of the United States to maintain the two metals on a parity with each other upon the present legal ratio, or such ratio as may be provided by law." This was generally interpreted to mean that the person asking for coin might make his choice, which would presumably be gold. The clause was soon to assume considerable importance.

Crisis and the endless chain. During the three years the new law was in operation $156 million of treasury notes was issued. Since business was stagnant most of the time, such expansion was not needed; in fact it was ill-timed, and caused considerable anxiety because upset conditions abroad and at home were causing an outflow of gold that depleted the treasury's gold reserve. This was supposed to be kept above a minimum of $100 million, and it was feared that redemption might have to be made in silver if the gold reserve continued to fall. Although this would have been quite legal, resort to the less valuable metal would have meant abandonment of the gold standard, a sharp fall in the value of the dollar, and perhaps even financial chaos. When panic broke out in 1893, President Cleveland announced that notes would be redeemed in gold as long as gold lasted and urged Congress to repeal the Sherman Silver Act of 1890. Congress complied with considerable reluctance and by a purely sectional vote. Silver advocates felt that this was silver's opportunity and that once again the cheaper metal had been unnecessarily sacrificed for the benefit of gold.

Repeal ended the threat of inflation but could not undo the harm that had already been done. Nor did it restore prosperity as some had prophesied it would. Public revenues dried up to such an extent that the treasury had to pay ordinary bills out of its gold reserve, and by January, 1894, that fund had fallen to $66 million. During the next two years four large loans totaling $262 million were arranged to replenish the reserve fund, which was continually wasting away because of the operation of a so-called "endless chain." Bonds were sold to obtain gold, but some of the purchasers presented notes for redemption in gold to buy the bonds. Not only that, but the government itself, hard pressed for funds, continued to pay out the notes to meet its expenses. These notes were again presented for redemption, the gold reserve was further diminished, a new loan had to be arranged, and so the chain continued. The successful but expensive help of the Morgan-Belmont syndicate, which agreed to secure gold abroad and take steps to prevent its outflow here, did much to slow down the chain. Returning prosperity finally ended the government deficits and created a need for the additional money supply.

The Free Silver campaign. The question of whether the Secretary of the Treasury should use a dubious authority to negotiate loans or should use his clear authority to redeem treasury notes in silver did much to keep the topic of free silver in the headlines. Furthermore, the depression and continued downward trend of prices stimulated the activities of the inflationary elements. The new Populist party, a union of various Farmers' Alliances and other groups, with a platform somewhat like the Granger movement's, had made a strong showing in the West in 1892 by championing free silver. It continued to grow and in 1896 nominated William Jennings Bryan, a pro-silver Democrat, for the Presidency. Bryan had already captured the Democratic nomination and the public eye by an oration in behalf of silver as a means of ending falling prices, which concluded with the lines, "You shall not press down upon the brow of labour this crown of thorns, you shall not crucify mankind upon a cross of gold." The Republican party, which had itself enacted the Sherman Silver Act in 1890, nominated William McKinley and demanded the gold standard.

Bryan wanted free coinage of silver at 16 to 1, although the market ratio had by now slipped to 30 to 1; in other words, the cost of enough silver to make a silver dollar was 52 cents. Republicans claimed that to install bimetallism at 16 to 1 under the circumstances would create financial chaos and cause prices to skyrocket. Some silverites replied that American adoption of bimetallism at this ratio would of itself create such a demand for silver that the world market ratio would return to 16 to 1. In campaign speeches Bryan frequently pointed to the fact that wheat was selling in the West at 50 cents a bushel and argued that by adopting free coinage of silver the price of wheat might easily be raised to $1.00. The argument made a strong appeal to the debtors and farmers of the West. But in the end Bryan was decisively defeated, although not without coercion, such as warnings by some employers on payday before the election that their men need not bother to return if Bryan won. Perhaps, too, the extraordinary rise in the price of wheat to almost $1.00 a bushel by early November without the aid of silver but because of a crop failure in India dampened some of the inflationary ardor.

Prices tend upward. The question of free coinage of silver did not again worry the American public until another generation had passed. The year 1896 was the low point in the downward sweep of prices after the Civil War. Wholesale prices rose a fifth by the next presidential election, and a half by 1914. Numerous explanations have been advanced for the change, but the most generally accepted is the increased gold supply resulting from important discoveries of gold and from the invention of the cyanide process of refining low-grade ores. This made possible a three-fold increase in demand deposits. Deprived of their chief grievance, the silver advocates were no longer able to maintain enthusiasm for their program and so finally abandoned it. The Gold Standard Act of 1900 legally and beyond any further doubt placed the country on a single gold standard and ordered the Secretary of the Treasury to set apart "a reserve fund of $150,000,000 in gold coin and bullion, which shall be used for such redemption purposes only." Moreover, the Secretary was to hold back notes presented for redemption until gold was exchanged for them again, and was also authorized to negotiate loans to maintain the reserve fund. Thus a repetition of the "endless chain" experience was rendered unlikely.

In conclusion, it should be admitted that the farmers and debtors of the West did suffer unduly for a generation from falling prices and that their program of silver purchases may have moderated the downward trend of prices. Yet at the same time it should be emphasized that the advocates of free silver contained silver mineowners and inflationists whose main interest was making it easier to pay their debts or to sell their silver or crops at a better price, a modest enough desire to be sure, but they had no plan of controlling inflation and probably even less inclination to do so. While it is not within the province of an historian to prophesy what might have been, it does seem likely that the silverites, if given a free hand, would have repeated with modifications some of the disastrous experiments already witnessed in pioneer sections of the country when the scarcity of capital was keenly felt.

Commercial banking. When extra capital is needed, it should be sought from banks rather than from the treasury. Commercial banks, however, should be cautious about the number of long-term loans they make. Walter Bagehot, long editor of the London *Economist,* once said that a commercial banker must first of all learn to distinguish between a mortgage and a promissory note, his business being concerned with the latter. Bankers have repeatedly ignored this distinction, often with disastrous consequences. Pre-Civil War banks frequently tied up their capital in land mortgages and railroad securities, which could not be liquidated on short notice without great loss, and then found themselves helpless when panics like those of 1837 and 1857 broke upon them. Their assets were "frozen." Bitter experience has taught that a bank should, if possible, keep its assets in a reasonably "liquid" form; that is, it should be able to convert them into cash quickly. One of the best types of loan from this viewpoint is the 30-, 60-, or 90-day loan to finance the purchasing of raw materials to be processed, or to pay for stocks of goods. In either case the sale of the goods will supply the funds for repayment. Such a loan is said to be self-liquidating.

In order to perform these services banks loan their own liquid capital, the money of depositors, and, most important, *they loan their credit.* Such credit has taken two principal forms: first, a bank note, which is nothing more than the bank's own demand promissory note, which is generally recognized by the public as money and hence acceptable where an individual's promissory note would not be. The other and more recent method a bank has of lending its credit is to create on its books a deposit to the borrower against which he may draw checks at will which the banks will honor immediately. Of course a bank had to keep some specie (roughly $\frac{1}{5}$ to $\frac{1}{3}$) available to pay persons who presented notes for redemption or wanted checks cashed, but experience showed that nowhere near complete backing in specie was needed, and if the rest was in short-term commercial paper or could be turned into cash shortly, the bank was safe enough.

National banking system. The period from 1833 to 1866 comprised the "dark decades" of American banking. Bank-note detectors published every week were needed to identify counterfeits and notes often circulated at a discount. Reliance on such bank currency in many parts of the country increased business risks and hence the cost of goods. As markets widened, the demand grew for a more dependable bank currency such as a few regions, like New England or Louisiana, enjoyed. Finally the Civil War supplied a second motive for reform. The federal government was making strenuous efforts to sell its bonds and saw in the popular state banking system known as "free banking" a way to improve the currency and sell bonds at the same time. One essential of free banking was that the bank should buy state bonds with some of its capital, exchange the bonds for bank notes obtainable from a state official, and then use the notes in its business. If the bank's loans were unwise and the bank failed, the state official was empowered to sell the bonds and use the proceeds to redeem the notes. The federal government adopted this idea and drew up in 1863 what was called the National Currency Act because it was expected to provide a stable, uniform, national currency. Later the name was changed to National Banking Act.

Many of the details of the early provisions of the National Banking Act are of little interest and so it will be described as of 1874. Banks were encouraged to secure their charters from the federal government, but those doing so had to meet certain requirements and insert the word "national" in the bank's title. The minimum capital permitted was $50,000 for national banks located in towns of under 6000 persons, and this requirement was graduated upward to a minimum of $200,000 in cities of over 50,000. Half of this had to be paid in immediately and the other half within six months. Stockholders stood liable to lose their investment and up to par value of their stock in addition in case of insolvency; in other words, liability was "double." All banks had to subscribe to at least $30,000 or as much as one-third of their capital, whichever was larger, in government bonds, but in return, as under the free banking system, they might obtain bank notes up to 90 per cent of the par value of the bonds. These notes could then be loaned to customers, thus assuring the banks double interest on this portion of their capital. Notes of all national banks were to be receivable at all other national banks at par. Loans on real estate and on the security of the bank's own stock were forbidden and no loans of over 10 per cent of the bank's capital might be made to a single borrower. The new system was obviously framed to eliminate many banking abuses, but it was such a strict and excellent law, especially with regard to note issues, that most state banks preferred not to join. The measure also failed in its immediate purpose of being a stimulant to bond sales.

The government, however, determined that it would succeed in its chief purpose of providing uniform currency. Consequently, Congress passed a law in 1865 placing an annual tax of 10 per cent on the notes of all state banks, beginning July 1, 1866. The number of national banks jumped from 139 in 1864 to 1582 in 1866 and the number of state banks dropped from 1089 to 297. An important corollary consequence was a speeding up of the trend away from making loans in the form of bank notes and toward making them in the form of deposits subject to check, a system already popular in some older and more settled areas. Because of the 10 per cent tax on notes this was the only way state banks could lend their credit; moreover, national bank reserve requirements against notes, particularly before 1874, were so strict in comparison to requirements against deposits, that national banks for this reason also regarded the latter method with favor. Once these advantages were fully realized the number of state banks increased rapidly. They enjoyed certain advantages from the bankers' viewpoint: they could be started and operated with less capital; they had more lenient deposit reserve requirements; they could lend on real estate, and they were less restricted in other respects. By 1895 there were a few more state banks than national banks, although their combined capital and surplus was only one-third as great as those of the national banks. Fortunately, state governments had begun to improve their banking laws by this time.

Defects of national banks. Although definitely superior to the haphazard system that had prevailed before the Civil War, the national banking system did have serious faults and it was not long before these became apparent.

(1) The notes were "inelastic"; that is, the number available for lending did not readily expand at times when business was more active and then contract when a dull period occurred. The notes were backed by government bonds, and if bond prices were high, banks were inclined to sell the bonds and would then have to retire the notes; and if bond prices were low, banks might invest in bonds and then have notes they were anxious to lend. Bond prices and the possibility of lending notes often had little relation to each other. Moreover, the steady retirement of the national debt, especially in the 1880's, cut the supply of bonds available to back bank notes and so reduced the circulation of bank notes.

(2) Since national banks could not lend on real estate, they were of little assistance to the agricultural classes, who had to go without national bank aid and secure high-priced assistance from state banks or private capitalists. Interest rates on loans from these sources were very high.

(3) Perhaps the most important defect was the decentralization of deposit reserves. The law provided for three classifications of banks according to the size of the city in which they were located. The "country" or small city banks might keep part of their deposit reserves in the middle-sized city or large city banks. And the middle-sized city banks might keep part of their deposit reserves in the large city banks. Since the large banks paid interest on these deposits, the result was that the lesser banks made the most of this opportunity and a large portion of their reserve funds gravitated to the cities, especially to New York City. In order to pay the interest the large banks had to lend the money themselves, and they preferred to make short and well-secured loans. An obvious solution appeared to be the "call money market": in this market stockbrokers sought money, which they would repay on demand and would protect with their customer's securities until the customer paid them or ordered resale. Often the broker's customer was speculating and hoped to sell again at a profit. In short, a considerable portion of the

nation's banking reserves was being used to finance stock speculation.

On several occasions the failure of some well-known business concern precipitated a serious panic: outlying banks demanded their reserves, New York banks demanded early payment from brokers, call money rates soared, speculation costs rose, stock prices dropped because many persons were offering shares and few were buying, and general panic spread over the land, leading to runs on banks. A bank might have enough money on hand to stop the run, or it might not, but one thing was fairly certain—help was hard to obtain. No other bank would easily part with its precious specie reserve, because it, too, might have to face a run. Under the circumstances good banks as well as poorly managed banks suspended payments or sometimes went under. Crises occurred in 1873, 1884, 1893, and 1907. Finally, after the panic of 1907 a National Monetary Commission was appointed to study foreign banking systems and propose an adequate central banking system for this country. A central bank is fundamentally a bankers' bank, a source of funds in time of need if the credit of the appealing bank is sound. The Federal Reserve System, with twelve regional central banks, established in 1914, was the solution to the problem. It will be described in a later chapter.

Investment banking. It is through investment banks that demands for long-term capital are satisfied if large amounts are involved. In order to start a new business the promoters often need more funds than they can provide themselves, and in order to expand the capacity of a successful enterprise additional amounts are frequently required beyond what the company has saved. During the period under review the process of investment banking was crystallized into three steps. First, the standing and prospects of the firm were carefully investigated. Second, if these were satisfactory, the investment bank bought the securities after arranging with a syndicate of other investment banks to guarantee their sale above a certain price. The third step was the actual marketing of the securities to investors. During the Civil War Jay Cooke, an energetic Philadelphia banker, became the nation's best-known investment banker because of his high-pressure salesmanship of government bonds. By hiring hundreds and thousands of agents, resorting to the house-to-house canvass, and appealing to the patriotic motive he helped the treasury sell $2000 million worth of bonds. After the war he directed his financial talents toward the building of the Northern Pacific Railroad, but his failure in this undertaking precipitated the panic of 1873.

Cooke's place was later taken by J. Pierpont Morgan, who rapidly made a reputation at home and abroad as a shrewd and sound investment banker by disposing of a huge block of New York Central stock for William Vanderbilt, by helping to reorganize several tottering railroad systems, and finally in 1901 by setting up the country's first billion-dollar corporation, the United States Steel Corporation.

Meanwhile, John D. Rockefeller was erecting a mammoth organization in the speculative petroleum business. From the outset he insisted on the accumulation of large cash reserves so as to be in a position to purchase opportunely and also to be independent of banker control. Pursuance of this policy eventually necessitated investment of a portion of these reserves, which was done largely through the National City Bank of New York headed by James Stillman. Known as the "Standard Oil Bank," this concern was a worthy rival of J. P. Morgan's house by the end of the century.

The marketing of securities to finance gigantic trusts led to further expansion of the investment-banking mechanism. The funds of leading insurance companies controlled by financial leaders were unwisely invested, and two panics of this period were largely caused by the speculations of the rich. Finally in 1911, Kansas passed the first law to regulate the selling of securities and a year later Congress itself called in Morgan and others to testify as to the existence of a "Money Trust." The conclusion was reached that existing banking and credit practices resulted in a "vast and growing concentration of control of money and credit in the hands of a comparatively few men." Although public opinion was shocked by some of the findings, little was done to remedy the situation.

The stock exchanges. Whereas the investment banks sell new securities, the stock exchanges are a market where subsequent sale of many of these securities may occur. Daily records of the transactions on the floors of the exchanges provide information on the current value of securities. Throughout the century trading in bonds was several times greater than that in stocks; and of the stocks, railroads were most numerous and active. As late as 1898 there were only twenty industrial issues officially "listed" on the New York Stock Exchange, although between 1885 and 1910 the Unlisted Department facilitated trading in new industrials still considered too speculative to be formally accredited. Other big cities had stock exchanges, but their volume of trading was small compared to New York's.

Business cycles. Closely associated with the widespread use of credit, banking, capital accumulation, and the money supply, especially since the industrial revolution, is the phenomenon known as the business cycle. Only in the last generation have economists devoted much attention to this subject and relatively little is still known about it. The business cycle should be distinguished from the occasional crises which have occurred for various reasons but without pattern from the dawn of history. The business cycle consists of four recurring phases of (1) prosperity, culminating in overexpansion and speculation, (2) panic and liquidation, (3) depression, and (4) recovery, taking place in that order, although sometimes one phase and sometimes another is the more pronounced. There appears to be no established length of the cycle, the four phases sometimes lasting a few months and at other times a decade or more, although it would appear that three years is most common and that the worst panics occurred at about twenty-year intervals during the nineteenth century. For example, serious economic collapses are associated with the years 1819, 1837, 1857, 1873, 1893, and 1907, with the Civil War intervening in mid-century to explain the time shift.

Explanations of the business cycle are legion and the student should be as much on his guard against the economic diagnostician who advances one simple interpretation for all economic illnesses, as he would be against the doctor who has one explanation for the sicknesses of all his patients. Nonetheless, two broad and widely accepted interpretations of the business cycle merit some attention. Leonard Ayres of the Cleveland Trust Company believed that wars are the originating cause of many depressions and pointed to the fact that every major war has been followed shortly by a minor depression and about a decade later by a major one. For example, after the Civil War there was a minor depression in 1866 and a major one in the years after 1873. Critics reply that if one waits long enough two depressions can be found after any war and they inquire as to the causes of subsequent depressions. Professor Wesley Mitchell believes that the business cycle is self-generating: that is, each phase of the cycle contains within itself the seeds of the next one. The excesses of prosperity bring about panic followed by liquidation and depression, and the opportunities to produce at extremely low cost offered by depression start a recovery which develops into prosperity. Critics say that this is more descriptive than explanatory and want to know the nature and cause of the excesses of prosperity and what resemblances they bear to one another.

Conclusion. Issuance of greenbacks during the Civil War led to price inflation with attendant evils. After the war prices fell more or less gradually for a generation. Debtors, farmers, and some early labor unions, resisting its effects as well as desiring cheap capital, inaugurated first the Greenback movement and then the Free Silver movement. Although considerable quantities of silver were issued, other influences, like the industrial growth of the country, kept prices from rising or even becoming stabilized. After the failure of the Bryan "free silver" campaign of 1896 prices turned upward and the cheap money movement died out.

Whereas long-term capital is provided by investment banks, commercial banks are supposed to supply short-term capital and did so to an increasing degree as the century advanced. Commercial banks also provided more and more of the nation's money in the form of bank notes and of demand deposits against which checks might be written. The National Banking Act established a banking system superior to the heterogeneous mass of state banks in existence before. However, it, too, developed faults, chief of which were an inelastic note issue and decentralization of reserves, the latter being a positive menace in times of panic. A central banking system was obviously needed. The strict rules governing national banks stimulated the use of checks and this in turn was a factor in reviving the small state banks.

Part IV—World Power
1914-1946

CHAPTER XXVI

MECHANIZED AGRICULTURE

Agriculture in transition. Agricultural history since 1914 presents a kaleidoscopic picture, showing unparalleled fluctuations of prosperity and depression, and of governmental intervention to establish more orderly production and marketing. Changes were also taking place in agricultural organization and techniques. Census statistics do not show the many phases of these movements, but they do present the broad outline of changes in the number of farms and in the amount of farmland, and they may therefore be given at this point.

	1910	1920	1930	1940	1945
Number of farms (1000).	6,362	6,448	6,289	6,097	6,011
Land in farms (100 acres)	878,798	955,884	986,771	1,060,507	1,142,818
Per cent of land in farms	46.2	50.2	51.8	55.6	59.8
Average acreage per farm	138.1	148.2	156.9	173.9	190.1
Per cent of population that was rural.............	54.3	48.8	43.8	43.5	—

The facts of immediate interest that are revealed by these figures were the addition of 87,000 new farms between 1910 and 1920 and the much greater decrease in each of the following decades. Thus, there was a loss of 159,000 farms between 1920 and 1930 and of 192,000 farms between 1930 and 1940. At the same time there was a constant increase in the amount of land in farms. This meant of course that the size of the average farm was growing larger; the small farms were being consolidated or annexed by the big ones. And finally there was a steady movement of population from the rural to the urban areas, arrested only temporarily during the depression of the 1930's when unemployment in the cities sent many families back to the farms. This is the general

picture; a more detailed analysis is necessary to explain the
reasons for the changes.

Effect of World War I: Expansion. The outbreak of
World War I in 1914, by diverting the labor and capital of
Europe from normal productive pursuits to war, created an
immediate demand for raw materials, foodstuffs, and war
munitions by the chief belligerent countries of the world.
The United States was in much the same position that it had
been in during the European war in 1793 and the years following, in that it was the only neutral nation capable of
supplying these needs. Its position differed only in that in
1914 it did not possess a merchant marine adequate to carry
its expanding exports. The export of cereals, meats, horses,
mules, and other agricultural products increased enormously,
and at the same time prices rose so that farmers' profits were
very large. The only important exception was cotton, in the
case of which the cessation of the German demand caused
a fall in prices and an accumulation of stocks. The entry of
the United States into the war in 1917 stimulated demand
still further, while the ensuing inflation raised prices to yet
higher levels. Under the impulse of these forces much marginal land hitherto unimproved or in pasture was brought
under cultivation, machinery was used on a larger scale, and
the output was greatly enlarged. This increase was shipped
abroad to our allies and for our own troops. The great exports
were made possible also by self-denial on the part of American consumers in the form of meatless and wheatless days
and the more economical use of such things as sugar, tobacco,
chocolate, and other articles which were needed for the
soldiers.

Even after the Armistice, on November 11, 1918, the
European demand for American foodstuffs and raw materials
continued, that for cotton now being revived. Between 1914
and 1920 the exports of meat rose from $143,000,000 to
$353,000,000, those of wheat from $88,000,000 to $298,-
000,000 and those of cotton from $537,000,000 to $768,-
000,000. These supplies were necessary to start the mills
and factories and to feed the war-stricken peoples until they
could resume their normal peacetime activities. They were
sold, moreover, at record prices, partly because of scarcity and

more largely because of inflation, and brought in greatly increased incomes to farmers and planters. The situation was very much like that which prevailed in this country during the period of high prices before the end of the Napoleonic wars. Under the impetus of all these forces the American farmer, assuming that the foreign demand at high prices was permanent, still further expanded his operations and speculated wildly in farm land. In Illinois and Iowa land sold for $500 an acre and more. Much of the capital invested in land and farm machinery was borrowed and as a result 150,000 farmers placed mortgages on their farms between 1910 and 1920.

Agricultural depression. By 1920 conditions in Europe were more normal and the emergency imports from the United States fell off. With this decline the inflated prices of agricultural products fell precipitately to the prewar level. Between December, 1919, and December, 1920, wheat dropped from $2.15 a bushel to $1.44, corn from $1.25 to 68 cents, and cotton from 36 cents a pound to 14 cents. The farmers who had purchased land at high prices and even those owners who had held their land but mortgaged it suffered greatly, for prices of other products did not decrease as rapidly, and they were at a disadvantage both as debtors and as consumers. Production in the United States was not easily curtailed, however, and the American farmers were faced again with the problem which had created such profound discontent fifty years previously. This was the production of more goods than could be sold at prices sufficient to cover costs. But prices were falling, while costs remained high, in so far as they rested on interest and amortization charges on land bought or mortgaged before the war. Production, moreover, had been greatly stimulated by an abnormal foreign demand, by high prices, by government encouragement,[1] by farm mechanization, and by improvements in agriculture itself.

Demand, on the other hand, was lessened by several changes. In the first place, as was just pointed out, foreign demand fell off greatly. But so did domestic demand. The

---

[1] In 1917 the government practically guaranteed the farmers $2.20 a bushel for wheat, and $2.00 in 1918. In addition, some two million war gardens were planted, over a million acres in city lots being put under cultivation.

great decrease in the number of horses and mules as a result of the use of tractor-drawn farm machinery caused a decline in the consumption of feed crops. It has been estimated that the elimination of 8,000,000 horses and mules released approximately 25,000,000 acres from producing feed and added that much to land available for other crops. These other crops were not needed, however, for human consumption of certain foods fell off at the same time. Owing to more sedentary occupations, warmer buildings, and the spread of much advice as to dietetics, the consumption of cereals, meat, animal fats, and other staple articles declined, their place being taken by vitamin-rich vegetables, fruits, and dairy products, which need for their production much less land than meat requires. This situation was rendered even worse by ill-advised reclamation projects which brought into use additional land, without regard to established agriculture.

Production was very difficult to adjust to changing conditions. The process of production may spread over months, as in the case of most crops, or years, as in the case of orchard fruits and nuts and livestock. Increasing specialization and the use of particular machines limited the possibility of shifting from one line to another, while the inertia or ignorance of the farmers disinclined them to venture on unknown paths. Meanwhile, increased yields were constantly resulting from such biological and technological advances as better seed selection, the introduction of more productive varieties of disease-resistant varieties, of improvements in plant and animal breeding, and better systems of fertilization and spraying. The resulting disequilibrium might have been remedied by reduced production, but this was practically impossible under the individualistic system of American farming. A decade of suffering and experimentation was necessary before this last drastic remedy was resorted to in 1933.

The depression of 1920–1921 affected primarily the farmers, for industry and commerce recovered quickly, and between 1922 and 1929 the country experienced a boom. With the growth of prosperity the increased purchasing power of the people swelled the demand for manufactures and for services rather than for agricultural products, which are relatively non-elastic. Hence the farmers' sales failed to keep pace with those of other lines. It is a well-known economic law that as income increases, relatively less is spent on the primary wants. Thus food and clothing (both ultimately agricultural products) fell from 59 per cent of total production in 1914, to 44 per cent in 1929. It was difficult if not impossible for agriculture to adjust itself to such rapidly changing conditions.

Search for new uses. But if production could not be reduced, and the old channels of demand were closed, perhaps consumption could be increased by finding other uses for agricultural products. Accordingly, new markets, closer home, now began to be sought through industrial uses for agricultural products and through the utilization of agricultural by-products. This is a movement which had been carried far in the slaughtering and meat-packing industry, but the development of chemistry in the United States since World War I opened up new possibilities to agriculture in other fields.

Corn is already the raw material for several flourishing industries such as starch, alcohol, and others, but the manufacture of glucose or corn sugar from corn, of wallboard and paper from cornstalks, and of furfural from corncobs has just begun. Cereal grains furnish starch for sizing and finishing textiles and paper, dextrine adhesive, glucose used in the rayon and leather industries, and a whole series of industrial chemicals and solvents. Although 90 per cent of the soybean crop is used for human or animal consumption, an increasing proportion is utilized for adhesives, plastics, paint and varnish. From animal carcasses the processing industries obtain leather, glue and gelatin, soap, greases, glycerin, and fertilizers. Many valuable products are now being made from skim milk which was formerly fed to hogs or thrown away. Thus casein is extracted and used in the preparation of wallpaper, paints, and glue; under the name of karolith it is used in the manufacture of combs, brushes, buttons, etc. Flax straw is used in making carpets. About 40 per cent of the cotton consumed in the United States finds industrial outlets other than clothing, such as cordage, auto tires, explosives, bags, paper, packing and stuffing, and artificial leather. Cottonseed oil, obtained from the seeds, is used in making salad oils, oleomargarine, lard, and soap; the meal is used as a fertilizer or fed to the stock; and the hulls and stalks are used for the same purpose or in the manufacture of paper.

This new chemurgy has attracted federal support and four regional research laboratories have been established in different areas. Each devotes itself to the increased utilization of the agricultural products native to its region. Thus the laboratory at Peoria, Illinois, is studying the possible uses of corn, wheat, and soybeans, and such agricultural residues as cornstalks, corncobs, and straw. But in spite of this impressive list of achievements in the industrial use of agricultural products, the outlook for a solution to the farmers' ills along this line is none too favorable. Some markets are expanding, but others are shrinking. On the whole, non-farm products are preferred as raw materials because of variations in the quality of farm products and of their fluctuating prices. But more important than chemurgy which has increased demand, has been the impact of technology, which has cut costs.

Mechanization of agriculture. The improvement of agricultural machinery has passed through three stages in the United States. In the first period, between about 1830 and 1860, great changes were made in the character and efficiency of farm implements, but the motive power was still pretty much human muscles. The second wave of mechanical advance was the general adoption of horse-drawn machines between 1860 and 1914. The third stage is the mechanization of the farm by the use of power machinery; it is the application of engineering to agriculture. This involves a change in point of view and in farm organization and management, as well as the stepping up of the farmers' productive efficiency.

Steam traction engines were employed to draw agricultural machinery at the beginning of the twentieth century, but they were not very successful, and by reason of their weight tended to pack the soil. The use of the gasoline tractor began about 1905, but for a number of years spread slowly. As first developed the gasoline tractor was a large heavy-duty machine, but this was not very successful and was followed by the development of the caterpillar type, and finally by the light general-purpose tractor. In 1945 there were over 2,000,000 tractors on American farms.

The gasoline tractor has effected a revolution in agriculture comparable with that made by the steel plow and the reaper a hundred years earlier. It has made possible the use of more and bigger machines in preparing the land, and in cultivating and harvesting the crops. By its adaptability, economy, and effectiveness it has already forced changes in farm organization and management, which go farther than merely the substitution of machines for horses. Next to the tractor the most important machine is the combine or harvester-thresher. This is tractor-drawn to the field; there, in a single operation, the grain or other crop is cut, carried by means of a conveyor, threshed, and elevated to a bin on top of the machine. Today 50 per cent of the wheat acreage is harvested by combines, compared with 5 per cent in 1920. Other tractor-drawn machines are corn planters, pickers, plows, the rotary hoe, and many other specialized types of machines.

Economic results of farm mechanization. The consequences of this farm mechanization are numerous. It permits a more perfect execution of many operations. Thus, "Efficient tillage machinery accomplishes more effective cultivation, resulting in a larger product per acre. Shredders and silage cutters have made possible more efficient utilization of feeds. Mechanical sprayers and dusters are more effective than hand implements in applying safeguards against insect and disease devastation. Pasteurizers and fruit sorters make possible products of higher quality." [2]

The use of power machinery has eliminated millions of horses and mules, which formerly furnished the power. In 1920 the number of horses and mules on the farms of this country was 25,000,000; this was practically the maximum. By 1945 there were 8,900,000, the lowest figure since 1874. This means a saving in the amount of land and labor formerly required to grow forage for these animals, which ate whether they were at work or not. It is estimated that this has released 40,000,000 acres for other uses.

[2] *Encyclopedia of the Social Sciences, s.v.* Agricultural machinery, I, 552.

Farm mechanization has greatly increased the productivity of agricultural labor. It has cut production costs from one-third to two-thirds of the horse-farming costs, and has trebled the acreage which can be cultivated per man. Unit costs of production have been greatly reduced, largely as a result of the lessened labor requirements. On the great plains of the United States a unit of land and a unit of machinery, consisting of tractor, combine harvester-thresher, tractor drill, tractor tillage implements, and truck, produce wheat at new low levels of cost. "In Nebraska it cost 38¢ per bushel to produce wheat in Perkins County in the western part of the state with improved machinery as compared with 86¢ per bushel as an average for four eastern counties under the older methods.... In Montana the combine reduced production costs by about 15 or 20 cents per bushel." [3]

There is the same variation in per-acre costs between hand tools and mechanical equipment in raising cotton, as reported by the Mississippi Experiment Station:

1-mule ½-row equipment...............	$14.20
2-mule 1-row equipment...............	10.78
Tractor 2-row equipment..............	6.78
Tractor 4-row equipment..............	5.20

The mechanization of the farm has had notable effects on the organization of agriculture itself. There has been a geographic shift toward lands of relatively level topography and low rainfall, such as the western part of the United States. But the same movement has brought the cheap lands of Canada, Australia, and the Argentine into competition with our farms. This shift has affected disadvantageously the more humid and more rugged lands in other sections of our country, as in New England, and some of this is either going out of cultivation or is finding new uses.

The size of the profitable farm has been greatly enlarged. The census statistics report an increase in the average farm from 138 acres in 1910 to 190 acres in 1945, but these include the small cotton patches of the South. In the grain belt of the west north central states, where the new machinery is principally used, the average size was 258 acres in

[3] E. G. Nourse, in *Recent Economic Changes* (New York, 1929), II, 563, 566, 568.

1940. Competent observers are advocating a 640-acre farm in the corn belt as a family farm, and for maximum efficiency the farmer should operate 1000 or even 2500 acres. To obtain the greatest economies a combine outfit must be worked to nearly its maximum capacity, which would require about 1000 acres for a medium-sized machine. This puts a premium on large-scale farming. But with increasing mechanization the farmer has been compelled to invest more heavily in fixed plant and has perforce become a businessman as well as a producer; he must watch prices as well as output. This has made his economic position more precarious.

Social consequences of mechanization. Several momentous social consequences followed from this mechanization. In the first place, since not so much man power was needed on the farms, a great deal of labor was set free for other pursuits, and this sought employment in the developing manufactures. There was therefore a steady movement of population from the country to the city, resulting in a redistribution of the population and a readjustment of social organization and of living conditions. The proportion of the population living in towns of 8000 inhabitants or over grew from 7 per cent in 1830 to over 56 per cent in 1940. Some persons have viewed this movement with alarm and have cited several causes to explain it, such as the abandonment of farms, the smaller size of rural families, and the barrenness of rural social life.

The real explanation must be found in the greater productiveness of farm machinery and the setting free of labor formerly needed to raise our food supplies. In 1787, according to the National Resources Committee, the labor of 95 per cent of the population was required to raise the food and agricultural raw materials for the nation; today less than one-fourth is needed. The labor thus set free naturally gravitates to the cities where it is applied in industrial and commercial occupations to the production of other commodities. It is estimated that machine-farming improvements released over 30,000,000 workers from agriculture between 1850 and 1940. This must be regarded as a real economic gain, from a national standpoint. The shifts in occupations that have resulted are shown in the following chart.

Some of the changes have, however, resulted in hardships. Mechanization enabled a single man to operate a larger area, and there was therefore a tendency for the successful farmers to buy out their less efficient neighbors and increase the size of their farms. The dispossessed operators usually resorted to cheaper and therefore poorer land, from which

SHIFTS IN OCCUPATIONS, 1870-1930

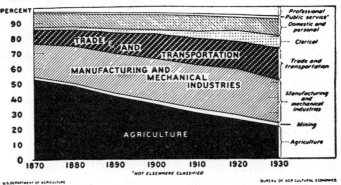

The decrease in the proportion of the population engaged in agriculture, made possible by the advances in technique, particularly the increase in power used per worker, resulted in a great cityward migration of young people from the farms, which was notably heavy from 1870 until 1930. Until about 1920 these rural youth as well as urban youth found increasing employment in manufacturing, mining, trade, and transportation, clerical work, and the various personal and professional services. But soon after 1920 a decline started also in the proportion of the population engaged in mining and in manufacturing and mechanical pursuits. As a consequence, trade and clerical work and the various services absorbed many of the young people no longer needed in the basic productive industries. Between 1880 and 1930 the proportion of the population engaged in trade doubled, while the proportion engaged in clerical work doubled between 1910 and 1930. The graph is adapted from a diagram by R. G. Hurlin and M. B. Givens, *Recent Social Trends in the United States* (New York, 1933), 284.

the former owners or tenants were in turn displaced. A vast migration was thus set in motion, with attendant loss and human suffering. The last, and least capable, in this succession of migratory farm operators were unable to obtain land on any terms and became wandering agricultural laborers—the "Okies" of novel and film. These high-cost—because inefficient—producers could probably be kept in operation by subsidies, but if a choice has to be made between low costs and subsidies the former is certainly to be preferred.

Depression of 1930 and after. The movement toward mechanization and large-scale farming ran into difficulties during the depression which began in 1930. The cumulative efforts of power machinery and improved methods resulted in keeping up agricultural surpluses, in spite of exhortations to the farmers to curtail production. But this was something which the individual farmer could not do; to be effective it must be of national scope. On the side of demand the conditions grew progressively worse, especially as regarded foreign trade. The exports of some of the leading agricultural products are shown in the following table:

AVERAGE ANNUAL EXPORTS OF AGRICULTURAL PRODUCTS (*In millions of dollars*)						
Products	1910-1914	1915-1919	1921-1925	1926-1930	1932	1940
Meats	67.3	360.2	139.8	78.0	18.9	21.7
Animal fats and oils ...	76.7	133.5	138.5	109.2	37.9	13.1
Bread grains..	147.3	460.4	474.3	318.6	51.7	76.4
Fruits	28.0	41.8	81.4	119.3	77.3	34.4
Tobacco	44.8	83.4	164.6	144.5	65.9	44.0
Cotton	551.9	669.8	805.0	765.7	345.1	213.4

Statistical Abstract of the U. S., 1930, 510-20; 1931, 528-38; 1936, 466-77; 1941, 557-67.

It is evident from this table that, while there had been a great decline in agricultural exports in the period 1926–1930 as compared with the previous half decade, by 1932 there was a complete breakdown, the exports falling below even the prewar level; by 1940 the situation was still worse, but the demands of war soon changed the picture.

Domestic demand is difficult to determine accurately, but a few items may be mentioned. The domestic consumption of raw cotton by mills fell from 7,091,000 bales in 1929 to 4,866,000 bales in 1932; that of tobacco from 796,626,000 pounds to 674,896,000 pounds for the same dates; that of federally inspected meat from 11,184 million pounds to 10,659 million pounds. The explanation of this decline is to be found in the general depression which had overtaken the country and which now affected city wage earners even more disastrously than the rural population and greatly curtailed general purchasing power. Indeed, after 1930 no distinction can be made between rural and urban distress, for all areas were affected.

As factories began to close and unemployment to increase there began a reverse movement of the population from the city to the country. Professor Hibbard estimated that between 1930 and 1934 probably 3,000,000 people "have gone back, not exactly to the land, but to the beds and boards of their relatives and friends." [4] The migration from the farm to the city was, however, resumed after 1934, at the rate of about 300,000 annually.

Tenancy. The tendency toward an increase of tenancy, which had already been noted, continued unabated in the two and one-half decades 1910–35, the proportion of farms operated by tenants rising from 37 per cent of all farms in 1910 to 42 per cent in 1935; it fell back to 39 per cent in 1945. During World War I there was a slackening in the rate of increase in tenant farming, owing on the one hand to high prices obtained for farm products and the consequent profits accruing from operation by the owner, and on the other hand to the withdrawal of labor from agriculture into industry and into the army. The next decade, however, saw a strong movement in this direction. It is difficult to generalize for the United States as a whole, for conditions differ so in different sections. The greatest increase occurred in the South and in the west north central division. Tenancy in the South, where practically three-fifths of the tenant farms were situated, was intimately connected with the labor problem of that section. As has already been pointed out, it was found impossible after the Civil War to re-establish the plantation system with Negro labor; hence, the freedmen were set up as tenants on small tracts of land and furnished with the necessary capital. This system has maintained itself to the present as well suited to existing conditions. In the Northwest, on the other hand, the increase in tenancy must be ascribed to the fact that this section most nearly reproduced pioneer conditions and tenancy was regarded as a stepping-stone to ownership. In other regions there was little increase

---

[4] B. H. Hibbard, "A Long Range View of National Agricultural Policy," in *Journal of Farm Economics* (January, 1934), XVI, 15.

and even in some cases a decrease. Many factors contributed to this situation, of which a few may be mentioned.

The rise in the price of land, the larger-sized unit that could profitably be operated by one family, and the cost of the equipment in those parts of the country where agricultural machinery was largely used—notably in the Northwest—all required a larger capital investment on the part of the owner. Thus the average value of a farm in the United States rose from $2896 in 1900 to $8400 in 1940, almost trebling. This made it more difficult for a young man to climb the agricultural ladder and become an owner. Moreover, it was not at all certain that it would be profitable for a young man to buy a farm and borrow the money by placing a mortgage on it. The low rents as compared with the high rates of interest seemed to make it advisable for such a person to invest his capital in stock and equipment and become a tenant rather than sink his capital in the land. One of the motives that had previously led farmers in the United States to invest in land was the likelihood that it would increase in value. Under existing conditions the future course of farm land prices was very uncertain and this factor no longer had much weight. Many tenants moved "up the ladder" by expanding their operations on rented land, while remaining tenants. Finally, there seems to have been a change in attitude on the part of the farmers themselves. Instead of saving to buy land, they now preferred to raise their standards of living and to spend their incomes on immediate consumption goods, such as automobiles, radios, washing machines, and forms of entertainment.

Tenancy is found in greatest degree in the rich agricultural districts where the price of land is highest and where consequently it is difficult for a young man to purchase land of his own. It seems best suited to cash crops where only a small investment of capital is required, such as cotton, tobacco, and vegetables; but where the investment is larger and a longer time elapses between seedtime and harvest, as in the case of fruit, livestock, and dairy products, tenancy is less usual. Tenancy is found also to have resulted in those sections where specialization in cereal or cotton production has proceeded farthest: that is, where a standardized routine agriculture is practiced; on the other hand, where diversified farming is carried on, ownership is more general. Owners tend to be more progressive while tenants follow the beaten track.

The general attitude in this country toward the increase in tenancy is one of dislike or dismay. But there is usually not a simple choice between tenancy and ownership; the alternative is more likely to be either renting out the land to tenants or a larger investment in fixed capital and perhaps a mortgage on the farm by the owner. In periods of depression the position of the tenant is often superior to that of the owner, who must meet fixed charges whatever the price may be that he obtains for his produce. Since it is clear that tenancy is a stubborn fact in our agricultural economy, suggestions have been made for lengthening the lease contract, which usually runs for a year, and thus giving the tenant a greater interest in good farming and soil conservation. Congress, on the other hand, has tried by legislation to convert tenants into owners. The Bankhead-Jones Farm Tenant Act of 1937 authorized loans to farm tenants, farm laborers, share croppers, and other persons who obtained a major portion of their income from farming, in order that they might purchase farms. Very few of the persons enumerated took advantage of the act. Whether tenancy is to persist as a permanent phenomenon will probably depend upon the character of agriculture which the future may develop in the United States.

Regional specialization. It seems scarcely necessary to trace again in detail the regional specialization of agriculture, as World War I introduced few important changes and the subsequent years simply confirmed tendencies already in operation. If a line be drawn from about Washington, D. C., to the southeast corner of South Dakota, it will be found that most of the area to the northeast of this line is devoting itself to the production of rather perishable commodities, which cannot stand distant transport; such are milk, fresh vegetables, potatoes, and fruit, serving the great urban industrial population of this region. Directly southwest of this line is the corn and meat belt, which produces primarily for the domestic market but which disposes of about 15 per cent of its pork products on the foreign market. Northwest of this area is the wheat belt, which is still more dependent on the export market, and still farther west is the cattle-raising country. South of all these areas lies the cotton belt, about half of whose products are exported. The failure of the foreign market in recent years is the most important reason for the centering of agricultural discontent in these regions. (See map on page 453.) The only section whose farm economy has been disturbed by recent changes is the South, and this calls for a more detailed explanation.

The dominance of cotton in the agriculture of the South has been a striking feature for a century, but this was profoundly affected by the depredations of the boll weevil, and has undergone a veritable revolution in the past fifty years. The beetle migrated from Mexico into Texas in 1892, and since that time has spread over practically the entire cotton-growing area of the United States. The destructiveness of the boll weevil and the cost and difficulty of combating it forced the southern farmer in the infested regions to give up or reduce the planting of cotton and to diversify his crops. This was so beneficial that the effects of the boll weevil cannot be said to have been altogether bad; indeed, the town of Enterprise, Alabama, erected a monument to the boll weevil because it compelled the abandonment of the one-crop system. Production of food for home consumption has greatly increased, and the "cow, hog, and hen" program, urged by the state experiment stations, is being more generally adopted. Cotton has moved steadily westward until today Texas, Arkansas, and Oklahoma produce nearly two-fifths of the entire crop.

A definite limit has always been placed upon the production of cotton by the necessity of picking it by hand; in other words, a man can plant and cultivate more cotton than he can pick. Efforts have long been directed to the invention of a cotton picker, over 800 patents having been granted for such a machine. But finally John R. and Mack D. Rust, Texas cotton planters, seem to have developed a practical one, which picks as much cotton in an hour as a good worker does in one week, namely, three bales. If generally introduced this will mean more efficient harvesting, but it will effect a revolution in Southern agriculture as momentous as that which followed the introduction of the cotton gin. "The whole social, political, and economic structure... still rests upon a tripod, whose three legs are the Negro, the mule, and the plow."[5] If this is overturned the consequences are apt to be revolutionary.

Because of the specialization in products among the different regions, agriculture has necessarily been commercial rather than self-contained, and has been based upon interdependence and exchange. When this process of interchange is interrupted, as it was by the depression of 1930 and subsequent years, then all branches suffer. The difficulties under which the farmer was laboring were greatly increased by this disaster, and in an attempt to help him solve some of his problems Congress turned first to his financial troubles.

Farm relief: easy credit. The earliest steps taken by the federal government in granting relief to the farmer were those providing for easier credit. Agriculture had become a capitalistic enterprise and called for a larger investment than the average farmer could command; he was therefore forced to borrow the necessary capital and to rely increasingly on banks and other lenders. The farmer borrowed money for various purposes. Because of the slow turnover of agricultural products, varying from about six months in the case of crops to perhaps three years in the case of cattle, he frequently needed to borrow on short time to finance his operations until he could sell his products. The national banks were forbidden to loan on real estate, so he obtained accommodation from state banks, local merchants, or private lenders. To buy farm machinery and equip his farm he often found it necessary to borrow for somewhat longer terms, and for this purpose he obtained funds from the sources just named or from agents of farm machinery companies. For long-term loans, to pay for his land, he turned to mortgage companies or eastern investors. But the farmer complained that he was ill served by all these agencies. The cost of the short-term credit was unduly high, amounting to 15 or 20 per cent, and for the longer period the average

[5] William H. Clark, *Our Farms and Farmers. The Story of American Agriculture* (Boston, 1945), 274.

mortgage, running for only five years and loaded with heavy charges, was equally unsatisfactory.

It was evident that the banking and credit system of the country had conspicuously failed to meet the financial needs of agriculture. Some efforts were made to liberalize bank credit after the establishment of the Federal Reserve System, but these were inadequate, and the farmers' demand for assistance became insistent after the agricultural depression of 1921 and even more so after 1929. The difficult financial situation of many farmers called for remedial measures, which the new administration was prompt to give. The government proceeded to grant greatly increased agricultural credit, and at the same time to provide an effective comprehensive system.

Following the pattern of the Federal Reserve System, the government in 1916 set up a separate system of Federal Land Banks to provide for financing farm mortgages. The Federal Reserve Banks could make certain short-time loans to farmers, and these new banks could extend long-time credit. The gap between these was filled in 1923 by the establishment of twelve Intermediate Credit Banks which cared for medium-term loans of six months to three years. These and other banks and credit institutions, which had been created under earlier legislations, were now brought together under the Farm Credit Administration, which was created for the purpose of providing agriculture with a complete and co-ordinated system of credit. It made available to farmers long-term mortgage loans and short-term credit and also provided intermediate credit facilities for farmers' co-operative purchasing, marketing, and business service organizations. During the seven years ending in June, 1940, it made loans amounting to $6300 million, of which $3100 million was still outstanding at the latter date. Although the government was now furnishing farmers with the cheapest and most convenient credit they had ever enjoyed, this was not considered enough and agrarian pressure forced the steady lowering of interest rates until in 1935 they were fixed at 3.5 per cent. Credit was now being furnished the farmers at less than cost, and by 1940 interest subsidies amounted to nearly $170,000,000.

Mortgage troubles. The period of falling prices for agricultural products which followed the collapse of 1920, and especially the period of deflation after the panic of 1929, made heavier the burden of indebtedness resting upon the farmers. Since they received less for their produce, they were compelled to give more wheat or cotton or other things to meet a fixed sum in interest or principal.[6] Moreover, the number of farms mortgaged and the amount of debt both increased between 1910 and 1930. Although the number of owned farms fell off between these two dates by 380,000, the number of mortgaged farms grew by 186,000, the proportion increasing from 33 to 42 per cent. It was estimated in 1930 that the total farm mortgage debt was then about $9600 million. Nor was this situation helped by the easy credit policy adopted in 1916, for by this the farmers were encouraged to borrow more. The pressure of these debts, the failure of the various relief plans to achieve satisfactory results, and the growing number of foreclosures of mortgaged farm property all brought the farmers to a rebellious frame of mind.

A striking manifestation of this discontent was the nullifying of foreclosure sales by groups of farmers in many parts of the Middle West by intimidating serious buyers at a sheriff's sale, bidding in the property for one cent, and then turning it back free of encumbrance to the debtor. Another example was furnished by the "farmers' holiday" movement, which placed an embargo on the sale of agricultural products at the prevailing low prices and sought to enforce it by dumping the contents of milk trucks into the ditches and preventing the shipment of produce into the cities.

Such a situation called for action, and in 1933 the Farm Mortgage Foreclosure Act was passed, which was designed to facilitate the repurchase of foreclosed farm property, the provisions of which were made still more favorable to debtor farmers by the Frazier-Lemke Mortgage Moratorium Act of 1934 for farm bankrupts. The purpose of this measure was to grant extension of time to distressed farmers for payment of their existing debts and mortgages and to permit them to retain possession of their property, under the control

[6] See charts on p. 757.

of the courts, during the period of readjustment. Although this was declared unconstitutional by the Supreme Court in 1935, it was quickly replaced by another act of similar intent, but which avoided the Court's strictures. Under these circumstances there was little inducement for private lenders to operate in this field. By 1941 over 40 per cent of all farm mortgages were held by government agencies, and it was predicted that ultimately the government would be the sole lender. The mortgage debt had, however, been reduced to $6,586 million, and the proportion of farms mortgaged had fallen to 39 per cent of all.

Price stabilization. The cheaper credit provided by these acts proved not to be the remedy needed to lift the farmer out of his depression. Indeed, by making it easier to borrow at a time when prices were falling, they tended to increase the load of mortgage and other indebtedness. What the farmers really wished was higher prices for their products. Two different plans were proposed to achieve this result, the first of which was contained in the McNary-Haugen bill, and the second in the Farm Board Act of 1929, but both were based on the principle of stabilizing prices at a high level by more effective marketing.

The McNary-Haugen plan provided for the organization of a gigantic corporation, to be backed financially by the federal government, which should purchase the leading agricultural products of the farmers at prices profitable to them and dump abroad the surplus at the best prices possible, distributing the loss from such transactions among those farmers benefited, by means of an equalization fee. This plan was incorporated in the McNary-Haugen bill, which was twice passed by Congress, in 1927 and 1929, but was vetoed each time, first by President Coolidge and second by President Hoover.

Failing to provide the desired relief by this method, Congress by the Agricultural Marketing Act of 1929 established a Federal Farm Board to stabilize prices. A revolving fund of $500,000,000 was allotted it, half from the federal treasury. The Board was given power to buy and store surpluses and to set up stabilization corporations. In pursuance of this purpose it created marketing agencies and entered into contracts with existing associations that dealt in agricultural products. In an effort to check falling prices a Grain Stabilization Corporation was organized which in three years acquired over 900,000,000 bushels of wheat. A Cotton Stabilization Corporation bought 1,300,000 bales of cotton in the same futile effort. In spite of the accumulation of these huge surpluses, the Board was unable to exercise any effective control over prices, which continued to slump to lower levels. Finally, in 1933, the reserves of wheat were handed over to the Red Cross and other relief agencies for distribution among the needy and the affairs of the Farm Board were wound up. The experiment had cost the government $360,000,000.

Reducing the surplus. Neither of the two methods of relief by easy credit or by price stabilization having improved the condition of the farmers, a third method was put into operation in 1933, as part of the so-called "New Deal" program. The theory underlying this legislation was that overproduction was the real cause of the agricultural depression. Since overproduction is producing more than can be sold at a price that will cover cost, it can be cured in either of two ways. One is to raise prices and the other is to cut costs. The administration preferred the first of these methods. In order to raise prices production had to be curtailed. The administration believed that the farmers might be persuaded to do this if it was made profitable for them. Accordingly, the Emergency Farm Relief Act of May 12, 1933, put into effect a domestic allotment plan of control for seven "basic" agricultural commodities, namely, wheat, cotton, corn, hogs, milk, tobacco, and rice, to which other commodities were added later. This was in reality nothing but a government-sponsored agricultural "trust" and it was often justified on the ground that industry had its trusts and skilled labor its unions or labor monopolies and the farmer must be allowed equal power to protect himself. To administer this new farm program the Agricultural Adjustment Administration was set up. Those farmers who agreed to cut their acreage according to a scale set up by the Department of Agriculture were paid sums proportionate to the estimated returns from the crops or animals not grown. By July, 1934, the wheat acreage had been cut 7,500,000 acres, and benefit payments of almost $100,000,000 had been made to wheat growers, while the price of wheat was doubled; 10,000,000 acres of cotton land were taken out of production, reducing the crop by about 4,000,000 bales and raising the price from 5½ cents to 9½ cents a pound, while planters received some $200,-000,000 in benefit payments.

The funds thus distributed were obtained by a processing tax on millers, packing houses, and other manufacturers who converted these products into food. The processors were expected to pass the taxes on to the consumers, thereby raising the prices of these commodities. The object lesson of plowing under every third row of cotton, and the purchase and threatened destruction of over 6,000,000 pigs, raised strong doubts in the minds of many citizens as to whether artificial scarcity was the proper solution to the farmers' difficulties, especially in a period of general depression and distress. The pressure of public opinion finally forced the distribution of the pigs to public relief agencies instead of destroying them.

Whatever may be said for such an allotment system, by which crops were apportioned among the states on the basis of their production for the past ten years, as an emergency measure, it was open to serious objection as a permanent policy. One of the characteristic features of American agriculture has been its readiness to move to new areas where conditions are most favorable for production. But this scheme froze production to existing areas. In the process of reducing acreage the sub-marginal or poor lands were not the ones to be forced out of use, but a given percentage of each area including good and poor land. Even more fundamentally faulty, of course, was the policy of inducing scarcity as a means of promoting prosperity. The forcing of domestic prices up above world levels lost us a considerable part of our cotton export market.

In 1936 the Agricultural Adjustment Act was declared unconstitutional by the Supreme Court, but Congress quickly responded with the Soil Conservation and Domestic Allotment Act, under which crop regulation could be continued. The emphasis was now placed on the improvement of soil fertility and protection against erosion. The payment of farm benefits was continued, but was conditioned on the diversion of farming operations from the production of soil-depleting to soil-conserving crops and on the use of methods designed to conserve soil resources. That such a measure of soil conservation was desirable seemed indicated by a report in 1945 of the Soil Conservation Service of the Department of Agriculture that nearly 1,000,000,000 acres, or 90 per cent of the country's farm lands, needed soil conservation treatment as protection from soil erosion and to maintain fertility. A promising start has been made through the organization of voluntary soil conservation districts controlled and operated by farmers living in those districts, with the advice and technical guidance of the Service just mentioned. A new feature was the expressed determination to "reestablish the ratio between the purchasing power of the net income per person on farms and that of persons not on farms that prevailed during the five-year period August 1909–July 1914." This came to be known as "purchasing power parity."

This law failed, however, to provide effective means of crop curtailment, and farm surpluses in the important crops continued to depress prices. The system of reducing the acreage planted did not work because farmers were able by improved seed selection and shrewd use of fertilizers to increase production even on their smaller allotments. A striking illustration of increased yield from improved seed is furnished by the case of "hybrid corn," whose partial use increased the national corn production by 1800 million bushels during the four years 1942–45. This law was accordingly replaced in 1938 by a new and comprehensive Agricultural Adjustment Act, which combined most of the provisions of previous legislation with much that was new. This was hailed by Secretary of Agriculture Wallace as a "complete charter of farm equality." Government regulation was now applied to the production of basic crops, not to the acreage. The Secretary of Agriculture was authorized to fix the acreage; if unexpectedly large crops should materialize he was to restrict sales by marketing quotas, but if the crops were below normal he was to make "parity payments" to the growers. Provision was also made for loans to farmers in good years on their crop surpluses, which were to be kept off the market by being stored. It was expected that in bad years, when prices were higher, the stored-up surpluses would be released for sale. This was the "ever-normal granary" plan of Secretary Wallace.

Owing partly to the perversity of nature and partly to that of the farmers themselves, there were bumper crops in the next three years, and low prices continued. Exuberant production in other countries and restrictions on international trade prevented disposal of the surpluses in foreign markets, so they piled up at home. Some relief in the disposal of the surpluses was found in their diversion to relief agencies, and in 1939 the food-stamp plan was introduced, according to which the surpluses—or the products made from them—were sold to persons on relief at reduced prices through regular marketing channels. Loans were made to growers on stored wheat, corn, cotton, tobacco, etc., sometimes amounting to more than the market price, and the government held enormous quantities of these commodities, paying meantime heavy storage charges. In addition, millions of dollars flowed to the farmers from the federal treasury in parity payments. Agricultural adjustment, originally justified as a relief measure in a time of crisis, had degenerated into government largesses to a maximum number of farmers in response to the political pressure of agricultural interests. These had moved a long way from the Populist demand of "special privilege to none."

A change in agricultural policy was made in 1941. Secretary Wallace's ever-normal granary was replaced by Secretary Wickard's ever-normal food supply. Henceforth the emphasis was to be shifted from the five basic crops that had been subsidized and placed upon vitamin-rich or "protective" foods, such as meat, fats, dairy products, poultry and eggs, fruit and vegetables. The food needs of Britain and other European countries and our own domestic requirements, as well as the failure of previous schemes, seem to have dictated this change in policy. Farmers were advised to make the necessary shifts in their crop programs, and government control was extended to ensure compliance. Under pressure of patriotism and profits the farmers responded promptly to this appeal, especially in such crops as soybeans, peanuts, pigs, and other products.

Effect of World War II: Increased output. The entrance of the United States into World War II in December, 1941, sharply altered the picture, though it did not change the policy of increased production. During the war years American farmers achieved almost miraculous results in the raising of agricultural products. Despite a drain of over 5,000,000 men by selective service and industry, they raised more food each year, and in the peak year of 1944 their production exceeded the 1935–39 average by 36 per cent. The explanation of this seeming miracle must be found in the larger use of farm machinery to replace the workers. The one-man, all-crop combine, the self-propelled grain harvester, corn pickers, shredders, and huskers, and other power-driven machines made it possible for one man with their help to farm alone a larger area and to raise more produce than he had previously been able to do with hired help. This contribution of the farmers was materially aided by the planting of 20,000,000 Victory gardens, approximately ten times as many as were planted in 1918, which produced 42 per cent of all the vegetables raised in the country. There were various reasons why this vast increase was necessary. Owing to the wartime dislocation of agriculture and trade throughout the world we were almost the only major source of supply for our Allies. The American armed forces, both at home and abroad, consumed more than they had as civilians. And the people at home, who had more employment and received larger incomes, increased their consumption of food.

The needs of our allies were great, but they did not have the money with which to buy the desired supplies. Accordingly, in March, 1941, the plan of lend-lease was instituted, by which the President was empowered to provide goods and services to those countries whose defense he deemed vital to the defense of the United States and reciprocally to receive a return in so-called "reverse lend-lease." The total value of goods transferred to our allies under this arrangement was over $50,000 million by August, 1946, of which about one-sixth consisted of agricultural products. About 98 per cent of lend-lease aid went to the British Empire, the

U.S.S.R., China, and France, mostly to the two first named. During the war these exports, and supplies furnished our armed forces, were the greater part of our exports of food.

© International Harvester Company.

THE HARVESTER THRESHER

The modern self-propelled harvester-thresher moves across the field and carries out the threshing operations under its own power. It can be operated by one man, and one engine furnishes all the power.

Such a drain called for corresponding restriction of domestic consumption and in May, 1942, the system of rationing was introduced, beginning with sugar and gradually extending until a year later it covered 95 per cent of our food products. The "point system," generally adopted in European countries during World War I, insured fairer distribution of limited supplies. The Office of Price Administration (OPA) was also set up to control prices by placing a "ceiling" price on most goods. Rationing was largely discontinued after V-J day, but price administration continued throughout 1946. Additional restrictions were imposed in special cases: thus the use of alcohol, needed for the manufacture of munitions, was restricted for liquor distilling, as was that of grain for brewing. When it was belatedly discovered in 1945 that there would be a shortage of wheat, largely owing to a misguided policy of using it for cattle feed, millers were required to grind more flour from each bushel of wheat. This made a slightly darker flour but it was estimated to save 25 million bushels of wheat during the first six months of 1946.

After the conclusion of the war with Germany on May 7 and with Japan on August 14, 1945, we directed our efforts to the work of relief and rehabilitation of the war-torn countries. For this purpose the United Nations Relief and Rehabilitation Administration was set up, to which the United States pledged about three-fourths of the $3,671 million subscribed by various nations. Relief supplies consisted primarily of consumer goods, such as food, clothing, fuel, and medicines, but of these food made up three-quarters of all, most of which went from this country. Rehabilitation took on the task of furnishing the countries in need of them with seeds and farm implements, and other equipment for the reconstruction of fisheries, factories, and transportation. Chief among the recipients of UNRRA assistance were China, Italy, Greece, Yugoslavia, and the U.S.S.R.

Conclusion. The objective of American agriculture has, during most of our history, been simply to bring more land under cultivation and to produce more. The public domain was got rid of as rapidly as possible, and most of the arable land was put into the hands of farmers, together with much that was suitable only for forestry or grazing and some that was not good even for such use. It seems clear today that this process went on too rapidly, with disastrous consequences to the farmers and to the nation. That such a continued expansion of production could take place at all was due to the European market, which absorbed the agricultural surplus above our normal domestic needs. The distress of the farmer was largely owing to the fluctuations of this European demand, expanding enormously during World War I and afterward falling off until by 1940 the foreign markets were almost closed to our agricultural products. The outbreak of World War II again altered the situation and created a new demand for foodstuffs, cotton, and other agricultural commodities. Prices rose and farm income reached new highs.

There was much to be said for the early emergency measures which were designed to assist the farmers in a national crisis and to facilitate their recovery. By 1936 the improvement in the economic position of agriculture had ended this phase, and thereafter emphasis came to be placed increasingly on measures which tended to put farmers in a privileged class. After this date reform took the place of relief and an effort was made to reconstruct our farm economy according to plans made in Washington. A new national agricultural policy was set up which looked to an economic balance between the agricultural output and the demand for these products, and also between agriculture and other industries. The objective of this "New Deal" was to bring about an equilibrium in which a more perfect adjustment might be obtained among these different interests.

Before endorsing or rejecting such a course we must make up our minds as to the purpose of our agricultural program. Shall we strive for a maximum of efficiency in the utilization of the land or for the maintenance of as large a number of farm families as possible? The former involves the use of improved machinery and scientific technique, by which a larger product can be raised with less labor, thereby releasing both men and land for other uses. This is the method pursued in industry, according to which the more efficient low-cost plants crowd out the less productive ones. Dr. O. E. Baker concludes that the elimination of 28 per cent of the lowest income-producing farms would involve a loss of only 3 per cent of the commercial farm product. In the interests of efficiency these high-cost marginal farms should probably be closed down, but the removal of a million and a half farmers from the land presents a nearly insoluble problem, and makes such a plan impracticable. It is too narrow a view, however, to look at this question solely from the economic standpoint, for it has many facets. "The men of theory," writes Trevelyan,[7] "failed to perceive that agriculture is not merely one industry among many, but a way of life, unique and irreplaceable in its human and spiritual values." Let us not make this mistake.

[7] G. M. Trevelyan, *English Social History* (London and New York, 1942), 554.

CHAPTER XXVII

MANUFACTURES

Growth of manufactures. Three events had a profound influence on American manufactures during the period 1914–46. The first was World War I, the second was the great depression following the panic of 1929, and the third was World War II. Before taking up an analysis of the causal relationships it is desirable to present the facts. The dominating position of manufactures in our national economic life is easily shown. In 1914 the value added to materials through manufacturing was $9.2 billion, compared to cash income from farm operations amounting to $6.1 billion. On a dollar basis, therefore, manufacturing was 50 per cent more important than farming. By 1943 it was three times as important as farming and worth six times as many dollars as in 1914.[1] Manufacturing also excels farming when measured by the number of persons engaged in the two occupations. In 1914 farmers and farm laborers totalled 12,000,000, which was twice the number of wage earners in manufacturing; but by 1943 there were 10,000,000 engaged in agriculture compared to 14,000,000 wage earners in manufacturing. Between 1910 and 1940 three-quarters of the country's increase in population took place in urban communities (places with more than 2500 people) where manufacturing and other industrial pursuits concentrated.

The growth of manufactures as a whole is shown in the table on page 630. Since at this writing the usual biennial census of manufacturing has not been taken for seven years because of the war, the data for the period since 1939 are not complete. The outstanding fact shown in the table is the fluctuating and yet definite growth that has taken place.

[1] The more exact figures were $19.9 billion for cash farm income in 1943 compared to an estimated $60 billion for value added in manufacturing. Total value of manufactures was $140 billion and value added has in recent years been about 43 per cent of that.

Between 1914 and 1919 it was extraordinarily rapid; the next decade saw recession and advance, while the 1930's witnessed a sharp decline followed by a partial recovery. World War II has produced another remarkable upward trend.

GROWTH OF MANUFACTURES, 1914-45*					
	Number of estab-lishments	*Annual average number of wage earners*	*(In millions of dollars)*		
Year			*Wages*	*Cost of materials*	*Value of products*
1914	173,656	6,478,713	3,783	13,824	23,066
1919	210,426	8,431,157	9,673	36,284	60,054
1921	192,275	6,484,447	7,468	24,446	41,749
1925	184,108	7,879,508	9,994	35,194	60,926
1929	206,811	8,380,536	10,910	37,441	68,178
1931	171,450	6,136,144	6,689	21,229	39,830
1935	167,916	7,203,794	7,311	26,441	44,994
1937	166,794	8,569,231	10,113	35,539	60,713
1939	184,230	7,886,567	9,090	32,160	56,843
1943	—	13,930,000	30,397	—	148,700
1945	—	11,810,000	26,216	—	140,000

* *Statistical Abstract of the U. S., 1944-45* (Washington, 1945), 794, and the 16th Census. Figures are only for establishments having products valued at $5000 or more. 1943 and 1945 figures for wage earners and wages are from the Bureau of Labor Statistics; figures for value of materials are manufacturers' shipments as reported by the Department of Commerce. See *Survey of Current Business*, February, 1946, 12.

Effect of World War I upon manufactures. When the war began in 1914 American industries were in a depressed state, but the urgent demand from the European belligerents for war supplies of every sort quickly led to revival and expansion. Our exports to the five leading nations of the Entente Allies grew from $.9 billion in the fiscal year 1914 to $2.4 billion in 1915 and $3.0 billion in 1916. These foreign orders were for explosives, iron and steel, copper, brass, bronze and zinc, automobile parts, boots and shoes, canned goods, meat and dairy products, and similar articles. As a result, manufacturing industries which could produce munitions and war supplies expanded and prospered greatly. With the diversion of labor and capital into war industries, however, other enterprises suffered correspondingly. Building operations were almost at a standstill and in many cities factories were shut down, while unemployment and high prices showed that the war prosperity was very unevenly distributed.

The same thing was true in even greater degree after the United States entered the war in April, 1917. In order to mobilize the industrial forces of the nation and direct all efforts to the single task of winning the war, there was early created a War Industries Board. Its functions were to obtain materials for military purposes with the minimum dislocation of industries; to restrict non-war production; and to fix maximum prices. Through the War Priorities Board, fuel, transportation facilities, labor, and even credit were assigned first of all to war industries, while those producing luxuries or dispensable goods were forced to curtail or even to suspend their operations. Government contracts were made with private contractors on the basis of cost plus a profit of 10 per cent or more, an extravagant but effective method of speeding up production. Profiteering was checked when too shameless, but the whole system of war production was necessarily wasteful, since normal safeguards on cost were disregarded under the influence of war needs and rising prices.

Postwar changes. The resumption of peacetime activities after the armistice compelled a readjustment of industry along many lines. Those industries which had served war demands and essential needs—munitions, food, and clothing—had expanded greatly, and now faced the problem of finding a profitable use for their enlarged facilities. This was solved for some by the renewal of activities in those lines which had been starved during the war, such as residences, office, store, and factory buildings, roads, and public works of all kinds. There were added a few new lines such as the dye and chemical industries, of which before the war Germany had had a practical monopoly. Considerable shifts also took place in domestic manufactures. The expanding automotive industries practically ruined the wagon, carriage, saddle, and harness business, and cut seriously into that of railroad construction; the radio diminished piano making; rayon partially supplanted cotton in the textiles.

Other changes, still more fundamental, were taking place. Down to the period of World War I the expansion of manufacturing had always been based upon the availability of a large body of wage earners. But war put a premium on the use of laborsaving machinery greater than ever before, and manufacturing plants came then and afterward to depend more on technical equipment and skill than on mere numbers. Professor Mills concluded [2] that "in the six years 1923–29 the technique of physical production reached a higher development than at any other time in our history." During this period the value of the manufactured product increased 13 per cent but the number of wage earners in these industries declined 7.4 per cent, while the productive efficiency, that is, the per capita productivity, increased 22 per cent. Such a change involved an increasing amount of industrial displacement and readjustment with an increase of unemployment, unless the displaced labor could be absorbed in new lines or by the expansion of old ones. There is a soothing economic theory which asserts that this will always take place, but events in the United States for the next few years demonstrated that considerable time is needed for the adjustment and that in all probability the worker whose skill has been displaced by a machine will never be as well off again. Many persons simply blamed the unemployment of the depressed 1930's on such technological changes. They forgot that every invention which has contributed to our high standard of living has done so by increasing the buying power of many in a small way although injuring the livelihod of a few in a big way. That the small gains of the many outweigh the heavy losses of the few is attested by our generally rising standard of living. The causes of the depression to come were deeper than mere technological unemployment.

Another industrial change in the 1920's and one probably contributing more to the depression was the change in articles demanded by the public. In the previous chapter it was shown that as income increases the percentage spent on primary wants—food, clothing, and shelter—tends to decline. But the demand for goods that gratify less imperative needs is likely to fluctuate considerably. For example, automobiles, radios, washing machines, and refrigerators, to name only a few, were each the object of a tremendous demand at some

[2] F. C. Mills, *Economic Tendencies in the United States* (New York, 1933), 530. See also p. 630.

periods in the 1920's. For a vast market of well over 100,-000,000 enjoying the highest standard of living in the world these products had to be turned out in enormous quantities. Production on a large scale is cheapest by machine methods and consequently a great deal of labor and capital must first be invested in instruments of production. In order to satisfy the immediate and apparently insatiable demand it is easy to expand plant facilities beyond the capacity needed to produce for a more normal market. The customer may want one refrigerator badly but not desire a replacement for many years. Likewise automobile companies had to expend many millions on advertising and on real or make-believe improvements for each new model to maintain the demand for cars. Products of this character absorbed a constantly growing proportion of the national income down to 1929. Manufacturing becomes highly unstable as demand fluctuates in response to advertising, to changes in income as in 1920–22, or to the export market. Even some of our most important exports were of this character. The crisis of 1929 and the subsequent depression lend support to the thesis that during these years too large a proportion of our labor and capital was being sunk in fixed capital equipment and plant expansion in certain industries. The same over-investment in fixed forms of capital took place that had led to the panics of 1873 and 1893, only in those cases the over-expansion was in railroads and now it was in some lines of industrial plant and equipment.

Concentration in large establishments. The same tendency toward the growth in size of the single plant, which began in the last period,[3] continued after 1914. Indeed, to such an extent was the size of the typical individual establishments being enlarged that after 1914 the census bureau ceased collecting statistics of establishments turning out products with a value of less than $5000 a year. The next larger group, with products of $5000 to $20,000, also showed a falling off absolutely in this same period, as did all others relatively up to the largest group of all, comprising those establishments with products of $1,000,000 or more. This

[3] See page 475.

group, which in 1914 turned out 49 per cent of all manufactures, was producing 69 per cent in 1929, and almost the same in 1937.

Year	SIZE OF AVERAGE MANUFACTURING ESTABLISHMENTS*				
	Average value of product (dollars)	Average cost of materials (dollars)	Average horse-power	Average number of wage earners	Index of volume of production per establishment
1914	135,500	80,000	126	38.9	100
1919	289,800	174,000	137	45.3	104
1925	335,370	175,000	196	44.8	153
1929	333,800	182,000	203	41.8	154
1931	240,000	122,000	—	37.2	123
1935	267,860	156,400	—	42.8	142
1937	363,500	212,800	—	51.3	185
1939	308,900	174,500	278	42.3	157

* *U. S. Census Reports*, except for column 6 which is from Temporary National Economic Committee, Monograph No. 27, *The Structure of Industry*, 4. No additional material available because of cessation of biennial manufacturing censuses.

The indexes of growth given above tell the same story. Between 1914 and 1929 the average number of wage earners per establishment increased from 39 to 42, the amount of horsepower from 126 to 203, and the value of product from $135,000 to $334,000. The conclusion is irresistible that large-scale manufacturing was continuing to expand at the expense of the small producer, though the rate of growth had begun to falter even before 1929. After that year there was a marked falling off, due, not to a multiplication of small plants, but to the contraction of production in general. There is observable here, however, the same tendency for the extension of large plants to slow up or even for a reverse movement in favor of small ones to take place in times of prolonged depression that was noticed in the case of large-scale farming. With the revival of prosperity in 1937, however, the production per establishment spurted to a new high. There can be no doubt that a still higher peak was reached during World War II. For example, in the four years following June, 1940, some 33 big corporations each received government orders totaling $1 billion or more. These giants were also entrusted with the operation of the bulk of $12 billion worth of new government-built plants. In 1939 the

250 largest manufacturing corporations owned 65.4 per cent of the nation's total manufacturing capacity, in 1945 they held 66.5 per cent, and this capacity was 50 per cent greater than it had been in 1939.

The general reasons for the growth of the large establishment have already been described, but certain tendencies became more pronounced in this period. The outstanding ones were the technical and mechanical improvements in organization and machinery, and the greater use of mechanical power. All this required more capital and further stimulated the use of the corporate device. These tendencies call for further analysis.

Power in manufacturing. In the period 1914 to 1939 the amount of power furnished by prime movers and electric motors more than doubled, growing from 22,000,000 h.p. to 51,000,000 h.p. Of this great increase, steam furnished only a small fraction, and many of the steam engines, moreover, were used to generate electric power within the plant. The victory of electricity was complete. Electric power was desired for the speed it gives motors as well as the energy it generates. "Acceleration rather than structural change is the key to an understanding of our recent economic development," reported the Committee on Recent Economic Changes to President Herbert Hoover's conference on unemployment in 1929.

During World War II manufacturing plants redoubled their power requirements in order to turn out the great amount of war matériel they were called upon to produce. Electric power requirements of the nation as a whole were 73 per cent higher by 1944 but the capacity of power plants to meet this load was only 26 per cent greater. It took brownouts in the big cities and other economies and some expert pooling of power resources by the War Production Board to avert a power famine. Yet chiefly as a result of the tremendous supplies of power available to industry the nation was able to more than double its physical production of goods in World War II, a much better record than that made in World War I, as the table on the next page shows.

It is largely in power plus other capital equipment that we find the explanation of the increased productivity of the

American workman, and the speed which characterized practically all lines of production. Notwithstanding the reductions in the length of the working day, productivity per worker in manufacturing was double in 1939 and more than triple in 1943 what it had been in 1899.

United States Physical Production Index in Manufacturing in Two Wars			
World War I	Index	World War II	Index
1914	100	1939	100
1915	117	1940	116
1916	139	1941	154
1917	138	1942	194
1918	137	1943	237

* National Industrial Conference Board, *Economic Almanac*, 1946-47, 93.

Quite as significant as the growth in amount have been the changes in sources and character of the power. In 1906 about 85 per cent of our energy was derived from coal but by 1940 only 50 per cent came from coal and 30 per cent from oil. As to changes in character the improvement of electrical devices and the introduction of the gasoline engine added new sources which revolutionized not only manufacturing and transportation, but our social life as well. Both of these can be furnished at any point desired, in any quantity and for any length of time, and can be applied in small units. The location and technique of factories was profoundly affected by these changes. Also the equipment of the modern kitchen and home laundry with their many electrical appliances virtually made miniature factories of the up-to-the-minute home. If the horsepower stated in the figures given above be expressed in term of man power at the rate of ten men to one horsepower, then in 1939 each factory worker had at his command 68 iron slaves and by 1943 roughly 81. Such an addition to our productive capacity made the genii of Aladdin's lamp appear mere shadow men.

Scientific management. Such a mechanization of manufacturing could not take place without corresponding changes in the organization and equipment of the factory. Perhaps the most striking feature was the arrangement of the factories on the flow-sheet design, so that the raw materials moved steadily from one operation to another, in a continuous stream, until they emerged as finished goods.[4] The most spectacular illustration of this principle was the assembly line in the Ford automobile factories, in which a conveyor, moving six feet a minute, carried to the workmen, each of whom performed only one operation, the parts to be assembled. The Chevrolet and Ford motor companies demonstrated the same method to thousands of observers at the Century of Progress Exposition in Chicago in 1933 and 1934.

But not merely was the machinery arranged in a fashion to produce the most efficient results; the job itself was analyzed and an effort was made to obtain maximum production from the worker. The expression "scientific management" was applied to a system first proposed by F. W. Taylor toward the end of the nineteenth century, but which has been greatly expanded and refined by his successors in the twentieth. Taylor analyzed each operation to determine the maximum speed at which the work could be done and what was the most efficient type of tool for it and how that tool should be used; later he emphasized factory layout and shop organization. Science was to supplant the old rule-of-thumb methods. That there was need for a more careful analysis of methods of management was shown by a report of the American Engineering Council in 1921 entitled *Waste in Industry*. This report estimated that, for the six representative industries studied, 50 to 80 per cent of the responsibility for waste rested upon faulty management. A single but significant illustration may be given. It was found that there existed a chaotic variety of sizes and shapes of materials that was both unnecessary and uneconomic. Investigation showed, for example, that there were 287 kinds of tires which could be reduced to 32; 210 different shapes of bottles, reducible to 20; 175 kinds of automobile wheels, reducible to 4; 66 shapes of bricks, reducible to 7. The savings to manufacturers from the adoption of the simplifications proposed were estimated at $600,000,000 annually. National co-operation in an efficiency program of this sort marked a new departure in the conduct of industry.

[4] For a description of this method and its application to various industries, see E. L. Bogart and C. E. Landon, *Modern Industry* (rev. ed., New York, 1936).

Industrial research. Factory organization and management were only aspects of a much broader development that was going on; namely, the use of scientific methods in industry. The application of science in order to perfect industrial technology was belated, but the twentieth century has already witnessed the conversion of the American businessman, and frequently of his plant or factory. Practical application was made of the latest researches in biology, chemistry, physics, and other sciences, and many of the leading scientists like Edison, Bell, Steinmetz, and others, devoted themselves to the industrial utilization of scientific discovery. So important did invention become in modern industry that progress along these lines is no longer left to the unaided efforts of some talented individual. Most great manufacturing plants today have their research departments in which experiments are being carried on at an expense far beyond the means of an individual inventor. In 1938 the total industrial research bill of some 30,000 scientists and their laboratories was estimated at $180,000,000, and during the war the federal government contributed toward private industrial research at the rate of $60,000,000 a year. This does not include most of the $2 billion spent in developing atomic energy. The leading industries in research before the war were the chemical, oil, and electrical equipment industries. During the war a great deal of expert skill and money was also devoted to the development of a satisfactory synthetic rubber and in 1942, according to Professor Marvel, as much progress was made as in the preceding thirty years. In general, only the big companies or the government can afford to spend large amounts on research: two-thirds of the industrial research workers before the war were employed by only 140 companies.

Some of the results of this research activity are startling indeed. Out of the lowly soybean are now made glycerin, explosives, waterproof goods, soaps, printing ink, and so many automobile parts that Henry Ford once boasted that some day he would make the entire car out of soybeans. Women's nylon stockings are now made out of coal, air, and water; rayon can be substituted for wool in the manufacture of rugs and carpets; glass can be transformed into yarn and woven into cloth on standard textile machinery; celotex, which is increasingly used in building houses, comes from what was formerly refuse in refining sugar; enough good-quality synthetic rubber was produced from petroleum in the five war years to take the place of most of the natural rubber we could no longer import; more and better gasoline is obtainable from petroleum through catalytic cracking, hydrogenation, and other processes; the radio industry with its frequency modulation and television is on the threshold of extraordinary improvements; the airplane is continually made cheaper and safer; and, to sum it all up, this country leads all others in the number of patents registered.

The new technology, based upon the knowledge of chemistry and the use of electricity, the internal combustion engine, the radio, and the airplane, is inaugurating economies and social changes even more momentous than those introduced by the invention of the steam engine over one hundred and sixty years ago. For example, as chemistry teaches man to satisfy his needs from simple and easily obtainable raw materials, the race for such natural riches as rubber, petroleum, and metals may slacken and a strong incentive for wars be lessened. Or, as it becomes possible to transmit power long distances, and as radios, automobiles, and airplanes are improved, the need and desire for concentrating much of our economic activity in large cities may be abated. These illustrations are quite within the realm of possibility, although the trends are not yet clearly discernible.

Capital formation and the corporation. This increased use of power and other capital equipment, the scrapping of old machinery in order to replace it by new inventions, and the introduction of streamlined methods were all costly. Where did the money come from for this new capital? According to Simon Kuznets the net capital formation between 1909 and 1941 was above 8 per cent of the national income. Much of this was accumulated by corporations which regularly plowed back part of their earnings to improve the efficiency and enlarge the capacity of their plants. The table below shows the extent of these savings between 1916 and 1942. In addition, persons with incomes over $2000 and especially over $10,000 a year contributed heavily. Many of these savings were routed to industry through purchases of life insurance, through deposits in savings accounts, and through investment in securities.

CORPORATE SAVINGS* (billions of dollars)	
Period of years	Average each year
1916-20	3.1
1921-25	1.2
1926-30	.8
1931-35	—4.7
1936-40	— .5
1941	2.8
1942	5.5

* National Industrial Conference Board, *Economic Almanac*, 1946-47, 51.

How corporations grew in size and importance is shown in the accompanying table. The number of manufacturing establishments almost doubled between 1914 and 1939. Not only did corporations do a lion's share of the manufacturing business (92 per cent in 1939) but a few big corporations did the bulk of all corporate business. By 1933 it was estimated that less than 600 of the country's largest corporations owned over one-half the corporate wealth.

GROWTH OF THE CORPORATE FORM OF BUSINESS IN MANUFACTURING*		
Date	Per cent of business enterprises that were corporations	Corporations turned out the following per cent of total value of products
1904	23.6	73.7
1909	25.9	79.0
1914	28.3	83.2
1919	31.5	87.7
1929	48.3	92.1
1939	51.6	92.4

* Twentieth Century Fund, *Big Business: Its Growth and Its Place* (New York, 1937), 15, and Sixteenth Census, *Manufacturing, Types of Organizations*.

As the corporations grew in size, the number of stockholders increased enormously, until by 1928 the number of book stockholders of American corporations totaled 18 million and it was estimated that from 4 to 7 million individuals held stock. Much of this change took place in the five-year period between 1916 and 1921, when people of large incomes sold a sizable portion of their ownership of American industry to people of more moderate means. World War I produced this revolutionary change by imposing heavy income and excess profits taxes on the one hand, and on the other hand by educating thousands to invest in securities. In 1938 the United States Steel Corporation had 168,400 stockholders, the Pennsylvania Railroad, 213,300, and the American Telephone and Telegraph Company, 644,700. In no one of these concerns did the largest stockholder own as much as even 1 per cent of all the shares outstanding.

The question will doubtless occur to most students at this point, "Who controlled such corporations and how was it done?" In a small corporation the controlling individual or element must have 51 per cent of the stock to be safe, but in the case of large companies whose stock is widely dispersed and whose stockholders are extremely difficult to organize effectively, a much smaller percentage is all that is necessary. Control of corporations is sometimes exercised by subtle legal devices; for example, only a small proportion of the stock may carry voting privileges. An investment of about $2,000,000 in such stock of Dodge Brothers, Inc., enabled Dillon, Read and Company to control this $130,000,000 concern in 1925. But the most popular method is known as management control and is based on the use of proxies. In 1930, 44 per cent of the 200 largest companies in the country made use of this device, whereas only 5 per cent depended on majority ownership.[5]

Important in general as were increased use of power, scientific management, and industrial research, all made possible by greater use of capital through wider use of the corporation, probably the best way to understand the progress and changes taking place in manufacturing is to trace developments in particular industries.

Iron and steel. In the basic iron and steel industry can be studied in detail the features which characterized manufactures in general in this period. The following table shows the major movements, except for the period of World War II, for which comparable figures are still unavailable.

[5] This material was drawn from A. Berle and G. Means, *The Modern Corporation and Private Property* (New York, 1932), Part I, Chap. 5.

			(In millions of dollars)		
Year	Number of establishments	Annual average number of wage earners	Wages	Cost of materials	Value of products
1914	587	278,072	210.9	855.1	1,263.3
1919	695	416,748	711.4	2,301.9	3,623.4
1925	595	399,914	660.3	2,429.4	3,711.4
1929	591	419,534	731.0	2,514.4	4,127.2
1933	466	288,945	270.4	876.0	1,357.6
1937	497	502,417	817.8	2,378.6	4,003.0
1939	498	418,529	639.0	2,071.4	3,406.3
1943	—	531,975	1,183.7	—	—

CRUDE IRON AND STEEL ROLLED PRODUCTS, 1914-43 *

* *Statistical Abstract of the United States* (Washington, 1942), 815; Nat. Ind. Conf. Bd., *Econ. Almanac*, 1944-45, 241.

Although the iron and steel industry had lost its pre-eminence of leadership among American manufactures which it held in 1900, having sunk to second place in 1914, third in 1929, and fifth in 1937, it was still one of the most important, for it was basic to many others. Whether measured by the value of the product or by the number of wage earners, it showed a great expansion between 1914 and 1937. The most rapid development occurred during and as a result of the two world wars when we supplied a large part of the needs of our allies as well as our own needs for war materials. Production of pig iron, ferroalloys, steel ingots and castings increased about 70 per cent between 1939 and the 1944 war peak. At the war's end we were turning out about three-quarters of the world's production of iron and steel.

This industry also reflects the major and minor fluctuations of this period. That is better illustrated by the iron and steel production index, which shows the ups and downs in response to business conditions. From a level of 88 in 1919, it fell to 50 in 1921 as a result of the depression of that year, recovered to 110 in 1923, dropped to 92 the following year, after which it showed a fairly steady rise to 135 in 1929. The next decade showed even wider fluctuations—from a low of 33 in 1932 it rose to 114 in prosperous 1937, then dipped to 68 in 1939 and climbed to a peak of 214 under the influence of World War II. Only one other major industry, namely auto-mobiles, showed a more temperamental behavior.

Iron and steel is an industry of decreasing costs; that is, the cost per unit decreases as plant equipment increases. It requires an extremely large investment of capital in order to realize the maximum economies, and is therefore a large-scale industry. There has been a constant tendency toward concentration in large plants, as is shown by the reduction in the number of establishments from 695 in 1919 to 497 in 1937. Of the 497 establishments in 1937, 123 employed over 1000 wage earners each. Four companies produced about 64 per cent of the iron and steel output of the whole country in 1938, over half of this being turned out by the largest of them all, the United States Steel Corporation. However, it is not true that the larger a plant the greater its efficiency—at any time there is probably an ideal size. For that reason the large companies often found it more profitable to expand by building new modern plants or buying out competitors. Merging of competing plants is called horizontal combination.

Vertical combination or integration was also characteristic of the iron and steel industry; that is, the bringing together under one control of the various stages from the mining of the ore to the turning out of the finished product. This had already been effected during the previous period by the United States Steel Corporation, which owned its own mines, railroads, steamship lines, blast furnaces, rolling mills, and plants to produce other finished commodities. But the present period saw a still further movement in this direction. Even during the depression these integrated companies held their gains.

Within the steel industry changes were taking place. During World War I coke produced in by-product ovens increased from 27 per cent to over two-thirds of the nation's total output of coke and today the figure is 93 per cent: the wasteful and smoky beehive oven is almost a relic of the past. Open-hearth steel passed Bessemer steel around 1908 and by 1944 its production was sixteen times as great. Since the coming of the open-hearth furnace the character of the raw material for making steel has also changed. Scrap iron and steel collected in cities, factories, and railroad yards have grown steadily in importance until by the 1940's they supplied almost as much tonnage as pig iron did. In this period also electric steel completely displaced crucible steel for fine tools and cutlery, although the high cost forbade its general use.

Despite the low level of operations during the 1930's the steel industry made extraordinary advances. Mr. Edward R. Stettinius, Jr., Chairman of the United States Steel Corpora-

ROLLING MILL

The three principal methods of working metals are founding, forging, and rolling, and of these three methods that of rolling has been chiefly instrumental in extending the use of iron and steel for structural purposes to its present enormous proportions. Rolling consists in working metal ingots into rails, bars, plates, rods, and structural shapes by passing them repeatedly when intensely hot between cylindrical rolls. Usually each set of rolls has two or more grooves, each of which approaches more closely to the form of the finished piece than the set of grooves preceding it, and the metal is passed through these grooves in order. Commonly also several sets of rollers are employed, each set bringing the piece closer to its final form than the set preceding. In the illustration a white-hot ingot is shown going through a set of rolls.

tion, testified before the Temporary National Economic Committee in 1939 that "it must be realized that the steel industry has been through a revolution since the early 1920's." Modern rolling mills produced a new kind of sheet steel from which all-steel automobile bodies and one-piece tops could be made; a new steel pipe was devised which made it possible to drill oil wells to a depth of 15,000 feet; and advances were made in the manufacture of structural steel and of tin plate to aid the preservation of foods. But perhaps the most important technical improvement was the widespread use of ferroalloys, such as titanium, manganese, tungsten, and others, by means of which light, tough, springy, and hard forms of steel were produced. For example, out of the new high-tensile steels faster, lighter, and yet more comfortable trains were manufactured. Up to 1939 there was a noticeable tendency for the per cent output of lighter steel to increase at the expense of the heavy steels like rails, pipes, and structural shapes. World War II of course stimulated the demand for heavy steels again and also resulted in the building of many new blast furnaces and open-hearth furnaces. The new equipment, however, increased producing capacity only about one-sixth by 1945, most of it merely replacing obsolete or worn-out furnaces.

Motor vehicles. The most spectacular and far-reaching event in the annals of both manufacturing and transportation in the twentieth century was the rise of the automobile industry. Not mentioned in the census of 1900, it ranked first in 1929 with a total product of $3723 million, and has ever since remained at or near the top. This epic of modern industry is only partially portrayed in the cold census figures of growth, which are given below.

Year	Number of establishments	Average annual number of wage earners	(In millions of dollars)		Factory sales of automobiles and trucks
			Cost of materials	Value of products	
1914	300	79,307	293	503	573,000
1919	315	210,559	1579	2388	1,876,000
1925	297	197,728	2108	3198	4,266,000
1929	244	226,116	2402	3723	5,358,000
1931	178	134,866	1044	1568	2,390,000
1935	121	147,044	1815	2391	3,947,000
1937	131	194,527	2394	3096	4,809,000
1939	—	—	—	—	3,577,000
1941	—	—	—	—	4,839,000

GROWTH OF AUTOMOBILE INDUSTRY, 1914-41 *

* *Statistical Abstracts of the United States.* Comparable data for 1939 and after were not available at time of publication.

Since the automobile has exerted its most transforming influence upon transportation, the story of its development will be reserved for a later chapter; here only those aspects that pertain to its manufacture will be considered. Not only does this industry turn out a larger value of products than any other, but it supports a host of dependent industries. Thus in 1939 it consumed 90 per cent of the gasoline product, 80 per cent of the rubber, 75 per cent of the plate glass, 68 per cent of the leather, 51 per cent of the malleable iron, 34 per cent of the lead, 23 per cent of the nickel, 18 per cent of the steel, 14 per cent of the copper, and a vast amount of cotton, lumber, aluminum, and other materials. It has created the hard roads and yet employed more than 3,600,000 railroad cars in 1939. The industry claimed that it gave employment directly and indirectly to about 6,500,000 workers.[6]

Automobile manufacture is both greatly concentrated and highly integrated. Three giant corporations account for 90 per cent of the production—Ford, General Motors, and the Chrysler-Dodge combination. The Ford Company represents the highly centralized type of organization, practically owned and certainly operated by a single family. It is a vertical combination, embracing all steps in the making of an automobile, from the ownership of iron mines, blast furnaces, and railroads, to the control of selling agencies. Started with a meager capital of $100,000 in 1903, it has been built up by plowing back into the business profits which, in the prosperous years 1923–25, ran up to $100,000,000 a year. Henry Ford, its founder, exhibited great organizing ability, carried standardization to the limit, and introduced the famous system of the assembly line. By these methods he was able to produce a low-priced car, the Model T, of which the fifteen-millionth was turned out in May, 1927, and driven in state across the country. The competition of other cheap yet more attractive cars, together with the rise in the standard of living and the demands of the public, twice forced him to alter his model radically. Once in 1927 he closed production for several months and then presented his more modern Model A to the public, and a second time in 1932 drastic alterations were made and then the greatly improved Model V-8 was brought out.

Another great automobile giant is the General Motors Cor-

6 *Automobile Facts and Figures*, 1940 (Detroit, 1941).

poration, dating from 1908 but wholly reorganized in 1920. This represents a decentralized type of organization, for each of its producing units—such as Chevrolet, Pontiac, Oldsmobile, Buick, Cadillac, and others—retains its independent identity. It is a horizontal combination, formed by bringing together under one general control a number of formerly competing units. This company has adopted the policy of furnishing the public with practically all types of cars in each price class, and therefore makes many kinds. Within each plant, however, there exist the same economies of large-scale production and efficient organization that characterize all the large automobile establishments.

Necessary as they have become in our modern economic life, automobiles are still sufficiently a luxury to be subject to a highly fluctuating demand. The manufacturing production index,[7] starting with a low of 42 in 1921, jumped to 105 in 1923, and then rose to 139 in 1929; from this high point it fell precipitately to 36 by 1932. It climbed steadily to 125 in 1937, dropped sharply to 65 in 1938, and then skyrocketed to a new high in mid-1941. While the automobile industry affords an extreme case, it was symptomatic of the fluctuations of the business cycle in this confused period.

In February of 1942 the industry ceased production of automobiles for civilians and turned all its attention to the manufacture of war supplies. How very important this industry was in the war effort may be seen from the single fact that in the first ten months of 1944 alone it provided $14.4 billion worth of war matériel or over one-quarter of all the war products produced by all metalworking industries. It turned out vast quantities of army trucks and jeeps, tanks, airplanes and parts, ship parts, and much other needed equipment. At least 4,000,000 cars were junked during the war and many more became antiquated, so that the postwar outlook for the industry looks bright. Strikes unfortunately cut output to less than half of what had been anticipated in 1946.

Localization of industry. The tendency of manufacturing to localize became less marked as the industrialization of the country became more general. New England and the Middle Atlantic states lost their monopoly, and the east central section

[7] *Federal Reserve Bulletin*, esp. Aug., 1940, 830.

seized the industrial leadership. The six states of New York, Pennsylvania, Illinois, Ohio, Michigan, and New Jersey together produced about half the total manufacturing output, ranking in the order named. The reason was not the absolute decline of the former centers, but rather the general dissemination of manufactures over the whole country, so that almost no section any longer controlled an industry. Relatively, New England fell back and the Far West advanced. This became more pronounced during World War II with the building of more steel plants in such areas as Colorado, Utah, and California and with the great increase of shipbuilding and aircraft factories on the west coast. The South, too, has made great industrial advances since 1914, but her growth did not subtract from the manufactures of other sections, except in the cotton-goods industry. Finally, the extreme concentration of certain industries in favored centers has become less marked. There have been several reasons for this. One is industrial research. For example, before 1900 the cement industry was heavily concentrated in New York and Pennsylvania where the right mixture of natural cement could be quarried; now cement plants are found outside most large cities because the proper mixture of limestone and clay (common enough ingredients) is well known. Likewise discoveries of ways to make good coke out of coal, formerly considered unsuitable, have reduced the concentration of the iron and steel industry in the Pittsburgh area. Westward movement of grazing land and of manufacturing capital and greater use of the refrigerator car probably explain the relative decline of Chicago's share in the slaughtering and meat-packing industry.

Industrial combinations and trusts. The growing mechanization of industry brought with it an increasing tendency toward combination and monopoly. Machine industry, involving the use of large amounts of capital, operates under conditions of decreasing costs; that is, it realizes the greatest economies when conducted on a large scale. Strong pressure is therefore exerted to eliminate competition by combination, and to hold up prices by monopoly control. Business organization for the control of industry has been quite as significant as technological improvement in the industries themselves.

World War I hastened the tendency toward combination. There was strong pressure for increased production, and for the most efficient utilization of resources, capital, and labor. It was found that this could best be achieved in most instances by co-ordination under strong central control. Indeed, the government took the lead in this direction. The railroads were taken over by the federal government and operated as a unified system by an all-powerful Director General. The War Industries Board was set up to prevent competition among agencies purchasing war supplies and to regulate production under practically dictatorial powers. Standardization was enforced among private manufacturers, and even governmental price-fixing was employed to some extent.

After the war there was a strong reaction from the extreme governmental regulation, and an insistence upon a return to private ownership and operation. But the events of the war period had two effects: they demonstrated to the public the advantage of co-ordinated industry, and thus modified the hostile attitude toward the trusts. As a result of all these forces there occurred a new era in the combination and trust movement. Between 1919 and 1930 some 8000 independent concerns in manufacturing and mining alone disappeared in merger or other combination arrangements. This movement reached its peak in 1927-29, which was known as the era of consolidations. It exceeded in magnitude the earlier combination movement of 1898-1903. In the decade 1919 to 1928, 4500 public-utility enterprises were combined, chiefly under holding companies. There was also an increase in banking mergers and consolidations, the motion-picture industry was steadily consolidated, and there was a marked tendency toward the development of chains of retail stores. Except in 1931 the merger movement declined during the 1930's.

There was renewed merger activity with the outbreak of World War II. The last quarter of 1945 saw the largest number in manufacturing and mining since 1931, and 1946 was expected to produce a still larger crop. Although many of the recent mergers represent horizontal combination—8 large steel companies bought up 35 smaller ones; 1 big drug company took over 31 lesser concerns—many also were conglomerate in character. Large companies sometimes acquired small firms making auxiliary or even unrelated products. The motives were various: to lessen taxes, to make a profit on some promising venture, to eliminate the middleman by buying up a supplier, or simply to lessen competition. But at least one great monopoly lost ground, namely the Aluminum Company of America, which once controlled 99 per cent of the country's aluminum production but which now has two sizable competitors.

There have developed other methods of eliminating competition besides the merger, methods so subtle that for a time they almost defied detection by commissions and courts. These might be achieved by the leaders of an industry or through a trade association. Two devices will suffice to illustrate: the first is the basing point system, and the second is "price stabilization" as encouraged by trade associations.

The prime example of the basing point system is the "Pittsburgh Plus" method of pricing used in the steel industry previous to 1924 and continued with modifications thereafter. The steel trust took the lead and other concerns saw fit to follow. Most steel products were priced as if produced in, and shipped from, Pittsburgh. The effect of the practice was that there was virtually no price competition anywhere. The older steel trust plants in the Pittsburgh area were protected against outside competition, and the plants of the trust or of independents elsewhere enjoyed a huge profit from the "phantom freight" charges paid them. Everyone but the consumer liked it. The practice has also been found in the cement, copper, sugar, maple flooring, and numerous other industries.

Price stabilization is little better than a polite name for price-fixing, although trade associations strive earnestly to draw a distinction. They urge members to "co-operate," they lecture on the disadvantages of price-cutting, and they sometimes publish price lists and other information indicating supplies available and sales recently made. The association's information is considered most successful when the prices of certain leaders are copied by the majority of the industry. On occasions steps are taken against concerns that do not play this game: they may be expelled from the association, find it difficult to secure credit, or suffer disparagement or predatory price-cutting at the hands of association members.

Anti-trust legislation. Under President Wilson a Federal Trade Commission had been created in 1914 to administer anti-trust laws and prevent unfair methods of competition. During the next decade the commission performed valuable service by its "cease and desist" orders in preventing such unfair acts as misbranding goods, making false claims in advertising, price discriminations, and discrediting competitors. Adverse court decisions and executive hostility, however, as well as business opposition, forced the commission after 1925 to confine its activities largely to false advertising. In the meantime, however, it had adopted the plan of calling trade-practice conferences of the leading concerns in a given business to formulate codes of fair trade, and in this way tried to introduce a policy of self-regulation; but the effectiveness of this plan declined during the depression. In recent years the commission has been given the responsibility of administering new fair trade laws. Chief criticisms of the commission are that it acts in the dual role of both prosecutor and judge and that it keeps secret the terms of settlement with firms against whom proceedings are begun and then dropped.

The other law passed in 1914 was the Clayton Anti-trust Act, which specifically defined as unfair practices price discrimination among different purchasers, exclusive dealer and tying contracts, one corporation's holding the stock of another where this would lessen competition substantially, interlocking directorates, and relations of railroads with construction companies. After more intimate acquaintance with the methods of big business during World War I, the public began to realize that not all combinations were bad. When the Transportation Act of 1920 was passed, therefore, the earlier restraints upon railroad combination were removed and a policy of encouraging consolidation was adopted, subject to regulation through the Interstate Commerce Commission.

In two other respects the legislation with regard to combinations was made more liberal. It was felt that the fullest possible co-operation among merchants engaged in foreign trade was desirable, if they were to compete in foreign markets on a basis of equality with merchants from other countries. Accordingly the Webb Export Act of 1918 provided that American exporters might organize associations for conducting export trade without thereby rendering themselves liable for violation of the anti-trust laws. The same principle was applied also in the Co-operative Marketing Act of 1922, which recognized the right of farmers, ranchers, and growers to combine for the purpose of obtaining more efficient distribution of their products.

The National Industrial Recovery Act. The legislative trend of the prosperous 1920's was favorable to combinations and trusts in that little was done to hinder their growth, and the depressed 1930's at first continued that policy. One of the outstanding new laws of the Franklin Roosevelt administration was the National Industrial Recovery Act of 1933,[8] whose aims were to reduce unemployment, to increase purchasing power, and to insure just rewards to both capital and labor by eliminating unfair competition. Here we are concerned only with the last-named feature. The "rugged individualism" of President Hoover had failed to restore prosperity, and the business leaders had in many instances been discredited. The ethics of business deteriorated under the pressure of increasing competition, and reputable producers felt forced to adopt the practices of their less honorable competitors. In order to survive, firms had also repeatedly cut prices and granted rebates, but seemingly without gaining much for themselves and yet often hurting the market for their product. When an industry was overexpanded and had to be partially liquidated, price-cutting, so painful to the seller, was a necessary part of the process. Virtually the only alternative was some form of monopoly with price-fixing and production controls. American industrialists had reached a point where they were ready to unite against unfair or unpopular practices, chief of which, in the eyes of many, was price-cutting.

The National Industrial Recovery Act suspended the anti-trust laws and authorized industries to organize representative associations and to frame codes of fair competition, which,

---

[8] This act was known as the N. I. R. A., and the body set up to administer it, the National Recovery Administration, was known as the N. R. A.

upon approval by the President, should become binding upon the whole industry. An approved code constituted the standard for an industry or trade, and violations were deemed an unfair method of competition within the meaning of the Federal Trade Commission Act. The President was also given authority to impose codes on industries which refused or failed to frame acceptable codes for themselves, and also to move to punish violators of codes that had received his approval. By the end of the first month of the N.I.R.A. over 400 codes had been filed and eventually the total reached 677, including activities ranging from steel production to pants pressing, although unfortunately, many of the codes were too hastily drawn. The cotton-textile code was the first to be signed and its great achievements were the setting of minimum wages and the abolition of child labor. After this it was not difficult to write similar provisions in all other codes.

It should not be surprising under the circumstances that some industries drew up codes that gave them monopolistic powers. For example, the copper and petroleum codes provided for the limitation of output by means of plant quotas; the textile industry and nearly sixty others controlled production by limiting the number of hours machines might be operated; and many codes had provisions forbidding sales below cost. In the soft-coal industry a generous minimum price was set which so stimulated the industry that more coal was produced than could be disposed of at that price, agreements were broken, and the code had to be abandoned.[9] This illustrates a truth that supporters of price-fixing often overlook, namely, that cutting prices is one of the chief ways by which the more efficient producer enlarges his market at the expense of his less efficient rival and is one of the secrets of the improving American standard of living.

N.I.R.A. was destined to be short-lived: in May, 1935, the Supreme Court unanimously declared it unconstitutional in the famous Schechter case involving violations of the Live Poultry Code. Thus ended an experiment in self-government by business, and with its close, existing anti-trust legislation was once more restored. N.I.R.A. did much to improve busi-

[9] G. M. Modlin and A. M. McIsaac, *Social Control of Industry* (Boston, 1938), 179-92.

ness ethics and among other things it was a step in the outlawing of child labor, but it also represented the extreme in legislation favorable to monopoly in this period. Soon the trend was to be the other way.

Recent anti-trust activities. Two new laws affecting trusts were enacted in 1936 and 1937. The first was the Robinson-Patman Act of 1936, an amendment to the Clayton Antitrust Act, which sought to define more clearly the forms of price discrimination that are illegal and to eliminate some that involve intrastate commerce. It forbade price discrimination between buyers where the effect is to limit competition substantially and tend toward monopoly. The act was intended principally to lessen the buying advantages of chain stores over smaller rivals who cannot enjoy the economies of volume buying. The other law was favorable to big business. This was the Miller-Tydings Act of 1937, which permitted resale price maintenance on the ground that the choice of any brand as a "loss leader" hurt the reputation of the brand, hence the manufacturer, and also disturbed local business conditions. The act legalized price-fixing from manufacturer to consumer. Although the evils it seeks to remove are real, its elimination of some price-cutting may create more serious problems.

The recession of 1937 brought on a renewal of trust prosecutions. Proceedings were begun against the country's then outstanding trust, the Aluminum Company of America; the Federal Trade Commission attacked the basing-point system of the Cement Institute; the Attorney-General pointed to the need of a monopoly-curbing program to reduce prices of materials required for a public works program; the President stressed the need of revising and improving the anti-trust laws; and finally on June 16, 1938, Congress by joint resolution authorized the appointment of the Temporary National Economic Committee (T. N. E. C.) to find a way to reconcile existing anti-trust legislation and the growing concentration of economic power and to recommend appropriate legislation to Congress. The T. N. E. C. conducted extensive hearings and submitted its final report in March, 1941, but war broke out before any legislation was enacted.

Just as in World War I, anti-trust prosecutions were suspended for the duration of hostilities. But with the coming of peace the Department of Justice commenced anti-trust investigations of the activities of about 122 large companies.

Conclusion. One of the outstanding developments of the last generation has been the tendency for the business unit to increase in size whether measured by number of wage earners or by value of product, and for the number of plants to decline. In the steel and automobile industries three or four major concerns were responsible for more than one-half the production. Public attitude toward combinations underwent several changes: World War I brought a slackening of anti-trust feeling and activity, and combinations were allowed to multiply rapidly in the prosperous 1920's; the depression produced an awareness of the wasteful aspects of competition and resulted in temporary suspension of the anti-trust laws when the government set up the N.I.R.A. and encouraged co-operation not only in better business practices but in price-fixing and determining the amount of output; then the death of N.I.R.A. and business revival saw a renewal of anti-trust activity in the late 1930's, which was temporarily suspended by the advent of World War II. Along with increased size certain other tendencies became more pronounced, such as increased use of power in manufacturing, technical improvements in factory organization, known as "scientific management," a strong interest in industrial research, and more extensive use of the corporate device. Great advances in the knowledge of chemistry resulted in the making of new products like plastics, light steels, and synthetic fibers from readily available raw materials. New mechanical developments produced long-distance transmission of power, the radio, the airplane, and the internal combustion engine. All these bid fair to revolutionize the life of the coming generation and perhaps to alter international economic rivalries.

CHAPTER XXVIII

POPULATION AND LABOR

Population growth. The tremendous advances in manufacturing described in the last chapter were made possible not only by the growth of capital but by the existence of an adequate supply of labor. This depends on population. When population is small, as it was in early America, the nation's industrial development is handicapped by the shortage of labor; when population is excessive, as in China, industrial development is also hampered because the cheapness of labor makes laborsaving devices seem hardly worth while and capital is hard to accumulate. There is a happy medium in the matter of population and labor supply as compared with natural resources, and the United States perhaps comes as close to striking it as any nation in the world today. How strong labor's bargaining position is and therefore how large a slice of the national income labor is to receive depends on population.

The population of the United States grew from 92 million in 1910 to 140 million in 1946. The rate of increase was thus less than half of what it had been a century before when the population doubled every twenty-five years. The declining rate of growth may be attributed to the disappearance of good cheap land, to immigration restrictions, and to the rising standard of living which generally means smaller families. The birth rate fell from 19.8 per 1000 in 1910 to 18 in 1940, and the average American family declined from 4.5 persons in 1910 to 3.85 in 1940. Population increased despite the declining birth rate largely because of the even more rapidly falling death rate. This dropped from 13.6 per 1000 in 1912 to 10.8 in 1940. Thanks to advances in medical science the expectation of life at birth increased from 50 years to about 65 years at the present time. Never before in history had such rapid progress been made. But not only is the size of a nation's population important, but also its composition, by which is meant its age, racial characteristics, and distribution.

Other population trends. At least three important changes in the composition of the population have occurred within the last generation. In the first place, the percentage of white population that was foreign born declined from 16 per cent in 1910 to 9 per cent in 1940. Our immigration restrictions and a prolonged depression were responsible for this drop.

		THE POPULATION OF THE UNITED STATES, 1910-40*				
Date	White	Negro	Total	Immigration during decade ending with year	Percentage of growth of population during decade ending with year	Percentage of total in towns of 8000 inhabitants or over
1910	81,736,957	9,827,763	91,972,266	8,796,308	21.0	38.7
1920	94,820,915	10,889,705	105,710,620	5,705,811	14.9	43.8
1930	108,864,207	11,891,143	122,775,046	4,107,209	16.1†	49.1
1940	118,213,287	12,865,518	131,669,275	528,431	7.2	56.1

* The column labeled "Total" contains a small number of Indians, Japanese, Chinese, and others who are not comprised in either of the two preceding columns.

† Owing to the change of the census-taking date from January 1 to April 1 this figure is somewhat distorted. The census bureau has recalculated two decades on the basis of 120 months each, which gives 15.3 for 1920 and 15.7 for 1930.

The rate of increase of the Negro population surpassed that of the white population by 1940. If those rates continued the whites would fail to reproduce themselves by 5 per cent each generation and non-whites would gain by 7 per cent.

Still a third change which has made itself apparent in recent years is the aging of the population owing to the declining birth rate and virtual cessation of immigration. This is clearly revealed in the table on page 658. Notice however that, throughout, the most productive age group of 20 to 44 has not varied widely. Before World War II these shifts in age groups were already starting to necessitate adjustments: for example, enrollment in elementary schools had begun to decline. It was only half-jokingly suggested that in the future the market for wheel chairs might outsell that for perambulators, doctors would find more business if they specialized in cardiac diseases instead of obstetrics, and the country would show the effects of the conservatism of age and of the loss of youth's daring. These ideas seemed outdated during the first half of World War II when the number of marriages increased sharply and the birth rate rose from 17 per 1000 in 1939 to a peak of 21.5 in 1943. Since then, however, the trend has been downward, although it is still above the pre-war figure. In the long run the bulge that appeared in the war years is not likely to have much effect on major population trends.

Our Aging Population, 1850-1980			
Age groups	1850	1940	1980 (est.)
Below 20	54%	34%	25%
20 to 44	32	40	40
45 to 64	10	20	24
Over 65	4	6	11

Finally, in spite of the fact that the population is more than 140,000,000, this country must be regarded as but thinly settled when compared with the states of Europe. If the United States in 1930 had been as densely populated as France it would have had a population of 560,000,000, while if it had numbered as many people per square mile as Germany it would have had 1,065,000,000.

Geographical trends. The changes thus far enumerated have to do with the growth and composition of the population, but other movements and regroupings were taking place. The geographical shift from east to west had not wholly spent itself; it still caused the western states and particularly those on the Pacific coast to grow more rapidly than those to the east or south. There was, however, a backwash to industrial centers like Detroit and Pittsburgh, and the new manufacturing districts of the South expanded greatly. For part of this period, too, there was a steady drift of Negroes from southern plantations to northern mills and factories. The number living north of the Ohio and east of the Mississippi tripled between 1910 and 1940. Perhaps the most striking shift in the distribution of the population came about through the growth of large cities, which absorbed the major portion of the immigrants and in some states even occasioned a decrease in the rural population. While the movement from country to city is nationwide in scope, it proceeded most rapidly in the industrial states, and tended to swell the size of the largest commercial and manufacturing centers; nearly one-third of the population in 1940 lived in 96 cities of over 100,000 inhabitants and over one-half in towns of over 8,000. Industrial factors alone, however, do not explain the popularity of Miami and Washington, D. C., the fastest-growing cities in the decade ending with 1940.

Immigration. As a reason for population increase and as a source of labor, immigration has declined in importance in the last generation. Six million immigrants have come to this country since 1914 but 2 million have returned, leaving us a net gain of 4 million. During the period of World War I the country gained half a million immigrants; in the 1920's about 3 million more, and in the 1930's and early 1940's another half million. This net immigration of 4 million is in sharp contrast with 16 million for the generation before 1914. The reasons for the decline are not hard to find.

Restrictive legislation. The arrival of approximately a million immigrants each year just before World War I, particularly immigrants not easy to assimilate, alarmed many Americans. In 1917 the head tax upon each immigrant admitted into this country was raised to $8.00 and immigrants were required to know how to read and write either English or their own language. In 1921 for the first time an absolute limitation upon immigration was imposed; the so-called "quota" law restricted the yearly immigration of any nationality to 3 per cent of the number of such persons resident in the United States in 1910. The reasons which led to this legislation seem to have been, first, the fear of a flood of emigration to this country as a result of the efforts of European citizens to escape the heavy taxes and hard living conditions in their homes which resulted from the war; second, the fear on the part of organized labor that the standard of wages would thereby be lowered, especially in view of the widespread unemployment in the United States at the time; and third, the presence here, as disclosed by World War I, of some 10,000,000 unnaturalized aliens, whose Americanization seemed necessary before further additions were permitted.

Another act of 1924 still further reduced the quota by changing the apportionment to 2 per cent of any nationality residing here in 1890, and by forbidding the immigration of Japanese. The last ungracious provision was deeply resented by the Japanese and was hardly necessary since virtually the same end could have been accomplished under the quota system. The "national origins" provision of the act of 1924 assumed superiority of the "Nordic" race and therefore sought to limit the non-Nordic immigration; the total immigration under this law was limited to 150,000 annually and immigration from Northwestern Europe was favored by selecting 1890 as the base year. The law was slightly modified in 1927, but not essentially changed, by making the population of 1920 the base. This legislation did not apply to our neighbors in the Americas. The one-time stream of immigration dried to a mere trickle. Evidently an end has come to the original idealism which asserted that America had "room about her hearth for all mankind."

As a result of the decline in immigration the nation has had some opportunity to assimilate the "little Italys," "little Hungarys," etc., which had grown up in many of our big cities. There was less fear of alien sabotage in World War II than in World War I. Also, as the immigrants have become more used to American ways, many have joined trade unions and become less of a threat to those growing organizations. With immigrant labor no longer the main source of cheap labor for big industry, mines, and other large-scale operations, new sources have had to be tapped. Mexicans have streamed across our southern border to help harvest the crops of the Southwest, especially sugar beets. As already indicated, the Negro population of the North has greatly increased as tens of thousands have taken industrial and other jobs in such cities as New York, Chicago, and Detroit. And textile industries have moved to the Southeast to avail themselves of the cheaper and more amenable labor to be found there. In time the result of all this may be more equal wage levels throughout the country. These are some of the consequences of our restrictive immigration policy.

The American Federation of Labor. The decline in immigration just described was only one reason for the greater scarcity of labor in the last generation. It is a well-known economic truth that any factor of production, whether land, capital, or labor, is rewarded in proportion to its scarcity. The 140 per cent rise in factory workers' real wages between 1914 and 1946 (see page 675) is ample evidence that labor had become relatively scarcer. This scarcity was not apparent in the depressed 1930's but it is for the period as a whole. What have been some of the other developments that account for the greater labor scarcity? A second one is the growing accumulation of capital mentioned in the previous chapter, and a third, affecting factory labor but not labor as a whole, is the increase in trade-union membership. Unions have been encouraged by the government in the three great crises that have occurred since 1914, namely, two major wars and a staggering depression.

The outstanding labor organization in the period has been the American Federation of Labor which in 1914 practically stood alone except for the Railway Brotherhoods. At that time it consisted of 110 national and international unions plus numerous state, city, and local unions, the membership totaling 2,000,000. The A. F. of L. was essentially a skilled white man's organization; in other words, it had very few Negro or women members and only a small number of unskilled. Most of the national unions were built on individual skills like those of the bookbinders, the coopers, the cigarmakers, or on an amalgamation of similar skills like the Amalgamated Association of Iron, Steel, and Tin Workers.

World War I and labor. The period of World War I was one of tremendous opportunity for organized labor and unions prospered accordingly. By 1920 the membership of the A. F. of L. had almost exactly doubled, although the number of constituent national and international unions remained the same. The A. F. of L. announced in 1917, "This is labor's war. It must be won by labor and every stage in the fighting and final victory must be made to count for humanity." But at the same time the labor leaders warned that in all previous conflicts labor had been stripped of its defenses against capital under the guise of national defense, that this time labor should be given representation on the important councils of national defense, and that "the government must recognize the organized labor movement as the agency through which it must cooperate with wage earners." Furthermore "service in government factories and private establishments and transportation agencies all should conform to trade union standards."

Many of these aims were substantially accomplished: President Samuel Gompers of the A. F. of L., who was already on the National Council of Defense, was appointed to the War Labor Board, and the A. F. of L. was given representation on the Emergency Construction Board, the Food Administration Board, and the War Industries Board, to name just a few. The recognition of union standards was gained first in the railway industry and in government work and then extended to other employments. Labor kept the right to organize, virtually won the eight-hour day, equal pay for women, and recognition of union standards, but gave up restriction of output and to a considerable extent the right to strike. Employer opposition to organized labor fell off. Employers needed more workers to fill their many orders, they were relieved of much of the anti-trust regulation, and they no longer faced the necessity of meeting a competitive price because many goods were sold to the government on a basis of cost plus a fixed fee, usually 10 per cent. Membership in machinist unions doubled, that of boilermakers and electrical workers tripled, and that of railway clerks increased tenfold. When the war ended, organized labor was proud of its record and accomplishments and expected the good times to continue.

Postwar readjustments. More than a year of prosperity followed the Armistice. During it one after another war board was discontinued, returning soldiers were demobilized, the cost of living soared, and a few severe strikes broke out in some of the heavy industries like steel, railroads, and coal. As conditions returned to "normalcy," business leaders determined to rid themselves of the labor organizations that had mushroomed in their plants. A short but severe postwar depression beginning in mid-1920 facilitated this weeding out program. No longer did the government interpose to maintain a basic eight-hour day, to protect union standards, or to uphold the right to organize non-union employees. Labor received a rude awakening. A steel strike in 1919 was broken, an anti-Bolshevist hysteria swept the country, and an open-shop drive begun by two leading employer associations achieved startling success. Kansas went so far as to forbid strikes, requiring arbitration in businesses "affected with a public interest." Between 1920 and 1923 A. F. of L. membership declined from 4,100,000 to 2,800,000.

The decade of the 1920's is associated with prosperity, but it was the employers, not the unions, that prospered. A. F. of L. membership remained stationary after 1923. There were several reasons for this. The high money and real wages prevailing blinded workers to the necessity of organizing. Even many union officials were content to let well enough alone and enjoy a comfortable white-collar-class existence. In the South organizing campaigns were often based on the policy of securing the good will of employers. Meanwhile, employers became more and more powerful as corporations merged into larger business units. Strenuous efforts were made to keep the workers happy, and often the simple method of fair treatment was adopted, but the unions were generally feared. Shrewd and effective policies were devised in dealing with them. On the one hand welfare measures including everything from athletic fields to pension plans and profit-sharing encouraged the workers to be loyal to their companies; on the other, legal restraints such as threatened anti-trust prosecutions, injunctions, yellow-dog contracts, or harsh practices like the use of labor spies and the discharge of union members frightened workers and made the task of the union difficult. Many industries set up company unions which lacked strike funds and, of course, independent leadership. On top of all this, technological changes were every year making it easier to substitute the combination of machines and semi-skilled workers for various skills.

The Great Depression. The economic collapse that began in 1929 witnessed a rapid decline not only in the strength of unions—A. F. of L. membership fell from 2,900,000 in 1929 to 2,100,000 in 1933—but also in the workers' standard of living. Three dependable authorities estimate that by

1932-33 one out of every three workers was without a job, and of course many of these had to lean upon relatives and friends fortunate enough to have kept theirs. Bread lines appeared in cities and, although strikes were infrequent, mass discontent grew steadily. The Hoover administration was largely a political victim of these economic circumstances.

The advent of Franklin D. Roosevelt's "New Deal" coincided roughly with an upturn in business recovery and the two greatly stimulated organized labor. Famous section 7-A of the National Industrial Recovery Act of 1933 granted workers "the right to organize and bargain collectively through representatives of their own choosing" and added that "no employee and no one seeking employment should be required as a condition of employment to join any company union or refrain from joining, organizing or assisting a labor organization of his own choosing." This was succeeded in 1935 by the National Labor Relations Act, sometimes called the Wagner Act, which gave the same protection and forbade various "unfair" labor practices of employers. Under the stimulus of these laws the A. F. of L. membership rose to 3,400,000 in 1936, the highest since 1921. But unions organized by industries gained 132 per cent while those built on craft lines rose only 13 per cent between 1933 and 1935. Why were industrial unions becoming more popular?

Changing industrial organization. The craft union was now over a century old and in the opinion of many was out of date. It had originated even before the coming of the factory system and when carried into the factory it chiefly benefited the skilled worker. The histories of the Knights of Labor and the Industrial Workers of the World related in Chapter XXII show that slow progress was being made in improving the lot of the unskilled and semi-skilled workers through labor organizations. But as time passed and markets widened, more products were factory-made and factory tasks became increasingly specialized. This greater specialization meant that *less* skill was needed to perform them. Many jobs could be learned in a few days', hours', or even minutes' time. The proportion of unskilled and semi-skilled workers steadily increased and skilled workers lost ground.

This was bound to have its effects on the type of labor

organization prevailing. Some crafts merged or amalgamated rather than wither away. An amalgamated union is an organization of skilled workers using more or less the same materials. It is a compromise between a craft union and an industrial union. Other unions went all the way and admitted to membership thousands who boasted little skill at all until some critics were asking how the A. F. of L. could insist "that the man who has become a living screw-driver is a skilled mechanic." These industrial unions were fast-growing and aggressive.

Out of these gradual changes in industrial organization, union structure, and union membership at least two major difficulties developed. First, jurisdictional disputes were a constant source of ill feeling among unions. For example, in railroad repair shops, where there were seven A. F. of L. shop unions, the boilermakers, sheet metal workers, blacksmiths, machinists, and electricians were in frequent conflict. Should a boilermaker or a sheet metal worker install the all-important crown sheet in the engine's firebox? Who should attach the headlight on the locomotive? Second, there was rivalry between skilled and unskilled and semi-skilled workers. This was the rock on which the Knights of Labor had once wrecked itself. Now the skilled workers in some unions were in constant fear that they would lose control. Likewise, within the A. F. of L. the leaders of the more purely skilled organizations were jealous of the growing power of industrial unions. In turn the leaders of industrial unions like the United Mine Workers and various garment workers' unions became impatient with the old-fashioned tactics of the craft organizations. Repeatedly they urged that all laborers in any factory should belong to one union since that would present a united front to management and lessen jurisdictional disputes. They bitterly resented attempts of craft unions to apportion members of newly formed industrial unions among themselves, or refusals to organize at all if it had to be along industrial lines. For example, William Green, president of the A. F. of L., told Gerard Swope, head of the General Electric Company, that the A. F. of L. would not organize workers in that company unless it could divide them into fifteen separate crafts. It was out of such conflicts over union structure that the Committee for Industrial Organization sprang.

The Committee for Industrial Organization. The C. I. O. came into being when the majority of the A. F. of L. delegates at the annual convention in Atlantic City in 1935 voted against the organization of workers along industrial lines in mass-production industries. A large minority revolted and founded the C. I. O. on November 10, 1935, with eight unions and one million members. John L. Lewis, head of the United Mine Workers, the largest constituent union, became president. Most of the other unions were from the textile trade. The C. I. O. had the same kind of federal framework as the A. F. of L.; the chief structural difference was the organization of local unions by industry instead of by craft. Partisans of industrial and craft methods of organization hurled arguments at American labor and the public for many months. The A. F. of L. leaders shouted that the C. I. O. leaders were guilty of dual unionism, a high form of labor treason because it means divided forces where there should be a united front before the employer. The C. I. O. leaders replied that the reactionary element in the A. F. of L. was itself guilty for prohibiting industrial unionism and would rather wreck organized labor than lose control. Craft organization was archaic in a factory economy, they insisted, and was the reason why only one-tenth of the working population was enrolled in unions after two generations of the A. F. of L. Within another two years the C. I. O. had partially organized the automobile, steel, oil, and rubber industries and boasted 32 national unions and 3,700,000 members. In 1938 it adopted the new name of Congress of Industrial Organizations.

The methods and conduct of the unions in this new giant organization sometimes showed more spirit and ingenuity than respect for the law. Rejoicing in their new-found strength, the unskilled and semi-skilled workers were anxious to make up for lost time. The head office had difficulty controlling the national union leaders and these in turn were sometimes unable to restrain the enthusiasm of their membership. Public opinion, although sympathetic toward the workers, was repeatedly shocked by the new union's excesses.

The story of the General Motors strike of 1937 will serve as an illustration.

Detroit sit-down strike. Most of the workers in the automobile industry were barely semi-skilled, since four jobs out of five could be learned in two weeks' time. But life on the assembly line was dull, tedious, and very wearing; some were unable to stand the pace which they claimed was constantly being speeded up. Although the pay was at times high on a per diem basis, work was not steady and the yearly wage was not high. Furthermore, numerous labor spies made organization hazardous, and company policy based on the strategy of "divide and rule" encouraged dissension among the unions that did exist. After the "New Deal" began, the United Automobile Workers, which was at first an A. F. of L. industrial union, grew in power, then deserted to the C. I. O., put on a vigorous organizing campaign under the leadership of Homer Martin, and in December, 1936, endeavored to negotiate with company officials for recognition and certain concessions. When the officials refused to negotiate, a strike began at a Fisher Body plant and spread. The workers sat down in the factories and refused to move, their attitude being that they were protecting their jobs. The corporation stressed that the men were trespassing, often destroying property, and preventing the operation of valuable equipment whose enforced idleness was very costly. A court order was secured ordering the men to vacate, but was not enforced largely owing to Governor Murphy of Michigan, who feared there would be bloodshed. Instead, he tried desperately to secure an amicable settlement and at last succeeded. The strike was won: the union achieved recognition, a survey of speed-up abuses was agreed to, time and one-half for overtime was to prevail, and there was to be no discrimination against unionists.

The sit-down strike was novel and highly effective at a time when the union needed victories to give the membership self-confidence. It was subsequently declared illegal beyond any doubt in the Fansteel case of 1938, but C. I. O. strikes continued to make the headlines.

Independent unions. Not all members of unions belong to either the A. F. of L. or the C. I. O. Since 1914 approximately one unionist in five to one in ten has not. Most famous of the independent unions are the Big Four Railway Brother-hoods: the engineers, firemen, conductors, and trainmen, who are sometimes referred to as the "aristocracy of American unionism" because of their conservatism, the high caliber of the men, the age of their organizations, and their independ-ence of the rest of the labor movement. Other railway workers have independent unions, as do also a few groups in manufacturing and a considerable number of workers in the government service, particularly in the post-office department. Finally, between 1942, when John L. Lewis led his United Mine Workers out of the C. I. O., and 1946 when he led them back to the A. F. of L., that great union of 400,000 members was an independent organization.

World War II and organized labor. Despite labor's new powers and privileges there were 10 million unemployed as late as 1940. The war then solved the unemployment prob-lem and created such acute labor shortages in the country that labor made further stupendous gains. Membership in labor unions grew from 8.2 million in 1939 to 14.5 million in 1946, with the C. I. O. claiming 6 million members and the A. F. of L. 7 million. The majority of industrial workers now belonged to unions; it was largely the non-industrial workers, three times as numerous, who were unorganized. Various devices were extensively employed to force workers into unions or to keep them there. The closed shop or union shop obliged them to join to keep their jobs, or the principle of maintenance of membership deprived them of their jobs if they tried to resign from the union after having joined it, and the check-off provided that the employer would deduct union dues from their pay checks and turn the money over to the union, thus keeping members in good standing. With such controls union treasuries swelled and the power of union leaders expanded. Organized labor was, moreover, repre-sented on many of the major war councils, like the War Production Board and the War Manpower Commission, just as it had been during World War I. Even more significant, organized labor was admitted at the policy-making level on the federal and numerous regional War Labor Boards.

Despite the autocratic character of the union machinery,

few workers objected because of the numerous benefits they received. Between January, 1937, and April, 1945, average weekly earnings of all manufacturing workers doubled. This was partly owing to the fact that the prewar 40-hour work week was retained during the war and overtime rates were paid when work schedules exceeded 40 hours. But it was partly owing, also, to wage increases. While labor's officialdom took a no-strike pledge in 1941 and wages were stabilized for the duration of the war on October 3, 1942, the war period witnessed both strikes and rising wage rates. Strikes and strike threats in coal mines, steel plants, airplane factories, and other industries brought pay adjustments from sympathetic War Labor Boards. Under the Little Steel formula a 15 per cent pay increase was allowed to offset the rising cost of living. In the coal strike further wage increases were permitted under the guise of "portal-to-portal" pay: for the first time miners were paid from the moment they entered the mine property until they left. Finally, vacation with pay, sick benefits, seniority rules, and other privileges were obtained in many factories as new trade agreements were negotiated. In short, World War II brought great gains to organized labor. However, unorganized labor, particularly in the white-collar classes, experienced a decline in real wages.

Aside from some unsavory strikes the war record of labor as a whole was one in which the vast majority could take pride. Almost as many civilian goods were produced as in peacetime and yet unbelievable quantities of planes, tanks, and other war matériel were turned out. Many laborers accumulated sizable savings in the form of war bonds.

Labor and reconversion. It was foreseen that reconverting industry from the production of war goods to the production of peacetime goods would be difficult, but opinions differed widely as to what the chief difficulties would be. Government forecasters feared falling prices and widespread unemployment. Many economists were afraid prices would spiral upward unless great quantities of civilian goods were produced to sop up the billions of dollars of purchasing power created by the war. Workers were tired of the wartime pace and dissatisfied because, when the war ended, overtime work became less necessary and the size of pay checks was reduced. Thus many laborers were in a mood to take a vacation, call it a strike, and trust that it would restore the wartime "take home" pay. President Truman publicly reasoned that wage increases were possible without price increases because of technological improvements developed during the war and because of the economies of full-scale production. Management resisted union demands because it saw profits squeezed thin between rising wages and continued price ceilings. Strikes were numerous and prolonged with great losses to both sides, to other industries, and to the public. More man-days were lost through strikes in the first half of 1946 than in any year of our history, indeed more man-days were lost than in all the five previous years. Reconversion was seriously delayed.

MAN-DAYS LOST THROUGH STRIKES AND LOCKOUTS IN THE UNITED STATES, 1927-JULY, 1, 1946*

(*Unit:* 10,000,000 *man-days*)

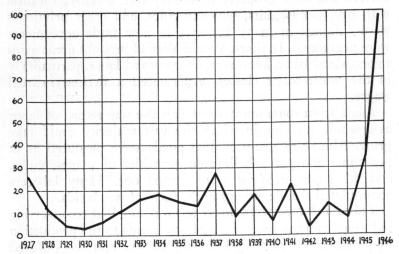

* Source: *United States Bureau of Labor Statistics.*

Organized labor saw gains of the first part of the year melt away as black markets, poor-quality merchandise, shortages, and finally abandonment of price ceilings raised the cost of living over 17 per cent in a few months' time (between January and mid-November, 1946).

Weapons of capital and labor. While the vast majority of trade agreements between employers and employees are amicably negotiated, occasionally issues can be settled only by resort to economic pressure. In these struggles between organized capital and organized labor the weapons would seem to be fairly evenly divided. Since each side has some weapons that are vicious, it behooves the public to establish and enforce a decent set of rules. There has been the rub. Although the government has outwardly tried to do that in the last half century, the tremendous political and economic power of the two contesting classes has made progress painfully slow. The rules have first favored one side and then the other.

Before 1933 the advantage in industrial conflict usually lay with the employer. He could maintain an anti-union open shop by using the yellow-dog contract or he could refuse to bargain with union representatives; he could use such insidious weapons as the blacklist and labor spy, or he could employ the injunction which was probably the most effective of all. Police would generally protect strike-breakers and often break up picketing demonstrations. On the other hand, unions were denied the use of the secondary boycott and were subject to prosecution under the anti-trust laws. Under the circumstances it is not surprising to find that organized labor's membership declined during the prosperous 1920's, a period in which it might normally have been expected to gain membership.

Beginning in 1929 a serious and prolonged depression accompanied by mass unemployment resulted in an overturn of the Republican administration whose sympathies had been with the employer. The incoming Democratic administration was keenly interested in raising wages and otherwise strengthening the hand of labor. Through legislation which will be discussed shortly many abuses were corrected. Unfortunately, the situation was overcorrected until labor was as much favored in the 1940's as capital had been in the 1920's. Union membership skyrocketed in the depression-ridden 1930's, a period in which it might have been expected to decline. What were some of the laws responsible for these startling changes and gains?

Labor's bargaining powers increased. Even before the election of Franklin D. Roosevelt to the Presidency, a Democratic Congress passed the Norris-La Guardia Act in 1932. One purpose of this measure was to free unions from prosecution under the anti-trust laws, something the Clayton Act of 1914 had not succeeded in doing. The Norris-La Guardia Act did not specifically exempt unions from prosecution under the anti-trust laws, but it made legal most of the things for which unions had previously been prosecuted under those laws. Federal courts were virtually forbidden to issue injunctions against unions engaged in labor disputes. The yellow-dog contract was rendered unenforceable, and the secondary boycott was made legal again. Safeguarded beyond doubt were the unions' rights to strike in their own behalf, to encourage sympathy strikes in the same industry, to picket peacefully, and to pay strike benefits. Within the next decade nearly half the states passed similar laws.

The next important piece of federal labor legislation was the National Labor Relations Act or Wagner Act of 1935, often called "labor's Magna Carta." This set up a three-man board with two basic functions: first to prevent employers from engaging in certain "unfair" labor practices, and second, to conduct elections among employees to determine what union should represent the workers in bargaining with management. The board forbade, as unfair to labor: using labor spies, employing professional strikebreakers and sluggers, circulating propaganda against unions in such a way as to cause laborers to fear for their jobs, and discharging employees for engaging in union activities. Employers were also required to bargain in good faith with the representatives chosen by their employees. The consequence was to outlaw the anti-union open shop and to encourage some form of the closed shop, or at least a subsequent compromise for the closed shop known as maintenance of membership. By 1941 approximately 10 per cent of all workers were in closed shops and by 1945 about 30 per cent were in closed shops or covered by maintenance of membership. The Wagner law was obviously and admittedly intended to curb the employer and promote the aims of labor. At least ten states passed laws resembling this act. The United States Supreme Court upheld the National Labor Relations Board at practically every turn.

The Fair Labor Standards Act of 1938 also improved labor's bargaining position by instituting the 40-hour week with a minimum wage of 40 cents an hour and by outlawing child labor in all establishments producing goods for interstate commerce. The result was to equalize to some extent costs in union and non-union shops and to reduce any economic advantage the non-union employer might have.

Probably even more important than the laws on the statute books was the attitude of the various organs of government toward labor. From 1932 until about 1946 this attitude was largely sympathetic. Pro-labor municipal and state government authorities repeatedly allowed mass picketing, even though it was clearly illegal. These mobs denied admission not only to any persons who might want to continue to work in the striking plants but in some cases kept even the owners out. There can be no doubt that this made strikes more successful. The President discouraged Congress from passing laws to curb unions and did not enforce the law (Smith-Connally Act) against wartime strikes that was passed. None of the pro-labor legislation described above was held unconstitutional by the Supreme Court; indeed that Court has not held any act of Congress unconstitutional since 1937. Finally, during and since the war the government made it a practice to seize strike-bound plants engaged in production essential to war or reconversion. The strikers then returned to work, but generally on terms close to what they were striking for. To repossess the plants the owners had to meet those terms.

While many of the reforms that have come since 1932 were long overdue—such as limiting the use of the injunction, outlawing yellow-dog contracts, blacklists, and labor spies, and enforcing collective bargaining—the American public came to the opinion after the war ended that the balance of power had shifted too far in labor's favor. There were too many strikes and too many labor monopolies. Just as the Robber Barons of industry and transportation of two generations ago—men like Gould, Vanderbilt, Rockefeller, and Frick—abused their powers under laissez-faire, so likewise had the modern czars of labor—men like Caesar Petrillo of the musicians' union or John L. Lewis of the United Mine Workers—abused their power after most of the curbs on labor were removed. The nation was learning something it should have known all along, namely, when the rules of making a living in any occupation are relaxed, the men who come out on top are those who exploit their advantage to the utmost. Therefore, laws adequate to protect the public should be impartially enforced on both management and labor. It was evident that reforms were forthcoming after the Republican victory in the 1946 elections and after John L. Lewis' arrogant demonstration in the coal strike of the power of one man heading one union to paralyze the nation's economy.

Wages. The real wages of the workingman have risen appreciably since 1914 although the increase has not been steady nor the gains equally distributed among all classes of workers. During World War I the real wages of men engaged in transportation and manufacturing rose noticeably despite the inflation, which usually has a tendency to lower real wages. Other groups that gained were coal miners, unskilled laborers, and farm hands; those who lost were chiefly white-collar groups, teachers, ministers, and workers in the building trades. Following the war all but the coal miners, unskilled workers, and farm hands gained, some like the teachers and building-trades workers being especially fortunate. By 1923 the real wages of manufacturing workers were about 30 per cent higher than in 1914, at least half of this increase occurring in the preceding three years. After 1923, according to the Bureau of Labor Statistics, real weekly wages in manufacturing changed very little until the depression which lowered them by about 10 per cent in 1932. That was not unduly severe for the workers who kept full-time jobs and had no unfortunate friends or relatives to support, but it was very hard on the 12 to 16 million unemployed, the millions more who were partially employed, and the additional millions who were helping their less fortunate fellow workers. This situation does not show up in most real-wage statistics. After 1932 the unemployment situation improved somewhat and real wages rose steadily except for 1938. The coming of World War II solved the unemployment problem and pushed real wages up sharply in certain manufacturing and mining industries. By the summer of 1946 manufacturing workers were getting about 25 per cent more real wages than they got in 1939, 100 per cent more than they got in 1925 and 140 per cent more than they got in 1914. The well-organized bituminous coal miners did better than that; they doubled their real wages between 1939 and 1946. Farm laborers, although unorganized, more than doubled their real wages because they were scarce. But non-unionized white-collar groups generally experienced a sharp decline in real wages as prices rose.

Labor's share of the national income rose from about 60 per cent in 1914 to 69 per cent in 1939 and to about 74 per cent in 1943, according to the National Industrial Conference Board. During this period the output per laborer nearly tripled. Labor's declining skill and shorter hours were more than offset by the greater amount of capital equipment at the disposal of each wage earner. However, it should be borne in mind that labor's share of the national income depends fundamentally on its scarcity relative to the other agents of production, land, capital, and management. This tends to set the upper limits to total wages beyond which even union efforts cannot readily raise them. Labor was very scarce during World War II and so its share of the national income rose.

Hours and working conditions. In 1915 the nine-hour day was the average for all industry, although the worker in unionized manufacturing industries enjoyed a work week that was less than this average and a good day shorter than that of his non-unionized brother. The war period witnessed about one-half a day's reduction in hours, more in the non-unionized fields than in the unionized. During the prosperous 1920's Saturday half-holidays became more common; in fact, in the building trades, which have often led the way, the five-day week prevailed, and the very long hours in the steel industry were reduced. The depression necessitated spreading the work among the workers to some extent, but this lessening of hours was accompanied by sharing the payroll. It was not until the advent of the N.I.R.A. and its codes in 1933 that the shorter workday with undiminished pay came into vogue again. Half of the employees under N.I.R.A. enjoyed the basic 40-hour week, and only 7 per cent had to work more than 48 hours a week. The Fair Labor Standards Act of 1938 provided that after 1940 the 40-hour week should be basic in all industries shipping goods in interstate commerce. During World War II the 40-hour week remained basic, but millions worked 48, 54, or even more hours per week and received 50 per cent more pay for the overtime hours.

Working conditions have been improved in countless minor and major ways in the last generation. Progress in lighting, ventilation, lubrication and shock-absorption techniques, the substitution of electric for steam power, improved lunchroom, restroom, and dispensary facilities, and increased use of safety devices, such as caging of exposed and dangerous machine parts, have all helped to eliminate much of the risk and unpleasantness of factory work. Industrial injuries in manufacturing per million man-hours worked declined from 20.8 in 1926 to 15.4 in 1939, but increased during the war period when many inexperienced persons had to be hired. Death injuries to railroad employees fell from an annual average of 3273 in 1911-15 to 513 in 1938 but doubled again during the war. Despite these and other encouraging gains in many industries there still remains the very definite menace of occupational diseases and ailments, such as tuberculosis in the very dusty or humid trades, lead poisoning among painters, "hatter shakes" (from mercury) among makers of felt hats, and "brass chills" (from zinc fumes) among workers in brass foundries, to name just a few. The Metropolitan Life Insurance Company's statisticians estimated in 1930 that the industrial worker had a shorter than average life expectancy because of the hazards of his occupation.

Security. One of the most common desires of human beings is for security against the impact of unforeseen events. Making ready for a rainy day costs money, and on a small income this necessarily requires much intelligence and more will power, so that many families are completely at the mercy of the economic tide. In recent years the government has helped the worker gain more adequate protection against unemployment, against personal injury, and against poverty-stricken old age.

According to the 1930 census, a man was definitely unemployed if he was "out of a job, able to work, and looking for a job." This did not include unemployables, idle rich, the sick, those with part-time employment or temporarily laid off without pay, and some other categories. In general, unemployment may be seasonal, such as among harvest workers, canners, and formerly in the automobile industry, or it may be secular as when new machines are introduced, such as the linotype, automatic bottle machines, or the McKay shoe machines, or it may be cyclical as when a depression necessitates curtailment of production. Of the three types, the cyclical has been far the most serious. During depressions in the last fifty years the number of unemployed has ranged between 1 and 16 millions, this peak figure being reached in March of 1933 near the bottom of the great depression. Until this depression the federal government did very little to relieve the plight of the unemployed; in fact, the vast outpourings of federal funds took place after the worst of this depression was over, nearly $14,000 million being spent on unemployment relief between 1934 and 1939. Whether in the form of direct relief, work-relief projects, or Civilian Conservation Corps camps for young men, the remedies were visualized originally as emergency measures.

Many experts accept unemployment as a misfortune along with other accidents, see no likelihood of eliminating it, and favor steps to spread the risk; that is, to insure against it. Although attempts have been made by companies and by unions to insure against unemployment, until recently this has not been done on a wide scale. Before the depression-ridden 1930's, states were reluctant to impose such a program lest their industries be frightened away or be handicapped in competition. It remained for the federal government to undertake the responsibility, and this was done in 1935 with the passage of the Social Security Act. A basic purpose of this law, however, was to stimulate the states to pass laws of their own and by July, 1937, all states had such laws. The federal government levied a 3 per cent pay-roll tax on employers for unemployment compensation. Individual states might repossess nine-tenths of these funds for payment of unemployment benefits by enacting state legislation in conformance with federal standards. To use Illinois as an example of the law's workings, an employee in a plant there hiring six or more persons is eligible for a benefit of $10 to $20 a week for a maximum of 26 weeks after he has been out of work for one week. In order to help the unemployed and lessen the drain on funds, an effective employment agency is essential, and this machinery was provided in the United States Employment Service, created under the Wagner-Peyser Act of 1933.

The nightmare of being tossed out onto the "industrial scrap heap," and the fear of spending his last years in the poorhouse have beset the worker for years. Non-governmental agencies were not able to meet this problem and progress by the states was slow. Arizona passed the first state old-age pension law in 1914, but it was declared unconstitutional and it was not until 1925 that Wisconsin enacted a successful one. It was becoming obvious that the national government must assume the responsibility. Great Britain had enjoyed such a law since 1908 and was imitated by a number of other countries before Congress took over the problem in 1935. The Social Security Act of that year, discussed above, provided not only the unemployment insurance, but also financial assistance to states possessing adequate old-age plans of their own, and most important, it set up an enormous old-age insurance scheme. The funds for old-age insurance were to be provided half by employers and half by employees, each to contribute equal small fractions of the payroll. At present every eligible 65-year-old worker is entitled to receive between $10 and $56 monthly and if he has a family they may be entitled to secondary benefits which will raise the total to something between $20 and $85. These are not large sums and the law is still faulty and will need numerous improvements. The essential fact, however, is that an old-age-pension system has been started at last.

A third type of security needed by the family breadwinner is protection against accidents. The modern theory has been that the cost of industrial accidents should be regarded as part of the cost of the product. Almost every state has either a compulsory or elective accident insurance law for employers yielding from 20 to 100 per cent compensation to employees.

Conclusion. The years since 1914 have witnessed two world wars, each of which afforded organized labor opportunities to improve its bargaining position and raised some doubt as to whether real wages decline in a modern war-produced inflation. Because the growing mechanization of industry has eliminated many skills and the craft organizations had little interest in unskilled labor anyway, a new type of labor organization built on industrial rather than craft lines was born in 1935 and quickly rivaled the A. F. of L. in size and power. Another important change was the friendlier attitude of government, particularly in periods of crisis, whether war or depression. In the 1930's the government compensated in part for the fall in real wages of labor as a whole by passing numerous laws shortening hours, giving the worker greater security against unemployment and old age, and increasing labor's bargaining weapons. By 1946 evidence in the form of arrogant labor monopolists and a tremendous increase in strikes indicated that labor's new powers needed some modifications.

CHAPTER XXIX

NEW AGENCIES OF TRANSPORTATION
AND COMMUNICATION

Development of transportation. The history of transportation in the United States has been one of constant improvement and change—rivers, roads, canals, railroads, each in turn served to raise to a higher level of efficiency the methods of transport. The twentieth century witnessed the advent of another agency, the automobile. The effects of this on the older forms, and on our social life, constitute the most marked change in this field since the railroad superseded the canal. This period has also seen the transformation of the airplane from an experiment to a commercial success, but the full utilization of this method belongs to the future. It should be noted, however, that no form of transportation in use has ever disappeared; as other methods have been developed they have been added to existing agencies, and have frequently quickened the older ones to renewed activity.

During World War I there was an almost complete cessation of new railroad building as the free capital of the country was diverted into war channels; and since that event other circumstances have combined to discourage additions to existing lines. Among these may be mentioned the insufficient earnings of the railroads during the years since World War I, the competition of automobiles, busses, and motor trucks, and the practical completion of necessary facilities. On January 1, 1944, the railroad mileage was only 228,557 or an actual decrease of 31,000 miles since the high-water mark in 1916; a greater mileage was abandoned than constructed during that subsequent period. Most of the new building after the opening of the twentieth century was in the South and Southwest, which were least well supplied with railroad facilities at the beginning of the period. The greatest mileage of any state is in Texas. An interesting addition to new mileage was the completion in 1923 of the Alaska Railroad, about 500 miles in length, which was built and operated by the federal government.

Effect of World War I. The vast expansion of industry during the years of our neutrality put a great strain upon the railroads, and after the entrance of the United States into World War I the railroad service began to break down. An effort was made in 1917 to co-ordinate the operations of the railroads in order to obtain greater efficiency in the utilization of the railroad plant by creating a Railroad War Board, consisting of a group of railroad presidents. This proved unsuccessful because the roads, fearful of reduced earnings and rising costs, refused to co-operate fully without any increase in rates. Even more confusing was the issuance of conflicting priority orders by various government departments, which caused serious congestion on the railways at ports, in shipyards, and at other points. It became evident that some form of centralized control was necessary and this was obtained by the operation of the roads of the country as a unit during the period of the war. Government operation was substituted for regulation.

During the twenty-six months from December 28, 1917, to February 29, 1920, the railroads were under federal administration, at the head of which was placed first William G. McAdoo, then Secretary of the Treasury, and later Walker D. Hines, and the problem of control became one of efficient administration. It was possible for the government, by the unification of all the railroads under one management, to effect many economies and to utilize the transportation facilities to better advantage than the separate organizations had been able to do. Short routing of traffic, unification of all facilities including ticket offices and terminals, rolling stock, etc., reduction in passenger service, expeditious movement of freight by sending solid trainloads, standardization of freight cars and locomotives, were a few of the economies introduced. The last-named is a striking case; before the war there were some two thousand styles of freight cars and nearly as many styles of engines, but these were reduced to twelve standard types of freight cars and six standard types of locomotives of two weights each.

So far as traffic operation was concerned the results of federal administration were praiseworthy, but the financial results were not so satisfactory. The excess of operating costs over revenues for the twenty-six months of government operation was estimated by Mr. Hines in 1920 at $900 million, an estimate which has since been raised to $1200 million. Part of this deficit is attributable to the mounting costs of labor and supplies, part to the subordination of profits to the requirements of war, part to the previous rundown condition of the railroads, and a large part to the failure to raise rates in proportion to the increase in wages and prices. The loss must be counted as one of the costs of the war, rather than as evidence of wasteful government administration, though it has frequently been used as an argument against government ownership and operation.

The Transportation Act of 1920. The war period of federal administration had pointed some valuable lessons both to the owners and to Congress, and the terms upon which the railroads were to be managed in the future were different from those which had prevailed before. Those conditions were laid down in the Transportation Act of 1920, which to some extent reversed previous railroad policy. The powers of the Interstate Commerce Commission were greatly enlarged and authority was given it to regulate railroad capitalization, car service, and consolidation. But the most important provisions of the act were those dealing with rates and with labor. On all these points railroad legislation before World War I had been insufficient. There had been no control over the issuance of securities except that exercised by the state commissions, nor had consideration been given to service. Attention had been concentrated mainly on questions of rates and discrimination. The machinery for the settlement of railroad disputes was also inadequate. On the other hand, the legislation had been unduly restrictive along other lines and had vainly attempted to enforce competition.

The idea that competition must be enforced among railroads was abandoned in this act. Pooling, forbidden under the original law in 1887, was now legalized under the supervision of the commission. Consolidation of the railroads of the country into a few great competitive systems was planned, and several comprehensive schemes were drawn up. It was hoped that by consolidation the costs of operation could be considerably reduced and that the combined systems would be enabled to earn a fair return on their investment. No government action was taken to enforce consolidation, but in the next twenty years a number of voluntary regroupings was made, without, however, materially changing the railroad map of 1920. On the other hand, real progress was made in the integration and co-ordination of the facilities of the railroads with those of motor carriers. The combination of American railroads into regional monopolies, as in Britain, or into a single unified system, as in Germany and France, seems unlikely.

With regard to rates, the Transportation Act of 1920 introduced a new principle; namely, the responsibility of the government, if it controls rates, to bear in mind their effect on earnings. The commission was given the power to fix both maximum and minimum rates: the former would protect the interests of shippers; the latter, those of investors and also of competitors such as water carriers.

The labor provisions of the act contained two kinds of tribunals to adjust difficulties; both had been set up during World War I. After several experiments a law was passed in 1934 which provided for a National Board of Adjustment of thirty-six members, which was divided into four parts. These considered controversies, but had no power to fix wages or to determine working rules. If they were unable to reach a decision, the matter was referred to a new Railroad Mediation Board of three members who endeavored to obtain a settlement or, failing this, to have the dispute submitted to arbitration. The new machinery has worked satisfactorily and has been held up as a model for handling industrial relations.

In addition to this, legislative provision has been made for a dismissal wage, for retirement allowance or old-age pensions, and for unemployment insurance. By the Railroad Retirement Act of 1937 all employees were made eligible to retirement annuities at the age of 65; and those 60 years of age might retire if they had completed thirty years of service or had become permanently disabled. The costs of the system were borne by contributions of the employees and of the carriers. Partly because of their economic strength, and partly by reason of their political power, the railroad unions have succeeded in substantially improving their wages and working conditions during the past twenty-five years. But they have not been able to protect themselves against the effects of decreasing employment in the railroad industry as a whole.

The Transportation Act of 1920 imposed upon the Interstate Commerce Commission new duties in fields formerly defined by regulatory legislation and gave it new responsibility. In order to enable this body effectively to discharge these added functions the membership was increased from nine to eleven members. This act, together with other prior legislation, has rehabilitated the commission and it is now recognized as a necessary and effective instrument of federal control. By its decisions it has developed a body of more or less authoritative rules for the regulation of railroads; the right of the federal government to control them, at first disputed, has now been thoroughly established; and finally there has been created a system of machinery for dealing with them which can easily be enlarged or entrusted with greater powers if that seems desirable. The growing development of public control in this field, wrote Professor Sharfman,[1] "is the most striking manifestation in the entire economic sphere of the changed relationship between government and business which has accompanied the industrial development of recent decades ... the traditional emphasis upon individualism is clearly subordinated to the achievement of conscious ends."

Agitation for government ownership and operation of our great railroad systems has thus been forestalled. This would surely have arisen in this country, as it has in Europe, had not an adequate and successful system of government control been devised, which has checked the worst abuses and won the confidence of the people.

Government regulation. In the development of regulation and control which has been described there was little room for state control. With the growth of the great railroad systems the state governments have become clearly inadequate

[1] I. L. Sharfman, *The Interstate Commerce Commission* (4 vols., New York, 1931-37), I, 283.

to cope with the problems involved, and, while the state commissions have done valuable service, broader powers of control were seen to be necessary. These could be exercised only
by the federal government.

After the United States entered World War I, the federal
railroad administration proceeded with little regard to the
rights of state commissions. But after the armistice state
commissions insisted upon their rights and the question of
final authority came before the Supreme Court, which in
1919 upheld the authority of the federal administration as
a war power. Finally the Transportation Act of 1920 confirmed the superior authority of the Interstate Commerce
Commission over the state commissions as a permanent peace
policy. There has been a gradual tightening of national control upon the entire transportation system until today the
states have little effective rate-making authority and in other
respects are subordinated to federal authority. On the other
hand, the scope of the state commissions has generally been
broadened so as to include the regulation of state and local
public utilities (such as street railways, electric light, gas, and
water companies) over which the federal government has no
control. Their names have usually been changed from railroad to public utilities commissions to correspond with their
new duties, and their chief usefulness in the future will probably be found in this field.

Railroad prosperity and depression. After their return to
private operation, the railroads enjoyed a long period of
prosperity, sharing in the industrial expansion of the times.
Roadbeds, tracks, and terminal facilities were improved;
curves were straightened and grades eliminated; unprofitable
lines and trains were discontinued; and passenger and freight
schedules were speeded up. The most promising improvement
was the electrification of some lines, especially of the suburban
railroad service to the larger cities and of terminals and
switching yards. On the heavy mountain grades of the Cordil-
leran region electric power is far superior to steam and here,
too, it was gradually being introduced.

Down to 1929 the freight business and the revenues of the
railroads steadily increased, only the passenger business falling off on short distances. The depression affected the rail-

roads adversely along with other industries, and they began to clamor for relief. Congress apparently took the view that the railroads should reduce their own costs of operation and improve their efficiency before asking for relief. In order to effect these results the office of Federal Co-ordinator of Transportation was created by act of June 16, 1933, and Joseph B. Eastman, for thirteen years a member of the Interstate Commerce Commission, was appointed to this post. His first efforts were directed at reduction of fixed charges, financial reorganization where possible, and better enforcement of the labor provisions.

Railroads are public carriers invested with a public function and are compelled to operate in bad times as well as good. They are not permitted to close down their plant during a period of depression, but must render their services even at a loss. During the business depression of the 1930's the net income of Class I railroads was transformed from a surplus of $897,000,000 in 1929 to a deficit of $123,000,000 in 1938. So serious did the situation become that the Interstate Commerce Commission granted temporary rate increases in certain commodity freight rates in 1932 and again in 1935, and the government through its agencies loaned the railroads over $800,000,000 to meet taxes and fixed charges. Railroad labor, too, made its contribution by accepting a temporary reduction in wages of about 10 per cent between 1932 and 1935; after the latter date the wage scales were gradually restored. Some help was also given in 1940 by relieving the land-grant railroads of the requirement that they should perform certain services for the government at low preferential rates; in return the roads restored to the government some 8,000,000 acres of land received under the early grants, which were added to the public domain. Thus ended an eventful chapter in American railroad construction. The close connection between railroad prosperity and industrial production is clearly shown in the graph on page 688.

The 1940's ushered in a new swing of the pendulum. The outbreak of the war in Europe, our own defense program, the passage of the Lend-Lease Act in March, 1941, together with the policy of all-out aid to Britain, increased tremendously the amount of freight to be carried and placed a severe

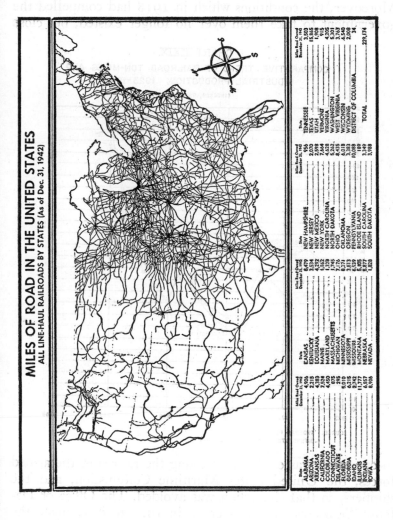

Ass'n of Amer. Railroads, *Railroads in this Century* (Wash., D. C. March, 1944).

strain upon the facilities of the railroads. Fortunately the railroads were in good condition; between 1923 and 1941 they had spent over $5,000 million rehabilitating and modernizing their plant with scarcely any increase in their capital debt. Moreover, the conditions which in 1918 had compelled the government to take them over no longer existed, but close

CHART XXIX

'COMPARATIVE TREND OF RAILROAD TON-MILES AND INDUSTRIAL PRODUCTION, 1923-1944

(INDEXES, 1935-1939=100)

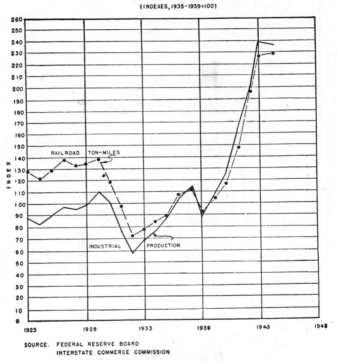

SOURCE. FEDERAL RESERVE BOARD
INTERSTATE COMMERCE COMMISSION

co-operation was established among the railroads, the armed forces, the United States Maritime Commission, and the shippers, so that congestion was avoided. The Office of Defense Transportation was set up in 1941 to co-ordinate the activities of these various groups, with Joseph B. Eastman, chairman of the Interstate Commerce Commission, as director. Although the railroads in 1944 had one-third fewer locomotives and passenger coaches and one-fourth fewer freight cars than they had had in 1924, they hauled more freight and carried more passengers. A partial explanation for this seeming miracle was the 13 per cent increase in the average capacity of the freight cars, a 33 per cent increase in the tractive effort of the locomotives, and a 50 per cent increase in the length of the average haul; thus the "Big Boys" on the Union Pacific, with a rating of 135,000 tractive effort, are capable of hauling a mile-long freight train more than a mile a minute.

But even more important was efficient and patriotic management. Orders were hurriedly placed for additional cars, but the shortage in steel and other essential materials prevented full delivery. The burden placed on the railroads was further accentuated by the delivery of oil tankers to the British, by the diversion of vessels from the coastwise trade to ocean traffic, and by the cessation of the intercoastal shipping traffic early in 1942. In spite of all difficulties they maintained their plant, equipment, and organization at relatively high standards during the war. Not only did they carry a greatly increased amount of normal traffic and the bulk of the war production traffic and the movement of troops, but in many instances took over services previously rendered by other agencies. A case in point was the movement of petroleum when the tankers were being sunk by submarines. Quicker routing and turn-around of railroad freight cars and the prevention of their use for storage purposes, the assignment of short hauls and way-freight services to trucks and the better organization of these into efficient lines, and the increased use of our waterways for bulky and slow-moving commodities were some of the methods by which the record-breaking traffic of the war years was cared for. Three-fourths of the commercial freight traffic and also of the passenger business was carried by the railroads, which were the backbone of the transportation system.

Motor traffic and improved roads. In the history of transportation in the United States there has run one primary purpose, that of providing the people with the most effective facilities yet developed. The next turn of the wheel in this kaleidoscopic picture revealed the internal combustion motor vehicle as the latest important commercial method of transportation. In 1941 there were registered 32,453,000 automobiles, of which about seven-eighths were passenger cars and the rest trucks or busses; this was 71 per cent of the world registration. The proportion of cars to population was thus about one car to every four persons; that is, theoretically, every family could go riding at one time. Nothing evidences better the high standard of living of the American people and their quick acceptance of new methods than the widespread use of the automobile.

When World War I began the motor-vehicle industry was just passing out of the experimental stage and it played only a minor part in that struggle. The number of cars produced in a single year first passed the million mark in 1916, but after that it increased rapidly. By the time we entered World War II our productive capacity was equal to the task presented by the demands of the armed forces. For the highly mechanized type of warfare, requiring mobility and rapid movement, new types were developed—jeeps, tanks, bulldozers, amphibious landing trucks, and others—which contributed largely to victory. Automobile plants were confined to the making of war vehicles or converted to the production of munitions, and the manufacture of private cars ceased. Those in existence, moreover, faced difficulties. Gas rationing was introduced in May, 1942, as vast amounts of gas were shipped abroad and as sinkings by submarines along the Atlantic coast reduced shipments by tankers, but this deficiency was met. This danger was eliminated by greater use of railroads and by building new pipe lines. Even more serious was the shortage of parts and of rubber. A synthetic-rubber industry was developed which partially cared for deteriorating tires, but the cars on the highways slowly diminished in number and reliability. This latter factor was reflected in a rising accident curve. By the war's end the average car was ten years old instead of five as before. The output of new cars was temporarily delayed by a series of strikes.

The effect of this popular, convenient, and mobile system of transportation has been even more revolutionary than the electric railway, for it has brought the country districts in close touch with the cities and towns and has done more than any other single factor to break down rural isolation. It is impossible to overestimate the social importance of motor vehicles, which have linked city and country, with benefit to dwellers in each section. Automobiles are today a necessity for the farmers, of whom practically a third are car-owners. The general use of motorized vehicles has also produced minor social changes: less is spent on housing and clothing, fewer books are read, church is neglected, and more time is spent in the open. Motor busses have put the trolley lines in many of the smaller communities out of business and have cut seriously into the passenger business of the interurban electric railway and of the steam roads. In addition to the busses it is estimated that in some years intercity travel in private automobiles amounted to more than 250,000 million passenger miles, which was almost double that of all other transportation agencies combined.

Motor trucks first appeared in quantity in 1904, but did not give much promise of becoming an important agency in intercity commercial transportation until about 1914. The early trucks were heavy, clumsy, and costly to operate, but under the pressure of war needs and of civilian demands they were steadily improved in all these respects. Today they possess certain distinct advantages over railroads in their flexibility, low cost, smaller loss and damage to goods in transit, door-to-door collection and delivery, ability to give rush-hour service when needed, and other features. They have been most successful in capturing the traffic of commodities that take high rates by rail, such as the movement of perishable fruits and vegetables, but also do an increased business in handling household goods and in the delivery service of retail stores. It is estimated that 75 per cent of the less-than-carload traffic that is carried into and out of Chicago within a 60-mile radius is moved by truck, and that 49 big cities receive all their milk by truck. With the improvement of roads, moreover, the area of profitable operation of motor trucks has steadily widened and now reaches 200 miles or more. They have extended the market areas of manufacturers and commercial houses and have shortened the distance and time between producers and consumers.

The attitude of the railroads toward this new competitor has undergone several changes. At first the railroads paid little attention to trucks and busses, but when these began to cut into railroad traffic they fought them and asked for protection. Finally, they realized that co-ordination offered the best solution and today some railroad lines are meeting this new competition by establishing motor service of their own. Most of the traffic handled by motor carriers and private automobiles, however, is new business, and has been developed by this latest agency. There are today in the United States 54,000 communities which have no other form of transportation at their command than the motor vehicle. This form of transportation supplements and does not supplant the older agencies.

Another result of the general use of the automobile has been the revival of an interest in good roads which is extending a system of hard roads across the country; to this purpose were applied revenues amounting to some $20,000 million for the period 1921–45, derived from automobile licenses and the practically universal gasoline tax. Since 1916 the federal government has revived the policy of federal aid for roads, which had lain dormant since the National Road was built in 1817. Federal appropriations for internal improvements were declared unconstitutional by Andrew Jackson when he vetoed the Maysville Road bill, appropriating federal money for a road in Kentucky, but today, in response to an urgent demand for good roads, the Constitution is found flexible enough to permit such appropriations. As a result of these improvements it is now possible to drive from the Atlantic coast all the way across the continent on paved roads, while a constantly increasing network of good roads crosses the country in every direction. Whereas in 1914 there were only 257,000 miles of surfaced roads in the United States, by 1943 there were over 1,500,000 miles of such roads, or more than six times the total railroad mileage. These are supplemented by about 1,600,000 miles of non-surfaced highways. The neglect of a century had been more than repaired in a generation.

Aviation. The airplane in the United States may be said to date from 1903 when the Wright brothers succeeded in remaining in the air with their heavier-than-air flying machines. The development of airplanes was greatly accelerated

The general location of routes of the recommended interregional highway system. Total length of the system is 33,920 miles.

by their use for military purposes during World War I, and after that event equally striking progress was made in their utilization for commercial purposes.

The expansion of aviation in this country is clearly set forth in the following brief table:

SCHEDULED AIR-CARRIER OPERATIONS IN THE UNITED STATES				
Year	Planes in service	Miles flown (millions)	Passengers (thousands)	Express carried (tons)
1927	128	5.9	8.7	23
1932	456	45.6	474.3	517
1940	358	108.8	2959.5	6,250
1945	411	215.0	7502.5	41,500

These figures relate only to domestic commercial air transportation, but American planes penetrate far beyond our national boundaries. Among the more notable extensions of passenger service may be listed the opening of routes between the United States and Central and South America (1932), the beginning of service across the Pacific (1936), and also of commercial travel across the Atlantic (1939). This expansion was facilitated by the provision of airway facilities, mostly by the federal government, by the building of airports, mostly by municipalities, and especially by improvements in the airplanes themselves. These have grown bigger and faster and safer. Among the advantages of air service that of speed [2] must be given first place, though this is partially offset by the time lost in getting to and from the airports, which are usually located at a distance from the centers of population; it has been estimated that little time is saved in airplane trips under 300 miles. There is also the saving in the expense of a track, but against this must be set off the outlay for landing fields, wireless installations, weather-reporting service, and the marking, lighting, and signaling of routes. The basic disadvantage of the airplane is that it is a poor weight carrier and must therefore charge high rates for passengers and express. The investment is, moreover, large, operating expenses are high, and the useful life of an airplane is short. The reliability and safety of airplane travel

---

[2] An 11-hour service between New York and London is promised for the near future.

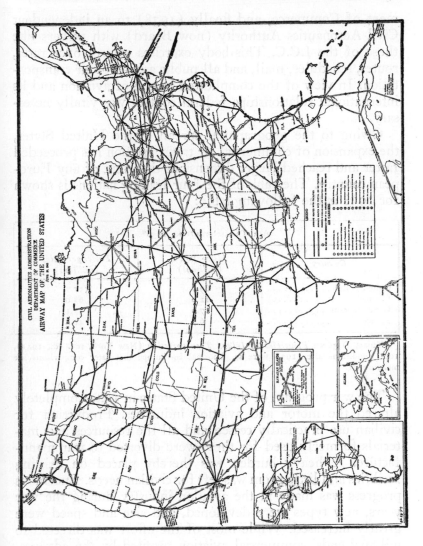

CIVIL AERONAUTICS ADMINISTRATION
DEPARTMENT OF COMMERCE
AIRWAY MAP OF THE UNITED STATES

had been notably improved—fatalities per 100,000,000 passenger miles flown on regularly scheduled commercial air
lines declined from 4.5 in 1932 to 2.9 in 1945 and to 2.0 in
1946. Travel by private automobile was more dangerous;
travel by train or bus was safer in 1946.

The government control of air service was first entrusted
to the Post Office Department, then (1926) to the Depart-

ment of Commerce, and finally (1938) to an independent Civil Aeronautics Authority (now Board) with powers like those of the I.C.C. This body exercises control over rates, routes, schedules, mail, and all public aspects of air transportation. In view of the complicated nature of aviation and its international relationships federal control was vitally necessary.

Owing to the geographical spread of the United States, the expansion of commercial air transportation has proceeded faster and reached larger dimensions than that of any European country. The rank of the four leading nations is shown for 1938 in the following table:

AIR TRANSPORTATION, 1938*		
Country	Miles flown (millions)	Passenger-miles (millions)
United States	69.7	557.7
Germany	12.0	63.0
Great Britain	7.9	37.1
France	6.7	41.2

* Stuart Daggett, *Principles of Inland Transportation* (New York, rev. ed., 1941), 107. Conditions after 1938 were so abnormal in Europe that later comparisons are meaningless.

The war program of the United States in 1941 completely altered the motor and aviation industries. Production for civilian use practically ceased and all the resources and materials formerly used for these were diverted to war manufacture. A heavy burden was thereby placed on existing facilities and little room was left for civilian needs. Enormous progress was made in the aviation industry during the war years, new types were developed, and size and speed were greatly increased. While most of the effort was directed to military ends, commercial aviation profited by the advance, and though it is unlikely that the same rate of progress will be maintained, the commercial movement on a large scale of passengers and mail, and even freight, must be reckoned with in the future. New speed records have been established that forecast undreamed-of possibilities. A commercial plane flew on January 20, 1946, from New York to Lisbon in 10 hours and 6 minutes, another made the trip on March 29, 1947, from Long Beach, California, to New York City in 6 hours and 47 minutes, while a jet-propelled fighter plane a year previously covered the same distance in 4 hours and 13 minutes. These performances give point to the statement often made in aviation circles: "No spot on earth is more than 60 hours' flying time from your local airport."

One thing is fairly certain—airplane production will never mushroom into a great industry, as the automobile industry did a generation ago. It is surprising how much traffic can be carried by a few planes. It has been estimated that 600 airplanes carrying 36 passengers each and operating 3500 hours yearly could have handled all the Pullman travel in the United States in 1940, and also have had space for cargo and mail. High capital and operating costs will limit their private ownership and use. The idea that cheap plastic planes could be stamped out like cookies has been abandoned, as has the hope of a helicopter in every home. To be successful the industry must be highly concentrated and, in view of its international complications, under strict governmental control.

Inland water transportation. The river trade, which was thought to be almost dead, experienced a great revival after 1914. Before that date the packet boats had almost disappeared from the rivers, the barge trade was just about holding its own, and only the rafting of logs was increasing, and most of these were floated down the Pacific coast rivers. Explanations of this decadence were to be found in the non-co-operation and even hostility of the railroads, but more especially in the lack of modern equipment and facilities for handling traffic on the rivers. The transportation needs of the war period, however, put a burden on the railroads which they could not adequately meet so resort was had again to water transportation.

Barge building was undertaken by private capital and also by the federal government, and soon strings of modern 2000-ton barges towed by powerful tugs made their appearance on the Ohio, the lower Mississippi, the Missouri and the Warrior rivers. A single tug towed 15 to 20 barges, representing as many freight-train loads. Most of the traffic was of heavy, bulky, and low-cost articles—wheat, cotton, logs, coal and coke, petroleum, stone, and iron and steel products downstream, and sugar, petroleum, gravel and sand, and sulphur upstream. The total river traffic in 1943 was 198 million tons.

The five Great Lakes comprise a chain of natural inland seas on which transportation resembles ocean transport. These lakes cover more than 90,000 square miles and contain half the fresh water of the world. Traffic on the lakes consisted largely of iron ore, coal, grain, and petroleum and to carry this heavy freight special types of vessels were developed, such as larger and faster tankers and ore boats. Shipments and receipts at all lake ports, almost entirely domestic trade, increased steadily to 1929, when they were 150 million tons, but during the early 1930's they fell to half that amount. By 1943, however, they were up to 340 million, a record high. This reflects the prosperity of this period.

Even the canals shared in the rehabilitation of the water traffic. Three main purposes seem to have led to this movement: (1) to give cheaper freight to shippers; (2) to provide effective competition with the railroads; (3) to relieve the railroads of the excessive volume of heavy freight. Barge companies did not pay for the costs of their roadbed; these were borne by the taxpayer. Canal traffic was confined almost entirely to the New York State Barge Canal and to coastal canals like the Cape Cod Canal and the Houston Ship Canal in Texas. Standing in a class by itself was the Saint Mary Falls Canal (Sault Sainte Marie), which connects Lake Superior with Lake Huron, with a tonnage in 1944 of 117,000,000 tons.

The completion of the Panama Canal, which was first opened in 1914, brought about a partial shifting of the routes of trade. By providing an all-water route between the two seaboards of the United States the canal diverted considerable traffic from the transcontinental railroads and developed the intercoastal trade. Freights to and from the Pacific and Atlantic coasts have been cheapened and industry in the Pacific section has been stimulated. The west coast of South America —Peru and Chile—was brought much nearer the United States, and an advantage was given our merchants over their European competitors in trade with them and also with the

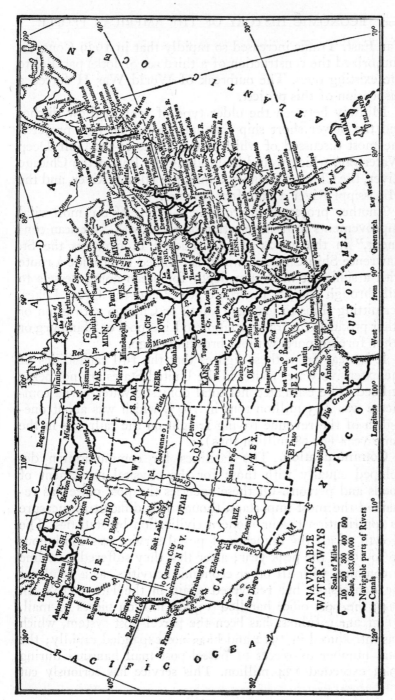

The heavy lines show the navigable waterways, in which the water is three feet deep or over. The length of these is some 28,000 miles.

Far East. Traffic increased so rapidly that in 1939 Congress authorized the construction of a third set of locks parallel to the existing ones. The outbreak of World War II forced a suspension of this project.

Midway between the older type of long shallow ditches and the newer short ship channels lie certain new projects, the most discussed of which is the Lakes-to-the-Gulf Deep Waterway, which would build along the line of the Chicago River, the Chicago Sanitary Canal, the Illinois River, and the Mississippi River a nine-foot channel.

Another projected improvement—"one of the most vital improvements to transportation on the North American continent," in the words of ex-President Hoover—is the St. Lawrence Ship Channel, which is planned to provide a route with a sufficient minimum depth for ocean-going vessels to sail through the St. Lawrence River and the Great Lakes, permitting ships to load at Duluth or Chicago with grain or other products for transportation to Liverpool or Hamburg or other foreign ports without breaking cargo.

It is clear from these figures that the full capabilities of the extensive water routes in the United States are not being utilized. The estimated net total domestic water-borne commerce was 453 million tons in 1943, which was about one-eighth of the revenue-paying freight on the railroads in the same year (3158 million tons).

Communication. The facilities for communication developed equally with those for the physical movement of goods and persons. Of these agencies the post office has remained the most important, though it is difficult to measure its contribution to our modern civilization by statistics. The growth of all the branches of postal service was continuous up to 1929, the peak year; after that they suffered a decline in common with all other economic activities, as a result of the depression, but recovered again in the late 1930's. In 1943 the post office handled 33,000 million pieces of mail. Of great usefulness has been the parcel-post system, which was introduced in 1912 and has since expanded rapidly; the total number of pieces of parcel-post mail handled during 1943 exceeded 734 million. This service has seriously cut

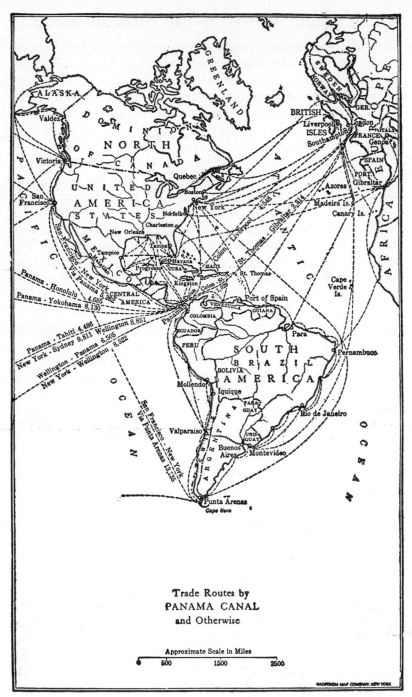

Trade Routes by
PANAMA CANAL
and Otherwise

Approximate Scale in Miles

500   1500   2500

RACHFERGUM MAP COMPANY, NEW YORK

into the business of the express companies, but has been of great utility to business houses and individuals. The one service of the post office which expanded during the depression was the postal-savings business. As distrust in commercial banks grew, increasing use was made of these government guaranteed agencies, in spite of the low rate of interest (2 per cent). During the prosperous 1920's other forms of investment were preferred and deposits grew slowly (from $43 million in 1914 to $154 million in 1929), but during the depressed 1930's they expanded greatly (to $2600 million in 1945 with over 3,500,000 depositors).

The growth of the telegraph and telephone kept pace with the expansion of business and at the same time aided it. The cost and time of transacting business were reduced, middlemen were eliminated, and merchants were enabled to operate with smaller stocks of goods—"hand to mouth buying," it was called. The number of telegrams sent—the best index of its importance—increased from 107 million in 1912 to 230 million in 1944.

Radiotelegraphy, introduced about 1900, was first used for land messages, but by 1913 transoceanic communication was possible and its uses were broadened. It competed with the seemingly impregnable cable systems and offered lower rates.

The telephone was steadily perfected and extended. In 1915 long-distance messages were first sent from New York to San Francisco; in 1923 the first picture was transmitted over telephone wires; and in 1930 teletyping was perfected, by which typewritten messages are sent over telephone lines and are automatically reproduced. In 1945, the peak year, there were 28,000,000 telephones in use in the United States, triple the number of 1915. Even more than the telegraph, the telephone has increased the speed and area of business.

The most spectacular of recent inventions is the radio. It has outdistanced even the automobile in the rapidity of its growth. First definitely established between 1920 and 1922 as a regular means of entertainment, it is estimated that in 1945 there were nearly 60,000,000 receiving sets in use in the United States. Its importance is social as well as economic, for it is used to bring music, lectures, news, and other forms of entertainment, as well as financial news or advertising, to radio audiences. It was the last step needed to break down the isolation of rural communities.

The main agency for the dissemination of information and the molding of public opinion is after all the printed page, although its importance has been somewhat reduced by the radio. Most people limit their reading to newspapers and magazines, and these have undergone changes to win popular demand. Larger newspapers, made possible by technological improvements and the production of cheap paper, have been offered for the same price, but most of all by the expansion of advertising. The newspapers have grown in popular appeal through their various news services, but the power of the editorial has declined. In 1940 there were 1998 English-language daily newspapers with a combined circulation of 43,000,000 copies. Some 2300 monthly magazines, mostly of the pulp type, had the astounding circulation of 135,000,000.

Conclusion. It is hazardous to predict the future of transportation, but certain things seem fairly clear. The railroad network will probably contract further as a result of the abandonment of unprofitable branch lines and duplicate mileage. The railroads are peculiarly adapted to the carriage of commodities in large quantities between important shipping points, and when there is a sufficient volume of traffic to permit economical train loading the railroad is the most economical type of carrier for such traffic. To the low-cost but slow water routes have been assigned the heavy, bulky, and cheap goods. The motor trucks have captured a considerable portion of the light-weight freight, such as milk, and less-than-carload lots. It is estimated by the Interstate Commerce Commission that motor trucks carry nearly 25 per cent of all traffic moved by land. To these agencies should be added the pipelines of the country, with a total length of over 138,000 miles in 1944. There is a division of traffic among the various types of carriers according to their "inherent advantages." The outlook for passenger traffic is not so clear, for the airplane has introduced a revolutionary and unpredictable element in travel, but the railways are meeting this competition by improvements in comfort and in other ways. As between the different agencies of transportation there has gone on and is still continuing a lively competition and readjustment of traffic so as to obtain the most efficient service. We may conclude that transportation, like agriculture and industry, never stands still. It assumes new forms, performs new services, and continually advances.

CHAPTER XXX

WIDENED HORIZONS OF DOMESTIC AND FOREIGN COMMERCE

Domestic commerce. The systems of transportation and communication which have been described are after all not ends in themselves, but agencies by which persons, commodities, and information may be transferred from one place to another. Transportation and trade are complementary to each other and move parallel in their expansion and contraction. The volume of our domestic commerce can only be approximated, but if the estimates already given [1] are carried forward we find that the movement of freight increased from 2000 million tons in 1914 to a high of 4012 million in 1943; the values of the trade for these two dates were approximately $30,000 million and $100,000 million. This was over ten times the value of our foreign trade, and more than triple the foreign commerce of the world, which was estimated by the League of Nations at $28,000 million for 1938. The domestic commerce of the United States is clearly much more important than our foreign trade, although the latter attracts greater attention.

The growth in extent and importance of this traffic, and the vital service which transportation played in bridging the gap between areas of production of raw materials and areas of their manufacture into finished goods, may be illustrated by tracing the movement of some of the more important branches of internal trade. Over three-fourths of the railroad freight traffic consists of coal, gravel, lumber, iron, grain, petroleum, and livestock, and these will be selected for purposes of illustration.

Two-thirds of all the coal mined comes from the four states of Pennsylvania, West Virginia, Illinois, and Kentucky, and five-sixths of all the iron ore is produced in the Lake Superior region with an additional tenth from Alabama. These two materials are brought together by rail and water in the range of states bordering on the south shore of the Great Lakes, where 80 per cent of the blast furnaces and over 60 per cent of the steel plants are located. From these the finished steel and iron products are distributed to all parts of the United States. Most of the lumber cut today in this country is either yellow pine, which is highly localized in the southern states, or Douglas fir, which grows exclusively in the Pacific coast and northwestern states, yet the principal area of utilization is the Middle West. The production of grain and livestock is rather widely distributed throughout the country, yet there exist well-defined regions where they predominate, so that we speak unhesitatingly of the wheat belt, the corn belt, etc. But the chief areas of production are, in general, far removed from the centers of manufacture, which in turn are highly centralized and equally far from the centers of consumption in our great industrial cities. Of the seven groups of commodities named in the preceding paragraph one only—clay, gravel, sand, stone, etc.—is so heavy and so cheap that it cannot stand the costs of distant transportation.

Even this brief survey shows that the production of our most basic commodities is concentrated in restricted districts, and that even where production is widespread, as in the case of livestock, there is frequently a concentration in a primary market for processing. In each producing area great commercial cities have grown up, where the surplus commodities are gathered, manufactured, and distributed. The areas of production may change, as is illustrated by the exhaustion of the lumber along the Erie Canal, by the opening up of better sources, as in the case of the iron deposits of the Lake Superior region, or by the discovery of new products, as in the case of petroleum, but whatever the occasion domestic commerce quickly adjusts itself. This territorial specialization, with its widespread exchange of commodities, has greatly increased production, lowered and equalized prices, and brought within reach of all groups in the nation a constantly enlarging supply of necessities and conveniences. The expansion of domestic commerce has also had important social and political effects, for the ease of movement has made for standardization and homogeneity of type. We eat the same food, wear the same clothes, read the same magazines, see the same motion pictures, and travel by standardized automobiles over highways lined with national advertising.

This commercial development took place in a system of free enterprise, in which the government entered the market to only a small extent, either as purchaser or as producer. The effect of war, however, was greatly to enlarge government participation; trade movements of all types, domestic as well as foreign, departed from their normal pattern under the stress of a war economy. For instance, in 1944 the proportion of the gross national income sold to or produced by the government was 40 per cent. While this proportion was greatly reduced after the war, the government will undoubtedly always constitute a more important figure than it did in prewar days.

Barriers to interstate trade. It was long our boast that the United States constituted the "greatest free trade area in the world" in which could be achieved all the advantages of the territorial specialization just described. Recently, however, this has been threatened by the legislation of states which desire to protect their own interests even at the expense of national benefits. Although restricted by the commerce clause of the Constitution, which confers the power to regulate interstate commerce upon the federal government, the states have been able to erect barriers which constitute a serious menace to national freedom of intercourse. In order to protect industries carried on within the state against outside competition differential taxation has been imposed, or public authorities are required to purchase all needed materials from producers within the states; thirty-one states had such laws in 1939. Home merchants are protected by curbing traveling salesmen representing outside sellers, and by legislation restricting the operation of department stores, mail-order houses, and chain stores. Interstate trucking has been checked and rendered more expensive by contradictory laws regulating and taxing motor trucks. In 1945 it was estimated that there were over 1000 restrictive measures directed at out-of-state trucks alone. The farmers have been given a near monopoly on some home markets by oleomargarine legislation, milk-market restrictions, and quarantine and inspection laws.

The purpose of these restrictions has been in part to raise revenue, in part to give protection, and in minor degree to protect health and prevent the spread of plant diseases and insect pests. The extreme to which legitimate objectives have been perverted is illustrated by the requirement of a certain state that milk brought into the state from outside must be colored pink; this law was promptly declared unconstitutional. The effect of these interferences with the free movement of goods has been to prevent regional specialization and to raise costs. It was part of a "buy American," "buy at home" movement carried to an extreme localism, but seems already to have begun to ebb. The fundamental issue is constitutional as well as economic, and this is whether the guarantee of freedom of trade among the states can or should be evaded by subterfuge.

Wholesale trade. The wholesaler is a middleman who stands between the producer on the one hand and the retailer or consumer on the other. He is being affected, usually adversely, by changes in the methods of distribution and by those in consumer demand. The census figures illustrate the first point. In 1939 there were 200,000 wholesale establishments in the United States, but only half, or 101,000, were solely wholesalers, most of the others being bulk tank stations, manufacturers' sales branches, manufacturers' agents, brokers, commission merchants, and selling agents. In other words the manufacturers, producing now on a large scale and under severe competition, are by various devices trying to dispense with the middleman and to establish direct communication with retailers and consumers. They maintain regular selling departments, sending out agents to get orders and often sending goods on approval direct from the factories. Such a movement is facilitated by improvements in transportation, better credit-rating facilities, and by national advertising which familiarizes the consumers with standard brands.

Changes on the side of demand also are rendering the services of the middleman less necessary. The splitting up of the old general store into specialty stores makes it easier to establish direct contacts between manufacturers and retailers. The growth in the size of metropolitan stores and of chain stores means larger orders which the manufacturers find it worth while to seek directly. And finally, the rapid changes in style, the hand-to-mouth buying of retailers, and the shift of much of the risk and storage functions back to the manufacturer, make it necessary for him to keep in close and direct touch with consumer demand and put an emphasis on what is called "merchandising."

New York is the greatest wholesale distributing point for imported goods, but probably yields first place to Chicago for domestic wares. The latter is the center of the grain trade, followed by Minneapolis, Duluth-Superior, Kansas City, St. Louis, and other cities; it is also the leading meat-packing city, although hard pressed by St. Louis, Kansas City, and Omaha. Most of the dairy and poultry products also pass through Chicago. Boston and Philadelphia on the Atlantic coast and San Francisco on the Pacific coast are important distributing points for foreign trade, while Cleveland and Detroit are important for iron and steel and automobiles. Houston, Galveston, and New Orleans handle most of the cotton. Louisville is one of the most important tobacco markets in the world. Pittsburgh is an iron and steel and coal center, and Los Angeles is a great assembling and distributing point for lumber and petroleum, having larger intercoastal trade than any other city.

Retail trade. The census of 1930, for the second time in a century,[2] collected statistics of the retail business of the country. This showed that there were approximately 1,500,000 stores, restaurants, filling stations, and other retail establishments in the United States in 1929. By 1939 the number of stores had grown to 1,770,000. Sales fluctuated with the business cycle, reaching $50,000 million in 1929, falling to $42,000 million ten years later as a result of the long depression, but jumping to a record high of almost $70,000 million in 1944. Here was a prize worth striving for. Different types of retail establishments endeavored to capture for themselves as much of the trade as possible, large pro-

2 See page 311.

ducers sought to by-pass the middleman and to sell direct to retailers, and consumer demand was informed and whetted by an enormous growth of national advertising.

The type of organization that represented the greatest relative expansion was farmer and consumer co-operative stores, though actual figures for stores (3700 in 1939) and of sales ($224 million) were small. Co-operatives have appeared at different times in our history, never very successfully, but after World War I they gained new significance, especially among the farmers. Down to about 1920 co-operation was carried on by members of independent associations, but after that date the local units began to be centralized in national organizations. State and federal funds were allotted to farmers' co-operatives, which handled an increasing share of the members' sales and purchases. By 1930 such associations sold one-quarter of the wheat, one-third of the cheese, and 85 per cent of the citrus fruit of California. Although the farmers did not buy as much co-operatively as they sold, they used this method in the purchase of farm machinery, gasoline, and similar lines. In the cities co-operation was never widespread nor successful, perhaps because of the efficient service rendered by other retail outlets. Our experience in this respect differs markedly from that of Britain, France, Germany, and other European countries, where co-operatives transact a large part of the wholesale and retail business.

The chain store showed a vigorous growth, the number of stores in chains increasing from 24,000 in 1914 to 160,000 in 1929. After that the number declined and there was a tendency toward concentration, as in the super-market. Success brought denunciation by hard-pressed or incompetent independent storekeepers, and anti-chain legislation was passed by some of the states. The economies to consumers of this method of retail distribution were, however, too obvious for such a movement to succeed, and the more reasonable independents began to organize their own systems of co-operative buying, and to introduce other economies in selling and credit.

Mail-order houses play only a small part in the nation's system of distribution, though in rural districts they are important. The large mail-order stores of Montgomery Ward and Sears Roebuck began in 1926 to establish branch stores in the more important trading cities, both to hold their rural clients and to attract new urban customers. Other smaller mail-order houses entered the field, especially for the sale of ready-made clothing, but they all experienced rough sledding during the depression years after 1929. The mail-order catalog is best suited to a market where prices are stable, but during this period prices were fluctuating and price lists had to be corrected constantly.

Independents far outnumbered all other types of retail business put together, constituting 92 per cent of all in 1939. They practically monopolized such businesses as the sale of men's and boys' clothing, women's ready-to-wear garments, furniture, radios, motor vehicles, and filling stations. The average establishment was small, frequently run by the proprietor alone; even including large department stores, there was for the whole country, an average of only two employees for each store in addition to the proprietor. Annual sales averaged only $20,000. But independents carried on three-quarters of the retail business of the country and are still the most important element in our retail trade organization, in spite of the competition of other types.

Probably no part of our economic system is undergoing more far-reaching changes and readjustments than is the organization of the retail trade. This has been called the "last great frontier of business." One marked change is the extension of the trading area. The increasing use of the automobile and the construction of good roads have widened the trading area from perhaps 5 to 150 miles. This has meant a shift from the village store to one located at a larger town, where motion picture shows are also to be enjoyed.

Advertising was used on a grand scale to stimulate the sale of goods and to assist in their distribution. Newspapers and periodicals were the chief media by which consumers were advised of the superior excellence of the goods advertised, though in more recent years the radio has been a favorite instrument. Newspapers and periodicals derive a larger part of their income from advertising ($845 million in 1939) than from sales ($486 million). Defenders of the expenditure of these vast sums point to the educational value of advertising, and insist that the costs are met by the economies of large-scale production made possible by increased sales. Advertising has helped to eliminate the traveling salesman and to shorten the route between producer and consumer. It combines ballyhoo with education, and makes it easier to sell nationally advertised products. The consumer was until recently poorly protected against misrepresentation, but the Food, Drug, and Cosmetic Act of 1938 compelled honesty of statement in advertising these three lines.

The decade of the 1920's saw a great expansion of instalment buying. An investigation by Professor E. R. A. Seligman showed that about 13 per cent of the total retail sales in 1925–27 were made in this way, especially in the case of automobiles, radio sets, washing machines, vacuum cleaners, and mechanical refrigerators. The crisis of 1929 and the subsequent depression put a damper on this method of trade expansion, which was still further accentuated by our entry into World War II in 1941.

Perhaps the most striking feature of our present system of merchandising is its costliness. A recent estimate [3] of these costs as revealed by the 1929 census put them at 59 per cent of the total cost of the goods. In that year the goods brought to market were valued at $65,600 million but it cost $38,500 million to distribute them, of which the chief part went to retailers. In other words, it cost more to distribute the goods than it did to produce them. This feature of the distributive process has called forth considerable criticism on the ground that it is both inefficient and wasteful. It is a truism of economic history that, as specialization has proceeded, the route between the producer and the ultimate consumer has lengthened. Part of the increased cost of distribution is certainly offset and more than offset by the economies of territorial specialization, although this involves longer hauls and more handling. The multiplicity of retail stores is also condemned on the ground of wastefulness, but this is counterbalanced by the convenience to consumers. And, finally, it may be urged that the elimination of the middleman could

[3] The Twentieth Century Fund, *"Does Distribution Cost Too Much?"* (New York, 1939), 12.

not get rid of the function which he performs; this would be possible only if we were willing to return to a system of family self-sufficiency and household production. It must be concluded, however, that any change in methods which can reduce expenses and eliminate waste should be welcomed.

Foreign trade and World War I. World War I had various transforming effects upon our foreign trade, of which one of the most striking was its enormous expansion. After the first temporary disorganization upon the outbreak of the war, orders began to pour in from Europe for foodstuffs, for raw materials of all kinds, and finally for actual munitions of war. This increased demand was not due to the superior excellence or cheapness of our goods, or to the capture of foreign markets by well-planned selling methods. It was caused rather by the cessation of peacetime industry in Europe, which caused the Allied belligerents to turn to this great neutral country for material assistance. The excess of exports over imports, which had remained fairly steady for a decade, now jumped from $470 million in the year ending June 30, 1914, to $1000 million for 1915, to $2000 million in 1916, and to $3600 million in 1917. Not only was the volume greatly expanded, but the character of the trade also underwent a remarkable change. The expansion took place, as might be expected, primarily in the group of commodities which ministered directly to war needs, such as explosives, munitions of every sort, canned goods, meat and dairy products, and similar items. As during the Napoleonic wars, when the United States had supplied the wants of the belligerents, so now the industries of this country were organized to meet the new situation. On the other hand, our imports from the belligerent countries fell off, as their energies were absorbed more and more fully by their own immediate needs. The statistics of merchandise exports and imports for selected years since 1914 are given in the table on page 714.

As a neutral nation the United States insisted upon its right to trade with any of the belligerents or with other neutrals. Owing to the early disappearance from the seas of Germany's merchant marine and the blockade of her ports little was furnished direct to the Central Powers, though a considerable quantity of American munitions and other supplies found its way to them through neutral ports. British interference with this trade, though irritating, never resulted in a diplomatic breach between the two countries. But when German submarines began the policy of sinking American merchant vessels trading with belligerents hostile to that country, President Wilson declared that a state of war with Germany existed. As in 1812, so again in 1917, the leading neutral nation was forced by the aggression of foreign belligerents to take up arms in defense of its commercial rights on the high seas.

FOREIGN TRADE OF THE UNITED STATES, 1914-46 *(In millions of dollars)*					
Year ending Dec. 31	Exports of merchandise	Imports of merchandise	Excess of exports over imports	Percentages of total exports formed by	
				Agricultural products	Manufactures
1914	2114	1789	325	40.0	31.1
1920	8228	5278	2950	42.3	34.7
1925	4910	4227	683	36.9	37.5
1930	3843	3061	782	31.5	50.2
1935	2283	2048	235	29.4	43.5
1940	4021	2625	1396	13.0	57.9
1946	8000	4900	3100	—	—

With the entry of the United States itself into the war, there was a slight falling off in the figures of our foreign trade, for some of the supplies which we had formerly sold to the belligerents were now shipped with the American Expeditionary Force, and some of the ships which formerly carried goods were now used as transports. Under the control of the War Trade Board, moreover, ships as well as exported goods to the neutral countries were strictly rationed, while imports were limited by the lack of cargo space. Over 60 per cent of all the exports went to our European Allies, but comparatively little was bought from them, since they had little to spare.

After the signing of the Armistice there was a cessation in our shipments of war supplies, but this was more than counterbalanced by the heavy exports of foodstuffs, raw materials, and manufactured goods to the former belligerents. The need of Europe for these supplies was so desperate and so urgent that they were bought up in large quantities at inflated prices. The high point, both of exports and of imports, was reached in 1920, but the crisis of that year halted the expansion. After that there was a decline until 1928.

Foreign trade and the depression. Beginning with 1930 there was a steady and rapid fall in our foreign trade, exports declining even more rapidly than imports. The intense nationalism that was developing in the European states, as well as in our own country, led to the enactment of hostile tariff legislation, the deflation in the United States put additional obstacles in the way of our export trade, while the general world depression reduced purchasing power. At the same time we ceased lending to European countries, especially Germany, money with which to buy our goods. World trade in 1932 fell to a half of its amount in 1928. The commerce of the United States suffered severely, and no branch was harder hit than the exports of foodstuffs whose value dropped in 1932 to one-tenth their high in 1920. Meat products fell to one-fifteenth the 1920 figures, wheat and flour to one-sixteenth, and even tobacco and cotton declined to one-quarter and one-third respectively.

Exports and imports. The basis for our trade with the rest of the world is found in large measure in the wealth of our natural resources. Although the United States contains only 6 per cent of the world's population and 7 per cent of the land area, it produces over two-thirds of the world's supply of natural gas, petroleum, sulphur, and Indian corn, and over one-half of the copper, aluminum, zinc, mica, and cotton. On the other hand, we lack certain minerals, as tin, nickel, tungsten, platinum, and some others, and of course cannot grow tropical products like rubber, or foodstuffs like tea, coffee, bananas, spices, and similar things. These differences in natural endowment and in climate guarantee permanent and growing trade between the United States and foreign lands.

The six leading exports from the United States in 1939, in the order of their importance, were the following: machinery, petroleum, automobiles and parts, raw cotton, iron, steel, and copper and its manufactures. The contribution of our factories to the war in Europe is clearly evidenced in this list, which also testifies to the industrial maturity of our manufactures. Missing are such important exports of the peace years as tobacco and wheat and flour. The most spectacular growth in exports—as also in domestic production—has been in automobiles. Not mentioned in 1900, automobiles, parts, and accessories made up over one-fourth the exports of manufactures in 1929 and over one-ninth of all exports. Since then there has been a relative decline.

Although the total exports of the United States exceed in value those of any other country, our per capita exports are comparatively small. Our exports in 1929 per capita were only $42 as compared with $132 for Canada, while our imports per capita amounted to only $35 as compared with $134 for the Netherlands. In 1939 our exports amounted to only $23 per capita. It is possible that foreign goods do not constitute more than 5 per cent of the commodity consumption of the average American. Nevertheless, Professor Heilperin [4] found that in 1929 some 17 industries were exporting from 30 to 60 per cent of their output, and that an additional 18 exported between 10 and 30 per cent. For these industries foreign markets were undoubtedly important, although the exports made up only a small portion of our total exports. Evidently the exporting interests are not yet sufficiently dominant to effect a change in our traditional tariff policy.

The imports present a very similar picture and yet show the extent to which we rely on the rest of the world for goods which we either do not produce at all or produce in insufficient quantities for our needs. The most important imports in order of value in 1939 were the following: crude rubber, coffee, paper and its manufactures, sugar, raw silk, and wood pulp.

The character of the imports into the United States serves after all to give additional proof of the development of American domestic manufactures, almost all the increase being confined to crude materials for use in manufacturing, or to foodstuffs. Most of these are on the free list, and the tendency therefore is for other nations which buy our exports

---

[4] M. A. Heilperin, *Foreign Trade and Free Enterprise* (New York, Bristol-Myers Company, 1945), 11.

to pay us back in the things that we are most willing to take.

The shift in our interests between 1860, when we exported raw materials and imported manufactures, and 1940—or, indeed, today—when we exported manufactures and imported raw materials, is well illustrated in the following table.

PERCENTAGE OF EXPORTS AND IMPORTS, 1860-1940	Exports		Imports	
	1860	1940	1860	1940
Crude materials for use in manufacturing....	64	11	11	39
Manufactures ready for consumption........	11	58	49	16

A shift in our exports from agricultural to manufactured commodities occurred in the twentieth century, and as a result our trade with Europe, whose industries are similar, has declined relatively; in 1940 we sent only 40 per cent of our exports there and received only 15 per cent of our imports from that section. European countries, too, were raising tariff barriers against American manufactures. Trade with Canada, Cuba, and Mexico grew more rapidly than that with Europe, but that with the Far East, especially Japan, which in 1939 ranked fourth as a buyer of our exports and second as a supplier of our imports, showed the greatest relative expansion.

This was the picture before the outbreak of World War II; on the whole, regional specialization had taken place and different countries were exchanging their surplus commodities with one another to the benefit of all. War interrupted the plan and distorted the picture. Imports came from countries that could spare them, exports went to those that could be reached. Freedom of intercourse no longer existed and statistics of foreign trade measured military and naval strength rather than willingness to buy or excellence of wares. Our foreign trade was made to serve political as well as commercial ends, and it became increasingly an instrument of economic warfare. Wartime fluctuations in both exports and imports, but especially exports, came to bear little resemblance to any peace pattern.

As the national defense policy of the government developed, and then after the United States entered the war, measures of commercial strategy were adopted which directly affected our foreign trade. Exports of certain materials were subjected to licensing and the government imported needed wares on its own account. But the most far-reaching innovation was the establishment of lend-lease with our Allies, according to which the government furnished them with munitions and other supplies and they repaid these grants, so far as they were able, with "reverse" lend-lease in the form of food, housing, and other things. Commencing in March, 1941, the major portion of American exports went abroad under lend-lease arrangements, as is shown in the following table:

UNITED STATES FOREIGN TRADE, 1940-45 *(millions of dollars)*						
	1940	1941	1942	1943	1944	1945
General imports	$2,625	$3,345	$2,745	$3,372	$3,913	$4,130
Exports, incl. re-exp.	4,021	4,408	3,147	2,756	3,528	5,108
Lend-lease	—	739	4,932	10,219	10,831	4,313
UNRRA	—	—	—	—	—	361

In addition to lend-lease large exports of food and other supplies were sent to UNRRA for relief of the people in

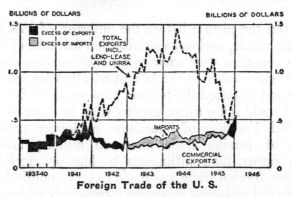

Foreign Trade of the U. S.

war-torn countries; these were augmented by expenditures abroad for relief purposes by the War and Navy departments, by the American Red Cross, and by other organizations. Some, but not all, of these are reflected in the statistics of foreign trade.

The balance of payments. During most of the years after 1914 the merchandise balance sheet of our foreign trade showed an excess of exports over imports, but the size of this surplus and the uses to which it was put have varied. It has been estimated that at the outbreak of World War I the people of the United States were indebted to the people of Europe to the amount of about $6000 million. During the next three years our favorable balance of trade amounted to over $7000 million, and it may be concluded that this enormous sum canceled the foreign investments and wiped the slate clean of the accumulated debts of past years. After our entrance into the war the government of the United States advanced to our Allies some $10,000 million, nearly all of which was lost through the failure of reparations and the repudiation of the war debts. During the 1920's private loans and investment of American capital were made in Europe, especially Germany, in Central and South America, and in other parts of the world to an amount of some $10,000 million.[5] These were of course reflected in increased exports. Unwise extension of credit, the outbreak of a general crisis in Europe, which affected Europe as well as this country, and other factors, resulted in default or loss of about $2000 million of these private loans, so that in 1939 the people of the United States were creditors of the citizens of other nations for a sum estimated in round numbers at about $14,600 million. From this should be subtracted, however, about $9600 million of foreign capital invested in this country. Most of this had fled to the United States during the troubled 1930's and more came in the subsequent war years, as this seemed the

---

[5] According to Dr. Max Winkler our total foreign investments and their distribution in 1930 were as follows:

Europe	$ 5,108,000,000
Canada	4,389,000,000
Central America	2,936,000,000
South America	2,786,000,000
China, Japan, and Philippines	926,000,000
Miscellaneous	459,000,000
Total	$16,604,000,000

"Prosperity and Foreign Investments," in Foreign Policy Association *Information Service*, Vol. VI, Supplement No. 1 (May, 1930), 4.

safest refuge from the uncertainties of Europe. So large were the receipts of gold and silver that our total imports (merchandise plus the precious metals) exceeded our total exports during the three years 1939-41. But the movement was reversed at the end of the last-named year and since that time exports have greatly exceeded imports.

The countries devastated by war are hungry for American goods, and the problem is not so much to gain markets for exports as to find ways for other people to pay for these exports and persuade the American people to accept payment in the form of imports. This situation can hardly be expected to be permanent and sooner or later, as in the case of all creditor nations, the merchandise balance of trade will become "unfavorable." To be a creditor nation, we must stand ready to import more than we export. If we are to collect from our customers and debtors we must abandon our traditional attitude of hostility to imports.

Leading ports. The widening geographical lines of our foreign trade during this period were owing not only to the extension of the sources of supply of our imports and the expanding markets for our exports, but quite as much to the internal development of the country. All these factors have affected the routes taken by our exports and imports and have given prominence to different ports at different times. In 1860 the greatest value of domestic merchandise exports left the country through New Orleans, owing to the great value of the cotton crop; New York City ranked second, but was followed by three other southern ports, Mobile, Charleston, and Savannah. By 1900 New York City and New Orleans had changed places and third rank was taken by Galveston; then followed Boston, Baltimore, Philadelphia, and San Francisco.

The imports were much more concentrated in the Atlantic ports than were the exports, though this dominance lessened somewhat as the origin of our imports widened. In 1860 New York handled 70 per cent of the country's entire import trade; this proportion was 63 per cent in 1900 and 45 per cent in 1943. As the point at which converged the chief ocean steamship lines, and from which radiated the important railroad lines, this city offered unrivaled opportunities as a distributing center.

The merchant marine. American shipping had steadily declined between 1860 and 1914, and as a nation we had come to rely to an ever greater extent upon foreign vessels to carry our ocean trade.

World War I created new conditions and new opportunities. Within two weeks after its outbreak Congress eliminated the five-year age limit on vessels seeking American registry, permitted such vessels to retain their foreign officers, and in other ways modified the former exclusive policy. Under these liberal provisions about 175 vessels sought the protection of the neutral American flag, bringing the tonnage under American registry up to 1,871,543 in 1915, and 2,191,715 in 1916. The disappearance of the German merchant marine from the sea, the diversion of British and French vessels into war service, and the sinking of many of these by German submarines, all greatly reduced the number of vessels available for carrying our commerce, which was at the same time increasing by leaps and bounds. What was needed was an immediate increase in ships and the construction of new tonnage.

Congress responded in 1916 by the creation of the Shipping Board, which was given important regulatory powers over shipping, and was authorized to acquire merchant vessels and to sell or charter them to citizens of the United States. Immediately after we entered the war it organized the Emergency Fleet Corporation for the purpose of building new ships. An ambitious program, calling for the delivery of 3256 ships of 18,249,520 dead-weight [6] tons, was laid down, and after a time-wasting debate over the relative merits of steel, wood, and concrete ships, construction was finally begun in earnest. The race between the submarines and the shipbuilders ended with the Armistice of November 11, 1918, but the construction of vessels for the Emergency Fleet Cor-

---

[6] A gross ton equals 100 cubic feet of space in a merchant ship, virtually all enclosed spaces in the vessel being counted. Dead-weight tonnage is the weight of fuel and cargo that will depress a ship to the load line from its empty, but equipped, state. Dead-weight tonnage should be reduced by one-third to make it comparable with gross tonnage.

poration continued until some 1500 vessels had been launched. By 1920 the total seagoing merchant marine of the United States consisted of 4889 vessels of 13,789,874 gross tons, but five-sixths of these had been built after the Armistice. Included in this number were some of the former German ships, which were turned over to this government after the war. The United States was now second only to Great Britain as a shipping nation.

The antagonism of private shipping interests to government ownership and operation of the Shipping Board vessels resulted in the passage of the so-called Jones Merchant Marine Act of 1920, which provided for the lease or sale of these vessels to private shippers. The concrete and wooden vessels were scrapped and their value was written off as a cost of the war. Eventually, many of the better steel vessels were sold to private companies, about 10 per cent of the original cost being recovered by the government.

Other methods of stimulating shipbuilding were mail subsidies and the granting of federal loans at low rates of interest for new construction or reconditioning, but neither was effective. The mail contracts were tainted with fraud and little new building was undertaken. Meanwhile the wartime merchant fleet was becoming obsolete, and the usable tonnage was declining.

In 1936 a new Merchant Marine Act was passed. Under the terms of this act the federal government was authorized to pay part of the cost of building new ships and to loan most of the balance at 3.5 per cent interest. Operating subsidies were also to be given. Ships receiving such aid would automatically become available for national defense. The purpose of this act was not so much to enlarge the merchant fleet as to replace the rapidly aging and obsolete vessels with modern ships of reasonable cargo capacity and speed. In spite of this encouragement the demolition and retirement of old ships went on faster than new building and there was a steady decline in the number and tonnage of United States vessels. The development down to 1945 is shown in the table on page 724.

The defense program of 1940, and especially the entry of this country into World War II in December, 1941, completely changed the situation. Two months later the government took part, as it had done in World War I. It created the War Shipping Board, to which was given the acquisition, operation, maintenance, allocation, control, and insurance of the ocean-going fleet, and the Maritime Commission, to which was entrusted its construction. Merchant ships were built and launched at the rate of one a day to keep open the "bridge of ships" between this country and Britain. Some of these were standardized stopgap craft, quickly built, but most of them constituted permanent additions to the merchant marine— seagoing ships, tankers, Great Lakes carriers, and other types.

The Liberty ships, freighters of 10,000 dead-weight tons capacity, were the first built. The design for these was furnished by Britain, which had ordered 60 of them in 1940, and this model was adopted by the Maritime Commission in order to lose no time. Rivalry between different yards to lower man-hours and cost of construction resulted in the spectacular exploit of the Oregon yard, which delivered a Liberty ship in less than twelve days after the keel was laid. Later, Victory and other types, more difficult to build but with greater speed than the Liberties, were preferred. All the better vessels were powered with steam turbines or diesel engines. The end of the war found the United States possessed of a merchant marine of about 33 million gross tons, of which about half are Liberty ships. These are not economical cargo boats in international trade because of their slow speed, but some of them may be used at home or sold abroad for local use. It is estimated that we shall have a surplus of about 20 million gross tons in 1946. No better use could be found for these surplus vessels than to sell them to Britain, Norway, Sweden, Denmark, Holland, and Belgium. For all of these countries, shipping is a major economic activity, and their merchant fleets suffered severely during the war. From a purely economic standpoint we could profitably still further reduce our merchant marine and hire these nations to carry our trade, at lower rates than we can do it. But so long as the fear of war persists we must, from the standpoint of security, maintain an adequate mercantile fleet and shipyards.

No estimate of our merchant marine would be complete that did not take into account shipping used in the coastwise trade, for vessels in this trade and in that for foreign service are largely interchangeable. Indeed, one of the reasons for confining coastwise shipping to United States vessels was to provide a reservoir of national ocean-going ships. The vessels that ply between the Atlantic and Pacific coasts via the Panama Canal—defined as coastwise trade—equal most of those in foreign trade both in size and speed. Nor are the great freighters on the Great Lakes much inferior. Their relative importance during the eleven years 1929–39, inclusive, is indicated by the fact that the movement of freight by coastwise shipping was 40 per cent of all, and that of the Great Lakes and foreign traders was 30 per cent for each. Today the merchant marine engaged in foreign service has outstripped both of the others in tonnage.

THE AMERICAN MERCHANT MARINE*					
(1000 gross tons)					
	Sailing and Other		Steam and Motor		Total
Year	No.	Tons	No.	Tons	No.	Tons
1915	10,753	2446	15,948	5,944	26,701	8,390
1920	9,369	2501	18,814	13,823	28,183	16,324
1925	7,730	2430	18,637	14,976	26,367	17,406
1930	6,099	2300	19,115	13,768	25,214	16,068
1935	6,424	2118	18,495	12,535	24,919	14,653
1940	7,708	2665	19,504	11,353	27,212	14,018
1945	7,025	2566	22,772	30,247	29,797	32,813

* Bureau of Marine Inspection and Navigation, U. S. Department of Commerce.

Tariff legislation. The Underwood Tariff of 1913, which had somewhat moderated duties, never had a fair chance to demonstrate its virtues, for imports were reduced and deranged during World War I. Just as during the War of 1812, when foreign goods were cut off and new domestic industries sprang up, so now the manufacture of articles formerly obtained from Germany and other countries was given an opportunity to develop with little competition. After the Armistice there was a sharp rise in imports, mostly of commodities on the free list, but this was seized upon by the "war babies" and the established industries as an excuse to demand more protection.

Upon the inauguration of a Republican president in 1921 the dominant party at once proposed a revision of the tariff upward. The great fall in the prices of agricultural products in 1920 and the consequent hard times for the farmers led to a demand for protection to farm products. Accordingly, the so-called Emergency Tariff was passed in 1921 which imposed duties on wheat, corn, meat, sugar, cotton, wool, and many other agricultural products. This was replaced the following year by the Fordney-McCumber Act, which raised the level of duties above that of the Underwood Act, but below that of the Payne-Aldrich Tariff, or to about 38 per cent. The principle already enunciated in the Republican platform of 1904, that "the measure of protection should always at least equal the difference in cost of production at home and abroad," was further elaborated, and a new argument advanced to meet the new conditions in Europe. This time it was urged that, owing to the depreciation of foreign currencies, the countries with cheap money enjoyed an advantage in manufacturing over the United States, which alone had maintained its currency on the gold standard; import duties would therefore have to be increased in order to protect American industry against cheaply produced foreign goods. The comprehensive character of the act may be judged by the boast of Senator McCumber that "every industry in the country is fairly and justly protected."

Continued agrarian discontent, which was now well organized and militant, forced another revision of the tariff in 1930. Originally designed as a partial revision to afford protection to agricultural products, the House bill was seized upon by manufacturing interests to obtain special favors for themselves in every direction. Determined opposition of the agricultural bloc in the Senate, however, eliminated many of the increases to manufactures except to some depressed industries, but retained the higher rates on agricultural products. Hides and cement were removed from the free list, but the flexible provision, allowing the President to make certain changes upon recommendation of the tariff commission, was retained. As finally passed, the Hawley-Smoot Act fixed the average rate of duties at above 40 per cent.

Protests against this measure were immediate and showed

a revulsion against continued tariff favors to the manufacturing group. A petition signed by over 1000 economists
urged the President to veto the bill because of the obstacle
it would place on exports, the likelihood of tariff reprisals
by other countries, and the strain it would put on international relations. That these fears were not idle was shown
by the prompt action of Canada in raising rates on goods
which were imported principally from the United States.
Other countries put up their bars against American exports,
by high duties, quotas, or other methods. Even Great Britain,
the citadel of free trade, enacted protective legislation, and
the depression revived interest in reciprocity. No effort was
made to revise the tariff, but in 1934 a Trade Agreements
Act was passed. The President was given power, without re-
ferring the matter to Congress and its pressure groups, to
make reductions of tariffs and other trade barriers in return
for trade concessions from other countries. This was called a
"Yankee swapping" measure, and was essentially a bargaining program with the objective of increasing our trade with
foreign countries in both directions by reducing excessive barriers on both sides. Initiated by Secretary of State Cordell
Hull the act has been repeatedly extended and now goes to
1951. Average duties have steadily fallen and trade with
agreement countries, which now carry on over 80 per cent of
the world's trade, has increased more than with others. By
the end of 1949 some 33 countries had made such trade agreements with the United States.

Neutrality legislation. Even while these efforts were being
made to increase our foreign trade, events were occurring that
threatened to curtail if not to destroy it. The outbreak of the
war in Europe and a strong peace movement in this country
led to legislation designed to emphasize our isolation and our
neutrality. In 1934 the Johnson Act had forbidden loans to
governments in default on their debts to us, and an amendment of 1936 imposed an embargo on loans to all belligerents. The non-interventionist policy found expression in the
Neutrality Act of 1937, which aimed to exclude American
citizens as fully as possible from any commercial or financial
dealings with belligerents that might involve this country in
war. This prohibited the export of arms, ammunition, and

implements of warfare to belligerents, repeated the embargo on loans, and laid down the "cash and carry" policy for our export trade. According to this, exports to belligerents were not permitted until title to the goods had passed to the foreign buyer, who must then carry the goods away in a foreign vessel. This policy was intended, in the words of Senator Borah, "to avoid all risks, all danger . . . but to get all the profits." But the climax of our isolationist attitude was reached in the Neutrality Act of 1939, which forbade American vessels to trade with belligerents, withdrew government protection from American citizens venturing into combat zones, and made it unlawful for vessels in the merchant marine to be armed. This abdication of our rights as a sovereign nation on the high seas "gave the green light to international gangsters to go ahead," but did not protect us. It was repealed on November 17, 1941, just three weeks before Japan, Germany, and Italy declared war on the United States. The policy of isolationist neutrality had proved a dismal and dangerous failure. The principle of freedom of the seas was, however, reaffirmed in the Atlantic Charter, to which we subscribed the following year.

The United States as a world power. The isolationists had not realized to what an extent the interests and activities of the people of this country had become enmeshed in those of a world economy. The war with Spain resulted in the acquisition of the non-contiguous territories of Puerto Rico, the Philippines, and Guam. In the same year we also annexed the Hawaiian Islands, valuable as sugar and pineapple producers and as a military outpost, and in 1899 we acquired part of the Samoan Islands as a coaling station. The territorial expansion of the United States had now assumed an aspect strikingly akin to the imperialism of Europe, and this was lent confirmation by the method of our acquisition of the Canal Zone in Panama, which was brought about by strong-arm tactics on the part of President Theodore Roosevelt, who was impatient of the dilatory methods and demands of Colombia, within which the proposed canal was located. When the Colombian Senate rejected a treaty ceding the necessary strip of land, a revolution occurred which led to the establishment of the republic of Panama. The administration in Washington at once recognized the new republic and, with what seemed to many unseemly haste, made a treaty by which the United States acquired practical sovereignty over a strip five miles wide on either side of the canal route, excepting the cities of Colón and Panama at either end. The next addition to our national domain came in 1917 by the purchase of the Virgin Islands from Denmark.[7]

This territorial expansion was paralleled by the development of a foreign policy in keeping with it. The traditional course of the United States had been formulated by Washington, who warned against permanent political alliances, and by Jefferson, who gave currency to the phrase "entangling alliances," against which later statesmen have so frequently cautioned this country. A generation later, in 1823, the Monroe Doctrine warned foreign nations against encroachments on the American continents. The western hemisphere was to be reserved for a series of American republics, freed from alliances with Europe and working out their destiny in their own way. We guarded the Americas with the help of the British fleet in the nineteenth century; alone in the early twentieth century. This attitude of self-defense and non-intervention was abandoned after the building of the Panama Canal, which gave the United States new and vital interests in the Caribbean area, and made it necessary that this region be safeguarded from the intrusion of foreign powers. A specialized Caribbean policy was accordingly developed which asserted, in effect, that in this "American Mediterranean" the interests of the United States were paramount. This assumption of international guardianship carried with it the suppression of "international nuisances," in the picturesque phraseology of Theodore Roosevelt, which might become dangerous to American peace and safety. Under this principle the United States, having paramount interests in the Caribbean, assumed the authority to compel the smaller states of that region to fulfill their international obligations in order to prevent interference by European powers. In some cases it landed marines, appointed financial officials, and admin-

---

[7] The price of real estate had gone up since 1803, when we paid approximately three cents an acre for the Louisiana Purchase; for the Virgin Islands we paid $300 an acre.

istered the revenues until the finances were straightened out and civil order established.

The decade 1930-40 saw a reaction from this imperialistic attitude, which found expression in the adoption of the "good neighbor" policy, a promise of independence to the Philippines (carried out July 4, 1946), a repudiation of the Theodore "Roosevelt corollary" justifying intervention in Latin America to insure payment of foreign-owned debts, and in other ways. The "good neighbor" policy in effect rewrote the Monroe Doctrine into something like a Pan-American doctrine of collective security.

It is difficult to speak of an American policy, for the attitude of the government has varied from one administration to another. The gamut has been run from the frank imperialism of Theodore Roosevelt through the idealism of Wilson and the legalistic theory of Coolidge to the nonintervention policy of Hoover and the "good-neighbor" doctrine of Franklin D. Roosevelt. The last seems to represent fairly the public attitude and to mark a long step forward toward the realization of more friendly relations with our neighbors to the south.

World War II, beginning in 1939, brought with it the possibility that the Axis powers would seize the colonial possessions of the enemies situated on the western hemisphere. This danger was met by the Havana Convention of July 30, 1940, according to which the United States and all the Central and South American republics except Argentina, Bolivia, Chile, Uruguay, and Venezuela agreed to joint administration of European colonies and possessions in the Americas by an emergency committee in case of a sudden crisis. The policy of joint action was carried still further after the declaration of war against the United States by Japan, Germany, and Italy in December, 1941. All the American republics made common cause and broke off diplomatic relations with the Axis powers, except Argentina and Chile. Some of them even showed their solidarity by declaring war. Common danger at last brought a recognition of their common interests and led to unity of action such as had never before been achieved.

The active participation by the United States in World

War II, the acquisition of bases in the Pacific, and commitments in Europe and the Far East have given the nation a new international status with accompanying responsibilities. Involvement in world affairs through the spread of commerce and investment in other countries has now been reinforced by political and military considerations. Disclaiming imperialistic ambitions, we yet claim recognition of our interests as one of the leading world powers.

Conclusion. It is evident that the United States has traveled a long way since the days of Jefferson and no entangling alliances. Become a world power through irresistible territorial and industrial growth, the nation has been compelled to modify its traditional policy of aloofness and to take part in ever-increasing degree in world affairs. Today it is enmeshed in the problems of world peace and international trade and finance by a thousand ties. During the period when American capital was being heavily invested abroad, the United States, under the influence of the business community, gradually changed its policy of non-interference into one of frequent intervention in those countries where American interests were considered paramount. After 1929 American investments lessened and our foreign policy became more pacific. In European affairs the United States refused to take part, and the refusal to join the League of Nations undoubtedly reflected the popular view, although Americans participated helpfully in conferences for the settlement of the reparation problem and other international questions. By the Kellogg Pact and participation in international conferences for disarmament we gave, moreover, proof of our earnest desire for peace and of our intention to devote our economic resources to the improvement of economic conditions in the world rather than to the work of destruction. It is ironical that today we are custodians of the most destructive force ever developed by man, but the existence of such an agency has brought a determination that our civilization shall not again be threatened with destruction by war. "One World" was the plea of Wendell Willkie in his book by that title; "One World or None" is the alternative offered by a group of scientists describing the effects of atomic warfare. The isolation of which Washington approved has been steadily broken down as a result of the shrinking of the spatial world through improvements in transportation and the annihilation of distance through improvements in communication. National economy has inevitably yielded place to world-wide interdependence and integration, in spite of utterances to the contrary. In the modern world no nation can remain wholly aloof, but each must co-operate in the promotion of the best economic interests of all.

CHAPTER XXXI
FINANCING THREE EMERGENCIES

An era of emergencies. A baby born in 1914 would be in his early thirties today and would have spent two-thirds of his life in an atmosphere of national emergency. In his lifetime there have been four years of World War I, about ten years of the Great Depression, and six years of World War II. These three great emergencies dominate the period. In each emergency the nation was called upon to apply its ingenuity and resources to meet a tremendous crisis. Each required governmental expenditures far in excess of anything the people had been accustomed to. The government sought to meet these emergencies without making too drastic changes in existing financial institutions, and yet the emergencies necessarily had considerable effect on the direction and growth of those institutions. But before investigating how the three emergencies were financed and how financial institutions were altered in the process, a clear understanding of those institutions as they existed about 1914 is necessary.

The gold standard. The monetary system of the United States in 1914 was the gold coin standard. This had been in force ever since the resumption of specie payments in 1879 and before that it had prevailed in practice from 1834 to 1862. However, it was not until the Gold Standard Act of 1900 that Congress publicly committed the nation to the gold standard. A nation is said to be on the gold coin standard if its money contains a fixed amount of gold, if there is complete freedom to coin or export gold, if all other monies in the country are redeemable in gold, and if gold is full legal tender. Our gold coins contained 23.22 grains of pure gold per dollar. In 1914 we had $3.4 billion in circulation of which almost half were gold coins or gold certificates (a kind of paper money backed 100 per cent by gold coins). Silver coins and silver certificates were about half as numerous and the remaining $1 billion consisted of greenbacks and national bank notes. It was a heterogeneous collection of money, but since it was all redeemable in gold it made a sound money system in which the people had full confidence.

Being on the gold standard does not insure that a nation's price level will be rigidly stable. Evidence of this is found in the fact that prices in this country fell 24 per cent between 1879 and 1896 and then rose 50 per cent between 1896 and 1914. But a gold standard does virtually guarantee that ample warning will be served the nation if policies are adopted likely to lead to serious inflation. For example, in the 1890's the effects of extensive purchases and coinage of silver were quickly apparent. The outflow of gold under the operation of Gresham's Law gave warning that unless this tinkering with the nation's monetary system were stopped, redemption in gold would end, the gold standard would break down, and serious inflation might follow. The silver legislation was repealed, the issue was made clear to the public, and the choice of inflation was voted down. Thus the gold standard is primarily a device to protect the nation against powerful pressure groups within itself. There were to be times in the next generation when the gold standard would be more or less abandoned. This increased the chances of financial disaster and at the same time lessened the likelihood that the country would realize the danger in time to act.

Federal reserve banks. On top of the money system rested a system of commercial banks which provided the bank deposits against which checks were drawn. These were in some ways our most important form of money, for during the last generation about 85 per cent of all business had been settled by checks. The banks also provided the nation with much of its short-term capital and some of its long-term capital. In 1914 two-thirds of our 22,000 commercial banks had state charters and one-third had national charters. However, the national banks were bigger and owned over 70 per cent of the banking resources. Bank failures were more frequent among the smaller state banks but were unfortunately all too numerous among all banks. This was largely attributable to the fact that in times of crisis there was no central bank, that is, no bankers' bank, to which the banks could turn for help. Another fault of our banking system was the inelasticity of national bank notes. Based as they were on government bonds, they did not expand and contract automatically with the needs of business. This was explained in Chapter XXV. And finally, the agricultural classes could not easily borrow from the national banks because their charters forbade them to make loans on real estate which was the farmers' chief asset.

Beginning in the nineties criticism of our banking system grew and finally culminated in the appointment in 1908 of the National Monetary Commission, to investigate banking and currency systems throughout the world and to propose a plan for legislation. After five years of discussion of the general problem, the Federal Reserve Act was passed on December 23, 1913. It took some time to organize, but on November 16, 1914, the present Federal Reserve System went into effect.

All the national banks were compelled to join and state banks might do so if they conformed to Federal reserve requirements. Only a handful of state banks joined at first. Funds for the founding of the Federal reserve banks were obtained by selling stock to each member bank equal to 3 per cent of its own capital and surplus. The Federal Reserve System was thus privately owned although control of it lay largely in government hands. Twelve Federal reserve banks were established, each of which served the member banks in twelve regions of the country. At the head of the Federal Reserve System stood the Federal Reserve Board of seven men appointed by the President to administer the whole and give it a unity of policy.

The Federal reserve banks can best be understood by regarding them as bankers' banks. To begin with an individual rarely had dealings with them. More important, their relationship to member banks was and still is analogous to the member banks' relationship to customers. This is true in at least three major respects. First, customers deposit their idle funds in commercial banks for safekeeping; likewise member banks were required after 1917 to keep all their legal reserves against deposits in the district Federal reserve banks. Member banks' reserves are thus their deposits in the district Federal reserve bank. Second, a customer with good security but insufficient cash funds may borrow from his bank; likewise a member bank in the same circumstances may borrow from its district Federal reserve bank. This gives the member banks a place to turn for help in times of panic, although it should be emphasized that the Federal reserve bank will help only sound banks. And finally, just as commercial banks loaned their credit to customers—formerly in the form of bank notes and latterly in the form of deposits placed in their customers' names—so likewise Federal reserve banks make loans to member banks by issuing to them Federal reserve notes or by crediting the loan to the member bank's deposit at the Federal reserve bank. The Federal reserve notes issued by the Federal reserve banks were an elastic currency, for the member banks could obtain them in almost any amount by rediscounting the commercial paper (such as promissory notes) of merchants, manufacturers, and others to whom they had made loans. The supply of Federal reserve notes thus expanded with the greater needs of business; it also contracted as business needs declined. This was because the Federal reserve notes had to be backed at least 40 per cent by gold and the rest by commercial paper, or, in the absence of commercial paper, 100 per cent by gold. There is no profit for banks in circulating bank notes entirely backed by gold, so when customers paid off their promissory notes, member banks generally retired an equal amount of Federal reserve notes. In summary, the Federal Reserve System overcame two of the main evils of the national banks—inelasticity and lack of co-operation—and gave the United States its third experiment in central banking.

Other financial factors in 1914. The country was in a mild depression when war broke out in Europe in 1914 but it soon recovered from that. Actually the government was well prepared, from a purely financial point of view, for the coming world crisis. The national debt was slightly over $1 billion, the budget was regularly balanced every year, and the cost of running the federal government was less than $1 billion a year. The funds came equally from customs duties and internal revenue taxes. A constitutional amendment making possible a federal income tax had just been adopted in 1913, but as yet provided only an insignificant amount of revenue. Real national income, in terms of 1929 dollars, was $52.6

billion and per capita real income was slightly greater than just before World War II.

World War I. Two and a half years passed by, after the outbreak of war in Europe, before the United States was drawn into the conflict, but only in the last year did we make even meager military preparations. The nineteen months of our participation in the war thus saw us in a frenzy of activity. War is wasteful enough when one is prepared; it is even more so when one is not. Expenditures by our government at once rivaled and soon surpassed in magnitude those of the other warring countries. The total expenditures attributable to the war, including advances of about $10 billion made by the United States to our Allies, have been stated by the treasury as about $32.8 billion. This is twice as much as the total expenditures of the federal government during the first one hundred years of our national existence, including those for the War of 1812, the Mexican War, and the Civil War.

It has been emphasized before that the generation that wages a war must pay for it and that there are only three ways of doing that. These are by taxation, by borrowing, and by creating money, which last generally causes inflation. Taxation is the best but least popular method. Congress quickly increased taxes of all kinds, especially the newly created income taxes whose highest rates were stepped up from a mere 6 per cent in 1913 to 67 per cent during the war. Graduated income taxes and the related excess profits taxes became the government's chief revenue producers. However, the revenues raised by taxation during the war amounted to less than one-third the sums needed, the highest figure for any one year being $4.7 billion in 1919. The remaining two-thirds was seemingly raised by borrowing.

Five bond issues were floated, the first four of which were called Liberty loans, and the fifth, which was issued after the Armistice was signed, the Victory loan.

WORLD WAR I BOND CAMPAIGNS

First Liberty loan	$ 1,989,000,000
Second Liberty loan	$ 3,808,000,000
Third Liberty loan	$ 4,176,000,000
Fourth Liberty loan	$ 6,964,000,000
Victory loan	$ 4,498,000,000
	$21,435,000,000

These enormous sums were obtained from practically every class in the country, the number of individual subscribers running up to 22,000,000 persons in the fourth loan, when war enthusiasm was at its height. In addition to the bonds, whose lowest denomination was $50, war savings certificates for $5 and thrift stamps for 25 cents were sold. It is significant, however, that only about half of these bonds and stamps were paid for out of savings. The other half was procured simply by exchanging government promissory notes and bonds for credit at the banks. The treasury then wrote checks against these manufactured deposits as any bank customers would. The trouble was these war loans were not self-liquidating, hence not paid off soon. Nearly all the demand deposits therefore stayed in circulation.

Creating money, chiefly demand deposits, thus paid for a considerable part of the war. Between 1914 and 1920, when bills for immediate costs of the war ceased to flood the treasury, the following increases in money supply took place.

WORLD WAR I INCREASES IN MONEY SUPPLY* (in billions of dollars)				
Kind of money	1914	1916	1918	1920
Currency outside banks.......	$ 1.5	$ 1.9	$ 3.3	$ 4.1
Demand deposits	10.1	12.0	14.8	19.6
Total	$11.6	$13.9	$18.1	$23.7

* Fed. Res. Bd., *Banking and Monetary Statistics* (Washington, 1943), 34.

Notice that the most important kind of money, namely bank deposits against which checks may be drawn, increased by $9.5 billion. Yet, although our total money supply had approximately doubled by 1920, not many more goods were being produced than in 1914.[1] Indeed during the war fewer goods which the civilians wanted were produced and much of the war matériel was either shot up or of little value after the war. This increase in money was evidence that something

[1] National income in terms of 1929 dollars, according to National Industrial Conference Board estimates, increased from $49.6 billion in 1914 to $53.8 billion in 1920. The wartime peak was $59.4 billion in 1917. For wartime needs perhaps 20 per cent more money was justified but not 100 per cent more. *National Income in the United States, 1799-1938* (New York, 1939), 15.

unusual had taken place; it was evidence that about a quarter to a third of the cost of World War I had been paid for by creating money.

In the Civil War issuance of greenbacks met an estimated seventh of the cost of that war to the North. Unquestionably our methods of financing World War I were more subtle than those of financing the Civil War. Yet they hardly represented an improvement if the measure is the extent to which money creation and inflation were avoided.

Inflation in World War I. War usually brings about inflation in the general price level not only because more money is issued but also because fewer civilian goods are produced to spend it on. War orders from Europe had caused noticeable price rises as early as 1916. The belligerents had abandoned their gold standards and engaged in inflationary war financing and this had its effects on prices all over the world. In the autumn following our declaration of war on Germany President Wilson placed an embargo on the export of gold and discouraged its use by the public. This amounted to a suspension of the gold standard. Prices continued to rise in 1918, 1919, and early 1920, as the accompanying table shows.

WHOLESALE PRICES, 1913-25*	
Year	Wholesale prices
1913	100.0
1914	98.1
1915	100.8
1916	126.8
1917	177.2
1918	194.3
1919	206.4
1920	226.2
May, 1920	246.7
1921	146.9
December, 1921	139.8
1922	148.8
1923	153.7
1924	149.7
1925	158.7

* Statistical Abstract of the United States, 1926, 313.

Meanwhile the embargo on gold exports was taken off in July, 1919, bringing us back on the gold standard. Civilian production began to pick up about the same time, and the inflation period came to an abrupt end in mid-1920.

The World War I inflation was characterized by most of the inequities which have accompanied inflationary periods in the past. As the purchasing power of the dollar declined, debtors were able to repay their creditors more easily and the creditors received less valuable dollars than they had originally loaned. Widows and other recipients of some $3.5 billion worth of life insurance policies which were paid off between 1915 and 1920 also lost in this way. Farm prices rose more rapidly than the general price level, so that the farm population prospered. Business boomed: business failures were only a third as numerous in 1919 as in 1914 and the number of millionaires in the nation more than doubled. Labor shared unequally in this wartime prosperity. The money wages of organized labor employed in war industries and of farm laborers kept pace with prices and in some cases rose faster than prices. According to Paul Douglas, real annual earnings of wage earners in all industries, including farming, rose from 102 in 1914 to 108 in 1920. Thus the real wages of these classes of labor were not appreciably affected by the war. White-collar workers, on the other hand, men in the building trades, teachers and ministers, and many unorganized groups experienced a sharp drop in their real wages. Since wages are the source of most of the buying power in the nation, serious consequences followed. The standard of living for many was reduced.

Financial legacies of World War I. A period of liquidation and depression began in the middle of 1920 and lasted for about two years. At the end of the war, industry hastened to reconvert itself for peacetime production. The high prices being received for civilian goods promised generous profits. Prospects were deceivingly bright. Some merchants hoarded goods in anticipation of still higher prices while others ordered two or three times as many goods as they needed on the theory that manufacturers would send them only a fraction of what they ordered anyway. That was the way manufacturers had treated them during the war. As a result industry swung into full-scale production and store inventories began to pile up. Meanwhile, because people's real incomes had declined, they could not afford to buy as much as before. What seemed to be a "buyers' strike" took place, although it is a mistake to assume it was in any way organized. Merchants cancelled their orders with the factories, factories curtailed production and laid off workers, workers could now buy still less, and the downward spiral was under way. Business failures were four times as great in 1921 as in 1919. The only way out of this economic morass was for prices to fall back into line with wages or even below them for a while. That was what quickly happened, although again by no ordered plan. Merchants and manufacturers sold surpluses at sacrifice prices and the price level came tumbling down, falling from a level of 247 in May, 1920, to 146 a year later. Probably never before in the history of the country had such a sharp decline in prices occurred. Even at their lowest, however, prices did not reach the 1913 level.

By 1922 prosperity began to return. The drastic cut in prices noticeably increased the real incomes of those employed in 1921. This and the stimulus given the important automobile industry by the desire of millions of persons somehow to acquire a car of their own were chiefly responsible for the country's swift recovery. The price level was remarkably stable during the next seven years at a level about 50 per cent higher than before the war.

A third legacy of the war, in addition to an immediate depression and a higher price level, was a large public debt. It reached an all-time peak of $26.6 billion on August 31, 1919. This was $250 per capita. During the next decade we succeeded in reducing the total at the rate of about $1 billion a year until it stood at $16.2 billion in 1930. Andrew Mellon got most of the credit for this feat and at the time was hailed as the greatest Secretary of the Treasury since Alexander Hamilton.

Taxes too were higher as a result of the war. It is well known to students of public finance that it is easier to increase taxes than to reduce them. Our World War I experience is an excellent illustration. The federal government collected five to six times as much in taxes after the war as it had before. Servicing the debt at first took as much as had been needed altogether in 1914 and on top of that there was the billion dollars to reduce the debt each year, and other government costs that were over twice as great as before the war.

The graduated income tax provided most of the revenue and was obviously here to stay.

World War I also enhanced the popularity of two other financial institutions. One was the gold standard and the other was the Federal Reserve System. Sound money is never more appreciated than just after a period of inflation. That fact is reflected in our monetary policies following the Revolution, the Civil War, and World War I, and also in the monetary policies of most of the nations of the world in the 1920's. The United States was the first country to return to the gold standard. By 1928 virtually every important nation in the world was on the gold standard and the world enjoyed a brief period of sound money and relatively stable prices. The prestige of the gold standard was never higher.

As for the Federal Reserve System, the government and the people both wondered how they had ever got along without it. In the 1920's it was called upon to help the gold standard to do something a gold standard had never been able to do alone, namely, to maintain a stable price level over a period of years. The stable price level that prevailed between 1922 and 1929 was attributed in large part to the Federal reserve bank's open market operations which began in 1922. It is not necessary here to enter into the technical intricacies of these operations; it is sufficient to point out that they encouraged banks to lend when times were bad and to curb their creation of credit when expansion seemed to be getting out of hand. With this mechanism for controlling the money supply and presumably stabilizing the price level at the disposal of its financial leaders, the country seemed on the threshold of endless good times. A "new era" had apparently arrived. For several years nothing happened to dispel the illusion.

Background of the Great Depression. The final legacy of World War I was the subtle reaction of economic forces that undermined the prosperity of "the golden twenties" and finally precipitated the crash in 1929 thereby bringing on the Great Depression. A few of the more obvious of these forces may be mentioned although the events are still too recent and our understanding of business cycles is as yet too imperfect to weigh their importance accurately. To begin with there was too much money in the banks and elsewhere as a result of the war. The presence of these surplus funds and the existence of a more efficient credit and banking system lowered interest rates. Lower interest rates, plus improved industrial techniques and the tremendous demand for semi-luxuries like autos and radios, in sum, the general spirit of prosperity, led to increased borrowing and expansion. Many companies and some people, too, got deeply involved in debt. As the government paid off some of its debts, these funds were reloaned. About $4.5 billion was tied up in foreign long-term securities between 1921–29. Within the country public utilities and industries increased their long-term debts by $8 billion or by about 70 per cent. Lower interest rates also tended to raise the price of income-yielding property.[2]

Declining interest rates, rising property values, a continuing high demand for goods by a prosperous public, and a government not inclined to hamper business activity by rules and regulations—all these factors in time generated speculative activity. A boom took place in Florida real estate and collapsed in 1926. Samuel Insull made use of the holding-company device to gather together thousands of power and light companies and build a fabulous public utilities empire. The automobile, the radio, the chemical and the electrical industries, not to mention the bootleg liquor industry, enjoyed large profits and expanded in hopes of even greater gains. The public added to their hopes by spending not only much of its present income but $1 billion worth of future income by installment-plan buying. And in order to share in the prospective profits thousands and then millions of persons bought stocks in every project with a rosy future. Banks, too, entered the speculative melee, investing some of their own funds and encouraging customers to buy securities being offered by their investment bank affiliates, that is, investment banks in which they had a controlling interest. These sometimes unloaded their own poor investments on the unsuspecting customers. By 1928–29 many people were not only

[2] For example, in 1921 long-term interest rates were about 5 per cent and in 1928 they were around 4 per cent. In 1921 the capitalized value of a property yielding $5000 a year would tend to be $100,000, but in 1928 it would tend to be $125,000.

buying stock out of their savings but borrowing and leaving the stock as collateral. Note in the accompanying table that brokers' loans doubled and then redoubled between 1922 and 1929. As the stockbroker required only a 25 per cent margin, little capital was needed to start speculating. Common stock averages rose gradually at first and then soared to amazing heights as the speculative mania took hold and the volume of trading multiplied.

STOCK MARKET BEHAVIOR, 1922-32 (Prices of selected stocks)					
Name	1922	1925	1927	1929	1932
Commonwealth Edison Co.........	140	140	173	450	122
General Electric Co.............	190	337	586	1612	418
General Motors	15	150	282	429	35
Goldman-Sachs Trading Co.......	—	—	117(1928)	226	0
Radio Corporation of America....	31	67	101	549	13
September stock averages (1935-39 = 100)	77	98	135	238	61
Brokers' Loans—September—in billions	$1.8	$2.9	$3.9	$8.5	$.5
Annual volume (millions of shares)	261	460	582	1125	425

The above are all common stocks. High price for year is quoted. First three companies named were and are very reputable concerns. Goldman-Sachs was a flashy investment trust. Radio Corporation's stock was recognized as being speculative. Allowance has been made for stock split-ups. All fractions are omitted. Data are from Poor's *Ratings*.

In short, it was on the stock market more than anywhere else that the surplus money created to finance World War I had its last inflationary fling.

The Federal reserve bank controls which were intended to prevent just such an unhealthy expansion as this were probably not strong enough and certainly were not used soon enough to stop the boom. Before criticizing the financial heads too severely for dereliction of duty, it is well to remember that we now have the advantage of hindsight, that presumably competent economists then forecast a "new era of prosperity," and that the pessimist gets scant attention when times are good and is likely to be thrown out of power anyway if he persists in spoiling the fun.

The Great Depression begins. Unlike previous panics no one incident, no one concern's failure is credited with starting the 1929 financial holocaust. The truth probably is that enough people had come to realize that future business earnings could not possibly justify the high prices being paid for stocks on the stock market and that they had better cash in on their profits at once. A moderate amount of selling turned the market downward in September and then on two days in late October the market broke sharply. On October 29 over 16 million shares were sold and stock averages went off 40 points. Thousands of speculators operating on a thin margin, from telephone girls to millionaires, were wiped out and dozens of suicides were reported in the newspapers in the days that followed.

This was the signal that the economic tide had turned. No amount of cajoling by financial or political King Canutes could change it until its course had been run. It was to no avail that John D. Rockefeller publicly announced that he and his son thought the situation fundamentally sound and were buying common stock or that President Hoover exhorted that "any lack of confidence in the economic future or basic strength of business in the United States is foolish" and that "prosperity is just around the corner."

Matters steadily went from bad to worse. National income in terms of 1929 dollars declined from $83 billion in 1929 to $63 billion in 1932; manufacturing corporations reported a fall of net earnings from $4 billion profit to a $2 billion loss; and common stock prices fell to a quarter of what they had been at the peak. Loans to foreign nations virtually ceased and many nations defaulted on previous loans. Banks failed in droves: 4100 closed their doors between 1930 and 1932 and caused the depositors to lose a large part of the $3 billion put with them for safekeeping. It was remarked with more bitterness than humor, "Yesterday I got back a check stamped 'No Bank' instead of the usual 'No Funds'." The public was profoundly shocked by the apparent poor judgment and even downright crookedness of men who had been looked upon as pillars of respectability in their communities. High officials of some large financial institutions were investigated, and one, Richard Whitney, went to prison. Although the majority of bankers and business leaders were honest, these revelations and the hard times accompanying them brought the business world into very low repute. Big business became the scapegoat in the minds of some 12 to 16 million persons who were now unemployed, of millions of farmers whose real incomes had been cut in half since 1929, and of hosts of others who were affected by the Great Depression. The majority of people lost patience with the Hoover administration whose economic philosophy was that the depression was a problem every individual must solve for himself, that it was not a government responsibility. If this seems heartless it is well to remember that it was the philosophy by which all our previous depressions had been handled. In any event, the majority held the Hoover administration responsible and in 1932 elected in his place Franklin D. Roosevelt, the Democratic governor of New York, who had promised the country a "New Deal" and constructive action.

New Deal banking legislation. Few if any presidents have taken office under more dramatic circumstances than Franklin D. Roosevelt did. Between November, 1932, and March 4, 1933, over 2000 more banks failed. State governors were closing banks temporarily in one state after another and the crisis was mounting hourly as Inauguration Day approached. Almost as soon as he was sworn in, Roosevelt declared a four-day national bank holiday, and got Congress to enact emergency legislation closing all banks and permitting the reopening of only those in good condition. Another 2113 never opened their doors again. This was followed by the Banking Acts of 1933 and 1935 whose provisions somewhat overlapped and which for the purposes at hand may be considered together. Four reforms accomplished by this legislation stand out.

First, there was the establishment of the Federal Deposit Insurance Corporation which all member banks of the Federal Reserve System had to join and most other banks soon saw fit to join. By paying in $1/12$ of 1 per cent of its average deposits each year a bank could guarantee every depositor against the loss of his deposit up to $5000. In 1945 about 92 per cent of all banks belonged to it, 96 per cent of all depositors were protected, and 46 per cent of all deposits were protected. This agency probably did more than anything else to restore the public's confidence in banks and to eliminate the danger of runs on banks. Bank failures fell to 57 in 1934, to 9 in 1942 and to none in 1945. Yet it must be admitted that the F.D.I.C. would be unable even today to withstand the strain of a major depression without substantial assistance from the federal treasury.

Second, commercial and investment banking were henceforth to be divorced; there were too many abuses in the system of investment affiliates.

Third, more loans against real estate were permitted. It was hoped that this would encourage state banks to join the Federal Reserve System or at least enable member banks to compete with them more effectively. Also it would encourage banks to make more loans and thereby stimulate economic recovery.

Fourth, the Federal Reserve Board was reorganized and renamed the Board of Governors of the Federal Reserve System and granted greater powers of control over the nation's banking system. It could now raise reserve requirements for member banks up to twice what they had been and increase margin requirements on the stock exchanges. The over-all tendency was to increase government control of the Federal Reserve System and to lessen private control. The former was strengthened during World War II.

Along with reforms of the banks went two other laws regulating investment banks and stock exchanges, namely the Securities Act of 1933 and the Securities and Exchange Act of 1934. Designed to protect the buyer of securities, they required the registration of all new security issues, forbade the use of misleading statements in any form of advertising or the omission of essential facts, and put the administration of the law in the hands of a Securities and Exchange Commission. Registration with the commission did not of course guarantee the goodness of a security issue. The filing of numerous blanks and the fear of severe penalties for violation of these laws made big business leaders and distributors of securities realize that a revolution had taken place in their affairs; the old rule of "Let the buyer beware" had been supplanted by the new one of "Let the seller beware." Although fraudulent issues were largely eliminated, so also was the financing of some experimental projects, the success of which in the past had furthered the technical advance of the country.

Monetary experimentation. Falling prices was another problem the "New Deal" administration undertook to solve. Prices had been stable during the 1920's at about 50 to 60 per cent above the 1913 level, but the depression following the panic of 1929 saw them drop back to the 1913 level with many of the harmful consequences of deflation in attendance. Farmers suffered because the prices of their produce sagged more than those of the goods they bought, debtors found it increasingly difficult to pay their creditors, business was stagnant, and millions were thrown out of work. The deflation was a symptom of sickness in the body of the nation which would continue until certain poisons were purged from its system, in this case until overexpanded and inefficient business organizations were liquidated. A wise government, like a wise doctor, could ease the pain and perhaps speed recovery, but in the final analysis Nature was probably the most dependable healer. Many persons, however, regarded the low prices as a cause of the depression and believed that if prices could be restored to pre-depression levels, prosperity would return and would remain if the price level were kept stable. In order to achieve and maintain this higher and more stable price level they felt it was necessary to control and manipulate the amount of money and credit in circulation. President Roosevelt accepted these ideas and surrounded himself with advisers who also did. In his book, *Looking Forward,* he wrote, "The country needs and, unless I mistake its temper, the country demands bold, persistent experimentation."

The President was primarily interested in two aspects of this matter of falling prices. One was the problem of falling agricultural prices; the other was the burden of existing indebtedness. The two were closely related and it is necessary to understand the debt problem to see why the price problem was handled as it was.

The internal debts of the country stood at $120 billion.[3] Moreover, debts had increased 100 per cent between 1913 and 1928 while the production of wealth was up only 60

[3] Evans Clark, *The Internal Debts of the United States* (New York, 1933).

per cent. Assuming a 6 per cent interest charge, the annual interest payments would absorb about 15 per cent of our national income of $49 billion. The burden of these debts, it was claimed, was crushing industry and agriculture. But they were not merely heavy; they were also unfair, for they were incurred at a time when prices were high (that is, when dollars were cheap), and now, when prices were falling (that is, when dollars were dear) their payment required the giving up of more commodities or labor than the original value of the loan. Debts had, however, been incurred at different times and ran for various periods. How could equal treatment be accorded to all debtors? This was solved by taking the time center of mortgages and other debts created during the period of rising prices, which was estimated to be the year 1926. The objective was therefore to put prices back on the 1926 level, and the program adopted aimed at this end.

How, then, were prices to be raised to the 1926 level? There are only three ways of raising the prices of commodities: (1) increase the demand—but this was falling off; (2) lessen the supply—this was attempted in the agricultural program already described; (3) cheapen the money in terms of which prices are quoted. This last was the chief method adopted in dealing with the whole question of prices.

The "New Deal" monetary advisers believed that in order to raise prices to the 1926 level and hold them there by manipulating the money and credit supply, it would be necessary to go off the gold standard. They said that it was basing the value of the dollar on the fluctuating value of gold that had given us the shifting price level and caused the economic ills we were trying to cure. Abandonment of the gold standard was quietly accomplished by a series of measures. On April 5, 1933, the President ordered all gold and gold certificates turned in to the treasury. This was so that any profit from subsequent debasement of the gold dollar would accrue to the government. Then on April 19 an executive order prohibited the export of gold, and Secretary Woodin announced that we were off the gold standard. On June 5 the gold clause in all contracts, providing for payment of principal and interest in gold, was abrogated.

Gold had now been removed from all monetary use and placed under lock and key. The next step was to devalue the dollar; that is, to lower its value so that prices in terms of this cheaper dollar would rise. Authority for this was granted by the Thomas Amendment to the Agricultural Adjustment Act of May 12, 1933. This gave the President discretionary powers: (1) to authorize the Federal reserve banks to expand their credit by the open-market purchase of government obligations up to $3000 million; (2) to issue up to $3000 million in United States notes; (3) to devalue the dollar as much as 50 per cent; (4) to fix a bimetallic ratio between gold and silver and provide for unlimited coinage at that ratio.

The President chose to "reflate" the dollar, i.e., re-inflate, by using only the third one of the above methods, namely by devaluing or debasing the dollar.[4] On the theory that a gold dollar with, say, half as much gold in it would cause exchange rates and prices to double, the government lowered the gold content of the dollar to 59 per cent of what it had been with the expectation that this would promptly raise prices 69 per cent and thereby restore them to the desired 1926 level. Numerous involved steps were taken with this end in view, but the last and chief one was the passage of the Gold Reserve Act on January 30, 1934, which in effect cut the size of the gold dollar from 23.22 grains of pure gold to 13.71 grains. This gave a new mint price of $35 an ounce, for now 35 gold dollars of the smaller size could be coined from an ounce of gold. The law also amounted to a partial return to the gold standard although no smaller-sized gold coins were minted.

Despite all this experimentation, wholesale prices showed only a moderate tendency to rise, increasing from 96 in 1933

---

[4] Mention should also be made of the fact that senators from seven western silver-producing states did their utmost to restore bimetallism. This was the fourth inflationary method mentioned under the Thomas Amendment. Their chief accomplishment was the Silver Purchase Act of 1934 by which the treasury was required to buy silver until the government's stock of silver was a third as great as its stock of gold. Moreover it was to buy domestically mined silver at a price considerably above the world market price. The desire to raise prices by the free coinage of silver is reminiscent of the Free Silver movement of the last third of the nineteenth century, only this time it was the miners rather than the farmers who were chiefly interested in doing something for silver. And the miners were big copper-, lead-, zinc-, and gold-producing corporations for whom silver was merely a valuable by-product.

to 109 a year later and to a high of 126 in 1937; after this, there was a decline to an average of 115 the following year and little change occurred thereafter until 1941. The desired level of 146, which was the average for the pre-depression "normal" year of 1926, was not reached, and what early rise did take place was attributable in part to the higher costs required by NIRA codes, to the crop destruction plans of the AAA, and to the droughts of 1933–36. It was adequately demonstrated that in the short run more than changes in the gold content of the dollar and the amount of money in circulation are needed to alter the price level. Nature is unpredictable, businessmen must have confidence in the future or they will proceed very cautiously. If business is not active, the velocity of money and deposit currency—that is, the speed with which it passes from hand to hand through spending—is slow, and that is just as important as the amount in circulation.

What the long-run effect of the devaluation experiment will be remains to be seen, but it is noteworthy that because of the depression, and because of the 41 per cent reduction in the size of the dollar and of the consequent higher price for an ounce of gold, the gold holdings of the government in terms of dollars rose from $4.3 billion in 1933 to $22.7 billion in December of 1941. There was considerable fear of the ultimate inflationary power contained in this reserve even before World War II began.

Financing the New Deal. President Roosevelt sought to promote recovery in many other ways besides trying to raise the price level. Almost from the beginning he and his advisers took the view that the depression with its millions of unemployed constituted another national emergency such as World War I. Soon advocates of reform and recovery were vying with one another for the adoption of expensive programs. The theory was widely held in government circles that economic recovery would be promoted and unemployment reduced if the lag in private business activity were compensated by increased government expenditures. Accordingly, a Public Works Administration under the direction of Secretary of the Interior Ickes was established with an appropriation of $3.3 billion in 1933 and in 1935 Congress appropriated $4.9 billion for a second public works program. These sums were more awe-inspiring than they are today. Alphabetical agencies were spawned for every imaginable purpose, each with its grant of several millions or even hundreds of millions of dollars. Some were much-needed and sensible reforms, others were downright luxuries and thinly disguised make-work schemes. The total expenditures by the federal government between 1934 and 1939 were $27 billion greater than between 1924 and 1929 and the difference was almost entirely attributable to the cost of the "New Deal" program. This was a dollar cost approximately equivalent to that of all government outlays including wars between 1789 and 1916. Since the federal budget was never once balanced, the public debt, which had been so painstakingly reduced from $26 billion to $16 billion between 1919 and 1930, was increased to $40 billion by 1939.

The question arises, "Who paid for all this and how?" As with a war, the generation that suffered from the depression paid for it. And, as with a war, there were three methods of financing the emergency—taxation, borrowing, creating money. Government revenues, largely derived from taxation, paid for roughly *three-fifths* of the government expenditures. Of these taxes, about 40 per cent were collected in various kinds of internal revenue, and most of the rest in customs duties and Social Security taxes. The other *two-fifths* of this huge six-year outlay was obtained largely by government borrowing and represented a considerable increase in the public debt. Some government bonds were bought by wealthy men because the interest on them was tax exempt, by conservative investors and by insurance companies, but primarily by banks of every description. At the end of 1939 over 40 per cent of all earning assets of member banks were United States government obligations. Banks bought government bonds for various reasons, but an important one was that they were one of the best-paying investments available. Monetary inflation through the coinage of several hundred million more cheap silver dollars had a very minor part in financing the government's program. Paper money inflation was simply too crude for this modern age and although $3 billion worth of greenbacks was authorized by the Thomas Amendment to the AAA, they were not issued. Instead, a more subtle type of monetary inflation was employed, a type developed during World War I, inflation of bank deposits subject to check and to a lesser degree of Federal reserve notes. Demand deposits in member banks increased from $17.5 billion to $29 billion between 1934 and 1939, some of this rise being attributable to improved business conditions, but the bulk was written on bank ledgers to pay for government bonds. Only the increasingly sluggish turnover of these deposits prevented a noticeable price inflation.

The third great emergency. The outbreak of World War II in Europe in September of 1939 brought on the third great emergency which this country has had to face in the last generation. It came so fast on the heels of the second that it found us financially ill-prepared. A few comparisons between our situation in 1914 and 1939 are worth noticing. In 1914 we had a public debt of $1.2 billion, in 1939 it was $40 billion. The per capita real national income was actually less by a small amount in 1939 than in 1914. In both years a mild depression was in progress, but 1914 had been preceded by long years of almost unbroken economic growth and prosperity whereas 1939 was preceded by a decade of virtually uninterrupted depression during several years of which we had reduced our resources of capital. In 1914 we had a soundly functioning gold coin standard to serve as a buffer against inflation, but in 1939 we had a hybrid gold and managed currency standard whose chief virtue was that it was better than other nations' money standards. And in 1939 our banking system was loaded with what was even then regarded as the makings of a dangerous inflation, namely, large deposits arising from the purchase of government bonds.[5]

[5] It may be asked why created deposits loaned to merchants are regarded as desirable while created deposits loaned to the government are not. There would be no difference *if* the government devoted the funds to producing as cheaply as private industry goods and services people wanted and then paid off the loan promptly. But much was spent on wasteful "boondoggles" and the government's loans at the banks were not liquidated but constantly enlarged. The created deposits thus became a permanent part of the money supply without, it is to be feared, resulting in an equivalent increased flow of goods and services.

Financing World War II. The direct costs of war activities to this country in the form of cash expenditures from June, 1940, to December, 1945, were $261.5 billion.[6] Our 1939 public debt of $40 billion jumped to a peak of $279 billion by February of 1946. By the war's end the word "billion" had become commonplace and some people were beginning to talk in terms of trillions: the war was estimated to have cost the world at least a trillion dollars ($1,000,000,000,000). The immensity of such figures is almost beyond human comprehension. A billion dollars in $1 bills would fill 20 of the largest railroad boxcars, in $10,000 bills (the largest denomination there is) it would weigh 200 pounds; or— much more significant—a billion dollars would pay for 18 months' operation of all the country's colleges and universities in existence around 1940. Yet toward the end of the war this nation was spending a billion dollars for the war every four days!

World War II was financed in much the same fashion as World War I, namely, by taxes, borrowing, and the creation of money. Even before we entered the conflict income taxes and excess profits taxes were increased until in 1945 such taxes could take 95 per cent of the top earnings of a wealthy man but not to exceed 85 per cent of his total income. Whereas in 1939 only 7.6 million persons made income-tax returns, in 1945 nearly 50 million persons made them. Not only did income taxes go up but all sorts of excise taxes were increased and a variety of nuisance taxes were devised until these alone yielded several billions each year. How much more was finally paid in taxes by the American people may be seen in the table on page 754. Unfortunately, the greatest increases did not take place until late in the war. Before 1942 taxes no more than paid normal costs of running the government. During the last two years of the war, taxes provided nearly half the cash expended for purely war activities. For the entire period between June, 1940, and December, 1945, they yielded 31 per cent of the needed war funds.

[6] This is the period repeatedly cited in the *Survey of Current Business* and the cost of "war activities" therein mentioned.

FEDERAL TAX RECEIPTS AND EXPENDITURES IN 1939 AND 1945* (billions omitted)		
Receipts from	1939	1945
Income taxes on individuals...............	$1.1	$19.9
Income taxes on corporations..............	1.0	14.5
Other internal revenue taxes..............	2.6	7.5
Customs duties	.3	.4
Social security taxes	.7	1.9
Miscellaneous sources	.2	3.3
Total	$5.9	$47.5
Expenditures on	1939	1945
Civilian needs	$6.4	$ 7.8
War or defense measures..................	1.4	78.6
Servicing public debt....................	1.0	4.1
Total	$8.8	$90.5

* Source: Department of Commerce.

The remainder of the cash needed had to be raised by the sale of bonds or the creation of money. Bonds would appear, at first glance, to have been the answer, for the public debt increased $232 billion between June, 1940, and December, 1945. Everyone was urged to subscribe a share of his income and many war-plant workers and others arranged to have a certain percentage of their monthly pay check deducted for bond purchases. Eight nationwide bond drives were staged and all were oversubscribed, or at least none was declared at an end until the goal was exceeded. A total of $156.9 billion was raised by these drives, well over half being subscribed by corporations, savings banks, life-insurance companies, and other associations. Only a quarter ($43.3 billion) was subscribed by individuals, partnerships, and trust accounts, which was quietly admitted to be a disappointing proportion

In reality, a considerable part of the war was financed by creating money just as in World War I. Although bonds are presumably receipts for the loan of savings which are an accumulation of the past, not all bonds were actually paid for out of savings. Banks directly or indirectly created money to buy bonds. The bank or perhaps a big customer would get a bond and the government would be given a credit on the bank's ledgers which it could then spend for war supplies.

Such created demand deposits were sometimes referred to as "invisible greenbacks." Between June, 1940, and the end of 1945 commercial bank holdings of government bonds increased by $90 billion ($19.6 billion to $109.9 billion) and demand deposits increased by $44 billion. To that should be added the currency outside banks which in the same period grew by about $20 billion. It may be assumed that most of this $64 billion increase in money supply was created to pay for the war and that it will remain permanently in circulation just as similar but smaller increases in the Civil War and in World War I remained after those wars.

WORLD WAR II INCREASE IN MONEY SUPPLY* (billions omitted)				
Kind of money	June 1929	June 1940	Dec. 1945	Sept. 1946
Currency outside banks........	$ 3.64	$ 6.7	$ 26.5	$ 26.8
Demand deposits	22.54	32.0	75.8	80.9
Total	$26.2	$38.7	$102.3	$107.7

* Federal Reserve Board, Banking and Monetary Statistics (Washington, 1943), 34-35; Federal Reserve Bulletins.

In summary, the cash needed for war activities appears to have been raised about 44 per cent by the sale of bonds for savings, about 31 per cent by taxation and about 25 per cent by the creation of money in some form. The record as a whole was somewhat better than that of World War I, particularly in view of the facts that the second war lasted over twice as long and was much more costly.

Inflation in World War II. In the matter of controlling prices our record was definitely better than in the previous war. When this war began, we had a devalued dollar and a supply of money and demand deposits about 10 per cent greater than in the boom year of 1929 and were pursuing a policy of trying to force up the price level. Only the sluggish turnover of all this currency, caused in part by business distrust of government, had prevented the then desired rise in prices. On top of this already inflationary situation were piled the financial explosives of World War II already described. Under somewhat similar circumstances during the Civil War and World War I prices had more than doubled.

Yet between 1939 and the end of 1945 the wholesale price level rose only 39 per cent according to the Bureau of Labor Statistics. What kept it from increasing more than this?

The price level was apparently held down by several influences, two of them of major importance. First of all, more money will not cause prices to rise if there are more goods and services to buy. Between 1939 and 1945 the total amount of these produced in this country increased about 80 per cent. The United States did something that no other warring nation has ever done on a like scale: we provided ourselves with the vast war supplies we needed without having to curtail our normal production of peacetime goods more than about 15 per cent. While the war meant a lower standard of living for many, for others it did not, and for a very considerable number it actually meant a higher standard.

A second significant influence restraining prices was the extensive system of price controls put into effect early in 1942. In January the Emergency Price Control Act created the Office of Price Administration (OPA) and within four months that agency was functioning effectively. Its most sweeping and spectacular order was the General Maximum Price Regulation of April 28 which froze all prices, except those of combat items and farm products, at the March levels. Along with this went an extensive program of rationing scarce goods. At the same time rent controls were also imposed on areas containing two-thirds of the country's population. These two measures covered 80 per cent of the items which enter into the cost of living. Meanwhile, through the War Labor Board a somewhat similar but less effective effort was made to stabilize wages at existing levels or at least at not more than 15 per cent above them.

How extremely effective the OPA program was can be seen from the table below in which comparisons are made with farm prices which were not under OPA control and with the general price level in corresponding periods in the previous war when the price-control machinery was quite rudimentary. Notice in particular how very little prices rose after OPA took over during the war period. Presumably even more could have been accomplished if effective ceilings had been imposed on farm products and on wages. It was

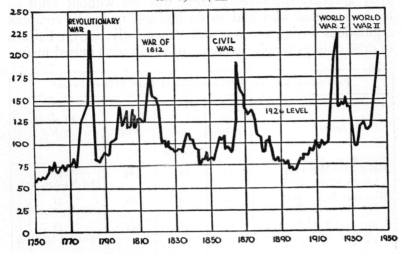

Prices during Revolution are in terms of gold.

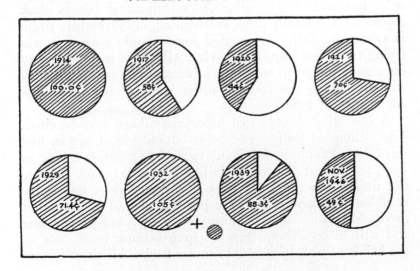

Based on wholesale prices, Bureau of Labor Statistics.

these, especially the farm prices, which caused the chief trouble and forced OPA to lift ceilings in one special case after another. Admittedly OPA was not without fault as many a person who had to do business under its complex regulations during the war will vehemently testify. Failure to raise ceilings despite evidence of rising costs caused manu-

PERCENTAGE RISE OF WHOLESALE PRICES OVER PREWAR LEVEL*				
Period	All prices	All commodities other than farm products	Farm prices	All prices W.W.I
August 1939-May 1942 (Before OPA began)	32	25	64	78 (Jul. '14-Apr. '17)
May 1942-August 1945 (In war, under OPA)	9	5	29	31 (Apr. '17-Nov. '18)
August 1945-November 1946 (As OPA declines, goes)	45	41	65	45 (Nov. '18-May '20)
Total	86	70.5	138	154

* Bureau of Labor Statistics figures. 1926 = 100.

facturers to cease making many products. OPA became unpopular with the public who were deprived of the goods or obliged to turn to high-priced substitutes or buy in black markets. OPA finally died, unlamented, in November, 1946. It cannot be fully appreciated until people realize it was trying to do the impossible. After all, there is no sure way for a government to enjoy the advantages of creating money without having the country suffer some of the usual disadvantages of inflation.

A few other factors that held prices down may be cited. The billions of dollars people saved, outside of bonds, had this effect. People saved at the rate of $37 billion a year in 1945 as contrasted with $4 billion a year in 1940. Because the dollar was the most trusted currency in a financially troubled world, millions were hoarded abroad or circulated there. Money circulated more slowly than before the war and still more slowly than in 1929 because much was in the hands of people who did not use banks. All these factors that held prices down spared us some of the worst evils of a changing price level during the war and reduced the cost of the war by many billions of dollars. We did much better in this regard than in the Civil War or World War I. The moderate inflation accompanying and following World War II has not of course been borne equally by all classes, as can be seen clearly in the accompanying table. Only those

Price and Wage Increases, August, 1946 over January, 1941	
Item	*Percentage increase*
Cost of living [1]	43
Wholesale prices (B.L.S.) [1]	60
Annual net income of farm operators, 1941-45 [1]	95
Farm workers [1]	220
Workers in all manufacturing industries [2]	69
Workers manufacturing non-durable goods [2]	84
Bituminous coal miners [2]	140
Workers manufacturing women's clothing [2]	145
Workers manufacturing automobiles [2]	42
Hotel workers [2]	73
School teachers, annual, 1939-46 [3]	31
Dividend and interest payments [1]	35

[1] OPA Handbook of Basic Economic Data, 2nd ed. (Washington, 1946).
[2] Also *Business Week*, November 9, 1946, 88, tables based on B.L.S. figures.
[3] *U. S. News*, December 27, 1946, 20. Wages are weekly earnings unless otherwise indicated.

groups gained whose increase in earnings was greater than the rise in the cost of living. On the losing side were of course creditors, as usual, for they got back less valuable dollars than those they loaned, although some probably recovered dollars they never expected to see again because fortune smiled on even the most luckless debtors. Other perennial losers in times of inflation were the pensioners, widows living on insurance payments, endowed institutions, and all other classes whose incomes were rather fixed. This doubtless covered a wide variety of professional and other white-collar workers on whose salaries statistics are not available. Judged by its dividend and interest payments business did not do as well as in past wars because of heavy taxes and price ceilings. On the other hand, true to form in a period of rising prices, the farmers prospered greatly and farm hands even more. Debtors gained; nearly everyone seized the opportunity to pay off his obligations, although the government got ever deeper in debt. But most surprising of all were the gains registered by organized labor. Almost all factory workers gained and some, like the bituminous coal miners or women's clothing workers, bettered their position phenomenally.

Conclusion. The country has faced three great emergencies since 1914. Despite some questionable solutions to their problems, we have weathered them all because we had a fair money system, a good banking system, a good tax system, and, most important of all, because we were a nation of tremendous energy and resources. The costs of these emergencies have been stupendous. World War I cost $33 billion; the "New Deal" program for bringing us out of the Great Depression cost $27 billion between 1934 and 1939 alone, and World War II necessitated cash outlays of another $261 billion between June, 1940, and the end of 1945. The cost of each of these emergencies has been met by borrowing, taxation, and the creation of money: we have relied upon them in about that order. Although the nation at this writing (January, 1947) is enjoying tremendous prosperity, the underlying financial situation can hardly be said to be as bright as it was in 1914. The accompanying table clearly reveals that our strength has not grown in proportion to the burden we have shouldered. In addition, our monetary standard,

FINANCIAL COMPARISON OF U. S. IN 1914 AND 1945 ON PER CAPITA BASIS			
Factor being compared	1914	1945	Per cent gain 1945 over 1914
Per capita national income [1] (current dollars)	$293.00	$1185.00	405
Per capita public debt (federal)[2]	12.25	2039.00	16,637
Per capita tax burden (federal)[2]	7.57	345.26	4,560

[1] National Industrial Conference Board estimates.
[2] From Statistical Abstract of U. S. for 1946-47.

although one of the best in the world today, is less reliable than the gold coin standard of 1914. Our commercial banks, whose business it should be to concentrate on self-liquidating short-term loans, have few of these and are literally loaded with government bonds. While these bonds are not exactly frozen assets, in the short run they can only be liquidated by resort to government printing presses, a very dangerous solution. Fortunately public confidence in our financial situation is high and this can perhaps help more than anything else to carry us through the critical years ahead.

CHAPTER XXXII
SOCIAL PROGRESS, 1860-1946

The situation after three centuries. The record of the economic development of the American people has been one of steady growth in material wealth and in the upbuilding of an enduring civilization. After three centuries of steady advance we have reached a position of pre-eminence as an industrial country. The situation may be stated somewhat as follows: We have large natural resources of almost every sort needed in modern production; a working population of some 60,000,000 persons, many highly trained; a supply of active capital of not less than $150,000 million; a highly efficient organization of industry, transportation, and finance, which permits very economical production and exchange of commodities; and finally, political and social institutions which are distinctly favorable to the production and acquisition of wealth and to a high standard of living. In the process of building up this great economic organization certain features have been developed which may be regarded as peculiarly American, and these may be described briefly.

An outstanding characteristic, which particularly impresses foreign observers, is the far-reaching mechanization of industry and even of agriculture. While this is typical of all modern industrial countries, it seems to have been carried farther along certain lines in the United States than elsewhere, and to have given a distinctive character to American methods of production, exchange, and even consumption. The scarcity of labor has always favored the invention and use of laborsaving devices, and it was soon found that these greatly increased the productivity of labor. What had been an expedient now became a national habit.

As the population grew and the market expanded, it was discovered that mass production was most economical along lines in which it was possible to market millions of units of identical products. Those industries in which standardization of product was feasible and for whose output an elastic demand existed were accordingly organized along these lines. Among these are included agricultural machinery, automobiles, boots and shoes, clocks and watches, canned goods, electrical fittings, hardware, ready-made clothing, sanitary porcelain, radios, automobiles, and many other articles. Where hand labor or careful artistic finish is required, Europe or the Orient still leads.

Large-scale production, interchangeable parts, and standardization are the trinity upon which American manufacturing has been built up. These have already been described,[1] but a word more on the social effects of standardization may be added. Lower costs are obtained by focusing on a few accepted models; danger of obsolescence is reduced; competition is made fairer, for the standard articles are comparable; and the best and most efficient design is usually worked out by careful research. Standardization has not merely reduced manufactured wares to a few patterns, but it has placed its impress upon consumption and social life. Mass production, national advertising, and chain stores, aided and abetted by a syndicated press, have given remarkable uniformity not merely to our automobiles, clothing, and cigarettes, but even to our amusements, manners, and speech. Even our mental processes have been standardized by a uniform system of education. "It is the age of the machine triumphant," writes a contemporary critic. "We are but ants in the machine; the wheels revolve and we revolve with them—alarm clocks, time tables, factory whistles, ordinances, rules, the lockstep of industrialism!" Cheap and plentiful goods, it is claimed, have been produced at the expense of individuality. The point remains, however, that they have been produced, and the standard of living of the people has been raised to ever higher levels. And, along with the increase of material goods, the working time is being shortened, and greater leisure is made possible.

The distribution of wealth. The great increase in the production of wealth is of course the most striking result of American enterprise. The period of the Civil War and of

[1] See Chapter XXVII.

the succeeding years to the panic of 1873 was marked by increasing concentration of wealth and the emergence of large fortunes. The first to reach $100,000,000 seems to have been that of Commodore Vanderbilt, who died in 1877. By 1889 it was estimated that six fortunes had reached that mark, but after this the rate of concentration seems to have slackened until the 1920's. "At the close of the [first] World War," wrote Charles and Mary Beard, "millionaires were almost as common in Detroit, Toledo, Indianapolis, Cincinnati, Denver, and Seattle as they had been in New York and Boston in the age of McKinley." In 1929 the Treasury Department stated that there were 513 persons in the United States with incomes of $1,000,000 or more a year, of whom 38 received incomes of over $5,000,000. By 1932 the depression had caused the disappearance of the multi-millionaire and had reduced the number of those with incomes of $1,000,000 to only 20. This number rose somewhat during the 1930's, and in 1941 was 57. The accumulation of large fortunes had evidently been checked by the depression and their dispersal hastened by the income, estate, inheritance, and other taxes. For instance, the federal income tax in 1940 took $697,000 from an individual income of $1,000,000, leaving to the recipient only $303,000. This was further reduced by state income taxes in certain states.

The ownership of the wealth from which these incomes were drawn has been investigated from time to time. An early estimate by the Massachusetts Labor Bureau in 1873 was that 2 per cent of the population owned 48 per cent of the wealth. Half a century later, in 1921, W. I. King, on the basis of a more careful study, concluded that 2 per cent of the population owned 40 per cent of the wealth, which would indicate a slight lessening of the concentration of wealth in the hands of a few. A more recent inquiry[2] reported that 1 per cent of the population owned 20 per cent of the wealth. It is evident that we have moved a long distance from the democratic conditions of comparative economic equality that existed in the days of Jefferson or De Tocqueville. And yet certain qualifications need to be made. Although there are many large fortunes in the United States, the members of

[2] R. R. Doane, *The Anatomy of American Wealth* (New York, 1940), 32.

the high-income group are a constantly shifting lot. Carried to great wealth by a boom, they shrink back again in depression; the permanent core is not large. There has also been a tendency for wealth to be distributed more widely, especially after the present income tax system went into effect. At the time of the Civil War the few wealthy were probably wealthier in relation to the mass than the larger number after World War I.

But the increase in wealth was not confined to the plutocrats, for the middle classes and the professions also shared generously. The real wages of the working population increased greatly, even more rapidly than the incomes of the middle classes, and many luxuries came within the purchasing power of the wage earners. Their command over goods and services which promote health, comfort, and pleasure was broadened and consumption became more democratic. The trend in expenditures as the nation became wealthier is illustrated in the following table:

PER CENT DISTRIBUTION OF FAMILY EXPENDITURES*		
Item	1900-09	1935-39
Food	43.1	33.9
Housing	18.1	18.1
Clothing	13.0	10.5
Fuel and light	5.6	6.4
All other	20.2	31.1
Total	100.0	100.0

* Source: Nat'l. Ind. Conf. Board, *Economic Almanac*, 1944-45, 98.

The national income at the first date was approximately $35 billion and at the latter about $75 billion, which showed a per capita gain from about $472 to $572 annually. As the annual consumer income increased and the standard of living rose, less proportionately was spent on basic necessities, such as food, and more was devoted to such things as education, automobiles, washing machines, radios, recreation, and other commodities and services usually regarded as semi-luxuries.

Averages, however, conceal some of the facts. Other studies revealed that one-half the families received annual incomes of less than $1160. Since an income of $1250 was held to be the minimum on which an adequate standard of living could be supported, it appeared that one-half of all American families were unable to purchase needed supplies of food, housing, clothing, and other necessities and comforts of daily life. It must be said, however, that the figures were gathered during a depression; much depended, moreover, upon the concept of what was deemed essential. Had these families been content to live upon the plane of comfort enjoyed by their grandparents in 1870, an income of $1160 might have sufficed. Or if the comparison were made with colonial conditions or with most European countries today, such an income might be considered satisfactory. But between 1870 and 1939 the standard of living had been greatly raised and included conveniences such as improved plumbing, lighting, better food and clothing, recreation, and other items un-dreamed of seventy years earlier. The stubborn fact remains, therefore, that in spite of past gains a distressingly large portion of the population has not shared proportionately in the advance. A long-run survey shows a steady improvement, especially after the middle of the nineteenth century. Per capita realized income, adjusted by the general price level, increased from $210 in 1799 to $237 in 1849, to $438 in 1899, and to $590 in 1929.[3] But even this gain is insufficient for general well-being; further progress is to be achieved primarily by an increase in total national income as a result of augmented production.

The standard of living. Economic advance cannot be measured accurately by statistics of wealth or of individual income alone. These need to be translated into the tangible commodities that we buy and the intangible benefits that we enjoy. Since all economic activity is directed in the final analysis to the satisfaction of human wants, we may fairly gauge our progress by noting how fully these have been met in some of the most important spheres of life.

Food. The most striking features in the history of food during the past two generations have been the increase in variety, the lengthening of the season, and the decrease in cost.

[3] National Industrial Conference Board, *Studies in Enterprise and Social Progress* (New York, 1939), 83.

Not merely was the table of the average man furnished with a greater variety of food in 1940 than in 1860, but the proportion that was fresh was much larger. Refrigerator cars, developed in the sixties, brought at first fresh meat and later fruits and vegetables to the cities; the rural population was less well served by such agencies, but many of this group provided fresh food for themselves. Perishable fruits and vegetables could be found in the larger cities every month in the year; improved transportation lengthened the season of consumption and made them available to those with modest purses. More recently automobiles, motor truck delivery, and chain stores have brought them within reach of the farm home.

Changes in consumption were also taking place. Less meat was eaten, corn meal was largely displaced by wheat flour, and in recent years this has fallen off, to be replaced by greatly increased consumption of milk, fruits, and vegetables. Partly responsible for this was the vast expansion of the canning industry, and partly the spread of education regarding the value of "protective" foods. Early experiments in scientific feeding had stressed the value of calories and proteins, but with the discovery about 1916 of vitamins, increasing emphasis was given to the need for minerals and other essential elements. The shifts in consumption are clearly shown in the annual per capita use of a few selected foods. Between 1899 and 1943 the consumption of meat fell off nearly one-fifth, especially beef (from 67 to 50 pounds) and pork (from 72 to 62 pounds); this was largely due to the fact that fewer people were now engaged in heavy physical outdoor labor and more of them lived in cities. Bread ceased to be the staff of life, the per capita consumption of wheat flour actually declining during the first half of the twentieth century. On the other hand, the increased consumption of certain semi-luxuries, while not of great food value, showed a greater use, a wider distribution, and a higher standard of living among the masses. Thus, between 1871 and 1943 the annual per capita consumption of coffee grew from 8 to 15 pounds, of sugar from 36 to 108 pounds, and of tobacco from 4 to 9 pounds; the consumption of distilled liquors more than trebled. Against this latter undesirable symptom may be placed the enormous expansion in the production of non-alcoholic beverages.

At the beginning of the eighty-year period 1860–1940 there was practically no governmental supervision or control of the manufacture and sale of food products; "let the buyer beware" was the slogan. This attitude worked little harm so long as most of the food was produced within the household, but when canning, baking, and the processing by factory methods of food for immediate consumption and the sale of various patent medicines became general, it proved dangerous. Agitation for federal pure food and drug legislation was initiated by Dr. Harvey Wiley in 1885, but made little headway against vested interests until the "embalmed beef" scandal of the Spanish-American War and the publication of Upton Sinclair's *The Jungle* disclosed the unsanitary methods of the meat packers. An outraged public opinion forced the passage in 1906 of a Pure Food and Drug Act which closed interstate commerce to foods which contained any added poisonous or harmful ingredient that might render them injurious to health, which were decomposed or unwholesome, which were debased without the inferiority being indicated on the label, or which were deceitfully labeled. In spite of opposition and of the inadequacy of the legislation much was done under this act to protect public health. Food manufacturers saw the publicity value of pure food and put clean packaged articles on the market, whose sale was promoted by national advertising. Finally, in 1938, a new Pure Food, Drug, and Cosmetic Act gave even greater protection to consumers.

Housing. In 1860 the typical dwelling was a frame structure, housing a single family. The destructive fires in Boston and Chicago in the 1870's led to fireproof construction in the cities, which was given further emphasis by the growing urbanization of the population. At the same time the building of multiple-unit houses gained ground, which in the larger cities led to congestion and the development of tenement districts. The dangers to health and morals from bad housing called forth remedial legislation to abate some of the worst evils. The New York Tenement House Law of 1867 was the first to set up minimum requirements as to light, air, sanitation, safety, and similar matters, and in 1901 a Tenement

House Department was established to administer it. This was copied by other states and cities, but so-called housing laws setting up general standards for a whole community were not enacted until 1911, the earliest being that of Columbus, Ohio. But regulatory legislation merely prohibited bad houses; it did not provide good ones.

One obstacle in providing good houses at a rental within the means of the low-income group was the high cost of construction. It was found difficult to apply machine methods to building construction, and this remained largely a hand industry. Materials, too, rose rapidly in price, and it became increasingly difficult for the wage earner to own his home or rent an entire dwelling. Another cause of higher costs and rents lay in the better standard of sanitation and comfort that was being demanded. Some of the largest cities provided water and sewer connections for the whole population, but in many towns and on farms these were lacking for large sections. Water was carried into the house from a hydrant or well, while backyard privies served from one to a dozen families. Only a few years ago St. Louis had 40,000 privy vaults, Philadelphia 60,000, and Baltimore 90,000, while such methods of sewage disposal were the general rule in farmhouses. A Mississippi investigation in 1921 revealed that 61 per cent of the white and 85 per cent of the Negro families did not have even privies; 85 per cent of the families in a Georgia survey in 1923 were without any sort of sanitary convenience; and even in Montana, where all the families were white and of an enterprising type, nearly one-quarter were in the same situation in 1919.

It was conditions such as this that led to the conclusion that one-third of the families in the United States were living in good homes, one-third in fair homes, partially lacking in conveniences, while the last third occupied houses that were designated as sub-normal. It must not be overlooked, however, that the standard against which this measure was taken was much higher than that of 1860.

Efforts to provide good housing at reasonable rentals were made by limited dividend companies, beginning in the 1870's, but these philanthropic organizations barely scratched the surface. The government's interest in the matter began during

World War I, when the close connection between good housing and productivity was realized as an aspect of preparedness. In 1932 Congress passed legislation that recognized the government's concern in low-cost housing as a matter of public health, and also as part of a relief-work program. Nearly one-half the states now have laws for establishing local or state housing authorities with power to own and operate low-cost housing projects.

Clothing. About the time of the Civil War the well-dressed man or woman wore more yardage of cloth than perhaps ever before or since in history. This was a consequence of the industrial revolution which made cloth more available to people at reasonable prices. People were able to advertise their greater prosperity by the greater amount of clothes they wore. It is perhaps an example of what Thorstein Veblen once called "conspicuous consumption." With the passage of years, however, cloth became so much cheaper that mere quantity of clothes no longer assured distinction. The heating of homes also made heavy clothing less desirable in winter, and certainly American summers offer little encouragement. No doubt, too, the triumph of common sense, the spread of co-education in schools and colleges, and the requirements of sport have done much to simplify women's clothes. One of the most noticeable changes is the greater use of silk in women's clothing that has come with the industrialization of the silk industry. And now rayon and nylon are replacing silk, lowering the price or improving the quality of what appears to be the same material. Another change has been the development of ready-made women's clothes following the invention of the sewing machine and of dressmaking by patterns, the latter first popularized by Butterick, around the middle of the century. As a result the working girl may now dress attractively on her wages and yet closely resemble the debutante in appearance. The once-obvious distinction in dress between social classes has largely disappeared. Rapidly changing fashions unfortunately prevent full realization of economies from these improvements.

For men, whether working on the farm or in the factory, the homely overall developed great appeal and is presumably here to stay. In the last century the business executive seeking distinction by his dress often wore somber and heavy broadcloth suits. Lesser individuals wore suits which have been aptly described as "ready-to-wear-whether-they-fit-or-not." Within the twentieth century the quality of ready-made suits has greatly improved, so that today nearly all businessmen seem dressed alike whether they be executives or clerks. Another article of attire that has left with the long coat and heavy suit are the beard and side-whiskers which gave our Civil War forefathers the appearance of more years than they actually possessed. Men still wear more clothes than women, although in recent years they have favored lighter-weight clothing in summer. And until lately men's clothing was undistinguished by any spark of color unless it was the necktie. But that man's attire is becoming less formalized and more comfortable is best illustrated by changes that occurred where the greatest conservatism might have been expected. The soldier's uniform of World War II was undoubtedly an improvement over that of World War I with its tight fit, choked neck, and wound leggings.

Health. For the individual, both as producer and as consumer, the preservation of health is of the first importance. It is essential because only physically healthy men can normally put forth their best powers as producers, and because illness and disease are in themselves a heavy burden and prevent the realization of a full life. During the period under review there was unprecedented advance in the prevention of disease and in the care of those needing medical attention. Certain diseases, such as smallpox, leprosy, yellow fever, tetanus, cholera, diphtheria, and typhoid have been practically abolished. A striking illustration of the advance along this line is furnished by the statistics of disease in the American Army. In the Spanish-American War 20 per cent of all the American soldiers were infected by, and 86 per cent of the deaths were caused by, typhoid fever. In World War I between September, 1917, and January, 1918, a period of about the same length, there should have been 150,000 cases if the same proportion had held; as a matter of fact, there were only 114 cases. As a result of pure water and pasteurized milk, typhoid deaths in the United States dropped from over 46 per 100,000 in 1890 to half of 1 per 100,000 in 1943. While the record is not so brilliant for tuberculosis, malaria, hookworm, and syphilis, these have been brought under effective control by the prevention of infection, by better understanding of and elimination of parasites, and by serum treatment. The prevention of the common cold and the more deadly influenza still baffles medical science. In spite of this record, we cannot afford to be too optimistic. A report of the Senate Subcommittee on Wartime Health on January 2, 1945, stated that 40 per cent of America's young men were unfit for military service and that about one-third of all selective service rejections were caused directly or indirectly by nutritional deficiencies.

The decline in the death rate is a most encouraging sign of the improvement in public health, indicating as it does a growing mastery over the dread enemy, disease. There has been a steady decline in the death rate in the United States, in those areas where records have been kept, from 19.8 per 1000 inhabitants in 1880 to 10.9 in 1943. The decline in the death rate is ascribable in the first place to the spread of general education in matters connected with health, resulting in better sewage disposal, purer water and foods, saner diet, and more attention to personal hygiene. The expectation of life at birth in 1860 was about 40 years; today it is about 65 years, though this is due primarily to a decrease in infant mortality. And the 65 years of the present generation will be clouded by less suffering and disease than the 40 years of the earlier period. Life expectancy is perhaps the best index of national health just as the increase in the per capita income is of an improving standard of living. Judged by both these tests we have made an undeniable advance. The gain of the past two generations is greater than that of the previous two thousand years.

Responsible for this advance was a phenomenal improvement in medical science and in surgery. Increasing emphasis has been placed upon preventive medicine in all its forms. Medical schools enforced higher standards and co-operated with hospital clinics to turn out experienced doctors. Nurses' training schools in connection with hospitals began in the seventies and are today universal. Not only was the quality of hospital care improved by these developments, but the number of hospitals greatly increased and equipment became more specialized and expensive. Between 1909 and 1944 the number of beds in hospitals in the United States practically quadrupled, increasing from 421,000 to 1,930,000; this growth was more rapid than that of the population.

Health became a matter of public concern in the sixties as disclosures of bad housing and other evils in the cities aroused the public conscience. New York City established a health department in 1866, and three years later Massachusetts founded a state board of health. Today all the states and most of the cities in the United States have such organizations, and in 1912 the federal Public Health Service was set up. The early health authorities endeavored by the exercise of the police power to protect the public against unsanitary environmental conditions, polluted food, and the dissemination of communicable diseases. As better sanitation and improved medical science conquered these dangers, the concept of public health was broadened from prevention of the spread of disease to one of responsibility for the development of a good environment and of healthful habits on the part of individuals. The role of medical care was also enlarged; it was to prevent disease as well as to cure it. Health education was introduced into the schools and is now widespread. Unfortunately, the cost of medical service is high, though group medicine and possibly compulsory health insurance might ultimately provide everyone with proper medical care. The broadened concept of public health thus raises economic and social problems. Disease is associated with poverty and ignorance; to banish the former it is necessary to grapple with the latter. Fortunately, progress along these lines has been steady.

Leisure. Foreign visitors to America in the middle of the last century frequently remarked that the American was too absorbed in the serious business of making money to relax and play. A writer in the first issue of the *Atlantic Monthly* in 1858 queried, "Who in this community really takes exercise —even the mechanic confines himself to one set of muscles, the blacksmith acquires strength in his right arm—but the professional or business man, what muscles has he at all?" The average worker in 1860 worked eleven hours a day, with Sundays and holidays off but with no paid vacations. His leisure has been estimated at twenty-four hours a week, but household routine in those unmechanized days often required much of this time to be spent on chores. Amusements for the upper classes in the 1860's consisted of attending a horse race, a musical recital, or a theater, possibly to see *Uncle Tom's Cabin* or a Shakespearean tragedy, followed by a farce, as a chaser to lift their spirits. Croquet and archery were popular in the afternoon, mixed bathing was coming into vogue in the summer, and there was the hunt in the South. The common people had begun to appreciate baseball, P. T. Barnum was attracting thousands to the circus, and such other spectator sports were beginning to appear as foot races, prize fights, and sailing regattas. Along the Mississippi dazzling showboats occasionally tied up at port towns bringing melodrama, musical extravaganza, and minstrel shows from the outside world. Country people found entertainment at church gatherings, county fairs, picnics, and sleighing parties, but co-operative jamborees like barn-raising and husking bees were dying out as the frontier advanced westward. Intellectuals founded local lyceums to bring in prominent lecturers to talk on philosophy, prison reform, and women's rights; among college students debating societies were prominent and sports lacking, which may explain the frequency and severity of student riots. But on the whole, sports and leisure occupations were on a simple plane, for people had little time to devote to them.

Today people have more leisure than ever before. The 40-hour week prevails normally in many occupations, which means not only that the working day is three hours shorter than in 1860, but the work week is at least half a day and often a day shorter. Holidays are more numerous and many persons in white-collar occupations receive at least two weeks' paid vacation a year. The worker's leisure was estimated to be thirty-six hours in 1931 and is doubtless more now. Countless gadgets and household improvements have reduced the time needed by both the worker and his wife to perform household chores, making available much spare time for relaxation. Between 1924 and 1942 the amusement industries of the nation averaged an income of over $1000 million a year. New forms of recreation have appeared: the theater and the vaudeville have given ground to the movie in the last generation; the radio, unknown twenty years ago but now found in most homes, has largely replaced concerts and lectures and even affected reading habits; and dancing, no longer frowned upon as immoral, is a favorite pastime.

One of the greatest changes has been the growth of sports, especially organized sports, until today the great athlete is admired and worshipped as much as he was in ancient times. One sport after another introduced by society leaders has been taken over by the masses. For example, baseball was begun before the Civil War, college football in 1869, lawn tennis in 1874, bicycling and polo both about 1876, and golf around 1888. Every year, often in numbers of fifty or one hundred thousand at a time, millions are attracted to the huge stadiums to watch baseball and football games. Although millions watch, millions also engage in some kind of competitive sport themselves. Girls have invaded almost every kind of sport and in some achieved close to equality with men. Public parks, picnic grounds, beaches, and forest preserves have been set aside in every section of the country so that the city dweller may escape the heat and monotony of city streets. Entire states, like Maine and Florida, advertise themselves as the playgrounds of the nation and cater to summer or winter vacationists. According to Frank Menke's *Encyclopaedia of Sports* the American people spent $4 billion in 1938 on sports, most notably on fishing, hunting, motorboating, and golf. World War II demonstrated conclusively, if the testimony of many army and navy officers is accepted, that organized sport had contributed greatly toward strengthening the body and character of the military recruit. During the war millions more were spent by the services on sports equipment to increase the men's endurance still further and to build morale.

Public services. The citizen of 1860 rarely complained that the government was interfering in his affairs or competing with his business, for the spirit of *laissez faire* was dominant. The services rendered by the various governments seem meager when measured by our present-day standards. The federal government provided Army and Navy protection against foreign invasion and domestic insurrection, maintained courts, enacted necessary laws, and had created two new cabinet posts since the nineteenth century began. The Post Office

Department was given cabinet rank in 1829 and the Department of the Interior was set up in 1849 to handle such miscellaneous bureaus as the public land office, pensions, Indian affairs, and the decennial census. A Department of Agriculture without cabinet rank was founded in 1862, a Bureau of Education was begun in 1867, and many of the land-grant colleges originated in the 1860's. But as yet there were no regulatory commissions, little thought of protecting the consumer against fraud, and no concern for the unemployed, injured, overage, or child laborer. In the advanced states public schools were free, but elsewhere parents of school children paid fees. Local governments provided police and maybe fire protection and a few minor services. The most tangible thing a citizen might receive from his government was cheap or free land, but the best of this was obtained by big business and speculators rather than by the little man. However, since taxes totaled only about 2 per cent of the national income, perhaps the above was service enough for the price.

Before the outbreak of World War II our various governments absorbed about 20 per cent of the national income and during the war as much as 62 per cent in the peak year of 1944. The bulk of this was for military protection. Even after the war government expenditures were expected to total over 25 per cent. Since the Civil War our various governments have taken upon themselves many new responsibilities as *laissez faire* has waned and something resembling mercantilism has returned. Four overlapping groups have been the objects of government concern; namely, consumers, workers, small businessmen, and the poorer classes among the general public. Since the Granger Movement of the 1870's more and more businesses have been declared "affected with public interest"—railroads, grain elevators, gas and electric companies, streetcar lines, insurance companies, and stock exchanges—and have had their rates and activities placed under commission regulation. The Pure Food and Drug Act passed in 1906 has since been repeatedly improved. With the advent of the "New Deal" billions of dollars were poured out to relieve victims of the depression; unemployment insurance and old-age pension systems were set up under the Social Security Act of 1935 and accident insurance laws were started. About the same time the AAA and succeeding programs endeavored to prevent the small farmer from hurting himself by ruinous competition and to increase his income. The people have received more dollars of free income from public schools and state universities than any other non-military public service. In 1944 the state governments expended over $2 billion on these. Highways are also provided by our state governments; there were 1,421,000 miles of surfaced roads in 1942. Our millions of acres of beautiful national parks, founded since 1890, were visited by 21,000,000 persons in 1941. Local police and fire protection have been improved and supplemented by many other services, like hospitals and libraries, as state and local governments tripled their per capita expenditures between 1890 and 1924. Professor Douglas estimated that the American worker in 1924 enjoyed a 7 per cent gain in real income from free services over his father in 1890. Between 1924 and 1940 per capita expenditures by our various governments quadrupled, so that a very considerable portion of our real income now comes to us through government services.

Education. One of the basic assumptions of democracy is that the people will think intelligently about the issues of the year and elect reasonably competent representatives to carry out their wishes. Thus, for democracy to succeed the people must be educated. Growing recognition of this fact has produced a steadily improved educational system, especially during the last seventy-five years. By 1944 the nation was spending over $3 billion on its public schools, colleges, and universities each year.

In 1860 most schools were of the rural one-room type, in many states schooling was not yet free, the curriculum often consisted of little more than the three R's—readin', 'ritin' and 'rithmetic—which quite likely were "taught to the tune of a hickory stick" wielded by a stalwart schoolmaster; he had to be strong to cope with the big boys. One result of the Civil War was the hiring of many more women teachers, who brought to the schoolroom a slightly more humanizing influence. There were perhaps three or four hundred high schools in the country, and 250 colleges, many of them inferior to a present-day good preparatory school but beyond the reach of the average youth. The impracticability of Latin, Greek, and other classical studies, the chief subjects taught in these colleges, had started an "Industrial Movement" which in 1862 produced the Morrill Act for the establishment of colleges in each state primarily "to teach such branches of learning as are related to agriculture and mechanic arts... in order to promote the liberal and practical education of the industrial classes in the several pursuits and professions of life." The land-grant colleges which were thus spawned in the 1860's and have since become our great state universities were at first supported by the proceeds of the sale of lands set aside by Congress for this purpose. At this time co-education was in its infancy, not only in colleges but also in high schools, none of which prepared a girl for college because girls' colleges were so very rare. Graduate work was just being inaugurated at Harvard, but the master's degree was the highest attainable. As for Negroes, it was illegal to teach them to read in the South, and there was little provision for their education in the North.

PUBLIC SCHOOL DEVELOPMENTS*				
	1870	1900	1920	1942
Percentage of children 5-17 enrolled in public schools.....	57	72.4	77.8	84.2
Average number of days annually attended per enrolled pupil..	78.4	99.0	121.2	149.6
Percentage of youths 14-17 in high school	—	10.3	26.4	81 (1940)
Average salary of public-school teacher	$189.	$325.	$871.	$1507.
Average educational expenditure per school pupil in average attendance	$15.55	$20.22	$64.16	$110.03

* *Statistical Abstract of the United States, 1946* (Washington, 1946), 128; *World Almanac, 1944*, 553.

Today the picture has altered greatly. There are now thousands of well-equipped brick schools with a separate room for each grade. Only 4 per cent of the population are illiterate instead of 20 per cent as in 1870, an illiterate person being defined as anyone over nine who cannot write in any language. The three R's have been supplemented by other useful subjects; most schools are on a co-educational basis; there are classes for the very young children, and Negroes receive an education just like other citizens. The first trade-school was founded in 1880 and after World War I vocational education grew rapidly in popularity. Schools have been founded for the blind, deaf, feeble-minded, crippled, and others needing special attention. Four-fifths of the youth of high-school age attend high schools and either prepare for college or take a more practical curriculum that includes such subjects as typewriting and shorthand to help them get a job. The great state universities virtually carry the possibilities of free public schooling through four years of college and beyond. Thousands now do work at the graduate level to prepare themselves as doctors, lawyers, scientists, and educators. University libraries are among the finest in the country and millions of dollars have also been put into experimental laboratories. Like the one-room schoolhouse, the ungainly one-building college has largely vanished.

The education gains made in just the last generation should not be lost sight of in making the above long-term comparisons. The American soldier of World War II was a much better-educated person than his father in World War I had been, as can be seen from the accompanying table, and was perhaps therefore a more skilled fighting man. And judged by the millions of dollars now being expended to give a col-

DEGREE OF EDUCATION OF DRAFTED MEN (WHITE)*		
Education	World War I Per cent	World War II Per cent
Some college education	5	11
High-school graduates	4	30
High-school non-graduates	12	28
Grade school and no schooling	79	31

* National Industrial Conference Board, *Economic Almanac, 1944-45,* 27.

lege education to returning GI's, many of whom never expected to have that opportunity, the future American will be still better educated.

Social control. Down almost to the end of the nineteenth century the prevailing economic philosophy of the American people was one of *laissez faire,* of almost unrestricted indi-

vidualism. With practically free land and apparently boundless national resources the economic virtues called for were
initiative, enterprise, energy, and skill to develop these resources and to convert the raw land and materials into con-
sumable wealth. So long as there was enough for all, little
disposition was manifested to curb the activities of the enterprisers who were building railroads, drilling oil wells, opening
mines, cutting lumber, ranging the public domain, and in other
ways building up their fortunes. But in the inevitable clash
of conflicting interests that developed, protests began to be
raised against the less defensible practices of these despoilers,
and when the first national inventory of our natural and
human resources ever made [4] revealed a startling depletion of
our patrimony, the protests swelled into a cry for regulation
and control.

The new point of view is well stated by a competent French
observer.[5] "Little by little the successes of the heroic age
diminished, and a reaction against exploitation set in among
business men. By the end of the century the West was no
longer a land of adventure beyond the frontier of civilization.
People had begun to adopt the idea that industry and commerce were more or less public functions involving responsibilities and duties toward the community. In a sense this was
a Puritan tradition, but the [first World] War hastened this
evolution by putting industry for the first time at the service
of the nation. Production was now looked upon as a unit, and
as a national rather than an individual affair."

The first protests after the Civil War had been made by
the farmers who felt themselves aggrieved by high freight
rates and who demanded public regulation of the railroads.
While the Granger legislation was extreme it set a clear
precedent, which was followed by the federal interstate commerce acts, lukewarmly at first, but with increasing vigor as
public approval was manifested. Today the *laissez-faire* doctrine has been practically abolished in this segment of economic activity. Business and industrial monopolies were next
brought under control by the Sherman Anti-trust Act of
1890, in order to preserve competition. As the advantages of

---

[4] *Report of the National Conservation Commission* (Washington, 1909).
[5] André Siegfried, *America Comes of Age* (New York, 1927), 171.

large-scale industry and of co-ordinated management came to be recognized more clearly, the Clayton and other acts were passed to define more carefully combinations in restraint of trade and to restrict these when necessary in the public interest. The Federal Trade Commission was established to insure fair dealing, and the pure food law still further extended the regulation of private business in order to protect consumers from the harmful practices of the unscrupulous few. Credit control and price stabilization are being increasingly employed by the Federal Reserve Board and by other newly created federal agencies, in an effort to control the business cycle and to prevent inflation.

Increasing safeguards have been thrown around labor, though by state rather than by national legislation, in order to insure it against exploitation. Laws prohibiting child labor, limiting the field of employment and hours for women, regulating dangerous trades, prescribing minimum wages, workmen's compensation laws, and general factory acts have been passed by most of the states. The federal government has, moreover, endeavored to protect the standard of living through restriction of the supply of labor by restrictive immigration legislation. A more positive step in eliminating conditions detrimental to the health, efficiency, and well-being of workers and of oppressive child labor was the enactment of the Fair Labor Standards Act of 1938, popularly known as the Wage and Hour Law. This set a minimum wage of 40 cents an hour (1945) and a work week of 40 hours. The early assumption of capitalism was that the existing system was divinely ordained and that the determination of wages and working conditions rested solely with the employer. This was bluntly stated by one capitalist—George F. Baer—as follows: "The rights of the laboring man will be protected and cared for, not by labor and agitation, but by Christian men to whom God in His infinite wisdom has given control of the property interests of this country." It is evident, from the present lack of sympathy with such a point of view, that the pendulum has swung a long way from unrestricted freedom of economic action toward government regulation.

But the departure from *laissez faire* has been marked not only by the control of harmful practices, but also by constructive aid along a number of different lines. The post office, the only business enterprise carried on by the federal government, has been made to serve the public and even to compete with private business by the extension of free rural delivery, and the establishment of the parcel post and postal savings banks. To no group has more government assistance been granted than to the farmers, both by the guaranteeing of easy credit and the organization of more efficient marketing agencies, and by helpful advice and guidance through state agricultural colleges and experiment stations and county advisers. Even industry, usually distrustful of government interference, has long accepted tariff favors.

The tendency to enlarge the functions and powers of government has been proceeding steadily for the past fifty years. Federal and state governments have not only set up many regulatory commissions, but have also greatly expanded government enterprises and have entered many fields previously occupied by private industry. The federal government owns and operates a railroad in Alaska, a barge line on the Mississippi River, electric power development plants, and at one time owned and operated a considerable merchant marine. During World War II the government also built and operated aluminum, steel, and other plants. State and local governments operate practically all sewage-disposal plants, most of the water works, and many other public utilities, such as lighting and electric power.

The greatest departure from our traditional policy of individualism was made under the so-called "New Deal" of President Franklin D. Roosevelt. By this, conscious and deliberate government action was taken to help, control, and direct economic activities. In Russia such action was designed to abolish the competitive system, but in the United States the existing price and profit system remained with only a somewhat greater degree of control. The pendulum has swung far from a regime of *laissez faire* in the direction of increasing powers of regulation and operation. The long struggle between freedom of enterprise, with its attendant risks and disequilibriums, and security, even at the sacrifice of a certain degree of freedom, seems about to end in at least a partial defeat of the former. The outbreak of World War II greatly accelerated the movement toward social control, as the necessities of total war subordinated private interests to national safety. It is improbable that we shall soon move back very far toward the "rugged individualism" of Hoover. A new era is in the making.

Further reforms. It is easier to chronicle and criticize than to suggest constructive remedies, but certain conclusions may be stated. Monopoly and special privilege must be prevented or, where inevitable, brought under strict social control. Not only this, but society should also assert its rights to all unearned values by ownership, by special taxation, or by other methods. Limited natural resources must be saved to future generations, and this should be done by the means that seem most feasible under the particular circumstances, whether this be government ownership, regulation, fixing of rates, or assistance. Although the old ideal of a free farm or unrestricted access to natural resources ended with the close of the last century, the door of economic opportunity along other lines must be kept open as wide as possible for all alike. To effect this there is no better method than education.

This book has related the story of the economic conquest of a virgin continent by man, of the appropriation of its resources to his uses, and of the development of a highly efficient industrial organization for the production of wealth. In the pursuit of these aims we have neglected the study of the most rational utilization of this wealth, or expenditure of income, but among all the reforms suggested this would probably yield the greatest immediate improvement in economic conditions. Education in consumption, in the art of spending, has lagged behind, but is scarcely less necessary both to prevent waste and to achieve greater economic satisfactions from existing wealth. This may be obtained by greater wisdom in the expenditure of his income by each individual, by the greater socialization of wealth, as in the form of public libraries, art galleries, parks, swimming pools, and golf links, and by the shortening of the working day, whereby leisure, one of the greatest boons of our material civilization, will be more generally distributed. We may trust to education to teach the best use of this leisure.

By means of better education, especially along vocational

lines, increased individual efficiency can be obtained and economy in national production augmented. The new technology is, moreover, making greater demands upon science and scientific training, which are being steadily strengthened in our schools and colleges. Better distribution of wealth requires that production be kept at its present high level or increased. The future holds grave responsibility for the wise and conservative solution of this and other economic problems, but also great promise if we maintain the high ideals of the first settlers on these shores.

BIBLIOGRAPHICAL NOTES

GENERAL

While some of the more readily accessible books are listed in the accompanying topical bibliographies, the student may want more extensive assistance. He should consult H. P. Beers *Bibliographies in American History* (New York, 1942), Chapter 5. A great deal of monographic material may be dug out of the *Annual Reports* of the American Historical Association between 1906 and 1937, most of them edited by Grace Griffin. E. Channing, A. Hart, and F. J. Turner, *Guide to the Study and Reading of American History* (Boston, 1912), although devoted chiefly to history and only up to 1910, is still a helpful bibliography. On government publications and their use probably Anne Boyd, *United States Government Publications* (New York, 1941), is most helpful. Excellent bibliographies of current books and periodicals are to be found in the *American Historical Review* (quarterly since 1895), the *American Economic Review* (quarterly since 1910), the *Journal of Political Economy* (since 1892), *Agricultural History* (since 1927), the *Southern Economic Journal* (since 1933), the *Mississippi Valley Historical Review* (since 1914), and the newly founded *Journal of Economic History* (semi-annually since 1941). Also valuable is the now defunct *Journal of Economic and Business History* (Cambridge, 1928–32).

At this point it may be helpful to list the few collections of source material, a study of which is indispensable to a thorough understanding of the economic history of the country. E. L. Bogart and C. M. Thompson, *Readings in the Economic History of the United States* (New York, 1916). G. S. Callender, *Selections from the Economic History of the United States, 1765–1860* (Boston, 1909). F. Flügel (Ed.), *Documents Relating to American Economic History, 1651–1820* (Berkeley, 1927). F. Flügel and H. U. Faulkner, *Readings in the Economic and Social History of the United States, 1773–1929* (New York, 1930). N. S. B. Gras and H. Larson, *Casebook in American Business History* (New York, 1939). H. S. Commager, *Documents of American History* (New York, 1940).

For a quick summary of almost any American history topic accompanied by a brief bibliography consult *The Dictionary of American History* (6 vols., New York, 1940). The biographies of famous Americans, now dead, may be found in *The Dictionary of American Biography* (21 vols., New York, 1928–37). Briefer information on the less famous and more recently deceased is available in *Who Was Who in America* (Chicago, 1943), which covers all who have appeared in *Who's Who in America* since 1897. *The Encyclopaedia of the Social Sciences* (15 vols., New York, 1930–35) contains scholarly articles on practically all the topics covered in this book, and should be consulted both for subject matter and further references. A great deal of valuable current information may be obtained from the publications of the various departments of the federal government at Washington. Among these may be mentioned the annual Statistical Abstracts of the United States, the year books and bulletins of the Department of Agriculture, the reports of the Bureau of Foreign and Domestic Commerce and of the Census Bureau of the Department of Commerce; the publications of the Bureau of Labor Statistics; the monthly and annual publications of the Board of Governors of the Federal Reserve System; the annual reports of the Geological Survey, of the Bureau of Mines, of the Interstate Commerce Commission, of the Treasury Department, and of other bodies. Important reports of national commissions on various problems are frequently published. All these government documents can be purchased at a nominal charge from the Superintendent of Documents, or may sometimes be obtained free from the Congressmen of the district. Valuable economic history studies and statistics are also published by such privately endowed organizations as The National Industrial Conference Board, whose *Economic Almanac* (New York, annually since 1940) is particularly recommended, The Twentieth Century Fund, The Brookings Institution, and The National Bureau of Economic Research.

For a pictorial presentation of the economic development of the nation, the student should consult R. Gabriel, *Pageant of America* (15 vols., New Haven, 1925–29), the first five volumes, elementary but good. Newer but somewhat less suited to the economic historian is J. T. Adams (Ed.), *Album of American History* (3 vols. to date, New York, 1944–46). Also helpful is L. Hacker and others, *The United States: A Graphic History* (New York, 1937). The best historical atlases for American economic history are C. O. Paullin, *Atlas of the Historical Geography of the United States* (Washington, 1932) and C. L. Lord and E. H. Lord, *Historical Atlas of the United States* (1944). Interesting illustrations of particular phases of our economic development may sometimes be obtained from historical novels. A list of American historical novels with an economic bearing was compiled by the senior author and published in the *History Teacher's Magazine*, Vol. VIII (September, 1917), 226–231.

THE ECONOMICS OF COLONIZATION

(Chapter I)

The search for new routes and the discovery of America have been described many times, and a few only of the most accessible books need be given. A general view is given in J. Brebnor, *The Explorers of North America*, 1492–1806 (New York, 1933). E. J. Payne describes early voyages in *History of the New World Called America* (2 vols., Oxford, 1892–99). More popular, but excellent, is John Fiske, *Discovery of America* (2 vols., Boston, 1892). Scholarly but much less readable is Justin Winsor, *Narrative and Critical History of America*, Vol. II (8 vols.,

Boston, 1884–89). The best account in English of trade between Europe and the Orient and of trade routes is E. P. Cheyney, *European Background of American History* (New York, 1904), retold more briefly in C. J. H. Hayes, *A Political and Social History of Modern Europe*, Vol. I (New York, 1936).

On the development of geography see J. N. L. Baker, *A History of Geographical Discovery and Exploration* (London, 1932), C. R. Beazley, *The Dawn of Modern Geography* (3 vols., London, 1897–1906); Edward Heawood, *A History of Geographical Discovery in the Seventeenth and Eighteenth Centuries* (Cambridge, 1912); and Jas. E. Gillespie, *A History of Geographical Discovery* (New York, 1933); and on the art of navigation, W. H. Tillinghast's chapter in J. Winsor's *Narrative and Critical History of America*, Vol. I (8 vols., Boston, 1884–89).

A good introduction to a study of colonization is H. C. Morris, *The History of Colonization from the Earliest Times to the Present Day* (New York, 1900). Other general works are A. G. Keller, *Colonization: a Study of the Founding of New Societies* (Boston, 1908), and H. E. Bolton and T. M. Marshall, *The Colonization of North America*, 1492–1783 (New York, 1925), which pays due attention to non-English settlements.

The Spanish colonial system has been carefully described by W. Roscher, *The Spanish Colonial System* (translated from German, New York, 1904). An older book, though still valuable, is H. Merivale, *Lectures on Colonization and Colonies* (London, 1839; new ed., 1861). These are severely critical, as is also Bernard Moses, *The Establishment of Spanish Rule in America* (New York, 1898). More sympathetic is E. G. Bourne, *Spain in America* (New York, 1904). An excellent treatment is given by H. I. Priestly, *The Coming of the White Man*, 1492–1848 (New York, 1929).

For French colonial policy the general reader may be referred to the scholarly and dramatic works of Francis Parkman, *France and England in North America* (complete ed., 12 vols., Boston, 1898); of these, *Pioneers of France in the New World* describes the life of the missionary and trader and *The Old Régime in Canada*, the economic conditions. A good short account is W. B. Munro, *Crusaders of New France* (New Haven, 1918). Other regional studies are H. P. Bigger, *The Early Trading Companies of New France* (1901), L. P. Kellogg, *The French Régime in Wisconsin and the Northwest* (Madison, Wis., 1925), and N. M. M. Surrey, *The Commerce of Louisiana during the French Régime*, 1699–1763 (New York, 1916). H. A. Innis, *The Fur Trade in Canada* (Toronto, 1930), describes the role of the Indians in this trade and English rivalry.

The brief chapter of Dutch colonization in America is interestingly told by John Fiske, *Dutch and Quaker Colonies in America* (2 vols., Boston, 1899), and by T. A. Janvier, *The Dutch Founding of New York* (New York, 1903). Irving Elting, *Dutch Village Communities on the Hudson River* (1886), and L. M. Salmon, *The Dutch West Indies Company on the Hudson* (Poughkeepsie, 1915) are careful studies.

English colonization is briefly covered in the general histories. The best short survey of the colonial period is M. W. Jernegan, *The American Colonies* (New York, 1928). C. M. Andrews, *The Colonial Period of American History* (4 vols., New York, 1934–38), gives considerable attention to the English background, forms of colonization, the land system, and English mercantilist policy. Economic and social conditions are also described in T. J. Wertenbaker, *The First Americans*, 1607–1690 (New York, 1927), in J. T. Adams, *Provincial Society*, 1690–1763 (New York, 1927), and in E. B. Greene, *The Revolutionary Generation*, 1763–1790 (New York, 1943). Especially good is C. P. Nettels, *Roots of American Civilization* (New York, 1938). A stimulating account of the intellectual background is V. L. Parrington, *The Colonial Mind*, 1620–1800 (New York, 1927). The most complete treatment is contained in *The Cambridge History of the British Empire* (5 vols., 1929–40).

The economic features of English colonization are more adequately treated in W. B. Weeden, *The Economic and Social History of New England* (2 vols., Boston, 1891), and P. A. Bruce, *Economic History of Virginia in the Seventeenth Century* (2 vols., New York, 1896). A good picture of social conditions is given by Edward Eggleston, *Beginners of a Nation* (New York, 1897) and *Transit of Civilization* (New York, 1900).

Companies and proprietors as methods of settlement are described by Cheyney and Andrews, already cited, by William Cunningham, *Growth of English Industry and Commerce, Modern Times* (3 vols., Cambridge, 1896–1903), by G. L. Beer, *The Old Colonial System* (New York, 1912), and by F. Rose-Troup, *The Massachusetts Bay Company and its Predecessors* (1930).

The West Indies are discussed as a part of the British colonial empire by A. P. Newton, *The European Nations in the West Indies*, 1493–1688 (New York, 1933), F. W. Pitman, *The Development of the British West Indies*, 1700–1763 (New Haven, 1917), and Richard Pares, *War and Trade in the West Indies*, 1739–1763 (Oxford, 1936).

COLONIAL POLICY, REVOLUTION, AND CONSTITUTION

(Chapters VII, VIII)

The general setting and background for a study of English colonial policy should be sought in a study of conditions in England as well as in America. For the former the best general accounts are *Cambridge Modern History*, Vols. V, VI (14 vols., London, 1902–12); E. Lipson, *The Economic History of England* (3 vols., London, 1920–1931); J. R. Seeley, *Growth of British Policy* (2 vols., New York, 1895); A. D. Innes, *Britain and Her Rivals in the Eighteenth Century* (London, 1895); H. E. Egerton, *A Short History of British Colonial Policy* (2nd ed., Oxford, 1906); J. A. Williamson, *A Short History of British Expansion* (3rd ed., New York, 1931); and L. H. Gipson, *The British Empire before the American Revolution* (6 vols., Caldwell, Id., 1936–46), which is especially good on economic themes: Vol. II, Chap. 3 (tobacco), Chap. 7–9 (sugar islands), Chap. 10 (African slave trade); Vol. III, Chap. 8 (iron), Chap. 10

(fisheries), Chap. 11 (British colonial policy). An authoritative account of British colonial policy to 1763 is contained in Vol. I of *The Cambridge History of the British Empire* (5 vols., Cambridge, 1929–40).

For the colonies, see the books cited in the previous chapter; also E. Channing, *A History of the United States* (6 vols., New York, 1905–25), Vols. I, II; E. B. Greene, *Foundations of American Nationality* (New York, 1922); and E. A. J. Johnson, *American Economic Thought in the Seventeenth Century* (London, 1932). The last volume of C. M. Andrews, *The Colonial Period of American History* (4 vols., New Haven, 1934–38), deals with mercantilism.

A scholarly appraisal of the theory of mercantilism is G. Schmoller, *The Mercantile System*. Transl. from the German by W. J. Ashley (New York, 1896). More recent are J. W. Horrocks, *Short History of Mercantilism* (London, 1925), and E. F. Heckscher, *Mercantilism* (2 vols., London, 1935). The historical setting is given by L. B. Packard, *The Commercial Revolution*, 1400–1776 (New York, 1927). A valuable contemporary account of the workings of the system is found in Book IV of Adam Smith, *Wealth of Nations*.

The best study of the English colonial policy is G. L. Beer, *The Commercial Policy of England Toward the American Colonies* (New York, 1893), which the author later amplified by more extended studies: *Origins of the British Colonial Policy*, 1578–1660 (New York, 1908); *The Old Colonial System*, 1660–1754 (New York, 1913); and *British Colonial Policy*, 1754–1765 (New York, 1907). The English viewpoint is given by W. J. Ashley, "Commercial Legislation of England and the American Colonies" in *Surveys Historic and Economic* (London, 1900). A thoughtful volume based on a more careful study of the sources is H. E. Egerton, *A Short History of British Colonial Policy* (2nd ed., Oxford, 1909). An unprejudiced survey is that by the Italian economist, Ugo Rabbeno, *American Commercial Policy* (2nd ed., New York, 1895). The influence of the colonial policy on British shipbuilding is set forth in L. A. Harper, *The English Navigation Laws; a Seventeenth Century Experiment in Social Engineering* (New York, 1939). The best accounts of the Board of Trade are O. M. Dickerson, *American Colonial Government*, 1696–1765 (Cleveland, 1912), and A. H. Basye, *The Lord Commissioners of Trade and Plantations, commonly known as the Board of Trade*, 1748–1782 (New Haven, 1925).

Special studies of the attempts to regulate manufacturing are E. L. Lord, *Industrial Experiments in the British Colonies of North America* (Baltimore, 1898), and A. C. Bining, *British Regulation of the Colonial Iron Industry* (Philadelphia, 1933).

The history of the American Revolution has been reappraised and rewritten since about 1900 by the application of more scientific methods. The newer point of view has been the study of the colonies as an integral part of the British empire rather than as an oppressed section, and this is well brought out in the general histories of C. M. Andrews, *The Colonial Period* (New York, 1912); C. L. Becker, *The Beginnings of the American People* (New York, 1915); E. B. Greene, *Foundations of American*

Nationality (New York, 1922); E. Channing, *A History of the United States*, Vol. III (6 vols., New York, 1905–25), and C. H. Van Tyne, *England and America: Rivals in the American Revolution* (New York, 1927). C. Altschul, *The American Revolution in Our School Text-Books* (New York, 1917), traces the changes in treatment.

A number of excellent studies have been made of the Revolution, of which the more recent may be cited. G. E. Howard, *Preliminaries of the Revolution*, 1763–1775 (New York, 1906), and C. H. Van Tyne, *The American Revolution*, 1776–1783 (New York, 1905), give considerable attention to the economic factors. Another volume by Van Tyne, *The Causes of the War of Independence* (New York, 1922), is mainly political. The economic basis of colonial discontent is carefully studied by Allen Nevins, *The American States during and after the Revolution*, 1775–1789 (New York, 1927), and by Matthew Chamberlain, "The Revolution Impending," in J. Winsor, *Narrative and Critical History of America*, Vol. VI (8 vols., Boston, 1884–89). S. G. Fisher, *The Struggle for American Independence* (2 vols., Philadelphia, 1908), is iconoclastic. Shorter is C. L. Becker, *The Eve of the Revolution* (New Haven, 1918). H. E. Egerton, *The Causes and Character of the American Revolution* (Oxford, 1923), is a fair and balanced study by an Englishman, which can scarcely be said of Sir George Trevelyan's brilliant *American Revolution* (4 vols., New York, 1899–1907), as it is strongly biased by the author's party affiliations. Older but still good is W. E. H. Lecky, *American Revolution*, 1763–1787 (Ed., J. A. Woodburn, New York, 1898), also by an Englishman. Two more recent books are J. C. Miller, *Origins of the American Revolution* (Boston, 1943), and R. B. Morris (Ed.), *The Era of the American Revolution* (New York, 1939).

The best books for an understanding of the economic causes leading to the Revolution are those of George Louis Beer, of which only two need be named here: *The Commercial Policy of England Toward the American Colonies* (New York, 1893), and *British Colonial Policy*, 1754–1765 (New York, 1907). W. J. Ashley follows Beer and criticizes the popular view as to the injurious effects of the colonial policy in "Commercial Legislation of England and the American Colonies, 1660–1760" in his *Surveys Historic and Economic* (London, 1900). The books listed in the previous chapter should also be consulted here. An interesting presentation of the constitutional aspects of the Revolution is given in C. H. McIlwain, *The American Revolution: A Constitutional Interpretation* (New York, 1923), who argues for it, and R. L. Schuyler, *Parliament and the British Empire* (New York, 1929), who opposes. D. M. Clark, *British Opinion and the American Revolution* (New Haven, 1930), describes contemporary views.

The financing of the Revolution may best be studied in D. R. Dewey, *The Financial History of the United States* (12th ed., New York, 1934). More diffuse and less scientific is A. S. Bolles, *Financial History of the United States* (3 vols., New York, 1879–86). Good material very badly arranged is to be found in W. G. Sumner, *The Financier and Finances of the American Revolution* (2 vols., New York, 1891). Better is S. P. Oberholtzer, *Robert Morris, Patriot and Financier* (Philadelphia, 1903).

Other special studies are C. J. Bullock, *Finances of the United States, 1775–1789, with Especial Reference to the Budget* (University of Wisconsin Bulletin, Madison, 1895); and R. A. Bayley, *History of the National Loans of the United States* (Tenth Census of the United States, 1880, Vol. XIII). For further references Dewey may be consulted.

Among specialized studies may be mentioned A. M. Schlesinger, *Colonial Merchants and the American Revolution* (New York, 1918); C. M. Andrews, *The Colonial Background of the American Revolution* (New Haven, 1924); the brilliant study by C. H. Alvord, *The Mississippi Valley in British Politics. A Study of the Trade, Land Speculation, and Experiments in Imperialism Culminating in the American Revolution* (2 vols., Cleveland, 1917); L. W. Labaree, *Royal Government in America: a Study of the British Colonial System before 1783* (New Haven, 1930); T. P. Abernethy, *Western Lands and the American Revolution* (New York, 1937); and V. G. Setzer, *The Commercial Reciprocity Program of the United States, 1774–1829* (Philadelphia, 1937).

The period of the Confederation and the Constitution are adequately treated in the standard historical works. The best general histories of this period are George Bancroft, *History of the United States* (6 vols., New York, 1883–85); J. Fiske, *The Critical Period of American History, 1783–1789* (Boston, 1888), popular and interesting but not authoritative; J. B. McMaster, *History of the People of the United States from the Revolution to the Civil War* (7 vols., New York, 1883–1914), with much valuable and suggestive material drawn from current newspapers; A. C. McLaughlin, *The Confederation and the Constitution, 1783–1789* (New York, 1905); and E. B. Greene, *The Revolutionary Generation, 1763–1789* (New York, 1943).

Economic conditions should be studied in the books by contemporary observers, of which the following may be named: J. P. Brissot de Warville, *New Travels in the United States* (2 vols., 2d ed., London, 1794); François J. Chastellux, *Travels in North America, 1780–1782* (2 vols., London, 1787; 2nd ed., 1828); Lord Sheffield, *Observations on the Commerce of the American States* (2nd ed., London, 1784); Tench Coxe, *A View of the United States of America* (Philadelphia, 1794); David Ramsay, *The History of the American Revolution* (2 vols., Philadelphia, 1789). More statistical are Timothy Pitkin, *Statistical View of the Commerce of the United States* (New York, 1816); and Adam Seybert, *Statistical Annals of the United States* (Philadelphia, 1818). Of especial value for the northern states is W. B. Weeden, *Economic and Social History of New England, 1620–1789* (2 vols., Boston, 1890).

The economic phases of the movement for the constitution are treated in C. A. Beard, *An Economic Interpretation of the Constitution of the United States* (New York, 1913). An enlightening chapter from a similar point of view is contained in A. M. Schlesinger, *New Viewpoints in American History* (New York, 1918). C. Warren, *The Making of the Constitution* (2nd ed., Boston, 1937), minimizes the economic influences in the framing of the Constitution. Emphasis upon an economic explanation is also found in Orin G. Libby, *The Geographical Distribution of the Vote* of the *Thirteen States on the Federal Constitution*, 1787–1788 (Madison, 1894). The standard works on this subject are Max Farrand, *The Framing of the Constitution of the United States* (New Haven, 1913), and R. L. Schuyler, *The Constitution of the United States* (New York, 1928). The former also was editor of *The Records of the Federal Convention of* 1787 (3 vols., New Haven, 1911). C. Read (Ed.), *The Constitution Reconsidered* (New York, 1938), attempts to reconcile the conflicting viewpoints.

AGRICULTURE

(Chapters II, XI, XIX, XXVI)

The best books on the natural resources and geographic areas are A. P. Brigham, *Geographic Influences in American History* (Boston, 1903); Ellen C. Semple and C. Jones, *American History and Its Geographic Conditions* (New York, 1933); and H. R. Muelder and D. M. Delo, *Years of This Land: a Geographical History of the United States* (New York, 1945). Another helpful book is A. B. Hulbert, *Soil: Its Influence on the History of the United States* (New Haven, 1930). Excellent also are Isiah Bowman, *Forest Physiography*, which is best on geographic regions, and J. Russell Smith, *Men and Resources: a Study of North America and Its Place in World Geography* (New York, 1937), on land uses.

An adequate description of English agriculture during this period may be obtained from any of the numerous manuals on English economic history. More specialized treatment is given by W. H. R. Curtler, *A Short History of English Agriculture* (Oxford, 1909), and R. E. Prothero (Lord Ernle), *English Farming, Past and Present* (5th ed., London, 1936). Bibliographies for the study of American agriculture are given in E. E. Edwards, *Bibliography of the History of American Agriculture* USDA Bibliographical Contribution 32 (Washington, 1939), and L. B. Schmidt, *Topical Studies and References on the Economic History of American Agriculture* (Philadelphia, 1923).

On Indian agriculture the most scholarly work has been done by Lyman Carrier, *The Beginnings of Agriculture in America* (New York, 1923). Good accounts have also been given by L. Farrand, *Basis of American History* (New York, 1904), G. K. Holmes, "Aboriginal Agriculture: The North American Indian," in L. H. Bailey, *Cyclopedia of American Agriculture*, Vol. IV (New York, 1909), and J. W. Powell, "The North American Indians," in N. S. Shaler, *The United States of America*, Vol. I (2 vols., New York, 1894). Especially good accounts of the southern Indians are given in C. C. Jones, *Antiquities of the Southern Indians* (New York, 1873), and of the western agricultural methods in F. H. Cushing, *Zuni Breadstuff* (U. S. Bureau of American Ethnology, Washington, 1896).

Colonial agriculture has been most carefully and fully described by P. W. Bidwell and J. I. Falconer, *History of Agriculture in the Northern United States, 1620–1860* (Carnegie Institution, Washington, 1925), and by L. C. Gray, *History of Agriculture in the Southern United States to*

1860 (2 vols., Carnegie Institution, Washington, 1933). Good accounts are given by T. N. Carver, "Historical Sketch of American Agriculture" in L. H. Bailey, *Cyclopedia of American Agriculture*, Vol. IV, and O. C. Stine, *American Rural Life* (Boston, 1927). Older but usable is C. L. Flint, "One Hundred Years of American Agriculture" in *Eighty Years' Progress* (Hartford, 1866), 30–130; the same article was reprinted in *Annual Report, United States Department of Agriculture*, 1872, and in *21st Annual Report, Massachusetts Board of Agriculture*, 1873. A popular but carefully written book is A. H. Sanford, *The Story of Agriculture in the United States* (Boston, 1916). Reference may also be made to N. S. Shaler, *The United States of America*, Vol. I, Chapters V to VII (2 vols., New York, 1894). Scattered references are made to New England Agriculture in W. B. Weeden, *Economic and Social History of New England, 1620–1789* (2 vols., Boston, 1890), and a more careful and detailed study of agriculture in the South is found in P. A. Bruce, *Economic History of Virginia in the Seventeenth Century* (2 vols., New York, 1895); a scholarly but more specialized study is A. O. Craven, *Soil Exhaustion as a Factor in the Agricultural History of Virginia and Maryland, 1606–1860* (Urbana, Ill., 1926).

The best contemporary account of colonial agriculture, though written at the end of the period, is the anonymous *American Husbandry* (2 vols., London, 1775; reprinted by Columbia University, New York, 1939); this was the work of a scientific observer and is attributed to Dr. John Mitchell, an English physician and naturalist, who lived some time in Virginia. Another excellent book is that by the Swedish botanist Peter Kalm, *Travels into North America*, 1748–1750 (3 vols., London, 1770–71). The outstanding work by a contemporary American is Jared Eliot, *Essays upon Field Husbandry in New England* (Boston, 1760), reprinted by Columbia University (New York, 1934). W. L. Brooke (Ed.), *The Agricultural Papers of George Washington* (Boston, 1919) contain much of interest.

Land tenure is treated in most of the authorities cited above, but special studies have been made by M. Egleston, *The Land System of the New England Colonies* (Baltimore, 1886); R. H. Akagi, *The Town Proprietors of the New England Colonies* (Philadelphia, 1924); F. Harrison, *Virginia Land Grants, a Study of Conveyancing* (Richmond, 1925); and J. C. Ballagh, *Introduction to Southern Economic History—The Land System* (in Report Amer. Hist. Assn., Washington, 1897). A general account is given in A. C. Ford, *Colonial Precedents of Our National Land System* (Madison, Wis., 1910). H. L. Osgood, *American Colonies in the Seventeenth Century* (3 vols., New York, 1904–1907), contains a thorough analysis of the land systems of New England and the middle colonies, and W. R. Shepherd describes that of Pennsylvania in his *History of Proprietary Government in Pennsylvania* (New York, 1896). An excellent account of one phase of landholding is given by B. W. Bond, Jr., *The Quit Rent System in the American Colonies* (1919). Later repercussions from the patroon system of landholding in New York are described in Henry Christman, *Tin Horns and Calico: A Decisive Episode in the Emergence of Democracy* (New York, 1945); and in D. M. Ellis, *Land-*

lords and Farmers in the Hudson-Mohawk Region, 1790–1850 (Ithaca, 1946).

Agriculture between 1789 and 1860 is described in histories of agriculture cited above, but some new references may be added. Territorial specialization was now developing and this is reflected in the literature. Conditions in the West are well portrayed in F. J. Turner, *The Rise of the New West,* 1819–1829 (New York, 1906), James Caird, *Prairie Farming in America* (New York, 1859), and J. G. Thompson, *The Rise and Decline of the Wheat-Growing Industry in Wisconsin* (Madison, Wis., 1909). Southern agriculture is described by M. B. Hammond, *The Cotton Industry* (Publ. Amer. Econ. Assn., New York, 1897); by E. C. Brooks, *The Story of Cotton* (Chicago, 1911); by J. A. B. Scherer, *Cotton as a World Power* (New York, 1916); and by Ulrich B. Phillips, *Plantation and Frontier,* 1649–1863, being Vols. I and II of *A Documentary History of American Industrial Society* (Cleveland, 1910). That of the East by P. W. Bidwell, *Rural Economy in New England at the Beginning of the Nineteenth Century* (Trans. of Conn. Acad. of Arts and Sciences, Vol. XX, 1916), and *The Agricultural Revolution in New England* (Amer. Hist. Rev., Vol. XXVI, 1921). An interesting study by W. C. Bagley, Jr., *Soil Exhaustion and the Civil War* (Amer. Committee on Foreign Affairs, Washington, 1942), attributes the war largely to the soil exhaustion of southern plantations.

The development of livestock can best be studied in the articles under the appropriate name in L. H. Bailey, *Cyclopedia of American Agriculture* (4 vols., New York, 1907–1909). Sheep- and wool-raising have received more attention than other branches; reference may be made to D. E. Salmon, *Report on the History and Present Condition of the Sheep Industry of the United States* (U. S. Dept. of Agric., Washington, 1892), and to C. W. Wright, *Wool Growing and the Tariff* (Cambridge, 1910). For swine, see F. D. Coburn, *Swine Husbandry* (New York, 1897).

The history of agricultural machinery must be traced in many separate studies, but two may be mentioned here. I. P. Roberts, *The Fertility of the Land* (10th ed., New York, 1907), contains an excellent discussion of the improvement of the plow from the earliest times, and M. F. Miller, *The Evolution of Reaping Machines* (U. S. Dept. of Agric., Washington, 1902), is good on this topic. A study of the plow and the reaper is made by L. Rogin, *The Introduction of Farm Machinery in its Relation to the Productivity of Labor* (Berkeley, 1931). Farm machinery is also discussed by H. W. Quaintance, *The Influence of Farm Machinery on Production and Labor* (Publ. Amer. Econ. Assn., New York, 1904). A popularly written book is H. N. Casson, *The Romance of the Reaper* (New York, 1908). W. C. Neely, *The Agricultural Fair* (New York, 1935), describes an important institution in disseminating knowledge of the new machines.

Unfortunately the books of Bidwell and Falconer and of Gray end with the year 1860, so for developments after that date we have to depend upon less authoritative sources. The *Twelfth Census* (Washington, 1900), contains a suggestive article "Agricultural Progress of Fifty Years, 1850–1900," and F. A. Shannon, *The Farmers' Last Frontier: Agriculture,*

1860–1897 (New York, 1945), covers the same period. The best general account is that by E. E. Edwards in the 1940 *Agricultural Yearbook*. A local study of agricultural changes is R. P. Brooks, *The Agrarian Revolution in Georgia*, 1865–1912 (Madison, Wis., 1914).

The farmers' movements are covered in S. J. Buck, *The Granger Movement* (Cambridge, 1913); his *The Agrarian Crusade* (New Haven, 1921) is a slighter treatment. Nathan Fine, *Labor and Farmer Parties in the United States* 1828–1928 (New York, 1928) is more political. John D. Hicks, *The Populist Revolt: a History of the Farmers' Alliance and the People's Party* (Minneapolis, 1931) pays due attention to economic factors. An earlier treatment was F. L. McVey, *The Populist Movement* (New York, 1896).

On cereal production the standard work for this period was T. F. Hunt, *The Cereals in America* (New York, 1907). More popular and historical is E. C. Brooks, *The Story of Corn and the Westward Migration* (Chicago, 1916). Good surveys of certain aspects of agriculture are covered in articles to be found in the Census. The *Eighth Census* (Washington, 1860) treats "Agriculture," "Meat," and "Tobacco," while the *Tenth Census* (Washington, 1880), has an excellent report on the "Cereal Production of the United States," by W. N. Brewer.

Good books on the cattle industry are E. S. Osgood, *The Day of the Cattlemen* (Minneapolis, 1939); P. I. Wellman, *The Trampling Herd* (New York, 1939); E. E. Dale, *The Range Cattle Industry* (Norman, Okla., 1930); Louis Pelzer, *The Cattleman's Frontier* (Glendale, Calif., 1936), and R. A. Clemen, *The American Livestock and Meat Industry* (New York, 1923).

J. A. Widtsoe, *Dry Farming* (New York, 1911) describes agriculture in the arid regions. Irrigation is described by Elwood Mead, *Irrigation Institutions* (New York, 1909); F. H. Newell, *Irrigation in the United States* (New York, 1906); R. P. Teale, *Irrigation in the United States* (New York, 1915); and G. W. James, *Reclaiming the Arid West: the Story of the United States Reclamation Service* (New York, 1917). Good summaries are provided by *The United States Reclamation Service: Its History, Activities and Organization*, Service Monographs of the United States Government, No. 2 (Washington, 1919), and J. W. Haw and F. E. Schmidt, *Report on Federal Reclamation to the Secretary of the Interior* (Washington, 1935).

Farm tenancy is analyzed by C. L. Stewart, *Land Tenure in the United States, with Special Reference to Illinois* (Urbana, Ill., 1916). See also E. L. Bogart, "Farm Tenancy," in *Jour. of Pol. Econ.*, Oct. 1908. Southern tenancy is discussed in C. O. Brannon, *Relation of Land Tenure to Plantation Organization*, Dept. of Agric. Bull. No. 1269 (Washington, 1916), and in *Plantation Farming in the United States* (Census Bulletin, Washington, 1916), and also in the books already cited on southern agriculture. A recent book is E. Q. Hawk, *Economic History of the South* (New York, 1934). Carey McWilliams, *Ill Fares the Land* (Boston, 1942), describes tenancy in a graphic account of the agricultural revolution in the South.

Agricultural education is described in two federal reports: A. C. True, *A History of Agricultural Extension Work in the United States, 1785–1923*, Dept. of Agric. Misc. Pub. No. 15 (Washington, 1928), and his *A History of Agricultural Education in the United States, 1785–1925*, U. S. Dept. of Agric. Misc. Pub. No. 36 (Washington, 1929). An optimistic interpretation of developments in scientific agriculture is given by W. S. Harwood, *The New Earth* (New York, 1906) and K. L. Butterfield, *The Farmer and the New Day* (New York, 1919).

As we approach recent events, more dependence must be placed on official reports, such as the *Census* and the various publications of the United States Department of Agriculture, and on periodical literature. Among the official publications mention should be made of the *Yearbook* and *Bulletins* of the Department of Agriculture, of the *Annual Report of the Secretary of Agriculture*, and the *Bulletin of the Office of Experiment Stations*. The census reports furnish abundant statistical material, which is conveniently summarized in the *Statistical Abstract* (Washington, 1879–). Interpretive books are still largely lacking. Fortunately, excellent bibliographies of current books and periodicals are to be found in the *American Economic Review* and the *Journal of Economic History*. *The Encyclopaedia of the Social Sciences* (15 vols., New York, 1930–35) contains scholarly articles on practically all of the topics covered in this book, and should be consulted both for subject matter and for further references.

The development and problems of agriculture since 1914 are discussed in the following books: Harold Barger and H. H. Landsberg, *American Agriculture, 1899–1939. A Study of Output, Employment, and Productivity* (New York, 1942); W. H. Clark and L. C. Page, *Farms and Farmers: the Story of American Agriculture* (Boston, 1945); E. E. Edwards, *American Agriculture: the First Three Hundred Years*, USDA Yearbook Separate No. 1730 (Washington, 1941); R. W. Howard, *Two Billion Acre Farm: an Informal History of American Agriculture* (Garden City, 1945); Joseph Schafer, *The Social History of American Agriculture* (New York, 1936). Two excellent but more specialized studies are J. C. Malin, *Winter Wheat in the Golden Belt of Kansas: a Study in Adaptation to Subhumid Geographical Environment* (Lawrence, 1944), and W. P. Webb, *The Great Plains* (Boston, 1931), which describes the readjustments forced on the pioneers from the humid East.

Some of the more recent problems of American agriculture in a world economy are treated in the following: Karl Brandt, *Reconstruction of American Agriculture* (New York, 1945); Ferdie Deering, *USDA, Manager of American Agriculture* (New York, 1945), highly critical; O. M. Kile, *The New Agriculture* (New York, 1932). E. G. Nourse, *American Agriculture and the European Market* (New York, 1924); C. J. Schmidt, *The American Farmer in the World Crisis* (New York, 1941); H. A. Wallace, *America Must Choose* (New York, 1934). The 1940 Yearbook of Agriculture, *Farmers in a Changing World* (Washington, 1940), contains valuable historical material. A single volume in the field of farm machinery may be mentioned: R. L. Ardrey, *Our Agricultural*

Implements: a Review of Invention and Development in the Agricultural Implement Industry of the United States (Chicago, 1944).

Land utilization is treated in J. B. Morman, *The Place of Agriculture in Reconstruction: a Study of National Programs of Land Settlement* (New York, 1919), and R. P. Teale, *The Economics of Land Reclamation in the United States* (New York, 1927). The related subject of farm tenancy is discussed in E. A. Goldenweiser and L. E. Truesdale, *Farm Tenancy in the United States*, Census Monographs, No. 4, (Washington, 1924); President's Committee, *Report on Farm Tenancy*. Prepared under the auspices of the National Resources Committee (Washington, 1937); and H. W. Spiegel, *Land Tenure at Home and Abroad* (Chapel Hill, 1941). A critical account of the vacillating federal land policies is the *Supplementary Report* of the Land Planning Committee to the National Resources Board, Part III (Washington, 1936).

Conservation, especially from the standpoint of erosion, is discussed by H. S. Person, *Little Waters. A Study of Little Waters and Other Streams, Their Use and Relation to the Land*, Sen. Doc. No. 198, 74th Cong., 2nd sess. (Washington, 1936); Russell Lord, *To Hold This Soil*, USDA Misc. Pub. No. 321 (Washington, 1938); P. B. Sears, *Deserts on the March* (Norman, Okla., 1935); and USDA Yearbook, *Soils and Man* (Washington, 1938).

Agricultural marketing has been the subject of much discussion. Among the books on this subject are G. G. Huebner, *Agricultural Commerce* (2nd ed., New York, 1924); T. Macklin, *Efficient Marketing for Agriculture* (New York, 1921); J. E. Boyle, *Marketing of Agricultural Products* (New York, 1925); and F. E. Clark and L. D. H. Weld, *Marketing Our Agricultural Products* (New York, 1925). On the allied topic of co-operative marketing may be cited C. L. Christensen, *Farmers' Co-operative Associations in the United States,* 1929. USDA Circular No. 94 (Washington, 1929); two reports by R. H. Elsworth, *Agricultural Co-operative Associations, Marketing and Purchasing*, 1925. USDA Technical Bull. No. 40 (Washington, 1928), and *Co-operative Marketing and Purchasing*, 1920–30. USDA Circular No. 121 (Washington, 1930); Federal Trade Commission, *Co-operative Marketing*, Sen. Doc. No. 93, 70th Cong., 1st Sess. (Washington, 1928).

The various plans for relief of the farmers have called forth a voluminous literature, of which only a few books can be mentioned: O. M. Kile, *The Farm Bureau Movement* (New York, 1921); J. D. Black, *Agricultural Reforms in the United States* (New York, 1929); J. E. Boyle, *Farm Relief: a Brief on the McNary-Haugen Plan* (New York, 1928); J. S. Davis, *The Farm Export Debenture Plan* (Stanford, 1929); E. A. Stopdyk and C. H. West, *The Farm Board* (New York, 1930); W. Gee, *American Farm Policy* (New York, 1934); E. G. Nourse and others, *Three Years of the Agricultural Adjustment Act* (Brookings Institution, Washington, 1937); and Carter Goodrich, *Migration and Economic Opportunity* (Philadelphia, 1939). A good criticism of the parity price idea appears in R. F. Martin, *Income in Agriculture, 1925–1935*

(Nat. Ind. Conf. Board Studies, New York, 1936). Clear and restrained is S. D. Black, *Parity, Parity, Parity* (Cambridge, 1942). The federal farm loan system is discussed by A. C. Wiprud, *Federal Farm Loan System in Operation* (New York, 1921); J. B. Morman, *Farm Credits in the United States and Canada* (New York, 1924); Frieda Baird and C. L. Benner, *Ten Years of Federal Intermediate Credits* (Brookings Institution, Washington, 1933); and L. J. Norton, *Financing Agriculture* (Danville, Ill., 1940). On farmers' organizations the best books are E. Wiest, *Agricultural Organization in the United States* (Lexington, Ky., 1923); S. A. Rice, *Farmers and Workers in American Politics* (New York, 1924); C. B. Fisher, *The Farmers' Union* (Lexington, Ky., 1920); P. R. Fossum, *The Agrarian Movement in North Dakota* (New York, 1925); and J. D. Hicks, *The Populist Revolt* (1931). For agricultural education reference may be made to the two monographs by A. C. True, listed in Chapter XX. An interesting account of the work of American agronomists is P. de Kruif, *Hunger Fighters* (New York, 1928).

WESTWARD MOVEMENT

(Chapters X, XXVI)

The significance of the westward movement is best interpreted by F. J. Turner in *The Frontier in American History* (New York, 1921), especially Chapter I. In his *Rise of the New West*, 1819–1829 (New York, 1906), the same author gives an excellent picture of the movement and its effects upon politics. F. J. Turner and F. Merk, *List of References on the History of the West* (rev. ed., Cambridge, 1922) and E. E. Edwards *References on the Significance of the Frontier in American History;* U. S. Dept. of Agric., Bibliographical Contributions 25 (Washington, 1935), are indispensable bibliographical aids. The history of the West is given in F. L. Paxson, *History of the American Frontier,* 1763–1893 (Boston, 1924). The westward migration is portrayed by L. D. Branch, *Westward* (New York, 1930), and R. E. Riegel, *America Moves West* (New York, 1930). The early advance is described in Justin Winsor, *The Westward Movement,* 1763–1798 (Boston, 1897). A vivid picture is given in J. B. McMaster, *History of the People of the United States* (6 vols., Philadelphia, 1883–96), Vol. II, 144 ff.; Vol. III, 100–42, 459–96; Vol. IV, 381–428; Vol. V, 166 ff. A popularly written book is E. E. Sparks, *The Expansion of the American People* (Chicago, 1900). The influence of the West in bringing about the War of 1812 is told in J. W. Pratt, *Expansionists of 1812,* (New York, 1925). Theodore Roosevelt, *The Winning of the West* (4 vols., New York, 1889–96), has a somewhat misleading title, but is written with vigor. Edward Channing, *A History of the United States* (New York, 1921), Vol. V, Chap. 2, may be mentioned among the general histories.

The settlement of the West is best studied in the writings of contemporary travelers and residents and in the gazetteers of the period. Among the most valuable of these are: Timothy Flint, *Recollections of Ten Years'* *Residence in the Valley of the Mississippi* (Boston, 1826), and *History* *and Geography of the Mississippi Valley* (2 vols., Boston, 1828; 2nd ed., 1832); James Hall, *Letters from the West* (London, 1828) and *Statistics of the West* (Cincinnati, 1836); Harriet Martineau, *Society in America* (2 vols., New York, 1834–36); J. W. Monette, *History of the Discovery and Settlement of the Valley of the Mississippi* (2 vols., New York, 1846); J. M. Peck, *A Guide for Emigrants* (Boston, 1831, 1837) and *New Guide to the West* (Boston, 1836, and Cincinnati, 1848); H. S. Tanner, *Geographical, Historical, and Statistical View of the Central or Middle United States* (Philadelphia, 1841); M. Birkbeck, *Notes on a Journey in America* (Philadelphia, 1817); R. G. Thwaites (Ed.), *Journals of Lewis and Clark* (7 vols., Cleveland, 1904–1905), and *Early Western Travels* (32 vols., Cleveland, 1904–1907). Thwaites is well indexed. The far western advance is portrayed in the voluminous and uneven histories of H. H. Bancroft. These may be supplemented by G. P. Garrison, *Texas* (Boston, 1903), and *Westward Extension, 1841–50* (New York, 1906); W. P. Webb, *The Great Plains* (Boston, 1931); E. N. Dick, *The Sod-House Frontier, 1854–1890* (New York, 1937) and *Vanguards of the Frontier* (New York, 1941); George W. Fuller, *A History of the Pacific Northwest* (rev. ed., New York, 1945); and F. L. Paxson, *The Last American Frontier* (New York, 1910). A popular account is Emerson Hough, *The Passing of the Frontier* (New Haven, 1918).

Territorial expansion is pictured in C. Goodwin, *The Trans-Mississippi West, 1803–1853; A History of Its Acquisition and Settlement* (New York, 1922) and in Chapters, 9, 11, 13, 19, and 24 of C. A. and M. R. Beard, *Rise of American Civilization* (2 vols., New York, 1927, 1931). The influence of rivers and mountains on the westward movement are well told by E. C. Semple and C. Jones, *American History and Its Geographic Conditions* (Boston, 1933). Most attention to economic factors is paid in Katharine Coman, *Economic Beginnings of the Far West* (New York, 1930), and in H. M. Chittenden, *The American Fur Trade of the Far West* (3 vols., New York, 1902). Pioneering to California is described in R. G. Cleland, *Pathfinders* (Los Angeles, 1929), and the gold rush in S. E. White, *Forty-niners* (New Haven, 1918); O. C. McCoy, *The Great Trek* (Los Angeles, 1931); and Leonard Kip, *California Sketches with Recollections of the Gold Mines* (Los Angeles, 1946). J. E. Ware, *The Emigrants' Guide to California* (St. Louis, 1849; Princeton, 1932) was widely used by those who crossed the plains in wagons. On Oregon, see K. Coman or C. L. Skinner, *Adventurers of Oregon* (New Haven, 1920).

The public land policies in colonial times are to be found in C. R. Nettels, *Roots of American Civilization* (New York, 1938) or, in more detail, in C. M. Andrews, *The Colonial Period of American History* (4 vols., New Haven, 1934–38); B. W. Bond, Jr., *The Quit Rent System in the American Colonies* (New Haven, 1919) and R. H. Akagi, *The Town Proprietors of the New England Colonies* (Philadelphia, 1924). The importance of the land cessions is well brought out by H. B. Adams,

Maryland's Influence on Land Cessions to the United States (Johns Hopkins University Studies, Baltimore, 1885). A full account is contained in B. A. Hinsdale, *The Old Northwest* (2 vols., New York, 1888; rev. ed., 1897). See also F. A. Ogg, *The Old Northwest* (New Haven, 1919). The public land policies have attracted much attention and have been fully treated. Thomas C. Donaldson, *The Public Domain, Its History with Statistics* (Washington, 1884), is a government report that has been heavily drawn upon by later writers. This was soon followed by Shosuke Sato, *History of the Land Question in the United States* (Baltimore, 1886), a careful work. The most complete account is B. H. Hibbard, *A History of the Public Land Policies* (New York, 1924). Other studies are P. J. Treat, *The National Land System*, 1785–1820 (Boston, 1910); R. G. Wellington, *The Political and Sectional Influence of the Public Lands*, 1828–1842 (Cambridge, 1914); G. M. Stephenson, *The Political History of the Public Lands from 1840 to 1862, from Pre-emption to Homestead* (Boston, 1917). The latest and most comprehensive study is R. M. Robbins, *Our Landed Heritage: The Public Domain*, 1776–1936 (Princeton, 1942). The extent to which lands fell into the hands of speculators rather than pioneers is well told by Paul W. Gates, "The Homestead Act in an Incongruous Land System," *American Historical Review*, July, 1936, and also *Frontier Landlords and Pioneer Tenants* (Ithaca, 1945). How railroads disposed of the lands granted to them is discussed in P. W. Gates, *The Illinois Central Railroad and Its Colonization Work* (Cambridge, 1934); and R. C. Overton, *Burlington West* (New York, 1941). A well-written defense of the railroads is R. S. Henry, "The Railroad Land Grant Legend in American History Texts," *Mississippi Valley Historical Review*, September 1945, to which replies and a rejoiner will be found in the March and June 1946 issues. A popular account of land speculation throughout our history is given in A. M. Sakolski, *The Great American Land Bubble* (New York, 1932).

Conservation is perhaps best told in C. R. Van Hise and L. Havemeyer, *Conservation of Our Natural Resources* (New York, 1930) and may be supplemented by J. Ise, *The United States Forest Policy* (New Haven, 1920) and *The United States Oil Policy* (New Haven, 1927); by the *Report of the National Conservation Commission*, Sen. Doc. No. 676, 60th Cong., 2nd sess. (Washington, 1909); and more recently by the many reports of the U. S. National Resources Committee (Washington, 1934) and the Energy Resources Committee (Washington, 1939).

In recent years doubts have been cast on the truth of the theory that free or cheap land has served as a safety valve in time of depression or has even raised the American wage level. For this view see C. Goodrich and S. Davison, "The Wage Earner in the Westward Movement," *Political Science Quarterly*, June 1935; Fred A. Shannon, "The Homestead Act and the Labor Surplus," *American Historical Review*, July 1936; and "A Post Mortem on the Labor-Safety-Valve Theory," *Agricultural History*, January 1945; and Clarence Danhof, "Economic Validity of the Safety Valve Doctrine," *Journal of Economic History* Supplement (1941).

Source material may be found in E. L. Bogart and C. M. Thompson,

Readings in the Economic History of the United States (New York, 1916); G. S. Callender, *Selections from the Economic History of the United States*, 1765–1860 (Boston, 1909); A. B. Hart, *American History Told by Contemporaries* (New York, 1911), Vol. III; and F. Flügel and H. U. Faulkner, *Readings in the Economic and Social History of the United States*, 1773–1929 (New York, 1929).

MANUFACTURING

(Chapters III, XV, XX, XXVII)

The best and most complete study of manufacturing is Victor S. Clark, *History of Manufactures in the United States*, 1607–1929 (3 vols., Washington, 1929), one of the series published by the Carnegie Institution on the economic history of the United States. In addition to much detailed information on our major industries, it contains an extensive bibliography in the third volume. An older book is J. Leander Bishop, *A History of American Manufactures from* 1608 *to* 1860 (3 vols., Philadelphia, 1866); although valuable on the colonial period the organization of the material is faulty. Carroll D. Wright, *The Industrial Evolution of the United States* (Meadville, 1897), is merely a compilation, drawn largely from Bishop and the *Census*. Uncritical collections of interesting facts are: Albert S. Bolles, *The Industrial History of the United States* (Norwich, Conn., 1878); B. J. Lossing, *History of American Industries and Arts* (Philadelphia, 1878), and Chauncey M. Depew (Ed.), *One Hundred Years of American Commerce* (2 vols., New York, 1895). More helpful but sometimes sketchy is M. Keir, *Industries of America: Manufacturing* (New York, 1928), which may be supplemented by the same author's *Epic of Industry* (New Haven, 1926, one of the Pageant of America series), a pictorial portrayal of our industrial growth. Rolla M. Tryon, *Household Manufactures in the United States*, 1640–1860 (Chicago, 1917), is the authority on this one-time main aspect of manufacturing. Material on the South may be found in James C. Ballagh (Ed.), *Economic History of the South* (Vols. V and VI of *The South in the Building of the Nation*, Philadelphia, 1910). Callender's *Selections*, Flügel and Faulkner's *Readings*, and Bogart and Thompson's *Readings* contain a variety of source material on manufacturing.

There are no general histories of manufacturing limited to the colonial period: that aspect of colonial development has been relatively neglected. One must therefore rely on the general accounts already cited; on period sectional histories, contemporary descriptions, and histories of particular industries. Two excellent sectional histories are William B. Weeden, *Economic and Social History of New England*, 1620 *to* 1789 (2 vols., Boston, 1890), and Philip A. Bruce, *Economic History of Virginia in the Seventeenth Century* (2 vols., New York, 1895).

The best contemporary accounts of colonial industry are given by Andrew Burnaby, *Travels through the Middle Settlements in North America*, 1759–1760 (London, 1798; reprinted, New York, 1904). Peter Kalm,

Travels in North America (2nd ed., London, 1772); William Douglass, *British Settlements in North America* (2 vols., London, 1760); and Edmund Burke, *An Account of the European Settlements in America* (London, 1757). The excellent collections of source materials in E. B. O'Callaghan (Ed.), *Documents Relative to the Colonial History of the State of New York* (15 vols., Albany, 1856–87), and the New Jersey *Archives* (First series, 28 vols., Newark, 1881—; Trenton, 1893) should especially be mentioned. A compilation from contemporary newspapers, is A. C. Prime, *The Arts and Crafts in Philadelphia, Maryland, and South Carolina*, 1721–1785 (Topsfield, Mass., 1929).

For the next period, between the Revolution and the Civil War, there are a few general studies but all are old and for the most part mere compilations of information about particular industries. The best summaries of our industrial development are given in the introductions to the volume on manufactures of the *Eighth Census* (Washington, 1860), and in the volume on manufactures of the *Tenth Census* (Washington, 1880). Also worth while is Thomas P. Kettel, *Eighty Years' Progress* (New York, 1861), although it lacks a comprehensive grasp. Vera Shlakman, *Economic History of a Factory Town: A Study of Chicopee, Massachusetts* (Northampton, Mass., 1935), has written an interesting case study. A regional study is I. Lippincott, *A History of Manufactures in the Ohio Valley to the Year 1860* (New York, 1914).

The most reliable accounts of manufactures during this second period, however, are to be found in government documents. In addition to the *Census* accounts already mentioned, Alexander Hamilton, *Report on Manufactures* (1791), probably the ablest state paper on this subject, may be found in any edition of his *Works*, in *American State Papers, Finance*, Vol. I, and conveniently in F. W. Taussig, *State Papers and Speeches on the Tariff* (Cambridge, 1892), 1–107. This may be supplemented by A. H. Cole (Ed.), *Industrial and Commercial Correspondence of Alexander Hamilton, Anticipating His Report on Manufactures* (Chicago, 1928). Two other official reports are Albert Gallatin, *Report on Manufactures* (1810), in *American State Papers, Finance*, Vol. II, in *Writings*, in *Niles Register*, in Condy Raguet's *Banner of the Constitution*, and in F. W. Taussig, *State Papers and Speeches on the Tariff*, 109–213; and Louis McLane, *Report on Manufactures*, House Doc. No. 308, 22nd Congress, 1st sess., (2 vols., Washington, 1833). Both of these contain descriptive material of considerable value, although the statistics which they present are worth little.

Good statistical presentations, often of data not easily found in official documents, are contained in Tench Coxe, *A View of the United States* (Philadelphia, 1794); Timothy Pitkin, *A Statistical View of the Commerce of the United States* (New Haven, 1835); and Adam Seybert, *Statistical Annals*, etc. (Philadelphia, 1818). Tench Coxe made a careful digest of the material on manufactures in the census of 1810, printed in *American State Papers, Finance*, Vol. II (Washington, 1814), 666–812.

The works of travelers and observers in the United States during this period often contain interesting material on industrial conditions; among the best of these secondary though contemporary sources of information are Daniel Blowe, *A Geographical, Historical, Commercial, and Agricultural View of the United States of America* (London, 1820); John Bristed, *The Resources of the United States of America* (New York, 1818); W. Winterbotham, *An Historical, Geographical, Commercial, and Philosophical View of the United States of America* (1st Amer. ed., 4 vols., New York, 1796). The biographies of two interesting contemporaries are K. W. Rowe, *Mathew Carey: A Study in American Economic Development* (Baltimore, 1933), and Broadus Mitchell, *William Gregg, Factory Master of the Old South* (Chapel Hill, 1928).

For the era since the Civil War the closest approach to a period study of manufacturing developments is E. D. Durand, *American Industry and Commerce* (New York, 1930), which is based largely on census material since the author directed the 1910 census. A clear conspectus of the development of manufactures is *A Graphic Analysis of the Census of Manufacturing, 1849–1919* (New York, 1923) by the National Industrial Conference Board. The statistical bases for original study are the decennial *Census Reports*, especially those of 1880 and 1900, which should be supplemented by the intercensal reports of 1904 and 1914, and the biennial census of manufactures between 1921 and 1937. A survey of general economic conditions is given in *Recent Economic Changes* (2 vols., Bureau of Economic Research, New York, 1929), of which a brief summary is presented in E. E. Hunt (Ed.), *An Audit of America* (New York, 1930).

Many authors have written books presenting a clear picture of industrial developments at a particular time or over a short period and in so doing have incidentally touched on historical developments. Among these may be mentioned the following: P. Leroy-Beaulieu, *The United States in the Twentieth Century* (New York, 1906), by a French economist; B. Baruch, *American Industry in the War* (New York, 1941); G. B. Clarkson, *Industrial America in the World War* (Boston, 1923); J. C. Malin, *The United States after the World War* (Boston, 1930); E. Greenwood, *Aladdin U. S. A.* (New York, 1928); R. G. Cleland and O. Hardy, *March of Industry* (Los Angeles, 1929); A. B. Adams, *Our Economic Revolution* (Norman, Okla., 1933); P. T. Warshow, *Representative American Industries* (New York, 1928); E. L. Bogart and C. Landon, *Modern Industry* (New York, 1936); E. B. Alderfer and H. E. Michl, *Economics of American Industry* (New York, 1942); J. G. Glover and W. B. Cornell, *The Development of American Industries: Their Economic Significance* (New York, 1941); E. G. Nourse and Associates, *America's Capacity to Produce* (Brookings Institution, Washington, 1934); H. Jerome, *Mechanization in Industry* (New York, 1934); and Temporary National Economic Committee, *The Structure of Industry* (Washington, 1941). On the period of World War II material is necessarily still fragmentary and ephemeral in nature but some ideas of the colossal industrial task performed may be obtained from the reports of the War Production Board chairman, especially *War Production in 1944* (Washington, 1945) and *Wartime Production Achievements and the Reconversion Outlook* (Washington, 1945). Books on invention often contain valuable material on technological changes. Probably the best of these is W. Kaempffert (Ed.), *Popular History of American Invention* (2 vols., New York, 1924). Others are George Iles, *Leading American Inventors* (New York, 1912); E. W. Byrn, *Progress of Invention in the Nineteenth Century* (New York, 1900); Holland Thompson, *The Age of Invention* (New Haven, 1921); B. A. Fiske, *Invention, the Master-Key to Progress* (New York, 1921); and E. Cressy, *Discoveries and Inventions of the Twentieth Century* (3rd ed., rev., New York, 1930). Standard biographies of outstanding inventors like Thomas Edison or Cyrus McCormick should also be consulted. For some of the misuses of the patent system consult Temporary National Economic Committee, *Patents and Free Enterprise* (Washington, 1941) and for some far-reaching effects see U. S. National Resources Committee, *Technological Trends and National Policy* (Washington, 1937).

When we turn to writings on particular industries, we often find a wealth of material; this is particularly true of textiles so that it will be possible to mention only a few. The tedious business of making cloth in the colonial home is well described in Alice M. Earle, *Home Life in Colonial Days* (New York, 1898). Of contemporary works of the nineteenth century the most important are Nathan Appleton, *The Introduction of the Power Loom* (Lowell, 1858); R. H. Baird, *The American Cotton Spinner* (Philadelphia, 1851); Samuel Batchelder, *Introduction and Early Progress of the Cotton Manufacture in the United States* (Boston, 1863); James Montgomery, *Cotton Manufacture of the United States Compared with that of Great Britain* (Glasgow, 1840); George S. White, *Memoir of Samuel Slater, The Father of American Manufactures* (2nd ed., Philadelphia, 1836); Levi Woodbury, *A Report upon the Cultivation, Manufacture, and Foreign Trade in Cotton*, Exec. Doc. No. 146, 24th Cong., 1st sess. (Washington, Feb. 29, 1836), and in *Works*, III, 248. Later books are: William R. Bagnall, *The Textile Industries of the United States* [1639–1810] (Cambridge, 1893); M. T. Copeland, *The Cotton Manufacturing Industry in the United States* (Cambridge, 1912); C. F. Ware, *The Early New England Cotton Manufacture* (New York, 1931); N. S. B. Gras, *Casebook in Business History* (New York, 1939), which contains a valuable chapter on Samuel Slater and his textile mills; Broadus Mitchell, *The Rise of Cotton Mills in the South* (Baltimore, 1921); and also, with G. S. Mitchell, *The Industrial Revolution in the South* (Baltimore, 1930); and Boris Stern, *Mechanical Changes in the Cotton Textile Industry*, 1910 to 1936 (W.P.A. National Research Project, Philadelphia, 1937).

On textiles other than cotton some of the standard treatises are: A. H. Cole, *The American Wool Manufacture* (2 vols., Cambridge, 1926); S. N. D. North, *A Century of American Wool Manufacture*, 1790–1890 (Boston, 1895); Boris Stern, *Mechanical Changes in the Woolen and Worsted Industries*, 1910 to 1936 (W. P. A. National Research Project, Philadelphia, 1938); A. H. Cole and H. F. Williamson, *The American Carpet Manufacture* (Cambridge, 1941); P. H. Nystrom, *Textiles* (New York, 1916); and W. C. Wyckoff, *The Silk Goods of America* (New York, 1880).

On the iron and steel industries there is likewise an extensive literature which can only be sampled here. The standard work on iron is J. M. Swank, *History of the Manufacture of Iron in All Ages, and Particularly in the United States from Colonial Times to* 1891 (2nd ed., Philadelphia, 1892). Some interesting early accounts are B. F. French, *The History of the Rise and Progress of the Iron Trade of the United States,* 1621–1857 (New York, 1858); J. P. Lesley, *The Iron Manufacturers Guide* (New York, 1859); J. B. Pearse, *A Concise History of the Iron Manufacture of the American Colonies up to the Revolution, and of Pennsylvania until the Present Time* (Philadelphia, 1876). Other historical accounts are: J. R. Smith, *The Story of Iron and Steel* (New York, 1913); F. W. Taussig, "Iron Industry in the United States," in the *Quarterly Journal of Economics,* XIV, 143–70, 475–508; A. C. Bining, *British Regulation of the Colonial Iron Industry* (Philadelphia, 1933); Kathleen Bruce, *Virginia Iron Manufacture in the Slave Era* (New York, 1930); S. J. Goodale, *Chronology of Iron and Steel* (Pittsburgh, 1920); J. G. Butler, Jr., *Fifty Years of Iron and Steel* (Youngstown, 1923), by an industrialist; J. B. Walker, *The Story of Steel* (New York, 1926); and H. N. Casson, *The Romance of Steel* (New York, 1907). H. B. Vanderblue and W. L. Crum, *The Iron Industry in Prosperity and Depression* (Chicago, 1927) touch on the "feast or famine" character of the industry. A popular discussion of nineteenth century iron discoveries and of progress in iron and steel manufacture is S. Holbrook, *Iron Brew* (New York, 1943).

Closely related to the iron industry is coal, on which the material is plentiful but unorganized. Brief surveys will be found in Keir, in Taylor Thom, *Petroleum and Coal* (Princeton, 1929), and in H. Eavenson, *Coal Through the Ages* (New York, 1935). On coal fields and production, see H. Eavenson, *The First Century and a Quarter of the American Coal Industry* (Pittsburgh, 1941) or M. R. Campbell, *Coal Fields of the U. S.* (Professional Paper 100A, U. S. Geological Survey, 1922). Other helpful authorities are Walton Hamilton and H. Wright, *The Case of Bituminous Coal* (New York, 1926); Walter Voskuil, *Minerals in Modern Industry* (New York, 1930), and the U. S. National Resources Committee Report on *Energy Resources and National Policy* (Washington, 1939). Since 1928 the American Mining Congress has published a *Yearbook* on mechanical progress.

On the oil industry, see Thom and the Resources Committee just mentioned, and also George W. Stocking, *The Oil Industry and the Competitive System* (New York, 1925), which was long the standard work. Two later books contain much picturesque detail: Paul H. Giddens, *The Birth of the Oil Industry* (New York, 1938) and S. W. Tait, Jr., *The Wild-Catters* (Princeton, 1946). Annually, the American Petroleum Institute makes a report in its *Quarterly* on the petroleum reserves of the nation and this is widely quoted. Helpful suggestions may also be found in many government reports, geological surveys, and of course the biographies of John D. Rockefeller and many others.

The shoe industry, which so well illustrates the evolution of the factory system, is covered in Blanche Hazard, *Organization of the Boot and Shoe Industry in Massachusetts before* 1875 (Cambridge, 1921), of which a brief version was printed in the *Quarterly Journal of Economics* for February 1913; Frederick J. Allen, *The Shoe Industry* (New York, 1922), which is the standard work on the industry; and in a quaint little volume by Fred A. Gannon, *Shoe Making: Old and New* (Salem, Mass., 1911). The automobile industry, whose rise was so phenomenal in the twentieth century, may be studied in R. C. Epstein, *The Automobile Industry: Its Economic and Commercial Development* (Cambridge, 1928); L. H. Seltzer, *A Financial History of the American Automobile Industry* (1928); T. F. McManus and N. Beasley, *Men, Money, and Motors* (1929); E. P. Norwood, *Ford, Men, and Methods* (1931); and R. H. Graves, *The Triumph of an Idea* (New York, 1934). Useful factual information is available in the Automobile Manufacturers Association, *Automobile Facts and Figures* (Detroit, annually since 1919).

A scholarly volume on the forest industries is R. G. Albion, *Forests and Sea Power* (Cambridge, 1926). A more general but less careful work is J. E. Defebaugh, *History of the Lumber Industry of America* (4 vols., Chicago, 1906–1907). Interesting material is contained in A. L. Cross, *Eighteenth Century Documents Relating to the Royal Forests, the Sheriffs, and Smuggling* (New York, 1928), and in Eleanor L. Lord, *Industrial Experiments in the British Colonies of North America* (Johns Hopkins University Studies, Baltimore, 1898), which devotes most attention to naval stores.

The fisheries have been best described in two government reports: Lorenzo Sabine, *Report on the Principal Fisheries of the American Seas* (Treasury Department, Washington, 1853), and G. Brown Goode and associates, *The Fisheries and Fishery Industries of the United States* (7 vols., Washington, 1884–87). Other good accounts of the fisheries and of whaling are Harold A. Innis, *The Cod Fisheries, the History of an International Economy* (Toronto, 1940); R. McFarland, *A History of the New England Fisheries* (Publ. Univ. of Pa., Philadelphia, 1911); W. S. Tower, *A History of the American Whale Fishery* (Publ. Univ. of Pa., Philadelphia, 1907), E. P. Hohman, *The American Whaleman* (New York, 1928), E. K. Chesterton, *Whalers and Whaling* (Philadelphia, 1926); and T. Jenkins, *A History of the Whale Fisheries* (New York, 1921).

Other significant studies of particular industries are: R. A. Clemen, *The American Livestock and Meat Industry* (New York, 1923), C. B. Kuhlman, *Development of the Flour Milling Industry in the United States* (Boston, 1929); Malcolm MacLaren, *The Rise of the Electrical Industry during the Nineteenth Century* (Princeton, 1943); E. C. May, *The Canning Clan* (New York, 1938); W. G. Lathrop, *The Brass Industry in the U. S.* (Mt. Carmel, Conn., 1926); J. A. Guthrie, *The Newsprint Paper Industry* (Cambridge, 1941); and T. A. Rickard, *A History of American Mining* (New York, 1932).

Often the best description of an individual industry is found in one of the general treatises by Clark, Bishop, Keir, Glover and Cornell, or Alderfer and Michl. Monographic material may be found in the *Encyclopaedia of Social Sciences* (15 vols., New York, 1930–35). Among the W. P. A. National Research Project publications on recent changes in industrial techniques are studies on mechanization in the brick, cigar, lumber, and a variety of other industries, and on productivity in selected industries and on mining technology (Philadelphia, 1937–39). Good popular accounts of various industries are also to be found in *Fortune* magazine, published monthly since 1930 and indexed every third year, and more scholarly accounts in the *Journal of Economic and Business History*, published in Cambridge between 1928 and 1932. H. P. Beers, *Bibliographies in American Histories* (New York, 1942) contains a long list of bibliographies on specific industries, pp. 143–47.

On the subject of power to run industries comparatively little has been written. The best summary is to be found in Keir and there is scattered material in Clark, in the many writings on specific industries, and of course in those on coal, oil, and electricity. Also, there are: Oliver Evans, *The Young Mill-wright and Miller's Guide* (9th ed., Philadelphia, 1836), a technical contemporary work containing some helpful plates in the appendix; Marion Rawson, *Little Old Mills* (New York, 1935); "The History of the Steam Engine in America," in the *Journal of the Franklin Institute*, Vol. 72, pp. 253–68; C. R. Daugherty, "Horsepower Equipment in the U. S., 1869–1929," in the *American Economic Review*, Vol. 23 (1933), 428–40; C. R. Daugherty, A. Horton, and R. Davenport, *Power Capacity and Production in the U. S.*, U. S. Geol. Survey Water-Supply Paper No. 579 (Washington, 1928); R. B. Fuller, "United States Industrialization," in *Fortune*, February 1940; and the Federal Power Commission, *Industrial Electric Power*, 1939–46 (Washington, 1946).

Localization of industry has been rather widely investigated by theorists (Alfred Marshall, Alfred Weber), economic geographers, and economic historians. Clark, Keir, Durand, and the *Encyclopaedia of Social Sciences* all have helpful discussions of the subject. A fine early study is Frederick S. Hall, "Localization of Industries, 1890 and 1900," in the Twelfth *Census* in the volume on *Manufactures*, Vol. 7 (Washington, 1902), 190–214; a sequel to this by Joseph D. Lewis may be found in the *Census of Manufactures* of 1905 (Washington, 1905), and, as part of the Fifteenth *Census*, Tracy Thompson prepared a pamphlet, *Location of Manufactures, 1899–1929* (Washington, 1933). Also noteworthy are F. B. Garver, F. M. Boddy, and A. J. Nixon, *The Location of Manufactures in the U. S., 1899–1929* (Minneapolis, 1933); Glenn McLaughlin, *Growth of American Manufacturing Areas* (Pittsburgh, 1938); Edgar M. Hoover, Jr., *Location Theory and the Shoe and Leather Industry* (Cambridge, 1937) and D. B. Creamer, *Is Industry Decentralizing?* (Philadephia, 1935).

Since capital has been discussed in the chapters on manufacturing references on that will be cited here. The subject has received but little attention until recent years. Much that has been done in the field is either of dubious value or quite technical in a statistical way, and there is little material on the nineteenth century. The attempts of the Census Bureau to measure manufacturing capital were, statistically speaking, of questionable value. Probably the most scholarly work has been done by Simon Kuznets in his *National Income and Capital Formation, 1919–1935* (New York, 1937), his *Commodity Flow and Capital Formation* (New York, 1938)

and his *Capital Formation*, 1879–1938 (Philadelphia, 1941). More useful for the layman are 20th Century Fund, *America's Needs and Resources*
(New York, 1947), and Carl Snyder, *Capitalism the Creator* (New York,
1940). Useful estimates on savings between 1850 and 1910 appear in W. I.
King, *The Wealth and Income of the People of the United States* (New
York, 1915), 132. Revealing anecdotes may be found in the biographies of
men like Carnegie, Frick, Rockefeller, and Ford, who started with nothing
and built up tremendous fortunes. Pig iron production was once considered
a fair index of capital formation and Standard and Poor's Corporation,
Basic Statistics (New York, 1938) has information back to 1884. Valuable
statistical material is available in The National Industrial Conference
Board, *The Economic Almanac*, published annually (New York). Likewise essential is Cleona Lewis, *America's Stake in International Investment*
(New York, 1938).

The idea that the depression was caused by excess savings is developed
in two books put out by the Brookings Institution: Maurice Leven, H. G.
Moulton and C. Warburton, *America's Capacity to Consume* (Washington,
1934) and H. G. Moulton, *The Formation of Capital* (Washington,
1935). A brief but pungent answer to these is Benjamin M. Anderson, Jr.,
"Eating the Seed Corn," *The Chase Economic Bulletin*, Vol. XVI, No. 2
(New York, 1936). An excellent article is M. Abramowitz, "Savings and
Investment: Profits vs. Prosperity," in *American Economic Review* (Supplement, June 1942).

The development of the corporation likewise has received but little
attention. Probably the best general account is C. C. Abbott, *The Rise
of the Business Corporation* (Ann Arbor, 1936). This may be supplemented by more specialized studies like J. G. Blandi, *Maryland Business
Corporation*, 1783–1852 (Baltimore, 1934); R. C. Larcom, *The Delaware Corporation* (Baltimore, 1937); and S. Livermore, "Corporations
and Unlimited Liability," *Journal of Political Economy*, XLIII, 674 ff.
L. Steffens, "New Jersey: A Traitor State," *McClure's Magazine*, XXV,
41 ff., is illuminating but should be used with care. Useful statistical
material on large corporations is available in Twentieth Century Fund,
Big Business: Its Growth and Its Place (New York, 1937). For the
more constitutional and legal aspects of corporation history, see A. A.
Berle and G. S. Means, *The Modern Corporation and Private Property*
(New York, 1932); G. C. Henderson, *The Position of Foreign Corporations in American Constitutional Law* (Cambridge, 1918); and A. C.
McLaughlin, "The Court, the Corporation and Conkling," *American Historical Review*, XLVI, No. 1 (October 1940).

TRUSTS

(Chapters XXI, XXVII)

The trust movement has a voluminous literature and only a few general
works can be cited here. A good book to start with because it is clear and
fairly complete is Eliot Jones, *The Trust Problem* (New York, 1924).

A more thorough approach is through the Sherman Anti-trust Act of 1890, the background of which is furnished by the *Report on Investigation of Trusts,* House Rep. No. 3112, 50th Cong., 1st Sess. (Washington, 1889). The history of this act is told by A. H. Walker, *History of the Sherman Law of the United States of America* (New York, 1910); and O. W. Knauth, *The Policy of the United States Towards Industrial Monopoly* (New York, 1914). Volumes I and XIX of the *Report of the Industrial Commission* give a view of the situation at the dawn of the century. L. H. Haney, *Business Organization and Combination* (New York, 1913) gives especial attention to the forms of organization. John Moody, *The Truth About Trusts* (5th ed., New York, 1929) is written by an experienced businessman; his *Masters of Capital* (New Haven, 1919) is a popular account of some of the highlights of the period. J. W. Jenks and W. E. Clark, *The Trust Problem* (5th ed., New York, 1929) is a useful survey. Further helpful information is available in H. R. Seager and C.A. Gulick, Jr., *Trusts and Corporation Problems* (New York, 1929); W. Z. Ripley (Ed.), *Trusts, Pools, and Corporations* (rev. ed., Boston, 1916); W. H. S. Stevens (Ed.), *Industrial Combinations and Trusts* (New York, 1913); M. W. Watkins, *Industrial Combinations and Public Policy* (New York, 1927); H. W. Laidler, *Concentration of Control in American Industry* (New York, 1931); and A. R. Burns, *The Decline of Competition* (New York, 1936). A good summary is Twentieth Century Fund, *Big Business: Its Growth and Its Place* (New York, 1937).

Regulation and control of trusts, including changes in federal policy, are discussed in C. R. Van Hise, *Concentration and Control* (rev. ed., New York, 1914); G. C. Henderson, *The Federal Trade Commission* (New Haven, 1924); and M. W. Watkins, *Public Regulation of Competitive Practices in Business Enterprise* (New York, 1940). G. M. Modlin and A. M. McIsaac, *Social Control of Industry* (Boston, 1938) is an excellent short study. On the N.I.R.A. consult L. S. Lyon, P. T. Homan and others, *The National Recovery Administration* (Brookings Institution, Washington, 1935); and H. S. Johnson, *The Blue Eagle from Egg to Earth* (New York, 1935), by its first director. A philosophical and semi-popular treatment of the subject by a prewar trust buster is Thurman Arnold, *Folklore of Capitalism* (New Haven, 1937).

Of particular combinations most attention has been directed to the Standard Oil Company, on which may be consulted Ida M. Tarbell, *History of the Standard Oil Company* (2 vols., New York, 1904), a fearless exposé; John T. Flynn, *God's Gold* (New York, 1932), a popular and not unsympathetic biography; and finally Allan Nevins, *John D. Rockefeller* (New York, 1940), which is perhaps the best balanced. Studies of other combinations have been made by H. R. Mussey, *Combinations in the Mining Industry: a Study of Concentration in Lake Superior Iron Ore Production* (New York, 1905); Abraham Berglund, *The United States Steel Corporation* (New York, 1907); A. Cotter, *The Authentic History of the United States Steel Corporation* (New York, 1916), a favorable account; *Report of the Commissioner of Corporations on the Steel Industry* (Washington, 1911); Eliot Jones, *The Anthracite*

Coal Combination in the United States (Cambridge, 1914). F. A. Fetter, *The Masquerade of Monopoly* (New York, 1931) is an exposé of the oil and steel trusts among others by one who believes competition can and should be restored and maintained. The findings of numerous official investigations are to be found in the *Reports* of the Federal Trade Commission. The notes of Clarence Barron, long publisher of the *Wall Street Journal*, have been edited by A. Pound and S. T. Moore as *More They Told Barron* (New York, 1931) and give an idea of how some of the business tycoons of a generation ago regarded one another and played the game.

Monographs printed for the use of the Temporary National Economic Committee include No. 16, *Antitrust in Action*; No. 18, *Trade Association Survey*; No. 21, *Competition and Monopoly in American Industry*; and No. 43, *The Motion Picture Industry—A Pattern of Control* (Washington, 1941), all carefully reviewed during 1941 in *The American Economic Review*.

CURRENCY AND FINANCE

(Chapters VI, XIV, XXV, XXXI)

There are only three significant financial histories of the United States that cover all or most of the years since the founding of the first colonies. They are Albert S. Bolles, *Financial History of the United States, 1774–1885* (3 vols., New York, 1879–86); Davis R. Dewey, *Financial History of the United States* (12th ed., New York, 1939), for many years the standard reference; and W. J. Shultz and M. R. Cain, *Financial Development of the United States* (New York, 1937), which is the best today. These may be supplemented by the voluminous literature on the history of money, of commercial, central, or investment banking, or of government finance. See also M. Masui, *A Bibliography of Finance* (Tokyo, 1935).

Wampum, the Indian money, is described by W. B. Weeden, *Indian Money as a Factor in New England Civilization* (Johns Hopkins University Studies, Baltimore, 1884). Metallic money is described in D. K. Watson, *History of American Coinage* (New York, 1899); S. S. Crosby, *A Historical Account of American Coinage* (Boston, 1875); G. S. Evans, *Illustrated History of the U. S. Mint* (Philadelphia, 1891); but is best depicted in Nei! Carothers, *Fractional Money* (New York, 1930); A. B. Hepburn, *History of Coinage and Currency in the United States* (New York, 1903, rev. ed., 1915); and C. Nettels, *The Money Supply of the American Colonies before 1720* (Madison, Wis., 1934). There is also much material on this in the various money and banking texts mentioned below.

On bimetallism and the silver movement, there is a mass of controversial literature but little of permanent value. In addition to Hepburn and Carothers see J. L. Laughlin, *History of Bimetallism in the United States* (New York, 1900); F. W. Taussig, *The Silver Situation in the United States* (New York, 1893); A. D. Noyes, *Forty Years of American Finance* (New York, 1909); and H. B. Russell, *International Monetary Conferences* (New York, 1898). On more recent silver developments, consult

R. B. Westerfield, *Our Silver Debacle* (New York, 1936); N. Carothers, *Silver in America* (Bull. No. 11, prepared for the Association of Reserve City Bankers, Chicago, 1936), or the many but elusive writings of Herbert M. Bratter. Money and banking texts are also helpful here. The gold standard may be understood by consulting E. W. Kemmerer *Gold and the Gold Standard* (Princeton, 1944) or *Kemmerer on Money* (New York, 1934), or the various money and banking texts. The arguments for a managed currency are in G. F. Warren and F. A. Pearson, *Prices* (New York, 1933); Irving Fisher, *Stabilizing the Dollar* (New York, 1925); or F. D. Graham and R. Whittlesey, *Golden Avalanche* (Princeton, 1939). Other books dealing with recent monetary events are L. Pasvolsky, *Current Monetary Issues* (Brookings Institution, Washington, 1933); J. P. Warburg, *The Money Muddle* (New York, 1934); C. O. Hardy, *Is There Enough Gold?* (Washington, 1936); O. M. W. Sprague, *Recovery and Common Sense* (Boston, 1934); and J. D. Paris, *Monetary Policies of the United States, 1932–38* (New York, 1938). Some of the implications of these monetary changes are discussed in *Money and the Law* (New York University Law Review Supplement, 1945).

Writings on paper money are very voluminous despite the fact that this kind of money is only 250 years old. For the colonial period see Henry Phillips, Jr., *Historical Sketches of the Paper Currency of the American Colonies* (2 vols., Roxbury, Mass., 1865); W. G. Sumner, *History of American Currency* (New York, 1884); C. J. Bullock, *Essays on the Monetary History of the United States* (New York, 1900), and R. Lester, *Monetary Experiments* (Princeton, 1939). There are also valuable suggestions scattered through W. B. Weeden, *Social and Economic History of New England* (2 vols., Boston, 1890) and C. Nettels, *Roots of American Civilization* (New York, 1938). Colonial monetary and financial history is best studied in the separate colonies, since conditions differed in the various sections, and for this purpose the following list of specialized works is suggested: W. McF. Davis, "Currency and Banking in the Province of Massachusetts Bay," in *Publications of the American Economic Association*, Third Series, Vol. I and II (New York, 1900–1901); *Colonial Currency Reprints* (4 vols., 1910–11); C. H. J. Douglas, *Financial History of Massachusetts to the American Revolution* (New York, 1897); H. Bronson, *Historical Account of Connecticut Currency* (Papers of New Haven Colonial Historical Society, I, New Haven, 1865); S. S. Rider and B. R. Potter, *Some Accounts of the Bills of Credit or Paper Money of Rhode Island, 1710–86* (Historical Tracts, No. 8, Providence, R. I., 1880); D. L. Kemmerer, *Path to Freedom* (Princeton, 1940), for New Jersey; T. K. Worthington, *Finances of Pennsylvania* (Publ. Amer. Econ. Assoc., II, 1890); C. P. Gould, *Money and Transportation in Maryland, 1720–65* (Baltimore, 1915); W. Z. Ripley, *Financial History of Virginia, 1609–1776* (New York, 1895); P. A. Bruce, *Economic History of Virginia* (2 vols., New York, 1896); and a vigorous contemporary account by William Douglass, *Discourse Concerning the Currencies of the British Plantations in America* [1740] (Studies of Amer. Econ. Assoc., II, No. 5, 1897).

For the period from 1789 to the Civil War our paper money was in bank notes; consequently, the bibliographical selections will be found under the topic of banking for that period. Indeed, the Greenbacks are the only form of treasury bill issued since the adoption of the Constitution. The outstanding book on them is W. C. Mitchell, *A History of Greenbacks* (Chicago, 1903), but in addition there are: E. G. Spaulding, *History of the Legal Tender Paper Money Issued During the Great Rebellion* (Buffalo, 1869); Don Barrett; *The Greenbacks and Resumption of Specie Payments, 1862–1879* (Cambridge, 1931); J. J. Knox, *United States Notes* (New York, 1894); and A. D. Noyes, *Forty Years of American Finance*, already mentioned. Southern finance is described in E. A. Smith, *History of the Confederate Treasury* (Richmond, 1901) and J. C. Schwab, *Confederate States of America* (New York, 1901).

There was little if any banking in this country in the modern sense before the Revolution. The best introduction to the history of modern banking is through those money and banking texts that use the historical approach. The best of these include Horace White, *Money and Banking* (New York, 1895; rev. ed., 1935), concise and pungent; L. A. Rufener, *Money and Banking* (Boston, 1934); R. B. Westerfield, *Money, Credit and Banking* (New York, 1938), which is almost encyclopaedic; F. A. Bradford, *Money and Banking* (New York, 1941); and H. E. Miller, *Banking Theories in the United States before* 1860 (Cambridge, 1927). Longer studies are D. R. Dewey, *State Banking before the Civil War* (Washington, 1910) and R. E. Chaddock, *The Safety Fund Banking System in New York*, 1829–66 (Washington, 1910). Two valuable contemporary studies of a century ago are Condy Raguet, *A Treatise on Currency and Banking* (Philadelphia, 1840) and W. M. Gouge, *A Short History of Paper Money and Banking in the United States* (New York, 1835).

On the national banking system consult A. M. Davis, *The Origin of the National Banking System* (Boston, 1910) and the various specialized reports made to the National Monetary Commission, such as G. E. Barnett, *State Banks and Trust Companies* (Washington, 1911); O. M. W. Sprague, *History of Crises under the National Banking System* (Washington, 1910); D. Kinley, *The Use of Credit Instruments* (Washington, 1910); and J. G. Cannon, *Clearing Houses* (Washington, 1910). The text of the law and its numerous amendments appear in *Laws of the United States; Concerning Money, Banking and Loans, 1778–1909* (Washington, 1910) and in A. S. Pratt and Sons, *Federal Banking Law Service* (Washington, 1936).

Our central banks, including the First and Second Banks of the United States and the Federal Reserve System, and to a lesser degree the Independent Treasury System, have been intensively studied. The First Bank is described by M. St. C. Clarke and D. A. Hall, *Legislative and Documentary History of the First Bank of the United States* (Washington, 1832). D. R. Dewey and J. T. Holdsworth wrote *The First and Second Banks of the United States* (Washington, 1911) for the National Monetary Commission. The standard treatise on the Second Bank, however, is

R. C. H. Catterall, *The Second Bank of the United States* (Chicago, 1903). David Kinley, *The History, Organization and Influence of the Independent Treasury of the United States* (New York, 1892) is still best on this topic. Since both the First and Second Bank and the Independent Treasury System were important political issues in their day, considerable space is devoted to them in the history books on the period and in the biographies of such persons as Alexander Hamilton, Thomas Jefferson, Albert Gallatin, Andrew Jackson, Henry Clay, Martin Van Buren, James K. Polk, and others.

The Federal Reserve System is clearly explained by E. W. Kemmerer, *The ABC of the Federal Reserve System* (rev. ed., Princeton, 1938). Authoritative are H. P. Willis, *The Federal Reserve System* (New York, 1923), by the former secretary of the Federal Reserve Board; W. P. G. Harding, *The Formative Period of the Federal Reserve System* (New York, 1925), by a former member of the board; Carter Glass, *An Adventure in Constructive Finance* (New York, 1927), by one of the framers of the Federal Reserve Act; and P. M. Warburg, *The Federal Reserve System: Its Origin and Growth* (2 vols., New York, 1930), by a competent adviser. The workings of the system are described in a number of special studies, among which may be mentioned E. A. Goldenweiser, *The Federal Reserve System in Operation* (New York, 1925); W. R. Burgess, *The Reserve Banks and the Money Market* (rev. ed., New York, 1936); and S. E. Harris, *Twenty Years of Federal Reserve Policy: Including an Extended Discussion of the Monetary Crisis*, 1927–33 (Cambridge, 1933). More recent changes are explained in the money and banking texts by Bradford or Westerfield already mentioned. For current events see the *Federal Reserve Bulletin* (Washington, monthly since 1915) and the annual *Reports of the Board of Governors* (Washington, since 1915). Statistics from the *Bulletin* for over twenty-five years are compiled in *Banking and Monetary Statistics* (Washington, 1941), and the latest regulations are available in Pratt's *Banking Service* mentioned above. Two other statistical sources on banks are the *Annual Report of the Comptroller of Currency* (Washington, since 1864) and the *Annual Report of the Federal Deposit Insurance Corporation* (Washington, since 1934).

For a simple explanation of the beginnings of investment banking, see J. Moody, *Masters of Capital* (New Haven, 1921). Fuller information is found in H. P. Willis and J. I. Bogen, *Investment Banking* (New York, 1936) and Margaret Myers and others, *The New York Money Market* (4 vols., New York, 1931–32). Supplementary material is available in L. Corey, *The House of Morgan* (New York, 1930); E. P. Oberholtzer, *Jay Cooke, Financier of the Civil War* (2 vols., Philadelphia, 1907); and H. Larson, *Jay Cooke* (Cambridge, 1936). The money trust investigation is probably best studied in the original, *Investigation of Financial and Monetary Conditions in the U. S.—before a Subcommittee of the Committee on Banking and Currency* (3 vols., Washington, 1913). The shameful abuse of public confidence by some Wall Street magnates is well told in Ferdinand Pecora, *Wall Street under Oath* (New York, 1939), by the man who conducted the complex investigations. A good recent study is Charles C. Abbott, *The New York Bond Market*, 1920–30 (New York, 1937). The specialist is referred to the United States Securities and Exchange Commission, *Annual Report* (Washington, beginning 1934) and other releases and regulations.

The history of the stock market appears in M. G. Myers, *The New York Money Market*, just mentioned; J. E. Meeker, *The Work of the Stock Exchange* (New York, 1930); S. S. Pratt, *The Work of Wall Street* (New York, 1926); New York Stock Exchange, *Year Book* (New York, 1938); and A. D. Noyes, *The Market Place* (Boston, 1938). Henry Clews, *Fifty Years in Wall Street* (New York, 1908) is anecdotal. J. G. Martin, *A Century of Finance* (Boston, 1898) has material on the Boston exchange. The spirit of the prosperous 1920's is obtained from reading the notes of the former publisher of the *Wall Street Journal* in Arthur Pound and S. T. Moore, *They Told Barron* (New York, 1930).

On business cycles, see first the very brief summaries of year-by-year economic conditions, which appear in W. L. Thorp, *Business Annals* (Nat. Bur. Econ. Research, New York, 1926). Fuller accounts appear in O. C. Lightner, *History of Business Depressions* (New York, 1922); C. A. Collman, *Our Mysterious Panics*, 1830–1930 (New York, 1931); R. C. McGrane, *The Panic of 1837* (Chicago, 1924); and W. C. Mitchell, *Business Cycles* (New York, 1927), which is more theoretical but is one of the most authoritative works on the subject. Leonard Ayres' views on the Great Depression are set forth in *The Economics of Recovery* (New York, 1933). The specialist should consult J. A. Schumpeter's monumental *Business Cycles* (2 vols., New York, 1939).

Government finance in colonial times is treated in Dewey's *Financial History* mentioned in the first paragraph and in some of the financial histories of the individual colonies. On the Revolution, see Dewey or Bolles and also W. G. Sumner, *The Financier and Finances of the American Revolution* (2 vols., New York, 1891); E. P. Oberholtzer, *Robert Morris* (New York, 1905); C. J. Bullock, *Finances of the United States, 1775–1789, with Especial Reference to the Budget* (University of Wisconsin Bulletin, Madison, 1895); Henry Phillips, *Historical Sketches of American Paper Currency, Second Series* (Roxbury, Mass., 1865–66); Birch, *Historical Sketch of Continental Paper Money* (Philadelphia, 1843); and R. A. Bayley, *History of the National Loans of the United States* (Tenth Census of the United States, Vol. XIII, 1880). For the beginning of the national period biographies of Hamilton and Gallatin may be profitably consulted. Hamilton's and Gallatin's reports and papers are contained in *American State Papers, Finance* and in their respective works. A significant special work is E. G. Bourne, *The History of the Surplus Revenue of 1837* (New York, 1885). War financing in the last century is best studied in the standard financial histories but may be supplemented by F. C. Howe, *Taxation and Taxes in the United States under the Internal Revenue System* (New York, 1896) or Harley Lutz, *Public Finance* (3rd ed., New York, 1936) and by the memoirs or biographies of those who directed public affairs during this period, among whom may be mentioned: H. D. Capers, *The Life and Times of C. G. Memminger*

(Richmond, 1894); A. B. Hart, *Salmon Portland Chase* (Boston, 1889); H. McCullough, *Men and Measures of Half a Century* (New York, 1889); and John Sherman, *Recollections of Forty Years* (Chicago, 1895). On World War I finance, consult E. L. Bogart, *Direct and Indirect Costs of the Great World War* (Washington, 1920) and *War Costs and Their Financing* (New York, 1921). A. D. Noyes, *Financial Chapters of the War* (New York, 1916), and *The War Period of American Finance, 1908–1925* (New York, 1926), treats the subject from the standpoint of the money market. L. H. Kemmel, *Federal Finances, 1923–1933* (Nat. Ind. Conf. Bd., New York, 1933), discusses the subject from the standpoint of public finance. A valuable theoretical treatise is J. M. Clark, *The Costs of the World War to the American People* (New Haven, 1931). The annual *Report* of the Secretary of the Treasury contains essential statistical material. For further study reference may be made to W. G. Leland and N. D. Mereness, *Introduction to the American Official Sources for the Economic and Social History of the World War* (New Haven, 1926).

Material on depression financing and World War II financing is still fragmentary, so that chief reliance must be placed on official sources. Chief among these are the *Treasury Bulletin* (Washington, monthly); *The Survey of Current Business* (Washington, monthly); and the *Federal Reserve Bulletin*; the February 1946, issue of the latter summarizes the results of the war bond drives. There is of course a mass of special articles in the magazines and journals of the last few years that can be tracked down through the various magazine guides.

Prices in the colonial period may be studied in A. H. Cole, *Wholesale Commodity Prices in the United States, 1700–1861* (Cambridge, 1938). For the early west, see T. S. Berry, *Western Prices before 1861: a Study of the Cincinnati Market* (Cambridge, 1943). Other early nineteenth century price series are briefly available in N. Silberling, *Dynamics of Business* (New York, 1943). Price series for more recent times appear in Warren and Pearson, *Prices*, in the *Statistical Abstracts*, and in the National Industrial Conference Board's *Economic Almanacs*. Current data are published in the *Survey of Current Business*, the *Monthly Labor Review*, and in the *Federal Reserve Bulletin*.

POPULATION AND IMMIGRATION

(Chapters IV, XVI, XXII, XXVIII)

Population in the colonies is described by a statistical expert, F. B. Dexter, "Estimates of Population in the American Colonies," in *Proceedings of the American Antiquarian Society*, N. S., V. 22–50, and by a scholarly historian, E. B. Greene, *American Population before the Census of 1790* (New York, 1932). For the period since 1790, the primary source is the decennial *Census Reports*, which constitute mines of valuable statistical information. *The Statistical Abstract of the United States* (Washington, annually) regularly carries some of the basic census figures. For a general picture of population trends, see *A Century of Population Growth*, 1790–1900 (Census Bureau, Washington, 1909) or the U. S. National Resources Committee, *The Problems of a Changing Population* (Washington, 1938).

The first question to be settled in discussing immigration is where colonization leaves off and immigration begins. This is treated in H. P. Fairchild, *Immigration* (New York, 1925), which also contains a good general history of immigration to this country. Other helpful general accounts are J. R. Commons, *Races and Immigrants in America* (New York, 1907); P. F. Hall, *Immigration* (New York, 1906); I. A. Hourwich, *Immigration and Labor* (New York, 1922); G. M. Stephenson, *History of American Immigration* (Boston, 1926); Richmond Mayo-Smith, *Emigration and Immigration* (New York, 1890); Edith Abbott, *Historical Aspects of the Immigration Problem* (Chicago, 1926); and M. L. Hansen, *The Immigrant in American History* (Cambridge, 1940). For official reports and source material, consult the *Preliminary Report on the Eighth Census* (Washington, 1863); S. H. Collins, *The Emigrants' Guide to and Description of the United States of America* (Hull, England, 1830); Edith Abbott (Ed.), *Immigration: Select Documents and Case Records* (Chicago, 1924); and the comprehensive *Report of the Immigration Committee*, Sen. Doc. No. 747, 61st Cong., 3rd sess. (42 vols., Washington, 1911).

In addition, there are numerous studies of special aspects of immigration, most of them with self-explanatory titles, such as H. Jerome, *Migration and Business Cycles* (New York, 1926); R. L. Garis, *Immigration Restriction* (New York, 1927); L. G. Brown, *Immigration: Cultural Conflicts and Social Adjustment* (New York, 1933); Carter Goodrich, and others, *Immigration and Economic Opportunity* (Philadelphia, 1936); and M. L. Hansen, *The Mingling of Canadian and American People*, J. B. Brebner, Ed. (New Haven, 1940). M. L. Hansen, *The Atlantic Migration* 1607–1860 (Cambridge, 1940) shows well why the immigrants left home. Biographies of successful immigrants are legion but two may be mentioned, *The Autobiography of Andrew Carnegie* (Boston, 1920) and Edward Bok, *The Americanization of Edward Bok* (New York, 1920). R. G. Albion, *Square-Riggers on Schedule* (Princeton, 1938) has a chapter describing conditions on an immigrant ship of a century ago.

LABOR

(Chapters IV, XVI, XXII, XXVIII)

Voluminous though it is, the literature on labor is none too satisfactory for it is usually partisan: the student must constantly be on guard against extreme statements.

A full and scholarly general history of labor is J. R. Commons and Associates, *History of Labour in the United States* (2 vols., New York, 1918), which unfortunately does not go beyond 1896. To this two more volumes have been added by his colleagues, namely, *History of Labor in the United States*, 1896–1932 (New York, 1935), Don D. Lescohier treating "Working Conditions" and Elizabeth Brandeis discussing "Labor Legislation" in Volume 3, and Selig Perlman and Philip Taft handling "Labor Movements" in Volume 4. An abridged version of Commons is Selig Perlman, *History of Trade Unionism in the U. S.* (New York, 1922). A more recent complete study is H. A. Millis and R. E. Montgomery, *Organized Labor* (New York, 1945). Two brief but now somewhat dated studies are S. Orth, *Armies of Labor* (New Haven, 1921) and Mary R. Beard, *A Short History of the American Labor Movement* (New York, 1920). A modern text packed with facts is C. R. Daugherty, *Labor Problems in American Industry* (New York, 1941). Among the other general histories of labor may be mentioned Richard T. Ely, *Labor Movement in America* (New York, 1886), a pioneer work; A. Bimba, *The History of the American Working Class* (New York, 1927), a radical treatment; F. T. Carlton, *History and Problems of Organized Labor* (New York, 1920); G. G. Groat, *Introduction to the Study of Organized Labor in America* (New York, 1926); G. S. Watkins, *Labor Problems* (New York, 1929); W. J. Lauck, *Political and Industrial Democracy, 1776–1926* (New York, 1926); W. D. Savage, *Industrial Unionism in America* (New York, 1922); M. Keir, *Labor's Search for More* (New York, 1937); H. U. Faulkner and M. Starr, *Labor in America* (New York, 1944); and Florence Peterson, *American Labor Unions: What They Are and How They Work* (New York, 1945). A. M. Simons, *Social Forces in American History* (New York, 1911) presents an economic interpretation.

For government reports and source materials, consult first of all the materials Commons collected and on which he based his studies, namely, J. R. Commons and Associates, *A Documentary History of American Industrial Society* (10 vols., Cleveland, 1910). Of these, Vols. I and II edited by U. B. Phillips, are devoted to *Plantation and Frontier*, 1649–1863; Vols. III and IV and Supplement, edited by J. R. Commons and E. A. Gilmore, to *Labor Conspiracy Cases*, 1806–1842; Vols. V and VI, edited by J. R. Commons and Helen L. Sumner, to *Labor Movement*, 1820–40; Vols. VII and VIII, edited by J. R. Commons, to *Labor Movement*, 1840–60; and the last two volumes cover the period, 1860–80. The industrial and social results of the factory system are described and defended by Carroll D. Wright, *Report on the Factory System of the United States* (U. S. Census, 1880, Vol. II, pp. 529 ff.). The first comprehensive government investigation of labor conditions is the *Report of the Industrial Commission* appointed by President McKinley in 1898 (19 vols., Washington, 1900–1902). This may be supplemented by the *Report of the Commission on Industrial Relations*, Sen. Doc. No. 415, 64th Cong., 1st sess. (11 vols., Washington, 1916). The publications of the Bureau of Labor (after 1913 the Bureau of Labor Statistics) are invaluable for current information as to conditions of labor; these include the annual *Report of the Commissioner of Labor* from 1884 to 1913, the monthly *Bulletin*, and the monthly *Labor Review*. Comments by foreign observers on labor conditions in this country are found in Michael Chevalier, *Society, Manners and Politics in the United States* (Boston, 1839); Harriet Martineau, *Society in America* (2 vols., New York, 1837); P. Leroy-Beaulieu, *The United States in the Twentieth Century* (New York, 1906), and E. Levasseur, *The American Workman* (Baltimore, 1900).

The institution of indented servants in the different colonies has been studied by a number of authors. The following may be named: J. C. Ballagh, *White Servitude in the Colony of Virginia* (Johns Hopkins University Studies, Baltimore, 1895); J. S. Bassett, *Servitude and Slavery in the Colony of North Carolina* (*Ibid.*, 1896); E. S. McCormac, *White Servitude in Maryland* (*Ibid.*, 1904); K. F. Geiser, *Redemptioners and Indented Servants in Pennsylvania* (New Haven, 1901); and C. A. Herrick, *White Servitude in Pennsylvania* (Philadelphia, 1926). A special study is A. W. Lauber, *Indian Slavery in Colonial Times within the Present Limits of the United States* (1913). A related study is that of J. D. Butler, "British Convicts Shipped to American Colonies," in *American Historical Review*, Vol. II. The topic of Negro slavery is treated in a separate bibliography on pages 821-823.

For a picture of free labor in the colonies Commons' two-volume work is basic. A recent comprehensive study is R. B. Morris, *Government and Labor in Early America* (New York, 1945). Conditions in the northern colonies are described by Lucy M. Salmon, *Domestic Service* (New York, 1897) and W. B. Weeden, *Economic and Social History of New England* (2 vols., Boston, 1896). M. W. Jernegan, *Laboring and Dependent Classes in Colonial America, 1607–1783* (Chicago, 1931), is all too brief on free labor. R. F. Seybolt, *Apprenticeship and Apprenticeship Education in Colonial New England and New York* (New York, 1917), deals with a special aspect.

On the early labor movement again, see Commons' account and his source materials. Good brief accounts are to be found in Perlman and Orth. N. J. Ware, *The Industrial Worker, 1840–60* (Boston, 1924), presents a rather pessimistic picture of the period. John B. McMaster, *A History of the People of the United States from the Revolution to the Civil War* (Vols. I to V, New York, 1901), gives more attention to labor than the usual political history; his *Acquisition of Political, Social and Industrial Rights of Man in America* (Cleveland, 1903) is a sympathetic summary. In this same category is C. R. Fish, *The Rise of the Common Man, 1830–1860* (New York, 1927).

The social and humanitarian movements of the pre-Civil War period are described in several books, of which the following may be mentioned: A. J. Booth, *Life of Owen* (London, 1869); W. L. Sargant, *Robert Owen and his Social Philosophy* (London, 1869); Albert Brisbane, *The Social Destiny of Man, or Association and Reorganization of Industry* (Boston, 1840). W. A. Hinds, *American Communities* (Oneida, 1878); John H. Noyes, *History of American Socialisms* (Philadelphia, 1870); Charles Sotheran, *Horace Greeley and Other Pioneers of American Socialism* (New York, 1892); J. T. Codman, *Brook Farm* (Boston, 1894); Charles Nordhoff, *The Communistic Societies of the United States from Personal Visit and Observation* (New York, 1875). Ware has a good summary.

Since the Civil War the great national unions have occupied the spotlight. The first significant one of these, the Knights of Labor, is rather turgidly discussed by N. J. Ware, *The Labor Movement in the United States*, 1860–95 (New York, 1929). Perlman's account of the Knights is short but much clearer. George E. McNeill, *The Labor Movement— The Problem of To-day* (Boston, 1887) is written by one of the earliest state labor officials; Terence V. Powderly, *Thirty Years of Labor* (Columbus, Ohio, 1889) is semi-historical and semi-rhetorical but contains valuable information about the Knights of Labor of which he was Grand Master. On the American Federation of Labor, Perlman or Orth provide a good introduction. L. L. Lorwin, *The American Federation of Labor*, (Washington, 1933) and Leo Wolman, *Growth of American Trade Unions*, 1880–1923 (Bur. Econ. Res., New York, 1924), are more complete. Samuel Gompers, *Seventy Years of Life and Labor* (New York, 1925), is by the man who founded and for over 40 years led the A. F. of L. For more recent information, consult such general studies as Daugherty or Millis and Montgomery. The standard works on the I.W.W. are P. F. Brissenden, *The I.W.W., A Study of American Syndicalism* (New York, 1919) and J. S. Gambs, *The Decline of the I.W.W.* (New York, 1932). The early days of the C.I.O. are popularly and sympathetically described by Benjamin Stolberg, *The Story of the C.I.O.* (New York, 1938) and H. Harris, *American Labor* (New Haven, 1939) and *Labor's Civil War* (New York, 1940). For more recent facts, see Millis and Montgomery, *Organized Labor*, already mentioned.

The employers' association appeared almost as early as the union and is described in C. E. Bonnett, *Employers' Associations in the United States* (New York, 1922) and A. G. Taylor, *Labor Policies of the National Association of Manufacturers* (Urbana, Ill., 1928). Also see J. R. Commons, *Labor and Administration* (New York, 1913), which deals with management. Some of the many aspects of management-labor relationships are described in Felix Frankfurter, *The Labor Injunction* (New York, 1930); R. W. Dunn, *Company Unions* (New York, 1927); K. Page, *Collective Bargaining* (New York, 1922); H. C. Metcalf (Ed.), *Collective Bargaining for Today and Tomorrow* (New York, 1937); D. Yoder, *Personnel and Labor Relations* (New York, 1938); National Industrial Conference Board, *Employee Stock Purchase Plans in the United States* (New York, 1928); O. Tead and H. C. Metcalf, *Labor Relations under the Recovery Act* (New York, 1933); and W. McPherson, *Labor Relations in the Automobile Industry* (Washington, 1940).

Famous strikes are briefly described in Harris' *American Labor* and Keir's *Labor's March for More*. More detailed studies will be found in the *Report to the President on the Anthracite Coal Strike of May–October*, 1902 (Washington, 1903), by the Anthracite Coal Commission appointed by President Theodore Roosevelt; and U. S. Strike Commission, *Report on the Chicago Strike of June–July*, 1894, Sen. Doc. No. 7, 53rd Cong., 2nd sess., (Washington, 1894). The latter should be supplemented by Grover Cleveland, *Presidential Problems* (New York, 1904) and A. Lindsey, *The Pullman Strike* (Chicago, 1942). The story behind another important strike is found in the *Report of the Steel Strike of 1919* (New

York, 1920) by the Commission of Inquiry of the Interchurch World Movement. Louis Adamic's *Dynamite* (New York, 1935) is a popular history of labor violence. Conditions in the more recently industralized South are analyzed in B. Mitchell and G. S. Mitchell, *The Industrial Revolution in the South* (Baltimore, 1930); and A. Berglund, G. Starnes, and F. T. DeVyver, *Labor in the Industrial South* (Charlottesville, Virginia, 1930). The problem of the migratory worker is dealt with by Nels Anderson in *Men on the Move* (Chicago, 1940). For conditions among farm laborers, see Daniel Ahearn, *The Wages of Farm and Factory Laborers, 1914–44* (New York, 1945).

The plight of women and children in industry is described in John Spargo, *The Bitter Cry of the Children* (New York, 1906) and in A. M. Anderson, *Women in the Factory* (New York, 1922). There have been numerous articles in recent years on women in industry in the *Monthly Labor Review.*

Pre-eminent in the field of social insurance are H. A. Millis and R. E. Montgomery, *Labor's Risks and Social Insurance* (New York, 1938); P. H. Douglas, *Social Security in the United States* (New York, 1938); and Seymour E. Harris, *The Economics of Social Security* (New York, 1941).

On labor legislation in general, see J. R. Commons and J. B. Andrews, *Principles of Labor Legislation* (rev. ed., New York, 1936); Daugherty's *Labor Problems;* and Florence Peterson, *American Labor Unions* (New York, 1945). For current information, see the *American Labor Legislation Review* (New York, 1911—). The source for cases involving federal constitutionality of labor legislation is the *United States Reports.* The significance of each new case is briefly discussed in *The Monthly Labor Review,* 1915—, and in the *Labor Relations Reporter,* 1937—. Majoi aspects and trends may be studied in Commons and Andrews, just mentioned, and in Volume III of Commons. A later publication is C. Raushenbush and E. Stein, *Labor Cases and Materials* (New York, 1941).

The most scholarly synthesis of wage and hour studies is H. A. Millis and R. E. Montgomery, *Labor's Progress and Some Basic Labor Problems* (New York, 1938), which gathers its material on wages largely from A. H. Hansen's "Factors Affecting the Trend of Real Wages," *American Economic Review* (Vol. XV, March 1925), and from P. H. Douglas, *Real Wages in the United States, 1890–1926* (New York, 1930). Valuable material on wages and the cost of living is contained in the *Report of the Industrial Commission* (19 vols., Washington, 1900–1902). An uncritical collection of material is *History of Wages in the United States from Colonial Times to 1928* (Bulletin No. 499, Bureau of Labor Statistics, Washington, 1929). The first study of this kind was the so-called Aldrich Report on *Wholesale Prices, Wages, and Transportation,* 1840–1890, Sen. Doc. No. 1394, 52nd Cong., 2nd sess., (4 vols., Washington, 1893), but this was based on insufficient data and was faulty in interpretation. Two careful statistical studies are W. C. Mitchell and Associates, *Income in the United States, Its Amount and Distribution,* 1909–19 (Bureau of Economic Research, 2 vols., New York, 1921–22), and R. F. Martin, *National Income in the United States,* 1799–1938 (Nat. Ind. Conf. Bd. Studies,

No. 241, New York, 1939). Two other studies of wages for the latter part of this period, which supplement each other, are Whitney Coombs, *The Wages of Unskilled Labor in Manufacturing Industries in the United States*, 1890–1924 (New York, 1926), and P. F. Brissenden, *Earnings of Factory Workers*, 1899 *to* 1927 (Census Monograph No. 10, Washington, 1929). A later study is the National Industrial Conference Board, *Wages, Hours and Employment in the United States*, 1914–36 (New York, 1936). For more recent information see the *Handbook of Labor Statistics* (2 vols., Washington, 1941), the *Statistical Abstract*, the *Monthly Labor Review*, the National Industrial Conference Board's *Economic Almanac*, and other releases.

A brief bibliography on the influence of cheap land on wages in our economic history will be found at the end of the bibliography on the Westward Movement.

ECONOMICS OF SLAVERY

(Chapter XVII)

In a study of the economics of slavery it is even more necessary than in other problems to go to the sources. Fortunately, an excellent collection of such material exists in Ulrich B. Phillips, *Plantation and Frontier*, being Vols. I and II of the *Documentary History of American Industrial Society* (10 vols., Cleveland, 1910), edited by J. R. Commons and others. Selections from contemporary writers have been collected by E. L. Bogart and C. M. Thompson, *Readings in the Economic History of the United States* (New York, 1916), 558–97, by F. Flügel and H. U. Faulkner, *Readings in the Economic and Social History of the United States* (New York, 1929), and by G. S. Callender, *Selections from the Economic History of the United States*, 1765–1860 (Boston, 1909), 738–819. The introductions by Phillips and Callender are excellent brief surveys.

The contemporary literature on the subject of slavery is for the most part highly controversial and not always trustworthy; here will be cited only those works that show some appreciation of the economic aspects. One of the most thoughtful is John E. Cairnes, *The Slave Power, Its Character, Career, and Probable Designs* (2nd ed., enlarged, London, 1863), which was written by an English economist and is a powerful argument against slavery. Cairnes drew his information largely from Frederick Olmsted, who, though himself opposed to slavery, has furnished the fairest and most accurate pictures of economic and social conditions in the South before the war. Olmsted made long journeys on horseback through the South in the fifties and faithfully chronicled what he saw and heard. His observations are embodied in *A Journey in the Seaboard Slave States* (New York, 1856; new ed., 1904); *A Journey Through Texas* (New York, 1857); *A Journey in the Back Country* (New York, 1860). Parts of these books are reprinted in *The Cotton Kingdom, a Traveller's Observations on Cotton and Slavery* (2 vols., New York, 1861). His conclusions may be checked in Broadus Mitchell, *Frederick Law Olmsted:*

a Critic of the Old South (Baltimore, 1925). A balanced and careful book is George M. Weston, *The Progress of Slavery in the United States* (Washington, 1858).

Written from a pro-slavery standpoint, though quite valuable, is J. D. B. DeBow, *Industrial Resources and Statistics of the Southern and Western States* (3 vols., New Orleans, 1852–1853); these volumes are a collection of extracts from *DeBow's Review*, which should also be consulted. Important contemporary books written by pro-slavery advocates are David Christy, *Cotton Is King* (2nd ed., 1856); Daniel R. Goodloe, *An Inquiry into the Causes Which Retard the Southern States* (Washington, 1846); Thomas P. Kettell, *Southern Wealth and Northern Profits* (New York, 1861); *The Pro-Slavery Argument* (Philadelphia, 1853), a serious attempt by Harper, Hammond, Sims, and Dew to state the moral, political, and economic case for slavery. A vigorous book against slavery by a non-slaveowning white is Hinton R. Helper, *The Impending Crisis of the South, How to Meet It* (New York, 1857). Equally unbalanced is H. Wilson, *History of the Rise and Fall of the Slave Power in America* (Boston, 1872). Influential in molding public opinion in the North against slavery was Harriet Beecher Stowe, *Uncle Tom's Cabin* (Boston, 1852), which she afterwards attempted to document in *Key to Uncle Tom's Cabin* (Boston, 1853).

Travelers to the United States were many during this period and most of them recorded their impressions. Among the best are J. S. Buckingham, *The Slave States of America* (2 vols., London, 1842); Adam Hodgson, *Letters from North America* (2 vols., London, 1824); James Stirling, *Letters from the Slave States* (London, 1857).

Among the more modern books describing slavery and the South there is much valuable material in L. C. Gray, *History of Agriculture in the Southern United States to 1860* (2 vols., New York, 1941). W. E. Dodd, *The Cotton Kingdom* (New Haven, 1919) gives a fine survey, and Ulrich B. Phillips, *Life and Labor in the Old South* (New York, 1929) catches the spirit of the slave-holding South without yielding too many facts. His *American Negro Slavery* (New York, 1918) is more satisfactory. Others are Albert B. Hart, *Slavery and Abolition* (New York, 1906); Edward Ingle, *Southern Sidelights, a Picture of Social and Economic Life in the South a Generation before the War* (New York, 1896); Joseph A. Tillinghast, *The Negro in Africa and America* (Publications of American Economic Association, New York, 1902); Charles H. Johnson, *The Negro in America* (New York, 1930); C. H. Wesley, *Negro Labor in the United States, 1850–1925* (1927); R. R. Russell, *Economic Aspects of Southern Sectionalism, 1840–1861* (Urbana, Ill., 1923). How slavery existed in southern Illinois is told in N. D. Harris, *Negro Servitude in Illinois* (Chicago, 1904). Two highly significant articles on slavery are Alfred H. Stone, "Some Problems of Southern Economic History," *American Historical Review*, July 1908, and R. W. Smith, "Was Slavery Unprofitable in the Ante Bellum South," *Agricultural History*, January 1946. Sectional Studies are H. A. Trexler, *Slavery in Missouri, 1804–1865* (Baltimore, 1914); I. E. McDougall, *Slavery in Kentucky, 1792–1865* (1918); R. H. Taylor, *Slave Holding in North Carolina: an Economic View*

(Chapel Hill, 1926); R. B. Flanders, *Plantation Slavery in Georgia* (Chapel Hill, 1928); H. M. Henry, *The Police Control of the Slave in South Carolina* (Emory, Va., 1914).

The standard book on the slave-trade is W. E. B. DuBois, *The Suppression of the African Slave-Trade to the United States of America*, 1638–1870 (Harvard Hist. Stud., No. 1, Cambridge, 1896); more popular are John R. Spears, *The American Slave-Trade of the Southern States* (New York, 1904), and T. Canot, *Adventures of an African Slaver* (Garden City, 1928). A careful collection of source material is Elizabeth Donnan (Ed.), *Documents Illustrative of the History of the Slave Trade to America* (3 vols., Washington, 1930–32). The domestic slave trade is treated in H. C. Carey, *The Slave-Trade, Domestic and Foreign* (4th ed., Philadelphia, 1872), a prejudiced contemporary account. More balanced are W. H. Collins, *The Domestic Slave Trade in the United States* (New York, 1904), Frederic Bancroft, *Slave-Trading in the Old South* (Baltimore, 1931), and T. D. Jervey, *The Slave Trade* (Columbia, S. C., 1925).

The best brief accounts of slavery in the general histories of the United States are the following: Edward Channing, *History of the United States*, Vol. V, Chap. 5; John B. McMaster, *History of the People of the United States*, Vol. I, Chaps. 7–10; James F. Rhodes, *History of the United States from the Compromise of* 1850, Vol. I, Chap. 4, and Vol. II, Chap. 1; and A. M. Schlesinger, *Political and Social History of the United States*, 1829–1925 (New York, 1925).

On cotton, the best authority is M. B. Hammond, *The Cotton Industry* (Publ. Amer. Econ. Ass., New York, 1897). Also good is J. A. B. Scherer, *Cotton as a World Power* (New York, 1916). On tobacco see J. C. Robert, *The Tobacco Kingdom* (Durham, 1938).

There should also be noted an exhaustive *Bibliography of the Negro in Africa and America* (New York, 1927), by Monroe N. Work, which covers not mererly slavery but the whole problem from 1509 to 1922.

TRANSPORTATION AND COMMUNICATION

(Chapters XII, XXIII, XXIX)

For the study of transportation in the United States two important general works exist, to which reference should be made on all phases of this chapter. These are *History of Transportation in the United States before* 1860, prepared under the editorship of B. H. Meyer by Caroline E. MacGill (Washington, 1917), which embodies considerable research but is not well organized; and Seymour Dunbar, *A History of Travel in America* (4 vols., Indianapolis, 1915), written in popular style with abundant illustrations but containing much original material. Other good general accounts are contained in J. B. McMaster, *History of the People of the United States* (7 vols., New York, 1883–1914), Vol. IV, Chap. 33, Vol. V, Chap. 44; *Tenth Census* (Washington, 1880), Vol. IV, on Transportation; *Eighty Years' Progress* (Hartford, 1869), pp. 172–273.

Early roads are described in the preceding books, to which should be added A. B. Hulbert, *Historic Highways of America* (16 vols., Cleveland, 1902–1905), a series of books on the important trails, roads, and canals. A condensed picture by the same author is *The Paths of Inland Commerce* (New Haven, 1920). Among the better books in the first series is one on the Cumberland Road, which should be supplemented by T. B. Searight, *The Old Pike, a History of the National Road, with Incidents, Accidents, and Anecdotes Thereon* (Uniontown, Pa., 1894). Thomas Twining, *Travel in America One Hundred Years Ago* (New York, 1894), describes transportation 150 years ago. Detailed descriptions of wagons and wagoning are given in H. S. Hill, *The Conestoga Wagon* (Trenton, privately published, 1936). Regional studies of the movement for improved roads in the early nineteenth century are F. J. Wood, *Turnpikes of New England* (Boston, 1919), and J. A. Durrenburger, *Turnpikes, a Study of the Toll Road Movement in the Middle Atlantic States and Maryland* (Valdosta, Ga., 1931). Little more attention was paid to roads until the end of the nineteenth century, when the bicycle and the automobile forced improvements. A recent book is R. L. Kincaid, *The Wilderness Road* (New York, 1947).

River traffic took on new life with the advent of the steamboat. The trials of the early inventors of the steamboat are related in Thomas Boyd, *Poor John Fitch: Inventor of the Steamboat* (New York, 1935); J. T. Flexner, *Steamboats Come True: American Invention in Action* (New York, 1944); and H. W. Dickinson, *Robert Fulton, Engineer and Artist; His Life and Works* (New York, 1914). The story of the steamboat is brought down to 1900 in J. H. Morrison, *History of American Steam Navigation* (New York, 1903). On water transportation, mostly of the Mississippi and connected rivers, numerous government reports have been made. One of the first was I. D. Andrews, *Report on the Trade and Commerce of the British North American Colonies and upon the Trade of the Great Lakes and Rivers*, Exec. Doc. No. 136, 32nd Cong., 1st sess. (Washington, 1853). This was followed by a comprehensive survey in the *Tenth Census*, Vol. VIII (Washington, 1880); others by W. F. Switzler, *Report on the Internal Commerce of the United States*, House Exec. Doc. No. 6, Pt. 2, 50th Cong., 1st sess. (Washington, 1888); F. H. Dixon, *A Traffic History of the Mississippi River System*, National Waterways Commission, Doc. No. 11 (Washington, 1909); *Final Report of the National Waterways Commission*, Sen. Doc. No. 469, 62nd Cong., 2nd sess. (Washington, 1912). The relations of waterways to railroad competition are discussed in *Transportation by Water in the United States* (3 parts, Bureau of Corporations, Washington, 1909–10).

The proposed St. Lawrence Ship Channel has evoked a partisan literature. H. G. Moulton, *et al.*, present an adverse point of view in *St. Lawrence Navigation and Power Project* (Brookings Institution, Washington, 1929). A more sympathetic discussion of this project is found in T. Ireland, *The Great Lakes-St. Lawrence Deep Waterway to the Sea* (New York, 1935); and Geo. W. Stephens, *The St. Lawrence Waterway Project* (New York, 1930). Careful studies of the various plans have been made by the

Bureau of Foreign and Domestic Commerce of the Department of Commerce, Domestic Commerce Series No. 4, *Great Lakes-to-Ocean Waterways; Some Economic Aspects of the Great Lakes-St. Lawrence, Lakes-to-Hudson, and All-American Waterway Projects* (Washington, 1927); and by A. H. Ritter, *Transportation Economics of the Great Lakes-St. Lawrence Ship Channel* (Washington, 1925).

Fundamental for the study of railroads in the United States are the *Annual Reports* and *Statistics of Railways* of the Interstate Commerce Commission, since 1887. For the earlier period, consult *Hunt's Merchants' Magazine* (New York, 1839–70), *Commercial and Financial Chronicle* (New York, 1870—), and especially H. V. Poor, *Manual of Railroads in the United States* (New York, 1868—).

The best texts on railroad transportation are Stuart Daggett, *Principles of Inland Transportation* (rev. ed., New York, 1941); A. T. Hadley, *Railroad Transportation* (New York, 1886); Eliot Jones, *Principles of Railway Transportation* (New York, 1924); E. R. Johnson and T. W. Van Metre, *Principles of Railroad Transportation* (New York, 1920); and S. L. Miller, *Inland Transportation* (New York, 1933); H. G. Moulton and others, *The American Transportation Problem* (Brookings Institution, Washington, 1933); D. P. Locklin, *Economics of Transportation* (3rd ed., Chicago, 1947); T. V. Van Metre, *Transportation in the United States* (Chicago, 1939); K. T. Healey, *The Economics of Transportation in America* (New York, 1940); J. H. Parmelee, *The Modern Railroad* (New York, 1940). T. C. Bigham, *Transportation: Principles and Problems* (New York, 1946). All of these contain considerable historical material.

Early railroads are described in C. F. Adams, *Railroads: Their Origin and Problems* (New York, 1878); W. H. Brown, *History of the First Locomotives in America* (New York, 1871; rev. ed., 1894); A. T. Hadley, *Railroad Transportation; Its History and Its Laws* (New York, 1885); H. V. Poor, *History of the Railroads and Canals of the United States* (New York, 1860); J. L. Ringwalt, *Development of Transportation Systems in the United States* (Philadelphia, 1888). More popular and less valuable are S. Thompson, *Short History of American Railways* (Chicago, 1925), and J. W. Starr, *One Hundred Years of American Railroading* (New York, 1929).

The early abuses of the railroads are graphically described by C. F. Adams, Jr., *Chapters of Erie* (Boston, 1871), and *Railroads, Their Origin and Problems* (New York, 1878; rev. ed., 1893). A collection of material, including some chapters from Adams, is F. C. Hicks (Ed.), *High Finance in the Sixties, Chapters from the Early History of the Erie Railway* (New Haven, 1929). Bitter denunciations by contemporary writers are J. F. Hudson, *Railways and the Republic* (New York, 1886), D. C. Cloud, *Monopolies and the People* (Davenport, Iowa, 1873), and M. Josephson, *The Robber Barons* (New York, 1934). J. B. Crawford, *Crédit Mobilier of America* (Boston, 1880), gives a too-favorable account. More balanced is William Larrabee, *Railroad Question* (New York, 1893). H. G. Pearson, *An American Railroad Builder*

(Boston, 1911), describes events from the standpoint of the railroad builder, J. M. Forbes; and S. J. Buck, *The Granger Movement* (Cambridge, 1913), gives the agrarian background of discontent. Important for a picture of conditions at the beginning of the twentieth century is the census monograph *Transportation by Water*, 1916 (Washington, 1920). This may be supplemented by a report of the Bureau of Foreign and Domestic Commerce, Miscellaneous Series, No. 119, on *Inland Water Transportation in the United States* (Washington, 1923). A later government report on *Transportation on the Great Lakes* was prepared by the Corps of Engineers for Rivers and Harbors of the War Department in co-operation with the U. S. Shipping Board (Government Printing Office, Washington, 1926). Another regional report by the same authorities is *Transportation in the Mississippi and Ohio Valleys* (Washington, 1929). More general is M. E. Dimmock, *Developing America's Waterways* (Chicago, 1935).

River transportation is described in various regional studies: that of the Mississippi in W. J. Petersen, *Steamboating on the Upper Mississippi* (Iowa City, 1937); that of the Ohio in C. H. Ambler, *A History of Transportation in the Ohio Valley* (Glendale, Calif., 1931); that of the Missouri in H. M. Chittenden, *History of Early Steamboat Navigation on the Missouri River* (2 vols., New York, 1903). Popular accounts are H. and E. Quick, *Mississippi Steamboatin'* (New York, 1926), and G. L. Eskew, *The Pageant of the Packets* (New York, 1929).

Water transportation on the Great Lakes is described by Norman Beasley, *Freighters of Fortune* (New York, 1930); J. C. Mills, *Our Inland Seas* (New York, 1910); R. G. Plumb, *History of the Navigation of the Great Lakes* (Washington, 1911); and W. Havighurst, *The Long Ships Passing* (New York, 1942).

Canals have been given more attention than any other phase of transportation except railroads. An early picture is presented in Albert Gallatin's Report on Roads and Canals in *American State Papers*, Vol. I, (Washington, 1808), 724–921. Thirty years later another account was given by H. S. Tanner, *A Description of the Canals and Railroads of the United States; comprehending Notices of all the Works of Internal Improvements throughout the Several States* (New York, 1840). This should be checked by M. Chevalier, *Society, Manners, and Politics in the United States* (Boston, 1839), Chaps. 20, 21. A later study is W. F. Gephart, *Transportation and Industrial Development in the Middle West* (Columbia University Studies, Vol. XXXIV, New York, 1909). Canals in the most important states are described by N. E. Whitford, *History of the Canal System of the State of New York* (2 vols., New York, 1906); C. L. Jones, *The Economic History of the Anthracite-Tidewater Canals* (1908); A. L. Bishop, "The State Works of Pennsylvania," in *Trans. of the Conn. Acad. of Arts and Soc.*, Vol. XIII (New Haven, 1908); E. L. Bogart, *Internal Improvements and State Debt in Ohio* (New York, 1924); J. W. Putnam, *The Illinois and Michigan Canal: A Study in Economic History* (Chicago, 1918); and G. W. Ward, *The Early Development of the Chesapeake and Ohio Canal Project* (Baltimore, 1899). The best general account is

A. F. Harlow, *Old Tow Paths* (New York, 1926). For the Panama Canal, see A. K. Henry, *The Panama Canal and the Intercoastal Trade* (New York, 1929).

Internal improvements are graphically described in J. J. Lalor, *Cyclopaedia of Political Science, Political Economy, and the Political History of the United States* (3 vols., Chicago, 1881–84). Government investigations are those of the "Hepburn Committee," one of the first official inquiries into railroad abuses (New York State Assembly Document No. 38, Albany, 1880), and of the "Cullom Committee" of the United States Senate, which led to the passage of the Act to Regulate Commerce (Sen. Rep., 49th Cong., 1st Sess., Serial No. 2356, 2 vols., Washington, 1886). The results of a more general inquiry are contained in the *Report of the Industrial Commission*, especially Vols. IV, X, XVII, and XIX (19 vols., Washington, 1900–1902).

The combination movement is treated in two authoritative books by W. Z. Ripley, *Railroads: Finance and Organization* (Boston, 1915), and *Railroads: Rates and Regulation* (Boston, 1912). F. A. Cleveland and F. W. Powell, *Railroad Promotion and Capitalization* (New York, 1909), discusses primarily the financial aspects, and Stuart Daggett, *Railroad Reorganization* (Berkeley, 1908), the problems of receiverships. See also John Moody, *The Railroad Builders* (New Haven, 1920); J. Kennan, *E. H. Harriman, a Biography* (New York, 1922); and O. Lewis, *The Big Four* (New York, 1938), the story of the Central and the Southern Pacific railroads, for the human aspects.

The building of four of the transcontinental roads is carefully traced in Stuart Daggett, *Chapters on the History of the Southern Pacific Railroad* (New York, 1922); Nelson Trottman, *History of the Union Pacific* (Chicago, 1923); E. V. Smalley, *History of the Northern Pacific Railroad* (New York, 1883); and James Marshall, *Santa Fe, the Railroad That Built an Empire* (New York, 1945). R. E. Riegel, *Story of the Western Railroads* (New York, 1926), brings together the confused movements of this period. Another regional study is G. E. Baker, *Formation of the New England Railroad Systems* (Cambridge, 1937). Two books on an important railroad deserve mention: H. G. Brownson, *History of the Illinois Central Railroad to 1870* (Urbana, Ill., 1915), and P. W. Gates, *The Illinois Central Railroad and Its Colonization Work* (Cambridge, 1934).

Histories of particular lines are numerous, but only a few can be named. Among the best are M. Reizenstein, *The Economic History of the Baltimore and Ohio Railroad, 1827–1853* (Baltimore, 1897); Edward Hungerford, *The Story of the Baltimore and Ohio Railroad, 1827–1927* (2 vols., New York, 1928); U. B. Phillips, *A History of Railroad Transportation in the Eastern Cotton Belt to 1860* (New York, 1908); and F. W. Stevens, *The Beginnings of the New York Central Railroad* (New York, 1926).

Regulation and control are discussed in all the systematic treatises, but the following devote their main attention to this topic: F. H. Dixon, *State Railroad Control* (New York, 1896); B. H. Meyer, *Railway Legislation in the United States* (New York, 1903); S. O. Dunn, *The Regulation of Railways* (New York, 1918).

Regulation and control receive more attention in W. J. Cunningham, *American Railroads: Government Control and Reconstruction* (New York, 1922); F. H. Dixon, *Railroads and Government: Their Relations in the United States, 1910–1921* (New York, 1922); D. P. Locklin, *Transportation Since 1920* (New York, 1928); Roger MacVeagh, *The Transportation Act, 1920* (New York, 1920); and W. M. Daniels, *American Railroads: Four Phases of Their History* (Princeton, 1923). W. M. W. Splawn, *Government Ownership and Operation of Railroads* (New York, 1928); and L. G. Sorrell, *Government Ownership and Operation of Railroads for the United States* (New York, 1937), are opposed. More impartial is E. R. Johnson, *Government Regulation of Transportation Agencies* (New York, 1938). An excellent survey is I. L. Sharfman, *The Interstate Commerce Commission* (4 vols., New York, 1931–1937).

Government aid to railroads is described by L. H. Haney, *Congressional History of Railways in the United States to 1850* (Madison, 1908), and the same, *1850–1887* (Madison, 1910); J. B. Sanborn, *Congressional Grants of Land in Aid of Railways* (Madison, 1899); J. W. Million, *State Aid to Railways in Missouri* (Chicago, 1896).

Two unique experiments in transportation are described in L. R. Hafen, *The Overland Mail, 1849–1869, Promoter of Settlement, Precursor of Railroads* (Glendale, Calif., 1932), and L. B. Lesley (Ed.), *Uncle Sam's Camels* (Cambridge, 1929). The latter deals with an attempt to use camels in the semi-arid Southwest.

The electric lines have been described in a series of quinquennial reports by the United States Bureau of the Census, *Street and Electric Railways, 1902, 1907, 1912, 1917, 1922* (Washington). A careful study is D. F. Wilcox, *Analysis of the Electric Railway Problem Prepared for the Federal Electric Railway Commission* (Washington, 1921). Among books on the subject may be mentioned L. E. Fischer, *Economics of Interurban Railways* (New York, 1914), and H. W. Blake and W. Jackson, *Electric Railway Transportation* (New York, 1917).

Automotive transportation is described in Percival White, *Motor Transportation of Merchandise and Passengers* (New York, 1923); G. R. Chatburn, *Highways and Highway Transportation* (New York, 1923); G. W. Grupp, *Economics of Motor Transportation* (New York, 1924); T. F. MacManus and Norman Beasley, *Men, Money, and Motors* (New York, 1929); and E. P. Norwood, *Ford, Men and Methods* (New York, 1931); F. K. Edwards, *Principles of Motor Transportation* (New York, 1933); H. E. Stocker, *Motor Traffic Management* (rev. ed., New York, 1942); C. L. Dearing, *American Highway Policy* (Brookings Institution, Washington, 1942); and H. L. Barber, *The Story of the Automobile* (Chicago, 1917). On the automobile industry, see R. C. Epstein, *The Automobile Industry: Its Economic and Commercial Development* (Cambridge, 1928); L. H. Seltzer, *A Financial History of the American Automobile Industry* (New York, 1928); E. D. Kennedy, *The Automobile Industry: The Coming of Age of Capitalism's Favorite Child* (New York, 1941); and R. H. Graves, *The Triumph of an Idea* (New York, 1934).

Other agencies of transportation are described in T. H. Kennedy, *An*

Introduction to the Economics of Air Transportation (New York, 1924); John Goldstrom, *Narrative History of Aviation* (New York, 1930); P. T. David, *The Economics of Air Mail Transportation* (Brookings Institution, Washington, 1934); E. E. Freudenthal, *The Aviation Business: from Kitty Hawk to Wall Street* (New York, 1940); Henry L. Smith, *The History of Commercial Aviation in the United States* (New York, 1942), and *Airways* (New York, 1945); R. M. Cleveland and L. E. Neville, *The Coming Air Age* (New York, 1944), a good survey; C. E. Puffer, *Air Transportation* (Philadelphia, 1941); S. Paul Johnston, *Wings after the War: the Prospects of Post-War Aviation* (New York, 1945). The standard work is J. H. Frederick, *Commercial Air Transportation* (Chicago, 1946).

The history of the various agencies of communication is contained in special treatises, of which a few only can be named: H. M. Konwiser, *Colonial and Revolutionary Posts* (Richmond, 1931); D. C. Roper, *The United States Post Office* (New York, 1917); and an excellent study by W. E. Rich, *The History of the United States Post Office to the Year 1929* (Cambridge, 1934); W. K. Towers, *From Beacon Fire to Radio* (New York, 1924); H. L. Jome, *Economics of the Radio Industry* (New York, 1925); A. F. Harlow, *Old Wires and New Waves* (New York, 1936), covering the telegraph, telephone, and radio; H. N. Casson, *History of the Telephone* (New York, 1910); and M. Keir, *The March of Commerce* (Pageant of America Series, New Haven, 1927), with many good illustrations.

DOMESTIC AND FOREIGN COMMERCE

(Chapters V, XIII, XXIV, XXX)

The best general account of colonial commerce is E. R. Johnson, T. W. Van Metre, G. G. Huebner, and D. S. Hanchett, *History of Domestic and Foreign Commerce of the United States* (2 vols., Carnegie Institution, Washington, 1915). A good short account is found in C. Day, *History of Commerce* (4th ed., New York, 1938), and a less satisfactory one in W. C. Webster, *A General History of Commerce* (Boston, 1903; rev. ed., 1918). Chapters on colonial commerce may be found in E. Channing, *History of the United States* (New York, 1909 and 1912), Vol. II, Chap. 17; Vol. III, Chap. 13; Curtis Nettels, *Roots of American Civilization* (New York, 1938); M. Keir, *March of Commerce* (New Haven, 1927); E. B. Greene, *Foundations of American Nationality* (New York, 1922); and W. B. Weeden, *Economic and Social History of New England* (2 vols., Boston, 1890). An excellent popular account is Edward Eggleston, "Commerce in the Colonies," in the *Century* magazine, Vol. III, 61, 724; Vol. V, 431; Vol. VII, 873; Vol. VIII, 387.

On the Indian fur trade, consult W. S. Stevens, *The Northwest Fur Trade* (Urbana, Ill., 1928), C. A. Vandiveer, *The Fur Trade and Early Western Explorations* (1929), and H. M. Chittenden, *The American Fur Trade of the Far West* (3 vols., New York, 1902). The southern trade is described by V. W. Crane, *The Southern Frontier, 1670–1932* (Durham,

1928); and Katharine Coman, *Economic Beginnings of the Far West* (2 vols., New York, 1912), gives attention to that region.

Intercolonial trade has received inadequate treatment, but an excellent beginning has been made by Curtis Nettels, "The Economic Relations of Boston, Philadelphia, and New York, 1680–1715," in *Jour. of Econ. and Bus. Hist.*, Vol. III, 185–215. M. S. Morriss, *Colonial Trade of Maryland*, 1689–1715 (Baltimore, 1914), is a more specialized study.

Transatlantic commerce is discussed by G. L. Beer, though primarily with reference to colonial policy; among his books may be mentioned: *Origins of British Colonial Policy*, 1578–1660 (New York, 1908); *The Old Colonial System*, 1660–1754 (2 vols., New York, 1913); *British Colonial Policy*, 1754–1765 (New York, 1907). A brief summary of the main conclusions is contained in his *Commercial Policy of England toward the American Colonies* (Columbia University Studies, New York, 1893). Statistical information may be found in *American Husbandry* (2 vols., London, 1775); T. Pitkin, *Statistical View of the United States* (2nd ed., New York, 1817); Lord J. B. H. Sheffield, *Observations on the Commerce of the United States* (2nd ed., London, 1784); and David Macpherson, *Annals of Commerce* (4 vols., London, 1805).

On smuggling and piracy, see J. F. Jameson (Ed.), *Privateering and Piracy in the Colonial Period* (New York, 1924), a source book; John Esquemeling, *The Buccaneers of America* (New York, 1931); A. L. Cross, *Eighteenth Century Documents Relating to the Royal Forests, The Sheriffs, and Smuggling* (New York, 1928); G. F. Dow and J. H. Edmonds, *The Pirates of the New England Coast*, 1630–1730 (Marine Research Society, Salem, Mass., 1923); P. Grosse, *The History of Piracy* (1932); and E. S. Maclay, *History of American Privateers* (new ed., New York, 1924).

Certain aspects of colonial trade, not covered by the books already listed, are described by A. M. Schlesinger, *The Colonial Merchants and the American Revolution*, 1763–1776 (New York, 1918); E. Lonn, *The Colonial Agents of the Southern Colonies* (Chapel Hill, 1945); and R. B. Westerfield, *Early History of American Auctions: a Chapter in Commercial History* (New Haven, 1920).

There are few books dealing exclusively with domestic commerce between 1789 and 1860; recourse must be had to the works on transportation, already cited. Of these the most useful are W. F. Switzler, F. H. Dixon, and I. D. Andrews. The early commerce of the Mississippi is covered in F. A. Ogg, *Opening of the Mississippi* (New York, 1904). A special phase is described by W. A. Blair, *A Raft Pilot's Log: A History of the Great Rafting Industry on the Upper Mississippi*, 1840–1915 (Glendale, Calif., 1930). C. M. Depew (Ed.), *One Hundred Years of American Commerce*, 1795–1895 (2 vols., New York, 1895), may also be consulted, though the title is misleading.

Some material may be found scattered through the following books: Timothy Flint, *History and Geography of the Mississippi Valley* (2 vols., Philadelphia, 1828); James Hall, *Statistics of the West* (Cincinnati, 1836); W. F. Gephart, *Transportation and Industrial Development in the Middle West* (New York, 1909); F. J. Turner, *Rise of the New West*

(New York, 1905). E. S. Clowes, *Shipways to the Seas* (Baltimore, 1929), deals with the internal commerce from 1830 to 1860.

Josiah Gregg, *Commerce of the Prairies, or the Journal of a Santa Fé Trader* (2 vols., New York, 1844; also other editions) covers early commerce and transportation in the Far West; as do also H. Inman, *The Old Santa Fé Trail* (New York, 1898), and J. J. Webb, *Adventures in the Santa Fé Trade*, 1844–1847 (Glendale, Calif., 1931).

The movements of foreign commerce are fully presented in *American State Papers, Commerce and Navigation* (Washington, 1832–1839). After 1821 these were published annually in the *Report of the Secretary of the Treasury on Commerce and Navigation*. Statistical material is conveniently summarized in the book by Pitkin, mentioned above, and in Adam Seybert, *Statistical Annals: embracing...commerce, navigation...of the United States* (Philadelphia, 1818). Broader than its title is N. S. Buck, *The Development of the Organization of Anglo-American Trade*, 1800–1850 (1925). Another aspect of foreign trade is covered in F. L. Benns, *The American Struggle for the West Indian Carrying-Trade*, 1815–1830 (Bloomington, Ind., 1923).

The China trade is described by F. R. Dulles, *The Old China Trade* (Boston, 1930), by K. S. La Tourette, *Voyages of American Ships to China*, 1784–1844 (New York, 1927) and by S. E. Morison, already mentioned.

For an understanding of the difficulties of neutral trade during this period, two of the contemporary books, which exercised a tremendous influence at the time, should be read: James Stephen, *War in Disguise; or, the Frauds of the Neutral Flags* (London, 1805), and James Madison, *An Examination of the British Doctrine which Subjects to Capture a Neutral Trade not Open in Time of Peace* (Washington, 1806), in *Writings* (9 vols., New York, 1900–1910). More detailed, with citation of much original material, is Henry Adams, *History of the United States of America during the Administrations of Jefferson and Madison* (9 vols., New York, 1889–91). A more specialized study is S. F. Bemis, *Jay's Treaty: A Study in Commerce and Diplomacy* (New York, 1923).

The embargo has been made the object of careful study by W. W. Jennings, *The American Embargo*, 1807–1809 (University of Iowa Studies, Iowa City, 1921); and by L. M. Sears, *Jefferson, and the Embargo* (Durham, 1927).

The causes of the War of 1812 are described in J. W. Pratt, *Expansionists of 1812* (Baltimore, 1925); the War of 1812 is treated fully, though not particularly from a commercial point of view, by A. T. Mahan, *Sea Power in Its Relation to the War of 1812* (Boston, 1905).

Foreign trade to 1914 may be traced in the following books: A. L. Bishop, *Outlines of American Foreign Commerce* (Boston, 1923); J. T. and L. C. Ford, *The Foreign Trade of the United States* (New York, 1920); E. R. Johnson (Ed.), *History of Domestic and Foreign Commerce of the United States* (2 vols., Carnegie Institution, Washington, 1915); F. A. Vanderlip, *The American Commercial Invasion of Europe* (New York, 1902); C. M. Pepper, *American Foreign Trade* (New York, 1919).

Government aid to foreign trade is described in C. S. Donaldson, *Government Assistance to Export Trade* (Philadelphia, 1909); C. L. Jones, *The Consular Service of the United States: Its History and Activities* (University of Pennsylvania, Philadelphia, 1906); U. S. Bureau of Foreign and Domestic Commerce, *Government Assistance to American Exporters* (Washington, 1916).

Events since 1914 are covered in J. H. Frederick, *The Development of American Commerce* (New York, 1932); F. W. Taussig, *Foreign Trade* (New York, 1927); National Industrial Conference Board, *Trends in the Foreign Trade of the United States* (New York, 1930); E. D. Durand, *American Industry and Commerce* (Boston, 1930); E. B. Dietrich, *World Trade* (New York, 1939), and *New Directions in Our Trade Policy* (Committee on Foreign Relations, New York, 1941); H. Feis, *American Foreign Trade Policy and Position* (New York, 1945); C. B. Hoover, *International Trade and Domestic Employment* (New York, 1945); J. P. Young, *The International Economy* (New York, 1942); and C. W. Phelps, *Foreign Expansion of American Banks* (New York, 1927).

The American merchant marine has a considerable literature, but most of it is biased and controversial. The history of American shipping is best described by J. R. Soley, "American Merchant Marine," in N. S. Shaler, *The United States of America*, Vol. I (2 vols., New York, 1894). A valuable monograph on shipping and shipbuilding is J. F. Crowell, "The Shipping Industry of the United States and Its Relation to Foreign Trade," in *Monthly Summary of Commerce and Finance*, December 1900 (Washington, 1900). More popular, but trustworthy, is W. L. Marvin, *American Merchant Marine* (New York, 1902). W. J. Abbot, *American Merchant Ships and Sailors* (New York, 1902; rev. ed., 1919), also *The Story of Our Merchant Marine* (New York, 1919), and J. R. Spears, *The Story of the American Merchant Marine* (New York, 1910), give more of the romance. William W. Bates, *American Marine* (Boston, 1893) and *American Navigation* (Boston, 1902), are poorly organized pleas for bounties. Hans Keller, *American Shipping: Its History and Economic Conditions* (New York, 1913) is less prejudiced. A careful recent study is J. G. B. Hutchins, *American Maritime Industries and Public Policy, 1789–1914* (Cambridge, Mass., 1941).

More specialized, but well-written studies, are those of Arthur H. Clark, *The Clipper Ship Era, 1843–1869* (New York, 1910), R. D. Paine, *The Old Merchant Marine: A Chronicle of American Ships and Sailors* (New Haven, 1919); R. E. Peabody, *Merchant Ventures of Old Salem* (Boston, 1912); Helen la Grange, *Clipper Ships of America and Great Britain, 1833–1869* (New York, 1936); R. G. Albion, *The Rise of New York Port* (New York, 1939) and *Square Riggers on Schedule* (Princeton, 1938); S. E. Morison, *The Maritime History of Massachusetts, 1783–1860* (Boston, 1921); F. C. Bowen, *A Century of Atlantic Travel, 1830–1930* (1930); and C. C. Cutler, *Greyhounds of the Sea: The Story of the American Clipper Ship* (1930). The question of subsidies may be studied in Royal Meeker, *History of Ship Subsidies* (Publ. Amer. Econ. Assn., New York, 1905).

The present and future of our vastly expanded merchant fleet is discussed in the more recent literature: National Industrial Conference Board, *The American Merchant Marine Problem* (New York, 1929); E. J. Mears, *Maritime Trade of Western United States* (Stanford, 1935); P. M. Zeis, *American Shipping Policy* (Princeton, 1938); E. N. Hurley, *The New Merchant Marine* (New York, 1920); A. H. Haag, *An Adequate Merchant Marine* (Washington, 1928); G. W. Dalzell, *The Flight from the Flag* (Chapel Hill, 1940); and R. E. Anderson, *The Merchant Marine and World Frontiers* (New York, 1945).

Still more extensive and controversial is the literature on American commercial policy and the tariff, but works of a scholarly character are few. Foremost stand the books of F. W. Taussig, *Free Trade, the Tariff, and Reciprocity* (New York, 1920), *Tariff History of the United States* (New York, 1892; latest edition, 1930), and *Some Aspects of the Tariff Question* (3rd ed., Cambridge, 1931). Percy Ashley, *Modern Tariff History* (New York, 1920) is an unprejudiced presentation. Edward Stanwood, *Tariff Controversies in the Nineteenth Century* (2 vols., Boston, 1903), is strongly protectionist. Ida M. Tarbell, *The Tariff in Our Own Times* (New York, 1911) is more popular. P. W. Bidwell, *Tariff Policy of the United States: A Study of Recent Experiences* (National Council on Foreign Relations, New York, 1933) carries on the discussion. O. Fred Boucke, *Europe and the American Tariff* (New York, 1933) describes foreign repercussions. W. S. Culbertson, *Reciprocity—a National Policy for Foreign Trade* (New York, 1937), is a plea for better relatioss. D. L. Cohn, *Picking American Pockets* (New York, 1936), attacks our high tariff policy. F. B. Sayre, *The Way Forward: American Trade Agreements Program* (New York, 1939); J. D. Larkin, *Trade Agreements* (New York, 1940); and J. C. Pearson, *The Reciprocal Trade Agreements Program: the Policy of the United States and Its Effectiveness* (Cath. Univ. of Amer., Washington, 1942), all approve this method.

A considerable general literature exists on the foreign policy of the United States, though little is written from the economic standpoint. The following are among the best for the purposes of this book: J. H. Latané, *A History of American Foreign Policy* (Garden City, 1927); D. G. Munro, *The United States and the Caribbean* (Boston, 1934); Cleona Lewis, *America's Stake in International Investments* (Brookings Institution, Washington, 1938); B. H. Williams, *Economic Foreign Policy of the United States* (New York, 1929).

A neglected field in our economic history is the organization and methods of wholesale and retail trade and marketing. The historical development is only incidentally described in modern treatises, but there is a little in P. D. Converse and H. Huegy, *Elements of Marketing* (New York, 1946); H. B. Killough, *The Economics of Marketing* (New York, 1933); F. E. Clark, *Principles of Marketing* (New York, 1932); and C. S. Duncan, *Marketing: Its Problems and Methods* (New York, 1920). An analysis of merchandising under the codes is L. Valenstein and E. B. Weiss, *Business under the Recovery Act* (New York, 1933). A recent development is described by F. E. Melder, *State and Local Barriers to Interstate Commerce in the United States* (Orono, Me., 1937), and by F. V. Waugh, *Barriers to Internal Trade in Farm Products* (Dept. of Agric., Washington, 1934). The 1930 census for the first time gathered comprehensive figures on retail trade. The subject is treated systematically in P. H. Nystrom, *The Economics of Retailing* (New York, 1919); C. W. Barker and I. D. Anderson, *Principles of Retailing* (2nd ed., New York, 1941); D. J. Duncan and C. E. Phillips, *Retailing Principles and Methods* (Chicago, 1941); and David Bloomfield (Compiler), *Selected Articles on Trends in Retail Distribution* (New York, 1930).

A few books on related subjects may finally be cited: W. S. Hayward and P. White, *Chain Stores, Their Management and Operation* (New York, 1925); T. D. Clark, *Pills, Petticoats, and Plows; the Southern Country Store* (Indianapolis, 1944); R. Wright, *Hawkers and Walkers in Early America* (Philadelphia, 1927), about peddling; Frank Peabody, *The History and Development of Advertising* (Garden City, 1929); and N. H. Borden, *Economics of Advertising* (Chicago, 1942).

The history of accounting practice for the early period remains to be written. The two best American textbooks on bookkeeping were B. F. Foster, *A Concise Treatise on Commercial Bookkeeping* (2nd ed., Boston, 1837); Thomas Jones, *Principles and Practice of Bookkeeping* (New York, 1841).

SOCIAL PROGRESS

(Chapters XVIII, XXXII)

It is not easy to measure social progress, but the authors believe that they have selected vital economic indices. Of these the real income of the individual and his life expectancy at birth are the most important.

For the colonial period and the early national period we are compelled to rely primarily on the observations of travelers and the generalizations of historians, for statistical information is almost entirely lacking. The following are some of the best: Henry Adams, *History of the United States of America*, Vol. I, Chaps. 1–6 (9 vols., New York, 1889–98); C. A. and M. R. Beard, *Rise of American Civilization*, Vol. I, Chap. 16 (2 vols., New York, 1927); G. S. Callender, *Selections from the Economic History of the United States, 1765–1860* (Boston, 1909), pp. 617–33, 701–19; C. R. Fish, *The Rise of the Common Man, 1830–1860* (New York, 1927) pp. 88–136; Gaillard Hunt, *Life in America One Hundred Years Ago* (New York, 1914); W. C. Langdon, *Everyday Things in American Life*, Vol. I, 1607–1776, Vol. II, 1776–1876 (2 vols., New York, 1941); E. McClellan, *History of American Costume, 1607–1870* (2 vols., Philadelphia, 1904); J. B. McMaster, *History of the People of the United States*, Vol. I, Chap. 1, Vol. II, Chap. 17, Vol. V, Chaps. 42, 44, 50, Vol. VI, Chap. 66, Vol. VII, Chaps. 73, 74 (7 vols., New York, 1883–1914); E. W. Martin, *The Standard of Living in 1860: American Consumption Levels on the Eve of the Civil War* (Chicago, 1942); Allan Nevins (Ed.), *American Social History as Recorded by British Travellers* (New York, 1934); N. J. Ware, *The Industrial Worker, 1840–1860*

(Boston, 1924), pp. 1–71; T. J. Wertenbaker, *The First Americans*, 1607–1690 (New York, 1927).

Finally, a few references may be given on the topics covered in the concluding chapter. On *food:* U. S. National Resources Committee, *Consumer Expenditures in the United States* (Washington, 1939); R. O. Cummings, *The American and His Food* (Chicago, 1941), an excellent historical account. On *housing:* E. E. Wood, *Recent Trends in American Housing* (New York, 1931), a good general survey; D. T. Rowlands and E. Woodbury, *Current Developments in Housing* (Annals Amer. Acad. of Pol. and Soc. Sci., Philadelphia, March 1937); C. Aronovici (Ed.), *Americans Can't Have Housing* (New York, 1934) and *Housing the Masses* (New York, 1939). On *health:* M. P. Ravenal, *A Half Century of Public Health* (New York, 1921); Committee on the Cost of Medical Care, *Medical Care for the American People* (Chicago, 1932); and H. Cabot, *The Doctor's Bill* (New York, 1935). On *clothing:* A. B. Young, *Recurring Cycles of Fashion*, 1760–1937 (New York, 1937). On *leisure:* J. E. Steiner, *Americans at Play* (New York, 1933); J. A. Krout, *Annals of American Sport* (New York, 1929); G. A. Lundberg and Others, *Leisure* (New York, 1934); and F. R. Dulles, *America Learns to Play* (New York, 1940). On *public service:* President's Conference on Unemployment, *Recent Economic Changes in the United States* (2 vols., New York, 1929), "Consumption and the Standard of Living," by L. Wolman; and H. A. Millis and R. E. Montgomery, *Labor's Progress and Some Basic Labor Problems* (New York, 1938), 132–34. On *education:* E. G. Dexter, *A History of Education in the United States* (New York, 1904); E. P. Cubberley, *Public Education in the United States* (New York, 1934); and E. W. Knight, *Education in the United States* (Boston, 1934). On *distribution of wealth:* W. I. King, *The National Income and Its Purchasing Power from* 1909 *to* 1928 (New York, 1930); G. Myers, *The History of Great American Fortunes* (New York, 1937) and *Ending of Hereditary Fortunes* (New York, 1939), gossipy narratives; R. F. Martin, *National Income in the United States*, 1799–1938 (Nat. Ind. Conf. Bd., New York, 1939); R. R. Doane, *The Anatomy of American Wealth: the Story of Our Physical Assets (Sometimes called Wealth) and Their Allocation as to Form and Use among the People* (New York, 1940); and S. Kuznets, *National Income and Its Composition*, 1919–38 (2 vols., New York, 1942), highly theoretical. *General:* President's Research Committee on Social Trends, *Recent Social Trends in the United States* (New York, 1933); M. Leven, H. G. Moulton, and P. Warburton, *America's Capacity to Consume* (Brookings Institution, Washington, 1934); National Industrial Conference Board, *Conference Board Studies in Enterprise and Social Progress* (New York, 1939); and U. S. National Resources Planning Board, *The Structure of American Economy* (2 parts, Washington, 1939). For further information on these topics consult F. M. Williams and C. C. Zimmerman's bibliography, *Studies of Family Living in the United States and Other Countries* (Dept. of Agric., Misc. Pub. No. 223, Washington, 1935).

INDEX OF

MAPS, CHARTS, AND TABLES

PAGE

Air-Carrier Operations in the United States, 1927–45,
Scheduled 694
Air Transportation, 1938 696
Airway Map of the United States 695
Automobile Industry, 1914–41, Growth of . . 645
Bank Credit, 1829–60, Expansion of . . . 326
Bank Statistics, 1834–63, Local 333
British Possessions in North America, 1765 . . 167
Canals in the North, 1850 277
Circuit of Wind, Water and Commerce in the North
Atlantic 114
Claims of Nations, 1750 13
Claims of Nations, 1763–75 18
Claims of Nations, 1783 181
Colonial Commerce and Exchange 113
Continental Currency 177
Corporate Form of Business in Manufacturing, Growth
of the 640
Corporate Savings 640
Cotton, Average Annual Production and Exports of
American, 1790–1860 250
Cotton and Slaves, 1802–55, Prices of . . . 395
Cotton Kingdom in America, The 405
Cotton Manufactures, 1830–60 349
Cotton, Seasonal Distribution of Man Labor on . . 397
Crude Iron and Steel Industry, 1859–1909, Compara-
tive Summary of the 482

PAGE

Crude Iron and Steel Rolled Products, 1914–43   .   642

Cumberland Road, The   271

Drafted Men (White) in Two World Wars, Degree
of Education of   779

Duties under Tariff Acts, 1789–1861, Average Level
of   358

Exported from Great Britain, 1768–69   .   .   .   171

Exports and Imports of Merchandise, 1791–1860   .   205

Exports and Imports of the United States, 1789–1860   201

Exports and Imports of the United States, 1790–1816   192

Exports and Imports, 1860–1940, Percentage of   .   717

Exports from New England, 1763–66, Average Annual   118

Exports from New York and Pennsylvania, 1763–66,
Average Annual   118

Exports from Virginia and Maryland, 1763–66, Average Annual   119

Export of Agricultural Products, 1910–40, Average
Annual   611

Fall Line of Rivers, The   100

Family Expenditures, 1900–09 and 1935–39, Percent
Distribution of   765

Financial Comparison of United States in 1914 and
1945 on Per Capita Basis   760

Foreign Trade and Lend Lease   718

Foreign Trade of the United States, 1790–1816   .   192

Foreign Trade of the United States, 1860–1914   .   567

Foregin Trade of the United States, 1914–46 .   .   714

Foreign Trade of the United States, 1940–45 .   .   718

Immigration to the United States, 1840–1940, Foreign   510

Industries in 1860 and 1914, Rank of Leading .   .   468

Internal Improvement and Railroad Grants   .   .   288

Interregional Highway System, The Recommended .   693

PAGE

Iron Ore Shipping Routes 473
Iron Works, 1622–1800 67
Land Claims of States, 1783, Conflicting . . . 216
Land Entries, 1800–1934, Original 220
Land in Free and Slave States, 1860 399
Manufactures, 1849–1909, Growth of . . . 467
Manufactures, 1914–45, Growth of 630
Manufacturing in Two Wars, United States Physical
     Production Index 636
Manufacturing, Size of the Average Establishment,
     1849–1909 475
Manufacturing, Size of Average Establishments,
     1914–39 634
Merchant Marine, American, 1915–45 . . . 724
Money Supply, The World War I, Increase in . . 737
Money Supply, The World War II, Increase in . . 755
Occupations, 1870–1930, Shifts in 610
Plants of American Origin 30
Population, 1860, Distribution of 367
Population and Agriculture, 1870–1930 . . . 448
Population Growth, 1641–1775, American . . 79
Population Increase in the West, 1800–60 . . 229
Population of the United States, 1790–1860 . . 370
Population of the United States, 1860–1910 . . 508
Population of the United States, 1910–40 . . 657
Population, 1850–1980, Our Aging 657
Population per Square Mile, 1790 363
Population per Square Mile, 1840 365
Price and Wage Increases, August, 1946 over January,
     1941 759
Prices, Percentage Rise of Wholesale over Prewar
     Level 758
Prices, 1913–25, Wholesale 738

PAGE

Prices Since 1790, Wholesale 757
Products in the United States, Regional Distribution of 453
Public Lands, Disposition of the 441
Public School Developments, 1870, 1900, 1920, 1942 778
Purchasing Power of the Dollar, 1914–1946 . . 757
Railroad Ton-Miles and Industrial Production, 1923–
44, The Comparative Trend of 688
Real Wages, The Effect of the Civil War on . . 584
Regions of the United States, Humid, Semi-Arid, and
Arid 462
Roads and Trails into the Western Territory, 1792 . 229
Roads in the United States, 1942, Miles of . . 687
Routes of Discoveries 4
Slaves in the Southern States, Distribution of . . 407
Stock Market Behavior, 1922–32 743
Strikes and Lockouts in the United States, 1927–July,
1946, Man-days Lost Through 670
Tariff Acts, 1861–1913 579
Tax Receipts and Expenditures, 1939 and 1945, Fed-
eral 754
Territorial Growth of the United States, 1783–1853 . 235
Textile Fabric Industry, 1859–1909 485
Trade between Great Britain and the Colonies, 1774–
75 175
Trade of Colonies with England, 1770 . . . 112
Trade Routes by Panama Canal and Otherwise . . 701
Trade Routes, Medieval 2
"Trade, Three Cornered" 113
Urban Concentration, 1840 369
Waterways, Navigable 699
Wheat from Chicago to New York City, 1868–1910,
Average Annual Rates on 538

GENERAL INDEX

Accidents, security for, 527, 678
Accounting, 314
Act to Regulate Commerce, 493, 502, 503, 548-550, 682, 684, 685. *See* Interstate Commerce Commission
Acts of Trade. *See* Navigation Acts
Adams, C. F., cited, 542
Adams, J. T., cited, 161
Adams, John, 139, 187
Adams, Samuel, 174
Advertising, 703, 711, 712
Africa, trade with, 12, 114
Agrarian changes, 176
Agrarianism, 380
Agricultural: depression, 603, 604, 611; discontent, 449-52, 618; education, 265, 266, 464; experiment stations, 464; journals, 266; ladder, 613; research, 463
Agricultural Adjustment Acts, 620, 621, 622; Thomas amendment, 749
Agricultural credit in the South, 454, 455; effects, 456
Agricultural machinery, 258-62, 444-46, 606-10, 624; effects of, 263, 607, 608; contribution of, 447, 608; increased productivity, 608, 609; economic results, 607, 608; social consequences, 609
Agricultural Marketing Act, 619
Agricultural production, 34, 37, 42, 251, 253, 446, 447, 602, 624; effect of wars on, 179, 193, 194, 602, 624; European demand for, 193, 448, 602, 603, 611; expansion of, 438-65; domestic demand for, 477, 603, 611; search for new uses, 605; consumption of, 614
Agricultural products: corn, 29, 30, 31, 32, 33, 44, sod, 245, 457, 605, 614; hybrid, 602; cotton, 45, 247, 249, 251, 454, 605, 614; fruits, 37, 42, 46, 454-57, 614; hay, 37; indigo, 45, 80; potatoes, 29, 37, 614; rice, 45, 90, 153, 252; sorghum, 34; soybeans, 605, 624, 638; sugar, 154, 202, 252; tobacco, 30, 43, 44, 45, 118, 152, 251, 252; tomatoes, 420; wheat, 34, 41, 42, 43, 457, 608, 615
Agricultural Revolution, 242-47, 361

Agriculture, 27-52, 242-67, 438-65, 601-28; primitive, 32; colonial, 27-52, 33; English, 28; Indian, 31-35; New England, 36-41; middle colonies, 41-43; southern colonies, 43-47; extensive, 27, 34, 35, 245, 251, 267; self-sufficing, 43, 51, 244, 253; commercial, 49, 52, 252, 253, 254, 266, 447, 616; East, 253-55, 434; West, 242-45, 457-59, 614; Prairie, 244-45, 443; South, 246-53, 454-57, 615; scientific, 264, 265; Bureau of, 266, 464; Department of, 464; Far West, 459
Alaska Railroad, 681
Albion, R. G., cited, 204
Aldrich Report, 382, 384
Allotment system, 621
Aluminum Company of America, 650, 654
American Expeditionary Force, 714
American Farmer, cited, 266
American Federation of Labor, 519 ff., 661 ff.; membership, 661, 663, 664, 668
American Husbandry, cited, 35, 36, 39, 42, 46, 88, 117, 119
American Party, 366 n.
American Philosophical Society, 433
American Railway Union, 523
American Sugar Refining Company, 494, 497, 503
American System, 359
American Telephone and Telegraph Company, 641
American Tobacco Company, 494, 504, 505
Anarchists, 518
Anti-trust legislation: federal, 495, 502, 503, 504; state, 492, 495, 502-3; Supreme Court on, 504; prosecution, 503
Appleby, J. F., 444
Apprenticeship, 83, 373, 429, 470
Arid regions, farming in, 461
Arthur, C. A., 577
Articles of Confederation, 177
Articles of small bulk and large value, 1, 3, 539; heavy and bulky, 536, 705
Artisans, emigration from England forbidden, 75

Ashe, Thomas, cited, 310
Assembly line, 637
Assize of bread, 95
Association, 379
Assumption of state debts: 1791, 335, 336-37; proposed in 1842, 284
Astor, John Jacob, 239
Attitude of England toward colonies, 116
Auction system, 206, 309
Austin, Moses, 237; Stephen, 237
Automobiles, 552, 690-92; during World Wars, 690; effects of, 690. *See also,* Motor Vehicle industry
Aviation, 692-97; expansion, 694, 696; government control, 695; Civil Aeronautics Board, 696; speed records, 697
Ayres, Leonard H., cited, 599

Babcock test, 459
Bagehot, Walter, 592
Baker, O. E., cited, 628
Balance of trade: during Middle Ages, 1; colonial, 112-16; 1791-1860, 205; 1860-1914, 571, 572; 1914-1946, 719, 720
Ballagh, J. C., cited, 88
Baltimore, 41, 46. 297
Baltimore and Ohio Railroad, 284, 285
Bancroft, G., cited, 78
Bank: of England, 137; of Stockholm, 137; of Massachusets, 320; of New York, 320
Bank credit, expansion of, 326 ff., 592
Bank failures, 733, 744, 745, 746
Bank holiday, 1933, 745
Bank notes: explained, 319, 320; state, 322-23; contraction of, 323-24, 327; counterfeit, 329; detectors, 329, 593; national, inelastic, 595, 733; Federal Reserve, elastic, 735
Bank of the United States: First, 320, 321; Second, 320, 321
Bank statistics, 1834-63, 333
Bankhead-Jones Farm Tenant Act of 1937, 614
Banking, 316-38, 592-99; "free," 331, 332, 593-94; National Act of 1863, 332; commercial, 592; central, 595-96
Banks: colonial, 136-37; functions of, 319, ·320; state, 321-22, 326; "pet," 326; "wildcat," 328-29; faults of, 328 ff.; state-operated, 330-31; national, 593; state, 594; investment, 596-97; country, 595; runs on, 596; divorce of commercial and investment, 746
Baring Brothers, 336, 355
Barnum, P. T., 434, 774

Barriers to interstate trade, 706-8
Barter, 120, 128, 310, 311
Barton, Clara, 427
Basing point system, 650, 654; "Pittsburgh Plus," 650
Beard, C. A., and M. R., cited, 19, 388, 426, 764
Beehive oven, 483
Beer, G. L., cited, 152, 173
Belcher, Jonathan, 138
Bell, A. G., 557
Bellomont, Governor, 57
Berkeley, William, cited, 86, 428
Berman, Edward, cited, 522
Bernard, Sir Francis, cited, 148, 168
"Bespoke" work, 95, 344, 371
Bessemer process, 351, 352 n., 482, 484, 485
Bicycle, 551
Big Four Railway Brotherhoods, 668
Bills of credit, colonial, 134 ff.
Bimetallic standard, 316, 317, 587, 588, 590
Birkbeck, M., cited, 230-31, 383
Birth rate, 79, 507, 656, 772
Biscuit-making, colonial, 65
Bishop, J. L., cited, 75
Bland-Allison Act, 588
Blessing of the Bay, 107
Board of Trade and Plantations, 157, 165; on slavery, 93
Bog iron, 65
Boll weevil, 615
Bonds, Civil War, 585, 593-94, 596-97; World War I, 736; World War II, 754
Border States, 399
Boré, J. E., 252
Boston, 117, 174, 279
Boston Tea Party, 174
Bounties, 58, 75, 160, 179
Bowen, Francis, cited, 384
Boycott, secondary, 525
Breaking land, 245
Bridges, 102, 269, 270
Brisbane, Albert, 379
Broker, 562
Brook Farm, 374
Brooks, J. G., cited, 406
Bryan, William J., 590
Bubble Act, 139
Buck Stove and Range case, 525
Buffalo, 298
Building and loan associations, 477
Bundling, 422
Burke, Edmund, 61, 157
Burnet, Governor W., cited, 141
Business cycle, 334, 509-10, 598-99
Butter, 255, 459
Byrd, William, 104

Cairnes, J. E., cited, 391
California, 238-39; gold rush to, in 1849, 238, 240, 318
Call money market, 595
Camels, 293
Canals: in the North, 277-81; traffic on, 279, 280, 698; freight rates, 278; decline of, 553; rehabilitation of, 698
Capital: needed for colonization, 17, 19, 20, 23; described, 71-73, 353, 470; shortage of, 71; foreign, 73, 283, 336-37, 355; invested in internal improvements, 282; sources of, 353-54, 477; accumulation, 477, 639; in South, 393; growth, 356; importance of, 413; in agriculture, 443, 613; in railroads, 535; in industry, 633; confused with money, 582
Carey, Henry C., cited 292
Carlton, F. T., cited 375
Carnegie, Andrew, 477, 484-85, 498-99
Carnegie Steel, 498
Carpet industry, 487
Carrier, Lyman, cited, 33
Carrying trade, 192, 193; regulation of, 149
Carver, T. N., cited, 219, 259, 444
Central Pacific Railroad, 537, 541
Chain stores, 567, 709
Charcoal, 54, 350-52
Charleston: center of southern trade, 105, 107; commercial convention at, 204
Charleston and Hamburg Railroad, 285
Charter-mongering states, 478 n., 492, 494, 502, 503
Charters, corporation, 355
Chase, Salmon P., cited, 274
Chase, Solon, cited, 451
Cheap land, effects, 382-83, 399
Checking system, 594
Check-off, 668
Cheese, 255, 459; factory, 256
Chemurgy, 606
Chesapeake and Albemarle Canal, 212
Chevalier, Michael, cited, 327, 376-77
Cheves, Langdon, 323
Cheyney, E. P., cited, 14
Chicago, 299; Board of Trade, 308, 709
Child, Sir Josiah, cited, 117
Child labor, 371, 377, 514; laws against, 375, 526; in South, 481
China, trade with, 183, 184
Cider, 37, 417, 419
Cities, growth of, 363, 368-71, 508
Civil Aeronautics Board, 696
Civil rights, acquisition of, 414-16; by women, 415
Civil War, cost of, 584-85
Clark, George R., 180, 304

Clark, Victor, cited, 486
Clark, William, 236
Clarke, William, cited, 104
Class distinctions, 411; groups, 412; lessened after Revolution, 413
Clay, Henry, 359
Clayton Anti-trust Act, 504, 548, 651
Clearing land, 58 ff., 233
Cleavage, economic, 413; lines of, not fixed, 435
Cleland, R. G., cited, 184
Clermont, 273
Cleveland, 276, 280
Cleveland, Grover, cited, 524, 547
Clipper ships, 209, 210, 573; scheduled lines, 209; record runs, 210
Closed shop, 373, 381, 668
Clothing, 424, 770-71; homespun, 405; leather, 405; ready-made, 426, 770
Cloth-making, colonial, 61; dyeing, 62; fulling, 62
Coal industry, 353
Coastwise trade, 108, 212, 555, 575, 724
Cobbett, William, cited, 419
Coins: foreign, 317; subsidiary, law of 1853, 318
Coke, 473, 483; by-product, 483
Collective agreements, 381
Colonial control, obstacles to, 165
Colonial theory and policy, 146-63; changes in, 165-69; administration of territory, 165; enforcement of Acts of Trade, 166; prohibition of paper money, 166; tightening of taxation, 167
Colonization: economics of, 1-26; motives for, 5-11; effects of, on Europe, 12; Spanish, 14; Dutch, 15-16; French, 16; English, 17; as a business investment, 23
Columbus, Christopher, 4, 6
Coman, Katharine, cited, 323-24
Combination: common law on, 374; methods of, 493; horizontal and vertical, 495, 643; advantages and disadvantages, 500-2; unfair competition of, 501; and trusts, 643; hastened by war, 649
Combine, 444
Commerce, domestic: colonial, 98, 107, 108; 1790-1860, 295-315; 1860-1914, 559-67; 1914-46, 705-31; geographic conditions of, 295; early, 295; expansion of, 295-315; volume, 559, 705
Commerce, foreign, 98, 110-16, 206-8; 567-73, 713-21; geographic conditions of, 98; organization of, 119-21; in seventeenth century, 111; in eighteenth, 111; with England, 111, 171,

Commerce, foreign (cont'd)
175; after 1812, 200-8; geographical distribution of, 208; organization of, 1815-60, 200; reciprocal liberty of, 207, 208; expansion of, 568; and World Wars, 713, 717; in depression of 1930's, 715
Commercial banks, functions, 581, 592
Commercial legislation, 207, 208; treaties, 207, 208
Commercial Revolution, 1, 5
Commission merchants, 306, 307, 308, 562; functions of, 307, 562
Committee of Industrial Organization, 666; membership, 666, 668
Common store in colonies, 21, 22
Commons, J. R., 384, 528
Commonwealth v. Hunt, 374
Communication, colonial, 123; 1790-1860, 293; 1860-1914, 555; 1914-46, 700-3
Commutation, 439
Competition, 540, 682, 704; eliminated by trusts, 650
Compromise tariff, 358; of 1850, 397
Concentration in industry, 475, 497; in large establishments, 633
Confederate money, 583 n.
Congress of Industrial Organizations, 666-68
Congress of the Confederation, 186
Conkling, Roscoe, 478
Connecticut River, 99
Conservation, 57
Conspiracy, common law on, 374, 493
Constitution, 187, 188; economic forces behind, 187; struggle over, 188
Consumption, 604, 767, 783
Continental Association, 175
Continental Congress, 174, 175
Continental paper money, 178
Contract labor, 512
Cooke, Jay, 596
Cooking, 418, 423
Coolidge, Calvin, 619, 729
Cooper, Peter, 285
Co-operation, among colonists, 82; productive, 350, 517, 519
Co-operative Marketing Act, 652
Co-operative stores, 710
Corn. See Agricultural products
Corn laws of 1815, English, 201; repeal of, in 1846, 208, 299
Corporations, build the railroads, 254; 354 ff.; charters, 355; evolution of, 478; and capital, 479; and trusts, 492, 494, 502, 503; capital saving by, 640; growth of, 640; federal control of, 641
Cortés, Hernando, 6, 459

Cost of living, 670; and Civil War, 584
Costs, fixed, 490; operating, 490; overhead, 490; importance of, 505
Cotton, raw: production of, 45, 247, 249-51, 404, 615; exports of, 202-5, 250; sea-island, 247, 387; upland, 247, 387; gin, 248, 249, 346, 354, 387, 388; prices of, 250; methods of growing, 251, 396-97, 403; marketing, 307; recovery in production, 457; picker, 615; prices, 393, 404; westward movement of, 389
Cotton kingdom, 405
Cotton textile manufacturing, 341, 346-47, 468, 480-81, 485
Coxe, Tench, cited, 193
Cradle scythe, 261
Credit Mobilier, 541
Credit system, 1815-60, 206, 307, 309, 310; of land sales, 222; easy, for farmers, 616-19
Creditor nation, United States as a, 720
"Crime of 1873," 587
Criminals sent to colonies, 85
Crises. See Panics.
Crop notes, 131
Cropping system, 455
Crown lands, 215
Cumberland Gap, 229-30; Road, 270, 271
Currency, contraction after Civil War, 450
Currency Act of 1764, 168, 169
Cyanide process, 591
Cycle, business, 334

Dabney, Thomas, 400
Dairy industry, 254, 256; in East, 454; in Middle West, 458; revolution in, 256; cheese factory, 256
Davis, J. S., cited, 354
Davis, Jefferson, 293
Dearborn, Henry, 341
Death rate, 656, 772
De Bow, J. D. B., 403
Debs, Eugene, 525
Debt: imprisonment for, 375, 414, 415; mortgage, 450, 618, 619; national, 334-36, 735, 740, 751, 753, 754; internal, 747; time center of, 748; state defaults on, 283, 336
Debtor-creditor conflict, 127, 136, 140, 330, 582, 591
Declaration of Independence, 176
Declaratory Act, 170
Decreasing costs, in iron and steel industry, 643
Deere, John, 260
Deerskins, 104
Deflation, causes, 586; effects, 581, 591
DeLeon, Daniel, 521

Demand, domestic, 468; foreign, 469; fluctuating, for luxury goods, 632
Demand deposits, 581, 591, 594
Demonetization of silver, 587
Depression: colonial, 144; 1763-70, 171; 1784-87, 184; 1819, 323, 324; 1837, 327; 1857, 332; 1873, 597; 1893, 598; 1914, 735; 1920, 662; of 1930's, 663, 741-45; causes of, 742
De Tocqueville, Alexis, 764, cited, 267, 433
Detroit, 276, 299, 658; sit-down strike in, 667
Devaluation, 318, 749
Dewey, D. R., cited, 128, 329
Diet, lack of balance in, 419
Dingley Act, 491, 578, 580
Discontent: political, 186; of farmers, 449-52
Discoveries: of new routes to Orient, 4; of New World, 5; results of, 5, 12
Discriminations, railroad, 542, 543
Diseases, 771, 773
Dispersion of population, 49, 228, 234, 368; of industry, 296
Division of labor, 476
Dixie, origin of word, 331
Doctrine of continuous voyage, 196
Dollar: colonial Spanish, 127; American, 316, 317
Domestic animals. See Livestock
Double liability, 593
Douglas, P. H., cited, 739
Drummers, mercantile, 309
Dry farming, 461
Du Bois, W., cited, 92
Due process clause, meaning, 479, 528
Duryea, C. E., 552
Dutch: exploration, 11; colonization, 15-16, land policy, 15, failure of, 16; as farmers, 29
Duty Act of 1673, 156, 157
Dwight, Timothy, cited, 312, 433
Dye and chemical industries, 631

Earth butchery, 228, 246, 399
East India Company, British, 173, 174
Eastman, J. B., 686, 688
Edison, T. A., 570
Education, 427-31, 783; schools, 427, 429, 430, 777, 778; colleges, 428, 432, 778, 779; academies, 430; medical and law schols, 432; demanded by labor, 430; vocational, 779
Eight-hour movement, 516
Electric railways, 550-51
Eliot, Jared, 34, 41
Elkins Act of 1903, 503, 549

Embargo Act, 197-98, 342; effects of, 198
Emergency Fleet Corporation, 721
Employers associations, 374, 524; liability laws, 527
Enclosure movement in England, 10, 19
Endless chain, 589, 591
English: exploration, 7; colonization, 17, reasons for success, 17-19; colonial policy, 147, 149, obstacles to, 165, changes in, 165
English Orders in Council, 195
Entail, 177
Enumerated commodities, 151, 152, 153
Equality, 414, 416
Erie Canal, 276-79; effects of, 277, 298; freight rates on, 278, 298; improved in 1903, 553
Erie Railroad, 286, 541
Evans, G. H., 226, 380
Evans, Oliver, 272, 552
Evasion of restrictions by colonies, 161
Ever-normal: granary plan, 623; food supply, 623
Excess profits tax, 735, 753
Exploration: a century of, 2, 4; Portuguese, 4, 6, 10; Spanish, 4, 6, 11; French, 6, 8, 10, 11; Dutch, 11; English, 6, 7, 11; economic motives for, 5; religious motives, 10; political motives, 11
Export duties, forbidden by Constitution, 357
Exports, 99, 110, 111, 193, 202, 205, 568, 602, 715, 720; of New England, 17; of middle colonies, 118; of southern colonies, 119; regulation of, 151; leading, 1860, 568; in 1914, 569; in 1939, 715; per capita, 716; of agricultural products, 118, 602
Express companies, 539
Extractive industries, in colonies, 54

Factors, 119, 206
Factory: evolution of, 343-46; organization under Lowell type, 376; under Fall River type, 378; inspection laws, 527
Factory system, 345, 348; types, 375 ff.
Failures, business, 585
Fair Labor Standards Act, 673, 676, 781
Fairs, 109; county, 265
Fall line of rivers, 99, 100
Fall River, 486
Family, size of, 79, 507
Faneuil, Peter, 73, 91
Fanning mill, 262
Fares, passenger, on canals, 279; on railroads, 539

Farm: tools, 28, 40, 47; practices, 51; products, demand for, 447-49; labor, 463; mortgage indebtedness, 450, 618, 619; relief: easy credit, 616-19; reducing surplus, 620-23
Farm Board, 619
Farm Credit Administration, 617
Farm Emergency Relief Act, 620
Farm Mortgage Foreclosure Act, 618
Farmers Alliance, 590
Farming, large-scale, 444, 609
Farms: small, 37, 49, 609; size, 49, 455, 463, 601, 608; new, 441, 442, 601
Farr, Dr. William, cited, 511
Federal Bureau of Corporations, 503
Federal Co-ordinator of Transport, 686
Federal Deposit Insurance Corporation, 745
Federal Land Banks, 745
Federal Reserve: system, 596, 734, 741; banks, 733, as bankers' banks, 734, functions, 734-35, increased control, 746
Federal Reserve Board, 734
Federal Trade Commission, 504, 651, 652, 654, 781
Fences, 245; barbed wire, 443, 460
Fertilizer, 37, 251, 264
Feudal: privilege, abolition of, 176; tenure of land, 49, 176
Field, C. W., 557
Fifth amendment, 478, 528
Fillmore, M., 366 n.
Finance, 316-38, 583-85; government, 334-37
Financing: colonial wars, 143, 144; Revolution, 177-79; Civil War, 583 ff.; three emergencies, 732-61; war, by taxation, 736; by borrowing, 736, by credit money, 737
Fire department, 424
Fiscal agent, 321, 334
Fisheries, 7, 59-61, 180
Fitch, John, 272
Fitzhugh, William, 50
Fixed costs. See Costs, fixed
Flail, 262
Flour: export of, 42; price of, 194
Food, in colonies, 416-18; 1790-1860, 419; 1860-1946, 766-67
Food stamps, 623
Forbes, J. M., 542
Forbes Road, 229-30
Ford, Henry, 638, 646
Ford Motor Company, 646
Fordney-McCumber tariff, 725
Foreign exchange, 133, 206
Fourier, Charles, 379
Fourteenth amendment, 478, 528

Franklin, Benjamin, 64, 78, 79, 112, 123, 141, 173, 188, 265, 416, 433
Free artisans, 53, 83
Free coinage of silver stopped, 318; advocated, 587 ff.
Free enterprise, 707
Free silver movement, 582-83, 586 ff.
Free trade within the United States, 474
Freedom dues, 87
Freedom of contract, 526, 528
Freight: earnings on American vessels, 205; rates on railroads, 538, 539
French: exploration, 6; fur trade, 8, 103; colonization, 16; failure of, 16
French and Indian War, 18, 104, 161
Frontier, 442
Fulton, Robert, cited, 273
Fur trade, 8, 15, 16, 17, 103-7, 304; significance of, 106
Futures, dealing in, 564

Gadsden Purchase, 239
Gallatin, Albert, 270, 276, 335, 341; cited, 199
Gang system of slave labor, 398
Gary, Elbert H., 499
Gauge, railroad, 286
General Managers Association, 524
General Motors Corporation, 646
General store, 108, 311, 312, 565, 708
Genesee Road, 229-30
Gentlemen's agreements, 493
Georgia: slavery forbidden in, 90; as an outpost, 105
Germans, 29, 42, 442
Gibbons v. Ogden, 275
Gilbert, Sir Humphrey, 20, 23
Gimbel Brothers, 566
Gold and silver mines, 6, 7; discovery of gold in California, 304; rush to, 587
Gold Reserve Act of 1934, 749
Gold standard, 587, 589; begins, 317, 318, 319; makes for price stability, 733; abandoned, 732, 741, 748, 752
Gold Standard Act of 1900, 732
Gompers, Samuel, 520, 525, 662
Gould, Jay, 517, 542, 673
Government advances to Allies in World War I, 719, 736
Government aid: to roads, 270; to railroads, 532, 534, effects of, 534
Government aid to Allies in World War II. See Lend-lease
Government functions, 782
Government regulation of industry, 73-75
Grading grain, 446
Graduation Act, 226
Granger movement, 451, 543; legislation, 544

Gray, Asa, 557
Gray, L. C., cited, 94, 401 n.
Grazing, 459
"Great American Desert," 236
Great Atlantic and Pacific Tea Company, 567
Great Lakes, 275, 698; traffic on, 473, 555, 560, 575, 698; shipping on, 473
"Great Migration," 11, 23
Great Northern Railroad, 542, 547
Greeley, Horace, cited, 279
Green, William, 665
Greenback Party, 451; movement, 582, 585; and labor, 516; origin of name, 584
Grenville, George, 168
Gresham's law, 127, 130, 134, 138, 317, 318, 587
Griffiths, J. W., 209
Guthrie, James, 205

Hamilton, Alexander, 178, 316, 320; financial program of, 334, 335
Hammond, M. B., cited, 456
Hancock, John, 174
Hansen, A. H., cited, 529, 584
Harriman, E. H., 547
Harrow, 260, 446
Hasenclever, Peter, 73
Hat-making, 158; regulated in 1732, 75
Havana Convention, 1940, 729
Havemeyer, H. O., 491, 578
Hawkins, John, 43, 122
Hawley-Smoot tariff, 725
Haymarket riot, 518
Hayward, William, 521
Hazard, Blanche, cited, 343-46
Health, 426-27, 771-73; boards of, 773
Heating, 422
Heilperin, M. A., cited, 716
Helper, Hinton, 407
Henry, Joseph, 293
Henry, Patrick, 131 n.
Hepburn Act of 1906, 549
Hibbard, B. H., cited, 225
Hill, J. J., 542
Hines, W. D., 681, 682
Hoar, George F., cited, 541
Hoe, 41, 47, 66
Holding company, 494
Home market, 359
Homestead Act, 226, 439-41; effects of, 440
Hoover, Herbert, 619, 729; cited, 700
"Hot air" period of American history, 379
Hours of labor, 374, 381-82, 529, 675
Housing, 420-24, 768-70; cave dwellings, 420; log cabins, 420; frame, 421; brick, 421; lean-to, 421; furniture,

421, 422; heating, 422; slums, 424; cost of construction, 770
Houston, Sam, 237
Howe, Elias, 357
Howe, T. C., cited, 582
Hudson, Henry, 15
Hudson River, 99, 103
Hudson's Bay Company, 8 n., 13
Hull, Cordell, 726
Humanitarian movements, 378-81
Hussey, Obed, 261

Ickes, Harold L., 750
Illicit trade, 161, 172
Illinois Central Railroad, 288, 533, 534
Illiteracy, 428, 778
Immigration: after Revolution, 362; 1820-60, 364-66, 370, 378; German, 364; Irish, 365; and industrial growth, 469; increase, 509; changed composition, 510; advantages and disadvantages, 511; restrictive legislation, 512, 659; decline in, 657, 659; quota system, 659; assimilation, 660
Imports, 107, 111, 201, 202, 205, 570-73, 716, 720; regulation of colonial, 153, 154; leading in 1860, 571; in 1914, 571; in 1939, 716
Income tax, 735, 753
Incorporation laws, 354
Indentured servants, 22, 84
Independent treasury system, 337
India, European trade with, 2; route to, 5
Indians, 8, 31, 32, 33, 51, 103; fur trade with, 103-7; slave trade, 105; use wampum as money, 129-30
Industrial Commission, 491
Industrial organization: changing, 371-73; factors favoring growth, 469; leaders, 474; structure, 514; research, 638
Industrial Revolution, 339-61; prerequisites of, 340; in the South, 480, 486
Industrial Workers of the World, 521
Industries: infant, 339; rank of leading, 468; localization of, 479; migration of, 480
Industry: colonial, 160; home stage, 343; domestic stage, 344; handicraft stage, 344; factory stage, 345
Inflation: colonial, 134, 143, 144; by bank notes, 322, 324, 329, 332, 336; causes, 582; effects, 581, 584; during World War I, 738, 739; during World War II, 754, 755, 759
Ingle, Edward, 403
Inheritance, 50
Injunction, 524-25

Instalment buying, 712, 742
Insull, Samuel, 742
Integration of industry, 485, 498
Interchangeable parts, 342 n., 466, 471
Intercolonial trade, 107-8; restrictions on, 156
Interest rates, 450, 742
Interlocking directorates, 495, 504
Intermediate Credit Banks, 617
Internal improvements by states, 281-84; reasons for, 281; increase in indebtedness, 282; by corporations, rejected, 281; failure of, 283; sale of works, 284
Internal taxes, 169, 576, 577
Interstate Commerce Commission, 548, 682, 684-86. See Act to Regulate Commerce
Interstate trade: barriers to, 707; purpose of, 708
Intolerable Acts, 174
Inventions, 356, 470
Investment, agencies of, 355; by England, 356; long-term, 477
Iron and steel industry, 468, 481-85, 641-45; fuels for, 350; production index, 642; changes in, 643
Iron industry: in early Virginia, 53; colonial, 66-68; regulated by English in 1750, 75; restricted in colonies, 159, 160; cast, 349; wrought, 350; manufactures, 352; mines, 473, 484; shipping routes, 473
Irrigation, 461
Itinerant worker, 95, 343

Jackson. Andrew, 283, 325, 413, 692
James, Charles, 353
Jamestown, 20, 43, 46, 66-68
Jefferson, Thomas, 196, 197, 199, 207, 222, 226, 236, 260, 316, 317, 321, 356, 387, 429
Jennings, W. W., cited, 383
Jobber, 562
Johnson, Andrew, 226
Johnson, E. R., cited, 92
Jordan Marsh, 566
Judicial legislation, 504
Jurisdictional disputes, 665

Kalm, Peter, cited, 35, 79, 109
Kellogg Pact, 730
Kelly, O. H., 451
Kelly, William, 351, 352 n.
Kentucky: early settlement in, 223; claimed by Virginia, 215
Killough, H. B., cited, 308, 563
King, W. I., cited, 764
Kirkland, E. C., cited, 110

Knight, Mme., cited, 132
Knights of Labor, 512, 517; aims, 517; failure, 518; organization, 518
Know-Nothing Party, 366 n.
Kuznets, Simon, cited, 639

Labor, 362-85, 507-31, 661-78; scarcity of, 227, 340, 469; how overcome, 80; political demands by, 374; division of, 476; composition of labor force, 513; in South, 529; legislation, 525
Laborsaving machinery, 632
Labor unions: early, 373; awakening period, 374; effect of industrial changes on, 514; standards, 662
Laissez-faire, 488, 498, 505, 540, 780, 781, 782
Lakes to the Gulf Deep Waterway, 700
Lambert, John, cited, 198
Lancaster-Philadelphia turnpike, 270
Land: acquisition of, 47, 50, 52; colonial system, 48-50; claims of states, 1783, 215; cessions by states, 215; ordinances, 217; disposition of public, 219; companies, in Ohio, 221; in the Southwest, 222; speculation, 221, 226, 228, 323, 325, 330, 332; sales, 219; for cash, 222; on credit, 225; reform urged, 224; effects of cheap, 227; land grants to railroads, 288, 533, 534; for colleges, 464; value of, 399; policy of United States, 439, 627; of Dutch, 15; of French, 16; of English, 20, 22, 23; settlement, 440
"Land Bank Manufactory," 136-39; notes of, 136
Landis, Kenesaw M., 505
Large-scale production, 512; advantages of, 476
Law, John, 137
Lee, Daniel and Jason, 239
Legal tender, 316, 584
Leisure, 773
Lend-lease, 624, 686, 718
Lewis, John L., 666, 668, 674
Lewis, Meriwether, 236
Liability, limited, 355, 478; laws for accidents, 527
Life expectancy, 427, 676, 772
Life insurance companies, 477
Light, 422; candles, 422; lamp, 422; gas, 423; kerosene, 423
Liquors, 417; rum, 419; whisky, 419
Little Steel formula, 669
Livestock: cattle, 38, 39, 42, 46; beef breed, 255; milk breed, 255; trails, 460; range, 461; goats, 47; horses, 38, 39, 43, 47, 256, Narragansett pacers, 39, Conestoga, 43, 256,

Percheron, 257, decrease as result of machinery, 604, 607; mules, 253, 257; oxen, 39, 40, 47, 256; sheep, 38, 39, 42, 257, merinos, 257; Saxony, 257; swine, 38, 39, 42, 46, 257, 258, 259
Loan office, 136-38; notes, 136
Loans, during Revolution, 178; during World War I, 719
Localization: of production, 253, 559, 706; of industry, 352, 449, 647
Locomotive, first, 285
Log cabins, 29, 420, 421
London Company, 20; land policy of, 21; common store system, 21
Long Island Sound, 99
Longstreet, William, 273
Loom, automatic, 486
Louisiana banking system, 331
Louisiana Purchase, 234
Lowell, Francis C., 347, 354
Lowell, Mass., 347, 349, 376, 486
Loyalists, 176
Lucas, Eliza, 45
Lynn, Mass.: early shoe center, 63; iron manufacturing in, 66

Machinery, laborsaving, 470
Macy, R. H., 566
McAdoo, W. G., 681
McCormick, Cyrus, 261
McCulloch v. *Maryland*, 324
McKinley, William, 590
McKinley Act, 578, 580
McMaster, J. B., cited, 194, 197, 269, 341-42, 423
McNary-Haugen bill, 619
Madison, James, 207
Magellan, voyage of, 6
Mail service of railroads, 539
Maize. *See* Corn.
Mann, Horace, 375
Mann-Elkins Act of 1916, 549
Manning, William, 261
Manufacturing: restriction of colonial, 158, 159, 160; effect of Revolution on, 179; during depression of 1784-87, 185; growth of, 466, 629; large-scale, 467; size of establishment, 467, 475; value added by, 467, 469; geography of, 479; center of, 480; 1860-1914, 569, 570; 1914-46, 629-55; effect of World War I, 630; reconversion, 631; changes, 630; unstable, 633; indexes of growth, 634; reasons for, 635; power in, 635; scientific management, 636; industrial research, 638; iron and steel, 641-45; motor vehicles, 645-47
Maritime Commission, 1942, 733
Marketing, domestic: colonial organiza-

tion of, 108; 1815-60, 206, 307; 1860-1914, 561-63; 1914-46, 711; methods, 305; retail, 564, 709; wholesale, 561, 708; foreign, 572
Markets: colonies as, 9, 109; extension of, 295, 300, 559, 569, 711; become national, 514, 560; specialization limited by expansion of, 467-68, 471, 473, 477, 490; economies from combinations, 501
Marshall, John, 324, 330
Marshall Field, 566
Martin, Homer, 667
Martineau, Harriet, cited, 368, 369
Maryland: convicts in, 86; forces land cessions, 217
Marvel, C. S., cited, 638
Massachusetts Bay, 21, 22, 40
Massachusetts Land Bank, 138 ff., mint, 128
Mechanics' Free Press, cited, 377-78
Mechanic's lien law, 375, 415, 517
Mechanics Union of Trade Associations, 374
Medical: schools, 426; science, 772
Mellon, Andrew, 740
Mercantilism, 14-16, 73-75, 146, 147, 488; aim of, 148, 149; struggle with, 180
Merchant, 121, 206, 306; wholesale, 308; commission, 306, 307, 308, 562; merchant-capitalist, 372
Merchant marine, 193, 207, 208-10, 573-75, 721-24; Collins Line, 211; merchant marine acts, 722; Liberty and Victory ships, 733
Mexican cession, 235, 237
Mexican War, finances of, 337
Miami Company, 221, 225
Michigan State College of Agriculture, 266
Middleman, 306, 308, 515; elimination of, 562, 708
"Middle passage," 91
Migration of industries, 479-80
Milk, 255, 417, 419, 458, 614
Miller-Tydings Act, 654
Millionaires, 436, 764
Mills, F. C., cited, 632
Minimum wage laws for women, 526
Mint: colonial, 127-28; ratio, 317, 318
Mint Act, 1792, 317
Mississippi River, 100, 552; trade on, 300-3, 553, 560
Mitchell, Wesley C., cited, 585, 599
Molasses, 64-65, 114; Act of 1733, 154, 155, 168
Money: scarcity of, 2, 125, 135, 142; export forbidden, 126; commodity, 130,

Money (cont'd)
  133; paper: origin, 133, colonial, 133,
  134, 135, 139, 140, 142, 143, 166,
  167, 178, prohibition of, 139, 142,
  166, Continental, 178, issued by
  states, 185; defined, 130; forbidden by
  Constitution, 316; per capita, 588
Monopoly, common law on, 502
Monroe, James, 236
Montgomery, James, 382
Montgomery Ward, 566, 711
Moody, John, cited, 549
Moore, Thomas, 420
Moratoria, 185
Morey, Samuel, 273
Morgan, J. P., 499, 547, 597
Morgan-Belmont syndicate, 590
Mormons, 239, 240, 304
Morrill: Land Act, 464; tariff, 358, 576
Morris, Robert, 178, 320
Morse, S. F. B., 293, 357
Mortgage indebtedness, 450, 618, 619
"Mother of trusts": tariff, 491, 505; tele-
  phone, 492
Motor vehicle industry, 645-47, 689, 690;
  integration of, 646; production index,
  647; motor busses, 691; motor trucks,
  691, 703; traffic, 692. See also Auto-
  mobiles
Mower, 261, 262
"Muckraking," 502
Mulattoes, number of, 409

Napoleon's decrees, 195, 196, 236
National Banking Act of 1863, 332, 593
National Currency Act, 593
National debt, 334-35, 336. See also
  Debt
National income, 468, 744, 748, 765,
  776; labor's share of, 675
National Industrial Recovery Act, 652,
  664; codes under, 653; ended by
  Schechter case, 653; hours under, 675
National Labor Relations (Wagner) Act,
  664, 672
National Labor Union, 516
National Monetary Commission, 596, 734
National Pike. See Cumberland Road
Natural monopolies, 491 n.
Natural resources, 27, 783
Naval stores, 9, 53-56, 58-59, 153, 160
Navigable waters, monopoly of, 274, 275;
  extent of, 552
Navigation Acts, 107, 121, 149-57; en-
  forcement of, 168, 172
Negro population, 80, 92-93, 507-8;
  slavery, 89 ff., 386-410; free, 408;
  labor, 529-30
Nettels, C. P., cited, 122

Neutral trade, 190, 713; disregard of our
  rights in, 191, 714; blows at, 195
Neutrality, 190-96; legislation, 726, 727
"New Deal," 627, 745, 748, 782; financ-
  ing, 750
New England, 25, 32; agriculture in,
  36-41; land system of, 48; exports,
  112, 118
New England Workingmen's Association,
  380
New Jersey corporations, 479, 492, 494,
  503
New Orleans, 203, 204, 251, 300, 553,
  573
New York, 118, 203, 573, 709
New York Central and Hudson River
  Railroad, 544
New York State Barge Canal, 553, 554,
  698
New York Tribune, cited, 262-63
Newbold, Charles, 260
Newspapers: first colonial, 123; 1790-
  1860, 294; 1860-1914, 557; 1914-46,
  703
Nimmo, Joseph, cited, 460
Non-importation agreements, 169, 171,
  175
Non-Intercourse Act: of 1806, 197; of
  1809, 199, 342
Northern Pacific Railroad, 533, 547
Northern Securities Company, 503, 547
Northwest passage, 6, 8
Nystrom, P. H., cited, 311

Oberlin College, 415
Office of Defense Transportation, 688
Office of Price Administration, 626, 756
Ohio Company, 221
Olmsted, F. L., 392, 402
Omnibus, 292, 424 ·
One-crop system, 392, 399-400, 403
Open-hearth process, 482, 484, 485
Open price associations, 495
Orchards, 37, 255, 417
Orders in Council, English, 195, 196, 198
Ordinance of 1787, 387
Oregon territory, 235, 239
Ormsbee, Elijah, 273
Orth, S., cited, 380
Osborn v. United States Bank, 324
Ostend Manifesto, 399
Overseer, 398
Owen, Robert, 519

Packet boats, 209
Panama Canal, 548, 554, 698, 728
Pan-American Congress, 580
Panics, 333-34, 384, 596-98; of 1819,
  323-24; of 1837, 327; of 1857, 332;

of 1873, 597; of 1893, 598; of 1932, 663, 741-45
Paper-making in colonies, 64; 1860-1914, 480
Paper money. *See* Money, paper, Bills of credit, Loan office notes
Parson's Cause, 131 n.
Patents, 356-57, 471-472, 497, 639
Patrons of Husbandry, 451
Patroon, 15
Payne-Aldrich Act, 578
Peck, J. M., 231, 232
Peddlers, 109, 312, 313, 565
Peddling, by horse, 312; by boat, 313, 314
Penn, William, 47, 77, 104
Pennsylvania: population, 77; exports, 118; canal, 279; Railroad, 545, 641
Peoples' Party, 452, 590
Perlman, Selig, 519
Peto, S. M., cited, 471-72
Petrillo, Caesar, 673
Phalanxes, 379
Philadelphia: population, 80; foreign trade, 118; transportation, 270; canal, 279; market, 297
Phillipo, James M., cited, 432
Phillips, U. B., cited, 222
Piece of eight, 127
Pike, Zebulon, 236
Pilgrims, 21, 23, 40
Pine-tree shilling, 128
Pioneering, 221, 233, 243; on Great Plains, 443
Piracy, 121, 122
Pitkin, Timothy, 116, 179, 194
Pitt, Hiram and John, 262
Pitt, William, 182
Plantation system, 49, 90, 389, 396 ff.; changed after Civil War, 454
Plants: European, 28; native American, 29, 30; selection and adaptation, 33; improvement in, 34
Plow, wooden, 40; iron, 259, 260, 446; steel, 260
Plumbing, 421; water closets, 423
Plymouth, 21, 23; Company, 20; common store in, 22
Police power, 525, 528
Polygamy, 240
Pony express, 293
Pooling, 493, 546, 682
"Poor whites," 408
Population, 507-9, 656-60; growth of, 77, 362, 507, 656; colonies an outlet for, 9; distribution of, 80, 362, 367; dispersion of, 228, 234; increase in West, 234; Negro, 362, 370, 657; urban, 363, 368; ages of, 508, 658;

geographical shift, 508, 658; composition of, 507, 508
Populism. *See* Peoples' Party
Ports, 203, 204, 205; leading, 117, 720
Portuguese, discoveries of, 4; explorations by, 6
Postal system: colonial, 100, 123; 1790-1860, 293; rates, 294; stamps, 294; 1860-1914, 556; parcel post, 556, 700; savings banks, 556, 702
Potash, 59
Potato, white, 29, 37; famine in Ireland, 364
Potter, William, 137
Powderly, Terence V., 518
Power, sources, 70, 636; new kinds of, 353; in manufacturing, 472, 635, 636
Pownall, T., cited, 141
Prairie Farmer, 266
Precious metals, 6; in Mexico and Peru, 6, 7; need for, 7
Pre-emption, 224 ff., 439
Price control, by trusts, 501
Price cutting, 501
Price level, 581, 591; effects of changes in, 581, 591
Price-fixing, colonial, 96
Priests, 8, 10
Primogeniture, 50, 176
Privateering, 121, 122, 200
Privies, 769
Proclamation money, 127
Proclamation of 1763, 165, 166
Produce exchanges, 308, 564
Production, large-scale, 495, 497, 500; economies from combinations, 500, 501
Productivity of labor, 385; of machinery, 603, 609
Promoters' profits, 493, 499
Property-holding company, 494
Property rights protected, 528
Proprietary colonies, 23, 48
Propriety in New England, 48
Prosperity: 1787-89, 188; 1793-1807, 194; 1897-1914, 452; 1878, 577; 1919, 662; 1921-29, 742, 743
Proxies, 641
Public domain, 438-43; appropriation of, 438; settlement on, 441; settlers on, 442
Public services, 775-77
Public utilities commissions, 685
Public Works Administration, 750
Puddling iron, 351
Pullman: cars, 537; strike, 523
Purchasing power parity, 622
Pure Food and Drug acts, 712, 768
Puritans, 11, 22
"Putting out" system, 373

Quakers, 11, 104; views on slavery, 92
Quebec Act, 174
Quitrent, 50, 172; abolition of, 176

Radio, 702
Radiotelegraphy, 702
Railroad Retirement Act, 683
Railroad War Board, 681
Railroads, 284-92, 530-50, 680-89; construction, 285-86; opposition to, 287; state aid, 270, 287; building, 289, 532, 535, 680; economic effects, 290-92, 538; rates, 292, 473, 538, 539, 696; transcontinental, 490, 532; federal aid, 532, 534; track and equipment, 536; service, 537; air brake, 537; coupler, 538; abuses, 539-43; construction companies, 540; overbuilding, 540; competition, 540, 682; discrimination, 542; hostility to, 543; as natural monopolies, 544; consolidation, 545, 682; pooling, 545, 682; traffic associations, 546; combination, 547; community of interest, 547; regulation, 548-50, 684-85; during World War I: federal administration, 681, Transportation Act of 1920, 682-85; railroad prosperity and depression, 685; during World War II, 688, 689; freight traffic, 698, 705
Rails, manufacture of, 351
Raleigh, Sir Walter, 20, 23
Ramsey, James, 273
Randolph, John, 387
Read, Nathan, 273
Real wages. See Wages, real
Reaper, 261, 262, 444; self-binder, 444
Reaping, 41
Reciprocity, 579, 580
Réclus, E., cited, 218 n.
Reconversion, 631; and labor, 669
Recreation, 432-34, 774-75; community sports, 433; amusements, 434, 774; sports, 434, 775
Rectangular surveys, 217 ff.
Redemptioners, 85
Re-export trade, 192
Reforms, 783
Refrigeration, 420; car, 458, 537
Regenerative furnace, 483
Regional specialization, 452, 473, 479, 480, 614, 616, 717
Registry, American, of ships, 573, 575, 721
Regulated economy, 488
Religion, freedom of, 11
Repudiation of state debts, 283, 336; proposal to assume, 284
Revolution, American: economic causes of, 164-69; agrarian changes during,

176; financing, 177-79; cost of, 179; economic conditions during, 179; territorial gains after, 180
Rhode Island paper money, 136
Rice as money, 131
Richmond, 71
"Right of deposit," 234, 236
Ripley, W. Z., cited, 535, 541
Rittenhouse, William, 64
Rivers, navigable, 99, 100, 274-76, 552, 554, 697; barges on, 697
Roads: colonial, 100; ridge, 101; plank, 269, 272; corduroy, 272; good roads movement, 551; improvements in, 692; effects of automobiles, 692
Robinson-Patman Act, 654
Rockefeller, John D., 498, 673, 744
Rogers, Thorold, cited, 511
Rolfe, John, 43
Roosevelt, Franklin D., 664, 672, 745, 749
Roosevelt, Theodore, 502, 503, 727, 728, 729
Rotation: of crops, 29, 35, 251, 264; of fields, 36
Roundabout voyages, 121
Routes to the West, 228 ff.
Royal African Company, 91
"Rule of reason," 504
"Rule of War of 1756," 191, 196
Rum, 64, 114, 154, 419
Rust, J. R. and M. D., 615

Safety-fund bank system, 329
Safety valve theory of cheap land, 227
St. Lawrence Ship Canal, 700
St. Louis, 302, 304, 553; Board of Trade, 308; trade of, 302
St. Marys Falls Canal, 554, 698
Salutary neglect, policy of, 161
Sandys, Sir Edwin, 53
Santa Fe, 304
Savings: and capital, 477; national, 758; by corporations, 641; banks, 556, 702
Sawmills, 56
Schools, 375, 427, 429, 430, 777, 778, 779
Schooner, origin of, 60
Scientific management, 637
Scioto Company, 221
Scotch-Irish, settlement, 78
Scott, T. A., 545
Seager, H. R., cited, 497
Searight, T. B., cited, 271
Sears Roebuck, 711
Second Bank of the United States, 322-25, 355
"Second War of Independence," 200
Securities, early sales of, 355-56

Securities and Exchange Act of 1934, 746
Security: against unemployment, 676; against old age, 678; against accident, 678
Security holding company, 494, 499
Self-sufficiency, of colonists, 69-70; of agriculture, 43, 51, 244, 253
Seligman, E. R. A., cited, 712
Settlement, principal colonial localities of, 99; process of, 232, 233; western, 262, 298; of public domain, 441
Seven Years' War, 164-71
Seward, W. H., cited, 442
Sewing machine, 357
Shaler, N. S., cited, 407
Share crop system, 530
Sharfman, I. L., cited, 684
Sheffield, Lord John, cited, 114, 149
Sherman Anti-Trust Act, 502, 503, 504, 547; Silver Purchase Act, 588-90
Shipbuilding, 56, 107, 150, 193, 210, 573-75, 721-23
Shipping Board, 1916, 721
Shoe: factory, 343-46; machinery trust, 497; ready-made, 426
Showboats, 774
Shreve, Henry, 274
Silver Bank, 138
Sinclair, Sir John, 265
Sinclair, Upton, 768
Skidmore, Thomas, 380
Slater, Samuel, 189, 341, 347, 353-54, 361
Slaughtering and meat-packing industry, 458, 468, 480
Slave trade, 89, 91-92; Indian, 105; African, 114, 387, 401, 492; internal, 401-2; restrictions on, 401
Slaveholders, number of, 406 n.
Slavery, 386-410; sectional attitudes to, 92-93; forbidden in Northwest Territory, 210; and cheap land, 228; decline of, 1780-1800, 386-87; revival of, 389-90; economic reasons for, 390; advantages of, 390-91; disadvantages of, 391-93; economic cost to the South, 393; conditions necessary for, 396 ff.; effect of cotton production on, 404; social effects of, 406-9
Slaves: in factories, 397; prices of, 402; concentration of ownership of, 406; distribution of, 407; treatment of, 409; loyalty of, 409
Smedes, Susan D., cited, 400
Smith, Adam, 149, 165, 170, 488
Smith, Captain John, cited, 11, 21, 32, 53, 60
Smith, Joseph, 240
Smith, Oliver H., cited, 287

Smuggling, 121, 161
Snyder, Carl, 477
Social control, 779-83
Social progress: to 1860, 411-37; 1860-1946, 762-84
Society for Protection of Agriculture, 265
Sod houses, 443
Soil: exploitation, 245, 251, 399, 400; erosion, 246, 622
Soil Conservation and Domestic Allotment Act, 621, 622
Solidarity of colonies, 25
South, industrial development of, 480-81; status of slaves in, 530
South Carolina, 45, 47, 105; chief colonial crops in, 90; paper money in, 136, 137; and the tariff, 359
Southern Pacific Railroad, 533, 534
Southwest, settlement of, 221-22
Spanish: discovery of America, 5; explorations by, 6; colonial policy of, 14; silver dollar, 127
Specialization: in agriculture, 253, 254, 267, 452, 453, 604, 614, 616; in occupations, 303; in trade, 308; regional, 403, 452, 453, 559
Specialization limited by market, 68-69, 83, 94-95, 341-46, 372
Specie: defined, 128; payments suspended, 322-24, 327, 332; circular, 327
Speculation, 742. See Land speculation
Spiegeleisen, 351, 352 n.
Spindles, increase in, 347-49
Spinning machinery: in England, 247; in the United States, 346-47
Squatters, 224 ff.
Stabilization Corporation: for grain, 620; for cotton, 620
Stage coach, 292
Stamp Act, 169, 170
Stamp Act Congress, 169
Standard of living, 436, 507, 512, 530-31, 766
Standard Oil Company, 504, 505, 542
Standardization, 763. See Interchangeable parts
Stanford, Leland, 533
Stanwood, Edward, cited, 182
Staple crops, 396-97
State Banks, 321, 322
State debts, defaults of, 283, 336
Steam engine, first, 353
Steamboats, 272, 274, 275-76, 300; number on western rivers, 275; on Great Lakes, 275; significance of, 276
Steamship, iron, 210, 211, 272-76. See Merchant marine
Steel industries, 349-52; low costs of, in 1910, 484; trust, 498

Steffens, Lincoln, cited, 492
Stephens, Uriah, 517
Stettinius, E. R., Jr., cited, 644
Stevens, John, 273, 285
Stewart, A. T., 566
Stiegel, Baron, 68, 73
Stillman, James, 597
Stirling, J., cited, 244, 292
Stock exchanges, 356 n., 597
Stores: specialty, 565; department, 566; mail-order, 566, 710; chain, 567, 709, 710; co-operative, 710; independent, 711
Stoves, 422
Street cars, 292
Strikes, 662, 673; railroad, of 1886, 518; of 1877, 523; Pullman, 524; causes of, 524; sit-down, in Detroit, 667
Subordination of colonial interests, 172
Subtreasury system, 337
Suez Canal, 574
Suffolk banking system, 329
Suffrage, extension of, 414
Sugar Act of 1764, 168, 169
Sugar industry in West Indies, 155
Surplus, distribution of federal, 336
Swedes, 29; colonies of, 77
Swope, Gerard, 665
Sylvis, W. H., 516

Tariff Commission of 1882, 577; state, 186
Tariffs: described, 357-58; protective, 358, 474; revenue, 358; of Abominations, 358; level of duties, 358; sectional attitudes to, 358-60; economic significance of, 360; effect on industry, 474; and trusts, 491, 505; and silver, 588; 1860-1914, 576-80; 1914-46, 724-26
Task system of slave labor, 398
Taylor, F. W., 637
Taylor, John, cited, 251
Tax on tea, 171, 173
Taxation: colonial, 168, 169, 178; tightening of, 168; during Revolution, 178; of New Deal, 751; during World War I, 736; during World War II, 753
Taxes: federal income, 641, 735, 736; excess profits, 641, 736
Telegraph, 293, 357, 556, 702
Telephone, 557, 702
Temporary National Economic Committee, 641, 654
Ten-hour movement, 374
Tenancy, farm, 462, 463, 612, 613, 614
Tennessee: claimed by North Carolina, 215; early settlement in, 223

Territorial: division of occupations, 303; specialization, 560, 564, 706; expansion, 180, 707
Territorial growth, map, 235
Texas, 237
Textile: machinery in England, 247; industry in the United States, 1860-1914, 485-87
Three-cornered trade, 65, 91, 113, 303
Threshing machine, invention of, 261, 262
Thrift stamps, 737
Time zones, 537; center of debt, 748
Tinware, 312, 423
Tobacco: as money, 131; notes, 131. See Agriculture products
Toll bridges, 270
Tomatoes, 420
Townshend Acts, 170; repeal of, 171
Tractor, gasoline, 606, 607
Trade: of Europe with the Orient, 1, 3; routes to Orient, 3, 4; search for cheaper, 3, 4; reason for, 3, 5; with Baltic, 58; domestic, 98, 108, 295-315, 559-67, 705-13; colonial, 98; fur, 8, 104-6; Indian slave, 105; intercolonial, 107; coastwise, 108, 212, 555, 575, 724; three-cornered, 65, 91, 113, 303; with England, 111-15, 171, 175; Mediterranean, 183; East and West, 297, 560; East-South, 300, 560; West-South, 302; freedom of, 305; importance of, 305; wholesale, 306, 561, 563, 708; retail, 310, 564, 709, 711; routes of, 560; centers of, 117, 709, 720; costliness of, 712
Trade Agreements Act, 1934, 726
Trade unions, early, 373, 381
Trading companies, 15-23
Transcontinental railroads, 239
Trans-Missouri Freight Association, 503
Transportation, 99-100, 268-94, 523-58, 680-704; water, 99, 100; river, 99, 274-76, 697; road, 101, 269-72, 551, 692; turnpike period, 268-71; steamboat period, 272-76; canal period, 276-84; railroad period, 284-92; cost of, 101, 120, 270, 278, 292, 398; importance of, 268, 269; effects of, 557, 477
Transportation Act of 1920, 682-85; control over securities, 683; labor tribunals, 683; enlarged powers of the Interstate Commerce Commission, 684-85
Transportation revolution, 361
Treaty of Peace of 1783, 215
Trevelyan, G. M., cited, 628
Truck, payment in, 415
Truman, H. S., 670

Trusts, 488-506, 648-52; characteristics of, 497; narrow meaning of word, 480, 493; defined, 489-93; factors favoring, 490; peak of movement, 496; evils of, 500; profits of, 500; legislation, 502-5; dissolution of, 505
Tryon, R. M., cited, 69
Tucker, St. George, 400
Turner, F. J., cited, 176, 359 n.
Turner, J. H., 245
Twain, Mark, 275, 553
Tying contracts illegal, 504
Typographical Society, 373

Underwood tariff, 579, 580, 724
Unemployment, 632; insurance, 676
Union Pacific Railroad, 533, 541, 547, 689
Unions, types of: amalgamated, 615; business, 522; company, 663; craft, 664; independent, 501, 667; industrial, 521-22; national, 516; revolutionary, 522; welfare, 522. See American Federation of Labor, Congress of Industrial Organizations, Knights of Labor, Industrial Workers of the World
United Automobile Workers, 667
United Mine Workers, 665, 666
United Nations Relief and Rehabilitation Administration, 626, 718
United States notes, 583
United States Steel Corporation, 485, 495, 500, 597, 641, 643
Urban growth, 363, 368-71
Utah, 239, 240

Vail, T. N., 557
Van Buren, Martin, 374, 382
Vanderbilt, Cornelius, 413, 546, 673, 764
Vanderbilt, William, 597
Venice, trade monopoly of, 3, 5
Victory gardens, 603, 624
Virgin Islands, 728
Virginia, settlement of, 21; agriculture of, 32, 44; estates in, 49; slavery in, 90; tobacco exports, 118
Voice of Industry, cited, 377

Wage-earning class, growth of, 512-14
Wage system, 371, 512, 516, 522; in South after 1865, 455
Wages: colonial, 81; 1791-1860, 382, 383; real, 383-85, 529, 584, 674, 765
Wakefield, E. G., cited, 368, 390
Walker, Francis A., cited, 264-65, 507
Walker tariff, 358
Wallace, H. A., 623, 624
Wampum, 129
Wanamaker, John, 566

War: Industries Board, 631; Priorities Board, 631; Shipping Board, 723; Trade Board, 714
War finance: colonial, 143; Revolution, 177-79; of 1812, 335; Mexican, 337; Civil War, 583; World War I, 736-39; World War II, 753-55
War of 1812, 199, 200; causes of, 366; financing, 335, 336
War savings certificates, 737
Warden, D. B., cited, 342
Washington, Booker T., 530
Washington, George, 191, 265; cited, 188, 387
Waste in Industry, 637
Water power, 56, 353
Water supply, 424, 771
Water transportation, 107, 552, 697-700
Waterways, 99, 100, 552; lessened use of, 554
Watson, Elkanah, 265
Wealth: distribution of, 434-37, 763-66; increase in colonies, 435; tendency to inequality, 436; tendency to equality, 765; concentration, 764; utilization, 783
Weapons of capital, 671; yellow-dog contract and blacklist, 671; of labor, strike and boycott, 671, 672
Webb Export Act, 652
Webster, Daniel, 260, 397
Weeden, William, cited, 83
Weld, C. R., 384
Weld, Isaac, cited, 269
Wells, D. A., cited, 576
West India Company, Dutch, 15
West Indies, 24, 25; trade with, 55, 60, 115, 182, 203
Western: exploration, 106; migration, 186, 610; settlement, 242
Western Federation of Miners, 521
Westinghouse, George, 537, 570
Westward movement: colonial, 80; 1790-1860, 214-41, 366; three stages, 231
Whaling, 60; decline after 1857, 202
Wheat. See Agricultural products
Whisky, 419
White, Horace, cited, 136, 140 n., 328
Whitman, Marcus, 239
Whitney, Eli, 247, 248, 342, 346
Whitney, Richard, 744
Wickard, C. R., 623
Wilderness Road, 229
Wiley, Dr. Harvey, 768
Williams, Roger, 11, 129
Willkie, Wendell, 730
Wilson, Woodrow, 188, 241, 504, 580, 651, 714, 729, 738
Wilson tariff, 578, 580

Winthrop, John, 137
Women in industry, 513
Women's Rights Convention, 416
Wood, Jethro, 260
Woodbury, Levi, cited, 210, 247, 250, 313
Woolen industry, 487
Woolworth, F. W., 567
World power, United States as a, 727, 730
World War I, effect on: agriculture, 602; manufactures, 630; labor, 661; motor industry, 690; transportation, 681; foreign trade, 713; shipping, 721; government finance, 736; industry, 739; prices, 740; debt, 740

World War II, effect on: agriculture, 624; manufactures, 631; labor, 668; transportation, 688; motor industry, 690; marketing, 712; foreign trade, 717; shipping, 723; finance, 753
Wright, Frances, cited, 246
Wyatts, Nathaniel, 420

Yeoman farmers of South, 406-8
Young, Arthur, 265
Young, Brigham, 240